Ibsen's Kingdom

Ibsen's Kingdom

The Man and His Works

Evert Sprinchorn

Yale
UNIVERSITY
PRESS
New Haven & London

Published with assistance from the Ronald and Betty Miller Turner Publication Fund, and from the foundation established in memory of James Wesley Cooper of the Class of 1865, Yale College.

Set in Postscript Electra and Weiss types by Tseng Information Systems, Inc. Printed in the United States of America.

Frontispiece: Oil portrait of Ibsen by Erik Werenskjold, 1895, detail. (Fargetrykk av Henrik Ibsen i brei profilert svart treråme med gullkant inst. Photo: Sunnfjord Museum. https://digitaltmuseum.no/011025152667/trykk-i-ramme/media?i=18&aq=descname%3A%22Trykk+i+ramme%22)

Library of Congress Control Number: 2020933615
ISBN 978-0-300-22866-3 (hardcover : alk. paper)

A catalogue record for this book is available from the British Library.

This paper meets the requirements of ANSI/NISO Z39.48-1992 (Permanence of Paper).

10 9 8 7 6 5 4 3 2 1

[Critics] endeavor to make me responsible for the opinions expressed by some of the characters in my play [*Ghosts*]. And yet there is not in the whole work a single opinion, a single utterance, that can be laid to the account of the author. I took good care to avoid that.

Ibsen, Letter of January 6, 1882

If you want objectivity, study objects. You read me to get to know me.

Ibsen, c. 1872, Georg Brandes, *Levned*, vol. 2: *Et Tiaar* (Copenhagen and Christiania, 1907), 102

Ibsen, interrogated as to his meaning, replies, "What I have said, I have said." Precisely; but the point is that what he hasn't said, he hasn't said.

Bernard Shaw, *Plays: Pleasant and Unpleasant*, vol. 1 (London, 1898), xxii

[My next work] will be a book that will link my life with my works in an enlightening whole.

Ibsen, speech in Christiania, March 23, 1898. In Henrik Ibsen, *Samlede Verker: Hundreårsutgave*, ed. Francis Bull, Halvdan Koht, and Didrik Arup Seip, 21 vols. (Oslo, 1928–57), 15:412

Deep inside, a poem within the poem is hidden, and if you grasp that, my people, you grasp the song.

Ibsen, "Till de Medskyldige," c. 1864, *Samlede Verker: Hundreårsutgave*, 14:311

CONTENTS

Preface xi

Acknowledgments xiii

Introduction 1

PART ONE THE THIRD KINGDOM

A Contrary Spirit 9

A Divided Soul 16

The Apprentice 31

The Failure 41

God's Stepchild 54

Purity of Heart 64

Peer Gynt 81

Peer Gynt Meets Hegel 92

Falling Out with Bjørnson 102

Falling In with Brandes 111

The League of Youth 122

Particular Interests 135

Old Debts Repaid 143

Ibsen in Command 155

Those Little Devils 171

Anti-Brand 179

The Prudent Revolutionary 189

Emperor and Galilean 199

Ibsen the Mystic 214

Julian as Ibsen 220

Concordance of Opposites 227

Another Triumph 235

PART TWO THE DIVIDED KINGDOM

Changing Times 243

The Problem Play 256

Pillars of Society 261

The Road to *A Doll's House* 268

The Women Behind the Play 275

The Well-Made Play Transformed 284

The Ghosts at Rosenvold 295

Syphilis, the Unmentionable Disease 307

Public Enemy 320

The Slain Pegasus 334

The Wild Duck 345

The Past Recaptured 359

The Depths of the Sea 369

A Visit to Norway 382

Rosmersholm 395

After *Rosmersholm* 412

The Lady from the Sea 423

The Immoralists 438

The Unspoken *Hedda* 456

PART THREE THE LOST KINGDOM

World Fame 473

New Directions 485

Who Is Hilda? 490

The Story of Solness 501

The Man Behind the Mask 505

The Return of Nora 508

Solness as Superman 514

Conquering France 516

Little Eyolf 522

John Gabriel Borkman 535

Foldal and Hinkel 545

Seventieth-Birthday Celebrations 557

A Dramatic Epilogue 564

The Last Years 575

Notes 581

Bibliography 631

Credits 647

Index 649

PREFACE

In 1898 Henrik Ibsen's collected works were published in celebration of his seventieth birthday. This edition printed the plays not by genre—history plays, poetic dramas, realistic plays—but in the order in which they had been written. The first volume was prefaced by a personal note addressed "To The Reader" from the master himself, his copperplate handwriting reproduced, in which he expressed his pleasure in that arrangement. He complained that he was being misunderstood by most readers because they came upon his most famous plays without having read what came before. He insisted that only by studying his plays in the order in which they had been written could they be properly comprehended.

It was certainly true then and has been true ever since that almost all who study Ibsen intensely or read him leisurely for their great stories and complicated characters first come upon works like *A Doll's House* or *Ghosts* or *Hedda Gabler* without having read *Brand* or *Peer Gynt.* But Ibsen went even further, saying that it was not enough for the serious reader to catch up on the earlier plays; he insisted that they had to be read in the order in which they were written. Only then would the continuity between them become clear and only in that continuity would each individual work reveal its richness of meaning.

If so, why did he not complain earlier? Why wait until 1898? Well, if he had had his way, he might have been rather more forthcoming about his intentions as a writer and more willing to discuss the meaning of his plays. After the furor created by *Ghosts* and the hostility it created, Ibsen proposed writing his autobiography, which presumably would have had much to say about his work. It was his publisher Hegel who persuaded him to remain silent and distant. Acting as press agent, Hegel advised Ibsen to remain aloof from public discussion. He compared Ibsen to a statue who should not step down from his pedestal and engage with readers. He even encouraged Ibsen to destroy his notes, so that future scholars would have to puzzle out the meaning of his works. Ibsen took those words to heart and thus was born the taciturn, tight-lipped, enigmatic Ibsen, the Norwegian sphinx.

However, years earlier he had informed his readers what lay at the heart of his plays. In the preface to the re-issue of his very first play, *Catiline*, he said that the major theme of his works was the conflict between what one proposes and what is actually possible, the conflict between one's aims and one's capabilities. This is a subject that offers a bottomless well of possibilities, even more so than such common dramatic themes as revenge or sex. It was an inner conflict that nearly every person has experienced.

For Ibsen, his works were a transcription of his own struggles with this conflict. He never wrote a play just because he had found a good subject. He wrote because he was wrestling with a theme that obsessed him throughout his life. If the serious reader, taking up the plays in order, reaches *A Doll's House*, he will see that it is only superficially and incidentally about women's rights. The heroine Nora never talks about them.

In his plays Ibsen experienced inwardly the conflict between the two sides of his personality, leading outwardly a life of growing success while experiencing the inner qualms of the imperfect idealist. The inner and outer lives, art and reality, were perfectly coiled around each other. The present book attempts to explore that double helix as the source of Ibsen's creativity, a helix that raises him to the level of the philosopher-dramatist and made him the father of modern drama.

ACKNOWLEDGMENTS

First of all I am indebted to Åke Leander (1919–2003), Swedish poet and educator, who revealed to me the hidden splendors of Ibsen's plays. While I was studying theater at Columbia University I took his seminar on Ibsen and Strindberg. Under his guiding hand, *A Doll's House* was transformed from a social problem play with a couple of good acting parts into a multilayered dramatic poem, and the would-be actor into the nascent scholar.

Ryan Hart helped transfer my typewritten manuscript to the computer, and he prepared the diagram of Ibsen's poems.

The late Philip E. Larson, a fine Ibsen scholar and a diligent fact checker, was the first to read the manuscript and caught a number of errors. Above all, he especially approved of the passages filling in the cultural background to the plays.

Joan Templeton, author of the indispensable *Ibsen's Women*, perused the sections on Emperor and Galilean, and straightened out my tangled thoughts.

Gabrielle Cody, my colleague at Vassar College, read the manuscript for its narrative flow.

David Olivenbaum copyedited my manuscript, catching a number of inconsistencies.

My Norwegian cousin Karen Solberg kept me up to date on developments in Ibsen scholarship.

Ulf Bergström of Stockholm, Sweden, a friend since my happy days there, tracked down articles in Swedish newspapers.

John Kulka of Harvard University Press was the first editor to see merit in my manuscript and was instrumental in getting the work published.

Ibsen's Kingdom

INTRODUCTION

The career of Henrik Ibsen forms one of the most amazing success stories in the annals of literature, or of all art, for that matter. He emerged out of Norway, the *ultima Thule* of belles lettres, to become one of the two or three most famous creative personalities of the latter half of the nineteenth century and a major literary and theatrical influence on the twentieth. He was as readable as Dickens, as morally controversial as Tolstoy, as psychologically penetrating as Dostoyevsky, as inescapable as Wagner. He created the most vivid and varied array of dramatic characters since Shakespeare. The combination in his plays of a suspenseful plot, memorable characters, psychological insight, innovative stage techniques, and, not least, a disturbing examination of moral problems made him the unchallenged father of modern drama.

The impact of his plays was felt not just in the theater but wherever there were readers. His universal fame made Ibsen a household name. It was a guarantee of work of the highest possible quality. It appeared on Norwegian sardine cans sold on the international market. Anyone who read a newspaper knew he was someone to be reckoned with. Feminists read *A Doll's House* and hailed him as a prophet of women's rights. Young philosophers read *The Wild Duck* and weighed the ethical value of truth. Moralists pondered such matters as euthanasia and incest after having gone to a private performance of the banned play *Ghosts*, which excited the young Bertrand Russell "to a very high degree," and which shook the world as no other play in the postclassical era had ever done. The political right and the traditionally religious admired him in the 1870s as an upholder of ideals, a supporter of the monarchy, and then denounced him in the 1880s as an anarchist, a Darwinist, and an immoralist.

If he had been an English novelist who turned his hand to writing plays, as Shaw was to do, his achievement would have been remarkable enough. But Ibsen wrote in a minor language, and in a country in which there was at the beginning of his career no native drama worth mentioning. In the middle of the nineteenth century Norway was a cultural outpost. Its literary language was Danish, the theatrical troupes that toured its few towns along the seacoast were mainly Danish, and many of the plays they performed were Danish. The classic Scandinavian dramatist was Ludvig Holberg, who had been born in Norway in 1684 but lived and worked in Denmark. The combined population of Denmark, Norway, and Sweden at that time was about that of Greater London, and no Scandinavian writer could hope to support himself by his writings alone, even if he wrote popular novels. Moreover, there was not, either in Norway or elsewhere in the Western world, a reading public for plays apart from the classics: the Greeks, and Shakespeare, Goethe, Schiller. As in present-day Europe and America, people then did not read plays; they saw them in the theater. Only a few plays in the twentieth century have become best sellers in bookstores, plays like O'Neill's *The Iceman Cometh* and *Long Day's Journey into Night* and Albee's *Who's Afraid of Virginia Woolf?* (Albee's play sold 70,000 copies, both hard and soft covers. Bearing in mind the difference in size between the United States and Norway, nearly all of Ibsen's realistic plays sold as well.) Ibsen accomplished the miracle of turning plays into best sellers. Beginning in 1879, he produced one best-selling script after another, approximately one every two years for the next twenty. He wrote primarily with readers in mind, not actors, and avoided the technical jargon of theatrical scripts. Instead of writing, "Door in flat, 1st grooves. Manders enters from D.R.H. [door right hand]," he wrote, "Pastor Manders ... enters the conservatory from the garden." And he wrote with a deadline in mind. Once he had established himself as a writer, his plays were regularly published just before Christmas in order to take advantage of the gift-giving spirit of the season, often in first printings of 10,000 copies for the Scandinavian countries alone. The equivalent in the United States today would be 600,000. The first edition of his collected works in Dano-Norwegian, published 1898–1902, was printed in 15,000 copies. (For the collected edition of the works of Bernard Shaw, 30 volumes published 1930–32, only 1,025 copies were printed.)

In England and America, before the influence of Ibsen was felt, there was no reading public for plays. Writing in 1883, an English critic said, "No one reads plays at the present date, probably for the excellent reason that there are none, or so very few, to read. Modern plays are rarely published, or are printed almost exclusively for the use of the performers, and are addressed solely to theatre-goers: they seek no public among the readers of books."[1]

The unparalleled success of these plays did not depend on their power to amuse or to divert the mind from the problems of the day. They did not present the viewer in the theater or the reader in his library with a perilous situation that would be happily and incredibly resolved in the last act. The one thing that has always made plays popular, the power to make an audience happy or contented, was the one thing Ibsen's plays noticeably lacked. Often they ended with nothing resolved, with everything up in the air. The audience was left to wonder what would become of Nora after she slams the door on her husband and children at the end of *A Doll's House*. The unbearable anguish of Mrs. Alving as the curtain falls on *Ghosts*, when she must decide whether to end her son's life, is the last thing the audience sees. She remains frozen in time, her dilemma unresolved. No one before Ibsen had dared to write plays that had no endings, and when questioned about them, their grim author replied that his purpose was not to answer questions but to raise them. And even when his plays did come to a conventional end, with one or two dead bodies on the stage, the questions remained.

As the stages of nineteenth-century Europe became increasingly realistic, the imitations of life presented on them had to become more real also. And nothing was more true to life than unresolved problems and unanswered prayers. And, like the people who try to help us in times of trouble, Ibsen had a way of suggesting an answer and then turning it into another question. When Nora answered her husband by walking out on him, she declared her independence and won the admiration of feminists, making devoted followers of those who sought emancipation in a male-dominated society. Whereupon nonfeminists accused Ibsen of wishing to destroy the family, the mainstay of civilized life. Ibsen's reply to them was to write *Ghosts*, in which the wife listens to her pastor and remains at home, thus preserving the family as best she can by caring for a dissolute and diseased husband. That seemed to be answer enough to Ibsen's accusers. But Ibsen, typically, could not leave it at that. After the wife has become an independent woman, breaking free from her past, she finds herself burdened by a syphilitic son who demands that she put an end to his tortured existence. Against the cruel forces of nature, what good has her independence done her?

The unpalatable truth that life is not a theatrical entertainment, that it is a complicated business with no easy answers, brought out in play after play, made Ibsen an irresistible force among those who wanted more than amusement in the books they read and the plays they saw. Even the art of acting was transformed by his lifelike characters, who possessed a depth that could not be revealed by conventional posturing and declamation. The subtlest tragedienne of her era, Eleanora Duse, who believed that actors and actresses should all die of the plague because they poisoned the air and made art impossible, found only in Ibsen roles worthy of her genius.[2] When she went on tour to Christiania in 1906, she stood outside Ibsen's apartment house on a wintry day, hoping to catch a glimpse of the dramatist who had raised the modern theater to the level of the other arts. Unfortunately, he was then a dying man.

For people with intellects, reading Ibsen was more than entertaining; it was enthralling. Reading his plays is equivalent to a journey through nineteenth-century thought, its art, politics, and philosophy. Ibsen's collected works painted the intellectual landscape of his time as a magnificent panorama, which he traversed with a thoroughness unmatched by any other creative writer. He turned audiences into debating societies, theaters into political arenas, and drama into a chronicle of the times. What bliss it must have been to be young and impressionable when Ibsen wrote those masterpieces that revolutionized the drama and paved the way for Strindberg, Chekhov, Shaw, and the best playwrights of the twentieth century.

Although Ibsen's richest characters suggest the enormous potential in human nature, their promise is left unfulfilled, and even the best of them come to no good end. Brand, a prophet who wages war against hypocrisy and slackness of spirit, is abandoned by the few converts he has made and dies in an avalanche. Gregers Werle in *The Wild Duck* believes that the truth will set men free, but the truth when told results in the death of an innocent child. Hedda Gabler, superior intellectually and culturally to everyone around her, blows out her brains. One senses all too often in Ibsen that waste of the good in human beings which A. C. Bradley thought constituted the essence of that "painful mystery" called tragedy, and nothing was more painful to him than Shakespearean tragedy. But in Shakespeare the waste often derives from a conflict between good and evil, whereas evil seems to have lost its meaning in Ibsen's universe, or takes on the appearance of the good. Macbeth and Claudius are cold-blooded murderers who are punished for their crimes. In Ibsen destructive characters like Brand and Gregers Werle are monuments of rectitude.

Nothing is more characteristic of Ibsen's power to disturb than his forays into the no-man's-land between good and evil, right and wrong. He was, in the words of James Huneker, "the greatest moral artist of his century, Tolstoy not excepted,"[3] and as such he went beyond good and evil. He was the point man for Nietzsche (though the German philosopher did not realize it), in search of those heights where a superman might live and breathe. For him the tragic conflict was not between moral forces in the conventional sense but between the human and the superhuman, between man's capabilities and his aspirations. He was quite explicit about this. At the midpoint in his career, in 1875, he said that much of his work concerned "the conflict between one's aims and one's abilities, between what man proposes and what is actually possible."[4] What may appear to the casual reader as blatant contradictions were to Ibsen expressions of one personality and one unending struggle. The war within him never ceased, although the strength of the contending forces fluctuated. His major accomplishment was to see the great intellectual, political, and cultural conflicts of modern times as a mirror of his own inner contradictions.

Expressed abstractly like that, the conflict doesn't sound like the stuff of drama. But for Ibsen it was what life was all about. It was his own conflict, and for him victory meant immortality. It was a lifelong obsession with him. In 1867, while he was forging the immortal verses of *Peer Gynt* in the intense heat of an Italian summer, he told a painter friend that he wrote not just for his own time but for all time. The painter replied that, philosophically speaking, fame, however great, had its limits. Some geniuses might be remembered for a generation, some for a century, but in a thousand years all of them would be forgotten, even the greatest of them. Ibsen exploded, "Go to hell with your metaphysics! Take eternity from me and you take everything!"

The drama critic Brooks Atkinson once remarked that Eugene O'Neill had an infatuation with oblivion; Ibsen had the opposite longing, a passion for fame and honor. It was more than a passion—it was an obsession. And he got what he wanted. He became one of the immortals, his grasp matched his reach, and he attained his kind of heaven. But at what a price. And therein lay the tragedy of living as he saw it.

Part One

The Third Kingdom

A Contrary Spirit

At 2:30 in the afternoon, May 23, 1906, Henrik Ibsen, age seventy-eight, died in his apartment in the center of Christiania, Norway. He had been bedridden for some years, and a series of strokes had left him unable to write. His last creative effort, a play with the eerie title *When We Dead Awaken* (with emphasis on the *We*), had been published in 1899. According to one account, on the morning of May 23 his wife had come into his bedroom to inquire about his condition. The attending nurse had told her that he appeared to be resting more easily. Ibsen had stirred and said, "On the contrary" (*Tværtimot*).[1]

It is not clear whether these words were meant as a reply to the nurse or to some unspoken thoughts of his own. Not that it matters, since this anecdote must have been invented. It is too perfect. If, like an ancient Roman, he had carefully prepared the last words that were to cross his lips, he could hardly have chosen more fitting ones.

The contradictions warring within the man had provided the impetus for his dramas, and they manifested themselves after his passing as they had during his life. There was a general feeling that Tolstoy was Ibsen's only serious rival for the position of Europe's artist-philosopher left vacant by the death of Goethe. In Paris the obituaries praised him as a giant of the stature of Goethe, Shakespeare, and Michelangelo. In Germany he was hailed as "among the greatest spirits of the last century, a century that began with Goethe and Beethoven and ended with Wagner and Ibsen. He was universal. He was poet to the world. The news of his death strikes every cultured nation. No poet has ever been honored with equal recognition."

But this universally esteemed writer was passed over by the committee that awarded the Nobel Prize in Literature. They bestowed the prize on Sully Prudhomme (a French poet), Mommsen (a German historian), Bjørnson (Ibsen's

Norwegian rival as poet and dramatist and author of the Norwegian national anthem), Echegaray (a Spanish dramatist), and Sienkiewicz (a Polish novelist, author of *Quo Vadis?*)—and refused to honor Ibsen. In their assessment they said that while "all could unite in admiration of the author of *Brand, The Pretenders, Emperor and Galilean,* and other distinguished works," strong doubts had been expressed about Ibsen's "later productions, whose negative and enigmatic features have repelled even those who would have willingly given the world-famous author substantial recognition."[2] In other words, the plays that made Ibsen world-famous, plays such as *A Doll's House, Ghosts, The Wild Duck,* and *Rosmersholm,* were the ones that deprived him of the Nobel Prize.

The dilettantish English critic Max Beerbohm chimed in with the Nobel committee. "Mankind he simply could not abide. Indeed, I fancy he cared less for ideas as ideas than as a scourge for his fellow creatures.... He had a joy ... in the havoc he wrought."[3]

Beerbohm saw only one half of the Ibsen phenomenon. Ibsen was both a builder and a destroyer, a god and a demon, the alpha and omega of the nineteenth century. In France, a cultural arbiter summed him up as "the great demolisher of institutions who was to become one of the founders of the society of tomorrow,"[4] while the respected journal *La Revue* editorialized, "We can say, without being too rash, that here on the threshold of the twentieth century, alongside Renan and Tolstoy, Wagner and Nietzsche, [Ibsen] stands as a titanic creator, a fearless prophet, who cleared the broadest path toward the future."[5]

In Germany, the kaiser of dramatic critics, Alfred Kerr, stressed the contradictions between Ibsen's dour philosophy and the effect it had on the thinking world. The Norwegian playwright "was indeed an undeifier of the gods, but as such utterly forthright. He was the resolute man without hope, yet a miraculous consoling power lay in his resolution of the reasons for our disconsolation."[6]

While Ibsen's body lay in state, the bookshops in Christiania displayed his portrait wreathed in flowers. The telegraph lines were jammed with messages pouring in from all over the world. The day before the official burial ceremony, an honor guard composed of twenty-six students, artists, and writers presided over the bier, while twenty thousand people, nearly a tenth of the population of Christiania, filed past.

He was regarded by the Norwegians as the conscience of their nation and a scourge to their souls, their spiritual taskmaster who made them, notwithstanding their small numbers, "think big," encouraging them to surpass themselves. The king of Norway called on him as he lay dying, and the government paid the funeral expenses. The king was also present at the official burial ceremony, dressed in his admiral's uniform and wearing the Grand Cross of the Order of

St. Olav, which had been conferred on Ibsen, too, in 1893. Marching solemnly behind the casket as it was carried to the burial place was a state official displaying on a cushion all eleven medals that had been awarded to Ibsen during his lifetime.[7]

Yet in 1893 Ibsen had avowed himself "an anarchist and an individualist." In attendance at the service for this anarchist, who had once declared in a poem that he would gladly torpedo the ship of state, were official representatives of all the leading nations. In fact, the official cortege consisted only of government figures and functionaries—no writers or artists.

An anarchist in politics, Ibsen was an agnostic in religion, "the high priest of the unbelieving," as Kerr called him.[8] But the funeral service was a Christian one, conducted in Trinity Church, and the eulogy was delivered by Christopher Bruun, the minister who, many years before, had served as one of the models for Ibsen's uncompromising, idealistic pastor Brand. Bruun had come to Ibsen's deathbed to convert him to Christianity and save his soul from eternal damnation. The dying man had quickly shut him up: "Let me worry about that!"[9] But in Trinity Church Bruun had the last word.

The shade of Ibsen, hovering over the solemn services, must have relished the ironies apparent in these last rites. All the contradictions of his life were resolved, at least symbolically. The agnostic Ibsen had always respected the sacrificial element in Christianity, and the arch individualist and anarchist had always craved official recognition by the state. In a way, the gathering at these final ceremonies brought the whole of his life into focus. It was the perfect conclusion to all the years of struggle and suffering, the young years when his genius went unrecognized, the mature years when he was both reviled and honored by the establishment. Now all the inequities and injustices he had had to endure were corrected and set right—for the moment. And why should not the world that he had pictured so accurately and perceptively not gather at the end for a group portrait?

The Scandinavian countries had never witnessed such an outpouring of emotion and sentiment for a literary figure. Taking into account the difference in size between Scandinavia and France and the difference in temperament between the southern and northern nations, the public response to Ibsen's passing rivaled the extravagances in Paris in 1885 when Victor Hugo was laid to rest. On that occasion it was said that French women offered themselves to the nearest stranger, hoping to produce the next Hugo. Whether such stories were true or not, they seemed to fit the occasion. But nothing remotely like that would have been appropriate for Ibsen. Life flowed from Hugo, but not from Ibsen.

Seeing all those wreathed portraits of the great man, taking note of the darkened theaters, hearing the music Edvard Grieg composed for the death of Peer

Gynt's mother, and seeing the long line of ordinary citizens filing past the bier, an innocent observer might suppose that the dead man had been a loving and warmhearted soul, a father to his people. Yet to many of his contemporaries Ibsen was a formidably stern and unapproachable man, aloof in attitude, fastidious in his dress, punctilious in the observance of social manners, severely judgmental in his opinions, and uninterested in most of the pleasures of life. The sentimental Danish poet Holger Drachmann said, "Ibsen will always be a stranger to us Danes—cold, cold as stone, with dynamite under the frozen rock."[10]

In Sweden the music- and nature-loving Strindberg took an extreme anti-Ibsen position, viewing him as an inhuman troll and the incarnation of a godless age. After Ibsen's death, Strindberg unburdened himself in characteristically unrestrained terms.

"The proper epitaph for his tombstone came from Ibsen himself during an interview: 'He who rests here could tolerate neither flowers nor children nor music. . . .' He was a black soul. Thought to be a bringer of light, he came in fact from the dark and was always out of his mind, not knowing what he said or did."

The aging Strindberg, a Naturalist who converted to Swedenborgianism, abhorred the Darwinists, whom he labeled the "disciples of the Lord of the Flies," and Ibsen was their prophet.

"When he abjured the *deus caritatis* of his youth, he got a devil to watch over him. His own eyes were never opened to the truth; he merely kept on working at his own ruin. And the more stupidly he wrote, the wiser he seemed to the dwarfish Lords of the Flies. Finally he got such a fat head it burst. And then the light dawned on him, and he must have seen the error of his ways. People said he had lost his mind. He tried to deny that he had ever meant anything by his pronouncements. But to no avail. When he died, he was apotheosized. One of the eight beasts with crowns carried the mace, and the Babylonian whore followed behind."[11]

There is more than a grain of truth in these ravings. Strindberg had followed Ibsen's career closely and knew that Ibsen had felt uncomfortable with the materialism, determinism, and naturalism that underlay his most notorious dramas. He knew that, in struggling against them, Ibsen had more than once in his career evidently let himself be captured by them. He had indeed shifted positions radically. On several occasions he dissociated himself from Brand, the hero of the poetic drama that secured his fame in the Nordic countries. Every Ibsenite was stunned when this preacher of idealism portrayed the idealist in *The Wild Duck* as a neurotic man who destroys a happy family. What Strindberg did not perceive was that there was a unity to Ibsen's work that accommodated even such apparent reversals.

On the other hand, Strindberg was right to see Ibsen as a man who was at home only in the dark. This was not intuitive knowledge on Strindberg's part; it was a matter of record, and he could cite chapter and verse for his purpose. In a poem written before he became famous, Ibsen himself said that he had come to fear the light and that he gained courage when he hid himself under the veil of nightmares.

> Then I defy sea and flame;
> I fly as a falcon in the sky.
> I forget all anguish and pain
> Until the morning sun comes back again.
> Without the bastion of night
> I know not what I would do.
> If ever I accomplish a great deed,
> It will be a deed done in the dark.[12]

Where the ordinary person tends to identify light with the life-giving sun and dark with satanic forces, Ibsen did just the opposite. One thinks of the last horrifying moments in *Ghosts*, when the rising of the sun, flooding the stage with light for the first time after two hours of darkness and rain, signals the outbreak of madness in the syphilitic hero. It was always the dark that fed his creative energies; it was by being different from others that he found himself. He had to be the negative charge that produces positive results.

This was apparent in his very first play, *Catiline*, written in 1849 when he was twenty. He was already an apostle of the opposite, an affirmer of the negative. He was the young rebel who had broken with his family, separated himself from the teachings and beliefs of his childhood, a godless young man who had allied himself with the radical element in the small town where he was learning the apothecary's trade, and who was fired with enthusiasm for the revolutions that had swept through Europe in 1848.

"The February Revolution, the revolutions in Hungary and elsewhere, the Dano-Prussian War [of 1849] over Schleswig and Holstein—all this," wrote Ibsen, "had a powerful and formative effect on my development, however incomplete it remained for a long time thereafter. . . . While the big outside world was caught in the storm of great events, I found myself on a war footing with the little community where I felt I was being held back by my general situation and oppressed by circumstances in general."[13]

Exactly half a century after *Catiline*, Ibsen put an end to the oeuvre that began with it. All his important plays constitute chapters in an odyssey through the cultural history of modern Europe, to which *Catiline* is prologue and *When We Dead Awaken* epilogue. Shortly after he completed his last play he was stricken with erysipelas, and in 1903 a stroke—not the first he had suffered—left him unable to walk or write. It was as if the plays and their author sustained each other, as if they were written with his lifeblood. Throughout his career Ibsen insisted that he wrote only about experiences he had lived through inwardly. He meant more by this than simply seeing the characters and events with his inner eye, more than merely acting out all the parts in his mind. He meant that his obsessions were bodied forth in the characters and informed the plots of the plays.

"Everything that I have written," he said, "has the closest possible connection with what I have lived through inwardly—even if I have not experienced it outwardly. In every new poem or play I have aimed at my own spiritual emancipation and purification—for no man can escape the responsibilities and the guilt of the society to which he belongs. Hence I once wrote the following lines by way of a dedication in a copy of one of my books.

Living is a war with the trolls
In the depths of the mind and heart;
Writing means summoning oneself
To court, and playing the judge's part."[14]

When *The Master Builder* was published, Ibsen told a French interviewer, "No one other than myself inspires me and my thoughts, and no one influences my view. I find everything within myself; everything comes from my heart. That is because I have felt strongly the contradiction that we have created between human destiny and the society built by human beings—it is because of that that I have written what I have written."[15]

The consequence of this extraordinary self-involvement in his works is that they have an organic unity, each play growing out of the preceding one. His collected works form a trajectory arching over the last fifty years of the nineteenth century. He shaped his life into a work of art.

Conversing with a friend whom he had not seen in some time and who remarked that the intervening years had changed both of them, Ibsen interrupted him.

"I have not changed. People think I have changed my views with the passage of time. This is a great mistake. In truth, my development is unusually consistent. I can point out the thread that runs through my entire career, the unity of my ideas and their gradual evolution. And I am in the process of setting down some notes that will show how precisely I am the same as when I first found myself."[16]

This was said in the spring of 1881, when he was hard at work on *Ghosts*. Seventeen years later, on his seventieth birthday, he revealed his intention of writing a book that would "link my life and my writings together as an explanatory whole."[17]

At about the same time Ibsen wrote a brief preface for the first collected edition of his works in which he once again stressed their overall unity.

"Simultaneously with the production of my works another generation of readers has grown up, and I have often noticed with regret that their knowledge of my more recent works is considerably more detailed than of my earlier ones. Consequently, these readers lack an awareness of the mutual connections between the plays, and I attribute a not insignificant part of the strange, imperfect, and misleading interpretations that my later works have been subjected to in so many quarters to this lack of awareness.

"Only by grasping and comprehending my entire production as a continuous and coherent whole will the reader be able to receive the precise impression I sought to convey in the individual parts of it."[18]

Great as many of the individual plays are, their thought becomes more profound and their power to stir both heart and mind more overwhelming when they are studied as Ibsen wished, as chapters in an autobiography, as stages in the exploration of the human spirit by a mind that was able to grasp and assimilate all the significant ideas of his age. While providing irresistible dramatic entertainment, his plays embrace morality, religion, and philosophy. His organizing mind endeavored to reduce the chaos of his time to a single unifying vision, and in mapping the cultural landscape of nineteenth-century Europe he succeeded perhaps better than any other creative artist of his time in doing so. In their entirety his plays constitute one of the supreme artistic achievements of Western civilization, a *Divine Comedy* of the modern age, with hell and purgatory in a Victorian parlor and a glimpse of an icy paradise on the mountain peaks of Norway.

A Divided Soul

If Ibsen had written his autobiography, it would have resembled the present book in at least one respect: it would have treated the works as equivalent to the life, surveyed the major dramas as chapters in a fifty-year narrative, and seen the beginning of that saga in his childhood when his world fell apart. He spent the rest of his life trying to put it together again.

Although it may be true that dramatists are born and not made, it does seem that in the bourgeois age the greatest ones have all been irreclaimably shaped by unhappy social circumstances while quite young and impressionable. Emerson said, "All great men come out of the middle classes. 'Tis better for the head; 'tis better for the heart."[1] Among dramatists, it is true of Ibsen, Strindberg, Chekhov, and Shaw. But Emerson neglected to add that for a playwright, talent and a middle-class upbringing were not enough. There had also to be an untimely and fateful change in the family fortunes. A dramatist creates conflict by seeing both sides of a question, and a young person who sees his father fail in business goes through both the good and the bad sides of middle-class existence. And if he is to deal with the social concerns of his time, this can only serve him well as a writer. With painters and composers it is another matter. They have not needed conflict to create their masterpieces. Gauguin and van Gogh may have lived in humble circumstances, but they chose to do so, the latter deliberately sniffing out in his nomadic existence what he called "the dog's path through life."[2]

The dramatists suffered unfortunate falls that marked them for life. Chekhov's father, who ran a general store, had to flee his creditors when the business failed. Anton was a teenager at the time, but he survived relatively unscathed and went on to medical school, though he never had much good to say about his father. Shaw's father was a Protestant merchant with ancestors among the Scottish nobility. When his business failed, his son, not quite thirteen, was moved from a Protestant school to a nondenominational school where most of the students were Catholic and sons of workingmen. The shock of finding himself among poor Catholics was so great to young George's self-esteem that he could not bring himself to write about it until he was ninety years old.

Strindberg affords an instructive case, a variation on the theme. Since some of the facts of his childhood didn't fit the paradigm, he altered them. His father's business failed when Johan August was only four years old, too young and unaware to be scarred by the event. Besides, it came only as a short-lived jolt to the family's affairs. The father quickly regained his financial balance, and neither he nor his family suffered much. The necessary blow to August's psyche came later, when his mother died. August was then at the delicate age of thirteen, and his mother had been a waitress before she got married. Throughout his life he identified himself with her; when he wrote his autobiography, he called himself the son of a servant and greatly exaggerated the not-so-humble circumstances of his childhood, demoting himself to the lower class. He dressed up (or, rather, dressed down) the facts of his childhood and upbringing, giving a vivid picture of the poverty that he had to endure, "afraid and hungry," as a consequence of his father's business failure, and stressing the division that developed in his soul, formed as it was by a middle-class wholesaler and a lower-class barmaid. Strindberg made himself into a middle-class loser because he understood where the serious drama of his time lay. The social upheavals of the nineteenth century were the result of class conflict, and Strindberg placed himself in the midst of the changing times by creating the relevant character for himself.

These are imperfect examples. It is Ibsen who is the archetype of the middle-class serious dramatist. His descent into poverty was horribly real, as was the concomitant loss of social esteem. As a very young boy he enjoyed a life of privilege and culture. By the time he entered his teens, however, he was a poor lad cast out into the world to make his own living. The result was a deep, lasting division within the man. Part of him was the well-dressed and pampered rich boy; part of him was the downstart, who, as Shaw remarked of himself in similar circumstances, had the pretense of a culture without the reality of it. There was the Ibsen before the crash and the Ibsen after the crash, the rich boy and the poor boy. He came to recognize this as the determining fact of his life and of his artistic creativity. When he wrote his autobiography in the form of a play, *The Wild Duck*, he put the two halves of himself onstage: Hjalmar Ekdal, the seedy photographer with vain illusions of restoring the family honor, tenderly caring for his derelict father, and Gregers Werle, the rich man's son, the father-hating idealist who wants to destroy lies and banish hypocrisy.

It is hardly an exaggeration to say that all Ibsen's major dramas have their roots in his divided soul. Both his life and his works were devoted to patching up his ruptured psyche. The inner conflict affected even his physiognomy. The left half of his face was different from the right, especially the eyes, quite noticeable in some portraits, such as Erik Werenskiold's 1895 sketch.[3] And the difference became greater as he grew older, all the while struggling to bring the two halves of his conflicted soul into harmony with each other.

The artist Stephen Sinding, who was making sketches of Ibsen in the 1890s and having difficulty capturing the expression on the writer's face, asked him to remove his spectacles. He was struck by the difference in the eyes. "I had never seen two eyes like these," he said. "The one, the large one, was, I might say, frightening—that's how it impressed me—holding a whole world of mysticism. The other, noticeably smaller, as if half-closed, cold, clear, and inquisitive. I stood silent for a few seconds, looking at these eyes, and could not help thinking it would not be good to have him as an enemy. Then the expression in his eyes and in his whole being flared up, and I was suddenly reminded of the troll in the folktale, who jumps out of his hole and cries, 'Who's cutting wood in my forest?'"[4]

Those peculiar eyes impressed another Norwegian artist in much the same way. "One has to study Ibsen's face especially closely to get at its character. Generally, he keeps one eye wide open, the other half shut. The open eye is at one moment mocking, at the next friendly. Still, it is always alert and observant. But when he opens the other eye, it is intense and piercing, like that of a bird of prey, and his glance bores into one's soul. Then his whole physiognomy undergoes a frightening transformation."[5]

An equally distinctive feature of his physiognomy, apparent in many of his portraits, was his mouth. If his eyes were the outward manifestation of his divided soul, his mouth with its clenched lips revealed the moral disciplinarian. Bernard Shaw remarked on it: "What bulldog ever developed such grip and tenacity in the mouth? One understands at a glance the remark made about Ibsen by Charles Carrington: 'No man has the right to have such a mouth.' But no less a mouth is needed to carry such a forehead through the idealist wilderness of this world."[6]

Genetics may have had as much to do with the division as social factors. Ibsen's blood inheritance may have established the fault line where the fracture would occur when his world was shaken by financial misfortunes. Certainly his mother and father had different temperaments and formed a badly suited pair. She was artistic, loved music, and had strong religious feelings, whereas he was money-minded, skeptical in religious matters, and very gregarious, the life of the party. The marriage from the start was more socially than romantically right. Marichen (pronounced *Marchen*) Altenburg had not married the man she really loved. Her well-to-do parents had urged her to be sensible and to find a more practical mate.

Waiting in the wings was Knud Ibsen. He was the son of a sea captain, a short, blond young man, slight of build but well proportioned, an engaging storyteller, with eyes that either sparkled with wit or glinted with craftiness. He was obviously an enterprising fellow who seemed likely to succeed in business, and who, thanks in part to his marrying a propertied woman, certainly did succeed—for a while. All those unhappy marriages and mismatches that Ibsen depicts in his plays are based on the one that he observed firsthand as a child and young man. But his understanding of his parents shifted, depending on whether he viewed them as they were before or after the fall.

Strindberg remained emotionally attached to his working-class mother and had little to say about his father. O'Neill, to take another example of a playwright from the middle class, had a very narrow, singularly unchanging view of his parents: he always retained before his eyes a narcomaniac mother and a parsimonious father, neither of whom offered him the love he cried out for. Unlike Ibsen, however, neither O'Neill nor Strindberg experienced a precipitous social downfall. Ibsen was highly ambivalent about his parents. Their personalities altered, depending on their social status. There was a lovable father and a distant mother; there was also a hated father and an endearing mother. Put with them a young man who split himself into two diametrically opposed halves, often in the form of two women, and you have the basic cast for Ibsen's plays. The combinations available to the dramatist were almost inexhaustible. They could be, and certainly were, infinitely varied in Ibsen's fifty years of playwriting.

In his poetic drama *Brand*, the mother is an avaricious woman who married for money, and her son, reacting against her, is an uncompromising idealist who will not come to her even as she lies dying. *Peer Gynt*, written immediately afterward, presents the opposite view. There the son is an unprincipled rapscallion, who drifts from one vocation to another, who recalls his childhood fondly, and who bids farewell to his dying mother in the tenderest scene that Ibsen ever wrote. In *The Wild Duck*, written eighteen years later, everything is reversed. There it is the idealist Gregers who cherishes the memory of his mother and despises his domineering father, while his counterpart, the charming, impractical Hjalmar, dotes on his alcoholic and dowdy father and has virtually no memory of his mother.

This ambivalence on Ibsen's part is not the result of an inability to see his childhood and his parents clearly, to see them as they really were. It is rather the result of the effect they had on him, the contradictory impressions they made on him, and his recognition of the complicated nature of human beings and their relationships—and of the difficulty he had in resolving the conflicts within himself.

The tension between his parents can only be inferred from Ibsen's poems and plays. A purely factual account of the life of the young Henrik Ibsen must center

Figure 2. The Stockman house, Ibsen's birthplace.

on money and property and social standing. Knud Ibsen was born in 1797, with a mixture of Danish, German, and Scottish blood in his veins. His parents were comfortably off and mingled with the best families in Skien, an obligatory port of call for packet ships plying the coast of southern Norway. The town then had about 3,000 inhabitants (in a country that had a total population of 1¼ million). Of the 3,000, 38 were businessmen, 31 were shop- and tavern keepers, 67 were fishermen, and 111 lived on charity. The principal industry was lumbering, and ironworks were not far away. The town as Ibsen remembered it in his middle age was filled with the noise of the millrace, rushing waters, and the pounding of steam hammers. It had three schools and a lending library with 781 books. Looking back to his childhood, Ibsen recalled the lively social life, quite the opposite of what it was to become. There were many cultivated and well-to-do families living in the town and on nearby farms.[7] On a regular basis, traveling troupes of actors would arrive from Denmark to put on plays in the local banqueting hall.

Until he married, Knud had been in the business of exporting lumber to Denmark and England. In 1825 he married into the Altenburg family. It was a marriage more to the groom's liking than the bride's. Marichen Altenburg was in love with a schoolteacher, Tormod Knudsen, who added to his meager earnings by working as a clerk in the sheriff's office. Economically, Tormod and Marichen were not on the same level. Temperamentally, however, they had much in common. She was artistic, played the piano, and painted pictures, and he wanted to raise the cultural level of his fellow citizens.

The Altenburgs owned a fine house in Skien, a distillery in Lundetangen, two ships, a summer residence, and many acres of land. After marrying Marichen, Knud opened a general store specializing in imports, everything from wine to ivory combs, from mustard to capers, from woolen goods to whetstones. He operated the business out of the Stockman house, a fine residence in the center of town, opposite the church. Gradually he put more of his money into wine, and to expand that end of the business he floated a loan in 1828 from a bank in Hamburg, Germany. Henrik Johan was born in that year (a boy born in 1826 had died in infancy), and four more children were to follow. In 1830 Knud's enterprises expanded into another field when his wife inherited the Altenburg distillery after her mother died. From being an importer of wine, he became a producer of hard liquor. The Ibsen family now moved into the Altenburg house (Altenburggården) in Skien, with ten rooms, plus a kitchen and quarters for the servants. It became the scene of lively parties during the next few years.

"There was a steady succession of dances, parties, and musicales throughout the winter and summer," Ibsen recalled in 1881, when he contemplated writing his autobiography. "There were also many travelers who stayed with friends and relatives, since there were no hotels to speak of. We almost always had strangers staying in our roomy house. Especially at Christmas and during the fairs the house was filled with people, and open house was the rule from morning until evening."[8]

In *Peer Gynt*, Ibsen has Peer and his mother bring to mind those happy days, the festivities and the drunken brawls when the guests would smash their drained glasses against the walls. Those were the good years. In 1834 Knud ranked seventeenth on the Skien tax rolls. He was a prosperous businessman, father of a growing family, and generally well liked—"a merry old soul and a witty son-of-a-gun," as one of his friends described him years afterward.[9] He lived in a fine house, owned a distillery, and spent the summers on a farm in the parish of Gjerpen, some miles inland. The place was called Venstøp (the name means, roughly, good pasture on a slope), and he had acquired it for fourteen hundred specie dollars from Jacob Boyesen, a foreman at the Fossum ironworks. The farmhouse, still standing, lies on a rather high plateau, which drops off to the south. Lower down, a mile to the west, was the Fossum estate, owned by Viceroy Severin Løvenskiold, which included iron mines; behind it, as seen from Venstøp, is a rounded hill known as Ulvskollen (Wolf Hill), and toward the north are other mountains. It was in this setting as Ibsen recalled it years later that he first came to grips with his childhood and understood how it shaped his life.

Knud, a lieutenant in the volunteer army, a member of the local rifle club, would often go hunting with Henrick Müller, an apothecary. Little Henrik must

Figure 3. Venstøp, the Ibsen family summer home.

have accompanied them on some of these expeditions. In the scenes in *The Wild Duck* when the Ekdals, father and son, go hunting in the loft of their house, pretending rabbits are bears, and old Ekdal dresses up in his army uniform, Ibsen gleans from all his memories those happy days when father and son were close together.

For it was all too good to last, and when the troubles began they came not as single spies but in battalions. The distillery proved to be in outmoded condition and had to be modernized in order to turn a profit. Knud invested 2,000 specie dollars in this undertaking, and he had no more than done so when two disasters occurred, almost simultaneously. The government demanded payment of the alcohol tax, which had been accumulating, and the Hamburg bank from which Knud had borrowed money in 1828 called in the loan. Short on cash and with a house that already had a lien on it, Knud had no recourse but to sell the distillery, taking a huge loss, selling it for 310 specie dollars. This was in December 1834. Then, only a month later, the mortgage on the house in Skien was foreclosed, and the distillery had to be shut down. From being a well-to-do businessman one year earlier, a leading citizen hosting extravagant parties, he was now poor, unable to pay his taxes and with food so scarce that the potatoes in the storage room were carefully counted out for each meal. And worse was to come. Most of the furniture in the house in Skien had to be sold at auction, while the family took up permanent quarters at Venstøp. What had been bought in 1833 by prosperous

Knud as a summer retreat became in 1835 the Ibsen family home. Knud sometimes did business like a peddler, selling old iron and buying grain, at the estate of Severin Løvenskiold.

For little Henrik, Venstøp with its open fields, surrounding forests, and proximity to iron mines was a playground, a child's paradise. He put on marionette plays, often using paper dolls pasted on wood, for the neighboring children, whom he otherwise ignored. He attended school at nearby Fossum (the name means "by the falls"), a private school maintained for the children of the workers in the mines. The house, two stories high with spacious, well-lit rooms, had a romantic and mysterious aura that excited Henrik's imagination. It had once belonged to a sea captain, Niels Jørgen Hirschholm, who had been captured as a youth by Barbary pirates and held captive for six years before being freed by the English. Some of his possessions were still in the loft. The haunted spirit of this storage room was magically recaptured in *The Wild Duck.*

Since Knud Ibsen was employed in some capacity on the Løvenskiold estate, Henrik probably attended the private school and had access to Løvenskiold's private library. Young Henrik saw two different worlds at close hand: Venstøp and Fossum. When the middle-aged Ibsen wrote *The Wild Duck* he brought the two together, as representing the two sides of his nature. As an expert on Ibsen's early years has pointed out, the description of the set for act one fits the rooms at the Løvenskiold manor house down to small details, just as the storage room in the play has its counterpart in the Venstøp farmhouse.[10]

This idyll came to an end when Henrik began taking classes in 1841 in Skien, some three kilometers away, alternating between a private school and a middle-class school (*borgerskole*). He did not attend the Latin school; with a tuition fee of twenty-three specie dollars a year it was beyond the family's resources.[11] It was probably at this time that Henrik, thirteen years old, felt, as Bernard Shaw did under similar circumstances, the full impact of the family's decline and realized how it would affect his future. A son in a fine family would ordinarily attend the Latin school, although in Skien at this time the Latin school did not have a good reputation. Going to the middle-class school meant that Henrik would take practical courses and study for a trade, not prepare for a university degree by studying the classics.

One of his teachers described Henrik as "a quiet boy with unusual eyes [was the difference in them already noticeable?] and a better-than-average talent for drawing—otherwise without any pronounced quality or aptitude." Another teacher was more perceptive. He remembered Henrik as a "schoolboy with a good head, a deep understanding, a rather touchy disposition, a somewhat cutting manner, a sharp tongue and a satiric temperament, but at the same time friendly and companionable."[12] He was by all accounts better liked by girls his age than by boys. He liked to dance at parties, usually singling out one girl for his attentions. The boys probably felt the sting of his sharp tongue. At any rate, boys his own age sneered at him: "Get out of town and stay out, you meanie!"[13]

In 1843 Knud left the farm in Venstøp and moved back to Skien into a house that had been purchased by his half brother Christopher Blom Paus. Knud was determined to make a new start in business, this time with his younger son Nicolai helping out. He set up his office on the first floor, where there were also rooms for lodgers; the living quarters for the Ibsen family were on the second floor. Unfortunately, the business did not prosper, and Knud's social and economic decline continued, to the embarrassment of the family. The once-successful wholesaler now could do nothing right. Before leaving Venstøp, Knud had applied for the position of customs inspector in Skien. Instead he was appointed collector of the poor tax. In 1843 an administrative official, checking back through the tax records, found that Knud Ibsen had not collected from his fellow citizens the full amount of the poor tax during his tenure as relief officer, 1829 to 1843. Knud was legally responsible for what he had neglected to collect, but in 1843 he was virtually penniless. Predictably, he sought comfort in alcohol, and vented his frustrations by physically abusing his wife.

The fact that Henrik, who was the eldest son, did not join his father in the business venture suggests that he had already decided to leave home and family and pursue a career on his own. In October 1843 he was confirmed in the parish church in Gjerpen. Although he was perfect in his catechism, he was not allowed to be first on the church floor because his father could not afford to follow the customary practice of paying off the dean with a joint of veal.

Ibsen was determined to leave his oppressive home, and even if circumstances had not compelled him, he would have done so on his own initiative. If he could have had his way, he would have studied painting, for which he had a great passion and a small talent, inherited from his mother. In those days, a hopeful Norwegian artist would take up residence in Germany, in Dresden or Düsseldorf, to study the masters. Fortunately for the modern drama, there was no prospect of Ibsen doing that. Had he managed to make a career as a painter the world would have lost a superb dramatist; as it was, the world gained a dramatist with a keen visual sense who would make the sets for his plays speak almost as eloquently and tellingly as the characters.

Opportunity rather than desire determined which profession he would pursue. His father spoke to Mrs. Mülertz, now the widow of Knud's former hunting companion, and she arranged for Henrik to become an apprentice to an apothecary in the town of Grimstad, some eighty miles southwest of Skien. Now bent on a career as a doctor, Henrik sailed from Skien in the late afternoon of November 28[14] on the *Lucky Venture* (*Lykkens Prøve*), a thirty-five-foot-long packet ship with a crew of three, serving the towns along the coast.

As he lost sight of Skien on that cold, dark day, the heartstrings that bound him to his family snapped. In one of his poems, "On the Heights" ("Paa Vidderne"), written in 1859 when he was still an unknown, the narrator witnesses, horrified, the burning of his family home at Christmastime. But his traveling companion, his alter ego, watches the events through the hollow of his hand in order to compose the scene artistically, and the poet confesses to being enthralled by the effect of the bright flames against the night sky.

From that moment when the *Lucky Venture* sailed out of the Skien harbor during the Christmas holidays, there would always be two Ibsens warring against each other, one longing for things as they once were, the other longing to escape the stifling atmosphere of an unhappy home. From that moment he began to lift himself to those chilly heights where the artist's mind would control the heart.

He arrived in Grimstad on November 29, dressed in his best outfit, his confirmation clothes, including a jacket with two long tails. Grimstad lived up to its name (originally Grømstad). With only eight hundred inhabitants, it was considerably smaller than Skien. Its crooked streets were unlit at night. There was only one teacher in town, no water system, and the sewage ran down the middle of the street. Most of the inhabitants had investments in sailing ships.

The apothecary where Ibsen was first employed occupied the lower floor of a two-story frame house with small windowpanes. Ibsen's room was on the second floor. This shop was the only apothecary between Kristiansand and Arendal, a forty-mile stretch.[15] The owner, J. A. Reimann, sold liquors and spices, handled the mail, and functioned as a shipping agent. It was like a general store in a small town in the American West, a popular gathering place.

Ibsen told jokes, played cards, painted landscapes, and read a great deal. He was often up until two in the morning, reading and writing.[16] He quickly gained a reputation as an agnostic, a cynic, a spouter of paradoxes. With black bangs hanging down his forehead, he presented a rather sinister appearance that frightened children, while his irresistible urge to deflate pomposity and unmask hypocrisy disturbed his elders. A religious man, hoping to bring Ibsen back into the fold, gave him a book of sermons to read.

"I can never get my fill from reading this book," was his recommendation.

"If you can't get your fill," replied Ibsen, "it certainly can't have much nutritive value."[17]

On the subject of marriage he opined, "The ideal marriage is to have the two partners living on different floors, addressing each other formally, and seeing each other only at the dinner table."[18]

But the new man in town also found congenial friends. There was Captain Niels Peter Nielsen, through whom Ibsen had access to the local reading society (there was no public library), and Nielsen's son Lars, who purchased the Reimann apothecary. Ibsen ate his midday meal at the Nielsen house. The captain was a great talker, with a fund of tales about his adventures at sea. There were also young men of Ibsen's age who dropped in at the shop to relish his biting tongue and iconoclastic views. Two of them, Ole Schulerud (1827–59), a law student, and Christopher Due (1827–1923), a customs officer at the harbor and a would-be poet, were so impressed by Ibsen that they were directly instrumental in getting his first play published. Among others who befriended the newcomer was Andreas Isaachsen, son of a schoolmaster, who would later become an actor. There were elderly women, like pious Mrs. Nielsen, who sensed his genius, and Miss Georgiana Crawfurd, a Scottish woman, whom he met at Captain Nielsen's house. She opened her excellent library to him. In appreciation Ibsen gave her some of his poems to read. He also had access through his friends to the local readers' society, well stocked with the popular books of the time.[19] There were proper young women, such as Clara Ebbell, to whom he sent romantic poems. And in the natural course of things there had to be a not-so-proper young woman, who would bring trouble.

Her name was Else Sofie Jensen. She was a servant to the apothecary's family and lived above the shop, where Henrik also had his room. The cold of winter and the lack of any heating apparatus in their quarters undoubtedly stirred fires within the two young people. He was a callow teenager, and she was an experienced woman some ten years older. In October 1846 she gave birth in her parents' home to Ibsen's son and promptly applied to the authorities for child support, naming him as father. Ibsen's letter responding to the inquiry of the town judge, dated December 7, is a pathetic document.

"Called upon by Your Honor to declare whether I affirm or deny that I am father to the male child christened Hans Jacob last October 25 and born to the maid Else Sophie Jensdatter Birkedalen, I herewith respectfully inform you that, notwithstanding the fact that other men have had intercourse with the said maid during the time in question, I did have carnal connection with her, occasioned as much by her flirtatious behavior as by her residing with me in Apothecary Reimann's house.

"I am now in my twentieth year [he was actually eighteen, going on nineteen]. I have no possessions, apart from some ordinary clothes, shoes and linen. In the near future I shall be leaving the apothecary in Grimstad, at which place I have lived since the summer [*sic*] of 1843, with no other payment than my room and board. My still-living father, to whom I necessarily first turned for help, is one of the lesser merchants in Skien and finds himself in very moderate circumstances."[20]

As the father of an illegitimate child, Ibsen was compelled by law to help pay for its support for fourteen years, until it reached the age of confirmation: 8 specie dollars a year for the first eight years, lesser amounts in the following years, all adding up to 105 specie dollars. (A common laborer made about 50 a year.) Because of his poverty, he was usually in arrears and hounded by the authorities, even twice threatened with hard labor in prison (*Kronarbeide*), until 1862, when, age thirty-four, he made the last payment. The payments were a constant reminder to him of the wages of sin, and for the rest of his life he regarded physical sex as dangerous and frightening, not as a joy and consolation. In his first play, *Catiline*, about a political revolutionary, it is sex more than politics that undoes the hero. In *Peer Gynt* Ibsen immortalized Else Birkedalen as the Woman in Green (described as being in labor in the autumn), who seduces Peer, leading him down the path of dalliance away from his true love. In *Ghosts*, sex is both incestuous and insidiously destructive. And on those occasions when love is praised, it is always elevated, idealized, and detached from that particular carnal connection that added to the woes of the young Henrik. Though Ibsen would have a lot to say about love, he never wrote a truly erotic scene.

In 1847 he was certified as an apothecary, and though he may have entertained fleeting hopes of becoming a doctor, he had already set his mind on a career as a writer.

In 1848 in a poem, "Doubt and Hope" ("Tvivl og Haab"), Ibsen described himself as lost in a sea of doubt, no longer possessing the innocence of a child but hoping that he might find his childhood faith restored. At the same time, like a true romantic poet, he "had a burning desire for—I almost *prayed* for a great sorrow that might fill my existence, give meaning to my life."[21]

> Yet I must not let myself despair,
> Must listen to the promptings of my heart.
> Yes, there is hope, I must cling to that
> And have faith in my dear God.
> Though the storm winds howl and shriek,
> I shall fall asleep in peace—
> If only I might wake again
> Reborn in my childhood faith.[22]

When Ibsen left Grimstad for the capital city, Christiania, in the hope of entering the university there, the years that had the greatest impact on his psychological makeup came to an end. The humiliations he endured because of the collapse of the family's fortunes would never be completely banished from his thoughts, the mortification never forgotten. Although he tried to begin a new life by breaking with his family, he could never rid himself of his memories; they figure prominently in his dramas and explain his extraordinary sensitivity to social slights, real or imagined. The degradation suffered by himself and his parents in his youth had to be wiped out by the fame he would achieve, the honors he would receive, and the place he would take among society's aristocracy.

The early careers of Shakespeare and Ibsen are so uncannily similar as to be worth some comment. Shakespeare's father, John, married Mary Arden, of an old, established, well-to-do family. She inherited considerable property in 1556. John became a prosperous merchant and property owner during the period 1566 to 1577. He held various municipal offices and at one time owned two houses. His fortunes declined, rather suddenly, about 1577. In that year, at age thirteen, William had to leave school and find work. In 1579 John was forced to mortgage some of his wife's property. He lost his standing in the community, was fined for failing to keep the peace, sank ever deeper into debt, and was dismissed from his position as alderman. All this finds a close parallel in the early formative years of Ibsen's life. Both dramatists sought almost obsessively to restore the family honor. As soon as he possibly could, in 1596, Shakespeare secured a coat of arms for the family name. Ben Jonson, among others, ridiculed his rival playwright for trying to buy a place in the aristocracy. Similarly, Ibsen's vanity about the honors he had received, and sometimes begged for, was a source of amusement among those who knew him, especially when he pinned the medals on his chest instead of the ribbons, as was customary. Both men succeeded in making drama one of the highest forms of artistic expression. Both became rich.

The division within Ibsen between the poor boy and the rich boy created by the collapse of the family fortunes would always be a source of bitterness and of an ambivalent attitude toward both family and society, always leading him to hate and mistrust what he wanted to be part of. It was fame and immortality that would, in his mind, restore the family fortunes, redeem the Ibsen name, and allow him to enter the Eden from which he had been cast out. That was the social solution to his plight. But how to resolve the conflict within himself? That was to be the work of many years. His first effort along those lines was *Catiline*. When he had finished that, he knew he was destined to be a writer and not a doctor.

In April 1850, the month in which *Catiline* came off the presses, he traveled to Skien, sailing on the steamship *Prince Carl*, with the hope of borrowing money from his half uncle Christopher Blom Paus. This was not the first time he had returned to Skien after his departure in 1843. He had gone back in 1845 for the confirmation of his younger brother Johan and had stayed for a month. But his visit in 1850 was to be his last, and what he saw probably determined him never to return. He experienced firsthand the melancholy atmosphere of his parents' home. He could see how the breach between his parents had widened. His father, immune to the revivalist fever, was drinking heavily, borrowing money from his half brother Christopher, becoming cynical and sarcastic, resenting the success of others, unable to hold a position, and being repeatedly hauled before the civil court for nonpayment of his debts.

His mother had withdrawn from her original social sphere, and she and her children Hedvig and Johan had, perhaps as a consolation for their loss of standing in Skien, become involved in the activities of a pietistic sect led by Gustav Adolph Lammers, a tall, stately evangelist with an orator's voice. Influenced by the Moravian Brethren, he found many in Skien, mostly women, who were willing to listen to him as he urged them to abandon the official religion and to deny the efficacy of infant baptism. In the 1850s, thanks to Lammers, Skien became notorious for its pietism. A meetinghouse was built in 1853, and in 1856 Lammers left the state church and established his "free apostolic-Christian" congregation. His inflammatory sermons brought strife and dissension to the town's inhabitants. Ibsen's mother, his sister, and his brother Ole left the Lutheran church to join Lammers's movement.[23]

What Ibsen felt in 1850 probably informs some lines he wrote years later. When he caught sight of his mother's house, his chest tightened as he felt the "terror of home." He felt tied to something outside himself. Half his strength was taken from him under the pressure of having to belong. The great things he dreamed of doing became strangers to him. He became, in his own words, a shorn Samson in a harlot's lap.[24] And again years later, while meditating on *The Wild Duck*, he noted that a child's first and deepest sorrows "are not cares about love; no, they are family sorrows—the painful circumstances at home."[25]

The bitterness Ibsen felt toward his parents and his home is extraordinary, out of proportion to what a bare recital of the facts suggests. But his feelings are made clear in both his words and deeds. He looked upon his mother as a materialist who did not marry the man she loved, settling instead for a clever man with a knack for business. He rejected his father because his father's mistakes made him a poor boy. Yet he could not help but sympathize with his parents. They were part of a society in which such things happened. He saw the contradiction in his attitude: he disliked his father for losing money and his mother for marrying to keep it. This was bourgeois existence as Ibsen saw it. The only way to resolve the basic paradox of middle-class existence was to rise above it.

Before leaving Skien, he went for a walk with his younger (by four years) sister, Hedvig, the family member he was always closest to. They climbed to the top of a hill outside the town. As they stood there in the ruins of an old conventual church, he spoke to her of his dreams and aspirations.

"I want to reach the utmost limit in the way of greatness and insight."

"And when you have attained that, then what would you want to do?"

"Then I would want to die."[26]

His parents never saw him again. His father, as an aged, impoverished man, would stretch out his arms and cry, "Henrik, my dear boy, my son Henrik, come home to your old dad."[27]

He never sent money home, not even when he had become successful and prosperous. He did write to his father once, on February 25, 1875, a letter that does not survive because Knud caressed and fondled it out of existence. Like a holy relic, it disintegrated from being handled too much. He sent a reply to it, calling it "a rarity, since I haven't heard or seen anything of you, as you say in your letter, in 25 years." He says he has, however, heard from his son over the years through his works.[28]

Ibsen's bitterness toward his father and the childhood years of poverty festered in him. He never forgot that when he was a boy, his father had not paid him the promised dollar for planting potatoes.[29] And when he learned in 1886 that a large part of Skien had burned and the city was devastated, his satisfied comment was: "The citizens of Skien were quite unworthy to possess my birthplace."[30]

Time did little to temper Ibsen's bitter memories. In the 1890s in Christiania at a small party, Chamberlain Løvenskiold invited the world-famous author to visit him at Fossum. At first Ibsen accepted the offer, but a short while later he declined. It had become clear to him that if he stayed at Fossum, he would be obliged to visit Skien and relive those painful early years.[31]

The Apprentice

In the waiting room of the apothecary, Ibsen would often amuse fellow young people by making fun of some of Grimstad's senior citizens, drawing caricatures of them or improvising rhymed verses. But he was also composing serious poems, and by 1850 he had a portfolio of them. By this time he had decided to abandon medicine for literature. His good friend Christopher Due, who was the Grimstad correspondent for *Christiania-Posten*, placed one of the poems, "In the Autumn" ("I Høsten"), in the September 28, 1849, issue of that newspaper. It was a melancholy poem conjuring up gravestones and invoking lost hopes. But it made Ibsen happy. For the first time he saw one of his works in print. Due said that when Ibsen read the poem, he first turned pale, then glowed with satisfaction.[1] Ibsen commemorated the moment a few years later in a poem called "Building Plans" ("Byggeplaner").

> I recall so well, as if it were yesterday,
> The time I saw my first poem in print.
> I sat in my cozy room, puffing away,
> Smoking my pipe, so happy and self-contented.
>
> I hummed to myself and read for the twentieth time
> That page which I found so especially interesting.
> And my imagination played its part, ranging freely.
> Good Lord, dreaming is also part of life.[2]

In trying to improve his Latin in preparation for the entrance examinations, he read the speeches of Cicero. What he found in them was the direct opposite of what Cicero intended. The twenty-year-old Ibsen was a rebel who had broken with his family, separated himself from the teachings and beliefs of his childhood. He was a godless young man who had allied himself with the radical element in the small town where he was learning the apothecary's trade, and who was fired with enthusiasm for the revolutions that had swept through Europe in 1848.

When he read Cicero's speeches deprecating the rebel Catiline, Ibsen sided with the rebel. Slandered by the consuls in Rome and impeached by one of them, Catiline planned a coup d'état with some other disgruntled politicians. The plot was betrayed, and Catiline was arrested. Cicero presided over the trial and pronounced a harsh verdict that smacked more of vindictiveness than justice. The standard edition of Cicero used in Norwegian schools bore on its title page a motto from the Roman historian Sallust: "This history I consider particularly memorable by virtue of the unheard-of crimes and threats it presents." Young Henrik found a kindred soul in this rebel who fought for the underprivileged at a time when the Republic was in financial straits, with widespread unemployment and a large number of dispossessed peasants. If he came to power, Catiline promised, all debts would be forgiven and all wealthy citizens would be proscribed. As depicted by Sallust and Cicero in the accounts that Ibsen read, Catiline was a vicious, power-mad demagogue. Ibsen took the contrary view and saw "something distinctly great and significant" in the man "whom Cicero, that indefatigable spokesman of the majority, was careful not to tackle until circumstances had so changed that there was no longer any danger in attacking him."[3] Ibsen's position was that Catiline had been denigrated by history; his posthumous reputation lay entirely in the hands of his enemies. In Georgiana Crawfurd's well-stocked library, Ibsen may have come across Voltaire's dictum that recorded history is a pack of tricks with which we cheat the dead, a cynical view that would have won Ibsen's assent.[4] The ancient chroniclers, thoroughly conservative in outlook and squarely on the side of the landowners and officeholders, could hardly be expected to deal fairly with the insurrectionist who sought to overthrow them by armed force.

Ibsen's hero, however, is hardly an admirable man fighting for the rights of the populace. Although meant as a corrective to the prevailing image, his Catiline is far from a noble defender of the disenfranchised and dispossessed. His motives are highly selfish. He emerges from Ibsen's pen as a man determined to avenge himself on a world that has not treated him fairly. He seeks to destroy rather than build, to tyrannize over a society that does not submit to his views. *Fiat justitia ruat cœlum* (Let justice be done though the heavens may fall) could well serve as his motto, as long as it is understood that justice for him meant recognition of his greatness.

Doubtless, what appealed to Ibsen was Sallust's description of the revolutionary. "Lucius Catilina, scion of a noble family, had great vigour both of mind and of body, but an evil and depraved nature. From youth up he reveled in civil wars, murder, pillage, and political dissension, and amid these he spent his early manhood. His body could endure hunger, cold and want of sleep to an incredible degree; his mind was reckless, cunning, treacherous, capable of any form of pretence and concealment. . . . His disordered mind ever craved the monstrous, incredible, gigantic."[5]

Sounding like Hitler in his Berlin bunker, Catiline rants, "If the great Rome of the golden days cannot be raised again with this hand, the Rome of our days must perish! Soon, where now the marble pillars stand row on row, pillars of smoke will rise from crackling flames. Palaces, temples shall crumble into dust, and the Capitol itself shall topple from its height."

Resolving to lead the revolt, he draws his sword, shouting, "Revenge it shall be! Victory and long life to all my dreams of greatness, tyrannical power, and eternal fame!"[6]

Only later, in the company of his fellow conspirators, does he speak of a higher mission, freedom for the citizens of Rome. As a Norwegian critic has well argued, the structure of the play and its principal concern derive essentially from the contradictions in Ibsen's soul, not from his political views or his sympathy with the revolutions in Europe.

"It is not the social side of the February Revolution [of 1848] that is on display in this drama," comments the Norwegian scholar Francis Bull. "Henrik Ibsen, the son of a bankrupt businessman, felt like a déclassé aristocrat and would hardly have been inspired by an insurrection carried out by Roman plebes or slaves, such as Spartacus's. By contrast, Catiline was a revolutionary of the nobility who had been driven out of his proper social sphere. In his mouth Ibsen could put some of the anger and indignation that he felt toward the ruling pillars of society."[7]

Ibsen was drawn to the character of Catiline because it was sharply divided like his own. Catiline aimed high and embraced noble ideals, but the inner man and outer circumstances prevented him from fulfilling himself. Ibsen's Catiline is a self-portrait, that of a loner, an outsider, whose overriding desire is to win undying fame, whatever the cost. His impelling fear is that he will die without having done anything truly great and remarkable. The drama presents a state of mind, in the manner of Byron's *Manfred*, and the action can be staged as a subjective drama, the inner struggle of opposing forces, played out against an abstract set of black curtains or drapes, since the Roman setting counts for so little.

The conflict within Catiline is projected onto two women, Furia and Aurelia, both of whom he loves. Catiline invades the temple of the Vestal virgins in pursuit of Furia, whose mere glance has bewitched him. She vows to give herself to him if in return he will take revenge on the man who raped her sister. He swears to do so. Furia goads him into rebelling against society and taking up a life of resounding deeds and unremitting struggle. Like him, she has been deprived of the joys of youth, and because of that her hatred of the world is carried to the point of willful, malicious destruction. She wants vengeance and is able to enlist Catiline on her side because in part he is the cause of her unhappiness.

In a revelation that brings to mind Sophocles's *Oedipus Rex*, in which the criminal pursues himself, we learn that it was Catiline who defiled Furia's sister. This means he must take revenge on himself, a rather too neat demonstration of the self-consuming nature of vengeance. Calling her his Nemesis, Catiline recognizes Furia as his genius and the image of his soul.

Opposed to this dark angel is Aurelia, who speaks for the domestic life, urging Catiline to forget about great deeds and everlasting fame. But, driven by a need to overcome his disgrace, to wipe from the Roman faces the scorn and open contempt he sees there, and to punish Rome for its ingratitude to him, he chooses to follow his evil angel.

At the end of the play, Furia attempts to draw Catiline, a defeated man, betrayed by his coconspirators, into her realm of darkness, but Aurelia arrives on the scene to offer him love and affection. He repulses her because she offers him only a life of petty fears and inhibitions in which he would be a nonentity. While the heavens roar with thunder, he stabs her with his dagger. However, her love for him keeps her alive and dispels the darkness. As daylight breaks, Catiline hands the dagger to Furia, who thrusts it into his breast. He breathes his last on Aurelia's breast, while Furia literally fades away among the trees in the background.

"I lived my life at night, horribly lit by flashes of lightning," murmurs Catiline, "but the rose-colored dawn is my death."[8]

The symbolic import of *Catiline* is the same as that of the poem "Fear of the Light." Only in the dark can Catiline make a name for himself. As a first play, the work is remarkable in that the author's personality impregnates every line. Although the influence of the German romantics is obvious, none of them could have written this unrelievedly tenebrous and gloomy drama (nearly all the scenes take place at night, and Ibsen wrote it at night when his daily chores as an apothecary's apprentice were done). Even Francis Moor, the satanic villain in Schiller's equally youthful drama *The Robbers*, would have felt himself a stranger in Catiline's godless and conscienceless universe, in which the only sin is a sin of omission, failing to make an indelible impression on earth before taking leave of it.

Although Ibsen said he wrote *Catiline* to set the record straight and to give the Roman conspirator his due, his imagination created a series of events that have little to do with the known facts. As he admitted in a note tagged on to the end of the printed play, he abandoned the historical account in order to write a free improvisation on Catiline's fate. As such, it provides the perfect introduction to his later work, in which the history of European culture will form the background to the action. The play is set in a primordial, inchoate Europe without any firm sense of time or place, the Roman names notwithstanding. In *Catiline*, modern Europe is about to give birth to itself, while the newborn playwright finds a way of giving shape to his obsessions. Catiline's world is a bare, stripped-down, simple place, an anti-Eden, where death is ever present, where the only energizing forces are fame and revenge, and the closest approximation to peace and happiness is freedom from obsession. Even Ibsen was astonished when, twenty-five years after he had written it, he discovered that in it he had adumbrated the principal themes of his later works: the conflict between aspirations and ability, between dreams and reality. And many years later, in 1896, in his next-to-last drama, *John Gabriel Borkman*, Furia and Aurelia appear again in the guise of the twin sisters who fight for the soul of Borkman.

More precisely, what this play, as autobiography, tells us is that Ibsen will be on a war footing with society until he finds his Aurelia, his golden girl, his Stella. He will be a negative force, fighting against society and the establishment until he regains his rightful place in it, perfectly willing to destroy it if he cannot be a part of it. The real problem that Ibsen had to deal with was not the banal one of the possible in conflict with the impossible, of high hopes and mortal powers, but a more fascinating problem: How can the rebel at war with society become its hero? How can the negative force, bent on destruction, become a positive, creative force?

Ibsen's departure from Skien for Christiania was planned so he would arrive there in time to capitalize on the publication of *Catiline*. It was issued on April 12, and Ibsen arrived in the capital on April 28.

He joined his Skien friend and backer, Ole Schulerud, who had found lodging in a rooming house in an unsavory part of town by the waterfront. Their landlady, Mother Sæter, in addition to letting rooms, was a medical quack and bone setter. Evidently the two young men found their mean and shabby quarters unsuitable for a budding genius, and they soon moved to a better section of town.

Ibsen spent May, June, and July studying for the university matriculation examinations. Like many others he took a cram course at a private school. Among his fellow crammers was his future literary rival, Bjørnstjerne Bjørnson, who years later described his classmate in a poem.

> Overstrained and lean, the color of gypsum,
> Behind a beard, huge and coal-black, was Ibsen.[9]

If a candidate failed any part of the examinations but maintained a passing average in all three parts, he would be admitted to the university with the proviso that he make up the subjects he had failed. Although Ibsen failed Greek, oral Latin, and esthetics, his overall score entitled him to provisional matriculation, which meant that he could attend lectures. It also meant that he had earned the title of student, which in the Scandinavian caste system brought him up a rung or two on the social ladder. (His position as a *Student* almost certainly saved him from a period of incarceration for nonpayment of child support.)[10] Of the approximately one hundred candidates taking the examination in 1850, the overwhelming majority came from families in which a university education was traditional. Of the eight candidates, including Ibsen, who passed only conditionally, all came from less privileged families.[11]

Ibsen never attempted to make up the subjects he had failed. A university degree had never been his main object. He lacked the money, the social background, and the inclination to be part of the free-living university crowd. He had resolved to be a writer, and the move to Christiania was intended to put him in a literary environment.

Catiline was lauded in the student paper, possibly because of its novelty. It was the first original play to be published in Norway in seven years, and new literary works were not exactly plentiful. During the period from 1814 to 1847, the 441 belletristic works that came off the presses were far outnumbered by 591 works on theology.[12]

Encouraged by the praise the play received, Ibsen took to heart the admonition of the reviewer that he should mine the vein of the almost untouched Norwegian history rather than recycle the all-too-familiar Roman chronicles. Ibsen quickly dashed off a one-act play, *The Warrior's Barrow* (*Kjæmpehøien*), in which the Viking code of revenge clashes with the new Christian spirit of mercy. Unlike *Catiline*, it was written without conviction, meant to please others and not himself. It was the first of Ibsen's plays to be staged (1850).

Although he was destitute and deeply in arrears on his child-support payments, hounded by the sheriff and threatened with imprisonment, these were heady times for Ibsen. After the dreariness of Grimstad and the long hours spent in the apothecary, he was free to do what meant most to him: to write. He now had one play published and another performed. The students chose him to edit their paper. And he was keeping company with young men who provided him with the intellectual stimulus he needed. Among them were Paul Botten-Hansen (1824–69), an avid book collector, who eventually possessed the largest private library in Norway, fourteen thousand volumes when he died; and Aasmund Olavsson Vinje, an odd character, ten years older than Ibsen, with an ironic personality that appealed to him. The three of them were university irregulars, Botten-Hansen and Vinje being sons of tenant farmers, while Ibsen was the son of an uneducated and now impoverished businessman. Together they founded a satiric journal called *Andhrimmer* (in Norse mythology, Andhrimmer was the cook in Valhalla), which during its short life, January to September 1851, had an antiestablishment and prolabor point of view.

There were two wings to the labor movement, which now was becoming highly vocal and organized. The moderate wing, led by Theodor Abildgaard, a law student at the University of Christiania, believed in revolution by means of the ballot and called for universal suffrage. The radical and more aggressive wing was led by Marcus Thrane, the son of a prosperous self-made merchant. Abildgaard's device was "Brothers, love one another!" Thrane's was "Strength through unity." In the wake of the 1848 European revolutions, Thrane had brought eighteen thousand Norwegian workers into his movement, and thirteen thousand of them had signed a petition addressed to the king of Norway and Sweden asking for an extension of suffrage, better schooling for the common man, and property rights for tenant farmers (this at a time when three-fifths of Norway's population worked the land, and nine-tenths of them lived in rural areas). Thrane's objective was to gather all the workers—farmers, tenant farmers, factory employees, and artisans—into one association that he called the "third estate."[13]

In the latter half of 1850 Thrane grew more confident, knowing that two-thirds of the industrial workers were behind him.[14] At a congress in Christiania in August of that year he forced a vote on a question that would determine the direction the movement would take. Were they going to recognize the sacredness of property rights or not? They voted against property.

Ibsen became involved in the labor movement through his friendship with Abildgaard, whom he had met at Mother Sæter's rooming house. He tutored a class in Abildgaard's Sunday school for workers, and he contributed some unsigned articles for Abildgaard's paper.[15] In *Andhrimmer*, during the critical months of the labor movement in 1851, he and his fellow editors criticized Thrane for advocating open rebellion, for advancing too rapidly and outrunning the ordinary citizen. In old age, Ibsen said that although he had admired Thrane for his energy and commitment, he could not embrace his ideas, which shifted too often.[16]

It is true that the conservative reaction against the labor movement had been increasing as Thrane became more aggressive. A confrontation was inevitable. Misjudging both the mood of the populace and the strength of the reactionaries, Thrane and Abildgaard organized a demonstration at the opening of the Norwegian parliament to celebrate the third anniversary of the 1848 February uprisings. The Norwegian viceroy, Severin Løvenskiold (who owned the ironworks at Fossum where Ibsen had briefly gone to school), got wind of the demonstration and called in the police. This proved to be a turning point. The leading liberal in parliament, A. B. Stabell, sensed the change in the country's mood. He abandoned his support of the workers, signaling the end of both Thrane and Abildgaard. In July 1851 they and one hundred workers were arrested. Abildgaard was held in custody for three years before standing trial. Found guilty of crimes against the state, he was sentenced to four years at hard labor, as was Thrane.

Ibsen played only a small part in all this. Before the crackdown on the laborites, he wrote a political squib, *Norma*, based on Bellini's opera, satirizing the vacillations of the liberals. After the arrest of Abildgaard, Ibsen spent a few anxious hours, knowing that the police had broken into the labor leader's office in search of incriminating documents. Fortunately, the clever foreman of the printing shop had strewn most of the manuscripts on the floor as if they were trash.[17] But Ibsen, ever prudent, did not continue to teach at Abildgaard's Sunday school for workers.

As a political agitator, Ibsen was no Catiline. As a young poet and dramatist, remembering the rich boy who had come down in the world, he could fantasize about violent acts of rebellion and imagine himself destroying the pillars of society. In practice, he settled for a position above the fray where specific political issues, such as suffrage and the property rights of tenant farmers, played no part. He settled for innocuous platitudes and palatable generalizations. It was Abildgaard's rectitude that made a deep and lasting impression on him, not his specific proposals, and he had Abildgaard in mind when a quarter of a century later he wrote the concluding lines of *Pillars of Society*, hailing the spirits of truth and freedom as the true pillars of society.[18]

The only political demonstration in which Ibsen participated took place in Christiania in 1850 and concerned freedom of speech. A writer named Harro Harring was shipped out of Norway by the police for being the author of an antiauthoritarian play, *Testament from America*. Ibsen joined the crowd at the docks to protest his treatment.[19]

Having had his brush with the law and seen at close hand the dangers of involvement with the class conflict, Ibsen in his search for a worthwhile political cause moved to safer ground: Norwegian nationalism. It was a wise choice that would lead him back to playwriting.

As a consequence of the rearrangement of European states brought about by the Napoleonic wars, Norway had been under the Swedish crown since 1814. Although Norwegians had been allowed to promulgate their own written constitution, and although they had their own representative body, the Storting (parliament), they were always made to feel subservient to the Swedish king, who retained veto power over the acts of the Norwegian legislature. Recalling their days of glory, when their Viking ancestors ruled the seas from the Arctic Ocean to the

Mediterranean, and heartened by the recent burgeoning of their worldwide shipping interests, the Norwegians were fired by nationalistic zeal and determined to shake off their Swedish fetters. Beginning in the 1830s, as part of this assertion of national pride, there was an extraordinary upsurge of interest in painting and music, in historical and sociological studies, and in poetry and linguistics.

Ibsen took advantage of all of it. Jørgen Moe and Peter Christian Asbjørnsen gathered Norwegian folktales (1841–44); Ibsen found his Peer Gynt among them. M. B. Landstad collected native ballads that captured the soul of the people; Ibsen tried to do the same in lyric dramas like *Olaf Liljekrans*. The poets Henrik Wergeland and Johan Welhaven romanticized Norwegian nature in verse; Ibsen mimicked them in his own poetry. Painters like Fearnley, Cappelen, Tidemand, and Gude, though trained in Germany, rendered in oils the fjords and pine forests of Norway, the rocky plateaus and icy streams, the farmers and fishermen. Ibsen, as early as 1842, did an aquarelle of a farm near Skien, and later painted fjords and waterfalls and did sketches of peasant types. Ludvig Lindeman traveled the length of Norway setting down the music of Norwegian folk dances, paving the way for serious composers like Edvard Grieg. Ibsen asked Grieg to compose the incidental music for *Peer Gynt*. P. A. Munch compiled the history of Norway in eight thick volumes. Ibsen drew on them for his first masterpiece, *The Pretenders*. Ivar Aasen analyzed the different Norwegian dialects and edited a dictionary (1850). Ibsen preferred Dano-Norwegian, the literary language, and in *Peer Gynt* he ridiculed the nativists.

The virtuoso violinist Ole Bull, mainly self-taught but modeling his technique on that of Paganini, included Norwegian folk tunes in his repertory. His Scandinavian spirit brought something fresh into the violin repertory, and, touring Europe and America, he amassed a small fortune. Back in Norway, he was infected by the nationalistic fervor and decided to use some of his wealth to establish a theater in Bergen, his hometown. It was to be a Norwegian theater with Norwegian actors performing Norwegian plays, in opposition to the existing theaters that produced foreign plays with Danish actors. In its first season, 1850–51, the theater gave eighty-seven performances.

Having launched with his own money an enterprise that attracted the public, Bull applied to the Storting for a government subvention. When his request for funding was rejected, he appealed directly to the Norwegian citizenry for support. In September 1851 a fundraising campaign was launched in Christiania. At a meeting of the student literary society, Ibsen spoke for an hour urging the establishment of a national theater. At a party held in the Freemason Temple in October, hundreds filled the hall to overflowing for an evening of food, liquor, and entertainment. Ibsen wrote a "prologue" to celebrate the occasion, and also a poem, "The Power of Art" ("Kunstens Magt"), which was set to music by Bull.[20] The next morning the sponsors of the affair found they had cleared three hundred specie dollars, enough to guarantee a second season of theater in Bergen. A. O. Vinje, Ibsen's fellow editor on *Andhrimmer*, had introduced him to Bull, and now Bull assured the young writer that there would be a place for him in the new theatrical venture. On November 6, 1851, Ibsen signed a contract that would pay him twenty specie dollars a month for six months, with the understanding that he would write plays for Bull's theater.[21]

Five months earlier, in a play review in *Manden* (before it was called *Andhrimmer*), Ibsen had scorned the idea of a national theater on the ground that the public did not deserve one. If the tastes of the theatergoing public were to be gratified, then "Goodnight, ye muses!"[22] But in September the taste of the public was no longer a consideration, and willy-nilly the would-be journalist and lyric poet was forced back into the theater, if not by fate, then by financial pressures. The summer had not been productive, and Ibsen had written very little. He was often surly, morose, and ill-tempered, as it grew more obvious day by day that he could not support himself by his writing. The little money he had saved while in Grimstad by going without decent clothes—sans coat, sans stockings, sans underwear—had long since vanished. So was the money he had borrowed from his half uncle in Skien. And the income from *Catiline* had provided only one good meal for himself and Ole Schulerud, who, along with Christopher Due, had paid half the costs of printing. Out of the 250 copies printed, only as few as 30 or as many as 45 were purchased.[23]

Quite a few copies were sold as wrapping paper, and on the proceeds Schulerud and Ibsen dined out in style. Ibsen, reminiscing years later, said that for "the next few days we lacked none of the necessities of life."[24] Usually, however, they left their rooms at dinnertime to deceive their neighbors, only to return for a very modest supper of coffee, bread and butter, and cheese. The unhappy fact was that Ibsen in the autumn of 1851 was totally dependent on Schulerud for food and lodging. And always hanging over his head was the threat of imprisonment for nonpayment of the support money for his illegitimate child. In September the officers of the law were demanding six specie dollars from him. Nonpayment could mean 102 days at hard labor. From 1859 to 1864 there were thirteen legal proceedings against Ibsen for debt. A tailor's bill from 1858 was still not paid in 1860.

On October 16, Ibsen sailed with Bull from Christiania to Kristianstad, traveling first class. Bull paid the fare, six specie dollars each. Ibsen then proceeded alone to Bergen, arriving there on October 21, 1851.

THE FAILURE

Although Bergen was not the largest city in Norway—its population was only half that of Christiania—it was the proper place for a national theater. Its old buildings, including a Romanesque church and a fort dating back to the thirteenth century, were ever-present reminders of a heroic past when Norway ruled the northern seas and Bergen was a part of the Hanseatic League. With its natural setting on a promontory, its streets lined with linden trees, the hills surrounding the harbor dotted with houses painted red and yellow, it was the most attractive city in Norway. Fully aware of the natural charms of their city and of its historical significance, the native Bergenites were a proud lot, who spoke their own dialect of Norwegian and were notoriously unrestrained in expressing their feelings.

Praised as a tourist attraction in European travel guides, Bergen, only a few miles from the spectacular Hardanger Fjord, oddly enough lacked a decent hotel. The standard English guide, *Norway and Its Scenery* (London, 1853), highly recommended "the accommodations offered in the house of Mrs. Helene Sontum, who entertains travellers in all the comfort to be found in a well-conducted family." Upon his arrival in Bergen in October 1851, Ibsen found a room in this house and boarded there for several months. Subsequently, he was given two rooms in the theater building as living quarters, but he continued to dine at Mrs. Sontum's table during all his Bergen years. She became a mother to him, giving him both financial aid and spiritual comfort. He was to portray her later in his comedy *The League of Youth* as the full-bosomed, good-hearted Madame Rundholmen, and her granddaughter was to become the great love of Ibsen's last years. The Sontums served as a substitute for the family he had disowned. While he did not keep in touch with his own parents, he maintained contact with the Sontums his entire life.

Although Ibsen had been brought to Bergen to write plays, he was paid a salary as stage manager and assistant director. He had to share the work of putting on a play with Herman Laading, the principal of the Bergen middle-class school, fifteen years older than Ibsen, a tall, gentlemanly, well-educated native of the town, where all doors were open to him. Ibsen was his opposite in nearly all respects: a newcomer, poor, a bit disreputable, odd in figure and manner. He once tried to bridge the gap by challenging Laading to a duel. Years later, Ibsen described the difference in 1851 between his immature, insecure, gauche self and the urbane Laading.

"At that time I found myself in a state of ferment that did not allow me to commit myself completely and openly to anyone. Nor had I any real understanding of myself; and this may explain, though it does not excuse, a great deal of my tomfoolery and crazy doings. *You*, by contrast, were already a complete man, and that put a certain distance between us."[1]

The theatrical conditions under which Ibsen worked were undergoing a radical change in the mid-nineteenth century. Both acting and stage lighting became more realistic. The rapid turnover of a play about every week or two meant that each new production could be rehearsed onstage only three or four times, and performed perhaps two times. Actors had to be quick studies, but even so there was a heavy reliance on the prompter. Richard Wagner remarked that if one attended a performance of a play in the German provinces one could hear it twice.

Blocking the movements of the actors followed the old rules until the middle of the nineteenth century. An actor virtually never turned his back on the audience; rarely was less than one fourth of his face visible. If the scene required several actors to be onstage at once, they grouped themselves in a half circle downstage near the footlights. An actor would not leave this half circle except to leave the stage. Minor parts, servants and walk-ons, stood behind in a second half circle.[2]

These seemingly arbitrary and confining rules had their origin in very practical considerations. Before the introduction of gas lighting, it was impossible to illuminate the whole stage. Chandeliers with wax candles were suspended over the auditorium and over the apron of the stage (the part that projected in front of the proscenium arch). The chandeliers in the auditorium were raised but not extinguished during performances. Whale oil, which was much cheaper but reeked infernally, was used in the footlights and in the lamps attached to the backs of the wings of the set. Overhead lighting upstage of the apron was impossible, since that space was used for the shifting of the wings when the set was changed. Consequently, there was only a comparatively small section of the stage that was adequately lit. Even there, the light was not nearly as bright as modern audiences are accustomed to, and the performers had to employ a broad style of acting with

Figure 4. Actors on stage. Kristiania Norske Theater.

clear, standardized gestures. The modern realistic actor, with his nervous tics and subtle movements, would have been lost on that dim and rather mysterious stage with its flickering shadows.

Theatrical entertainment in Christiania, Trondheim, and Bergen (the theater in Bergen seated nine hundred) was popular, and the theaters kept up with developments in staging techniques. And no development was more significant and revolutionary than the introduction of gas jets to light the stage—first in London as early as 1817, in Paris in the 1820s, in Germany in the 1840s, and at the Royal Theater in Stockholm in 1854 and the Royal Theater in Copenhagen in 1857.[3] Norway kept abreast of this innovation; the Christiania Theater installed gas lighting as early as 1848. The light could now be regulated by remote control merely by turning a valve; there was no need to hang lamps on the backs of the wings; and most of the stage could now be used by the actors. The box set, which could enclose the stage space and make it look like a real room, became feasible. From Ibsen's blocking directions we can see that he experimented with the new possibilities, breaking up the conventional half circle as often as possible.[4] (And the wonderfully atmospheric scenes in *A Doll's House*, *Ghosts*, and *The Wild Duck* would not have been possible without gas lighting.)

Following the German system, the production of a play lay in the hands of two people: the literary man who would select scripts, cast them, and interpret the roles; and the practical man who would be in charge of sets, costumes, and the blocking of the actors. In 1851 the board managing the theater, having had no experience in the field, failed to define clearly the functions of the two parties, Laading, the *inspecktør* (or *rolle-instruktør*), and Ibsen, the *instruktør* (*scene-instruktør*). The latter was responsible for the sets, the properties, and the lighting; that is, he would find the most appropriate set in the scene dock and make the necessary alterations, and he would gather whatever props were needed. Functioning as stage manager, he would also record the placement and movements of the actors, seeing to it that they grouped themselves properly and meaningfully onstage. At rehearsals Ibsen was either too shy or possibly too keenly aware of his lack of theatrical experience to be of much help to the actors. Setting down everything neatly in the promptbooks, drawing costume sketches, and registering stage movements, he exceeded what was expected of him. Overskou, who was the *sceneinstruktør* at the Royal Theater in Copenhagen and with whom Ibsen studied, never kept books as thoroughly as Ibsen did.[5]

In the inevitable confusion of duties and responsibilities that resulted, Laading got bad notices in the papers, Ibsen was mortified by his inferior position as stage manager, and the two men nearly came to blows (the craziness mentioned in the 1875 letter). Trying to rectify the confused situation they had caused, the board members reduced Laading's salary to three hundred specie dollars, raised Ibsen's to three hundred, and provided him with a viaticum to study theater abroad. From April to August 1852 he was in Germany and Denmark, observing firsthand the backstage work in excellent theaters and meeting such notables as H. C. Andersen. Upon his return, the theater board drew up a new protocol redefining the specific duties and responsibilities of the two directors.[6]

For the first time in his life, Ibsen had a fairly secure position, a modest income, and the prospect of a career as a dramatist. Now in his midtwenties, he could think about regaining the social position that had been his as a child. The intervening years had, however, left part of him stranded in the past. Returning to provincial Norway, he put on the airs of an elegant man about town. Unfortunately, he could not carry it off convincingly. He dressed with great care, but the details were all wrong. His shirtfront was frilled, and his coat had unusually wide sleeves, the so-called *engageant* sleeves, the cuffs decorated with lacework. Yellow kid gloves sometimes complemented the outfit. He was overdressed for Bergen, and its stolid citizens laughed at this *démodé* Beau Brummel behind his back.[7]

Short in stature, only about five feet two, his brown-hued face encased in a full black beard and topped with black hair, Ibsen looked like "a little, shy groundhog," in the eyes of his future stepmother-in-law, who offered an unflattering but perceptive description of the young Henrik. "There was something funny, unattractive, rather awkward and anxious in his bearing and manner. He was afraid of appearing ridiculous, of giving himself away. He had not yet learned to disdain his fellow man, and he lacked self-confidence. Moreover, he had a certain unbounded respect for the finer things in life. He sensed that in the elegant world of those with ample means there was not the unrest and disquiet that he felt within himself. Instead there was a quiet beauty. He felt forlorn, ostracized, existing outside good society."[8]

This social misfit fell in love with an attractive fifteen-year-old girl, Rikke Holst, from the upper ranks of Bergen society, and he wooed her with some ardent and youthfully ebullient poems. Her father read them and was furious. He forbade Rikke to see the playwright. But she and Henrik continued to have their trysts, taking her five-year-old brother along as a chaperone. Ibsen even became engaged to her by linking his ring to hers and throwing both into the sea. This romantic gesture lacked conviction. When Rikke's father caught the two lovers together, he angrily raised his fist at Ibsen, who fled from the scene and abandoned his beloved.

The woman Ibsen married, Suzannah Thoresen, was of a different sort.[9] With his dichotomizing temperament, Ibsen divided women into two categories. There were those who stood for the fine life that had once been his, and there were those who could help him have it again. At this point, Rikke was the romantic one, the woman of his dreams, and Suzannah the practical one. She was the daughter of a clergyman, Hans Conrad Thoresen, newly transferred to Bergen. Interested in the drama, she was drawn to the new playwright in town and, unlike her fellow Bergenites, divined greatness in him. And Ibsen sensed in her the energy and commitment that he desperately needed. He married her on June 18, 1858. He was thirty; she was eight years younger. Her father died a week before the wedding.

Ole Bull had engaged Ibsen to make up for the lack of any native Norwegian drama. Ibsen was expected to write plays, one a year, that would treat Norwegian history in a way that would appeal to a wide audience. He quickly learned the craft of the well-made play, the *pièce bien faite,* which had been perfected by the French dramatists, notably Eugène Scribe, who regarded theater as purely for entertainment. It was a formulaic product that relied heavily on misunderstandings and the perfectly timed disclosures of important secrets. In fact, the art of the well-made play consisted mainly in holding back vital information until the critical moment. The German drama, in contrast, was less "theatrical," relying more on character development than on plot machinations. Ibsen himself in an 1851 review of a German play spelled out the differences very lucidly. What he had to say laid the groundwork for what he was to accomplish in creating modern drama.

> Between modern French and modern German [drama] there are significant differences. French drama . . . requires the medium of actors to establish contact with life; only thus does it come to exist. Drama, as it emerges from the hand of a French author, is still incomplete; only when it is linked to reality by dramatic *performance* is the concept fully realized. For a Frenchman modern drama can make no claim to be *read* as literature. . . . The German playwright on the other hand writes his drama without particular regard to its performance. If in the form it leaves his hand it can be performed in the theatre, well enough; if not, it can be read, and as such he sees it fulfilling the demands of drama equally satisfactorily. For in Germany drama finds its *raison d'être* as pure literature as much as it does as dramatic literature.
>
> From this it also follows very naturally that the German, when he writes for the theatre, believes he has quite different things to attend to than when writing a dramatic work without this special aspect. But this conflict between his general conception of drama and those demands he has to satisfy on some isolated occasion manifests itself in his work and disrupts the unity without which art is an impossibility. In order—as he supposes—to achieve reality, he depicts his characters and situations *in extenso;* but this is precisely what defeats his purpose, for he thereby transgresses the limits of drama. The German play then stands to the French as a *tableau vivant* to a painting; in the former, figures present themselves in their natural contours and natural colours; in the latter, on the other hand, they only *appear* as such to us—which is, however, the only right way. For in the realm of art, reality pure and simple has no place; illusion, on the contrary, *has.*
>
> This is not in any way to suggest that French drama has any advantage over German; for that depends on how far it too satisfies the demands it has set itself. Undifferentiated reality may well have no justification in art, but any work of art that does not bear reality *within* it is equally unwarranted; and this is the real weakness of French drama. Here the characters generally appear as pure abstractions; in order to achieve maximum contrast—the hobby-horse of French drama—they reveal themselves either as angels or as devils, seldom as people. Whereas if the German concerns himself with reality, which for the most part is not usually his field, he does so with a vengeance. He portrays not merely people but the most trivial, ordinary people such as we see and hear every day. But the ordinary person's character is by no means trivial from an artistic standpoint: as represented by art it is just as interesting as any other.[10]

In the years to come Ibsen gradually brought the German and French kinds of drama into a unity, an amalgam, combining the thought-inducing drama of Schiller with the gasp-provoking entertainments of Scribe—a union brought to utter perfection in *Ghosts*. In his Bergen years, however, he alternated between the two. *Midsummer Eve* (*Sancthansnatten*), performed in January 1853, was a lyrical play in which elves and human beings mingled. It was meant to tap into the Nordic folk spirit, on the theory that *das volk dichtet*, that the old stories were the fruit of the innate poetic genius of the people and contained the deep instincts and age-old truths of the nation or race.[11] It was a resounding failure.

In a lecture delivered to a Bergen literary society in 1857 and later published as "The Heroic Ballad and Its Significance for Literature" ("Om kjæmpevisen og dens betydning for kunstpoesien"), Ibsen accepted the then widely held theory that the old ballads were composed by social groups rather than by individual poets. In those works one could find the "sum total of the people's poetic force, the fruit of its poetic genius."[12] The problem for Ibsen as a dramatist was how to impose the artificial and sophisticated world of Scribe on the primitive and instinctual realm of the myth without crushing the latter; or, in other words, how to adapt the Norwegian soul to the French salon.

The broad public naturally preferred the Scribean play. Ibsen himself remarked that about half of the plays produced on the stages of Europe in the 1850s were of French origin. Of the approximately 150 plays staged at the Bergen theater while he worked there, 82 were French plays, 22 of them by Scribe and his team of collaborators; and at least half of those that were not French were by adepts of the Scribean school.[13] And it was not only the public that admired Scribe's cleverness; the critics and the tastemakers considered him the great master of dramatic economy for whose equal one would have to go back to Racine. Johan Ludvig Heiberg, the doyen of Danish critics and a successful playwright, was a disciple of Scribe; Kierkegaard, too, marveled at Scribe's dramaturgical dexterity, and even the German critic Hermann Hettner, who was calling for greater psychological truth in the drama, praised the French playwright's skill at holding an audience.

Before he was engaged as a practical playwright in Bergen, Ibsen had excoriated the French type of play, ridiculing "Scribe & Co.'s theatrical bonbons."[14] As *instruktør* he had to supervise the productions of dozens of these trifling works, and as playwright he found he had to write the same sort of piece. Ironically, as a leader of a new nationalistic Norwegian drama, he found himself serving his public French and Danish theatrical fare.

Those first years in Bergen were very discouraging. Nothing seemed to work out for him. The first two plays he wrote there, *Midsummer Eve* and *Lady Inger of Østraat*, which opened on January 2 to mark the anniversary of the national theater, proved unsuccessful. And as assistant director he was so remiss in his duties that the managing board was forced to notify him that it could no longer ignore his neglect of his responsibilities, softening the statement by assuring him that lack of experience rather than incapability or lack of interest was to blame. He seems to have been drunk frequently, and one winter day he fell into the icy waters of the Bergen harbor and nearly drowned.

In his next two plays, *Lady Inger of Østraat* (*Fru Inger til Østraat*, 1855) and *The Feast at Solhoug* (*Gildet paa Solhoug*, 1856), he shied away from the lyrical drama and chose the form of the well-made play. He quickly demonstrated his mastery of its tricks, its misunderstandings, and its contrived climaxes that depended on the revelations of secrets.

Lady Inger is set in the sixteenth century, when Norway was under the yoke of Sweden and Denmark. In 1855 the situation was much the same. Lady Inger believes it is her God-given task to unite the Norwegian peasants, and once the Swedish and Danish forces have been defeated she will place her son on the throne.

Her tragic error lies in the past, when she had put her sexual desire for Sten Sture, regent in Sweden, above fealty to her nation. By him she had an illegitimate child, which was taken from her at birth and whom she has not seen for years. Ever since this child was born, her life has been compromised by its existence. The peasants in Dalarne used it as a hostage to ensure that Inger would side with them; and fearing the Danes knew of its existence, she married a Dane whom she did not love. Now she intends to make her son Norway's king, while she will be the power behind the throne. Through a series of implausible complications, he has to find refuge in Lady Inger's castle. She takes him to be the legitimate heir to the Sture dynasty, standing in the way of her own son, and orders him killed. Only in the last minute of the play, when she recognizes the ring taken from the corpse, does she realize what she has done.

Although the political struggles in the play are drawn from history, the story of Lady Inger's illegitimate son was Ibsen's own concoction. A similar case of mistaken identity provides the substance of the plot of Verdi's *Rigoletto* (based on Victor Hugo's *Le Roi s'amuse*), which in the early 1850s was making the rounds of the opera houses of Europe. It may have inspired Ibsen when he set himself the virtually impossible task of infusing Scribe with the blood of the Norwegian people.[15]

Finally in January 1856 he scored a theatrical hit with *The Feast at Solhoug*, another work based on Norwegian history. Years later, when the play was issued in a new edition, Ibsen recalled the joy he felt on opening night.

"It was done supremely well and with rare feeling. Given with pleasure and enthusiasm, it was received in the same way. The 'Bergen poetic temperament' . . . rose to a high pitch in the packed theater that evening. The performance ended with numerous calls for the author and actors. Later the same evening I was serenaded by the orchestra, accompanied by a large part of the audience. I have an idea I was so carried away that I made some sort of speech to the assembled crowd; at all events I know I felt very happy."[16]

Of the four new plays he wrote between 1851 and 1857, the two best are the most Scribean: *Lady Inger* and *The Feast at Solhoug*. The latter gave Ibsen his first unqualified theatrical success. Furthermore, although he later repudiated two plays from this period, *Midsummer Eve* and *Olaf Liljekrans*, he kept the others in the official Ibsen canon.[17] At the time he wrote *Olaf Liljekrans*, he thought enough of it to paint technically proficient aquarelles of the costumes of the leading characters.[18]

In *The Feast at Solhoug* the plight of Margit, the central character, is that she must reconcile herself to a life without love when the man of her heart chooses to love someone else. It is generally thought that the play is a reflection of his abortive affair with Rikke Holst, who is also supposed to have served as model for the sentimental and romantic Eline, Lady Inger's daughter.

In both these works Ibsen drew on personal experience to pump some life into the artificial heart of the well-made play. He had much in common with Lady Inger. She, like Ibsen, had had an illegitimate child, which had forever compromised her social and moral position. Also like Ibsen, she felt she had been chosen by a higher power to do great things. Ibsen had been entrusted with the responsibility of creating a national drama. Lady Inger had been called on to unite the Norwegian people.

"I felt God's power in me," says Lady Inger, "and I thought, as many have since thought, that the Lord Himself had set his mark upon me and chosen me to fight for my country and kingdom. Was it pride? Or was it a revelation from above? I have never found out. But unhappy is he who has been given a great task to perform."[19]

Ibsen's great task was to rehabilitate the Ibsen name, and in Bergen he began to think he could accomplish this by creating a national drama, just as Lady Inger had been called on to reform the Norwegian nation and make it independent of Denmark. When Ibsen met his bride-to-be, he said, prophetically, "Miss Thoresen . . . You have the stuff in you for a Lady Inger," words that neither would ever forget.

Their first meeting was arranged by her stepmother, Magdalene Thoresen, who presided over the only literary salon in the town. She ignored Ibsen until she saw *The Feast at Solhoug*. Then she invited him to tea on a January afternoon in 1856.

Suzannah was a bit intimidated by the young poet whose face was half hidden by a fearsome beard, while he for his part felt ill at ease. He invited her to a ball, a proper thing to do, but not the best venue for two socially awkward people. He was not a graceful dancer, while the young gallants ignored her.[20]

She was a forceful, strong-willed woman, who as a child had preferred to take the male roles in amateur theatricals. Although she was only nineteen when she met Ibsen, she was not too young to sense in the twenty-seven-year-old playwright a man who would cut a wide swath in the world. Later in life she would remark that she couldn't "abide jelly men who can't do anything and can't will to do anything. The first requirements for being a man are energy and iron resolution."[21]

Having hitched her wagon to Ibsen's star, she always remained faithful to him, though their marriage was to be subject to severe strains when he sought to find in other women the qualities that Suzannah lacked. In 1870 Ibsen said of her, "She is a woman of great character, exactly the person I need—illogical, but with a strong poetic instinct, a broad and liberal mind, and an almost violent hatred of all petty considerations."[22]

To him she was a reincarnation of the old Viking spirit, and from her he drew the strength and courage to survive the most severe crisis of his life. Years later, in 1894, when Ibsen toasted Suzannah's stepmother on her birthday, the latter, who was an author in her own right, replied, "You had things made so easy for you, Ibsen. While we others had to slave and study for years to get what we wanted from the sagas, you had Suzannah as the living source, from whom you could get everything."[23]

A young Danish student who visited the Ibsens frequently in 1867 set down in his diary a trenchant but unsubtle and unvarnished description of Suzannah. "She is unfeminine, tactless, with a stubborn temperament, a combination of reason and stupidity, without feeling, lacking in humility and womanly love."[24]

She was the immediate inspiration for the first two plays he wrote after marrying her: *The Vikings at Helgeland* (*Hærmændene paa Helgeland*, 1858) and *Love's Comedy* (*Kjærlighedens Komedie*, 1862). *The Vikings* mines the legends of the Volsungs, the same rich veins that Friedrich Hebbel and Richard Wagner were exploiting for their epic dramas of the Nibelungs. Ibsen differs from them in his dramatic economy and his smaller focus. Whereas the Germans give the legend the scope of universal history and make the hoard of the Nibelungs the ultimate source of the tragic events, Ibsen concentrates on the psychological drama of the ill-fated lovers. Hjørdis and Sigurd (Wagner's Brünnhilde and Siegfried), who would have formed the ideal Viking couple, he a man of indomitable vigor and she a Valkyrie who exults in a life of violence, delights in razing towns, wants sex to be as thrilling as a Viking raid, and dreams of swooning "with a strange ecstasy" in a man's arms. Only once has she experienced this divine rapture, and that was when she was embraced on her wedding night. As in Wagner's music drama *Götterdämmerung*, there is something preternatural about this sexual embrace: the ecstasy was achieved without the lovers "going the limit," as Ibsen made it plain in a letter to a properly inquisitive director. As in Wagner, principles of honor and claims of blood brotherhood determine that either she or Sigurd must die. It seems that their union can take place only in the afterlife. This being the case, Hjørdis shoots Sigurd with an arrow before killing herself. Unfortunately, between the one act and the other she learns that Sigurd had converted to Christianity, and hence the lovers cannot meet even in the afterlife. He goes to meet the White God in heaven, and Hjørdis joins the Valkyries charging on their steeds across the stormy sky.

In Ibsen's sexual universe there is an iron law that keeps happiness at a minimum. Love and marriage cancel each other out, since domestic happiness and artistic creativity are incompatible. A series of works in verse, written from 1854 to 1862, demonstrate how this inviolable law operates.

"In the Picture Gallery" ("I Billedgalleriet"), probably written 1854–56 and printed in 1859, in twenty-three parts, most of them Petrarchan sonnets, contains what Edmund Gosse, one of the first English critics to take any notice of Ibsen, described accurately as "a strangely violent confession of distrust in his own genius."[25] This cycle was followed by "On the Heights" ("Paa Vidderne"), composed late in 1859. The hero in this remarkable poem moves from doubt about his calling in life to certainty, and from a concern for others to an absolute artistic egoism. On the barren, rocky moors, above the run of humanity, he finds God and freedom, and from his superior position he observes with an inhuman detachment his childhood home go up in flames, his mother consumed in them, and without shedding a tear sees his beloved marry another man. "My life in the lowlands has been lived through. Here on the uplands are freedom and God; down below grope the others."

To reach this point the narrator must abnegate erotic love, which is associated in the first part of the poem with elves and imps, and especially with the nixie, the water sprite.

"Each passion of the night, each wild desire, is driven from my mind. I am sound and strong. I stand close to my true self and my God."[26]

He urges his beloved to do the same and to forget the sexual episode that figured in their lives. He speaks of slaying the troll that bewitched him into making love. The girl now becomes a symbol of purity and asexuality, and for that the poet desires to sacrifice himself.

The poet Falk in Ibsen's next play, *Love's Comedy*, scandalizes his fellow citizens by announcing that marriage "has no more to do with love than mathematics has." He and his fiancée, Svanhild, realize that in marriage their love will decline into domestic complicity, into a togetherness "of fond solicitude, of domestic peace, of individual wills bowing to each other." Svanhild kisses her engagement ring and tosses it into the sea, rejoicing in the thought that she has played her part in the poet's life by inspiring him with the love of the ideal.

Although Ibsen said, "I have read very little of S.K. and understood even less," the influence of Søren Kierkegaard on this play is palpable and has received a great deal of critical attention.[27] When Svanhild tells her fiancé, "I have renounced you for this life, but I have found you for eternity," she is speaking like Kierkegaard: "When two people fall in love with each other and sense that they are destined for each other, then it is vital that they have the courage to break off—because to remain together is to lose all and to win nothing. This seems like a paradox, and so it is for the emotional life but not for reason."[28]

The lovers in his *Fear and Trembling* behave just like Falk and Svanhild, and in *Stages on Life's Way* we can read the story of a man who must break off with the woman he loves precisely because he loves her so much.[29]

What he found in Kierkegaard was a philosophical context for his own thoughts. In this satiric comedy, written in iambic pentameter and totally lacking in Scribean intrigues, Ibsen holds up a mirror to his own marriage. Suzannah seems to have had an aversion to physical sex, and Henrik feared its power of seducing him from higher concerns. Only one child was born to the couple, a year after their marriage, and from that point on, according to rumors heard in Bergen, the Valkyrie Suzannah banished her husband from her bed. After that first child she expressed loudly enough for the neighbors to hear her ungodly wish for no more children.[30] There is no indication that Ibsen fought against her wishes, and probably a tacit understanding about sexual intercourse was reached early in their marriage. Ibsen married Suzannah because she had faith in him when virtually no one else did, and she could provide him with the moral support and encouragement he needed. His own son said Ibsen was a lazy man: "He had the genius; she had strength of character," and without her he would never have survived. Suzannah observed, "Ibsen had no steel in his character . . . but I gave it to him."[31]

"Not until after I was married," said Ibsen, "did I take life more seriously. The first fruit of this change was the rather long poem 'On the Heights.' The desire for freedom that pervades this poem was not, however, fully expressed until I wrote *Love's Comedy*."[32]

The effect of the iron law of love is to keep happiness at a bare subsistence level.

In *The Vikings* love is thwarted by the bonds of blood brotherhood. In *Love's Comedy* love and marriage are seen as incompatible. For espousing sentiments that could undermine the social structure, the poet Falk is scorned and despised by the townspeople, whereupon he asks his like-thinking fiancée, Svanhild, to join him in a battle against bourgeois conventionality. They quickly realize, however, that in marriage their love will turn into a shallow domestic complicity, into a togetherness "of fond solicitude, of domestic peace, of wills bowing to each other." Given their belief that love is an unearthly ideal, they renounce each other.

"I have renounced you for this life," she says, "but I have won you for eternity."

Falk responds, "Just as the way to lasting life lies through the grave, so love first truly comes to life when it escapes from longing and desire, and flees to freedom in the memory."

These two poems and the play capture Ibsen's thoughts at a crucial juncture when Rikke Holst vanished from his life and Suzannah Thoresen entered it. To achieve greatness, erotic passion had to be suppressed, while a higher romantic love had to be held on to only as a memory to provide inspiration. Ibsen killed love in order to create, just as Falk deliberately kills a bird in order to compose a touching poem about its death.

(Years later, when a good friend commented that Svanhild should never have engaged herself to a businessman, Ibsen replied, "Console yourself, the next day she will have a rendezvous with Falk.")[33]

This freedom from human attachments was to become a major motif in Ibsen's works. Freedom meant becoming superhuman, rising above ordinary earthly and domestic concerns. "Freedom lies in answering your innermost call," says Falk. For Ibsen, God is that inner voice. But in "On the Heights" the divine spirit does not speak to him. The ascent to the solitary peak where he would meet his God would take several years, from 1859 when he wrote "On the Heights" to 1865 when he wrote *Brand*. Before he could begin the ascent he had to endure further humiliations and pass through the Slough of Despond.

God's Stepchild

In July 1857 Ibsen left the Bergen theater and accepted a position at the Norwegian Theater in Christiania. He looked forward to working in the capital city. In Bergen he had had limited responsibilities; in Christiania he would be in overall charge of the theater, serving as both artistic director, responsible to a governing board, and stage director, combining the functions of dramaturg and director. Now the burden of forging a national theater was placed squarely on his shoulders.

To an outsider who resided there in the mid-1860s, Christiania was a deplorably provincial city,

> a big, overgrown village, a hot-bed of slander and scandalous gossip, and its intellectual life was incredibly meager. . . . The standards of judgment were mean, petty, provincial. What the Germans call *Brodneid, i.e.*, professional envy, the desire to destroy every possible rival, was rampant in the upper as in the lower social strata. There was, indeed, no lack of superficial culture; and some few highly refined families were to be found, among whom life had a certain gloss, and the manners were good enough to pass muster anywhere. But outside of University circles there were no intellectual interests; and even in University circles these had a wholly professional flavour and betrayed none of that charming hospitality of mind and generous glow of enthusiasm for all that is beautiful in the domain of thought, which makes life delightful in London, Paris, and Rome. . . . There was no escape from the Philistine. He was ubiquitous and all-pervasive. He dominated society from top to bottom. He imposed his crude judgments upon all, and would tolerate no dissent.[1]

Ibsen's contract with the theater would give him an income of six hundred specie dollars a year, enough for a married couple to live on. He married Suzannah a year after he took up residence in Christiania, and he set about reforming the theater, raising the standards of acting, and introducing plays of some literary merit. Yet nothing went right. Competition with the rival Christiania Theater reduced box-office receipts. Needed renovations of the building turned out to be more expensive than anticipated and drove the theater into bankruptcy. Ibsen was criticized in the press for his choice of plays and for failing to raise acting standards. Comedies, farces, and vaudevilles (light plays with songs) were the regular fare, while tragedies and the classics in general were slighted, obviously because they were beyond the capabilities of the inexperienced and untrained actors. Moreover, Norwegian speech might sound all right on the street, but onstage it sounded crude and vulgar compared with stage Danish, which was heard at the rival theater.

Discouraged, Ibsen proved to be a poor administrator and an uninspired director. Sniping critics demanded his resignation as artistic director, and he had to spend much of his time writing defensive articles pointing out the practical considerations involved in running a theater and catering to an uneducated audience. The actors and the governing board accused him of neglecting his duties. Several times he was hauled before the board to be upbraided and scolded like a child (one of the board members was a schoolteacher). Rather than endure this humiliation, Ibsen chose to absent himself from the board meetings and often slunk off to a café. On one occasion the board sought him out in his lair and held its meeting in the restaurant.

During these desperate years Ibsen went deeply into debt, with thirteen claims filed against him by creditors; at one point he owed them the equivalent of a whole year's salary. He came down with a severe fever and was absent from the theater for three weeks. In 1861 some of his furniture was sold at auction. Although his salary was large enough on paper, it was frequently not paid, and eventually his possessions were distrained for nonpayment of taxes. The Ibsens moved several times, descending steadily into ever more shabby quarters. In 1862 and 1863 he and Suzannah lived in a derelict house by the railroad tracks, with scarcely a crust of bread to eat. She could be seen on the street carrying a grocery basket, a cloth over it to conceal its emptiness.[2] He was shabbily dressed. His coat lacked buttons, and he kept his hand on it to hold it closed. He lost interest in writing, dabbled in painting, and took to drink. He often came home late, physically supported by his less inebriated companions. He won a reputation as "the drunken poet," and on one occasion students returning from their late-night revels saw him lying in a gutter unconscious from drink.[3] There were those who were willing to set up a fund to send "the drunken author" out of the country.[4] He seemed bent on destroying himself. One night when he was out of his mind, either because of fever or alcohol, he slipped out of bed and in his nightshirt ran down to the nearest bridge, where he attempted to throw himself into the water.[5]

Probably nothing discouraged him more than the reception of *Love's Comedy*. He had invested all his genius in this play, a highly original satire in verse, not based on Norwegian history, full of wit, and lacking all the meretricious devices of popular plays. It was hardly surprising that the Christiania burghers grouped themselves solidly against this one-man attack on their establishment. Said one critic, "Bitter indignation is the basis of this poem, but such cannot be the basis of poetry." Another faulted the verse while recognizing its satiric force. He called the play "a modern Viking raid on the family institution." Ibsen said he felt "excommunicated," which was not an exaggeration. He was banned from the better homes in Christiania. Years later when he applied to the government for a poet's stipend, he was rejected by the Ecclesiastical Department specifically because of *Love's Comedy*. "The author of *Love's Comedy* deserves the stick rather than a stipend," said a professor at the university.[6]

Bjørnstjerne Bjørnson and Ibsen had known each other fleetingly when both were preparing for their entrance examinations at the university. But from the time Ibsen moved to Christiania, their paths were to become so inextricably entangled that they appear to exist in symbiosis, the one supplying what the other lacked. It was not long before their countrymen recognized what they stood for: Bjørnson was the heart of Norway, Ibsen was the mind of Norway.

While Ibsen's star was sinking, Bjørnson's was rising. While Ibsen was suffering one defeat after another, when even his attempt at suicide was a failure, when he was virtually ostracized from respectable society, his rival author and playwright was everywhere triumphant. A man of impressive physique, prodigious energy, an ingratiating personality, an eloquent tongue, and a facile pen, Bjørnson was almost cursed with talent. The only noticeable blemish in this titan was nearsightedness. With his play *Between Battles* (1856) and his novel *Synnøve Solbakken* (1857), he caught the Norwegian national folk spirit in a way that had eluded Ibsen. When Bjørnson took over the post that Ibsen had vacated at the Bergen National Theater, he proved to be an inspiring and untiring stage director, putting on twenty-five plays in his first season. And in addition to his theater work, he was composing lyric poetry and short stories, while also editing the *Bergen Post*. More significantly, he was an active politician, grooming himself as leader of the liberal forces. In the eyes of the younger generation, he was the voice of the future. When he took to the podium, all eyes were fixed on him. He radiated self-confidence; he was enthralling, compelling. As Strindberg said of him, "In possession of a supple but powerful voice, he knew how to build suspense in his enthusiastic audiences and how to bring them to laughter or tears."[7]

Figure 5. Ibsen, 1861–62.
The earliest photo of him.

Figure 6. Bjørnson in 1857.

He was everything that Ibsen was not. Bjørnson wanted to be part of the great mass of people, a popular leader, and believed that the individual realized himself through his contact with the broad public. He was, in short, a politician and a republican. Ibsen, on the other hand, saw the individual realizing himself only through opposition to the mass, rising above them to a place on the heights. Ibsen's closest friends in Christiania were Paul Botten-Hansen, who had been his fellow editor on *Andhrimmer;* Jakob Løkke (1829–81); and Michael Birkeland (1830–96). They formed a little social circle and called themselves the Learned Dutchmen, in deference to Botten-Hansen. His skill in finding choice items in the book stalls made an envious rival, Ludvig Daae, quote a line from a Danish classic, Holberg's *Jacob von Thyboe:* "Damn that Dutchman: he has his spies everywhere."[8] They were all government functionaries and bureaucrats who supported the monarchy. They regarded Bjørnson, who had never studied constitutional law, as a man of abysmal ignorance, while he called them "a pack of sneering, cynical theoreticians."[9]

Ibsen's sense of historical development and his belief in social justice aligned him with the political radicals, the socialists, but his aspirations for social recognition made him prefer the company of the conservatives. He later remarked that his association with the Learned Dutchmen "exercised a decisive influence on my later development, an influence that I have never in my innermost being rid myself of—never been able to nor ever wanted to."[10]

Bjørnson's main support as a literary artist came not from Christiania but from Copenhagen, the taste-setting capital of the north, in the person of Clemens Petersen. He was a failed actor turned critic who in 1858, at the age of twenty-four, became a regular contributor to the cultural columns of Denmark's leading newspaper, *Fædrelandet* (*The Fatherland*). Bjørnson had first met him in 1856, and the two young men had formed an alliance. They were often seen together at Bidstrup's Café on Kongens Nytorv, where the Copenhagen literati held their nightly revels from ten o'clock to two. (The philistines called it "the Madhouse.")

Inevitably, Bjørnson dominated these late-night causeries. One participant described him in action. "He overwhelmed his listeners with his magniloquence, astonished them with the novelty of his ideas and points of view, as well as by the manner in which he expressed them. If someone in the group spoke up with the voice of authority, he would quickly squelch him. Against those who were superior to him in intelligence, in clarity of thought, and a gift for subtle analysis, he set the imposing weight of his personality, which unfailingly gave him the air of the victor."[11]

But he behaved differently with Petersen. The two of them formed a striking contrast: Bjørnson personable, large-framed, boisterous, with a booming voice;

Petersen rather delicate of physique, reserved in manner, with a weak voice that had been the source of his failure as an actor, his plain features made plainer by an illness that had deprived him of eyebrows and eyelashes. Next to the brash and self-confident Bjørnson, Petersen seemed impulsive and flighty. "You know yourself," said Bjørnson, reproachfully, "you are as capricious as a happy young girl."[12] Bjørnson listened eagerly to Petersen's animadversions on the older school of Danish criticism, represented by Johan Ludvig Heiberg, and was impressed by the vigor with which Petersen reprobated all art that lacked an ethical content. Upon his return to Norway, Bjørnson expressed his fervent thanks to Petersen. "If I ever move ahead, it will largely be because solid fellows like you give me the horses I need. My dear friend I have cried with joy on reading your letters, and yes, I have held my head high like a soldier praised by his officer."[13]

In long epistles written 1857–61, Bjørnson discussed his latest literary projects and provided detailed reports on his reading of the classics, especially Goethe and Schiller. He was like an enthusiastic graduate student who had found the perfect mentor. "Never have I understood so fully what friendship is, as with you."[14]

He called Petersen his second conscience and said Petersen had infused his being with moral earnestness. The critic responded by saying that his conversations with Bjørnson had fired him with enthusiasm. "When I am in touch with you, I spark and crackle."[15] These almost amative declarations obviously signified more than a union of two minds that thought alike. Bjørnson admired Petersen for living in a purer atmosphere than himself, and said that the essential difference between them was that he was always falling in love, while Petersen did not even seem to understand what falling in love meant. The critic, concealing his homosexuality from Bjørnson and most of the world, saw more to admire in the author than literary talent, and the author saw more in the critic than a second conscience. Petersen wanted Bjørnson as a close friend, and Bjørnson wanted Petersen as a press agent.

Petersen promptly launched the Norwegian writer into Danish literature. In 1857 he became the first Danish critic to lavish praise on Bjørnson's novelette of peasant life *Synnøve Solbakken*, and thanks to him the book soon had more readers in Denmark than in Norway. In 1860 Petersen published in the Danish magazine *Illustreret Tidende* (October 7) the first biographical account of Bjørnson and found him worthy of comparison with the literary giants. "He gives his stories the impression of reality, and in this regard no one surpasses him, and only a few, such as Goethe and Dickens, measure up to him. It is not bookish learning, it is his own life and development that is transmuted into poetry in his soul."[16] Of Bjørnson's *Lame Hilda* (*Halte-Hilda*), a historical drama, Petersen said it was an epoch-making work deserving comparison with Goethe's *Götz von*

Berlichingen and Schiller's *The Robbers*.[17] In 1861, after the death of J. L. Heiberg, the twenty-seven-year-old Petersen quietly succeeded to his place as Denmark's cultural arbiter or, in Bjørnson's words, "the absolute monarch of Parnassus." In 1867 he proudly told Bjørnson that his views on matters artistic that had horrified proper citizens ten years before were now generally accepted. "The power is mine," he exulted.[18] Earlier Bjørnson had predicted, "The future is ours!" Now the words were coming true.[19]

It would have been astonishing if a man of Ibsen's disposition did not feel envious of his rival, two years his junior, graced with all the virtues, and accepting popularity and success as the proper perquisites of his God-given endowments. Bjørnson knew that Ibsen was jealous and sometimes spoke condescendingly of him. When Petersen lauded Bjørnson and dismissed Ibsen as a much lesser literary figure, Bjørnson replied, "As soon as Ibsen acknowledges that *he is small*, he'll make a rather lovable writer. I've told him this pretty clearly, but the result is, he is jealous....

"His poem 'Cry of the Sea Gull' I haven't read; I've heard that it is a rather affected thing, written because a Danish monthly said he is a lesser author than me. It's things like that that draw Ibsen away from what he should be doing. Add to this the fact that he is a rather small odd fellow, without a rump and without a chest; and so he feels, since he doesn't have a gift for oratory either, he has to carry on like mad when he writes."[20]

There was, however, one strong bond between them, and that was their dedication to the revival of Norwegian culture. In 1859 they were among the founding members of the Norwegian Association, established to promote nationalism. The speechifying Bjørnson served as chairman, and the taciturn Ibsen as—inevitably—deputy chairman. The club became for all intents and purposes an arm of the liberal party. During the years that followed, as the drive for independence from Sweden grew ever stronger, Bjørnson did perhaps more than any other individual to invigorate his people with nationalistic ideals and to unite the various forces under the liberal banner.

In June 1863, thanks in part to Bjørnson, Ibsen was invited to be the guest of the businessman and shipowner Randolph Nilson at a patriotic festival held in Bergen. Ibsen's effusive gratitude in a letter to his host thanking him for his "indescribable kindliness and friendliness" is a measure of the hostility, coldness, and inhospitality he had been subjected to in Christiania. The Bergen festival brought a profound change in Ibsen's spirit. Meeting his rival Bjørnson again, and hearing him speak, fired his imagination. Taking the growth of the national spirit as his theme, Bjørnson alluded to Håkon Håkonsson (1204–63), who had united the country in 1240, as Norway's greatest king, and then referred to Ibsen.

"Have I not had to see my friend Ibsen set up against me to hurt me, and I against him to hurt him?" The context left the clear impression that Bjørnson regarded himself as a modern Håkon destined to create a new Norway, independent of Sweden, and that Ibsen would be his right-hand man in the literary aspect of the campaign.

For Ibsen, it was public recognition of his status as a dramatist equal to Bjørnson. It was precisely the encouragement the despairing and unappreciated dramatist needed. Seizing on the idea planted in his mind by Bjørnson and recognizing the difference between himself and the born leader, Ibsen quickly sketched out a drama, *The Pretenders* (*Kongs-emnerne*), in which he set up a contrast between Håkon and Earl Skule, a claimant or pretender to the throne of Norway. Håkon had a great dream and was borne along by it, while Earl Skule was the man on whom fortune did not smile, a man consumed by doubts, as Ibsen was at this time. Here was historical material that corresponded to the reality of Ibsen's situation. He put his heart and soul into this drama on a grand scale, completing it within seven weeks in the summer of 1863. It was by far his most impressive achievement up to that time, a history play that could bear comparison with Schiller's *Don Carlos*.

Although Bjørnson was hounded by the conservative press and portrayed as an insurrectionary Jacobin, and had to care for his wife, who was deathly ill for a time, he never despaired, behaving always as if God had personally assured him of a happy end to his struggles. In describing Håkon as the greatest man because he is the luckiest, Ibsen clearly had Bjørnson in mind.

"The greatest deeds are done by him on whom fortune smiles, whose pulse beats with the needs of the time, whose intuition outstrips his reason and points the way that leads he knows not where, which nonetheless he takes because he must follow it, until he hears the people shout with joy and, looking round him with dazed eyes, sees that he has achieved a noble deed."[21]

In writing those lines, Ibsen may have been thinking of the impression that Bjørnson made in May 1859 with his first public speech, celebrating the victory of the liberal candidates in the Storting elections. Those who heard him never forgot the occasion.

"The responsibilities that Bjørnson laid upon us at that time have remained with us ever since.... That day was like the beginning of a new life for many of us."

"Like a sun god he stood there, his blond head held high and shining in the light, as his voice rang out over the spellbound multitude."[22]

"With his wonderful, sonorous voice, he appeared as a revelation from a world far different from that of our quiet, bourgeois existence."[23]

The story material for *The Pretenders* comes from the formative years of the

Norwegian nation in the thirteenth century when, after the age of the Viking raiders, there was much fighting among the claimants to the throne. Ibsen put much of himself into Earl Skule, Håkon's rival as leader of the Norwegian people. Influenced by the Mephistophelean Bishop Nicholas, Earl Skule determines to rebel against Håkon, presenting a more legitimate claim to the throne. But legitimacy does not stand up against Håkon's charisma. Skule cannot rally the people as effectively as Håkon can. When he examines the cause of his failure, he realizes that he is a brooding skeptic, consumed by doubts about his purpose in life, and therefore destined to be "God's stepchild." He has nothing to offer the people besides his title to the throne, while Håkon possesses the "kingly thought" of uniting the nation. "Norway was a kingdom; it shall become a nation.... All shall be one, and all shall know that they are one."[24] It is this ideal rather than any hereditary rights to the kingship that makes him an irresistible force, one of those people Shaw called vital geniuses.

Although Skule endeavors to appropriate this kingly thought, to make it his own, he is too fainthearted to commit himself wholly to it, and consequently he loses the battle in the field as he has lost it in his own soul. Ibsen dramatizes the conflict within Earl Skule by introducing a villain into the plot. The seeds of doubt are sown in Skule's soul by Bishop Nicholas, whose purpose in the scheme of things is purely destructive. A pathological case, he is obsessed by a compulsion to kill men and embrace women, intent upon acting out the first because he is impotent to do the latter. What faith Skule may have had in himself is destroyed by the bishop: he tricks Skule into burning a letter that would have proved conclusively whether Håkon had a legal right to the throne.

Nicholas sets Håkon and Skule against each other, hoping to see them destroy each other, and he dies contentedly in the third act knowing that he has spread hatred and dissension. Ibsen brings him back in the fifth act, as a ghost and a tempter, a messenger from Lucifer, "the oldest pretender in the world," who promises to take him to a high mountain and show him all the kingdoms of the world, and the glory of them.

Critics have condemned Nicholas's reappearance as an artistic fault. It isn't. Ibsen was right to bring him back, not only because the role is too superbly melodramatic to be truncated by an early death scene but because his presence is required at the end to bring about a change in Earl Skule. Skule is able to resist him now. He walks out of his sanctuary to let himself be slain by Håkon's soldiers. By dying, he serves the "kingly thought."

"I have no lifework for which to live. I cannot live for Håkon's either. But I can die for it."[25]

In *The Pretenders*, Ibsen came to terms with himself. By seeing himself as a foil to Bjørnson the magnificent human being, he made himself great as a dramatist. The young man who would rather destroy the world than go unrecognized by it, the young man who wrote *Catiline*, appears here as the envious Bishop Nicholas, and the Ibsen who for a time lost faith in himself is incarnated in Earl Skule.

Ibsen knew from an early age that he was a creature of the night and that he could not be God's chosen one. Skule comes to the same realization: "Some men were made to live, some made to die. My will always took the path that God did not designate for me; so I never saw things clearly—until now."[26]

"The great curse that has shadowed all my life," says Skule, "this—to stand so near the highest—only a ditch between—one leap and I would be across."[27]

"That is the curse that has hung over you," says Bishop Nicholas. "You wanted all paths open at all times before you. You don't dare to smash all the bridges, to leave only one, and to conquer or die *there*."[28]

After finishing *The Pretenders*, Ibsen knew in his heart that he had to make the great commitment. In the works leading up to it, we can see him burning his bridges, one after another. With "In the Picture Gallery," "On the Heights," and *Love's Comedy*, he cut himself off from family, denied himself romantic love, and renounced popular appreciation. With *The Pretenders* he resolved to be entirely himself, whatever that might mean.

Purity of Heart

The Pretenders, with its depiction of a confident and conquering hero, signaled a change in Ibsen's fortunes. Even before it was published in October 1863, Ibsen had been awarded a travel grant by the government, and when it was performed at the Christiania Theater the following January, it proved to be the greatest success he had known.

He was still in Norway because the travel grant was too meager to support him, his wife, and their small child abroad for a year. Moreover, as he said in his petition for the grant, he was in debt to the tune of 500 specie dollars. Bjørnson came to his aid. He had recently returned from an extended stay in Italy, living on a travel grant of 500 specie dollars awarded him in 1861. Ibsen had also applied in that year, but his request had been denied, mainly because of the animosity aroused by *Love's Comedy*. Now Bjørnson appealed to several individuals on Ibsen's behalf and scrambled together 700 specie dollars, which, added to the government grant of 400, made it possible for Ibsen to entrain for Italy in April 1864. His wife and son remained behind to be sent for when he had set up living quarters in Rome. In the meantime, his household possessions were sold off for 131 specie dollars. Ibsen reproached Bjørnson for having done nothing to prevent it.[1]

The first stop on his journey south was Copenhagen, and what he saw there proved to be the direct stimulus for an epic drama in verse, boldly and simply titled *Brand*, which immediately after its publication established Ibsen as the greatest Scandinavian poet of his generation. For the author it became the fountainhead from which flowed the rest of his dramas, and it was the work he revisited in his very last play.

While Ibsen was in Copenhagen, Prussian troops invaded the Danish province of Jutland and reduced the fort at Dybbøl, the *tête-de-pont* on the island of

Figure 7. Ibsen, 1863.

Asland, thus settling by force of arms the long-vexed question of Schleswig and Holstein. These were two duchies claimed by both Prussia and Denmark, the former pointing to the overwhelming number of German-speaking people in the disputed territory, the latter insisting that the duchies belonged to the Danish king by hereditary right.

The dispute had erupted into war in 1848, which fizzled out when Sweden sent troops and England, displeased at the prospect of Prussian tentacles reaching out toward the North Sea, exerted political pressure. The young Ibsen had taken a passionate interest in these events, writing in 1848 a poem in which he expressed a fervent hope that the Nordic countries, Sweden, Denmark, and Norway, separated since the thirteenth century, would soon be one again. And in 1849 he composed a cycle of twelve drum-thrumming sonnets, "Awaken Scandinavians," in which he appealed to the citizens of Sweden and Norway to secure Schleswig against a Prussian invasion, arguing that the duchy belonged to all Scandinavians, constituting its first line of defense. Addressing the king of Sweden directly, he calls upon him to defend not only Denmark proper, as he had promised, but also Schleswig. As is usual in jingoistic poetry, facts are treated cavalierly. Ibsen protests the suppression of Nordic culture and language in Schleswig; actually, the Danes were compelling the use of the Danish language in all state schools, although half the population was German.

In 1863, while Ibsen was writing *The Pretenders*, Sweden and Denmark entered into a provisional alliance that committed Sweden to the sending of twenty thousand troops if Prussia invaded Denmark. In November, King Frederik of Denmark died unexpectedly, and Charles XV of Sweden entertained hopes of being hailed as a hero by the Danes and offered the crown of a united Scandinavia. In an unguarded moment, in a private audience with a group of ardent Scandinavian unionists, he vowed to gather twenty-two thousand men in southern Sweden and lead them in person to Denmark, should the need arise. The conversation was meant to be confidential, but August Sohlman, a newspaper editor and leading unionist, decided to use the information to force the king to commit himself publicly. He sent a dispatch to the conservative Danish newspaper *Fædrelandet*, printed December 15, 1863, stating that the Swedish king had declared he would come to the defense of Denmark. The crucial telegram message was rendered as "On their way are 22,000 men and Himself." The Swedish parliament had to deny that any such commitment had been made. To the young Scandinavianists, Sweden's disavowal was a gross betrayal of Denmark in her hour of need, for the German Confederation had already resolved to invade Schleswig and Holstein, and five thousand Saxon troops were now assembled along the Danish frontier.

Norway's response to the plight of her sister nation was hardly more inspiring than Sweden's. Although the university students, who were the main advocates of unionism, called for Norway's immediate and active participation in the war, the politicians and businessmen urged prudence and discretion. The members of the Storting set down a number of conditions under which Norway might possibly send aid, and then quashed all the hopes of the unionists by passing a resolution declaring that "the great majority of the Norwegian people certainly do not want any closer ties with Denmark." The isolationists distanced themselves even further from Denmark by saying that Norway would send money but no men, and that even the money would not be forthcoming unless one of the great powers—that is, England—came to the aid of Denmark first.

For Ibsen, these were the times that try men's souls. The Dano-Prussian War revealed the true nature of his fellow men. Before the war broke out, he had believed that an attack by the Prussians would bring out the best in the Nordic people, unite them as they had not been united for centuries. In 1861 he wrote two poems in which he vowed that the Swedes and Norwegians would come to the aid of the Danes in their hour of need. In the concluding lines of "A Ship in Distress" ("I havsnød"), Ibsen said, "Tell the mighty German leaders that if you Danes must fight, you will receive a helping hand from us up north—and *first* from the *Norwegian* Nordics." In "A Poem for the Klingenberg Festival" ("Sang ved Festen paa Klingenberg"), he promised "woe betide those who offer only words as help to a brother in need."[2] In 1863, after the Swedish king had said in the Storting that Sweden and Norway could not venture into war without carefully weighing the chances of success, Ibsen offered in a poem called "A Brother in Need" ("En Broder i Nød") a stinging rebuke to the politicians whose promises to help Denmark were actually betrayals, Judas kisses.

This poem, Ibsen later said, "had no effect on the Norwegian-Americanism [commercialism] that had driven me back at every point. That's when I went into exile."[3]

On his way southward to Italy, Ibsen arrived in Copenhagen April 3, 1864, and remained for two weeks to be his with wife and son, who were staying with Suzannah's stepmother, Magdalene Thoresen. She arranged for Ibsen to meet Clemens Petersen, by then Denmark's most feared drama critic. In a letter to Bjørnson, Petersen recounted his impressions of Ibsen and Suzannah.

> Henrik Ibsen has been here in Copenhagen. He has called on me and I have met him elsewhere a couple of times. I saw in him a quiet, reserved and reasonable man, but I also noticed that he kept much of himself hidden [*han gik med lukket Vezir*]. A little incident opened up a different perspective. We were at Fru Thoresen's, he and I alone in the room. His little boy was asleep on the sofa, then fell on the floor, and though he didn't hurt himself, he naturally cried loudly out of fear. Then I saw the barely repressed ill-temper and total lack of gentleness that one finds only in very weak men; and not to have the ease and tact to smooth over such an insignificant situation in which a conversation is suddenly broken off by a child's cry is a sign of pettiness. . . . I have reviewed *The Pretenders* and, being as gentle as possible, have struck him where he deserves to be struck, because this work has little to do with art and nothing to do with poetry. He understood me well enough. . . . I have also met his wife. . . . Her soul is stiff with sham pretensions and her body with a corset. She licks her fingers when she eats, and to embrace her and look into her eyes would be like sinking into half-melted fat. Well, if Ibsen has drunk a lot and in his distressing life pursued unattainable ideals, it's no wonder, since there is not a spot on her that shines with beauty.[4]

Ibsen was in Copenhagen when Dybbøl fell, and with it went the last of his illusions about a Scandinavian union. In an ironic poem, "The Basis of Faith" ("Troens Grund"), he compressed into the final line the effect that the news from Dybbøl had on him. The poem begins with a reference to "A Brother in Need" as an alarm bell that everyone ignored. Having done what he could, Ibsen sails for Denmark. The ship, edging through the fog, is abuzz with reports from the war front. Many passengers have gathered around an elderly lady with silver hair, whose only son is a soldier. The women offer their commiseration, but the mother radiates confidence and hope.

"I am sure no harm will come to my boy."[5]

Seeing her, Ibsen realizes that the true Scandinavian spirit reposes with its women. Yet he must ask himself, what is the source of this faith and confidence? The explanation lies in a simple fact: her son is in the *Norwegian* army.

As he traveled south, he passed through Germany, where he was even more forcibly and cruelly reminded of the Swedish and Norwegian betrayal of "a brother in need."

"If I had stayed longer in Berlin," he wrote to Bjørnson, "where I saw the triumphal entrance in April, with the howling rabble, tumbling about among the trophies from Dybbøl, riding on the gun carriages and spitting into the mouths of the cannon—the cannon that received no help and yet went on shooting until they burst—I think I should have gone out of my mind."[6]

And to Magdalene Thoresen: "It seemed an omen that history will one day spit in the face of Sweden and Norway because of their behavior."[7]

His hatred of the Germans combined with his contempt for Scandinavian phrasemakers made a highly volatile mixture that would explode on the slightest provocation. In Rome he initiated a move to ban all Germans from the Scandinavian Society, which had about one hundred members. It was voted down mainly because the president of the club was German by birth. Then Ibsen called an extraordinary meeting of the officers of the society to demand that a German calendar be removed from the reading room. Every mention of Swedish courage raised his hackles. In one quarrel he declared that Swedes cloaked their cowardice by praising their old soldier-kings, long since passed away. When someone sought to defend the Swedes, Ibsen pounded the table and yelled, "Shut the hell up! You make me sick!"[8]

The view from Rome made the Norwegian national spirit seem mean and paltry. He excoriated the "deliberate hypocrisy of public life" and railed against those who spoke about "our great cause" yet who lacked the will and the sense of commitment to perform a great deed.

In Italy Ibsen, who had always seemed constrained and awkward in his public utterances compared with Bjørnson, became a voluble and impassioned speaker on the subject of the war. One witness vividly recalled being transfixed by his fervor. Newly arrived in Rome, Ibsen met with some Scandinavians at a tavern on the outskirts of the city.

> He began to tell us of the painful and moving impressions made on him during his journey by the recent turn of events in the war. But gradually and almost imperceptibly his narrative took on the character of an improvised oration. All the repressed bitterness, all the simmering indignation, all his ardent faith in the Scandinavian cause, all that he had for so long kept locked up within himself

> was now let loose. His voice grew firm as iron. In the dim light of evening one saw only his glowing eyes. And when he had finished, no one shouted bravo, no one raised his glass, but I am sure every one of us was left feeling that it was a Marseillaise of the North which that evening, heard by only a few, rang through the Roman night air.... And I know that I have never been, not even remotely, so gripped by the power of the spoken word as I was that evening.[9]

"I have stormed and raged and put things into a little better order," he wrote to his stepmother-in-law. "Down here I am afraid of nothing. At home I was afraid when I stood in that clammy crowd and sensed their evil smiles behind my back....

"Up there I could never lead a consistent life. I was one person in my writing and another outside it. And therefore what I wrote lacked wholeness. I know of course that I'm still at a halfway point, but now I feel solid ground under my feet."[10]

But as a poet and dramatist who had urged his countrymen to recall their past greatness, he felt himself implicated in an enormous fraud. The great cause was a great lie. In "To My Brothers in Guilt" ("Till de Medskyldige"), the poem in which *Brand* was incubated, Ibsen told his countrymen that their worship of the past was their besetting sin and the source of their moral corruption. As for himself, he determined to jettison both the soul-destroying illusions of a heroic past and the daydreams of Norway's future greatness in order to sail forth into the perilous mist of the contemporary world.

The behavior of Sweden and Norway in the Dano-Prussian War confirmed Ibsen in his belief that great deeds could not be accomplished without great sacrifice—that, in fact, it was necessary to lose all that one held dear in order to save oneself from all that was petty and contemptible. In losing the war Denmark had gained a spiritual victory; in saving their skins Sweden and Norway had lost much of their moral fiber.

The war afforded Ibsen the kind of cause that a man of his nature could make his own. In Norway he could never live a life that was consistent with his deepest beliefs. A positive personality like Bjørnson could rally the people around a kingly thought. He expected success, and his confidence and the public's natural preference for good news mirrored each other perfectly. Ibsen, having experienced one failure after another, and having since his adolescence been at odds with society, could not convincingly present himself as a leader of the troops. He was like Earl Skule, a loser. But the Dano-Prussian War revealed to him how fighting for a lost cause could make him a pretender to a throne in a nonpolitical realm. Loss and defeat fed his rage; the resentment against society he had harbored in his breast since childhood turned out to have been justified by the events; his efforts to make himself part of a larger political cause, the cause of Scandinavian union, had been inevitably delusive and insincere. What the Catiline in him wanted was the triumph of the individual, not of the state or of a party.

The journey from Norway to Italy was a revelation to him. Leaving Berlin in early May 1864, Ibsen made the most of his stipend by embarking on a cultural trek through a good part of eastern Europe. He traveled by train to Vienna, then on to Graz by way of the Semmering Pass; thence to Trieste. He spent a whole month in Venice, and visited Florence, Milan, and Genoa. He arrived in Rome on June 18.

With a cold and inhospitable north behind him, Ibsen now found himself in a land of sunshine. He was as overwhelmed by the lushness of northern Italy as Goethe had been when he descended from the Brenner Pass in 1786. The dramatic change left an indelible impression on Ibsen, which he recalled thirty-four years later.

"On the high mountains the clouds hung like vast dark curtains, and we rode underneath these and then through a tunnel until we suddenly found ourselves at Miramare, where the beauty of the south, a wonderfully bright glow, like shining white marble, all at once burst upon me and placed its stamp on all my future writings, even though everything in them is not beautiful."[11]

Once Ibsen had settled in, he sent for his wife and child, who arrived in November. They lived in a one-and-a-half-room apartment at Via Capo le Case, near the Trevi Fountain, paying nine scudi per month. Making do with very little, Suzannah sewed clothes for Sigurd out of pieces of Ibsen's discarded trousers and jacket.

This "feeling of having escaped from the darkness into the light, from the mists through a tunnel out into the sunshine" inspired him, in the strangely paradoxical way that is characteristic of the man, to write a work filled with darkness and bleakness and ever-increasing despair. It was not only the sunny climate of Italy that energized him, it was the distance from Norway that gave him the space and freedom he needed in order to write without regard to the political and social climate that had inhibited him in Norway.

And there were the glories of Italian art and architecture that cast a spell on the man who wanted most of all to be a painter. With his senses reeling before the power of Michelangelo, he had to reexamine his esthetic criteria. In the 1850s, when he had carefully studied the paintings in the galleries in Dresden, he had gone along with the standards of the time in exalting Raphael and Correggio as the greatest of painters, the unsurpassable masters. Now in Rome it was the Renaissance art of Michelangelo and Bernini that awed him. Raphael's angelic characters, too pure and innocent, seemed to belong to the prelapsarian days of man, while Michelangelo and Bernini "had the courage to do something crazy once in a while."[12] Reflected in his changing tastes was Ibsen's fascination with the exceptional individual who broke the rules, who put himself above and beyond his society, who deliberately violated conventions and created his own world, one unlike anything that had gone before. In his view, Michelangelo had sinned more against established conventions of beauty than anyone else; yet everything he gave shape to was full of beauty because it was full of character.

One statue in particular, *The Tragic Muse* (*Melpomene*) in the Vatican, conveyed to him the spirit of ancient tragedy, the highest form of drama. "No statue that I have seen in Italy has taught me so much. I would say that it has revealed the essence of Greek tragedy to me. That indescribably sublime, calm joy in the expression of the face, that laurel-crowned head with something supernaturally exuberant and bacchantic about it, those eyes that look both inward and yet through and far beyond the outward object they are fixed on—that is Greek tragedy."[13]

Faced with the example of Michelangelo, Ibsen aspired to do something equally great. The hero of the poem that was germinating in his mind would be a man like Michelangelo's Adam, created fully formed, muscular and dynamic, brought into being by God but just as powerful and every bit as big in scale as his creator. This hero, Brand, would raise himself above the common herd to become their scourge and prophet, calling upon them to risk their possessions in order to save their souls. It was the message of *Love's Comedy* translated from the erotic sphere to the political and religious. The lovers Falk and Svanhild will be forever in love because their love is never consummated. Bjørnson appealed to the people with the kingly thought of uniting them under the banner of a reborn nation. Ibsen said that there could be no kingly thought, nothing for the people to rally around without a great sorrow, and the Norwegians lacked "sufficient depth of soul to be able to feel sorrow." They regarded the downfall of the political state as the worst thing that could happen. "But the downfall of a *state* cannot be a reason for sorrow; and they do not understand what the downfall of a nation means. Denmark will not perish as a nation; for as long as a people can feel sorrow, so long will that people live."[14]

By identifying his own defeats and sorrows with that of a nation, Ibsen could overcome his doubts about his own claims to greatness and aim for heights that Bjørnson and his historical counterpart Håkon could not conceive of. The scorn and contempt for his fellow men that had become further tainted by malice during Ibsen's trying years in Christiania, when all seemed lost and when everyone was against him, were now given an impersonal basis. The bitterness he had secreted in his heart and mind for years spewed forth as he contemplated the events of the war. Enraged when he saw in Berlin "Kaiser Wilhelm's triumphal entry with trophies and war booty," Ibsen felt stirring within him "the embryo" of an epic drama.[15] Writing *Brand*, he likened himself to the scorpion he kept on his desk. When the creature grew ill, he fed it a piece of fruit, into which it emptied its poison and was well again.[16]

Brand began as an epic poem, in which the writer presents himself as the conscience of his country, railing at the Norwegians for their cowardice. But before the jeremiad gets well under way, Ibsen offers a psychological portrait of his hero. For the first time in his writings, he sees himself as a sharply divided personality, in which one half wars against the other. He sets up a contrast between two boys, both about twelve or thirteen, one fair-haired, the other dark-haired. They sit on a high ridge, overlooking a landscape that resembles the view at Venstøp, and exchange stories. The blond describes his happy life in a manor house with rosebushes in the front, children playing in the yard, guests constantly coming and going. The dark-haired boy believes none of this. His own home life is quite the opposite. He relates a nightmare that haunts him: on Christmas Eve his father dies and his mother strikes the corpse on its head, crying, "That's for ruining my life." The two boys stand for Ibsen before and after his father's business failure. It is the dark-haired boy who will mature into Brand.

Ibsen may have intended to continue the theme of *The Pretenders*, tracing the differences between himself and Bjørnson back to their childhoods. The poem was never finished. Both the conception of the hero and the form of the work changed in the winter or spring of 1865. In a letter to Bjørnson, Ibsen described what had happened to him.

"If I were asked . . . what has been the chief result of my stay abroad, I would say that it lies in my having purged myself of that esthetic point of view—existing in isolation and demanding that there be no other concerns in life—which formerly exercised a great power over me. Estheticism of this kind seems to me now as great a curse to poetry as theology is to religion. You have never been troubled about it. You have never gone about looking at things through the hollow of your hand," an allusion to the poem "On the Heights," the credo of the esthete.[17]

In Rome Ibsen met Fru Lina Bruun, mother of Christopher Bruun, a young Norwegian theologian who had volunteered in February 1864 to fight for the Danes. In April he had delivered an exhortation to the students in Christiania to volunteer as soldiers against the Prussians. In the following weeks 105 Norwegians signed up, along with 525 Swedes and 7 Finns.[18] Ibsen told Fru Bruun that if her son were slain in the war, he would raise a monument in verse to him that would also serve as a pillory of shame for the Norwegian people, exposing their cowardice and breach of faith. Fru Bruun, having like everyone else heard the rumors of the poet's alcoholism, and knowing him to be a rebellious sort who delighted in stirring up trouble, replied evenly, "If you do, *I* shall bury it with my own hands."

Tears welled up in Ibsen's eyes, profoundly touched as he was by this mother's refusal to have her son immortalized or eulogized at the expense of her country.

A little later, when the war in Denmark had ended, Christopher Bruun joined his mother in Rome, where Ibsen met him. They had many chats together that undoubtedly affected the characterization of Brand, particularly in the first act of the finished play, where the hero appears as a vigorous young man.

Abandoning the epic poem on which he had been working for a year, Ibsen completed the first four acts of the dramatic *Brand* in two months, thirty-six hundred tetrameters, iambic and trochaic, a prodigious achievement.

Brand is a parish priest who wants to reform his spineless countrymen by setting himself up as an example of a man who will not compromise his position as a savior of souls regardless of the cost to him personally. The God he adores is young, Herculean, a maker of miracles through sheer strength of will, not an ancient and remote god who is satisfied with the lip service rendered him by men who can put a price on things of the spirit. He rages against a peasant who will not risk his life for the sake of his dying daughter. Next he sails in a frail boat through a raging storm to offer last rites to a pitiable man who in a fit of mad despair had killed his starving child and then turned his hand against himself. To those who prefer the broad path to the straight and narrow this priest seems quite mad; to Agnes, however, who has been playing in the fields with an artist, Brand offers a glimpse of greatness. Hearing a voice that draws her out of the empty existence of a mere artist, she recognizes in Brand the new Adam who will fashion himself out of his own nature through sheer strength of will. She marries him, knowing that joined together they will both approach nearer to the God of infinite love and infinite sorrow.

But after three years of marriage she tells him that his kind of love, which allows no deviance from the straight and narrow, is so stern and hard that it hurts those he loves. His demand of "all or nothing" denies the weak the prospect of heaven. His reply to her calls for a transvaluation of love that will lead eventually to a transvaluation of all values.

> That which the world calls love I neither know
> Nor wish for, but I know the love of God;
> And that is not a soft and gentle thing,
> But stern as death's worst terrors. The caress
> It offers us may strike us like a blow.

What was God's answer in the olive grove,
When His own Son, in sweat of agony,
Begged and entreated, "Take this cup from me"?
Did he remove pain's chalice from His lips?
No, child, He made Him drink it to the dregs.[19]

When Agnes protests that no one in this sinful world can live up to such standards, that human beings must from time to time make compromises with their ideals, Brand replies that failure in the attempt is pardonable, while refusal to make the attempt is damnable. A doctor, a typical humanitarian, remonstrates with Brand: "In life's ledger, you've a large dose of man's will to your credit, but, priest, nothing's entered on the page of love."

Brand then launches into a tirade against the enfeebling effects of love, turning upside down the common idea that love inspires humankind and leads it upward to heaven, as in Dante and Goethe. As the German poet explained to Eckermann, Faust is saved at the end both by his positive deeds and by God's eternal love, showered on him from above—or, in more orthodox language, by works and by grace. Dante's pilgrim is impelled through life by a force loosely called love, "the love that moves the sun and the other stars." For Goethe, this was the "eternal feminine that draws us ever upwards." In contrast, for Brand, love is an excuse for failure, slackness, and sinfulness; even worse, it embraces them.

If the strait path too steep and slippery prove,
There's always the short cut that leads through love:
Or, if you choose on sin's broad road to move,
You never need despair—there still is love!
The man who knew his call, but never strove,
Will triumph in the end—because of love!
And if, with open eyes, astray you rove,
You'll still find shelter, in the arms of love.

Brand's point is that in a world and a society morally contemptible and spiritually lax there can be no place for love in the usual sense of the word. The war against spiritual indifference and moral slackness is a war against those qualities usually associated with humaneness, an understanding and an appreciation of the weakness inherent in human nature. Brand will have none of that. In his dichotomized world, to reach for something higher than present-day society means that the angel of love must be transformed into an angel of hate. In *Brand*, we glimpse just that transvaluation of values that underlies Nietzsche's philosophy. Ibsen's superman must be heroic not out of love for mankind as it is but for mankind as it might be. It also means that the reformation can come about only through the willpower of the chosen few, who are different from their fellow creatures, who live on the heights and want to climb ever higher, and who know that they must sacrifice themselves for this cause. Just as the Swedes and Norwegians should have honored their commitment to a brother in need not in order to save lives but to offer their lives for the cause of a Scandinavian union, so Brand must willingly put at risk all that he holds dear.

> First your will
> Must satisfy law's thirst for righteousness.
> First you must will—in great things and in small—
> Not just what's possible, or merely that
> Which costs some time and trouble to achieve.
> No, firmly, cheerfully, you must resolve
> To force your will through mustered hosts of fears.

"Law's thirst for righteousness" must first be satisfied before love can reign on earth; and this satisfaction can come about only through a willingness, a determination, to make the greatest personal sacrifices.

> To die in agony upon a cross
> Does not create a martyr; he must first
> Will his own crucifixion—be resolved
> To face it, while his flesh for mercy pleads
> And while the terror in his soul protests.
> Then only is redemption granted you.

The greatest impediment to the triumph of Brand's will is not other people but those hosts of fear that lurk within himself. Like Earl Skule, he is filled with doubts about his ability to live without compromising his ideals. A major part of the drama is devoted to scenes in which Brand must again and again overcome these doubts, and in those scenes Ibsen drew on his own inner conflicts. Brand is haunted by the bugaboo of inherited sin, and Ibsen could never cast off the memories of his childhood home. Ibsen's mother had married for money and not for love. So had Brand's mother. He recalls with horror a scene from his childhood when he witnessed his mother plundering the corpse of his father, grabbing a packet of coins, counting them, and groaning, "Is that all?" In his child's mind, she appeared as a falcon swooping down on its prey.

This memory never leaves Brand, and the extent to which it obsesses him is represented by recurring scenes in which a Gypsy girl and a bird of prey appear, never one without the other. The girl, fifteen years old, is the daughter of the man who had been rejected by Brand's mother, and the bird is explicitly called the Spirit of Compromise. Thus the source of his struggle against compromise and halfheartedness is psychologically linked to his childhood. Ibsen attributes both Brand's compulsion to achieve greatness and his self-doubts to the same cause: the materialism of his parents. For Ibsen, as for Brand's mother, what was true in his own home was true of bourgeois society in general. She says, "It's a time-worn custom here / To pay your heart and soul for property." Brand vows to pay her spiritual debt: "God's image, spotted and defiled by you, / In me shall be restored—cleansed by my will," and that vow leaves him no peace. It drives him to make inhuman sacrifices while his sense of inherited guilt undermines his faith in himself.

The last half of the drama puts Brand to a series of tests. Something must finally break the indomitable will of this man, and the suspense in the unfolding action lies in waiting for the moment, the crisis or turning point, that will prove a match for his indomitable will. What force or being or combination of circumstances will cause him to relent in his pursuit of the unblemished ideal?

His motto is "all or nothing," and when his mother is dying, he insists that she give up all her material possessions before he will come to her bedside. She holds back a tenth of what she possesses and, like Ibsen's mother, dies without seeing her son. In the next scene the tables are turned. Demanding no compromise from others, Brand must now let his own sickly son die if he remains as parish priest in a sunless valley. Like Abraham, but without the miraculous outcome, Brand does what his God demands and sacrifices his son.

Next he loses his wife, Agnes, who has wholeheartedly shared his belief in total commitment to the ideal. The manner of her death prefigures that of Brand himself. She treasures above all else the baby clothes of her dead child. When a poor Gypsy woman appears at her doorstep with a bedraggled child, Agnes knows that she must give up these priceless relics. Yet the imperfect spirit in her makes her hold onto the baby cap. Under Brand's stern eyes she forces herself through sheer willpower to surrender this too. Having fulfilled the principle of "all or nothing," she has achieved perfection, become one with her God, and so she dies.

Brand must take the same path, but as hero of the play he has a much more arduous course. Ibsen represents it as the long ascent up a mountain known as Black Peak. First he seeks to form his own church. He leads his followers up the mountain, but they quickly grow weary, and when they hear that a school of fish has been spotted in the waters below, they turn on Brand and stone him. "*Vox populi, vox dei*" is the ironic comment of the dean of the established church.

For Brand, nothing could be further from the truth. The mass of humanity has no understanding of true spirituality, which consists in the relation of the individual to God. Here, as in so much of *Brand,* Kierkegaard provides the appropriate commentary. Protesting against the general leveling characteristic of a democratic age, the Danish philosopher said it could be stopped only "if the individual separating himself through his individuality acquires the fearlessness of religion."[20] As Brand climbs ever higher, he comes ever closer to his God. All that now remains to be overcome are a series of temptations, projections of his inner doubts. A chorus of invisible spirits reminds him that no creature of flesh and blood can attain the perfection of godhead. Thereupon an apparition appears, calling itself Agnes, and pleading with him to abjure his principle of "all or nothing." He refuses to do so, and as the apparition vanishes in a clap of thunder, a voice is heard shrieking, "Die, then! The world has no use for you!" This is the last temptation, the temptation to question one's calling because of the sacrifices others have made to it.

When the apparition is transformed into the bird of prey, Brand knows he was right; the last temptation has been overcome. Gerd, the half-crazed girl, who embodies Brand's sense of inherited guilt, the source of his self-doubts, shoots the bird. The reverberations of the rifle shot set off an avalanche that hurtles down at Brand. Crouching beneath the snow, he calls upward, "Answer me, God, here in the grip of death, does not a measure of human will count toward salvation?"

As the snow covers him, making him part of the mountain that stands for his ideal, a voice is heard crying through the thunderous noise, "He is *deus caritatis*," usually translated as "He is the God of love."

The last verse of this extraordinary drama, the most discussed single line in Norwegian literature, is generally interpreted to mean that God condemns Brand for being unable to compromise, for failing to allow love to have its share in the reformation of the human spirit. That would put this God in agreement with the doctor who urged Brand to think about his love account in the ledger of life and make everything that Brand does in the second half of the play contrary to the spirit of God. Moreover, it would turn all the temptations that confront Brand in the last moments into inducements to do the right thing, whereas the author of the play clearly identifies them as evil temptations. It would in effect destroy every reason Ibsen had for writing the play.

It is not only the most discussed line, it is the most misunderstood, because the commentators will not follow where Ibsen leads them. They remain the humanitarians that Ibsen is castigating. As a philosophical work, *Brand* was so far ahead of its time that it confused readers. Even insightful and sophisticated readers misunderstood what was going on in Ibsen's head. The young, atheistic radical Georg Brandes in Denmark regretted the pietistic tendency in the work, labeled the author "Kierkegaard's poet," and found that Ibsen's moral indignation and social satire were undercut by Brand's being a poor representative of an ideal of any sort.[21]

Strindberg's response was probably typical of the time, and perhaps most readers today feel as he did. He read it when he was a student at the University of Uppsala, and he heard in it the clamorous voice of a modern Savonarola, denouncing a society that worshipped art. Writing about himself, he said it made

> a deep impression on his orthodox Christian [*gammel kristen*] soul, but it was hard and stern. The last line about *deus caritatis* left him unsatisfied, and the poet appeared to be too much on the side of his hero to allow him, merely for the sake of irony, to go down in defeat. Brand gave him a lot of trouble. He got rid of Christianity but held onto its asceticism. He demanded commitment to his old-fashioned teachings that no longer had any relevance; he scoffed at the current striving for fellow feeling and for compromise, but he ends by calling on the God of compromise, the spirit of accord. Brand was a pietist, a fanatic who dared to believe that he was right and the world was wrong, and he felt a kinship with this horrible egotist who on top of everything was wrong. Nothing halfway, just push head, break and bend anything that stands in your way, because you alone are right.... He was the last Christian who gave himself up to an old ideal; therefore he could not be a model for one who felt a dim stirring of revolt against the old ideals. The drama was a pretty plant without roots in time, and therefore belonged in a herbarium.[22]

In the same vein, Shaw read the play as an attack on idealism. Brand, he wrote, while "aspiring from height to height of devotion to his ideal, plunges from depth to depth of murderous cruelty." Most readers may perhaps agree with Shaw. But he saw in the drama what he wanted to see, not what actually happens. Describing the scene in which Brand forces Agnes to "sacrifice the relic to the ideal," Shaw says that Agnes dies brokenhearted. But this is a blatant misreading of what actually happens. (Just as Strindberg was mistaken in thinking that Brand calls on the Spirit of Compromise.) Far from dying brokenhearted, Agnes dies radiantly happy. Having surrendered the last object that bound her to the earth, she embraces Brand, an expression of sublime joy on her face, and exclaims, "I am free! Yes, I am free!" while Brand tries to console himself with the thought that to lose everything in the real world is to retain it forever in the ideal world.

To those who see Brand as a cruel monomaniac and Agnes as his deluded victim, this final embrace must seem like a *folie à deux*. To Ibsen it was transfiguration. Throughout the five acts of the drama Brand always gets the better of those who disagree with his uncompromising position. Ibsen is at one with his hero in every scene, and the satire in the last act is directed at those who think, with Shaw, that Brand's lonely ascent to perfection is a flight from reality.

"Brand is myself in my best moments," Ibsen declared,[23] and it is significant that he did not say, "Brand in *his* best moments is myself." In writing this epic drama, Ibsen purged himself, as he said to Bjørnson, of "the esthetic point of view—existing in isolation and demanding that there be no other concerns in life—which formerly exercised a great power over me." This was the position he had taken in "On the Heights." In *Brand,* he mounted far higher and came to recognize that only through sacrifice does life acquire a moral significance. To an esthete, explained Ibsen, "Christ is really the most interesting phenomenon in the world.... The esthete enjoys him as the glutton does the sight of an oyster."[24]

Ibsen told Bjørnson that while working on the drama, he read "nothing but the Bible—it has vigor and power." In the last act of *Brand* the hero comes more and more to resemble Jesus, the savior who had to resist one temptation after another and who at the end was transfigured at the top of a mountain. A voice out of a cloud said, "This is my beloved Son, in whom I am well pleased."[25] Ibsen draws an explicit parallel: in *Brand,* the voice cries out of a thunderclap, "He is *deus caritatis!*" and "he" cannot refer to the utterer of the words but only to Brand. (And the biblical God never refers to himself in the third person.) Those last words express fulfillment, not condemnation. They sound not an ironic and dissonant concluding chord but a perfectly harmonious resolution to Brand's struggles and an affirmation of the correctness of his views and his way of life.

But it does require an explanation. The transfiguration and sublimation of the man who assailed love as a weakness into the God of love at the very end is a mystery at whose center lies a definition and a dilemma. (Ibsen used the Latin phrase *deus caritatis* because he wanted to avoid the word "love.") He stated that he was using *caritatis* "as distinct from *amor*—earthly love, in order to express heavenly love, with the idea of mercy included" (letter to Michael Birkeland, May 4, 1866). Two kinds of love wage war with each other throughout the drama. Brand rails against the kind of love that makes the individual human being more important than a great cause, one's daily bread more important than the life eternal. In the Christian view, to manifest one's love for God one must subjugate the love for others. "He that loveth father or mother more than me is not worthy of me." The theologians define Christian love as transcending the love for creatures. St. John of the Cross avowed that the soul cannot be possessed of the divine union until it has divested itself of the love of created beings. Brand would accept this view. He takes on the attributes of a God who would call upon Abraham to sacrifice Isaac.

The dilemma that Brand confronts is that love and the law cannot be reconciled. There is no place on earth where light and life are one. He anticipates the final moments in the play when he tells Agnes in act three that mankind can be redeemed only when will has overcome every temptation to compromise. When that happens, love can reenter his life.

> If Will has conquer'd in that strife,
> *Then* comes at length the hour of Love;
> Then it descends like a white dove,
> Bearing the olive-leaf of life:
> But in this nerveless, slothful state,
> The true, the sovereign Love is—Hate![26]

When Brand perishes in the avalanche, the thrust of his whole life is spelled out symbolically. First Gerd, who represents the sins of Brand's mother, shoots the bird of prey, the Spirit of Compromise, that has hovered over his head whenever he has been called upon to make a crucial decision. Now Brand is at the end of a career devoted to atoning for the sins of his parents. The rifle shot sets off an avalanche, and the dead bird of prey vanishes into the snow, whose white flakes are transformed into the wings of a white dove, which in Christian symbolism stands for the Spirit of God.[27] Buried in the snow at the top of the peak that all along has represented the end of his quest, Brand becomes God. All this happens in response to his collapse. Having arrived at the top of the peak, the Ice Church, he can do no more, and he asks Jesus if he has not done enough to merit an end to his agony. When he breaks down and cries, which this stern man had never done before, the peak of ice dissolves into snow. The apostle of inflexible hatred is transformed into *deus caritatis*, the tolerant and forgiving God.

At the end, Ibsen came close to attaining, at least metaphysically, the goal that lies at the heart of his work as a whole. Opposites are united, compromise is defeated, Black Peak becomes white, hate is transformed into love. The possibility of transcending logical opposites in the real world would be a major driving force in his creative work.

PEER GYNT

There are 5,395 lines of rhymed verse in *Brand*, and there is no diminution of vigor from the first to the last of them. Hammered out in less than six months by a Jeremiah enraged at the poltroonery of his countrymen, a Norseman invigorated by the Italian climate, and a master builder awestruck by Italian art, they add up to one of the more astounding poetic achievements of the nineteenth century. Simply as an architectural feat, the fifth act, culminating in the bringing together of all the prior major themes, motifs, and symbols, and constituting one third of the whole poem, surpasses in ingenuity anything in Goethe and puts one in mind of the last moments of Wagner's *Ring* (which was still a few years from completion). In fact, Ibsen may have conceived the structure of that last act when in July 1865 he stood under the dome that Michelangelo had designed for St. Peter's and saw how all the lines springing from the foundation converge at the lantern that lets in the light of God. *Brand* in its entirety is planned like a cathedral: the first four acts are like the four arms of the Greek cross forming the foundation and designed to support the enormous dome. "One day," he said, "I strolled into St. Peter's . . . and there I suddenly saw strongly and clearly the form of what I had to say."[1]

The magnificence of the poem was in sharp contrast to the poverty and straitened circumstances of its author. While he was creating a lasting masterpiece, his personal possessions, left behind in Christiania, were sold at auction without his knowledge or permission. In the meantime, Bjørnson was exhorting his friends in the Norwegian parliament to grant a stipend for the destitute writer and trying to persuade a publisher to sign up the relatively unknown author. While Ibsen was composing the last act of *Brand*, Bjørnson prevailed on Frederik Hegel in Copenhagen to publish the play. Hegel assumed that this would be in the author's usual vein, perhaps another historical drama about the Vikings. The manuscript was delivered in sections, Ibsen evidently hoping to relieve his financial situation by being paid piecemeal for each part. The last sheaf was dispatched on November 16, 1865, a day after Ibsen received his contract. However, when Hegel saw that he had committed himself to publishing a drama in verse with a contemporary setting and much longer than he had anticipated—that fifth act alone would give him pause—he had second thoughts about publishing it. It was originally scheduled to be in print in time for Christmas. But the New Year was ushered in, the weeks passed, and still *Brand* did not see the light of day. Ibsen was in agony.

Humiliated by his inability to pay his debts and fearful that his book would not be published, he poured his heart out to his benefactor Bjørnson. "It seems to me as if I am separated from both God and men by an infinitely great void. Last summer when I was writing my drama, I was indescribably happy, even in the midst of all my pain and misery. I felt the exultation of a Crusader. I had the courage to face anything on earth. But there is nothing so enervating and exhausting as waiting hopelessly. I suppose this is only a transitional phase. Eventually I shall—I will score a victory. If the powers that be have been so unkind as to place me in this world and make me what I am, they must take the consequences."[2]

Shortly after this letter was sent, *Brand* came off the presses. Its success was unprecedented, with three more printings being called for within the year. Although controversy raged over the meaning of the work, no one denied its passion and grandeur. It was unlike anything else in Scandinavian literature. The younger generation especially was overwhelmed by it. The Danish enfant terrible Georg Brandes called it a mighty work of wrath and indignation written by a genius. He was caught up in the work because he had only a short time before gone through his Kierkegaard phase. Ironically, the man who next to Ibsen himself was most responsible for its appearance disliked it the most. Bjørnson said he was "ill from reading it." The politician in him protested. "Fie on this intoxication with principle, this mad enthusiasm for consistency that makes French Revolutions and German nonsense."[3]

Brand, however, made others realize what Bjørnson already knew: that Ibsen was a first-rate poet. In Norway during the next few decades, as Ibsen's fame spread to other countries because of his later realistic plays, no work was more closely identified with him. No work has enriched the Norwegian language with so many memorable lines: what *Hamlet* is to the English, *Brand* is to the Norwegians. It was the making of him as an artist, and it remained always in his own mind a monument to his creative powers and a reminder of his victory over the weaker side of himself. It certainly gave him a taste of the lasting fame he thirsted for.

In the early poem "In the Picture Gallery," written some time after his visit to Dresden in 1852 when he was still struggling to find himself, he expressed the awe he felt as he gazed at the artistic masterpieces of the past, the religious paintings of Correggio, Raphael, Murillo. And the reverential feeling was accompanied by a divine elation. "I feel that in myself is God. . . . I see the concept of God whole and clear, and within me is crushed the demon of doubt."[4] But that was only a fond hope. It was not until he wrote *Brand* that that demon was exorcised.

The years of obscurity, privation, obloquy, and illness were over. Where once he had been patronized as an insignificant poet, shunned as an alcoholic and deadbeat, and derided as a bohemian rebel unwelcome in the best homes, he was now showered with honors and embraced by the God-fearing members of the establishment, who, happily for Ibsen's monetary situation, read *Brand* as a religious poem.

Because of the popular success of his play *Sigurd Slembe,* Bjørnson had been granted a writer's stipend in April 1863, the Storting approving the grant by a vote of sixty-three to twenty-one. This was only the second time the government had granted a stipend to a writer. The committee dispensing these awards disapproved of such grants on the ground that it was impossible to assess the utilitarian value of fiction, and the award was given to Bjørnson only for the year. But with his growing popularity, the sentiments of the committee changed, and in 1865 it favored a regular annual stipend for Bjørnson; a resolution to that effect was passed by the Storting in January 1866, with only twenty-six votes opposed.[5] From 1863 to 1865 he received four hundred specie dollars annually.

Ibsen's application of 1863 had been rejected by the Ecclesiastical Department, which had jurisdiction over the grants. In April 1866, shortly after the publication of *Brand,* Ibsen's friends had telegraphed him, urging him to apply directly to the king of Sweden for the grant, while they would act on his behalf through their influence on members of the Norwegian Storting. Ibsen sent his petition to King Charles on April 15,[6] and on April 19, Ibsen's good friend Michael Birkeland, who as head of the National Archives was on the staff of the Ecclesiastical Department, drew up and signed a petition on the poet's behalf. Birkeland pointed to the enormous success of *Brand,* published just a month earlier, stated that the poet had lived for the past two years in Rome on a stipend of four hundred specie dollars, supplemented by monetary assistance provided by friends, and concluded with words that will strike a sympathetic note with any struggling young writer.

"With all due respect, we hope we may mention that Henrik Ibsen's living conditions have truly been that of a poet, that his career has been a ceaseless struggle for existence, and that he faces a future no brighter than his past. The honorariums that he may earn through his writings may perhaps be sufficient to keep a man from dying but would be all too little to give a poet a life."[7]

The matter had to be handled with dispatch to take advantage of the temporary absence from office of the head of the department, Minister Hans Riddervold. Ever since Riddervold had seen the church mocked in *Love's Comedy* and fancied himself caricatured as Pastor Strawman, he had been implacably opposed to any grant to Ibsen, who regarded him as his personal enemy.[8] Bjørnson may have attempted in 1866 to persuade Riddervold to relent, but his efforts, whether real or only rumored, had certainly had no effect. The Dutchmen were much more successful. After initiating in his weekly paper a campaign for an Ibsen stipend, Botten-Hansen, working with his friends, got the temporary head of the Ecclesiastical Department, Frederik Stang, to approve the stipend and bring it to the floor of the Storting. Two days earlier the same friends, busy behind the scenes, had managed to get twenty-eight members of the Storting to support a resolution for an Ibsen stipend. When the bill was brought in on May 12, it passed with only four votes cast against it.[9] Now each camp had its prize poet.

This grant provided him with an annuity of 400 specie dollars a year. Shortly thereafter, the Royal Norwegian Scientific Association of Trondheim granted him 100 specie dollars, and some weeks later the Norwegian government provided him with a travel grant in the amount of 350 specie dollars. Even the gods of fortune and chance seemed to smile on him. Not only had they arranged the convenient indisposition of Riddervold, but, as the government awards poured in, Ibsen also won money in the Danish national lottery—not just once, but twice.

Such success was bound to have its effect on the outer man. In Italy, when the telegram arrived informing Ibsen that he had been given a writer's annuity, his friends invited him along for a walk in the hills. Ibsen joined them for a short distance, then changed his mind, and sat down at a café for a glass of wine. When his friends looked for him again, the Ibsen they knew had vanished and in his place was the figure that the world was to come to know. The tattered bohemian in big hat, out at elbows, with worn shoes, untrimmed full beard, had stepped offstage and reentered as an elegant parvenu, smartly dressed in a tailcoat and handsome cravat, his full beard reduced to chin whiskers, neatly trimmed à la mode. Even his figure had become sleeker. The impetuous, garrulous, and argumentative social rebel had almost overnight been transformed into the somber, deliberate, rather incommunicative personage who weighed his public utterances as if they were meant to be inscribed in stone. Within a couple of months, from May to June 1869, the handwriting in his letters changed to conform with the personality of the new man. His former cursive, free-flowing, slanted style stiff-

Figure 8. Ibsen, 1866.
Photo by Fratelli Alessandrini, Rome.

ened into a severe verticality, with each page composed as if it were a copperplate engraving.[10]

With his newly acquired self-confidence, Ibsen went looking for a dramatic subject worthy of the author of *Brand.* His mind was drawn to individuals who, like himself, set themselves apart from society. He sifted through his notes on a fifteenth-century freebooter, Mogens Heinessen, who had begun to occupy his mind some years before, and he considered dramatizing the life of Julian the Apostate. Then, as was to happen more than once in his fabulous career, a hero presented himself unbidden. He stepped into his life through the pages of a book of Norwegian folktales. Ibsen had asked his publisher to send books that he could read to his seven-year-old son. Among these books was Asbjørnsen's *Norske Huldre-Eventyr og Folkesagn* (2nd ed., 1866). As he read these stories aloud, his mind teemed with visions of trolls that lived in the mountains, of wild rides on the backs of reindeer, of Askeladden (the Norwegian male counterpart of Cinderella), of sex-starved cowgirls on the upland pastures, of Soria-Moria castle, west of the moon and east of the sun, and of church bells whose tolling saved the souls of those under the devil's spell. But of all the strange characters that figure in these marvelous tales, which blended heathen legends with Christian beliefs, one—Peer Gynt—loomed larger than the others, not only because he was an outsider like Mogens Heinessen and Julian the Apostate but because he came from the same background as *Brand*.

Ibsen had met him once before. In 1862 the University of Christiania, eager to encourage the study of purely native culture, had given Ibsen a grant to collect Norwegian folktales and songs. Setting off in May of that year, he had tramped through the mountains and highlands and along the fjords, accompanied during part of the time by another hiker. The thirty-four-year-old Ibsen must have cut a strange figure, his suntanned face wreathed in a full reddish-brown beard, his short, stocky body encased in a wool jacket, a pack on his back, an old felt hat on his head, his trouser legs cut off at midpoint to form knee breeches convenient for hiking. In this outfit he rambled through 490 miles of rough terrain, and the sights he saw and the people he met provided material for *Brand*—the desolate landscapes, the Gypsies roaming the highlands, the pastor with the young wife and smiling baby living in a cabin under continual threat of an avalanche, their first house having already been destroyed by one. He met the mentally ill Ingeborg Hellesylt, who rolled boulders down the mountainside. He saw the "ice church," a hollow in a glacier large enough to hold thirty people. And it was also on this trek that Ibsen heard about Peer Gynt, a real person who had flourished around 1700 and about whom a number of legends had sprung up. Famous for the incredible adventures he attributed to himself, Peer was a Norwegian Münchhausen. He struck Ibsen as the incarnation of a nationalistic spirit that manifested itself in grandiloquence and tall tales rather than in great deeds. In 1866 when he encountered Peer Gynt once again, he saw a large part of himself in this incurable romancer, remembering that he had only wielded a poet's pen while others had served as volunteers in the Danish army and met the enemy face to face. As Ibsen now saw him, Peer Gynt was a Brand who went bad.

Writing *Peer Gynt* was one of the happiest experiences of Ibsen's life. He felt like "a rearing stallion about to leap." Both in Rome and on the island of Ischia he maintained a strict routine, up at dawn for his morning constitutional, a pot of coffee, then work at his desk from ten to twelve. After his siesta, he read over what he had written in the morning and clear-copied it, leaving the evening for relaxation. This routine was threatened first by a cholera epidemic in nearby Naples, and then by the siroccos that swept across the island and forced the thermometer up to 104 degrees Fahrenheit. In August the temperature rose to 115 degrees. Ibsen still worked on, showing the strain more and more. It was not the hot winds that dislodged him, however; it was an earthquake. The tremor rocked the church tower in Ischia and caused a crack to appear in it. Ibsen took one look at that fractured tower and left for Sorrento on the mainland the next day. It was there that *Peer Gynt* was finished in mid-October.

Peer is twenty when the play begins, a carefree, rambunctious lad who dreams up stories to compensate for the dreariness and emptiness of his real life. His father is dead; his mother, Aase, is impoverished; and Peer himself is the object of the neighbors' ridicule. At a country wedding, he meets Solveig and immediately falls in love with her. But she rebuffs him, and, disdained by her parents, Peer gets drunk and in a frenzy of despair abducts the bride-to-be and carries her off into the hills. Sobering up, he realizes that his behavior has offended his ideal love, Solveig. He abandons the would-be bride and by that act makes himself an outlaw. In a highland meadow, he meets three cowgirls with whom he has a drunken orgy. After this escapade, while his brain is swimming in alcohol and his body is reeling from exhaustion, he encounters the Woman in Green, who takes him to her father, the Troll King. Inside a mountain, the trolls meet and demand that Peer become one of them by having his left eye slit so that he will see things as they do, which means adopting the troll motto: "Be independent." A human being lives by the precept "Be true to thyself" ("Vær dig selv"); the troll motto adds one word, "nok," that changes everything. "Vær dig selv—nok": "Troll, be independent—of others." Ibsen is making use of an old Danish proverb, "No one is an island; each one of us has a need of others" ("Ingen er sig selv nok; den ene har altid den anden behov"). John Donne's "No man is an island" is the English equivalent. Refusing any such commitment, Peer is set upon by the trolls, from whom he is saved by the sound of church bells, rung at the behest of his mother.

Next, Peer meets up with the Bøyg, a shapeless ogre, who tells him to go roundabout, to avoid the straight and narrow. Attacked by birds, the Bøyg's companions, Peer calls on Solveig to strike them with her prayer book, and once again he is saved by church bells and a woman. These scenes with the Bøyg and the trolls take place in Peer's fevered mind.

On a snowy night Solveig comes to Peer in the forest, alienating herself from her family. At the same time the Woman in Green appears to confront Peer with his bastard child. Ashamed and unable to tell Solveig the truth about himself, Peer leaves Norway to find himself in a larger world. Before he departs, he calls upon his dying mother, and in the tenderest scene that Ibsen ever wrote, Peer bids her farewell, brightening her last moments by the power of his imagination.

There is just as much autobiography as folktale and legend in these first three acts of the drama. Ibsen said that when he described the life in the house of Peer's father, the rich Jon Gynt, he had the circumstances and memories of his own childhood before him. Like Ibsen's father, Peer's lost his money in speculation. Peer escapes into a world of tall tales and fanciful dreams, a life of the imagination, to make up for the loss of the comfortable, even luxurious, life that might have been his. Ibsen must have traced part of his storytelling gift back to those days when the good times vanished, when the festive lights went out, and the riotous parties, with emptied schnapps glasses hurled into the fireplace, were no more. Although Ibsen never went to his mother's side when she grew old, and never even wrote to her, the touching scene of Aase's death may be a tender reminiscence of a moment from childhood when he and his mother played at sleigh riding, pretending her bed was a sleigh, the cat was a horse, and the floor an ice-bound fjord. He did admit that Aase was modeled on his mother.[11] A scene so marvelously true in feeling must owe its power either to an actual experience or to a longing so deeply felt by the poet that the real and the imagined became one.

The scenes involving the trolls, the Woman in Green, Solveig, and the Bøyg may seem like pure folktale stuff, but they too are drawn directly from Ibsen's life. They capture, as in a nightmare, the inner reality of his bad times. The Woman in Green is Else Sophie Jensdatter Birkedalen, the mother of his illegitimate child, who would return to haunt him whenever the bailiffs sought him out demanding support money for the child. The harrowing scene in the hall of the Mountain King, in which Peer is nearly compelled to become a troll, and the even more harrowing scene with the Bøyg that ends with the flapping of birds' wings reflect as in an alcoholic delirium the degradation he experienced in Christiania, especially during the period from 1857 to 1861, when nothing worked out for him. These were the years when he made an effort in his position as director of the theater to become a breadwinner and a pillar of society. But he failed as a writer and he failed as a theater manager, and he took to drink. Often too inebriated to carry out his duties at the theater, so distraught that he came close to committing suicide, for a long time bedridden with fever, he was saved from complete shipwreck only through the unselfish solicitude and undeviating faith of his wife, Suzannah, who like Peer's beloved Solveig saw potential greatness where others saw only social hostility, bohemianism, and moral laxity.

Although the evidence is only circumstantial, Ibsen may have felt that he was unable to marry any woman until he had satisfied his legal obligations to provide support for his bastard child. It was not until a year or two before the end of this fourteen-year period that Ibsen married Suzannah Thoresen. Quite possibly he put off marrying her for the same reasons that caused Peer to renounce Solveig. Shamed by his affair with the Woman in Green, Peer considers himself unworthy of Solveig. Peer sees in her the image of perfection, an ideal that is not to be sullied by his sinful past. Reverencing her and deprecating himself, he puts the ideal beyond his reach, unlike Brand, and consequently he shuns any commitment in life. Confronted by the Bøyg, he goes round about. Instead of embracing his ideal, he pursues its shadow. For Peer, the secret of success is to avoid taking any irrevocable steps. A man must never burn his bridges. "That theory has kept me going and colored all my conduct, a theory that I inherited from my family when I was a child."[12]

One reason for writing *Peer Gynt* was to moderate the extremism of *Brand*. The abstract nature of the argument in *Brand* and the religious tone of the drama allowed the hero to avoid some difficult questions. The doctor inquires about Brand's "love account," saying it is quite bare compared with the will he invests in his cause. He should have asked about the cause itself. Ibsen implies that it does not matter what one's higher purpose is—all that matters is the extent of one's commitment. The worth of the cause is equivalent to the sacrifices made in serving that cause. Most of Ibsen's readers, taking the cause to be essentially Christian, did not question it. However, when Ibsen said that Brand's profession as a priest was incidental to the philosophical meaning of the drama and that Brand could just as well have been a scientist like Galileo, he left open other, less pleasant possibilities. Why not Brand as a Napoleon who sought to unite Europe and was responsible for the slaughter of thousands? Or as Hitler? When Brand sacrifices his son, when he calls upon his wife to give up all she possesses, when he says that hate must replace love until his goal has been reached, he sounds very much like the twentieth-century dictator. "If a people is to become free, it needs pride and willpower, defiance, hate, hate, and once again hate." Those were Hitler's words in 1923, but they could have been Brand's.

Ibsen's reply to any such suggestion would be that his poetic drama must be seen against the background of the event that immediately inspired it: the Dano-Prussian War. That war figures prominently in *Peer Gynt*, but it is seen from the Norwegian point of view. The trolls, creatures indigenous to Norway, are the farmers who made up the majority of the Norwegian people, and who, in the debates about the war, saw no reason why Norway should send its men and ships to fight in a foreign country in a hopeless cause. They were isolationists, whose watchword was the same as the trolls' motto: "Be self-sufficient" ("Være sig selv nok"). The phrase carried the same meaning as "America first" did in 1940.

In the first three acts of the play Ibsen put much of himself into the character of Peer. In the troll scenes Ibsen reminds himself that the patriotic poems—like the twelve-sonnet sequence he composed in 1849, "Awaken Scandinavians! A Proclamation to the Norwegian and Swedish Brothers" ("Vaagner Skandinaver! Et Opraab til de norske og svenske Brødre")—and the history plays he wrote encouraged the nationalism he now deplored. And just as the troll scenes are basically political, so too are the scenes with the Bøyg. The shapeless ogre that forces Peer to go roundabout is nothing other than—in the words of Ibsen's German translator—"the wretched dull mass that cripples the will of the individual."[13] Peer fights in vain against the many-headed Bøyg, which conquers without the use of force, just as Ibsen fought against the compact majority when he was head of the theater in Christiania.

The fourth act of the play, which Ibsen did not think was stageable, constitutes a series of cartoons in dramatic form. In this act Ibsen and Peer part company, when Peer becomes everything that Ibsen put behind himself. In the strange, seemingly disjointed scenes set in North Africa, Peer, now middle-aged, has a series of encounters with various individuals. These can all be identified as specific persons prominent in Norway's political and cultural life, and all are the subject of Ibsen's satire. To identify these people and to explain their relevance to Norwegian politics would require, as Ibsen himself said, "a whole book."[14] They represent the Norwegian nation and what led to its demoralization at the time of the Dano-Prussian War.[15]

The drama is divided into three distinct parts, each with its special purpose in the overall design. The first three acts portray Peer as the typical Norwegian, as Ibsen saw him. The long fourth act places Peer in the company of Peer's satirically depicted contemporaries. Without an intimate knowledge of the significant personalities of the time, it is impossible to appreciate Ibsen's skill as a caricaturist. The fourth act was meant as a picture of Norway in all its aspects. Peer becomes Mr. Norway, and he represents the Norwegian spirit in all its incarnations. Knowing who is being ridiculed in these figures provides an entrée into Ibsen's private thoughts and political opinions. For instance, Hussein, who slits his own throat with a pen, is the diplomat who eased Sweden out of a commitment to send troops to Denmark. Bjørnson, perhaps the most representative Norwegian figure, both as writer and politician, appears as the prophet of a new religion, Danish Grundtvigianism. The dark-hued dancing girl who flirts with him is Magdalene Thoresen, the stepmother of Ibsen's wife.

Magdalene was a "seductive Latin beauty whose fiery glance suggested a mixed heritage, possibly a gypsy origin," and she was described as having "a brown complexion like that of Ritra in Christian Winther's poem."[16] Bjørnson had an affair with this voluptuous and sexually experienced woman in the early 1860s, and inevitably his wife came to know about it. Ibsen learned about the breakup of the affair, perhaps through Georg Brandes, more probably through Suzannah, and so he has Anitra ride off with the prophet's horse, leaving Gynt-Bjørnson thunderstruck. The Anitra scenes take up a disproportionately large part of act four, and Ibsen must have enjoyed sketching Bjørnson as a playful, boyish lover, who believes he can instill a soul into this earthy beauty. Years later, Ibsen found in Magdalene material for a study of sexual compulsions.[17]

Figure 9. Magdalene Thoresen, 1866.

As drama, the fourth act slows down Peer's progress and is usually cut severely when the play is staged. Yet for Ibsen's purposes, and for the reader's understanding of his thoughts, it cannot be ignored. Mingling politics and philosophy, the fourth act serves as a bridge to the final act, in which Peer confronts, as it were, the neglected Brandian aspect of himself. The last two acts form a kind of cautionary tale, condemning the Norwegians and showing what Ibsen might have become if he had not resolved to be as much like Brand as possible.

Peer Gynt Meets Hegel

There is an extraordinarily deep subtext to *Peer Gynt*, and exploring it reveals how well Ibsen understood the main philosophical schools of his time. Although *Peer Gynt* is part autobiography and part political drama, at bottom it is a philosophical drama. In fact, it cannot be fully appreciated as a work of art unless it is read as a disquisition of sorts. The underlying conflict sets two systems of thought against each other, and in dramatizing it, Ibsen displayed his superb organizational skills.

Although both *Brand* and *Peer Gynt* were inspired by the Dano-Prussian War, *Brand* presented an abstract picture of the heroic ideal. Emphasizing its quality as a demonstration, Ibsen called it a "syllogism."[1] Now in *Peer Gynt* he intended to dig at the root causes of the war, to picture the unheroic citizen, to tell the unvarnished truth about his countrymen, and finally to set his whole argument on a firm philosophical foundation. Boldly, trenchantly, he placed on one side Hegel, the state philosopher of Prussia, along with Goethe, the poet laureate of Germany. In opposition to these giants he set Kierkegaard, the Danish philosopher who had assailed Hegel's system of thought, and himself, now the leading poet in Scandinavia: Nordic intellectual might against the Teutonic.

Emulating Goethe, he shaped *Peer Gynt* as a Norwegian *Faust*, employing a variety of verse forms, and giving it a loose, episodic structure. Its hero wandered roundabout, like Faust, yielding to impulses, experiencing life with little concern for others, and ending in the arms of Woman.[2] For Ibsen, Faust was the type of man who leads a life of ceaseless activity without any specified higher aim, and much of Peer's career parallels Faust's. Both are saved from despair by church bells. Faust falls in love with the ideal woman but seduces Gretchen. Peer falls in love with Solveig but has a child by the Woman in Green. The trolls in Ibsen correspond to the witches in Goethe. The pact with Mephistopheles has its counterpart in Peer's contretemps with the trolls, with Peer finding out eventually that a pact was made in spite of himself. Similarly, there is in *Faust* a huge gap between the first and second parts, between the small world and the great world of Faust's explorations, just as there is between act three and act four of *Peer Gynt*. Faust becomes prime minister, economist, scientist, artist, and engineer, while Peer becomes capitalist, prophet, archeologist, and historian. Monetary affairs in both Ibsen and Goethe end in explosions. As engineer, Faust drains a swamp; Peer dreams of irrigating a desert. Faust finds Helen; Peer has a deflating affair with the dancing girl. And Goethe's Classical Walpurgisnacht has a parallel in Gynt's plan to visit Babylon, Troy, and Athens.

Ibsen did not, however, choose to follow Goethe for poetic reasons; his concerns were political and philosophical. Goethe's superman wandered through life always in search of new experiences. As long as he was active and dissatisfied, the devil could not claim him. Stagnation was the only damnable sin. Goethe replaced the Christian God with the evolutionary spirit, and Faust, like the force of nature in Darwin's theory, proceeds by trial and error, mounting ever higher in the process, finally being lifted up to heaven by a God who appreciates his efforts and who indicates his approval by showering him with roses, signifying God's grace—a far cry from the apotheosis of Brand.

To Ibsen, the Ibsen fresh from *Brand*, this view of the passage through life was inane. It lacked the one thing that could give meaning and value to the life of the individual: suffering and sacrifice. Faust was a playboy who was willing to see others—like Marguerite, whom he loves and discards, and the aged couple Philemon and Baucis, whom he evicts from their house because it obstructs his view—suffer for the sake of his mundane ambitions and selfish desires. He had no higher purpose other than keeping himself busy.

Paralleling the political war between Prussia and Denmark was a philosophical war between Hegel, the supporter of the political state, and Kierkegaard, the advocate of individualism. Ibsen often downplayed the influence that Kierkegaard had on him, insisting that he had read little of Kierkegaard and understood less.[3] Unlike Strindberg, who wanted his readers to believe that he had read everything and understood it all, Ibsen would admit only to having read the Bible, Holberg's comedies, and the newspapers. But the weight of Kierkegaard's thought is already felt in *Love's Comedy* and in the poem "On the Heights," while the hero of *Brand* is virtually an incarnation of the Danish philosopher. In *Brand*, Ibsen followed Kierkegaard in finding that his paradox applied to life itself. Attaining one's goal means sacrificing what one loves. Everyone knows that nothing worthwhile is accomplished without paying a price. Those who give nothing of themselves are worth nothing. In the economics of the soul, materialist values are reversed. The greater the loss that the individual incurs, the greater his net worth. To esthetes, however, the Kierkegaardian paradox sounds like nonsense. For them the pleasure offered by what one loves is all that matters. Moralists, on the other hand, recognize that the gratification of the senses and concern for loved ones must at certain times yield to higher causes, such as devotion to one's country in time of war. But for Kierkegaard there was a still higher cause, the will of God, and in serving this cause the individual attained the religious stage of existence, where the paradox of love and sacrifice takes its cruelest and most pointed form. For Kierkegaard, Abraham's willingness to sacrifice his son at the behest of God demonstrated the "teleological suspension of the ethical." It went beyond family feelings, beyond social morality, certainly beyond logic. It put man in direct contact with a transcendent God. Only the man who has the true faith understands that "God, without injustice, and without denying his nature, which is love, might create a man equipped with unexampled powers, set him down in a solitary place, and say to him: 'Do you now live through and experience the human in unparalleled intensity; labor so that half the effort might suffice to transform an entire contemporary generation. But you and I, we are to be alone about all this; your efforts are to have no significance whatever for any other human being.'"[4] This is "the divine madness" that drives Brand.

When *Brand* was published, everyone recognized how close the poem was to Kierkegaard's thought—that is, everyone except Ibsen. He protested that *Brand* was being misinterpreted because the hero was a priest. The problem presented in the play was not a religious problem. "I could have found an equally satisfactory expression for the feelings that impelled me to create it, if instead of Brand, I had written of Galileo, say (making him of course hold his ground and not admit that the earth stands still)."[5]

However much Ibsen owed to Kierkegaard, he was right to emphasize how he differed from him. Kierkegaard had kept the Christian God at the center of things; Ibsen cashiered him and replaced him with the indomitable hero who becomes godlike (or rather God himself) by overcoming all temptations to compromise his principles. The black peak, the church of ice, in the last act of *Brand* is the goal of perfection, and when Brand overcomes the last temptation he literally becomes part of it. He is then at one with his God. The tragedy is that his reward, the gift of love, cannot be his as long as he is struggling to attain purity. In that respect, Brand is no different from the Christian who knows that his reward for living the good life comes after death.

By substituting an abstract principle for a God in heaven, Ibsen became an atheistic existentialist, perhaps the first. Just as Kierkegaard is considered a forerunner of existentialism, so *Brand* should be read as the first existential drama. As in Kierkegaard, the signs of Christianity are put in the service of a new dispensation. Like Nietzsche, another proto-existentialist, Ibsen contemplated the death of God and understood that henceforth the individual must make his own existence, his own ideal. "I will" replaces "Thou shalt." Like Sartre, Ibsen recognized that to find some permanent value and to escape contingency, the individual must form his "own foundation of belief, the *ens causa sui,* which theologians call God. Thus the passion of man is the reverse of that of Christ, for man loses himself as man in order that God may be born. But the idea of God is contradictory, and we lose ourselves for nothing. Man is a useless passion."[6] The Ibsen who wrote the final pages of *Brand* faced up to this harsh truth. His superman has not changed the world; his sacrifices appear to have been all in vain. Yet he would not have it otherwise. A materially better world, a redeemed sacrifice, eternal life in paradise—for Brand these are carrots to donkeys. For him, the reward must lie in the journey itself, the useless passion must express itself in nothing else, measuring its worth solely in terms of its own purity, its own forcefulness, its power over others and over itself.

The philosophical implications of *Brand* were not appreciated in the Anglophone world until after World War II, when existentialism became fashionable. Karl Jaspers developed the idea of *Existenzphilosophie* during World War I after reading Kierkegaard. The Danish philosopher was virtually unread in England and America until the 1930s. The failure to understand *Brand* as an existentialist work prevented Anglophone commentators from seeing what lies at the heart of Ibsen's works as a whole, and it led them to ignore Ibsen the philosopher, a subject prominent in German criticism but virtually untouched by English and American readers until Brian Johnston's *The Ibsen Cycle,* 1975.

To set the record straight, Ibsen had to estrange himself from Kierkegaard. But when he sought to lay a sound foundation for his radical existentialist views he turned again to Kierkegaard for material and studied him carefully. In the summer of 1867, when he was writing *Peer Gynt,* he borrowed Kierkegaard's major work, *Concluding Unscientific Postscript,* from the library of the Scandinavian Society in Rome and kept it for six weeks.[7] This book is a sustained attack on Hegelianism, and in examining the effect that the Dano-Prussian War had on Scandinavia, which was Ibsen's immediate purpose in writing *Peer Gynt,* he aligned himself and Kierkegaard against Goethe and Hegel. The German poet found the philosophical basis for his view of human progress in the Prussian professor, who saw all of history as a process by which mind or spirit realizes itself, refining and purifying itself as it seeks freedom from matter. Progress results from the conflict of two opposing views that generate a higher point of view, thesis and antithesis becoming absorbed in a synthesis that in turn generates its opposite. This system of triads, fundamental to Hegelian thought, is ridiculed by Ibsen at the beginning of the fourth act when the German businessman Eberkopf describes Peer as "nature's man and the cosmopolitan, amalgamated at the triad's top."[8]

In his admired discussion of Sophocles's tragedy *Antigone,* Hegel found an excellent example of how progress occurs in politics. Antigone stands for the right of the individual, the tyrant Creon for the social order and the necessary discipline maintained by the state. They represent diametrically opposed views, and neither will yield. The immediate consequence is that Antigone is executed and Creon loses his son. But Hegel believed there was a further consequence: out of this double loss came an improved model of the social organization. Both Antigone and Creon were wrong, that is, too one-sided. But by the mediation of opposites, out of the two wrongs came a right.

Ibsen would have none of this. If he had written about *Antigone,* he would have argued that the heroine was right and the despot was wrong, and that there was no middle ground between the two. Brand's motto was "all or nothing," and purity of heart consisted, in Kierkegaard's words, in willing one thing. Hegel represented the spirit of compromise that Brand sought to slay. Compromise was the method of politics; it was not the way that the individual could realize himself. In the Dano-Prussian War, Sweden and Norway had behaved like Hegelians, regarding themselves as the mediating spirit between Denmark and Prussia.

In the mid-1860s Ibsen regarded Germany as the cancerous focal point of moral corruption; it was the land of a false and deceitful philosophy. Goethe created a superman who could ride roughshod over weaker souls in savoring life to its fullest. Hegel constructed a system of thought that saw history as the mediation of opposites. But in reading Kierkegaard, Ibsen saw that the Hegelian system contained the seeds of its own destruction.

In an extraordinarily incisive poem, "Abraham Lincoln's Assassination" ("Abraham Lincolns Mord"), Ibsen controverted the Hegelian concept of history. Written just two weeks after the murder of the American president in 1865, it contrasts the cries of sorrow and howls of indignation aroused by the killing of one man in America with the silence and indifference that greeted far worse crimes in Europe. Thousands are murdered by armies ("a Prussian perpetration, a Dybbøl deed")[9] without protest from other nations. Treaties are ripped to shreds and the fields bloodied because of forsaken promises. Nothing will change, says the poet, until Germany, the Roman Empire of modern times, shall have fulfilled its destiny and extended its sway from pole to pole. The tyrant must first be apotheosized, the kaiser must be enshrined as a god. Only then will the mighty state edifice collapse like Nero's Colossus. The circuses, the palaces and temples, the columns will be trampled under the buffaloes' hooves. By playing on "boffelen" as meaning both boor and bison, Ibsen unites Europe and America in one image and envisions a world in which the middle class is completely triumphant. The stench of decay is everywhere; and if modern civilization is sinking into a morass, the poet will not lament its passing, for a new age is about to be born. In the concluding lines a serpent bodies forth both the Prussian state and Hegel's System. History will eventually pronounce judgment on Europe, but not until the corrupting monster has nothing more on which to feed.

> May the great serpent consume itself.
> Only when naught remains but an empty shell
> Will the world fall in upon itself.
> And may the "System" swallow its own tail.
> On Doomsday the avenging spirits will meet
> To pronounce judgment on this Age of Deceit.[10]

This poem provides a gloss on what happens at the end of act four of *Peer Gynt*. Ibsen is setting up Hegel as the philosophical father of the new world order and then turning the dialectics of the System against Hegel himself. Where Marx stood Hegel on his head, Ibsen turns him inside out. If each concept or position gives rise to its opposite, then Hegel's entire System, which includes the German state, must upon reaching its fullest expression negate itself. Ibsen's poem has the serpent consuming itself, leaving only its skin; the philosopher Begriffenfeldt in *Peer Gynt* speaks of Absolute Reason as going from itself and as becoming unskinned, like Münchhausen's fox that was flogged until it leaped out of its skin, or like the eel that is pinned to the wall and pulled out of its skin. Hegel himself had considered this eventuality in his *Phenomenology of Mind* in which he wrote that the "last stage of reason's function . . . is its very worst, and for that reason its complete reversal becomes necessary." When a state of soulless existence has been attained, "rational observation seems in fact to have also reached its culminating point, at which it must take leave of itself and turn right about; for it is only when anything is entirely bad that there is an inherent and immediate necessity in it to wheel round completely into its opposite."[11] For Hegel, Absolute Reason was the goal of the Absolute Spirit working itself out in history. Then it would follow in the gyre of the Hegelian System that reason, having attained absoluteness in the Absolute State, must pass over into its opposite, Absolute Unreason.

In the final scenes of act four, Ibsen shows how. (Ibsen chose Egypt as his setting because for Hegel, Egypt was the land of symbols.)[12] The whole drama attains its climax in these scenes in which Hegelian reasoning leads to absurdity and madness. All the inmates of the asylum have a connection with the Dano-Prussian War and its consequences. Huhu is Kristopher Janson, a writer who encouraged the development of rural Norwegian, the dialect of the farmers and quite distinct from Dano-Norwegian, the literary language. Ibsen saw this as isolating Norway from its neighbors in Scandinavia. The Fellah, an Egyptian peasant, is Johan Sverdrup, a liberal politician who voted against military aid to Denmark, who headed a movement that would unite the farmers (the trolls) as a political force, and who, like Janson, wanted a distinct Norwegian language. Hussein, who thinks of himself as a pen, is George Sibbern, the Norwegian minister in Stockholm, who was no more than a pen in the hands of the Swedish foreign minister, who failed to act when the Prussians invaded Denmark. He slits his throat with his pen in front of Peer, who faints at the sight and is crowned Emperor of Self. Confined in a cage, which represents Germany, are its ordinary citizens, Mikkel, Schlingelberg, Schafmann, and Fuchs.

Presiding over this asylum is "Professor, Dr. phil." Begriffenfeldt ("field of concepts"), who is transparently Hegel, the state philosopher of Prussia. (Ibsen gives him a Berlin dialect because Hegel taught there during the last years of his life.) When Peer and Begriffenfeldt first meet, the philosopher has been standing behind the Sphinx. This, like everything in act four, is significant. General Moltke, the commander of the Prussian forces in the war with Denmark, was known as "the strategical Sphinx." To Ibsen, Hegel's philosophy, which saw the Prussian state as the culmination of reason in history, was the complement of Prussian regimentation. And the Scandinavian countries had come under the spell of Hegel, in spite of Kierkegaard's admonitions. In the Hegelian System, when a state of existence reaches its fulfillment, it flips over to its opposite; so when Begriffenfeldt tells Peer that "Absolute Reason dropped dead last night at eleven o'clock," it means that from that moment Absolute Unreason reigns in the world. The new age, the age of Peer Gynt, is characterized by an avoidance of individual responsibility, a "going-from-self" (*Fra-sig-Gaaen*), as Begriffenfeldt expresses it. The result is a "complete revolution."

> At eleven last night the mad and witless
> Became the standard of mental fitness,
> In conformity with Reason's latest phase.
> And then in accordance with logic's ways
> It follows that all those whose heads were healthy
> Found at eleven last night bats in their belfry.[13]

Like everything in act four of *Peer Gynt*, "eleven last night" is a pointed reference to a specific event. It was the hour that the Danish troops retreated from the supposedly impregnable redoubts at Dybbøl on the night of February 5, 1864. The Night of the Retreat (*Tilbagetogsnatten*) was the single most devastating public event in Denmark in the nineteenth century.

Peer believes that he escaped from the trolls and that their guiding principle of "me first" is not his. But in the storm at sea that begins the fifth act, he lets the ship's cook drown to save himself. As Peer clings to the keel of the sunken ship, the devil in the guise of a strange passenger (who like Goethe's Mephistopheles can assume the shape of a dog) pops up, expressing an interest in Peer's corpse. "Have you even *once* in your life gained the victory that is given in dread?"[14] From this point the fifth act becomes a morality play, a modern *Everyman*, as Peer's life passes in review, with Kierkegaard replacing Hegel as the philosopher at work behind the scenes, and existential Angst serving instead of Absolute Reason as the guiding force. A key concept in Kierkegaard, Angst is the apprehension felt when the individual sees his life as meaningless and inconsequential. It is a state of mind that one wants to be rid of, but its very presence is an assurance that one's life has some substance. It is the anguish that animals do not feel and that raises the afflicted individual above his sensual nature. For Kierkegaard, it is a sign of spiritual redemption.

Here again, Ibsen takes on Goethe, faulting him for his lack of earnestness. The old Faust never experiences Angst; the closest he comes to it is when he confronts Care (*Sorge*), admits that he seized every pleasure that came his way, did not regret missed opportunities, and gave no thought to what lies beyond the world of men.[15] Approaching the end of his life, Peer realizes that he has never made any strong commitments, never given himself to a higher cause, always yielded to his impulses and whims, and that consequently he has no self. In the paradoxical realm of the spirit, to lose oneself is to gain oneself. In the famous onion scene, Peer peels off layer after layer, each one representing a phase in his career, and finds that there is nothing left of the onion, no kernel, no center, nothing at all. This scene takes place on the evening of Pentecost. The following morning, at the time that the Holy Spirit descended on the disciples, Peer's heart fills with remorse for a life without meaning. "I am in terror of being dead long ere my death." The realization that his life is empty of meaning fills him with the dread that signals the birth of a new man. In Kierkegaard, Angst casts a ray of light from the higher spiritual regions that both attracts and frightens. Simultaneously, Peer sees his faithful Solveig and recognizes that his kingdom lay with her and not with the Gyntish ego of desires and impulses that led to his being crowned Emperor of Self in Hegel's madhouse.

When he meets the king of the trolls again, now as old as Peer, he learns that in spite of having refused to league himself with the trolls, he has actually lived according to their motto. He has been self-sufficient all along ("Vort *nok*").[16]

Only once in his life did he sacrifice what he most loved, and that was when he could not bring himself to see Solveig, feeling himself unworthy of her. Solveig comes to represent the best element in Peer, "the whole man, the true man," and at the very end of his journey he returns to her, like a frightened child to its mother. Whether the good stuff in him will be melted down by the button molder and recast in a finer human being is left unclear.

Something mystical occurs at the end, similar to the last scene in *Brand* in that the hero becomes his own savior. When Peer asks where his true self has been, "the Peer who bore the stamp of God upon his brow," Solveig says, "In my faith, in my hope, and in my love."

"What are you saying? Don't play with words! To the boy in me you are the mother."

"Yes," says Solveig, "that is what I am. But who is his father? He who hears the mother's prayer and grants a pardon."

Then Peer understands that he himself is that father. Solveig, the pure, transcendental ego, the good material in Peer, is comparable to the Virgin Mother whom God used to create the Savior. Comprehending this, Peer sees that he himself must be father to the boy within, that is, it must be he himself who impregnates the source of life with purpose and meaning. Here, as in *Brand*, Ibsen is employing Christian mysticism to formulate an existential philosophy that makes the individual his own redeemer—to rid himself of Christianity, to subvert Kierkegaard, and to turn himself into God. He addresses her as "My mother, my wife, innocent woman" ("Min Moder, min Hustru; usklydig Kvinde"), echoing the words with which Faust is received in heaven: "Virgin pure from stain of earth, / Mother honour-throned, / Chosen Queen, and peer by birth / With the Godhead owned" ("Jungfrau, rein im schönsten Sinn, / Mutter, Ehren würdig / Uns erwählte Königin / Göttern ebenbürtig").[17] And Goethe, in turn, is echoing Dante's *Paradiso*. Earlier in the play, Ibsen, who regarded Goethe as a womanizer, had Peer misquote the famous last lines of *Faust*, "The eternal feminine draws us upwards" ("Das Ewig-Weibliche / Zieht uns hinan"), turning them into their opposite: "The eternal feminine attracts us" ("Das ewig weibliche ziehet uns an!").

Ibsen himself fell into the clutches of the Lean One, the devil who informs Peer that he is not even much of a sinner; he is only a nonentity, one of Dante's Trimmers, worthy of neither heaven nor hell, and doomed to exist in limbo. When the Lord called on Abraham to sacrifice his son Isaac, Abraham had to obey the religious imperative, however absurd. For Kierkegaard, this sacrifice came to signify the raising of man's spirit from the ethical to the religious sphere. A similar recognition came to Ibsen. The loss of Norwegian men in a hopeless war against the Prussians might seem absurd to politicians and to ordinary citizens. But to Ibsen there was a principle involved higher than the saving of lives. It was a matter of brotherhood and loyalty and the fulfillment of a promise made. Absurd, perhaps, but that principle formed the bedrock of the social organization.

Insisting that "everything I have written has the closest possible connection with what I have lived through *inwardly*," and emphasizing that in each new work of his he had aimed at his own spiritual emancipation and purification, Ibsen went on to say that "no man can escape the responsibilities and the guilt of the society to which he belongs."[18] And he came dangerously close to becoming a nationalistic troll with his plays glorifying Norway's Viking age. He succeeded, however, in refashioning himself as Brand when the Dano-Prussian War brought home to him, as nothing in his private life had done, the importance of sacrifice. The trolls represented the Gyntish part of himself, the indulgent part that had to be subdued. Brand, he said, "is myself in my best moments,"[19] implying that Brand is virtually faultless and thus answering those critics who think Brand is condemned at the end of the drama, while *Peer Gynt*, which he called "the antithesis of *Brand*,"[20] represented "the dregs and sediment" of his nature.

Living is a war with the trolls
In the depths of the mind and heart;
Writing means summoning oneself
To court and playing the judge's part.[21]

FALLING OUT WITH BJØRNSON

Peer Gynt began winning the hearts of readers from the day of its publication, a second printing being called for only two weeks after the first. In a newspaper review Bjørnson called it a magnificent poetic achievement, "a satire on Norwegian selfishness, narrow-mindedness, and smugness carried out so that I not only laughed aloud time after time but had to pause in my reading to say to myself, as I now say publicly, how much I thank the author for giving it to us."[1]

To Ibsen himself, Bjørnson was even warmer in his praise. "Nowadays I cannot talk of anything but your poem nor think of anything but you. . . . I love your devotion to the great aims we share, from the Danish cause to the loftiest ideals. I love you for being strong, I love you for being bold and reckless. It struck me like the fresh air of the sea after the suffocating atmosphere of the sickroom. My thoughts became filled with joy, became daring and rashly truthful, as the small things revealed themselves as trifles while the great things brightened my own yearnings."[2]

While Bjørnson was lauding the poem for the truths it revealed and the inspiration it offered, a brash young critic in Denmark was censuring it for lacking both truth and beauty. "The contempt for humanity and the self-hatred that have inspired it provide a poor foundation for poetry. How ugly and distorted a view of life it offers! What sour pleasure can a poet find in so sullying human nature?"[3]

With a little imagination one can see Ibsen dismissing the insignificant Danish critic and embracing his fellow Norwegian. Together he and Bjørnson could hope to reform the Norwegian nation, instilling in it the faith and courage it had lacked in 1864. Their disagreements of the past would be forgotten, and Ibsen would take his place beside Bjørnson to forge the Norwegian conscience. But here a little imagination goes the wrong way. Bjørnson's panegyric was to be followed by recriminations on the part of both men, leading to a rupture in their relationship that was not to be healed for more than eight years. It was the brash young critic, Georg Brandes, not Bjørnson, who was to become Ibsen's comrade in arms for the next twenty years.

The immediate occasion for the falling out was a review of *Peer Gynt* written by Clemens Petersen, and the story of the two Norwegian authors becomes in large part a tale of two critics.

Ibsen knew that in order to win renown in Denmark, which he wanted as much as Bjørnson did, he would have to have the support of Petersen. But Petersen, in spite of the fact that his esthetic philosophy stressed content over form, always faulted Ibsen's works on formal grounds. *Love's Comedy* in his view lacked drama;[4] similarly, *The Pretenders* was essentially epic, not dramatic.[5] Ibsen has misunderstood his own originality and capabilities, said Petersen, and suggested that Ibsen's true métier was verse imbued with symbolic meaning.[6]

Now, *Brand* was the kind of work that accorded with Petersen's appraisal of Ibsen's talents. The danger was that the critic might this time adhere to his philosophy and censure the matter while ignoring the form. To guard against this, Ibsen, feeling isolated from his countrymen and convinced that his future success depended on Petersen's commendation, appealed directly to the critic for a fair hearing.

> At Christmas there will appear a dramatic poem by me which I most urgently ask you to interest yourself in as far as your conscience will permit. The mean and hopeless spirit that prevails in my home country has formed me to examine myself and current conditions; the sentiment and the subject matter of the poem have developed from this. You once wrote of me that the versified form imbued with symbolic meaning was my natural mode of expression. I have often thought about that remark. I agree with you, and it is in accordance with that thought that the poem has shaped itself. But I have not been able to avoid hitting hard. I ask you, if you can, not to examine this aspect of the work under a magnifying glass. Your review will be a decisive factor in my countrymen's reception of the poem and of those truths that I have not been able to withhold; but of course I should like to avoid martyrdom as long as possible.
>
> The journalistic scribblers who practice criticism in Norway will not understand it. I therefore urgently ask that you give me your support, as promptly and as strongly as you possibly can, on all those points where you find either the subject matter or I myself deserve it. Should you have anything to communicate to me that does not find a place in your review—which I await with assurance and eagerness—I would thank you most warmly for a few lines. I am unbearably oppressed by the feeling that I stand all alone.[7]

In his review Petersen did find much to praise, especially with regard to the logic of the argument. Nevertheless, he found *Brand* too abstract, too far removed from reality. To Bjørnson he expressed a harsher opinion, calling the drama polemical and unpoetic. Bjørnson concurred: "*Brand* is no poem, and Ibsen is hardly a poet."[8]

A year later, Ibsen wrote to Petersen again. Ibsen was now composing *Peer Gynt*, and a good word from Denmark's leading critic would be helpful in the marketplace. But, transformed by the astonishing success of *Brand*, Ibsen now wrote to the critic not out of loneliness and despair but out of the self-confidence of one more inclined to bestow thanks than to ask for favors.

> Although I have confined myself—for nearly a year now—to expressing through a third person [Bjørnson] my gratitude for your review of *Brand* and the advantages thereby secured to me, it is certainly not from a lack of appreciation of your services. But you once took occasion to write a few words about undue intimacy after short and hasty acquaintance, and those words have left me somewhat shy. I feel sure, however, that there has been no such "affectation" in my appeals to you; yet the characteristic such as you interpret it is at any rate so truly Norwegian that I can easily see it was a Norwegian who gave you the opportunity for the observation and the remark.
>
> In spite of this, I still venture to send you my thanks for the review—both for the expressed criticism and for the implicit one. The first has been a great personal joy to me and of great help in establishing my position with the public; the latter has certainly not been any joy to me, but has for just that reason been all the more helpful in self-analysis, which cannot be shirked with impunity.
>
> But I have to thank you for more than the reviews of *Brand* and my other works. I want to thank you for every word you have written besides, and I hope that in my new work [*Peer Gynt*] you will acknowledge that I have taken an essential leap forward.
>
> I have been told that you once said you did not believe it would be of any use to review my works since I would not follow suggestions for improvement. Certainly I could not follow directions simply upon the strength of mere authority, for then I would not be true to myself; and such a blind acceptance of your suggestions would, I am quite sure, afford you no satisfaction either. But the step forward of which I speak lies precisely in the fact that hereafter it is no longer a question for me of "what to be" but of "what must be." You have helped me across that yawning gulf, and therefore I thank you now and shall always thank you.[9]

Ibsen's thanks were premature. Reviewing *Peer Gynt* two weeks after its publication, Petersen asserted that neither *Brand* nor *Peer Gynt* was an authentic poem since in trying to accommodate reality to art Ibsen had done violence to both. *Peer Gynt* was too allegorical; the characters had no depth; and there was no sense of an ideal vision behind the work. As a final touch he gibed at Ibsen's provincialism. Comparing *Peer Gynt* with the famous Danish satiric journal *The Corsair* (*Corsaren*), Petersen remarked that Ibsen's satire was not witty but emotional, not Danish but Norwegian.[10]

That Ibsen would be affronted by the supercilious tone of the review is not surprising. What is surprising is that he took Petersen's strictures as the beginning of a campaign against him by a whole league of enemies. One reason for his suspicion was that Petersen had praised Bjørnson as a writer perfectly in harmony with current literary standards and had counseled Ibsen to learn from his younger countryman. But only the presence of deep-lying predisposing causes—and the slowness of the mails—can explain the accusations that Ibsen leveled at Bjørnson. A month after the publication of *Peer Gynt,* Ibsen held in one hand Petersen's carping review and in the other Bjørnson's exhilarating letter. There could be no deceit in the letter, but there was, he felt, malice in the review. Regrettably, Ibsen had not yet read the issue of *Norsk Folkeblad* containing Bjørnson's own review. So, confronted with what he interpreted as the complicity of Bjørnson and Petersen, he tore up the letter of thanks he had just written to Bjørnson and wrote another, and, with barely repressed rage, impugned Petersen's motives while reproaching Bjørnson for temporizing with the truth.

> If I were in Copenhagen and had a friend as close to me as Clemens Petersen is to you, I would have beaten the life out of him rather than let him commit such a biased and prejudiced crime against truth and justice. Clemens Petersen has built his review on a lie—not in what he says but in what he refrains from saying. And he very deliberately refrains from saying a good deal. You are quite at liberty to show him this letter. As surely as I know him to be profoundly and seriously concerned with what really makes life worth living, so surely do I know that his review will someday burn and sear his soul; for one can lie as much by keeping silent as by speaking out.[11]

What Ibsen calls a "lie" was Petersen's pretense that the *Peer Gynt* review was based on esthetic principles when in fact Petersen was impugning Ibsen's philosophy and religious beliefs. Ibsen had grounds for suspecting that Petersen and Bjørnson were in collusion since they belonged to the same school, so much so that they echoed one another. Bjørnson said *Brand* "is no poem, and . . . the whole thing is an abstract experiment, an army of thoughts on maneuvers. . . . The characters don't gain an ounce of life for all their shouting and screaming. . . . Now we have to shield ourselves against the confusions, the abstractions that destroy the humanity of it all. I hate this book! I am sick from reading it."[12] Some of this feeling he conveyed to Ibsen himself. "Your *Brand* for all its genius and miraculous power is no poem. . . . Your *Brand,* which is my antipodes, has filled me with deep respect for your talent and your idealism. . . . [But] now I would like to see you draw real characters without their becoming mere abstractions and ideas."[13]

These words would have been in Ibsen's mind as he wrote to Bjørnson about Petersen's biased review of *Peer Gynt*. Ibsen's letter reveals the new man, no longer Earl Skule envying Håkon, but a man determined to claim his place in the world.

> My book *is* poetry. And if it is not, then it shall be. The conception of poetry in our country, in Norway, shall be made to conform to my book. There is nothing fixed and eternal in the world of ideas. The Scandinavians of this century are not Greeks. He says that the Strange Passenger represents the concept Dread. If I were on the verge of being executed, and if all it would take to save my life would be an explanation like that, it still would not occur to me. I never thought of such a thing. I stuck in the scene as a mere caprice. And as for Peer Gynt, is he not a completely rounded human being with an individual personality? *I* know that he is. And what about his mother, is she not? There are many things one can learn from Clemens Petersen, and I have learned much from him. But there is something that it might do him good to learn, and where I, even though I cannot teach it to him, have the advantage of him—and that is what you in your letter call "loyalty." That is precisely the right word! Not loyalty to a friend, or a program, or anything like that, but to something infinitely higher.
>
> However, I am glad of the injustice that has been done me. There is a divine dispensation in it; for I can feel my strength growing as my anger increases. If it is to be war, then let it be war! If I am no poet, then I have nothing to lose. I shall try my luck as a photographer. One by one I shall come to grips with my contemporaries in the north, as I have already come to grips with the Norwegian nationalist language reformers [in the character of Huhu in *Peer Gynt*]. I shall not spare the child in the mother's womb, nor respect the thought or feeling that lies behind the word of any living soul who merits my attention.
>
> Dear Bjørnson, you are a good, warmhearted soul. You have let me share more of your noble and fine nature than I can ever repay. But there is something in your nature that may easily cause your good fortune—precisely that—to become a curse to you. I have a right to tell you this, for I know that underneath the crust of my foolishness and swinishness, I have always taken life very seriously. Do you know that I have entirely separated myself forever from my own parents, from my whole family, because being only half understood was unendurable to me?
>
> This letter is somewhat incoherent. Adding it up, it comes to this: I will not be an antiquarian nor a geographer; I will not cultivate my talent for the furtherance of Monrad's philosophy; in short, I will not follow good advice.

> But one thing I will do, even though the powers without and the powers within drive me to pull the roof down upon my head—I will always, *so help me God*, be your faithful and sincerely devoted servant.
>
> Henrik Ibsen
> December 10
>
> I have slept upon the above lines, and have now reread them in cold blood. They are the expression of yesterday's mood, but I shall still send them.
>
> Let me tell you, calmly and deliberately, what will come of Mr. Clemens Petersen's article.
>
> I have no intention of yielding, and Mr. Clemens Petersen cannot oust me; it is too late for that. He may possibly oblige me to withdraw from Denmark, but in that case I intend to change more than my publisher. Do not underestimate my friends and my adherents in Norway. The party whose newspaper has opened its pages to calumnies about me will find that I do not stand alone. When things go beyond a certain point, I feel no respect for others; and if I am only careful to do what I am quite capable of, namely, combining this relentlessness of purpose with deliberateness in the choice of means, my enemies shall be made to feel that if I am not a builder, I am at least capable of destroying.
>
> ... Mr. Petersen's article ... will not do me any harm. The absentee has always a great advantage in the very fact of his being absent. But to write the article in such a style was imprudent. In his review of *Brand* he treated me with respect, and the public will not find anything in the intervening year that renders me deserving of contempt. The public will not permit Mr. Petersen to dismiss me as summarily as he has attempted to do. He ought to leave such attempts to those of his colleagues who live by their work as a critic. Until now I believed that Mr. Petersen lived *for* his.[14]

Unless one reads between the lines and understands what lies behind these threats to destroy his enemies, these intimations that he too has powerful friends, the letter is indeed "somewhat incoherent." The incoherence stems from the ambivalence of his attitude toward Bjørnson. While declaring war on Petersen's clique, he wanted to keep Bjørnson's support. Consequently, like Petersen, he refrained from saying a good deal. When Petersen pointed out the close connection between the Strange Passenger swimming beside Peer Gynt and Kierkegaard's concept of angst, as many commentators have since then, Ibsen, instead of admitting the obvious, chose to imply that it had no meaning at all. In his next letter to Bjørnson, Ibsen defended himself by arguing that with a little ingenuity, any dramatic character could be seen as symbolic or allegorical.[15]

To admit the truth would be to open the door to the Kierkegaardian philosophy of the play and to close it on Bjørnson's friendship. Behind Petersen's "lie" and Ibsen's subterfuge lay a religious and philosophical issue that was a continuation of the quarrel between the leading Danish theologian Nikolai Frederik Severin Grundtvig (1783–1872) and Kierkegaard. Bjørnson saw the issue clearly in *Brand*, and that is why he abominated it.

"What is it . . . if not a frenzied attack on religion? . . . It means nothing at all if it does not mean to hell with all religion. What survives in it? Does Brand die so that the truth might live on? No, because he carries too terribly much of the truth with him in his fall; this should have been clearly separated from him before he died if something were to remain for us to believe in."[16]

After the disaster of 1864, "the new evangel," as one scholar succinctly put it, "found in Grundtvig its prophet, in Rasmus Nielsen its philosopher, in Bjørnson its poet, and in Clemens Petersen its critic."[17] Nielsen (1809–84) became the chief strategist of this new alliance when he found a way of employing the uncompromising Kierkegaard to effect an ingenious compromise between faith and knowledge.

Looked at from Ibsen's point of view, this controversy had its roots in the 1830s when Johan Ludvig Heiberg had introduced into Denmark a simplified, easily assimilated variety of Hegelianism. Within a few years, Hegel had become the reigning philosopher in Denmark and Norway, and Heiberg the leading authority on all matters intellectual. Even the theologians, who had at first recoiled from the whiff of atheism in German metaphysics, soon found that Hegel's Absolute Spirit made congenial company. Their only objection to Heiberg was that he was too much a man of the Enlightenment. He put philosophy above religion and placed Hegel's Spirit at the top of the Holy Trinity. The compact between the speculative theologians and the esthetic philosophers aroused the ire of Kierkegaard, who proceeded to bait Heiberg for his dilettantism and to fulminate against Hegel for his failure to deal with the ethical options of the individual. The clash of these giants made the 1840s a glittering decade in Danish intellectual history.

The following decades belonged to the epigones. Heiberg's influence began to wane as a new generation of thinkers moved in where Kierkegaard had cleared the way. The question that faced these new thinkers was whether faith and knowledge could still be reconciled with each other in the light of the higher criticism of the Bible and the demythologizing of Christianity by Feuerbach and Strauss. Nielsen, who like Feuerbach had grown disenchanted with Hegelianism, adopted Kierkegaard's position that opposites could not be mediated. Faith and knowledge, theology and natural philosophy, which had recently been made compatible through Hegel's principle of mediation, were completely sundered by Nielsen's insistence that the two had absolutely nothing to do with each other.

Consequently—and this was his eagerly awaited contribution to the debate—they cannot come into conflict. The blatant fact that the conflict was raging all around disturbed Nielsen not a whit. Faith and knowledge, he averred, coexist naturally in the mind. Man's subjective spirit is independent of science and factual knowledge; hence it is possible for one to put a belief in God above all else and still devote oneself to science. His position was like that of some modern scientists, who, while accepting Darwin's theory of evolution and the Big Bang theory of the origin of the universe, contend that religion and science exist in separate spheres. Nielsen, however, insisted that despite their mutual independence, one ranked above the other; it was not possible to make the pursuit of scientific knowledge the absolute aim in life and still preserve one's faith. What Nielsen was actually saying was that scientific truth and revealed truth could never come into conflict if science would always consent to yield.[18] This expedient philosophy immediately won a wide following as Nielsen strengthened his position numerically by allying himself with Grundtvig, who had a broad basis of public support.

The obvious reply to Nielsen was the one Dietrich Bonhoeffer would have made: Christians who stand with only one leg upon earth also stand with only one leg in heaven. Had Kierkegaard, the foe of all compromise, been alive, he would have demolished Nielsen's jerry-built philosophy.[19] As it was, the Prussian army in 1864 gave a rude jolt to the accepted ideas. When the guns fell silent and the Danes took to examining the cause of the debacle, the skeptics among them felt they had been living in a house of lies and illusions, separated from reality.

The old ideals had retreated with the Danish army at the Dannewerk, and it was no longer possible to advocate a purely esthetic or speculative outlook. More than any other literary work, *Brand* signaled the change in attitude. A Danish critic in 1867, commenting on the new wave of ethical writers emerging from Norway and singling out Ibsen's play for its moral earnestness, remarked that "the spirit of the times will no longer tolerate the purely esthetic, the beautiful life that satisfies only the conventions of beauty."[20] It was because Petersen had adopted the same posture that Ibsen expected a sympathetic hearing from him.

To stem the spreading disillusionment the establishment was compelled to gird and secure itself. "The reconciliation of the ideal with reality" became its watchword. This was nothing more than a retreat to the Hegelian system, but with a different emphasis than it had had under Heiberg. Petersen quickly allied himself with those dualists who believed in the compartmentalization of science and religion, praised Nielsen for fulfilling the work started by Hegel and Heiberg, and extolled Nielsen as the greatest mind and philosopher of the age.[21] German philosophy had exhausted itself in speculation; it was now necessary to test speculations against reality, cognition against experience. Petersen neglected to say what would happen if they did not square with one another. The possibility that Science and Experiment would not accord with Faith and Revelation was not to be considered in a world that God had created.

Having been converted to Nielsen's teachings, Petersen set about winning more disciples. He found a willing novice in Rudolf Schmidt, two years younger than himself. While tutoring him through the university matriculation examinations, Petersen inculcated him with Nielsenism. Lacking both talent and originality, Schmidt knew his glory would have to be borrowed, and he quickly attached himself to Petersen to help propagate Nielsen's dualistic philosophy.

Falling In with Brandes

Among the religious skeptics was Georg Brandes, whose display of learning in philosophy and esthetics had won him a gold medal at the University of Copenhagen in 1863 and a *cum laude prœrcipia* in 1864, along with the admiration of his teachers, especially Carsten Hauch, professor of esthetics, whom he was expected to succeed. Brandes's opposition to dualism was rooted in Feuerbach's contention that God is a projection of the human mind, and since God cannot have a separate existence apart from and over and against man, faith and knowledge cannot be kept in separate compartments as Nielsen argued. It was obvious to Brandes that Danish philosophy was essentially theology and that sooner or later the naturalists would have to confront the divines. Brandes wrote to his teacher Hans Brøchner, a leading spokesman of the positivists and naturalists, urging him to controvert Nielsen's dualism. But Brøchner's health prevented him from doing so, and the twenty-three-year-old Brandes entered the lists in his place, stepping from the quiet halls of the university into the public arena where he was to remain for the rest of his life.[1]

His first contribution to the debate on faith and knowledge was a review, printed in *Fædrelandet* on January 13, 1866, of the book *Science and Conscience* (*Samvittighed og Videnskab*) by A. C. Larsen. This brought a rejoinder from Rudolf Schmidt to which Brandes in turn replied on January 20. Next to enter the controversy was Harald Høffding, another bright graduate student at the University of Copenhagen, a year younger than Brandes and destined to rival him as an intellectual force in Denmark. (Their long-lasting rivalry was to provide plot material for *Hedda Gabler.*) Høffding issued a pamphlet, *Philosophy and Theology* (*Filosofi og Teologi*), in which he surveyed the field of battle and announced that Nielsen was victorious. Brandes rebutted this in another newspaper article on

February 16. "I have asserted," wrote Brandes, "that Professor Nielsen is guilty of a contradiction when at the same time that he calls faith and knowledge two absolutely different principles, he speaks of their reconciliation in the mind of man."[2]

A few days later, on February 27, Brandes published yet another article against Høffding, "A Final Word."

> It is not a question of belief versus unbelief; rather, it is clarity that stands opposed to obfuscation. . . . There is only one point to be settled here: is Professor Nielsen involved in a contradiction when he states that faith and knowledge are absolutely different principles while averring that the two can be reconciled in the human consciousness with one being placed above the other, or is he not involved in such a contradiction? Clearly he is. For either they are not absolutely separate and distinct or they completely cleave the human consciousness; either they are not absolutely different or there cannot be any talk of higher and lower. It is useless for Høffding to meet this objection by declaring that it is one and the same individual who must relate to both of these separate and distinct principles, for the question is whether the human consciousness must not be irreparably split by them. . . .
>
> There is, he says, an opposition between Knowledge and Experience. In trying to realize the idea of the good in life, this opposition asserts itself, rational morality betrays its inadequacy, and one sees the necessity—not of religious morality, as one might have expected—but of religion. Now, I ask, what then is to be understood by religious morality? Is this a part of Knowledge, or is it only another name for the positive religious element? If it is the latter, why the confusing terminology? If it is the first, the matter is quite simple, and there is no confusion. For then by virtue of this same opposition between Knowledge and Experience, morality proves inadequate as soon as it is brought to bear on life itself, and recourse must be had to something higher. But, not to speak of what significance there can be in a morality that diminishes step by step to less than nothing, we have here a series of levels—knowledge, superior knowledge, super-superior knowledge, and so on—that does not say much for the ratiocinative processes of those who defend it. If to be a moral human being meant involvement in such logical complications, one can well understand that Herr Høffding must ask, can one be both ethical and scientific? Otherwise the question has no meaning. No, the point remains. If ethics provides a transition from philosophy to religion, then the absolutely distinct nature of the two is abandoned, and the best indication of the insupportability of this doctrine is the fact that Professor Nielsen has abandoned it not only in this instance but in many other instances, as I have shown. For example, he allows room for miracles in his book *The Logic of Basic Ideas*. The difference between the Absolute of philosophy and the Almighty God of theology is that the latter, in contrast to the

> Absolute, has its own peculiar condition, but this condition cancels out logic by asserting the possibility of miracles. In his logic one finds the same duality as in his ethics. Just as it is incomprehensible how religious morality can fail to have some retrograde and annihilating effect on rational morality, so it is inconceivable how the unconditioned human being by virtue of self-determination can raise himself above his conditions except by annulling them, that is, except by reducing the laws of nature and of thought to nothing, to illusion. I understand how, like Kierkegaard, one can support one's paradoxical faith by subjective knowledge, but I do not comprehend how anyone can, like Professor Nielsen, entertain no doubts about knowledge and still maintain his faith.[3]

Living in Rome, Ibsen followed the debate by reading the newspapers in the Scandinavian Club, and he learned more about Brandes in conversations with Ludvig David, a former schoolmate of Brandes. When David, unable to withstand the agonies of typhoid fever, committed suicide, Ibsen took it upon himself, as a member of the Scandinavian community in Rome, to relate, in extraordinary detail, the circumstances surrounding David's death. At the end of it he signaled his sympathy with Brandes's political views and hoped that the two of them might meet. Thus began a relationship that would eventually draw Ibsen down from the heights where he felt most at home and down into the valley where he would find fame and fortune.[4]

Ibsen was at the time nervously awaiting the publication of *Brand*, and it must have struck him as prophetic that just before the appearance of that work, with its call for a young and uncompromising god, a young critic named Brandes was assailing the established thought with the same kind of argument Ibsen had put into the mouth of his hero. Later Ibsen was to tell Brandes, in admonishing him not to construe *Brand* as a religious and reactionary work, that "had I been born a hundred years later I might with equal enthusiasm have written about you and your battle with Rasmus Nielsen's philosophy of compromise."[5] Like Ibsen, Brandes felt infinitely superior to those who condescended to him and treated him as an intellectual upstart. "I felt," said Brandes, "as if I had in my left side a well overflowing with contempt."[6] The difference between them lay in the fact that Ibsen had learned to respect the power of society, while Brandes, fourteen years younger, strode out like David to do battle with Goliath, heedless of the depth of the ranks of the Philistines.

Brandes read *Brand* as soon as it appeared and promptly submitted his review of it to *Fædrelandet*. The editor rejected it on the ground that Petersen, the paper's regular critic, had also chosen to write a notice about it. After Brandes's reply to Høffding, readers of *Fædrelandet* were evidently to be spared any more of his inflammatory ideas. He was forced to find a hearing elsewhere, and his review of *Brand* finally appeared on May 23 in *Dagbladet*, a less conservative and, in the eyes of some, a quite radical paper.

Five months later, on October 26, 1866, Brandes made his official debut as a writer with the publication of a small work—hitherto he had published only articles and reviews—called *Dualism in Our Newest Philosophy* (*Dualism i vor nyeste Filosofi*). Here again he pointed out the inconsistency in Nielsen's thought and challenged him to reply. The philosopher did not deign to do so, relying instead on Petersen and Schmidt to silence the young firebrand. When Ibsen asked a visitor from Norway about Schmidt, he was told that Schmidt belonged to a cabal that included Nielsen, Petersen, and Bjørnson; informed that Brandes, not Schmidt, was the coming man; and given a copy of *Dualism in Our Newest Philosophy*.[7]

In the meantime, Petersen had spent May and June in Norway cementing his friendship with Bjørnson. Reverencing Grundtvig for having restored his childhood faith, Bjørnson viewed the controversy over dualism with a jaundiced eye and did all he could to further the religious cause. In 1866 he became an adherent of dualism and a personal friend of Nielsen.

The following year Nielsen delivered a series of sixteen lectures at the University of Christiania on the question of faith and knowledge under the title "Obstacles to and Conditions for the Life of the Spirit in Our Times" ("Hindringer og Betingelser for det aandelige Liv i Nutiden"). These lectures were deemed the most significant intellectual event of the sixties in Christiania, and Bjørnson hailed Nielsen as the hero of the day. "He exercises a great attraction on the younger generation, and his ideas will undoubtedly carry forward into the future, for they promote Grundtvigianism, and therein lies the future."[8] At the same time Ibsen was confessing to his friends his admiration for Brandes's strength of conviction. Commenting on the "pen-and-ink war between philosophers and theologians," Ibsen said, "It is clear to me that this man will come to play a prominent part in the intellectual life of Scandinavia."[9]

And as Nielsen's auditors in Christiania were being exhorted to find a proper life of the spirit through the dualistic acceptance of faith and knowledge, the printers in Copenhagen were gathering the sheets of Ibsen's satire on the typical Norwegian who stood to lose his soul for putting conscience and behavior in separate compartments. Three days after Bjørnson called Nielsen the hero of the day, the shops were displaying *Peer Gynt*, the book that derided all that Nielsen and Bjørnson represented.

Almost simultaneously with the appearance of *Peer Gynt*, Brandes published in the pages of *Dansk Maanedskrift* a lengthy essay on *Brand* that marked the beginning of Ibsen's reputation as an eminent Scandinavian, rather than a merely Norwegian, poet. Brandes was now promoting Ibsen as Petersen had promoted Bjørnson.

At first Bjørnson took little notice of Brandes, dismissing him as "someone who has a machine all set up but who has nothing to produce."[10] But indifference changed to aggressive enmity when the machine produced increasingly effective antidualistic ammunition. When Brandes assailed Rudolf Schmidt's essay "Nielsen's Philosophy and the Grundtvigian View" ("R. Nielsens Philosophie og den Grundtvigske Anskuelse"), Bjørnson felt called upon to resist the evil. Høffding had accused Brandes of appearing on the battlefield without displaying his colors as a free thinker. Bjørnson entered the fray with an unsigned article in *Fædrelandet* on October 2, 1867, and aimed his blows at Brandes's Jewishness. He condemned Brandes's remarks on Schmidt as "un-Danish," "un-Christian," and "blasphemous," avowing that anyone who could set them down "had nothing in common with other Danes and lacked a Danish consciousness."[11]

The strength of the dualists had never lain in logic but in numbers, and their every effort was directed at swelling their ranks to prove the rightness of their convictions. At the end of the year, Bjørnson was still trying to convert Ibsen to Grundtvig, "the mightiest tree in the forest," and cautioned him against relying too much on Brandes. "There is something misleading in anyone who does not have a belief in God.—But there is someone else here, a growing giant, the philosopher Rudolf Schmidt . . . with a poetic soul that exalts his every thought. Rasmus Nielsen is a source of great joy to me. Be sure to look him up when you come this way. You will meet no one more sweet or more gifted on your whole journey."[12]

Though all this was meant as a conciliatory reply to Ibsen's accusations of disloyalty in his letter of December 9, it could only have brought home to Ibsen, who had in *Brand* vehemently mocked Grundtvigianism ("Vox populi, vox dei") and dualistic thinking ("Life's one thing; faith's a different matter"), that the gulf between him and Bjørnson was greater than he had imagined. Yet he answered with a letter of exceptional cordiality in which he even attempted to repair his line of communication with Petersen.

> Dear Bjørnson, Nothing in the whole wide world could have been more welcome than the greeting which your letter, received on Christmas morning, brought me.
>
> Thinking of that cargo of nonsense which I shipped to you in my last epistle left me without a moment of peace. The worst that a man can do to himself is to do injustice to others. Thank you, noble-minded man that you are, for taking the matter as you have. I could see nothing before me but trouble and bitterness

> for a long time to come, but now, looking back, I see it as only natural that you should take it just as you did. I read your letter over and over again every day to free myself from the tormenting thought that I have hurt you.
>
> Do not understand what I said in my former letter to mean that my conception of what is essential in poetry is entirely different from Clemens Petersen's. On the contrary, I understand and am pretty much in accord with him. But I contend that I have fulfilled the requirements. He says no.[13]

It is apparent that at this time Ibsen had no inclination to break off his relationship with Bjørnson over a religious controversy in Denmark. Though he did not share the beliefs of Bjørnson and his friends, he recognized their power to make literary reputations. If Ibsen did not find himself guilty of dualistic thinking at this point, it was only because what he wanted most was fame, honor, and respect. His effusive letter was a step toward securing this.

Yet it was the last letter he was to write to Bjørnson for many years. In the early part of 1868, something happened that made him turn violently against Bjørnson, something that made all the charges he had leveled against him upon reading Petersen's review of *Peer Gynt* appear all too true and the mollifying words of Bjørnson's Christmas letter all too false, something that threatened to deprive him of what he wanted most.

In Denmark, Ibsen and Bjørnson were little more than bystanders in the pamphlet war. In Norway, however, they were the principal figures in the controversy that smoldered there. In Denmark the immediate issues were religious and philosophical; in Norway they were political and social. Consequently, when the battle lines were extended across the Skagerrak Strait, they overlapped. In Norway, Bjørnson was becoming notorious as a liberal, while in Denmark he contributed to the most conservative paper, *Fædrelandet.* In Denmark, Ibsen was associated with Brandes, the most radical of the polemicists; in Norway he was a member of the conservative circle of civil servants and academicians. Bjørnson's paper in Norway was the republican *Norsk Folkeblad* (The Norwegian People), in which he voiced his opinions first as contributor and later as editor. Ibsen's paper was the monarchist *Morgenbladet*, the organ for many of his friends in the Dutchmen circle. The center of this circle was Botten-Hansen, who until 1866 had edited his own journal, *Illustreret Nyhedsblad.* Bjørnson abominated Botten-Hansen's political conservatism and skeptical philosophy, and through Jonas Lie, who had acquired a three-quarters interest in the paper in December 1861, constantly brought pressure on him to adopt a more positive attitude.[14] When Botten-Hansen refused to yield, Bjørnson, in March 1866, assumed editorship of the relatively new weekly *Norsk Folkeblad* and succeeded in driving *Illus-*

treret Nyhedsblad out of business. Ibsen was very close to Botten-Hansen, and he would not forget Bjørnson's ruthlessness.

Bjørnson saw his cause as the liberation of the Norwegian people. At the time they were in thrall politically to Sweden, culturally to Denmark, and spiritually to the state church. He believed in government by the people, the complete separation of Norway from the Swedish crown, and the possibility of realizing God's kingdom on earth through the education of the common man. His reform program called for universal suffrage, an end to the civil bureaucracy that was in fealty to Sweden, the founding of a free church to oppose the depressing pietism of the state church, and the opening of Grundtvigian folk schools to counteract the influence of the state schools. In a word, Bjørnson was combating the whole establishment: church, school, and administration. As a republican, he wanted to bring Norway abreast of England, and the political aims of the Norwegian liberals of the 1860s were almost identical with those of the English Chartists of the 1840s. As an educator, he wanted to break the grip of the schools that trained students only to fill places in the church or the civil service. As a religious reformer, he wanted to bring the Lutheran church into the nineteenth century and to stem the rising tide of pietism. To do so he turned to Grundtvigianism, which put simple faith above abstruse theological doctrines, and to Nielsenism, which brought out the limitations of both a science without faith and a theology without humanity.[15]

In contrast, Ibsen preferred the constitutional monarchy to a republic, and Kierkegaard to Grundtvig and Nielsen. He saw little reason in the extension of the franchise to the very people who put self-interest above principle when Denmark needed help, and none at all in the double conscience that contributed to the moral collapse of 1864. Most of his friends in the Dutchmen circle shared these views, but their opinion of Bjørnson was much lower than Ibsen's. They disdained Bjørnson for his arrogance, obtrusiveness, and naiveté. To them he was an intellectual lightweight, a social boor, and a political upstart.[16]

Bjørnson's opinion of them was no higher. To him the Dutchmen were sickly intellectuals whose political conservatism and religious skepticism held back the progress of Norway. When he had raised the money that enabled Ibsen to travel to Rome, Bjørnson had felt he was freeing him from cynical friends to whose pernicious influence the poet had succumbed only because he had been denied the good things in life. In 1864 Bjørnson could write, "The path you followed, and still more the company that gathered round you, has often worried me. When I meet [some of your Dutchmen friends] on the street, whispering in my ear, laughing, I feel like lashing out and destroying them. Your life was entirely dark, hidden from the sun, and in such conditions plants draw more water than light, more spongy matter than color. You lacked affection and love, and the chance to contemplate in tranquility the essential things in life, and—God be praised!—you have now got it, and we shall have the fruits of it."[17]

But the first fruit was *Brand*, which nauseated Bjørnson. The Dutchmen and *Morgenbladet* had recognized, however, that with *Brand* Ibsen had become Bjørnson's literary peer, and they had immediately taken action to seek for Ibsen the official recognition that Bjørnson enjoyed.

The following summer (1866) Bjørnson scoffed at the Dutchmen, saying they enjoyed Ibsen's wit and irony only because they lacked a genuine love for humanity, and kept aloof from politics because, having stood so long on the sidelines, they were incapable of positive action.[18] But Bjørnson's growing power called for action of some sort. As a rejoinder to the articles Petersen had written about Norwegian literature after his 1866 visit to Christiania, *Morgenbladet* published a series of anonymous articles ridiculing Petersen and his "Bjørnsoniades" and exposing the allegiances behind the men. Bjørnson had joined "Young Norway," Petersen, "Young Denmark," and the two of them were now carrying on a campaign to promote each other, with Bjørnson being printed in the Danish *Fædrelandet* and Petersen in the Norwegian *Aftenbladet*. This alignment of forces was labeled by *Morgenbladet* Western Scandinavianism, as opposed to Eastern Scandinavianism, which sought to continue Norway's ties with Sweden. After having pointed out that *Aftenbladet* printed every word praising Bjørnson but had omitted to print Andreas Munch's warm appreciation of Ibsen, the anonymous writer concluded that Bjørnson and Petersen and their coteries, Young Norway and Young Denmark, were impeding the natural development of Norwegian literature.[19] It was the familiar situation in which the political conflict between conservatism and liberalism reflects the conflict between the older and the younger generations.

When Bjørnson read *Peer Gynt*, he exulted over what he took to be Ibsen's conversion to the liberal cause of rousing the common man of Norway from his age-long torpor. Here he found not the spiritually debilitating irony of *Brand* but happy satire with the salubrious purpose of building a strong and independent Norway. Ibsen knew that Bjørnson's enthusiasm for *Peer Gynt* was sincere, but when he read Petersen's review, his immediate thought, based on Bjørnson's close friendship with the critic, was that Bjørnson had put his allegiance to Young Denmark and Young Norway ahead of simple truth and justice. Ibsen did not expect Bjørnson to coerce Petersen, only to controvert his esthetic argument. "All I reproach you with," he wrote, "is inaction. It was not kind of you to allow, through negligence, this attempt to sell my literary reputation to the highest bidder in my absence."[20]

Here Ibsen was needling Bjørnson for having inadvertently allowed Ibsen's household goods in Christiania to be sequestered and sold at auction for non-payment of debt in 1866 when Ibsen was living in Italy. In accusing Petersen of venality, Ibsen was not voicing paranoid suspicions. His grasp of the situation was firmer than Bjørnson's, and he knew that both he and Bjørnson as public figures were being used by the politicians and opinion makers to sharpen the conflict between Western Scandinavianism and Eastern Scandinavianism, between the old establishment and the league of the young.

> I am carrying on no correspondence with anyone at home. Nevertheless, I can give you a bit of news from there. Do you know what they are saying now in Norway wherever Carl Ploug's paper [*Fædrelandet*] is read? They are saying: "It is evident from Clemens Petersen's review that Bjørnson is in Copenhagen."
>
> If you have reviewed *Peer Gynt* in *Norsk Folkeblad*, they will be saying: "A diplomatic maneuver, but not clever enough." Some will say it in all good faith; others out of vindictiveness and resentment. The critics will divide into parties for or against. You will see.
>
> They will call Clemens Petersen's review a return for favors received. A man unknown to me wrote some articles in *Morgenbladet* lately, in which he unmercifully disparaged Mr. Petersen's literary work, while I was favorably mentioned. These associations and combinations will be recalled. I know how these fellows reason.
>
> Dear Bjørnson, do let us try to stick together. . . .
>
> You can see from the very fact that I write all this to you that I harbor no suspicion of you in this matter. I have never taken and never will take sides with my adherents when they are opposed to you. When I am opposed to your friends, that is another matter.[21]

Bjørnson seized on Ibsen's offer that the two of them should stick together, but, as a compulsive proselytizer, he could not refrain from propagandizing for his own particular cause, Western Scandinavianism.

"Hold on to Denmark, I tell you. You must see as clearly as I do that we have no other alternative. Denmark can represent culture to us in that our culture, because of us, won't become Danish but will be totally Norwegian and will therefore enrich our nature. Yet Denmark is our cultural metropolis, and the day we become someone else's parish, we are lost; we will be driven into the polar ice. . . . If *we two* lose Denmark, we will have lost much, and so will Norway."[22]

For Ibsen, however, who put loyalty to principle above devotion to programs and platforms, there was a third alternative. Without principle there could be no true understanding between individuals. In his letter of December 9–10, 1867, he had told Bjørnson, "I know that underneath the crust of my foolishness and swinishness, I have always taken life very seriously. Do you know that I have entirely separated myself forever from my own parents, from my whole family, because being only half understood was unendurable to me?"[23]

In his answer, Bjørnson played on the themes of friendship and seriousness. "As sure as God is One, you are lost if you return home and league yourself with [the Dutchmen], who did so much harm to your mind and soul before you left home. ... One thing you must not forget: that circle that gathered around me and would not open itself to you—more because the other circle had claimed you first and they saw the effect of it on you than because they undervalued you—that circle is now ready to welcome you; your seriousness of purpose and your profound spirit they recognize as their own, and you will certainly get in."[24]

Ibsen's reply glowed with gratitude for Bjørnson's friendship. But the warmth came from the banked fires of a rage that would soon burst into flames again. "Our friends," Ibsen had cautioned in his previous letter, "have often enough made life miserable for us and our struggle more onerous than it should be."

And such was to be the case in the following months. Observing Bjørnson's popularity grow with the swelling of the ranks of the liberal movement, the Norwegian conservatives endeavored to create a rift between the two authors, and Bjørnson and the leagues of Young Denmark and Young Norway provided them with the opportunity. Petersen evidently could not refrain from broadcasting some of Bjørnson's more condescending remarks. "Once Ibsen acknowledges that he is *a minor poet*, he will instantly become a rather endearing one. I have told him this clearly enough, but I am afraid he is jealous."[25]

When the *Morgenbladet* clique—especially Løkke and Birkeland, whom Bjørnson later implicated as the troublemakers and scandalmongers[26]—picked up comments like these, they were not reluctant to pass them on to Ibsen, despite the fact that Ibsen told Bjørnson he was not carrying on a correspondence with anyone in Norway. Ibsen's most frank and intimate exchange was carried on with Løkke. It was never published, though Birkeland copied out some parts of it. Løkke burned Ibsen's letters when Ibsen became famous, presumably in the late 1870s and clearly on instruction from their author.[27]

Bjørnson's sneers did not express his true feelings. In uttering them he was playing to the gallery of Nielsenites in Denmark, liberals in Norway, and Grundtvigians in both countries, while giving as good as he got from *Morgenbladet*.

Early in 1868, however, he went too far. At a meeting of Grundtvigian friends in Denmark, he referred to Ibsen as a "hired hand" (*træl*).[28] It was doubly contumelious, wounding Ibsen at his two most sensitive points: his desire for social esteem and his pride in being subservient to no one. What was actually no more than a verbal indiscretion Ibsen took as evidence of Bjørnson's arrant duplicity. In

November Bjørnson's enthusiastic letter had been followed by Petersen's biased review; now Bjørnson's conciliatory Christmas letter asking Ibsen to join him and the league of the young in Denmark and Norway was followed by his calumny. Ibsen had in effect spurned Bjørnson's invitation, and now Bjørnson was calling him the tool of the *Morgenbladet* clique. "He has infamously slandered [me] in the presence of a number of people, while at the same time, perhaps on the very same day, he has written [me] a long letter filled with ingratiating declarations of friendship."[29]

When Ibsen heard of Bjørnson's insult, his first and worst suspicions were confirmed. The rage he had felt in November returned, and in the first part of 1868 he felt, he said, "like a beast of prey, and with good reason."[30] He is referring to the impression he must have made on Brandes's friend Julius Lange, who had met Ibsen in Italy in 1868 and had written to Brandes on May 15 that Ibsen needed a strong dose of artistic studies to learn moderation and balance.[31]

It was now evident to him that he was to be ousted from the Danish literary scene for not having allied himself with the Nielsenites, the Grundtvigians, and the league of the young. The gauntlet had been thrown, and Ibsen intended to be as good as his word. The threats he had made earlier were not empty ones.

"When things go beyond a certain point, I feel no respect for others; and if I am only careful to do what I am quite capable of, namely, combining this relentlessness of purpose with deliberateness in the choice of means, my enemies shall be made to feel that if I am not a builder, I am at least capable of destroying. . . . I shall not spare the child in the mother's womb, nor respect the thought or feeling that lies behind the word of any living soul who merits my attention."[32]

The irate Ibsen now dashed off a brief note meant for Bjørnson: "Shut your mouth. I know you, and I can photograph you." The note was never sent, but its contents were made known to Bjørnson's friends. Fru Ibsen claimed she saw the note and remembered the exact words.[33] Bjørnson was probably referring to the same note when he wrote to Lina Bruun on August 15, 1870, "From Lieblein I heard that Ibsen had said he had sent me another letter in which he asked me not to spread stories and lies about him. Such a letter I never received; if I had, Ibsen would have had his answer soon enough."[34]

To Ibsen, photographing Bjørnson meant putting him into a play. Which is what he did.

The League of Youth

Wrath often galvanized Ibsen into creativity, and he now set about writing a play that would pillory those he saw as his enemies. Since Bjørnson in his last letter[1] had tried to appease Ibsen's rage by suggesting that the proper reply to those he disagreed with should be a comedy filled with humanity and dispensing with theoretical problems, Ibsen resolved to write a realistic comedy in which the characters would not be abstractions but recognizable figures from the contemporary scene, and the issues not metaphysical but political. And since Bjørnson in his big-brotherly way had told Ibsen not to violate the sanctity of belles lettres by answering his enemies in anger or bitterness, Ibsen determined to do precisely that. And, finally, to make his new commitment as clear as possible, at least to himself, he spurned Petersen's poetics and looked to Georg Brandes for advice. Admitting that he had "no definite ideas" on the theory of comedy, but desiring to give Brandes "no cause to complain of illicit intercourse with the muses," Ibsen consulted Brandes's *Aesthetic Studies*,[2] about the time he began writing the first draft of his play.

Though Ibsen thought the chapter on comic theory an "absolute gold mine,"[3] there was nothing in it about comic technique that Ibsen would not have already known from his intimate familiarity with the works of Holberg.[4] But *Aesthetic Studies* also contained Brandes's lengthy essay on Ibsen, the first comprehensive study of the Norwegian poet. Anxious not to lose the critic's support, Ibsen wanted to know what he expected in a comedy. Brandes was quite explicit. Laughter, he wrote, has its source not in our ethical sense but in our esthetic sense, and the feeling of freedom that is peculiar to comedy is due to the fact that as an esthetic being man is free. Our enjoyment derives from our sense of liberation. All art releases us from the pressures of daily life, but comedy lets us soar above the anxieties that we feel in most of the other arts. Since the comic appeals primarily to our esthetic sense, form and balance are crucial to its success, and since comedy must reflect general truths and not personal bias, the author must not allow any character to become his spokesman.

What Ibsen learned from this was that if his planned comedy was to meet with Brandes's approval, it would have to be an objective work freed of the passions that impelled Ibsen to write it. When he had finished his play, he wrote to Brandes:

> In my new comedy you will find I have stayed on the level of ordinary, everyday life—no strong emotions, no deep feelings, and, above all, no thoughts isolated from the main subject. Your just condemnation of the unmotivated and unprepared-for "remarks by the author" in *The Pretenders* has had its effect. Your article—and I am going to express the warmest thanks I can possibly give you—has been to me what Mons Wingaard's Chronicles were to Jacob von Thyboe: "I have read it sixteen times and sixteen times more, and hope to make use of it in sundry wars."[5]

What was conceived in rage was nurtured in contemplation. Between February and September 1868, Ibsen made at least two false starts on his new comedy.[6] Finally, in October, Bjørnson himself provided Ibsen with the subject he was looking for, and at the end of the month he could inform his publisher that his new play would "deal with movements and conflicts of the present day, and in spite of the fact that it takes place in Norway will be just as relevant in Denmark."[7] Young Denmark may have been just as much in his mind as Young Norway when he began composing the play, but in providing the local color necessary in a realistic comedy the political situation in Norway came to dominate it.

The republican movement that affected the major European countries did not make itself felt strongly in Norway until the 1860s. There was no aristocracy in the European sense, and political power was centered in jurists and clergymen. Representatives to parliament, the Storting, were chosen by electors who were nominated by the voting public. The franchise was restricted to landed proprietors, leaseholders, burghers, and civil servants.[8] Representation in the Storting favored the towns over the rural areas, and the business of government was in the hands of functionaries loyal to the Swedish crown. All this was to change in the Storting sessions of 1859, when Ole Gabriel Ueland and Johan Sverdrup—leaders, respectively, of the rural and urban representatives—pressed for the enforcement of a paragraph in the 1814 constitution that stipulated that the ratio of country to town representatives should be two to one. Immediately the landed proprietors and the leaseholders of farmland became potentially the strongest political force.[9] In the 1859–60 session of the Storting, representatives from country districts were increased from sixty-one to seventy-four, while urban representatives were lowered from fifty to thirty-seven.[10]

Now it was only a matter of organizing the farmers into a disciplined party. Before this time political parties in the modern sense, along with party platforms and party lines, did not exist in Norway. The conservatives looked upon the Reform Association (Reformforeningen) as an inflammatory, almost insurrectionary force. Christian Friele, the editor of *Morgenbladet*, called the association a Jacobin club, a group of conspirators who voted as a bloc and whose purpose was to "corral the convictions of the farmers and lead them like sheep." Bjørnson defended the formation of political parties, insisting they were necessary to bring about needed reforms. In a bitter controversy he launched a personal attack on Friele, "that little squirt" (*dette lille sprit legeme*), and demanded that the owner of *Morgenbladet* fire Friele. Friele replied by calling Bjørnson a "journalistic tramp," derided his articles as "gelatinous gobs of words," sneered at his lack of education, and predicted that it was Bjørnson who would be relieved of his job as editor of *Norsk Folkeblad*. He was right. Bjørnson's impassioned editorials calling for Norway's independence even at the risk of war with Sweden cost him his job.[11]

The old association of government servants and academicians, the party of the intelligentsia, to which Ibsen's friends the Learned Dutchmen belonged, soon found itself threatened by rural philistinism as well as by urban republicanism. Gaining power in the 1860s were, on the one hand, the "lawyers' party," the republicans; and, on the other, the farmers' party. The latter consisted largely of leaseholding farmers under the leadership of Søren Jaabæk. He had mobilized the farmers' representatives in 1864 when the Storting met in extraordinary session to defeat a resolution urging Norway's support of Denmark in the war with Prussia.[12] Continuing to hold together afterward on other questions and calling themselves the Farmers' Friends (Bondevenner), they constituted an electoral aggregate capable of determining the course of Norwegian politics. In the spring 1868 election Jaabæk embraced Sverdrup as a true friend of the people and praised him for having voted against military appropriations in the past. But Jaabæk and the Farmers' Friends were much less interested in republican reforms than Sverdrup and the "lawyers' party" were. The sessions of the Storting beginning in October 1868 would determine whether Sverdrup and Jaabæk would league themselves with one another. Bjørnson was well aware of this—"We stand at a turning point," he said[13]—and during the summer of 1868 he conferred frequently with Sverdrup. Finally he put the matter squarely before Jaabæk: either join the republican movement or step down as leader of the farmers. After some bargaining behind the scenes, Jaabæk made up his differences with Sverdrup and hailed him as "one of Europe's greatest political geniuses." Their joint forces now composed the powerful left wing in opposition to the constitutional monarchists.

The 1864 war had turned Ibsen against the farmers and the republicans, and in *Peer Gynt* he had represented the new political forces in the trolls (the farmers) and the Bøyg (the unprincipled and headless mob). In 1868 he saw the proposed reforms as giving further power to the individuals he had satirized in the fourth act of that play. But then his attack had been so well camouflaged that only his friends in the Dutchmen circle had been able to appreciate it, and as propaganda it had been ineffectual. In writing his new play he realized that he would not have the support of Petersen and Bjørnson, of Young Denmark and Young Norway, and that he neither needed it nor desired it. He could speak frankly, and he resolved to depict the contemporary scene in realistic terms, to become a photographer, as he had threatened in his letter to Bjørnson.

To Ibsen at this time, "photography" in the drama was the opposite of poetry in the drama. Having failed to satisfy Petersen as a poet, he said he would try his hand as a photographer. This meant he would write a realistic drama in prose, dispensing with the ideal vision that was thought to be essential to poetic drama. It also meant this was to be a play "for the stage" rather than for the library or parlor. And third, it meant he would create recognizable likenesses of actual people. In a play review written in 1857 ("'En Landsbyhistorie' paa Christiania Theater," *Samlede Verker: Hundreårsutgave,* 15:153–55), he commented ironically on the theater public's fascination with realism. The dominant tone in the play under review was poetic, and for that reason alone, said Ibsen, it would be held suspect by the populace. "There are indeed many reasonable people who hold that the play is both untrue and unsound because it does not bear to reality the same relation that a photograph does. To these people reality and truth are one and the same. If the first is not copied, the second is absent." The public's passion for detailed realism indicates the path that popular art will take: people want to see themselves in art.

In October, while Bjørnson was stumping the provinces for republicanism and the general franchise, Ibsen was finally able to begin writing the play he had been contemplating for eight months. While Bjørnson was nudging the farmers into the republican camp, Ibsen was exposing the left-wing politicians as opportunists and intriguers. In March 1869, when Ibsen was fair-copying his play, the liberal movement scored a momentous victory in the Storting, transferring power from the civil servants to the elected representatives. And when the curtain went up on Ibsen's play, which he called *The League of Youth,* Sverdrup and Bjørnson had fused the Farmers' Friends and Young Norway into a single political instrument.

After the plays of his apprenticeship, Ibsen always wrote out of a strong sense of personal involvement. The works of his maturity are always about himself. Although *The League of Youth* is first and foremost a political satire, it also offers a record of how he stood on the major issues of the 1860s and how he felt about the personalities who shaped the times. Knowing what lies behind the characters in the play is like hearing Ibsen carrying on over drinks among friends. He planted clues throughout the play, identifying the real people behind the stage characters, a fine example of Ibsen's fondness for revealing while concealing, practiced throughout his career. It was a method that made it possible for him at least to be honest with himself if not with his public. It enabled him to lampoon Bjørnson in *Peer Gynt* and have Bjørnson love the work.

The old order is represented by Chamberlain Brattsberg, a country squire and constitutional monarchist, and by Lundestad, who heads the agrarian forces. The upcoming forces are represented by Monsen, a business speculator new to the area who is endeavoring to make himself a political power by drawing on the discontented element. When Stensgaard, a thirty-year-old lawyer, arrives in town, both Lundestad and Monsen recognize in him a natural talent for the political game. His ability to sway his hearers with high-sounding phrases makes him a good campaigner, while his ambition and an unconcealed sensitivity to his own social inferiority make him a pliable instrument in the hands of those who wield the real political power. In Stensgaard's magnetic appeal to the young, Monsen sees a force that will rally the discontented, while the aging Lundestad recognizes in that youthful appeal the force that will hold the rural party together when he retires from office.

Stensgaard is motivated only by his desire for social recognition and advancement, and his entrance into politics is entirely fortuitous. Stung by finding the Brattsberg home closed to him, he impulsively leaps upon a table at a public gathering on Norway's Constitution Day (May 17) to exhort the young people to open the doors that have been shut on them and to free themselves from the "ghosts of the past." On the spur of the moment the League of Youth comes into being, and Stensgaard, who knows nothing about government, becomes a political leader. Having no convictions, he changes his politics to suit his social ambitions and his fiancées to suit his politics. Since only property owners are eligible for office, and since his only way of promptly acquiring property is by marriage, he proposes to and disposes of women in accordance with their financial status.

Ibsen involved this Peer Gynt of politics in an extremely complicated imbroglio fashioned out of a forged note, a confusion of letters, and at least three misunderstandings, all of which keep Stensgaard whirling like a weathervane.[14]

The first misunderstanding leads Brattsberg to think that Stensgaard in his improvised Constitution Day address to the young is insulting Monsen and not him, thus causing Brattsberg to change his mind about the brash young man and to look on him with favor. The second misunderstanding has the widowed, matronly mistress of the local inn thinking that Stensgaard is courting her when he is only serving as a go-between for Monsen's son in exchange for a like favor on the son's part with respect to Monsen's daughter, a girl with a fortune. And the third misunderstanding involves rumors about Monsen's bankruptcy. When the collapse of Monsen's enterprises makes his daughter unattractive to Stensgaard and the widowed innkeeper finds out the truth about Stensgaard's shy wooing, the upstart is defeated on all sides and disappears from the scene along with the parvenu speculator, leaving old Lundestad holding the political reins. The old order that he and Brattsberg represent refuses to yield place to the new—for the time being. But Stensgaard is irrepressible, and in ten or fifteen years, Lundestad predicts, he will be holding an elected office, either as republican or monarchist, or both at once, if necessary. And though he will be too old to call his followers the League of Youth, they will still be the League of the Undecided, "the pliable stuff out of which politics is made."

The success of the play was due in large part to Ibsen's photographic technique, the vivid presence of the characters, and the fidelity of the dialogue to the language spoken by real people. The first realistic Norwegian play on a contemporary subject, it marked an epoch in Norwegian literature. It took a closer look at real life than decorum had previously allowed, and it made controversial politics the subject of a work of art. In a word, there was so much that was novel in it that the public at first found it difficult to orient itself.[15]

There were some who thought the play was an artistic failure because it was not sufficiently realistic, not true to life: Ibsen had let the caricaturist in him overpower the photographer. The truth, however, was that the political reality was itself a caricature. Even the most outrageous remarks of Ibsen's characters were to be heard in contemporary political debate.[16]

In trying his hand as a photographer, Ibsen was of course compelled to use models, and two of them were so recognizable that when he first circulated copies of the play, Ibsen sought to forestall criticism on this point. "In Norway," he said, "they will perhaps say that I have portrayed actual persons and situations. However, that is not so. I have of course used models, which are just as necessary for the writer of comedies as for the painter and sculptor."[17]

Ibsen's point was that he was picturing movements rather than individuals and that he had created each of his characters by combining traits from various models. The question, however, was whether he had flattered or defamed them. Lundestad, the crafty politician, was meant to be Ueland, the leader of the agrarian association. Ibsen did little to conceal the identification: he gave Lundestad the name of Ueland's parish (Lund) and had him refer to his political testament; on March 12, 1869, when Ibsen was fair-copying the play, Ueland had delivered a speech that he called his political testament.[18]

If Lundestad represents the prosperous landowning class whose property has been handed down from generation to generation, Monsen represents the rising capitalist class. His father was a lumberjack, but Monsen has acquired a fortune through business speculations of a dubious sort. The change in standards introduced by the capitalists is expressed by Chamberlain Brattsberg: "One no longer asks how a man got his money or how long he has had it, but only how much has he got."[19] Monsen, the basest character in the play, is a disguised portrait of Jonas Lie, whom Ibsen at this time regarded as the incarnation of the materialist spirit for having, as mentioned above, through his investments, harassed Ibsen's good friend Botten-Hansen. Monsen is depicted as a swindler whose home life is as disreputable as his business dealings. Lie was a businessman and political liberal who was making a name for himself as a writer. His investments were imperiled in the mid-1860s, and at the end of 1868 his situation was so desperate that Bjørnson pleaded with several liberal politicians to donate money to save Lie from being hounded into the courts by creditors.[20] Lie's situation is meanly distorted in Monsen's plight at the end of the play when, having overextended himself and desperately in need of ready cash, Monsen is forced to flee his creditors and the sheriff. (However, it did come to pass that in 1871, Lie, finding himself in debt to the tune of twenty thousand specie dollars, took off for Italy.)[21]

The average Norwegian reader or theatergoer would not have recognized Monsen as Lie. Ibsen's friends, however, would have relished the sly intimations: (1) Jonas Lie was the son of Mons Lie, i.e., Mon-son. (2) Monsen's estate is called Storli, i.e., Big Li. (3) Lie, like Monsen, belonged to the liberal party, and Monsen's party is called Storlipartiet. (4) Monsen and Lie were both forced into bankruptcy; Lie entered a plea of bankruptcy in May 1868. (5) Monsen's father was a lumberjack; Lie lived in the middle of the lumbering area of eastern Norway, and his investments in lumber eventuated in his bankruptcy. (6) Monsen's house smells of bad tobacco; Lie was a heavy pipe smoker.[22]

Stensgaard, the dominant figure in the play, is a composite of at least four persons, three of them politicians: Bjørnson, Ole Richter, and Herman Bagger. Representing the republicans, Stensgaard had to be a member of the bar, since the republicans were popularly known as the "lawyers' party."

Prominent among them was the lawyer Richter, whose notorious pursuit of well-to-do women furnished Ibsen with one of the two main intrigues of the plot. Stensgaard is repeatedly called a fortune hunter, and Ibsen counted on the audience's recollection that in 1863, in a debate in the Storting, one of the assemblymen, hearing himself attacked as an apostle of materialism, turned on Richter and, pointedly alluding to him, said, "A materialist is one who seeks profits and rakes in his gains from all sides, looking for money and for rich women to marry."[23]

But Stensgaard's profile was distinctly Bjørnson's, and everyone who read or saw the play—including Bjørnson—knew it. His good friend Bernhard Dunker said that "Stensgaard is exactly Bjørnson if one separates the man from the poet. Stensgaard's speeches are completely like Bjørnson's."[24] The opening scene clearly alludes to Bjørnson's sensational political debut in Bergen on May 17, 1859. Bjørnson had a natural gift for oratory and an extraordinary power to spellbind the young, and, like Stensgaard, he reveled in his power. Though Ibsen added touches to the characterization of Stensgaard that derived from other republicans, the first impression the audience has of him is that of a mob-swaying public speaker. Bjørnson had established his reputation as one of Norway's finest orators in his Constitution Day speeches (years after hearing such a speech by Bjørnson, one of his auditors could recall it word for word).[25] Ibsen opens his play with a vivid picture of Stensgaard in action. In an impromptu speech on Constitution Day, he stirs the young and makes them band together, precisely as Bjørnson had done on similar occasions. Like Bjørnson, Stensgaard is given to such Grundtvigian utterances as "The wrath of the Almighty is within me. It is His will that you oppose!"[26] As Bjørnson mediated between the Farmers' Friends and the liberal party, so Stensgaard compounds with both Lundestad's agrarian party and Monsen's reform party. And much like Bjørnson, Stensgaard threatens to drive the newspaper publisher Aslaksen out of business if he does not print what he is told.

Bjørnson was deeply offended by what he could only take as a personal and vindictive attack. "This is an assault of the most shameful sort. . . . When Stensgaard gets wind in his sails, that is, when the lowness in him comes out in his stirring speeches, he [Ibsen] catches a neat strain of my form, so that anyone can get it. He might have, in that regard (the future, the political opposition), portrayed me—and comically—and I would have laughed myself; but assassin-like to make me part of ideas and plans of the worst kind of self-interest! Me, who lifted him out of the muck he lived in, contributed hundreds so he could travel, stood guarantor for him with Hegel [the publisher] until he made a name for himself in Denmark, took care of his family here [in Norway], offered him my furniture, my whole apartment that time I lived in Denmark, if only he would come home—I who as a man of the Opposition got him his writer's stipend—he is contemptible!"[27]

Although Ibsen did owe Bjørnson an enormous debt for helping him at the start of his career, Bjørnson claims more credit than was his due. The bits about the stipend and the apartment are obfuscations. Through negligence, Bjørnson had let Ibsen's household goods be sold at auction in 1864 in payment of debts Ibsen had acquired. When he wrote to apologize to Ibsen, who was in Italy, he sought to make amends by offering to put his own apartment at Ibsen's disposal at any time.[28]

Ibsen's fiction proved to be tamer than the facts. Stensgaard's threat to start a rival paper that will appeal to the broad public comes to naught, but as mentioned above, Bjørnson did take over the editorship of another paper and, by lowering prices and appealing to a larger readership, succeeded in forcing Botten-Hansen to close up shop.

The profits from the *Norsk Folkeblad*, the paper that Bjørnson edited, were supposed to go to a pension fund for the teachers in the Grundtvigian folk schools in Norway. But in underselling the competition, Bjørnson not only drove Botten-Hansen out of business but hastened the *Norsk Folkeblad* into bankruptcy, whereupon Bjørnson bought the paper and became editor-owner. Years later, after they were reconciled, Ibsen sought to extenuate the personal animus toward Bjørnson in *The League of Youth* by saying he had satirized a political type, not an individual, and Henrik Jæger defensively argued[29] that Stensgaard stood for those who imitated Bjørnson. What, then, is one to make of Monsen's son, who is depicted as imitating Stensgaard? Is he supposed to represent those who imitated those who imitated Bjørnson? Sverdrup has been mentioned by some[30] as having also contributed to the characterization of Stensgaard. Vinje in his review of the play (October 24, 1869) mentioned Bjørnson by name but added that there were two other models, both well known.[31] Vinje was probably referring to Richter and Sverdrup. Bjørnson, too, made a reference to Sverdrup: "A friend of mine, who has done Ibsen much good, has for obvious reasons been pointed out as prototype for the play's principal character."[32] However, the identification of Sverdrup with Stensgaard rests on the use of republican slogans and not on personality traits.

There is yet another source for Stensgaard's machinations. The forged promissory note that is placed in his hands to wield against Brattsberg derives from the exploits of a politician named Herman Bagger. He had once actually carried out what Stensgaard only threatens and had set up an opposition newspaper in order to further his own career. Bagger was first elected to office on a liberal platform and was subsequently reelected to the Storting with the support of the Workers' Union. Later, however, he had become an archconservative and was regarded in the 1860s as a traitor to the Thraneite labor movement. Stensgaard's ambition of moving from Monsen's party to Brattsberg's mirrors Bagger's opportunistic politics, and Stensgaard's future political career was to be the same as Bagger's past, which had found him indiscriminately serving the liberal and conservative causes. Bagger was reseated in the Storting in October 1868, when Ibsen drafted the outline for his antiliberal play.

What is more interesting is that Bagger was the representative from Skien, Ibsen's hometown. He had arrived there from Denmark in the 1830s and had become sufficiently friendly with the Ibsen family to stand as godfather to Henrik's younger brother Ole. A couple of years after Henrik left home, the friendship between Bagger and Ibsen's father, Knud, came to an end. Both men applied for the position of municipal accountant, but Bagger won the appointment by declaring his willingness to accept a cut in salary. Not long after this, he was nominated an elector, while Knud's fortunes rapidly declined. Henrik Ibsen never returned to his childhood home, but the entrance of Bagger into the scenario for his political satire stirred up memories, and his thoughts migrated from the current political scene to the scenes of his adolescence, that difficult time when the Ibsen family fell apart and Henrik was driven out into the world. As a result, *The League of Youth* is as much about Ibsen's younger days as it is about Bjørnson's progress through the 1860s, and beneath the political satire lies a human drama.[33]

Daniel Hejre is a deft sketch of Ibsen's father, each stroke of the pen adding another aspect to the portrait. Hejre's mordant wit, his fall from fortune, his insistence that he was never actually declared bankrupt, his malicious joy in the prospect that others will fall as he has fallen, and his license as community jester to blurt out indiscretions with impunity all add up to an image of Knud Ibsen in his decline.[34]

In the acting tradition of the part, Hejre is portrayed as looking and sounding a bit like a heron (*hejre*)—a thin, round-shouldered old man with a croaking voice and long, thin legs. Though he is no longer a force in the community, he still has the air of a grand seigneur, and in spite of his unbridled tongue he is a regular guest in the home of Chamberlain Brattsberg.[35]

Hejre makes himself at home there because of an injustice done to him by the Brattsbergs. Hejre's father had bought some land from the Brattsberg family, but since it was odal land (heritable land dating from feudal times), the Brattsbergs could legally reclaim it, which they did, thus hastening Hejre's downfall. Smacking his lips over his host's excellent sherry, Hejre can say, "It's a sheer delight to see my money so well spent," and derive some further pleasure from Brattsberg's embarrassed laugh. Ibsen borrowed the name Brattsberg from an estate near Skien that had once belonged to distant relations of his, but in the play Brattsberg stands for His Excellency Severin Løvenskiold, and the Brattsberg works correspond to the Fossum ironworks that Ibsen knew so well as a child. (Løvenskiold means "lion shield," and there is a reference in act two to "playing with lions" when Brattsberg's name is mentioned.) There is also a tradition in Skien that Knud Ibsen and Løvenskiold quarreled over the ownership of Venstøp,[36] the farm to which the family moved when Knud was threatened with bankruptcy.

The political drama of *The League of Youth* is cradled in a larger drama in which Ibsen relived the humiliation of his younger years. The town of Skien in which the Ibsen family had lost face and social standing became an image of that parochial Norway in which he had felt ostracized. Having lived abroad for

Figure 10. Knut Almlöf as Daniel Hejre.

over four years, he now saw his homeland and his former self in a new perspective. From the vantage point of his growing eminence and secure in his circle of politically conservative supporters, he could disavow his past and both mock and pity those who made up the little world he had escaped from. When examined as an autobiographical document, the play is more revealing than Ibsen's letters.

As Ibsen immersed himself in the past, the play became as much a story about Skien as about Christiania, as much about class distinctions as about political differences. Ultimately the conflict is "between patrician and plebeian," as one critic expressed it, "between inherited gentility and upstart headstrongness, between aristocratic reserve and parvenu aggressiveness, between the thumb-twiddling and complacency of the old generation with its straitlaced scorn for all that is new and the pursuit of happiness of the talented and enterprising young."[37] In the back of Ibsen's mind was the fall from fortune he had experienced as a child, and Stensgaard's efforts to make his way up the social ladder are no different from Ibsen's. In giving depth to Stensgaard's character and in explaining the source of his drive and ambition, Ibsen did not draw on his knowledge of Bjørnson; he created Stensgaard's psyche out of his own. "Through self-anatomy," he said, "I brought to light many of the characteristics of both Peer Gynt and Stensgaard."[38] He simplified the actual political situation in order to expand the story of a man who cares nothing about political progress and everything about social esteem. Paradoxically, this subjectivity gives the play the objectivity it must have lacked when it was first conceived as an attack on Bjørnson.

Stensgaard's bitterness and frustration are obviously not Bjørnson's but Ibsen's. The one person in whom Stensgaard can confide the truth about himself is his old friend Dr. Fjeldbo, the doctor at Brattsberg's ironworks. Fjeldbo was modeled on Michael Birkeland, a member of the Dutchmen circle and one of the few people to whom Ibsen unburdened himself.[39] He was the man who drafted the petition for a writer's grant for Ibsen. As pictured in the play, he is reserved and imperturbable, foppish in dress, somewhat unmanly in bearing and gesture, and a frequent guest in the best homes in Christiania. "A stiff-necked snob," Brattsberg calls him, and Stensgaard says to him, "You know what's wrong with you? You have never appreciated anyone. What did you do in Christiania but go from one tea party to another, passing the time by being witty. You pay for that sort of life. The feeling for the worthwhile things in life, for what is uplifting and inspiring—all that slips away and you're left behind, high and dry, fit for nothing."[40] Here Ibsen is echoing what Bjørnson said about the negative spirit of the Dutchmen, but when Stensgaard tells him of his bitterness, it is Ibsen who is speaking.

In a revealing passage in the last act of the play Ibsen contrasts Fjeldbo and Stensgaard and traces the differences in their temperaments not to heredity but to the influence of the homes in which they grew up. "I have known [Stensgaard] from childhood," says Fjeldbo. "His father was a dried-up, weak little good-for-nothing. He ran a small grocery store and had a pawnshop on the side—or rather his wife ran it. She was a completely vulgar woman, the least feminine woman I've ever met. She got her husband certified and put away; she was absolutely without heart. That was the sort of home Stensgaard grew up in. Then he went to school, took the college preparation course. 'He's going to get a degree,' said his mother. Going to be a first-class law clerk? Squalor at home, high hopes in school—mind and character, ambition and ability—all going in different directions. What could come of it but a man divided against himself?"[41]

Fjeldbo's young years were entirely different. "I had the kind of home life that brings a sense of security and balance. I grew up in perfect peace and harmony in a simple middle-class home. My mother was the complete woman, through and through. Nobody expected more of us than was possible. There were no extravagant hopes to be dashed on the rocks by a sudden change of the wind. Death didn't enter our happy circle to leave us empty and desolate. There was a love of beautiful things, and it was part of our life, not something apart from it. And nobody went to extremes either in their thoughts or emotions."[42]

This is an idealization of Birkeland's life, done for dramatic purposes. Although Birkeland came from a good family, he had known hard times. He had to abandon his studies at the University of Christiania for economic reasons and find employment as a tutor.

Stensgaard's upbringing is a grim version of Ibsen's, while Fjeldbo's life appears as a picture of what Ibsen's might have been if his father's business had never failed and family life had remained as genteel and pleasant after 1836 as it had been before. It was typical of Ibsen to represent the division within him, social and psychological, by two contrasted characters.

PARTICULAR INTERESTS

In the comic world of *The League of Youth* everyone is the victim of a society in which self-interest is assumed to be the greatest virtue and politics and government are only means of preserving such a society. When Chamberlain Brattsberg hurls after the departing Stensgaard the ultimate insult, "Rodhugger"—radical!—the cream of the jest, and of the whole comedy, lies in the fact that Stensgaard actually aspires to be part of the system and that the entrenched interests are so narrow in their outlook that they forget that the active desire to displace them at the top is a confirmation of their system and not a subversion of it. ("Rodhugger" was a term often applied to members of the liberal or "lawyers'" party.)

In the play the recurrent phrase "vor lokale Forhold" ("our particular situation" or "our local interests") is meant to convey the influence of the old families and what they used to maintain the status quo, the power of tradition and convention. Ibsen put the phrase in the mouth of the newspaper publisher Aslaksen, modeled on N. F. Axelsen from Ibsen's radical youth in Christiania. Although coined by the conservatives, the phrase had been turned against them by the republicans. In 1857, when a liberalization of the juridical system was pushed through the Storting, Ole Richter mocked the conservatives for arguing against innovations as being not suitable to "our local interests."

"Nothing," said Richter in a newspaper article,

> has performed such yeoman service for the conservative party as "our local interests." It is the magic formula by which a Chinese wall has with unbelievable success been raised time and again against the influx of new and civilizing ideas. Let anyone here at home put forward some suggestion for the improvement of our social or political affairs, and let him defend his proposal with all the means that genius and sagacity, backed up with hard common sense, can

> muster, then, even if the proposal has behind it the support of history and the happy experience of other nations, there will burst forth from his hard-pressed opponents the magic formula "our local interests," and these words will have the same awesome and petrifying effect on the public as Medusa's face had on those who unfortunately met its gaze.[1]

In *The League of Youth* Ibsen gave the phrase wider implications and applied it to all parties. Heard at the rise of the curtain and bringing down the curtain on the last act, "vor lokale Forhold" is repeated ten times in all as a constant reminder of the hidebound nature and essential illiberality of provincial Norway. In that sense it functions in the play as "vær dig selv nok" does in *Peer Gynt.* But it does more: it reaches out to indict political morality itself and to expose the naked self-interest beneath the cloak of party slogans. Removed from its political context and translated as "our local interests" or "our particular situation," "vor lokale Forhold" cannot have the satiric effect that Ibsen intended. Exactly what he meant is brought out in his comments on the German translation of the play in which the phrase was rendered literally as "lokale Verhältnisse." Ibsen said that this was wrong "in that it lacks the overtone of something comic and narrow-minded." He went on to say that the phrase "must be rendered as 'unseren berechtigen Eigenthümlichkeiten,' which in German is the precise equivalent of the corresponding expression in Scandinavia."[2]

The suggestion seems wrongheaded, and the German, English, and French translators have ignored it. Yet Ibsen's knowledge of German was good enough to make him feel at home in Dresden, where he was living when he wrote the play, and he certainly would not have insisted that "unseren berechtigen Eigenthümlichkeiten" ("our justifiable particularism") was the precise equivalent of "vor lokale Forhold" unless he knew what he was talking about. When a phrase is given comic meaning or satiric significance, the place to look for its proper equivalent in another language is not in the dictionary but in the thing satirized. "Vor lokale Forhold" was loaded with political meaning; so was "unseren berechtigen Eigenthümlichkeiten." The phrase became notorious among German liberals after Premier Otto von Bismarck and Kaiser William I used it in October 1866 to justify the annexation of certain territories. After defeating the Austrian forces in the Seven Weeks' War, Bismarck negotiated treaties of peace with several states in the German Confederation, but Hanover, Nassau, Hesse-Cassel, and the Free City of Frankfurt, which had displayed hostility toward Prussia, were ruthlessly annexed by decree. To the Diet of the German Confederation the kaiser declared that "political necessity compels us to unite in perpetuity those areas with our monarchy."

Bismarck vented his hatred of Frankfurt, a bastion of liberalism, by threatening to ravage and starve the city unless it paid an indemnity of 25 million gulden. In despair, the burgomaster hanged himself.

Particularism was the doctrine that defined the nature of the confederation of German states: each state was free to promote its own particular interests and maintain its own particular laws as distinct from those of the federated whole. When Bismarck was challenged by those who saw in the annexation of Frankfurt only "the right of conquest" and "open violence," he responded, "In this case the right of conquest rests on the right of the German nation to exist, to breathe, to become one." Particularism, which was originally intended to keep the German states only loosely united, was employed by Bismarck to justify the expansion of Prussia. With brutal cynicism he announced that "our justifiable particularism" demanded that Prussia take over these states to promote its own interests. It was the particularism of the wolf among the sheep.[3]

To Ibsen, "vor lokale Forhold" stood for the usurpation of the rights of others in order to maintain or promote one's own interests, which could always be sanctioned by the power that lay behind them. In *The League of Youth* he expanded his moral indictment of self-interest to the sphere of power politics. In the fourth act of *Peer Gynt* he had arraigned Bismarckian aggressiveness and Norwegian lack of principles. The motto by which Peer lived, "vær dig selv nok," meant to refrain from sacrificing oneself for any cause; in *The League of Youth*, "vor lokale Forhold" signifies the sacrifice of others to one's own interests. This meaning appears to be more clearly conveyed by the German phrase than by the Norwegian, and it is possible that "vor lokale Forhold" was chosen *faute de mieux*. "Unseren berechtigen Eigenthümlichkeiten" had just achieved notoriety in Germany when Ibsen wrote his play ("Is there not something in *The League of Youth* that smacks of Knackwurst und Bier?" asked Ibsen[4]); "vor lokale Forhold" was ten years old in Norway. Yet it was evidently still current in his homeland, and it served his purpose. He settled in Germany just in time to see how the stunning success of Bismarck's policies, based on "justifiable particularism," drew many liberals into the conservative camp, while in Norway the liberal republicans were compounding with the conservative farmers' associations for their own special interests.

William Archer, in translating Ibsen into English, said he found Ibsen's suggestion of no help at all, "especially when it is remembered in what context Aslaksen uses the phrase 'de lokale forhold' in the fifth act of *An Enemy of the People*."[5] But that is where the German would make perfect sense. Aslaksen proposes to enter into a collusion with Dr. Stockmann by which they can both snap up the virtually worthless shares in the baths before reassuring the public that the baths are safe. "You've got to take your food where you find it," says Aslaksen. Stockmann is so furious at this proposal that he chases Aslaksen out of the house. Bewildered, Aslaksen exclaims, "De, some bare kendte de lokale forholde—." Archer renders this as "if one only knew the local situation," adding that here "local situation" means "the lie of the land," a reading adopted in *The Oxford Ibsen*. This misses the point, however. What Aslaksen means here is what he meant when he used the phrase in *The League of Youth*. There is nothing "comic and narrow-minded" in having a man justify his conduct by appealing to the local situation or the lie of the land. The comic absurdity lies in having him justify his proposed swindle by ingenuously exclaiming when confronted by an honest man, "But my particular interests require me to cheat others."

While Ibsen was writing *The League of Youth*, Young Denmark and Young Norway appeared to grow stronger month by month. Clemens Petersen was described as being in high spirits "among his three sponsors and protectors: Bjørnson, Rasmus Nielsen, and [the editor Carl] Ploug."[6] Bjørnson praised him as standing head and shoulders above the other literary and theatrical critics: his "great, affirmative spirit creates as it criticizes."[7]

But there was also a swelling current of animosity toward Petersen. His youth, his blatant prejudices, his arrogance were resented by many writers, while the actors in the Copenhagen theaters regarded him as an untalented actor who requited his failure onstage in spiteful attacks on those who had succeeded there. In a typical anecdote of the time Petersen was introduced to a well-known thespian, who gave no sign of recognition at the mention of the critic's name.

"Don't you know who I am?" asked Petersen. "I write for *Fædrelandet*."

"Really," replied the actor. "I never read reviews. But wait a minute . . . Clemens Petersen! There once was an actor of that name. I'll never forget him."[8]

Furthermore, Johanne Luise Heiberg, the greatly admired actress and managing director of the Danish Royal Theater, disliked him not only for having draped himself in her husband's mantle as Denmark's leading critic but also for behaving as if he deserved it. This played into Ibsen's hand. *The League of Youth*, unlike *Brand*, was written expressly for the theater, where the Bjørnson-Petersen forces were weakly deployed. Fru Heiberg had staged Bjørnson's *Mary Stuart* at the end of 1867, but the atmosphere during rehearsals had been made tense by her knowledge that Bjørnson was a close friend of Petersen. After the play opened, she turned her back on Bjørnson, whom she thought boorish and vulgar, and, evidently infected by Petersen's spite, he did not try to make amends.[9]

Bjørnson's boisterousness often rubbed people the wrong way, and back in 1856 Fru Heiberg had shut her doors on him for some undisclosed impropriety.[10] In the high society of Copenhagen, the Paris of the north, this force of nature could seem like a bull in a china shop. As one critic said, "His striking appearance, the pithy terseness of his speech, and a certain *naïve* self-assertion and impatience of social restraints made him a notable figure in the polite and somewhat effeminate society of the Danish capital."[11] In the 1860s Brandes saw him as an imposing presence, loud and garrulous. "His manners went against the quieter style of Copenhagen. He gave the impression of a big, hulking, spoiled child."[12] Another Dane described Bjørnson's boorishness more wittily. "Bjørnson is one of those bears [*bjørne*] that doesn't always walk on two feet but sometimes gets down on all four and forgets that it is supposed to be a human being."[13]

Later, in the mid-1870s, by which time Petersen was out of the picture and Bjørnson had improved his social manners, Fru Heiberg succumbed to his ebullient nature and boisterous charm and enjoyed his company. More so than Ibsen's.

"I have talked with Ibsen on several occasions," she once remarked. "But he is as tightfisted as a miser and gives nothing of himself except in his works. I don't much like such locked-up houses, always on guard against thieves. A free spirit must move freely. It's very annoying to sit freezing next to so much fire."[14]

In 1869, however, the situation was different, and Ibsen was so eager to take advantage of the strained relationship between Fru Heiberg and Bjørnson that he offered his play royalty-free to her.[15]

In the meantime, Young Denmark was organizing itself for greater efforts. Rudolf Schmidt set about establishing a monthly journal, *For Idé og Virkelighed* (*The Ideal and the Real*), to advocate the dualistic philosophy. He signed on Nielsen, Petersen, and Bjørnson as contributing editors. At the latter's suggestion, Ibsen was also invited to serve. Since the last letter that Bjørnson had received from Ibsen, that of December 28, 1867, was full of expressions of friendship, he had no inkling of a change in Ibsen's attitude.

To Schmidt's invitation Ibsen replied on January 26, 1869, "I cannot bring myself to collaborate with men of whom I have the impression, based on experience, that at the first opportunity they will use their newspapers and pens against me. In the Norwegian *Morgenbladet* the Copenhagen correspondent writes that Bjørnstjerne Bjørnson has been named as probable coeditor. . . . That in itself would be decisive for me, even if there were not other reasons in abundance."[16]

Informed of Ibsen's reply, Bjørnson wrote to Frederik Hegel, the publisher they shared, "I have heard nothing from Ibsen except for an insult conveyed to me by a third party. I have no idea what I have done to deserve it and can't be bothered to find out. I'm fed up with him. Let the winds of his capricious nature waft him where they will."[17]

Precisely at this juncture, when Ibsen had decisively allied himself with

Brandes, both sides in the controversy were rocked by sexual scandals. Brandes had fallen in love with a married woman. On February 16 Fru Caroline David left her husband and six children to live with the Danish free thinker and defender of women's rights. This event became the talk of the town. But the elopement of the thirty-six-year-old emancipated woman with the twenty-seven-year-old Jewish radical would have had far greater repercussions among the Copenhagen artists and intellectuals if a second scandal had not distracted attention from the first.[18]

Only two weeks after the lovers eloped, Clemens Petersen was exposed as a pederast. Accused of molesting young boys at the school where he taught, Petersen resigned. If he had not won the enmity of a large part of the Copenhagen intelligentsia, he might have been accorded a measure of sympathy, and his penchant for young boys might have been passed over in silence, as was often the case with many others who shared his sexual predilections. As it was, he was persecuted and hounded out of the country.

Early in March he fled to Vienna, explaining to Rudolf Schmidt that he had to go to Italy to be treated for erysipelas. Schmidt suspected other reasons, since rumors had reached him that Petersen had either collapsed mentally (at the time, erysipelas was thought to cause mental imbalance) or had made obscene advances to the female students in his classes. Schmidt immediately wrote to Bjørnson on March 6, and then a week later sent Bjørnson another letter, informing him ominously that the truth was worse than the gossip. "For a long time to come a veil of suspicion will hang over us all: the cause of idealism [*Aandelighedens*] is crippled."[19]

Bjørnson was stunned by Schmidt's news. "That you don't tell me *what exactly* it is with Petersen, that you don't give me positive information, only some outbursts, that you carry on with a whole pack of stuff without doing that, appalls me, and I'll never forget it.—Give me the complete news, take the time to collect it and relate it, if only because he was our fellow worker in our dearest enterprise, he was my friend, and though I have cried and racked my brains, I can't find my way out of the spot you have put me in."[20]

With money provided by friends—Bjørnson immediately sent thirty specie dollars—Petersen exiled himself to America, settled in Brooklyn, eked out a living as a journalist writing on cultural affairs, met Walt Whitman, and did not return to Denmark until 1904. Admiring Petersen's fine intellect and esthetic sense, Bjørnson remained loyal to him over the years. In 1884 he said, "As long as I knew him, I had—none of us did—*any idea* that he had a predilection for pederasty. In spite of this failing, he was a good, yes, a sweet-natured person, with wide and strong interests."[21]

Brandes suffered little from the scandal in which he was involved, since in flouting a sexual morality to which he was opposed he was merely acting in harmony with his avowed principles. But the Petersen scandal staggered the Nielsenites and Young Denmark. It occurred just as they were awaiting the appearance of the first issue of the new journal that would serve to consolidate their position. The exposure of Petersen as a pederast suggested that their morality was as dualistic as their philosophy. Seeing reality overwhelming ideality, Rudolf Schmidt was compelled by his publisher to recall five hundred copies of the first issue of *For Idé og Virkelighed* that had already been mailed and to remove Petersen's name from the masthead.

To replace him, Schmidt and Nielsen turned to Bjørnson, who on March 28, 1869, quickly accepted the offer. But their cause was still one man short (and to make matters worse, Nielsen was seriously ill), and Bjørnson once again urged Schmidt to approach Ibsen. "He cannot turn us down," wrote Bjørnson, "when the cause is of the greatest importance, and when his services can benefit all of us who work for it."

Upon hearing about the Petersen scandal, Ibsen said, "I've always been darkly suspicious of his character; but something like this—!" And as for Bjørnson's accepting the position of editor, "I don't understand how he can want to occupy a seat still warm from the departed one."[22]

Bjørnson believed that Ibsen would have joined them earlier if he had been made welcome. Why, he asked, did Schmidt find Ibsen incompatible? As for Petersen, Bjørnson continued, "I had the distressing feeling that at the same time that Ibsen was being corrected [by the critic], which was of course necessary, he was also being rejected. In all essentials his goal is the same as ours. . . . I got more help from his last work, indeed I have never in my life (until recently when Nielsen's books appeared) got, or rather felt, such a helping hand from any other quarter as from *Peer Gynt*."[23]

These remarks show not only that Ibsen had assessed the situation accurately from the start but that Bjørnson was still unaware of the gulf that had opened up between them. Just how confused he was about the substantial issues is indicated by his next act. He sought a rapprochement with Brandes and asked for a discussion of possible collaborative efforts. Brandes promptly rejected the invitation and reported it to Ibsen.

"What you tell me about Bjørnson," Ibsen replied, "does not astonish me. For him there exist only two kinds of people: those he can make use of and those who might be an embarrassment to him. Furthermore, Bjørnson's cleverness as a psychologist when dealing with his own fictional characters is matched only by his inability to figure out real people."[24]

It was only after the scandal broke that Bjørnson came to realize that he had ingenuously allowed himself to be implicated in Petersen's vendettas and that he had been used as a stick to beat others.[25] That the critic's interest in him might have been homosexual never occurred to Bjørnson. He blamed Petersen's itch for young boys on an attack of erysipelas. "Isn't it terrible that a human being, most gifted and fine, should be afflicted with an illness that attacks him like a wild animal and forces him to commit acts that no one condemned more strongly than he? God preserve us all!"[26]

Bjørnson was always sublimely confident of his knowledge of people and in his powers of analyzing others. "If I am not disturbed and can receive direct impressions," he remarked, "I have a faculty for psychological observation the like of which I have never encountered, except once (in Clemens Petersen)."[27]

Old Debts Repaid

Although *The League of Youth* was not scheduled to be published until the autumn, advance copies began coming off the presses about June 1. To stimulate interest in his play, Ibsen discreetly circulated copies among theater managers, as well as among friendly readers. He wanted this play to achieve something that had so far eluded him—a smash stage success. He had written several plays for the theater in his apprentice years, but he had not established himself as a practical playwright. Employing all the techniques of popular comedy, *The League of Youth* was written to remedy that situation. Aiming for the best possible production with the finest actors, he offered the play free of royalty payments not only to the Royal Theater in Copenhagen but also to the Dramatic Theater in Stockholm. It was an unnecessary gesture. These national theaters were eager to stage a new work by the famed author of *Brand* and *Peer Gynt*, especially one that satirized the liberal movement.

The Stockholm theater mounted the play with great regard for the author's intentions. It was translated by Franz Hedberg, a professional dramatist in his own right. The director, Gustaf Fredrikson, who cast himself in the part of Stensgaard, consulted with Ibsen's friend Lorentz Dietrichson, who was residing in Stockholm, about Norwegian customs and Norwegian character types in order to enhance the local color.

Equal care was taken in Copenhagen. The censor for the Royal Theater found the plot of the play too difficult to follow and said it was completely unstageworthy. Fru Heiberg, who liked the complicated intrigue of the plot, put pressure on him, and he revised his opinion, remarking that what the play lacked esthetically it made up for as political satire.[1] Fru Heiberg herself directed the production, which proved to be an extraordinary success. Praising her for undertaking the production and Vilhelm Wiehe for his performance as Stensgaard, Brandes called the play "one of the most successful that has been staged at the Royal Theater in a long time."[2] Ibsen himself expressed his thanks to Wiehe, who played Stensgaard with a Norwegian accent, for the charm and vigor he brought to the part.[3] "You have grasped my intentions to the fullest and interpreted the part with genius."[4] The effect of the Norwegian accent would be rather like that of a southern accent in an American political play.

When *The League* proved itself onstage, the censor had another look at *The Pretenders*, which he had earlier rejected; it was performed in 1871, with Fru Heiberg again in charge.

What the critics and the public had to say about *The League* tells us a great deal about what a serious dramatist had to contend with in the middle of the nineteenth century. While the physical production impressed the critics, they were less happy about the author's conception of humanity. The severity of their strictures may disconcert a modern reader who does not know how strong was the resistance to realism, a resistance that the young Ibsen had supported in his theater reviews disapproving of "photography" onstage.

Ibsen's demeaning view of human nature dismayed the arbiters of taste; there was not a single character they could admire or sympathize with. Hejre was spiteful and destructive; Aslaksen crapulous and ineffective; Brattsberg smug and self-satisfied, naïve about people, and ignorant of the life of the intellect; his son Erik was motivated by greed; Monsen was even more greedy and only a little less scrupulous; and Lundestad, the cleverest of the whole assortment, pretended to be stupid only to preserve his interests. Forgetting that Ibsen was following classic comic theory in depicting people as worse than they really are, one Danish critic censured the play for offering "no enlightening prospect of that ideal horizon that is the only proper background for art." The characters, he said, exist in a world that is like "a hospital, in which all the patients are suffering to some degree or other from a moral defect and who owe their existence only to that defect—a hospital without healing waters and without doctors."[5]

In Stockholm, where the play had opened two months earlier than in Copenhagen, the critics were even harsher. "A comedy without any comedy." "From beginning to end nothing but a caricature." "A dark and despairing picture of nothing but meanness and wretchedness in all forms." The only human feeling aroused was one of commiseration "with our sister Norway for her miserable and ugly social conditions."[6]

Even Brandes was dispirited by the characters, believing them to be too base for comedy. "They are certainly natural and true enough, but alas! why is the truth so grim, the fun so heavy, and the good humor so restrained?"[7]

The Stockholm critics predicted a short life for the comedy, one of them declaring it was propaganda, a "pamphlet for our times rather than a play for the stage and for the future." The thought of seeing the play more than once was "morally inconceivable."[8]

This was one of those occasions when the public was ahead of the critics. It proved to be more sophisticated in its response to the satire and more advanced in its esthetic views. *The League of Youth* was an extraordinary theatrical success in both Stockholm and Copenhagen, and it was this work that established Ibsen as a practical playwright. In Norway it remained the most popular of his plays through the end of the nineteenth century. The main objection voiced by audiences had to do with the running time: three and a half hours. But they sat through it because of the theatrical brilliance of the characterizations. In Stockholm, Knut Almlöf, a gifted character actor, won most of the plaudits in the part of Daniel Hejre. His interpretation was unrelievedly satiric, and the heartlessness that the critics deprecated the audience applauded.[9] One Danish reviewer admitted that the spectators were "overwhelmed by the strong individualization of the sharply realistic characters and galvanized by the satiric current of the play." He went on to lament that Denmark possessed no Ibsen, who "after having depicted a spineless, characterless, egotistic phrasemonger, had the courage to end the play with the prediction that in ten years he would have a seat in parliament."[10]

Naturally, it was in the Norwegian capital, where the play had its premiere, that the satire cut deepest, with praise and censure strictly following party lines. Ibsen's friend Ludvig Daae, whose acerbity and vindictiveness earned him the sobriquet "chief of the *Morgenbladet* demons," was "mightily pleased," as were all those in the *Morgenbladet* clique.[11] The liberals were angered and shocked, Bjørnson's friend Dunker finding the characters "desolating . . . without a decent man in the bunch."[12] One liberal fumed at Daae and in a threatening voice declared that the play was "a gauntlet flung at the liberal party, but one that will redound on Ibsen, either in his face or on his rear." And a professor of literature who supported the liberals tagged the play "a *Morgenbladet* editorial in dramatic form," a description that the *Morgenbladet* board thought the finest compliment ever paid them.[13]

During the winter of 1868–69, when Ibsen was at work on the play, *Morgenbladet* intensified its campaign against Bjørnson, and as the liberals increased their numbers in the Storting, the attacks became increasingly scurrilous. Bjørnson was labeled "our national clown," ridiculed as a lout, denounced for traducing decent people and coercing critics to review his works favorably. He was accused of using threatening language against the man who succeeded him as chief of the Christiania Theater, a position he had lost through the machinations of the

Morgenbladet conservatives, who made up the majority on the theater's managing board. This unceasing editorial sniping further incensed the conservatives against Bjørnson, especially in Christiania, where half the population treated him as a leper.

All this was served up to Ibsen miles away in Dresden, where he had moved in the autumn of 1868. *Morgenbladet* was the only Scandinavian newspaper he subscribed to at this time, and reading Friele's editorials undoubtedly fueled his mordant imagination and emboldened him in his ridicule of Bjørnson. "*The League of Youth* is the result of a sort of tacit collaboration with *Morgenbladet*," says one Bjørnson biographer. "Sitting in a Dresden alehouse and reading these articles in which Ibsen recognized the accent and tone of his friends, he competed with them in comic inventiveness. He hurled his wit and sarcasms through Daniel Hejre, who is part Friele, part Ibsen's father, and of course Ibsen himself."[14]

With feelings running so high, the audience at the Christiania Theater on opening night, October 18, 1869, was surprisingly undemonstrative. Occupying the royal box was Norway's prime minister, Frederik Stang, who had supported the bill giving Ibsen an annual writer's stipend, and the *Morgenbladet* readers formed a substantial part of the audience. Daae, who had not attended a theatrical performance since Ibsen's *Pretenders* was staged in 1864, was almost as conspicuous by his presence as Bjørnson, who had managed the Christiania Theater for two difficult years and saved it from bankruptcy, was by his absence. He had left town two days previously, knowing the audience would be hostile toward him.

The theater was a bastion of conservatism, its public consisting of merchants, civil servants, and small manufacturers, who looked upon Bjørnson and the "lawyers' party" as troublesome radicals. But their response to Ibsen's satire was restrained by the liberal minority. When they attempted to express their approval of Ibsen's gibes, hisses silenced their applause. In the fourth act, when Monsen's son spoke of "the common people who have nothing, who are nothing, who lie in chains," some liberals expressed their disapproval by whistling rather timidly. They objected to this sentiment being expressed by the unprincipled Bastian Monsen, who was only mouthing Stensgaard's phrases, and these phrases were known to echo Bjørnson's. In a letter to a fellow republican, Bjørnson had stated the need for the support of the common man as a necessary political strategy.

"Programs or ideas must have people; people must have a banner; and I see no way of getting both other than by teaming up with those who stand together, ready for anything, because they have nothing and will get nothing unless they unite."[15]

Strong feelings were not vented until two nights later, when the play was given its second performance. By custom this was the author's benefit night, and the house was sold out. Some ten or twelve students from the university, where the republican movement had strong support, plotted to infiltrate the citadel and prevent the audience from enjoying this mockery of liberal ideals. As soon as Lundestad in the first speech of the play hurrahed Norwegian Independence Day, the students, sitting in the top gallery, the twelve-skilling gallery, began blowing on police whistles and through the holes of their door keys. The conservatives responded to the ear-piercing noise by clapping as loudly as possible. The pandemonium continued for several minutes, and when it gave no indication of abating, the manager of the theater brought the curtain down, stepped forward, and appealed to spectators for quiet in order that the play might go on. The next hour or so passed without any untoward incidents, but in the fourth act, when Monsen's son spoke of the common people, the whistling and clapping recommenced. As soon as the curtain came down on the last act, the manager turned off the gas in the house, dispersing the audience in darkness, while the clapping and whistling continued with dwindling force in the corridors, finally dying out in the street outside the theater.[16]

The students overstepped the limits of social propriety and theatrical etiquette in disrupting the performance with their whistles, whether they knew it or not. Nowadays whistling is an expression of enthusiastic approval. It was quite the opposite until fairly recently. Whistling was an expression of strong disapproval when it originated in France in 1680. A whistle was customarily used backstage in the seventeenth-century theater to signal the stage mechanic of a scene change. In 1680 a whistle from a spectator inadvertently brought down the curtain, and thenceforward those who wanted the show stopped would whistle, while those who wanted the show to go on would clap, pound with their shoes, and shout bravos. In Christiania there were legal limits on these demonstrations. A police regulation required the demonstrators to be silent after a third warning or face arrest, while social custom decreed that it was in bad taste to whistle in the middle of an act.[17] Johan Ludvig Heiberg in his discussion of the niceties of the hiss, the whistle, and the bravo noted that whistling is properly an expression of a general feeling of indignation shared by the whole assemblage, aroused by what they hold sacred, as, for example, an affront to the national honor.[18] The student whistling at *The League of Youth* was not in accord with Heiberg's dictum.[19]

The principal victim of the uproar was of course Bjørnson. Ibsen's protest that not Bjørnson "but his corrupt and 'lie-ridden' political clique served as my models" may have been half true, but to the knowledgeable public the other half was the whole truth.[20] Stensgaard was Bjørnson. The audiences knew it; Ibsen knew it; and Bjørnson knew it. (Later, about 1881, Suzannah Ibsen said bluntly that Stensgaard was drawn as a portrait of Bjørnson.)[21] Ibsen may honestly have thought that he had satirized a party and a movement, but the fact was that he had made Bjørnson the scapegoat. The worm of malevolence that had entered the play when he conceived it still lay coiled about its heart when it came forth into the world.

Upon his return from an extended tour of northern Norway, Bjørnson had first heard about *The League of Youth* from friends who had advance copies. Writing to Ibsen before the play was published or staged, he tried to snatch the fat from the fire by artfully turning the thrust of the play, whose deeper import he understood very well, against Ibsen and the *Morgenbladet* party. Ostracized by the Christiania intellectuals, Bjørnson cast them as the opportunists and political palterers, himself as the strong-willed and God-chosen idealist, and Ibsen as the victim of social circumstance. He changed the phrase "vor lokale Forhold" to "smaa Forholdes Forbandelse"—"the curse of small-town mentality." It is possible that the phrase was incorrectly reported to Bjørnson; it is much more likely that he saw a way of turning the satire against Ibsen. At this point he was probably unaware of how unmistakably Stensgaard resembled himself, and by referring to small-town mentality, he could shift the central significance of the play from the political struggle for power to the social struggle for esteem, an area in which Ibsen was peculiarly sensitive.

"I look forward with pleasure to *The League of Youth*," he wrote, "because in it I see what I have long waited for: your comedy. . . . The damnable thing about small-town mentality is that those caught in it, in fear of the stronger, in fear of not being 'independent,' fly into the arms of the mean-spirited—and often do so simply to irritate the one they know has been called, simply because he *has* the call."

Ibsen could hardly miss this glance at *The Pretenders*, written when he was in desperate circumstances and Bjørnson seemed the favorite of the gods, a play in which Håkon, the king-elect, was an incarnation of Bjørnson and Earl Skule was a reflection of an envious Ibsen.

"They have no commitment," Bjørnson continued,

> to an ideal that rises above their personal pleasures or needs, no sense of responsibility in public affairs. They are full of intellectual passion but lack passion of soul because they have no serious purpose, no sense of human solidarity that can save them from their eternal intellectualizing and compel them to have a true passion for what must be done, to set aside their own concerns for a moment, dare to acknowledge their aims, their party, their purpose. In their eyes the most esteemed is he who "belongs to no party," who straddles the fence, available for a price according to circumstances. In the meantime, however,

> *one* party has everyone's sympathy, the party that *wills nothing*, that says no to all spiritual progress and yes to all material progress, that puts everything in the hands of the state in order to free the hands of the townspeople who set the tone in this country (and first and foremost in Christiania).
>
> A man like *you* should be here at home to see all this and a lot more besides. I don't fear that you will fall into the clutches of Birkeland and those who think that *everything* in Norway is wrong and that the country can be saved only by being cursed and scourged and beaten until the Swedes come to our rescue and swallow us.[22]

The letter was a well-crafted preemptive strike. Virtually each sentence was an adroit thrust at Ibsen's most vulnerable points: his claim of standing alone, his rarefied and inhuman idealism, his failure to say in so many words what the good cause was, his philosophy of willing one thing and his practice of willing nothing. The unkindest cut of all was the repetition of the "hired hand" insult, the intimation that Ibsen belonged to no party in order to be available to any party that offered him the flattery and social standing that the small-town mentality made him crave.

But if he hoped that his letter might drive a wedge between Ibsen and his old conservative friends, he was mistaken. The ad hominem satire of *The League of Youth* caught Bjørnson by surprise. His "inability to figure out real people" had closed his mind to the meaning of Ibsen's long silence.

To Richter he wrote, "You presumably know of Ibsen's latest piece of swinishness, and you can see that he is an utter scoundrel.

"All the spite this town [Christiania] has to offer is out after me, like a pack of mad dogs. You can imagine how pleasant it is.

"But I regard it as all for the best. Now our victory is assured. One of the first issues of N.F. [*Norsk Folkeblad*, the paper that Bjørnson had just acquired] will carry your portrait and a biographical sketch of you by Jonas Lie. One of the following issues will carry a poem by me honoring Johan Sverdrup.... Ibsen will find himself isolated in the world he has created."[23]

Early in November the Danish actor Karl Mantzius gave a concert performance of an abridged version of *The League of Youth* in the ballroom of the Hotel Phønix in Copenhagen. Playing the lead, he gave Stensgaard a Norwegian accent and Bjørnson's mannerisms. As editor of *For Idé og Virkelighed*, Schmidt offered Ibsen a chance to protest against Mantzius's interpretation.

Belatedly replying to Schmidt, Ibsen wrote on December 27, "That Mr. Bjørnson's bad conscience makes him regard as his enemy the man whom he has infamously slandered in the presence of a number of people, while at the same time, perhaps on the very same day, he has written him a long letter filled with ingratiating declarations of friendship—all of which can be documented and corroborated by witnesses—I find quite natural.

"And when I consider that gang of cheap and common people Bjørnson has unfortunately got himself involved with—if such people were to put a foot in my house, I would have to air out the place—it seems every bit as natural that he should consider me just as base as that man who sets the tone for the behavior of the whole gang. . . .

"I can assure you that my desire to keep myself out of bad company would force me to choose a publication that does not list Mr. Lie among its collaborators."

The parting shot was reserved for Jonas Lie because Ibsen's suspicious nature led him to believe that Lie was Bjørnson's mouthpiece. In the summer of 1869 in Tromsø, Bjørnson had toasted Lie as "the poet of northern nature." "The fact that he has been hailed at Tromsø as an epic writer," concluded Ibsen, "does not raise him the slightest in my estimation."[24]

Schmidt gave Bjørnson the gist of this letter, characterizing it as "so full of scorn and hatred, of cheap arrogance and poisonous accusations against you and Lie, that it almost made me sick. I am not the sort that will readily add to an inimical or intemperate atmosphere, but I have to say that with this man no reconciliation is possible. It is obvious that he has held repressed a venomous, swollen grudge for many years, and *now* expresses it when he feels safe and secure."[25]

Ibsen had been traveling during October and November, and when he returned to his home in Dresden, he did not attempt to parry Bjørnson's thrusts. Instead he responded indirectly by sending letters to two of Bjørnson's friends.

Putting on an innocent face, he wrote to his publisher, Hegel, "I was prepared for the opposition [to my play], and I would have been disappointed if there had been none. But what I was not prepared for was that Bjørnson, from what I have heard, should feel that he was personally attacked in the play. . . . I shall write him today or tomorrow, and I trust that the matter, in spite of all our differences, will end in a reconciliation."[26]

Ibsen did not write to Bjørnson that day nor the day following, and his actions indicate that he was not eager for a reconciliation. There were scores to be settled. First, the events of two years earlier were to be carefully reenacted. Ibsen, too, had a little list, and everything on it was to be repaid in full: Bjørnson's insults, Bjørnson's condescension, Bjørnson's contempt for Ibsen's friends, and Bjørnson's duplicity.

Two years before, in December 1867, Bjørnson had sent Ibsen a warm and conciliatory letter, and within a month he had called him a "hired hand." Now the situation was neatly reversed. Two years earlier, Bjørnson had warned Ibsen against the smug, cynical, sneering *Morgenbladet* clique; now Ibsen could superciliously regret Bjørnson's involvement with those political opportunists of the liberal movement, "that gang of cheap and common people." Two years earlier Ibsen had held in one hand Bjørnson's letter enthusiastically praising *Peer Gynt* and in the other the coolly disapproving review by Bjørnson's close friend. Now Bjørnson stood with a letter from Hegel in one hand and the letter from Schmidt in the other: conciliation and balm in one, animosity and venom in the other. Even his duplicity was being precisely requited.

Bjørnson replied to Hegel's letter:

> Thank you for the good words you bear to me from Ibsen. I still like him in spite of all he says and does. His latest is that I have slandered him! Made up stories about him!! If you care to know more about this and to see how he says evil things about me at the same time that *to you* he is saying good things about me, then ask Rudolf Schmidt on my account to show you the letter Ibsen wrote to him about me and Jonas Lie!
>
> Beware of Ibsen! He is ungrateful, and ingrates are capable of anything.
>
> You are a kind and gentle soul, and so he writes kindly and gently to you about everybody; he thinks you would prefer that. But beware!—Now he can do what he pleases. He can no longer surprise me. But if he were to come to me again in good faith, I would welcome him as if nothing had happened. I am not the one who has wronged him, and therefore I can feel right about it all.[27]

No doubt Ibsen could have said the same thing. Yet his moral system differed from Bjørnson's in one important respect. Ingratitude may have been a heinous sin to Bjørnson; no less heinous to Ibsen was the deliberate putting of people into one's debt. A large heart could hold a lonely soul in spiritual bondage. In Ibsen's scale of virtues, gratitude was outranked by loyalty, "not loyalty to a friend, or a program, or anything like that, but to something infinitely higher."[28]

Bjørnson's poem in honor of Sverdrup appeared in the November 20 issue of *Norsk Folkeblad.* In it he alluded to *The League of Youth* as an assassination in "the sacrificial groves of poesy," and to Hegel he explained what he meant:

"Ibsen's play says that Young Norway is an intriguing, self-absorbed association that misuses the idea of freedom to conceal its own ambition and greed. He sets up a few persons and in them presumes to execute the young people of Norway. That is how it is taken here by his friends and all those behind him. This is what I mean by assassination, as do all those behind me. As for myself—if he intended to mix in some of my traits in just the worst places, so much the worse for him—I have nowhere defended myself. The former (the attack on Young Norway) is what I protested against, and it was absolutely necessary."[29]

Years later, in 1881, he said it had not been the satiric portrayal of real people that had offended him; it was that good men should have been treated so shabbily. Ibsen turned the young liberal party into a "gang of ambitious opportunists whose love of country could be dismissed as mere phrasemongering."[30]

Ibsen's play polarized the political conflict in Norway, driving many of the uncommitted younger men into the liberal camp. The students rallied to Bjørnson's side. They not only staged the demonstration in the theater but, some weeks later in a stormy meeting, elected him chairman of the Student Association by a huge plurality of 102 votes.[31] In meetings of the association, Bjørnson in his lectures on Grundtvig, Wergeland, and Michelangelo utterly captivated and hypnotized the young minds, for many of whom this brilliant lecturer was their "first revelation of true genius."[32]

Ibsen may have won a secure place for himself in the establishment, but he had lost the liberal youth of Norway. The question was, had he cut himself off from the future by spurning Bjørnson? He understood perfectly well that Norway would soon be swept up in the republican tide. What the "radicals" wanted in the way of democratic reforms, extended suffrage, the lowering of property requirements for holding office, yearly sessions of the Storting, and the introduction of the jury system had already been achieved in many European countries. As a matter of fact, nearly everyone was a liberal in one way or another, a point that Ibsen makes in the last act of his play.

> LUNDESTAD. [Stensgaard] finds being a liberal the easiest thing in the world.
> CHAMBERLAIN BRATTSBERG. I should have thought we are all liberal-minded.
> LUNDESTAD. Of course we're liberal-minded. No doubt about it. But you see, we're liberal only on our own behalf. Now this Stensgaard fellow comes along and is liberal on behalf of the others, too. That's the novelty.[33]

And the chamberlain, fearing to be thought unprogressive, intolerant, and out of touch with the times, ends by acknowledging that this is, after all, the age of political parties and joins the League of Youth.

Brattsberg's easy way with the new was not Ibsen's. As a satirist in the classic vein, he saw the changing political scene against the background of unchanging human nature. Although the republicans spoke ardently of bringing people together in a common cause, when a great cause lay before them, their spirit was selfish and divisive. They abandoned the Danes to the Prussians; they set Norwegians against Swedes, and Norwegians against Norwegians. Behind their talk of parties and unions, of humanity and justice, lay their "justifiable particularism," whatever it might be. "Vor lokale Forhold" stood for the egotism, the materialistic self-concern, and the noncommitment to larger causes and higher aims that

Ibsen had satirized in *Peer Gynt*. *The League of Youth* was a photograph picturing the outside of things as *Peer Gynt* had shown the inside, and the two political catchphrases "vor lokale Forhold" and "vær dig selv nok" represented exactly the same mental attitude. The growth of political parties encouraged the development of special interests and replaced regard for the individual with concern for the party, the result being not more spiritual liberty but less. In addition to all the masters that the ordinary man had to serve, the party man had one more: the party line. Inevitably, favors had to be returned, hypocrisies tolerated, and compromises countenanced for the sake of the party, not for the sake of principle. Sverdrup's republican organization was the first political party in the modern sense in Norway. In joining the party, that "lie-ridden political clique," Bjørnson could no more remain morally untainted than Ibsen could.

"If I were to go home now," Ibsen had written at the end of 1867, "one of two things would happen to me: within a month I would make an enemy of everyone there; or else I would worm my way back into favor again, using all sorts of disguises, and thus become a lie both to myself and others."[34]

Yet by writing about specific political issues and by depicting recognizable Norwegian personages, he had gone home again. By capturing his subjects in his photographic lens instead of distancing them poetically as in *Peer Gynt*, he had made enemies of the liberals and won the favor of the conservatives. He presumed to rise above politics for the loftier regions of the human spirit, setting principle against justifiable particularism. But no high ideal motivated him when he wrote *The League of Youth*. He was driven by the same craving for social esteem and independence that drove Stensgaard. Both Peer Gynt and Stensgaard were formed out of what Ibsen was later to call "the dregs and sediment" of his nature; Peer, however, sprang into being in search of an ideal, Stensgaard out of vindictiveness.[35]

The counterpart of the opportunism and democratism that Ibsen found in Bjørnson's politics existed in his philosophy too. Grundtvigianism and Nielsenism, republicanism and Farmers' Friends, all were manifestations of the two outstanding phenomena of the nineteenth century: in politics, the rise of the common man; in philosophy and religion, the triumphal march of science. Democracy and Christianity were to be united by the Grundtvigian notion "*vox populi, vox dei*," while science and religion were to be brought into harmony by baptizing reason. For Bjørnson, Nielsen's dualism was an extension of Grundtvigianism and consisted in "this simple point: that form of reason with which faith operates, initiated and baptized by it, is different from that with which science, the cold heathen reason, operates. . . . There is a difference between reason that has been baptized and reason that has not."[36]

This sort of muddled thinking offended Ibsen, and he saw it pervading Scandinavian culture. The philosophy of Young Denmark formed the politics of Young Norway. Where Nielsen's philosophy was all compromise, his religion was all politics. That was why Ibsen could tell his publisher, Hegel, that his play dealt with "forces and frictions in modern life and [that] though the action takes place in Norway, it is equally applicable to Denmark."[37] And that is why he first called the play "The League of Youth, or, The Almighty and Co." Hegel rightly caught the scent of blasphemy in the subtitle and urged Ibsen to drop it.

On the other hand, the play looked backward. He had evened the score with Bjørnson and remained true to his old reactionary friends. But it did nothing to advance his thoughts or even to strengthen the philosophical position he had reached in *Brand* and *Peer Gynt*.

While *The League of Youth* was germinating in Ibsen's mind, he was already looking for a kindred spirit, someone from the younger generation, someone who could challenge his mind and stimulate him. On July 7, 1869, his close friend and trusted mentor Paul Botten-Hansen, with whom he had in days gone by engaged in lively discussions, died, leaving Ibsen with a great sense of loss. Fortunately, there was someone who could take his place, a bright young man whom Ibsen had never met. Just at the time that Bjørnson sought to enlist him in the army of Grundtvig and to baptize him in the church of Nielsen, there appeared a man very like Brand in both name and spirit, who fought the dualists on their own ground and exposed the fatuity in their thinking. In Georg Brandes, Ibsen immediately recognized the man he needed. When he learned of Bjørnson's duplicity, he felt any debt he owed him was paid in full. He turned in fury from Bjørnson and embraced Brandes. Almost immediately after hearing of Botten-Hansen's death, Ibsen wrote to Brandes, "I thank you a thousand times for your friendship. It is a great blessing to have found a man of genuine and undivided character."[38]

Copies of *The League of Youth* were now in circulation. Ibsen had cut himself off from Bjørnson, Sverdrup, and Richter, the men who had given him the chance to leave Norway. In alienating himself from them and joining Brandes, he was leaving the backwaters of Scandinavia and venturing into the main currents of European thought.

Ibsen in Command

In the summer of 1869 Ibsen was nominated to replace one of the Norwegian delegates to the Orthographic Congress meeting in Stockholm at the end of July. These delegates, who met to discuss such matters as the use of Roman type instead of Gothic, the removal of capital letters from nouns, and the printing of *aa* as å, were advocates of Dano-Norwegian, the literary language of Norway, not *landsmål* or New Norwegian. This was the spoken language of the farmers and laborers, and the nationalists were promoting it. These recommendations were not officially adopted until many years later, the use of å not until 1938. Jakob Løkke presented the recommendations of the Stockholm congress to the Scandinavian Society in Christiania in October 1869, when they were vigorously opposed by A. O. Vinje, Ibsen's "troll king." Ibsen himself followed the recommendations in his own writings after May 1870.

Ever since their early days in Christiania, Løkke had been Ibsen's confidant and closest friend. It was he who was responsible for the playwright's last-minute appointment to the Norwegian committee. Ibsen's uncompromising position on the language question made him a natural choice, even though he was neither an academician nor a philologist; nor was he residing in Norway. It was clearly an honorary invitation, and he took advantage of it to leave Dresden in July 1869 and go hunting after other honors. He stayed on in Stockholm for two months after the last session of the congress, and made every effort to ingratiate himself with the social and literary aristocracy of the Swedish capital. As the author of *The League of Youth*, which was about to be published and performed in Stockholm, he was a welcome guest in those circles that meant the most to him. And he had a connection at the very center, Lorentz Dietrichson, his friend from their Italian days and now professor of esthetics at the University of Uppsala, who was tutoring the Swedish crown princess in Danish literature and history. He found a small apartment for Ibsen in the center of Stockholm and introduced him to members of the royal family and to Fru Fredrika Limnell, the Madame Récamier of Stockholm, the center of its literary elite. He spent several lovely days at her lakeside villa. A year later, he repaid her hospitality with his long poem "A Balloon Letter to a Swedish Lady" ("En Ballonbrev til en svensk Dame"), contrasting the poet's search for beauty with the materialism—and militarism—of the age.

On September 22 Ibsen hinted to Erik af Edholm, the director of the Royal Theater in Stockholm, that a "bit of green" in his buttonhole would look very nice. On the evening of September 28 at the theater, King Charles (Karl XV) called Ibsen to the royal loge, and after the performance he was escorted to the Royal Palace and decorated with the Order of Vasa, Ridderkors, an award neatly timed to coincide with the publication in Swedish of *The League of Youth*, which in effect canonized Ibsen as the poet of the conservatives. Edholm said Ibsen was "as happy as a child, and I can well believe it, since he is a rabid revolutionary."[1]

Obviously taken with the Norwegian dramatist, the king happily assented to the suggestion that Ibsen be sent as Norway's representative at the ceremonies attendant on the opening of the Suez Canal, scheduled for the following month. The idea originated with Ohan Demirgian, an equerry at the Swedish court who had arrived in Sweden along with some Barbary horses as a gift from the khedive, or vice ruler, of Egypt.

Ibsen returned to his Dresden residence; thence he entrained for Paris, where the guests for the Suez celebrations gathered before proceeding to Marseilles for the sea voyage to Egypt on October 9. Ibsen was one of sixty-five guests invited by the khedive. They formed a group of celebrities, separate from the official national delegates and selected to create publicity for the actual opening of the canal. They were sent on a twenty-three-day trip on the Nile, with all expenses paid, courtesy of the khedive, arriving on November 16 at Port Said, where a vast fleet of warships had been assembled. The next day the party went to the Sinai Peninsula, where the Jews had rested after the exodus from Egypt.

While *The League of Youth* was infuriating the liberals in Norway and delighting the conservatives, Ibsen by an odd stroke of fate was in that land of symbols, Egypt, that, thanks to Hegel, he had used as the setting for his satire on Norwegian politics in act four of *Peer Gynt*. He was lying in his tent at Ismailia, not far from Port Said, with two native servants on watch when news of the controversy that his new play had produced reached him.[2] His response was to write a poem, "At Port Said" ("Ved Port Said"), in which the Egyptian setting again prompted thoughts about his homeland. While waving his hat at the Swedish-Norwegian flag at the canal ceremonies, he imagined he was hearing the whistling and hissing of the hostile demonstrators at performances of *The League of Youth*, and the stinging flies of Egypt became his enemies in Norway.

> The flies stung. And their venom,
> Like thoughts of the past, made me ill.
> Praised be the stars in heaven,
> At home, it's all the same still.[3]

In Ibsen's most intensively allusive manner, the four-stanza poem, which was not composed until he had returned to Dresden, equates the gala banquet at Port Said with the feast of Passover, the invited guests with the biblical elect, the Suez Canal as an engineering marvel with the miraculous dividing of the waters, the Bitter Lakes through which the canal passes with Norway, the liberal party with the ancient Egyptians who drowned, and Moses with Ibsen.

The poem voices his newfound social assurance. Honored by the king, he could face with equanimity the fact that the republicans, far from vanishing like the Egyptians, were on the march and gaining power month by month. *The League of Youth* contributed to the polarization of forces in Norway. Bjørnson knew he had lost the support of the older generation and blamed Ibsen for betraying the republican cause, although he knew that Ibsen's views were strongly influenced by the *Morgenbladet* cabal.[4]

Ibsen, for his part, understood that Bjørnson, as an active politician living in Norway, had to play many roles. The difference was that where Ibsen was driven by a desire for social esteem and recognition by the ruling classes, Bjørnson sought political power in order to change the social structure. Ibsen's friend Michael Birkeland described Bjørnson as rushing "ahead with a political frenzy that is nearly incomprehensible. His ideal is power in all its various forms. His unending sorrow is that he does not occupy the social position that his ambition demands."[5]

Knowing that playing the game of politics compelled Bjørnson to equivocate and compromise, Ibsen could say, "I forgive Bjørnson with all my heart,"[6] while Bjørnson, knowing that Ibsen nursed a grudge against a world that had treated him as an inferior, could say, "Ibsen is an unhappy soul, and for that reason I can forgive him much."[7]

When Bjørnson asked Ibsen to show support for the republican movement by not accepting any decorations from the monarchy, he was asking the impossible. Ibsen's reply was less than honest. "I feel that by declining [decorations] I should be deceiving myself and others. If I had any real desire for such finery, I should certainly have refrained from playing the part of 'state satirist.' But if the finery comes my way, why make a fuss about it?"[8]

But he did make a fuss about decorations bestowed by the monarchy because he wanted them as much as a politician wants to hold office. His craving for honors was so great that he was willing to lower himself in his own eyes in order to raise himself in the eyes of the public. After he had been awarded the Order of Vasa from the Swedish king, he campaigned for a similar award from the king of Denmark, writing servile letters to a Danish lawyer with influence in the court.

"When I see how my Norwegian colleagues have been honored in a manner that makes an extraordinary impression on Norwegian public opinion, then it seems to me that justice should be done me. . . . And I might as well confess that I am simply greedy for any recognition that Denmark might bestow on me."[9]

At about the same time, he reminded Ohan Demirgian, who had arranged for the Egyptian trip, that "as Norway's representative at the opening of the Suez Canal, I should be among those to be decorated by His Highness the Khedive."

"This honor is highly flattering to me, and *it would also be of the greatest possible advantage in establishing my literary position in Norway.* It would also help make up the disregard I have suffered in my country when the order of St. Olaf was awarded to several artists, painters, composers, and musicians while I was passed over—in spite of the fact that I stand loyally by the government and support it with my pen and all my abilities.

"Since I saw your written word, I did not hesitate to mention the honor to my friends, and you can see how I have now been placed in an embarrassing position, which can only be relieved by your fulfilling your promise, or by the granting of an equivalent honor."[10]

It is difficult to see how a diplomatic award by the khedive could help promote Ibsen's literary position in Norway, and even more difficult to understand why Ibsen would desire an award earned through the connivance of Demirgian, a fortune-hunting Armenian, whose real name was Habib Bey and whose sinister influence on the Swedish king made him known in court circles as the Demiurge. Yet Ibsen pleaded sycophantically with Demirgian for "satisfaction." Half a year later he received his decoration, the Star of a Commander of the Medjidie Order, third class, and immediately expressed his delight with the "magnificent trinket" in a letter to his publisher, while putting himself in a special category by pointing out that the other Scandinavian representatives at the Suez ceremonies had received their decorations only in exchange for decorations they had delivered to Egypt.[11]

The medal Ibsen received was hardly an unusual honor. The khedive of Egypt handed out three hundred medals in connection with the opening of the Suez Canal. And Ibsen had to wait half a year for the medal to arrive because the king's ministers sought to restrain Demirgian's influence. They eventually had him locked up as insane.[12]

In the meantime Ibsen had collected, in January 1871, his Danish decoration, the Order of a Knight of Dannebrog, and thanked the Danish minister of culture in a letter in which he deplored the leveling tendencies of Norwegian politics, while venturing to hope that the award would inhibit any thoughts the republicans in Norway might have of depriving him of his writer's stipend.[13]

His greediness for medals was nourished by his neurotic feeling of insecurity, the fear that his world might collapse, as it had when he was a child, and that the eminent position he had attained since the publication of *Brand* might be claimed by someone else. At first Bjørnson had been less a rival to be feared than a fellow soldier to be admired, but when he called Ibsen a hireling, he overstepped the mark of guarded friendship and became a powerful enemy who might prevail on the republicans to deprive Ibsen of his government grant. He could hardly forget how difficult it had been for him to get his first stipend.

Actually, Bjørnson was going through a difficult period and was being hard pressed on all sides, while Ibsen was enjoying the kind of success he had always wished for. "If things are going against Bjørnson, they are going very well for Ibsen," wrote Fru Heiberg.[14]

For his interference in Danish politics, notably on the question of independence for Iceland, Bjørnson was losing the support of many Danes who had formerly respected him. He was thought to be too much the preacher, the self-appointed spokesman for God, an easily recognizable aspect of him that Ibsen had neatly hit off in *The League of Youth.* In Norway Bjørnson suffered both personal tragedy and public humiliation. His father died in August 1871, and his nine-month-old daughter a half year later. At the same time the theater company that he had tried to establish after being dismissed from the Christiania Theater failed.

During this time Ibsen, far from offering comfort, took advantage of Bjørnson's difficulties. After the publication of *The League of Youth,* both men, as might be expected, lost no opportunity to snipe at each other. Ibsen said Bjørnson was a second-rate author, and Bjørnson described Ibsen as "a hysterical" writer who "did not find himself as a writer until he wrote *Peer Gynt* because he is Peer Gynt."[15]

Ibsen's behavior was that of a man who has the enemy on the run and is pressing his advantage. Bjørnson said that Ibsen stole from him in writing *The Pretenders,*[16] and, when asked by his publisher to dedicate the new edition of the play to Bjørnson, Ibsen refused on the ground that Bjørnson's political activities had built up such strong opposition that a dedication to him would harm the sale of the book.[17]

The Christiania Theater affair exemplifies Ibsen's way of dealing with Bjørnson. Knowing that he had the support of the best actors there, Bjørnson asked the board of governors for a contract that would give him power over all aspects of the theater. The members of the board, most of them politically on the right, responded by inviting Ibsen to take the manager's position. It is doubtful that Ibsen ever considered the offer seriously, but he could not bring himself to recommend his rival. Instead he wrote, condescendingly, "As the sole artistic adviser, Bjørnson is not the most desirable man. But if all the practical details remained in the hands of a more skillful and sober-minded person, he might perhaps fulfill his duties. . . . Nor do I believe that Bjørnson under any circumstances whatsoever should be given absolute authority over the artistic aspects of the theater. He lacks, to a striking degree, any thorough knowledge of literature, and for that reason alone, he will never be able to build up a repertory with purpose and principle behind it."[18]

When the actors went on strike in support of Bjørnson, Ibsen played the tyrant's part, urging the governing board to punish the actors by hiring back only a few of them, and those few at a lower salary. "In ninety-nine cases out of a hundred the actors are indisputably in the wrong, and the management is right. . . . It would be acting most unpardonably toward the institution not to put a check on this spirit of rebellion on such an occasion as the present. An actor stands in a different position from other artists. He is not independent, he is part of a complicated machine in the working of which he is bound by law to take part, and if he has chosen to be an actor he must bear the responsibilities that go with the position."[19]

The stunning victory of the well-trained German soldiers over the French in August 1870 made everyone recognize that a new alignment of forces was taking place, the one that Ibsen had anticipated and feared in *Peer Gynt.* Bjørnson now exhorted the Danes to enter into a cooperative union with their traditional enemy, and Ibsen was quick to take advantage of Bjørnson's inept intrusion into Danish affairs. On September 12, 1872, at the obsequies for Grundtvig, probably the most influential figure in Danish culture in the first half of the nineteenth century, whose avowed program was a union of church and state, Bjørnson, who with characteristic modesty regarded himself as the prophet's successor (as Ibsen took note of in the Anitra scene in *Peer Gynt*), took it upon himself to extend Grundtvig's Aryan racism to the German question. He chided the Grundtvigians for hating the Germans. He declared that the Germans should be their ally in the great conflict that was engulfing Western civilization. This did not go down well with some of his listeners, who were Danes first and Grundtvigians second. Undeterred, he reaffirmed his position in articles and speeches. Rationalism and paganism have their roots in Voltaire's France; nihilism and its offspring, socialism and communism, are of Slavic origin. Germany was now the strongest military force in Europe, and now was the time for Denmark and Norway to extend the hand of peace to Germany, uniting Lutheranism with Grundtvigianism. It was time to "change signals" with respect to Germany.[20]

To Bjørnson the victory of the Germans made evident what Grundtvig had long understood: that the fundamental conflict was between the Germanic races on the one hand and the Latin and Slavic races on the other. A renewal of the Franco-Prussian War was inevitable, and a war between Germany and Russia could not be more than fifteen or twenty years in the offing. Hence the need for a reassessment of Denmark's relationship with its recent enemy.

As a prognosticator of things to come in Europe, Bjørnson, reading the future as wish fulfillment, was disturbingly prescient. But this time, as a practicing politician, he was no more astute than Stensgaard, and the predictable effect of his racist exhortations was precisely the opposite of what he had expected. In the controversy that ensued, the so-called Signal Controversy (Signalfejden), his Danish friends spurned him for selling out to Germany. The Grundtvigians, who had regarded him as an apostle, now considered him a clever opportunist who had exploited them in order to build his own politico-religious movement in Norway.

And now misfortune bred misfortune. His mother's health declined; his wife was brought to despair by the unhappy turn of events; and Bjørnson himself was at one point so troubled and humiliated that he could not bring himself to go to the barbershop, knowing he would be either laughed at or snubbed. In Norway, old friends and former supporters turned sharply against him. A typical political cartoon pictured him dancing arm in arm with the kaiser and Bismarck.[21]

In Denmark, Carl Ploug, spokesman for the national liberals and editor of the paper that had once been Bjørnson's platform, called him "a carnival figure" in affairs of state, "a raging berserker of hatred."[22] His admired Rasmus Nielsen described him as lacking any knowledge of human nature, as being blinded by an evil power, while his fellow dualist in philosophy, Rudolf Schmidt, immediately removed his name from the masthead of the journal they coedited. His most recent play, *Sigurd Jorsalfar*, was rejected by the Royal Theater in Copenhagen, while Ibsen's *Pretenders*, although not well acted, ran for nineteen performances.

Twelve years earlier Ibsen had known despair and suffered one defeat after another during the most trying time of his life, while Bjørnson had gone from success to success. Now fortune had reversed their roles. However, they were not played the same way. In 1858 and 1859 Bjørnson had offered a helping hand to Ibsen. Now Ibsen lost no time in adding insult to Bjørnson's injuries. Only a few weeks after the Signal Controversy erupted, Ibsen published in *Fædrelandet*, the Danish newspaper that had been Bjørnson's organ, a poem, "Signals in the

North" ("Nordens Signaler"), which begins with an evocation of the Danish soldiers who had been slain eight years before by the merciless Prussian army and ends with a comparison of the opportunistic Bjørnson to a weathervane. In the middle section Ibsen gibes at Bjørnson's speaking about reconciliation with Germany as if he were God's trumpet.

> No doubt about it! A poet has proclaimed it;
> Old Grundtvig and God Himself have ordained it.
> Good! Retreat! To the reconciling feast!
> On the dais stands Pan-Germanism's priest![23]

If Ibsen had remained true to the anti-Teutonism expressed in *Brand* and *Peer Gynt*, if he was still convinced that German militarism was a threat to the ideals he cherished, the poem might be read as part of his continuing indictment of the Prussian state and Hegelianism. But he had changed—a change that revealed once again the struggle between Brand and Peer Gynt within himself. In 1869 he had been welcomed and feted in Stockholm as the author of *Brand*. A year later he found the occasion to thank his hostess, Fru Limnell, for her hospitality with "A Balloon Letter to a Swedish Lady," one of his most revelatory poems, in which he reflected on current events, using his recent visit to Egypt for the opening ceremonies of the Suez Canal for a rumination on the course of history, a history that had culminated, as he sat at his desk, in the present victory of the German military over France.

Paris was now totally encircled by the German forces. The citizens of the French capital tried to maintain contact with the outside world by means of lighter-than-air balloons. In all, sixty-four balloons were sent aloft; the first one, released on September 23, 1870, carried twenty-five thousand letters (without envelopes). One balloon alighted in the Telemark region in southern Norway on November 25, after a fifteen-hour flight. The two balloonists were treated like heroes and feted at a gala banquet for nine hundred people in Christiania.[24] The news reached Ibsen in Dresden and, identifying himself with the citizens of Paris, in a genial conceit he thought of his poem as one of these balloon letters.

Fru Limnell was delighted with "A Balloon Letter to a Swedish Lady," and she knew that this philosophical and meditative work, one of Ibsen's longest and most original poems, was intended for a wide audience. She invited the intellectual elite of Stockholm to her salon for a reading of the work and called upon Lorentz Dietrichson, a Norwegian who could do justice to the sounds of Ibsen's verses, to deliver it. This privileged event became public when Ibsen sent a copy to the Norwegian *Morgenbladet*, which printed the "Balloon Letter" on January 8, 1871. Having posted the letter, the Gynt in him must have realized he had made an agonizing Brand-like commitment. The poem with its expressed hatred of Prussian militarism could now become available to German readers. He turned to his publisher, who in March assured him that common decency forbade such a thing.[25] But the influential journal *Im neuem Reich* printed a German translation.

At one of the Saturday-evening meetings of a Dresden literary society, which Ibsen regularly attended, he could sense the hostility in the room. The chairman stood up and in a voice shaking with indignation read aloud the most inflammatory and most rancorous stanza.

> Living here in Dresden, I find there is
> An encirclement like that in Paris.
> Brawny German boys yelling out of tune,
> Who would wrench the world to wrack and ruin,
> Singing under flapping flags, "The world is mine!"
> To the awful music of *Wacht am Rhein*.
> That is what besieges me.[26]

(A prophetic image of things to come. After the collapse of Hitler's Third Reich, *Die Wacht am Rhein* was forbidden in Germany.)

"Do you acknowledge, Herr Ibsen," asked the chairman, solemn as a judge, "that you wrote these lines?" Ibsen bowed quickly and left the room without saying a word.[27]

His reply came in the form of an open letter, dated November 23, 1871, and printed in *Im neuem Reich*. "Three years of my voluntary exile I have spent in Germany. My circumstances permit me to choose my place of residence as suits me best, and I chose Germany. My only son is enjoying the benefits of an education in a German gymnasium. Does this sound like hatred of Germany?"[28] In the recent war he had provided financial assistance to a poor widow whose two sons had served in the armed forces. And he had also supported an orphaned boy by paying his school fees.[29]

Writing to his German translator a few months later, Ibsen struck an even more pro-German note. "You are mistaken in thinking that I do not recognize the greatness of a man like Bismarck. But I also see in him an absolute hindrance to good and friendly relations between Germany and Scandinavia. The present tension is unnatural between two so closely related peoples. A closer alliance must be formed; the interest of both parties demands it. During my long stay in Germany I have in general changed my views on many matters."[30]

About the same time, he wrote in a private letter: "That my conception of German, or rather Prussian, politics is now quite different from what it was in Rome seven years ago when I wrote the poem about Abraham Lincoln goes without saying. It was not the successful war campaign against France that brought this change. I stood for a long time on the side of France, before I saw more clearly. But then came the great unification of Germany into a complete and living organism. That event is the mightiest and most significant one of our century. It was this that made me change my mind."[31]

Ibsen's stated position did not differ essentially from Bjørnson's. By 1872 Ibsen was as much a Pan-Germanist as Bjørnson, but the latter proclaimed his views in the public arena, while Ibsen expressed his in private letters. The crucial difference between the two lay in the reasons for their Pan-Germanism. Ibsen regarded Prussian Junkerism as a diabolical force that threatened to destroy not only the German confederation but the civilization of Europe. That force could best be checked and reined in by a Pan-Germanic union set up as a basis for an eventual European federation of states. His position on this matter was much the same as Bernard Shaw's clear-sighted examination of the causes of the 1914 catastrophe, *Common Sense About the War* (which, incidentally, made him the most unpopular man in England, coming as it did in the first year of the war). Where Bjørnson imagined the white forces of Northern Protestantism beset on all sides by the black forces of Latin Catholicism and Slavic barbarism, Ibsen saw the defenders of culture in Germany and Scandinavia under attack in their own countries by the militarists, the Junkers, and the zealous nationalists, the trolls, who could not see beyond their own borders except through the sights of their guns.

After the publication of "Signals in the North," Ibsen was again taken to task by those Germans who read the poem as a "*Hohngedicht*" (satire). He adroitly defended himself by avowing that his scorn and derision were directed at his fellow Scandinavians, not at the Germans.[32] This was perfectly true, but Ibsen did not enlighten his public on this point. Instead he left the impression that he took his stand with the nationalists who were still nourishing hopes that Denmark would be avenged for its defeat in the 1864 war. With the best will in the world it is not possible to understand how he could allow his privately expressed views to be misrepresented except to see in the publication of the poem a deliberate harassment of his younger rival. Ibsen had finally come out from under the shadow of Bjørnson, the writer who had created a distinct genre of Norwegian storytelling, who had brought Norwegian literature into Denmark, who had everywhere preceded Ibsen, who had even made it exasperatingly difficult for Ibsen to enter the English market because there, too, Bjørnson had come first and been so highly praised that no one thought Norway could possibly harbor another equally great writer. In his frustration Ibsen could not refrain from wishing that Bjørnson might be jailed. "People who permit... Bjørnson to be at large deserve to be locked up themselves."[33] However, in trying to smear Bjørnson, he wielded his brush too recklessly and tarred himself as well as his rival. The poem proved to be an embarrassment to both his conscience and his public image, and he took care not to include it in his collected poems.

Ibsen's rejection of Bjørnson was only one of many indications of the profound change that he underwent during these years of maturation. The rebellious young man became a middle-aged conservative. Politically, Ibsen, who had written revolutionary poems in his youth, was now a mugwump, surveying the shifting tides of politics from the lofty position of an eminent poet. His support now came from the establishment. His friends in Norway belonged to the *Morgenbladet* clique; in Sweden, to the literary *cénacle* of Fru Limnell; in Denmark, to the hieratic circle of Fru Heiberg. As a twenty-three-year-old, he had, in *Norma*, satirized the sudden conversion of the editor of *Morgenbladet* from opposition man to conservative. Now he himself could serve as a subject of such satire. In the same squib he had ridiculed Ueland, the leader of the farmers, but in *The League of Youth* he treated him with noticeable respect. During and after the Dano-Prussian War, Ibsen censured the Swedes for their false bravado, disparaged the Swedish king as ineffectual, and fulminated against Manderström, the Swedish foreign minister, for abandoning the Danes to the Prussian hordes. As late as March 1868, he railed against the Swedes as being Norway's "spiritual enemies" because of "the very foundation of their culture."[34] In 1869, however, while staying in Sweden and enjoying the company of the Swedish literati, he told his friend Snoilsky that he was no longer angry with the Swedes and no longer had any quarrel with Manderström's policies.

While at the Scandinavian Club in Rome in 1864–65, Snoilsky came across in a popular journal a picture of Manderström, who was his uncle; someone had drawn a hangman's noose on the portrait. Snoilsky asked Lorentz Dietrichson, the club's librarian, who the vandal was. Suspecting it was Ibsen, Dietrichson told him of Snoilsky's inquiry. Ibsen and Snoilsky met and had a frank discussion, with Snoilsky defending his uncle's policies. In 1869 when the two men met in Stockholm, Ibsen was happy to say that his opinion of Manderström had changed when he had learned more about the diplomat's position.

"Ah," said Snoilsky with a smile, "then I'm sorry to say that our reconciliation is still where it was. You see, I've since studied the diplomatic papers thoroughly and have changed my mind completely. So I stand now where you once stood."[35]

And in thanks for the Vasa order conferred on him by the Swedish king, Ibsen offered a poem, "Without a Name" ("Uden Navn"), lauding the king as a kind of poet, an idealist whose dreams were quashed by men without vision. Upon reading it, Bjørnson exploded. "Praising the king for not daring to take action in 1864 is, it seems to me, a criminal act."[36]

Nothing illustrates more unmistakably the change in Ibsen's views than his repudiation as a personal creed of the moral philosophy of *Brand.* Just at the time when he had firmly established himself as chief spokesman for a rigorous idealism in human affairs, he declined the role. In the 1870s, according to a young litterateur, for a young beau to give his girlfriend a copy of *Brand* or *The Pretenders* was more than a polite gesture. "Such a gift testified to the girl's intelligence and character, which the young valued more than beauty."[37] Yet in 1870 Ibsen could tell a woman who admired the poem (and who would later play a significant role in Ibsen's career) that *Brand* was "an artistic work, pure and simple, and not a bit of anything else. What it may have destroyed or built up is a matter of absolute indifference to me. It came into existence as the result of something that I had lived through, not simply observed. It was necessary for me to free myself from something within me that I had done with by giving it a poetic form, and when I had gotten rid of it, my poem no longer held any interest for me."[38]

If one is to believe this, Ibsen had retreated from the mountaintop and the Ice Church to the highlands of the coolly observant esthete (as in the poem "On the Heights"). He had exchanged the isolation of the individual for whom purity of heart is everything for the company of the social elite whose approval was a sine qua non. Instead of sticking to his former principles, Ibsen bent them to fit the occasion. In an 1860 poem, "On J. L. Heiberg's Death" ("Ved J. L. Heibergs Død"), he commemorated the passing of that arbiter of Danish culture by attempting to reconcile Heiberg's anti-philistinism (which suited Ibsen) with his pro-Hegelianism (which Ibsen reproved). He was unsuccessful. In 1870 he rewrote the poem entirely, reducing the original twenty-six couplets to six, and eliminated the discord by getting rid of his own anti-German sentiment. What remains, "To the Survivors" ("Til de Genlevende"), is a eulogy to the man who in trying to bring enlightenment to his country was destroyed by the philistines and the mob, those "inconstant trolls" (*døgnets trolde*), as Ibsen called them.[39]

Like Heiberg, Ibsen saw the authoritarianism of a monarchy as the only alternative to the despotism of the populace (which Marx called "the dictatorship of the proletariat"). Like Heiberg, Ibsen disapproved of political parties, seeing in them the means by which the public surrenders its responsibilities to demagogues. Like Heiberg, Ibsen believed in the rule of the educated minority. And just as Heiberg in 1840 had seen the liberals in Denmark gain the majority vote by joining forces with the farmers' representatives to legislate a constitutional reform, so Ibsen twenty-eight years later had seen the same thing happen in Norway.[40] And where Heiberg had written essays against the rising tide of democracy, Ibsen had written *The League of Youth*, which was just as relevant to Denmark as to Norway.

It was only natural that Fru Heiberg would recommend the production of Ibsen's political satire, and she overcame the objection, raised by the governing board of the theater, that the play lacked esthetic value by pointing out that it would compensate for that lack by proving to be effective propaganda against the liberal party.[41] The grateful Ibsen thanked Fru Heiberg by singing her praises in a poem, "A Rhymed Letter to Fru Heiberg" ("Rimbrev til Fru Heiberg"). Although he had seldom seen the now-retired actress perform, he wrote as if her classic roles were etched in his memory. After all, it was a poet's imagination that won him an invitation to the Heiberg salon.[42] She must have been more pleased by his poem than by his awkward presence at her parties, where he sat ill at ease, looking sour and glum.

Social recognition came to him in Sweden and Denmark, not in Norway, where the publication of *The League of Youth* had made him persona non grata with many of its leading citizens. Though he left his residence in Germany in 1869 to spend three months in Stockholm and four months in Copenhagen, he avoided his native country. Even the death of his mother in 1869 did not affect his determination not to call on the Norwegians until they called on him. A fitting occasion arose when Norway laid plans to celebrate its millenary in 1872. At Haugesund there was to be erected a monument, an obelisk seventeen meters high, surrounded by twenty-nine smaller obelisks representing the tribal districts united by Harald the Fairhaired in 872. Festivals were to be held in both Haugesund and Christiania on July 18.

Ibsen decided to participate in the celebrations. The gesture was eminently worthy of both the man and the occasion. However, the committee in charge of the arrangements thought differently. Its members were not particularly eager to invite him, and when Ibsen found out that Bjørnson would be the keynote speaker, he was furious. Why should the leading republican be allowed to celebrate one thousand years of that which he was bent on eliminating?

Using Michael Birkeland as messenger, Ibsen protested to the committee, which belatedly recognized that Bjørnson was probably not the right man for this particular occasion. Johan Lorange, the head of the Haugesund Committee, a civil engineer by profession and not a literary man, decided to approach both Ibsen and the novelist Jonas Lie. This set off a burst of accusations and retorts that ricocheted around Norway and between Christiania and Dresden. Ibsen found Lorange's letter to be insultingly terse, and instead of replying with a courteous retort, he took Lorange to task for mishandling the whole affair. Now it was the turn of the committee members to take umbrage, while Birkeland tried to soothe their ruffled tempers by explaining that Ibsen was a neurotically sensitive person.

"Ibsen is abundantly rich in that irritability that everyone agrees is part of a poet's nature. It has certainly been aggravated by the ups and downs of his life. I am inclined to believe that his share of misunderstandings and sorrows, not to say poverty, has been greater than anyone should be expected to bear. His situation in the last few years has of course been less harsh than before, but his feelings—all too sensitive—are still embittered in ways that affect him more deeply than anyone can imagine. Having for many years been his close acquaintance and friend, I have had many occasions to know whereof I speak."[43]

In the meantime, Ibsen's indignation was being further exacerbated. In February 1872 he had applied for a grant from the H. F. Schäffer fund, established particularly for writers and artists. This fund was administered by the Ecclesiastical Department of the government, where Ibsen's name was anathema. His application was rejected.[44] At the same time the reissue of his early play *The Vikings at Helgeland* received some unkind attention in the press, and to top off these insults he received an anonymous letter filled with calumnies. Since the nasty letter reeked of adolescent impudence and was written by three or four different hands on scraps of paper, Ibsen jumped to the conclusion that it came from students at one of the Grundtvigian schools and that Bjørnson had put them up to it.[45] Birkeland sought to placate Ibsen by noting that the letter had been mailed from Trondhjem and that Bjørnson could not possibly have been behind it.

The upshot of all this was that Ibsen did not attend the commemorative event. Instead he wanted his views to be made public in a poem that was to be read aloud at the unveiling of the monument in Haugesund and again at the festivities in Christiania. But even this was not to be. He proposed, but the committee disposed. The poem was read not at the unveiling of the monument but at the last course of the banquet that followed. In Christiania it was not read at all. It was distributed in a pamphlet along with poems by the anti-Scandinavianist P. A. Munch and the pro-Bjørnson Jonas Lie, men who stood for all that Ibsen opposed.

Fuming under this shameful treatment, Ibsen saw that his trust in the conservatives was misplaced, that they were manifestly incapable of standing up to the liberals, and that their weakness and compliance were signs of the times as much as the liberals' resoluteness and aggressiveness. He vented his feelings in a letter to his brother-in-law.

> They asked me to write a poem to be read at Haugesund. I wrote the poem. Then they omitted it from the festival program and sold it instead like a hawker's ballad, without considering it necessary to offer me the slightest explanation for their remarkable behavior. If they rejected the poem because reference is made in it to the separatists of our day, then all I can say is that the cause of order,

> culture, and progress is in the hands of men who are incapable of furthering it and ensuring its victory. And I shall regard it as my first duty, in my capacity of state satirist, to represent this party in all its wretched weakness, with all its lack of courage and determination, and with its absurdly naive belief that a sulky, passive resistance can possibly accomplish anything at all in the face of a well-organized, reckless, antagonistic party.[46]

Even if the members of the Haugesund Committee had been in complete accord with Ibsen's political views, they could hardly have been blamed for their reluctance to focus attention on his poem. It was a call for a powerful union of the Scandinavian nations, a transparent attack on the liberal party as the force of disunion, contrasting its present-day efforts to separate Norway from Sweden not only with Harald the Fairhaired's majestic confederating idea of a thousand years earlier but also with the contemporaneous unifications being achieved by Cavour in Italy and Bismarck in Germany. To use a national birthday for partisan purposes was not playing the game. Of course Ibsen had always made it plain that the game was beneath him, and on this occasion he was even more blunt than usual. The preamble to the poem, addressed to his countrymen, set the tone for what followed.

> My people, who gave me to drink in deep drafts
> That bitter, invigorating potion whereof
> I as poet, when success lay beyond my crafts,
> Gained strength to fight on, though the struggle seemed vain—
> My people, who gave me the staff of exile,
> A pack of sorrow, thin-soled sandals of pain,
> And a suit of melancholy for the road—
> I send you, my people, greetings from abroad.[47]

It was from the Swedes and Danes that Ibsen got the recognition he longed for. In Stockholm and Copenhagen from 1869 to 1871 he was admitted to the finest social circles and awarded the decorations he coveted. He had come out from under the shadow of Bjørnson and gloried in the medals that Bjørnson disdained. Ibsen knew as well as Samuel Butler that greatness wore an invisible cloak, and that was why it had to be adorned with something visible, like medals. As soon as he received word that he had been awarded the Danish order of a Knight of Dannebrog, he wrote to his publisher, "Now my countrymen will find my forthcoming volume of poems twice as good."[48]

With success came the desire to dress the part of a notable person, and for Ibsen that meant a gentleman of rank, not a bohemian poet. Nothing much could be done about his unimpressive stature except to give it the illusion of height by the addition of a high hat and built-up heels. But clothes could improve the man, the cut of his beard could be altered, and his handwriting transformed. The new man made his appearance before an astonished public in 1869. The asocial idealist who wrote *Brand* was seen to be a fop; the state satirist who wrote *The League of Youth* looked like a highly placed government official. He wore a black velvet jacket with satin lapels over a shiny white vest, and sported a cane with a gold knob. The style of his clothes was actually somewhat out of fashion, possibly a sign of his reactionary political views, more probably a subtle intimation that he was still his own man even in the world of fashion, and most likely an atavistic memory of a lost childhood, an attempt to join hands with the elegantly dressed rich boy who took dancing lessons in Skien. Ibsen himself, in a letter to Lorentz Dietrichson on June 19, 1869, wondered if those "who knew me in my bearded period will recognize me."[49]

The middle years of his extraordinary career were devoted to retrieving all that had been lost, to settling old accounts, and to fulfilling all those promises he had made to himself in those painful years when only dreams sustained him. The rich boy who had fallen into poverty would be rich again and wear fine clothes; the student who had never earned a degree would be honored as an artist; the playwright who had failed to create the Norwegian national drama would father the great Scandinavian drama; and those who had shut their doors on him would welcome him and marvel at the medals on his chest. And those who had ignored him and derided him and oppressed him would be caricatured by him, pilloried by him, and proscribed by him. Justice would have it so, and Fortune obliged.

By 1870 Ibsen had attained a position of considerable eminence in Scandinavia, and there were prospects of extending his fame to Germany and England. Not only had he made his mark as a poet, but with *The League of Youth* he had also achieved success as a commercial playwright. Already he belonged to that select group of writers who win their laurels both in the study and on the stage. *Brand* was being reprinted for the fifth time; *The League of Youth* had been staged fifteen times in its first season in Christiania, an exceptional number in those days, and in Stockholm it would be given sixty-three performances at the Dramatic Theater before continuing on at the Svenska Teatern.[50]

Those Little Devils

One of the oddities of Ibsen's career is that during what would normally be among the most creative and productive years for a writer, his forties, Ibsen spent much of his time revising earlier works. In 1868, when he was invited to contribute to the first issue of *For Idé og Virkelighed,* he declined to allow any of his early poems to be published on the grounds that they were from an early period and represented an abandoned position in his thinking. However, later that year he had second thoughts. A new anthology of Norwegian poetry, compiled by K. A. Winter-Hielm, contained fifty pages of Ibsen, only Johan Sebastian Welhaven being more abundantly present. The next year he asked Jakob Løkke and Lorentz Dietrichson to collect from newspapers and magazines his early lyrics, and when Bjørnson's collected poetry was issued in 1870 in a first printing of four thousand copies, Ibsen immediately seconded his publisher's proposal, which had been made early in 1868, to issue his own collected poems. This modest volume containing fifty-six poems was issued in May 1871 in a first printing of four thousand copies, selling for one and a half specie dollars each, with a second, enlarged edition coming out in December 1875.

In the early 1870s Ibsen consolidated his position as a best-selling author. In 1873 *Love's Comedy* appeared in a third edition and *The Vikings at Helgeland* was published in a new edition, with new printings called for within the next few years. *The Pretenders,* reissued in 1870, went through five printings during the following decade. In 1873 *Emperor and Galilean* was published, in an expensive volume, in two printings totaling six thousand copies. In 1874 his early play *Lady Inger of Østraat* was republished, and in 1875 his very first play, *Catiline,* appeared in a totally revised form. These figures testify to the eagerness with which Ibsen was being bought and read. A fellow Norwegian author said that Ibsen's books disappeared from the counters faster than any other author's. "At the very rumor that a new book by Ibsen is in the offing, the public is aroused to a point of expectation verging on hysteria, and when the book is out and being read, practically nothing else is talked about for a long time after."[1]

The idea for a volume of poems lay dormant while the dramatist worked on *The League of Youth*, but in 1870, encouraged by his friend Løkke, he revived it. Løkke did much of the spadework, digging up poems that Ibsen had written years ago. Of the poems he already had in his possession and those that Løkke unearthed, Ibsen weeded out about half. He then added some verses from his dramatic works and included some previously unpublished poems. He reworked some old poems so thoroughly they were virtually new, and he composed a few new ones especially for the collection.

In preparing the poems for publication, he also took a great deal of care with their arrangement. Besides recasting and condensing some, he took others out of their proper chronological order. For instance, "On the Heights," written at the end of 1859, was placed after the poems inspired by the war of 1864; "The Gully" ("Kløftet"), which was composed in 1864 and reads like part of *Brand*, was shifted from the chronologically correct fortieth position in the sequence to the fourteenth. The outcome of all these revisions and rearrangements was no hasty compilation of old poems but, like all the efforts of the mature Ibsen, an artful construct worthy of a place in his canon. To Brandes, he described the finished volume as "part of the story of my development" and as "forming something like a whole." Shakespeare might have said the same thing about his *Sonnets*, which is approximately the same length as Ibsen's *Poems*, and both sequences stand outside the dramatic works while forming a resource for understanding them. If Ibsen grouped the poems to show his "development," then it would appear he is showing it by considering certain themes and ideas rather than by following his progress from year to year or decade to decade.[2]

After 1868 the image of Ibsen was that of a man in complete control of himself. The poems, however, reveal inner tensions, the tightly coiled spring that provides the kinetic energy for his other creations. Insisting that his characters spoke for themselves and not for him, Ibsen was asked if that was true of the poems as well. Momentarily taken aback, he replied with an inscrutable smile, "Well, those little devils should never have been printed."[3]

In effect, the 1871 collection constitutes an autobiography written by a man who was abandoning poetry and was about to begin a new phase in his development. In this slim volume Ibsen assesses his life and works up to its midpoint, just as in his last four plays he would review and evaluate the last half of his career. To trace the artist's development, he made the poems part of a meaningful cycle and removed the temporal and transitory elements. "My Young Wine" ("Min unge

Vin"), which dates from the time of Ibsen's brief and abortive affair with Rikke Holst, becomes in the cycle a contemplation about the muse of poetry. "With a Water Lily" ("Med en Vandlilje"), which may have had its origin in Ibsen's suppressed love for his sister-in-law, is, by virtue of its placement in the cycle, less about an illicit love than about love as a temptation seducing the poet from his task. The water lily was also known as nøkkerose, the nixie's flower, because of its double nature, beautiful on the surface but drawing on sinister forces in the depths. "Gone!" ("Borte!"), which is assumed to have been written out of the sense of loss Ibsen experienced when the sister of an admired friend died at an early age, becomes an expression of the emptiness in the poet's heart when his hopes of fulfilling his task in life are dashed.[4] Similarly, the lines from *Brand* that found a place in the 1871 cycle are not the most poetic passages in the drama but are the ones required to carry forward the story of the artist's progress.

The sequence of fifty-six poems sets the aspiring, idealistic young man against the mature, successful, and somewhat disillusioned artist. The young poet dreamed of enjoying both the immortality of the gods and the domestic pleasures of ordinary people. But, like Yeats, he finds that one excludes the other. Again like Yeats, he hopes to invigorate his people with his poetry. He vacillates between elation and despair, and when his patriotic dream, the kingly thought, proves to be illusory, he replaces it with a larger vision. The world of art becomes his realm, and the adolescent dream of building a new Scandinavian nation is transcended by the desire to create a kingdom of beauty, transcending political and social issues.

Here, as in all his larger works, Ibsen displayed his architectural genius. The ground plan for the whole cycle shows the two-part division between the troubled political idealist and the increasingly skeptical and disillusioned poet who will create beautiful things as a defense against a world made ugly by politics. Schemas 1 and 2 outline the structure of the cycle.

The twenty-seven poems from Nos. 28 to 54, taken as a group, are the reverse of the first twenty-seven. The implication of this arrangement is that instead of politics and poetry working together to create a nation, they must be separated in order to create beauty. Several of the poems are strategically placed at what might be called turning points in the overall scheme.

"Terje Vigen," thirty-ninth in order, serves as a climax to the entire sequence. It rounds off the whole section dealing with Ibsen's quarrel with Norway. This long poem, forty-three stanzas, each with nine lines (ababcdccd—Ibsen's invention), is the only one that tells a story. It is a tale of a seaman's revenge. Among the common folk it was probably Ibsen's most popular work, and many a Norwegian sailor knew it by heart.

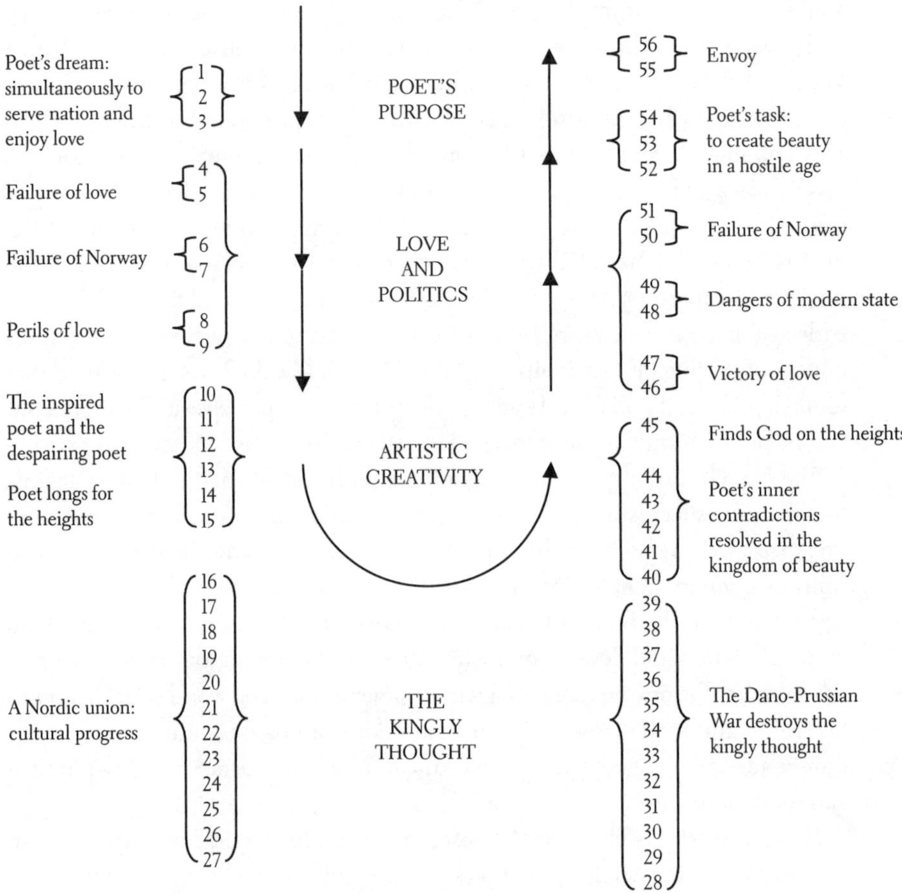

Schema 1. Themes in the 1871 Collection

During the Napoleonic wars, when the coast of Norway is blockaded by the English navy, Terje Vigen attempts to break through the English line to bring provisions to his village. Captured, he implores on his knees to be allowed to return to his wife and child. His captor turns a deaf ear to his pleas. Imprisoned for five years, he returns home to find that his wife and child have died. For years he lives a solitary existence, brooding on revenge. Fate finally smiles on him. The first mate who had taken him captive is now a rich gentleman sailing with his wife and child off the coast of Norway when his yacht runs aground. Terje Vigen puts them on his ship, and then at the very spot where his ship went aground and broke up years ago, he sinks his skiff so that it rests atop the old one. The English gentleman now recognizes in the old sailor the man who once begged to be set free.

	56. Burnt Ships (1871)
	55. In a Composer's Album (1866)
1. Fiddlers (1851)	54. A Rhymed Letter to Fru Heiberg (1871)
2. King Haakon's Guildhall (1859)	53. A Balloon Letter to a Swedish Lady (1870)
3. Building Plans (1853)	52. To Frederik Hegel (1870)
4. Wild Flowers and Potted Plants (1853)	51. At Port Said (1869)
5. A Bird Song (1853)	50. Without a Name (1869)
6. At Åkershus (1851)	49. To My Friend Who Talks of Revolution (1869)
7. The Eider Duck (1851)	48. Abraham Lincoln's Assassination (1865)
8. With a Water Lily (1863)	47. Thanks (1871)
9. Bird and Bird Catcher (1851)	46. Women's Prayer (1863)
10. The Miner (1850)	45. On the Heights (1859)
11. My Young Wine (1859)	44. The Invisible Choir (1866)
12. Fear of Light (1863)	43. In the Picture Gallery (1859)
13. The Poet's Song (1862)	42. A Church (?)
14. The Gully (1859–64)	41. From My Daily Life (?)
15. Life on the High Plateaus (1860)	40. Complications (1862)
16. On a Singers' Tour (1863)	39. Terje Vigen (1862)
17. A Swan (?)	38. Parliament House (1861)
18. Praise Be to Women! (1859)	37. Grounds of Faith (1864?)
19. 4th July 1859 (1859)	36. A Brother in Need (1864)
20. The School House (1858)	35. In Memory of Frederick VII (1864)
21. A People's Grief (1859)	34. Ørnulf's Eulogy (1858)
22. To Members of Parliament (1860)	33. To a Departing Artist (1863)
23. Greetings to the Swedes (1860)	32. Open Letter (1859)
24. To the Survivors (1860)	31. The Power of Memory (1864)
25. To Professor Schweigaard (1860)	30. Lines in an Album (1866)
26. Cradle Song (1863)	29. Agnes (1865)
27. Gone! (1864)	28. Stormy Petrel (?)

Schema 2. Poems in the 1871 Collection
(Dates of first versions, if known)

"Everything I held dear," says Terje, "you once held in your hand; and you let it go for the sake of glory. In one minute from now, revenge shall be mine!"[5]

The Englishman kneels. Standing over him, his hair flowing in the wind, Terje unburdens his heart of the pain and hatred that have been festering in him.

"Your wealthy lady is bright as spring
And her hand is as soft silk fine;
But my wife's hand was a calloused thing,
Yet for all that she counted as mine.
Your child is golden, her eyes as blue
As a little guest of our Lord;
My daughter was nothing worth pointing to,
Was thin, God help us, and sallow of hue—
What else can the poor afford?
. . .
"It's time for my vengeance to strike, beware—
For your turn to suffer comes round
To match all the pain of long years' despair
That bowed down my shoulders and whitened my hair
And buried my joy in the ground!"

Knowing that he is about to die along with his wife and child, the Englishman stands helpless, his arms at his side.

But Terje's forehead showed peaceful and fair,
His breast moved relaxed and free.
He set the child on its feet with care
And kissed its hands solemnly.
He breathed as though freed from a prison den,
His voice calm and level to say:
"And now Terje Vigen's himself again.
Like a rocky stream flowed my blood till then;
For I had to—I had to repay!"[6]

The high point in the artist's career as sketched out in the cycle comes with the forty-fifth poem, "On the Heights." The arrangement of the poems suggests how Ibsen viewed the arc of his career. The preceding poem, lifted from *Brand*, is an expression of the poet's despair. "On the Heights" celebrates the achievement of the poet-philosopher whose motto was "all or nothing." Immediately following is a passage from the earlier drama *The Pretenders* that contains the line "Now he wears the crown." In the forty-seventh poem, "Thanks" (Tak), Ibsen offers gratitude to his wife for her steadfastness and loyalty during his dark years. After that expression of appreciation, romantic love and the Scandinavian union are no longer concerns of the poet.

The two last poems serve as envoys. In No. 55, which dates from 1866 and was written in Edvard Grieg's album, Ibsen reaffirms in six strident lines the artist's resentment toward ungrateful Norway.

> Orpheus struck, with purest treble,
> Soul from beast and fire from pebble.
>
> Stones our Norway has no lack of;
> Wild beasts, too, we've many a pack of.
>
> Play, that stones may spark in wonder!
> Play, that hides may burst asunder![7]

At the last moment, just before his collected verse was to go to the printer, Ibsen added another poem. Bjørnson had concluded his recently published collected poems with a warm greeting to the Nordic people, "Good Cheer" ("Godt mod"). Realizing that he could not leave his readers with the harsh sentiments expressed in a poem from his earlier days, Ibsen composed a new one. "Burnt Ships" ("Brændte Skibe") is a parting shot, telling of the solitary poet, living in exile, who alienates himself from his people, although his thoughts are always of his homeland.

> He burnt all his ships,
> Smoke rose from the blaze,
> Arched cross the northern sky,
> A bridge of mist and haze.
>
> Toward the crofts snow-clad
> From southern strands sun-bright
> There gallops a horseman
> Who gallops each night.[8]

Those two last poems, opposite in sentiment, capture the division running through the whole collection, which in turn distills the essence of the man. In arranging his collected poems, Ibsen divides himself in two, as the structural scheme illustrates.

Taken as a whole, the cycle depicts the evolution of a poet who resolves the conflicts within himself by making the creation of beauty his ultimate goal, placing the artist above politics and love. The poet turns back on himself, returning to the pure estheticism of "On the Heights." In 1865 Ibsen told Bjørnson that he had purged himself of "that esthetic point of view—existing in isolation and demanding that there be no other concerns in life—which formerly exercised a great power over me. Estheticism of this kind seems to me now as great a curse to poetry as theology is to religion."[9] In a relatively short time, he had reversed himself.

ANTI-BRAND

The recycled poems tell of a radical reorientation in Ibsen's thought and a retreat from the position he had taken in *Brand*. Now that magnificent work, in which the artist Ejnar is an object of scorn, has become "an artistic work, pure and simple, and not a bit of anything else." This is an astonishing about-face. The Kierkegaardian poet has taken the position of an esthete. The Scandinavian cause now means little to him. Poetry is divorced from politics, and its purpose now is to stand up to the forces that drive the political state: mobocracy and militarism. In "Abraham Lincoln's Assassination" and "A Balloon Letter to a Swedish Lady," two of the most insightful political poems since Heine's, the kingdom of the artist is threatened by the sheer force of numbers, and beauty by the Prussian beast. Rudolf Schmidt, who as a member of Young Denmark was hostile toward Ibsen in the 1860s, praised him as having attained the highest point in Norwegian poetry in these two poems.[1]

"The importance of the state," said Otto von Bismarck, the German chancellor, "is measured by the number of soldiers it can put into the field of battle.... It is the destiny of the weak to be devoured by the strong."[2] For Ibsen, the greatness of a people was measured by the extent of their sacrifices, and a victory that was not a spiritual victory was a defeat. When the German armies pulverized France in 1870, Ibsen said that they lacked glory and that no poet could confer immortality on them.[3] Theirs was a victory by numbers, ensured when the German general Moltke in two weeks in July 1870 mobilized 370,000 men and massed them on the French and German frontiers with 1,200 guns, a feat unparalleled in military history up to that time. German efficiency had destroyed "the poetry of war," while Bismarck's political cunning destroyed the possibility of heroic conquests. No true poet, said Ibsen in a conversation, could "prosper in Prussia, the country of Bismarck, the enemy of beauty." When his interlocutor mentioned the brilliant and unfortunate Heinrich von Kleist as an example to the contrary, Ibsen retorted, "But that proves exactly what I said. He blew his brains out because he had the misfortune to be born in Prussia. He could not endure such a life."[4]

Prussian ruthlessness aroused animosity even in the other German states. In Bavaria, Bismarck's Northern Confederation was called the murder confederation, and many there felt it was better to be French than Prussian. Being Prussian meant paying taxes, serving as a soldier, and keeping one's mouth shut.

Still, if Prussian efficiency and discipline threatened an end to artistic creativeness and insight, the republicanism that was spreading through Europe offered no viable alternative for Ibsen. Like Balzac, Stendhal, Tocqueville, and Johan Ludvig Heiberg, he believed that the clamor of the populace tolled the end of culture. "The masses, both at home and abroad," he said to Brandes, "have absolutely no understanding of the higher things."[5] "The people" was for him a term of opprobrium. Furious with a printer who published one of his plays without permission, Ibsen reviled him as "a filthy scoundrel, who, by virtue of his filthiness, belongs to the people."[6] Ibsen regarded militarism and republicanism as two forms of the same curse: the rule of the mob, the reduction of all things that mattered to the lowest common denominator. It was the opposite of liberty and freedom. The state, says the dean of the church to the individualistic Brand, is especially fond of sameness but abhors liberty.

The state is, my innocent man,
Precisely half republican.
Freedom it hates like leprosy.
It dotes upon equality.
Now, to achieve precisely that,
Every hill must be leveled flat.[7]

To Ibsen, the Norwegian republicans and the Norwegian farmers stifled cultural development because they were concerned solely with their own material welfare. His low opinion of farmers never changed. "I have gotten to know the farmers of many countries, and nowhere have I found them to be liberal-minded and self-sacrificing. On the contrary, I have always found them to be extremely tenacious of their rights and very much alive to their own interests."[8]

In place of political factions that promoted various freedoms for the people, he put the noble, kingly idea. What he meant by poetry in the practical world was individualism as opposed to standardization and, on a more exalted plane, the unique deed that stirred a people to the depth of their souls. Political parties, though they might call for one sort of freedom or another, one liberty or another, actually inhibited the free spirit.

"Of course, it is a benefit," he told Brandes,

> to possess the right to vote, the right of self-taxation, and so on. But who benefits? The citizen, not the individual. Now, there is absolutely no logical necessity for the individual to be a citizen. On the contrary, the state is the curse of the individual. How did Prussia purchase its strength as a state? By absorbing the spirit of the individual into a political and geographic concept. The waiter makes the best soldier. [The dean of the church in *Brand* says, "The ideal leader for us all / Is nowadays the corporal"—a wicked premonition of Hitler's rise to power.]
>
> The state must be abolished! In that revolution I will take a part. Undermine the idea of the state, make willingness and spiritual kinship the only essentials for union—and you have the beginning of a freedom that is of some value. Changing one form of government for another is merely a toying with various degrees of the same thing—a little more or a little less. Folly, all of it.[9]

This was the language he used with his respected friend Brandes. He was even more nihilistic and anarchic in a poem, "To My Friend Who Talks of Revolution" ("Til min Ven Revolutions-Taleren!"), addressed to a Swedish politician who had chided him for joining the ranks of the conservatives.

> You say I have become conservative.
> Don't believe it, not while I'm alive.
>
> Moving pawns and bishops I've always spurned.
> What I want is: the board overturned.
>
> Only one revolution comes to mind
> That was not of the compromising kind.
>
> That revolution was played out in glory—
> Noah's I mean, the Flood, that sinful story.
>
> Yet that time too Lucifer got bested,
> When Noah as tyrant was invested.
>
> Let's redo it. This time let's not balk.
> We need men who can both act and talk.
>
> You flood the earth past the high-water mark,
> And I with joy will torpedo the Ark.[10]

In Ibsen's revolution the ship of state would be done away with and replaced by a fleet of small ships, loosely united by the currents that carried them. He constantly distinguished the state from the nation, the political federation from the spiritual union.

"A political state may be annihilated, but not a nation. Poland is not really a nation; it is a state. The aristocracy have their interests, the citizens [*Borgerne*] theirs, and the farmers theirs—all independent of, or even antagonistic to, each other. And Poland has no literature, art, or science with any special mission for the world's advancement. If Poland is made Russian, the Polish people will cease to exist. But we Scandinavians, even if we were deprived of our apparent independence, even if our countries were conquered and our states disintegrated, would still survive as a nation. The Jews were both a state and a nation; the Jewish state was destroyed, but the nation still lives."[11]

This to Bjørnson. A few years later he wrote to Brandes about the Jewish nation. "How has it managed to preserve itself—in its isolation, in its poetry—despite all the barbarity of the outside world? Because it had no state to burden it. Had the Jewish people remained in Palestine, it would long since have been negated in its construction [*være gået under i sin konstruktion*], like all the other peoples."[12] (Ibsen is using "construction" as defined in German speculative philosophy, meaning a union of abstract ideas gathered into a consistent whole. For Ibsen the political state is a construction in that sense.)

Consistent with the distinction he made between the state and the nation was the one he made between political liberty and the idea of liberty. To Brandes he wrote, "I shall never agree to making liberty synonymous with political liberty. What you call liberty I call liberties; and what I call the struggle for liberty is nothing but the steady, vital growth and pursuit of the very conception of liberty. He who possesses liberty as something already achieved possesses it dead and soulless; for the essence of the idea of liberty is that it continue to develop steadily as men pursue it and make it part of their being. Anyone who stops in the middle of the struggle and says, 'Now I have it,' shows that he has lost it. It is exactly this tendency to stop dead when a certain amount of liberty has been acquired that is characteristic of the political state."[13]

Actually, Ibsen's nihilism suggests that he had been reading Max Stirner at this time, and even earlier, at the time he wrote *Peer Gynt*. There is nothing in his pronouncements to Brandes that could not be found in Stirner's *The Ego and His Own* (*Der Einzige und sein Eigentum*), published in 1844. The number of similar passages defies coincidence. If he did not crib ideas from Stirner, he certainly found his own thoughts anticipated by him. A few examples:

Ibsen on religion and eternal values: "All religions will fall. Standards neither of morality nor of art are eternal. What is there that we are really obliged to hold on to? Who will vouch for it that two and two do not make five up on Jupiter?"[14] Stirner censured Feuerbach for not carrying his ideas to their logical end. Feuerbach had transferred the center of religion from heaven to earth, but Stirner insisted that religion should be entirely done away with to liberate man fully. This is in *The Ego and His Own*; elsewhere he says, "An intellect . . . is only unshakable because its object (2 × 2 = 4, etc.) cannot be questioned—this matter is said to be religion."

Ibsen on egoism: "What I recommend for you is a thoroughgoing, full-blooded egoism."[15] Stirner: "Seek for yourselves, become egoist, become each of you an almighty Ego."

Ibsen on the failure of the French Revolution: "We have been living on nothing but crumbs from the revolutionary table of the last century." Politicians "want only their own special revolutions."[16] Stirner: "The craving for a particular freedom always includes the purpose of a new dominion, as it was with the Revolution."

Ibsen on liberty as opposed to liberties: "The struggle for liberty is nothing but the . . . pursuit of the very conception of liberty. . . . This tendency to stop dead when a certain amount of liberty has been acquired . . . is characteristic of the political state."[17] Stirner said that freedom can only be the whole of freedom; a piece of freedom is not freedom.

Ibsen on the individual and the state: "The state is the curse of the individual."[18] Stirner: "I am free in no State."

Ibsen on the Prussian citizen: Prussia purchased "its strength as a state . . . by absorbing the spirit of the individual into a political and geographic concept. The waiter makes the best soldier."[19] Stirner: "'Every Prussian carries his gendarme on his breast,' says a high Prussian officer. . . . The bourgeoisie is nothing else than the thought that the State is all in all . . . and that the individual's human value consists in being a citizen of the state."

Ibsen on state and nation: The Jewish nation survived "because it had no state to burden it. . . . Undermine the idea of the state, make willingness and spiritual kinship the only essentials for union—and you have the beginning of a freedom that is of some value."[20] Stirner: "If a union has crystallized into society, it has ceased to be a coalition. . . . It has degenerated into a fixity; it is—dead as a union . . . it is society, community."[21]

Ibsen was not the thoroughgoing nihilist that Stirner was. The German philosopher believed in noncommitment; the Norwegian poet saw commitment as a moral virtue. Stirner envisioned an amoral universe; Ibsen recognized the existence of conscience and guilt as the inevitable concomitants of human social organization.

Skeptical of political liberties as the means by which parties exercised their will over the people, Ibsen looked upon liberalism as a force of oppression. When Brandes in 1872 had the sobering experience of finding himself effectively muzzled in Denmark, Ibsen offered him cold comfort.

"So the liberal press is closed to you! Naturally! I once expressed my contempt for political liberty. You contradicted me at the time. . . . Now you are more experienced. Dear friend, the liberals are the worst enemies of freedom. Freedom of thought and spirit thrive best under absolutism. We saw this in France, later we saw it in Germany, and now we see it in Russia."[22]

In 1870, when Rome was annexed and made part of Italy, Ibsen lamented, "They have finally taken Rome away from us and given it to the politicians. Where shall we take refuge now? Rome was the one sanctuary in Europe, the only place that enjoyed true freedom—the freedom from political freedom. All that was delightful—the unsophistication, the dirt—all that will disappear. For every statesman who crops up there, an artist will be ruined."

The paradox in Ibsen's view of political freedom was that, as he himself said, "the only thing I care about liberty is the struggle for it; I care nothing for the possession of it."[23]

Freedom to him was like pleasure to a sadomasochist. Neither could be enjoyed without its opposite coming into play. The strain that runs through all this is the mystical element in Ibsen's philosophy. Nothing significant could be achieved without sacrifice on the part of the individual. It was the masochistic streak that he had in common with Kierkegaard and the Christian saints. It was the substance of what he called poetry in human affairs as opposed to the prose of politics and the mathematics of militarism. The age that produced great speculators and great manipulators could not produce great poets because, in the words of a Victorian critic writing at just this time, the age "cannot give what it has not got. And it has not got the divine afflatus."[24]

In Prussia, true poets, like Kleist, killed themselves, while Moltke did away with the poetry of warfare. The Norwegian people had missed the chance for spiritual beauty and poetic greatness when they avoided national disaster and shrank from sacrificing themselves on the Dannewerk in the Dano-Prussian War. And the king of Sweden, Charles XV, became a poet when he sought to circumvent the diplomats, the ministers of state, and engage Sweden and Norway for a noble cause in that one-sided war.

In the 1871 *Poems*, Ibsen placed his encomium on the king, No. 50 in the sequence, immediately after the poem about torpedoing the ark not only because they were composed about the same time, 1869, but because their juxtaposition underscored the paradox in his position: the monarchist was an anarchist. In the last poems of the cycle he endeavored to resolve the contradiction by using the alchemy of poetry to sublimate both.

However, even as he was giving shape to the cycle and bringing order to his conflicted thoughts, events in Europe, whose echoes reached the street outside his window in Dresden, threatened to tear his poet's philosophy to shreds. In 1870 the poet saw the new alliance of German states, the North German Confederation, whose destructive potential he had accurately foreseen in act four of *Peer Gynt*, prepare for war against France and dreamed that now poetry would combine with power to defeat numbers and the mob mentality. France, the flower of European civilization, would make the great sacrifice and halt the German machine. Again, as in the Dano-Prussian War, it was not to be.

There may have been two kinds of victory for the poet, the victory of sheer numbers and discipline, and the victory of the divine afflatus, but now events made the first a hard fact and the latter a shattered illusion. In October, after the capture of the French army in Sedan, Ibsen, pacing his rooms in Dresden, could see from his window the growing number of ordinary French war prisoners, more than fifteen thousand of them, freezing and exhausted and housed in unheated huts, while their commissioned officers, in parade uniforms, caroused in the taverns and the noncommissioned soldiers were entertained by the Dresden burghers. The trophies of victory were paraded through the streets, and Ibsen heard the French soldiers joke about them.[25] His immediate response was to attribute the victory of the Germans to their discipline and the defeat of the French to their moral lassitude. What the poet in him loathed, the crushing of the individual beneath the juggernaut of the state, the tyrant in him admired. Only a few months before, he had urged the employment of stern means to break the actors' strike in Christiania. Now, noticing the indifference of the French prisoners of war to the fate of their homeland, he blamed them and found the lack of "proper discipline and order . . . perfectly natural in a revolutionary state."[26]

Gradually, Ibsen was compelled to reassess the Germans. His poet's hatred of them was increasingly mitigated by practical considerations. In 1867 and 1868, while residing in Italy, he openly expressed his detestation of the Germans and would have nothing to do with a ball organized by the German colony in Rome, all the while denouncing the German newspapers as filled with lies and deceit. Even in 1870 his attitude when among friends was anti-German, and as a resident of Dresden he was in an anomalous position. His acquaintances were Scandinavian, and his son, Sigurd, now eleven years old, was badgered by students at his school for not openly declaring himself a German. On at least one occasion he was thrashed by his classmates.[27] Yet Ibsen had voluntarily removed himself and his family from the Rome he professed to love for the Germany he once professed to hate, and, as he pointed out in answering his German critics, his actions betrayed an attachment to the Germans, if not to Teutonism. The superior schools in Dresden were undoubtedly a factor in his deciding to settle there at a time when his son's education had to be considered. On the other hand, there is no avoiding the fact that at this time Ibsen had determined to make a career for himself in Germany.[28]

Some of his works had been translated into German, and in the March 19, 1870, issue of the *Illustrirte Zeitung* there appeared the first German biographical account of Ibsen. Now the two sides of his nature clashed with each other. Brand spoke out against German militarism in the collected poems, while Peer Gynt assuaged German patriotic sensibilities with an open letter to the Germans in which he dissociated himself from opinions expressed in 1865. After the German students beat up his son, Peer Gynt humbly turned the other cheek and gave money for the education of a German orphan and supported a German widow whose sons were in the army.[29] This concern for others, this charitableness, was an aspect of Ibsen that had never revealed itself before. Was it loving-kindness or prudent self-interest?

In December 1870 he hit upon a solution to the philosophical dilemma that had been created in his mind by the emergence of the German states under Bismarck as the major power in Europe, and he tested his new idea in messages to Georg Brandes and to Fru Limnell. In his "Balloon Letter" to Fru Limnell, thanking her for the happy days he had spent in her *cénacle,* Ibsen adopted the position of a conservative, while in his letter to Brandes he was a dyed-in-the-wool radical. And with both he was equally sincere.

To Brandes he wrote: "How the old ideas will come tumbling about our ears! And high time they did. Up till now we have been living on nothing but crumbs from the revolutionary table of the last century, and I think we have been chewing on that stuff long enough. The old terms must be invested with new meaning and given new explanations. Liberty, equality, and fraternity are no longer what they were in the days of the late-lamented guillotine. This is what the politicians will not understand; and that is why I hate them. They want only their own special revolutions—external revolutions, political revolutions, etc. But that is only dabbling. What is really needed is a revolution of the human spirit."[30]

As we have seen, Ibsen in his "Balloon Letter" compared his own position in Dresden, surrounded by Germans, with that of the beleaguered Parisians, and he likens the German bluster and über alles propaganda that he is forced to swallow to the rat stew that the starving Parisians must eat in order to survive. In such times, he says, a balloon letter is more symbolic of his hopes than the biblical dove. With Junkerism triumphant in Germany and liberalism gaining strength in Scandinavia, he sees himself stripped of armor, standing amid the "ruins of broken dreams," while his thoughts drift back to his journey down the Nile, undertaken just after he had departed from Fru Limnell in Stockholm. Out of these shattered hopes he forms a new one based on the idea that setbacks in man's development are only apparent.

> History's course is fixed and binding:
> Up an endless spiral staircase,
> Inward turning, always winding,
> Mankind climbs a narrow space,
> Never ceasing to aspire,
> Its goal rising ever higher.[31]

In Egypt he had stood on the pharaoh's ground, and now in the helix of history the Germany of Bismarck stands precisely over the Egypt of the pharaohs. Which means that the master of military strategy Moltke (the Sphinx) will be defeated by his own cleverness, and the empire builder Bismarck (Memnon), lacking the life-giving dew of poetry, will crumble and vanish in the desert sands. Yet only a few months after writing "A Balloon Letter," Ibsen was confronted by the discomfiting fact that Germany was not going to be canceled out by an equal and opposing power or by its inner contradictions, à la Hegel, as he had believed in 1865 when he wrote "Abraham Lincoln's Assassination." If Germany was the Egypt of the modern era, the implication was that it would last for thousands of years. In January 1871, King William of Prussia was proclaimed emperor of the new German Reich. Under Bismarck's leadership, twenty-five states had been welded into a German Empire. This empire was the equivalent of the great Scandinavian union that had inspired the young Ibsen. But Bismarck's empire was a fact, and the Nordic union had proved to be an illusion. By 1872 Ibsen's perspective had changed so much that his only objection to Bismarck was that he was an obstacle to better relations between Germany and Scandinavia.[32] (Yet in the same year, in his poem "Signals in the North," Ibsen rebuked Bjørnson for pressing for closer relations between the Nordic countries and Bismarck's empire.)

As a unionist, he was compelled to approve of Chancellor Bismarck's achievement in creating a nation out of twenty-five states, while as an individualist and anarchist he could only anathematize the Prussian police state that was the basis of the union.

Within a few years after having impugned Bismarck's militarism in *Brand* and *Peer Gynt*, Ibsen had become quite thoroughly Germanized. In 1875 he was described as "a somewhat older gentleman, assured in manner and in his opinions, and entirely partial to . . . Bismarck's theories of society and discipline. . . . There is a consistency in that, as in his writings. As a politician, he would have been a fanatic."[33]

At about the same time, however, Brandes described him as anti-Bismarck. Discussing the chancellor's quarrel with the Catholic Church and his efforts to free the public schools from the grip of the clergy, Brandes wrote, "Characteristically, the only one here [in Germany] whom I have heard was definitely on the side of the church is the Norwegian Henrik Ibsen in Dresden, who is remarkably receptive to all kinds of reactionary influences."[34]

His views of Bismarck's policies appeared paradoxical only because he made the nation—that is, the people—distinct from the state. Why would he, as a nonbeliever, praise Bismarck for bringing the German people into an organic unity while faulting him for trying to wrest power from the spiritual union that was the church? Obviously because he deemed one unifying force of greater worth than the other, and his putting the church above the state made him a reactionary in Brandes's eyes. On this crucial point Brandes never understood Ibsen, and eventually it placed him, philosophically, as far on one side of Ibsen as Bjørnson was on the other.

THE PRUDENT REVOLUTIONARY

The young outspoken rebel who had narrowly escaped arrest in 1851, when the police rounded up the leaders of the workers' movement, had matured into the enigmatic literary lion who prudently took advantage of his position in the establishment to await in bourgeois comfort the coming of the revolution. What he wrote for publication about the great change that loomed on the horizon was couched in terms so abstract that it could not offend the conservatives any more than the Sermon on the Mount, while the liberals were galled by his failure to say explicitly and publicly what he must be thinking privately.

The relationship of Ibsen and Brandes illuminates the difference between an armchair revolutionary, pacing his well-furnished rooms, thinking daring thoughts, and the firebrand, the radical agitator, proclaiming the new era from a public platform. At first Brandes believed that Ibsen would be the leader, but he misunderstood Ibsen's nature and temperament. What in Ibsen should have inspired him soon disappointed him. Brandes proved to be the leader, and Ibsen had to follow him to keep up with the changing times. As might be expected, Ibsen preferred to remain the observer, discreet, cautious, while Brandes mounted the ramparts.

Although they saw themselves as comrades in arms, they fought in two different armies. In esthetic matters, for instance, they were always a little out of phase with each other. At first Brandes objected to the moralist and polemicist in Ibsen. In *Brand,* the religious element was too prominent; in *Peer Gynt,* the satire was inhuman; both works lacked the harmony and agreeableness of great art. Ibsen's rejoinder was that there was more objectivity and far less religiosity in *Brand* than anyone had perceived, and that in *Peer Gynt* he had followed the laws of beauty while possibly violating its ever-changing and temporal conventions.

Brandes's doctoral dissertation at the University of Copenhagen was on French esthetic theory, *Den franske Æstetik i vore Dage* (*Contemporary French Aesthetics*), centering on Hippolyte Taine. Ibsen chided Brandes for being an esthete unconcerned about practical matters and political events. It was a reproof wide of the mark. Brandes's involvement in the dualist controversy left him with few friends in Denmark, and he spoke of his sense of isolation to Ibsen. In response, Ibsen first congratulated him on his degree and offered him the consolation that friends were "an expensive luxury" that a man whose capital is invested in a calling could not afford to have.

"The expense of keeping friends does not lie in what one does for them, but in what one refrains from doing out of consideration for them. The result is that one's intellectual and spiritual development is stunted. I know this from personal experience, and there were, consequently, many years in my life during which it was not possible for me to be myself."[1] This remark struck the right note and strengthened the bond between the two men, with Ibsen now frankly taking the fatherly position of counselor.[2]

After being awarded his doctoral degree, Brandes traveled to Italy for a well-deserved rest. There he contracted typhoid fever and lay desperately ill for weeks. As he recovered, he indulged his senses, feasting on Italian art and wine, while his mind was occupied with thoughts about the great political and cultural change that he felt was coming. The sensual arts of Italy, both Roman and Renaissance, stimulated him as none of the ancient writers could. Gazing at the Sistine Chapel paintings, he saw a vision of what might be again—in Denmark. Michelangelo's biblical figures were for him an expression of a renewal of the pagan world. And in the paintings he saw in Pompeii he found heroism, youth, freedom: "No prohibitions, no fear. No temptation, no snake. No Fall."[3] With those images before him, he was determined to make war on the puritanism and narrowness of mind in Denmark.

The first person outside his family that Brandes wrote to was Ibsen. Ibsen answered with one of his boldest letters, predicting an earthshaking revolution and calling on Brandes to take the lead in the great spiritual and cultural struggle that lay ahead.

Writing at the end of 1870, when the Franco-Prussian War dominated his thoughts, Ibsen declared that "what is really needed is a revolution of the human spirit. And in this *you* shall be one of those who take the lead."[4]

This challenge to radicalize the world induced a nervous excitement in the still-feverish Brandes. In his hospital bed in Rome, on the night of January 10–11, 1871, he answered Ibsen's call with a four-stanza poem in which he addressed Ibsen as general of the army that would raise the spirit of revolution, while assigning himself the role of armor bearer.

> Greetings, comrade! To you all thanks.
> You are meant to play the leader's role,
> While I shall fight as soldier in the ranks.
> Together, united heart and soul,
> We shall rouse the spirit of rebellion.[5]

The middle-aged Brandes was a little embarrassed by this youthfully ardent poem. He dismissed it as "dilettante work . . . typhoid poetry" and equivocatingly pointed out that he did not say Ibsen was *his* leader.[6] But these rationalizations cannot conceal the deliberation with which the young Brandes weighed his words before writing to Ibsen, nor the fact that his disillusionment with Ibsen as a revolutionary leader came after the poem was written.

By morning his ardor had somewhat cooled, and then came second thoughts, as he reconsidered Ibsen's stunning ideas of liberty and revolution. He deliberated for a month before mailing the poem, and he sent it off on February 11 with a letter expostulating with Ibsen for his illiberal views.

Although Ibsen was absorbed in the revision of his collected poems, he replied promptly, ostensibly accepting the role assigned him by Brandes. His letter was a pre-Nietzschean call for a reevaluation of all values, as he explained what he meant by revolution and how he distinguished between the political state and a spiritually united people.

> Undermine the idea of the state. Make willingness and spiritual kinship the only essentials for union—and you have the beginning of a liberty that is of some value. Changing one form of government for another is merely a matter of toying with various degrees of the same thing—a little more or a little less. Folly, all of it. . . .
>
> The great thing is not to allow oneself to be frightened by the venerableness of institutions. The state has its roots in time; it will reach its height in time. Greater things than it will fall: all religion will fall. Neither standards of morality nor of art are eternal. What is there that we are really obliged to hold on to?[7]

These nihilistic views had the desired effect of overcoming Brandes's reservations regarding Ibsen's religious inclinations and political conservatism.

"Ibsen's radicalism goes beyond everything imaginable," he wrote his parents. "I get dizzy reading how he wants to revolutionize everything. I am afraid that if he had the power and the means, or if he lived in another age, he would have won renown as more radical than Marat in one respect and than Proudhon in another."[8]

He was very much in Brandes's thoughts during the following weeks. In the spring Brandes received a copy of Ibsen's *Poems*, and the little book gave him "a violent state of nerves." The dissonances that sounded throughout the poems, the clash of ideas that found no resolution, jarred Brandes profoundly. Some of the poems called for revolution; others did not. Although the most daring ones had an anarchic ring to them, the cycle as a whole petered out in an appeal to beauty. The tensions that produced the drama of the cycle stirred Brandes but left him uncertain about Ibsen's commitment to political and social change.

"Most of the poems," he told his parents, "are obscure to the point of incomprehensibility.... Nearly all are poems of the intellect [*Forstandsvis*]."[9]

On July 14, 1871, the nihilist and the revolutionary met for the first time. The date, Bastille Day, was chosen by Brandes.[10] Eager to talk face to face with the poet of paradoxes, Brandes journeyed to Dresden. And Ibsen was equally eager to meet the only critic with whom he felt he could speak freely. He hung out of the window of his apartment in his shirtsleeves, waiting to catch sight of his visitor. When Brandes came into view, Ibsen quickly changed into a velvet jacket. Unusually demonstrative, he pressed Brandes to his chest, squeezing the breath out of him. Brandes, to his surprise, found the older man handsome, with "a matchless forehead, long, wavy hair, and bright eyes." They talked for two or three hours, and Brandes felt his faith in the poet restored. The end of their conversation found Ibsen in a belligerent mood. With a smile, he shouted to the departing Brandes, "You provoke the Danes, and I'll provoke the Norwegians."[11]

Brandes had great faith in Ibsen, because "of all my contemporaries in the Scandinavian literary scene, only one was my benefactor, the stern, deeply understanding Ibsen. He opened up new sources of thought in my mind, and perhaps once I did in his."[12]

Brandes left fully expecting the radicalized Ibsen to begin the campaign against the old order. But Ibsen was silent. In the middle of September, Brandes wrote a long, emotional letter (not extant), appealing to the poet to raise the banner of revolt. Waiting for an answer, he was in turmoil.

"Am I the one who *gives* the rallying cry?" he asked himself in his diary. "Does it really fall to me to be the leader of the young? ... Should I give a speech to the Student Association, issue a proclamation to the young? It seems to me that I *must*, that it is a duty and a necessity."

By the end of the month, he still had not received a reply from the poet. "This hurts and angers me."[13] Early in October, Brandes could read, with a sinking heart, Ibsen's reply, dated September 24, 1871. Instead of calling for a gathering of forces, Ibsen advised a withdrawal from the masses.

"What I recommend for you is a thoroughgoing, full-blooded egoism, which will force you to regard yourself and your work as the only things of consequence in this world, and everything else as nonexistent. . . . I have never really had a very great feeling for solidarity. In fact, I have allowed it in my mental cargo only because it is a traditional article of belief. If one had the courage to throw it overboard altogether, one would be getting rid of the ballast that weighs most heavily on the personality. There are actually moments when the whole history of the world reminds me of a sinking ship; the only thing to do is save oneself."

The ardent Scandinavianist who only a few years before had written *Brand* and who had advocated self-sacrifice for the sake of a noble cause now saw that nothing was worth that price. He diagnosed Brandes's "cry of distress" as the symptom of the very disease that he had passed through when he wrote his dramatic poem. It was a momentary crisis in an illness for which the cure was total self-interest. The letter confirmed Brandes's darkest suspicions about Ibsen, and he realized now that he himself would have to lead the younger generation in new directions. The twenty-nine-year-old Brandes had to dissociate himself from the older man's pessimism and aloofness.

In October Brandes wrote a lengthy review of Ibsen's collected poems, five months after the book had been published, a delay caused by the critic's difficulty in assessing them. Caught between his disappointment in the poems and his admiration for their author, he regurgitated what he had had to swallow in Ibsen's letter, giving the words a bitter aftertaste.

> Ibsen writes primarily out of his isolation. It is a secondary factor that he has isolated himself, unhappy at the thought that he has not been able to carry the masses with him.
>
> It is always the case that in a land where the cultural life is at a critical juncture and the younger generation stands ready to rally around the new ideas that the great, compassionate, and unifying thought comes from its poets. Here [in Denmark] I know well enough that such is not the case. But—now—under such circumstances the young reach out to the poet to carry the banner. They call on him to give the word. Although they know inwardly what they are fighting for, they want to hear it for the first time coming from the inspired lips of the poet. If he does not at the right moment give the answer they are waiting for, then it takes shape in the young without his help, and then it is the poet who is stopped and asked if he knows the watchword. If he does not know it, the young strike him down and move on.
>
> Now, when hopes and desires lie scattered about without a goal or central point, there can be no expectation of a gathering cry, and the poet will retire into himself. Ibsen's nature suits that situation and draws its strength from it. His power depends on the stillness of night around him, on the quiet darkness, in which he alone breathes easily. Not the twelve fair hours but the night's

dark hours stand grandparents to his poetry. Alone, he divides more than he unites. He shows everyone how to find the strength within oneself—without fear or regard for others—to fulfill one's own nature and follow one's own star. But the stars shine only at night. It does no good to ask Ibsen to raise a banner; he writes only for himself and for those who are constitutionally like him; for them he provides not a banner but an example. They will understand what he means when he says that if ever he creates a great work, it will be a deed done in the dark."[14]

While convalescing in Rome, Brandes had met with Carsten Hauch, professor of esthetics at the University of Copenhagen. Hauch, who was in poor health, had made it clear that he wanted Brandes to succeed him. Upon his return to Denmark the young radical applied for a position at the university. He was asked to give a series of probationary lectures, preliminary to his being appointed to an extraordinary position as docent in esthetics. By this time he was the most controversial critic in Denmark, if not in all Scandinavia. He was a Jewish freethinker who had taken on the leading philosophers and theologians and whose personal life was as shocking as his views on contemporary literature. He had made John Stuart Mill's *The Subjection of Women* available in Danish, and it was hardly a secret in Copenhagen that he was enamored of an older married woman, who was the mother of six children. One third of the overflow audience that came to hear the first of his lectures on November 3, 1871, consisted of women, eager to show their public support for this defender of women's rights.

Brash, brilliant, cocksure, Brandes devoted his first talk to a broad, unsparing denunciation of contemporary Danish literature. It was bold and tactless, designed to attract attention. It succeeded in doing more than that. The date of his first lecture marked a watershed between the old and the new in Scandinavian literature, beginning what came to be known as the Modern Breakthrough (*Det moderne gennembrud*).

Although he had chosen as his broad subject the main currents in European literature ("Hovedstrømninger i det 19, Arhundredes europæiske Litteratur")—a suitable topic for a future professor of esthetics—in his opening talk he made it abundantly clear that the tenor of his observations and his evaluations of literary works would be politically slanted. In a challenging tone, he declared that he would attack the forces of reaction and point to those works that might favor the liberal cause. Although he was being considered for a position as lecturer in esthetics, he was determined to evaluate literature in practical, social terms.

His very first words established the militant tone of the whole speech.

"Before I embark on this series of lectures, I feel it is necessary to ask your indulgence. This is the first time that I speak from this platform, and I bring with me all the faults and failings of inexperience. I lack as much in the way of ability as I do in the way of knowledge. What I thereby do or say to offend you will, I believe, be corrected as I gain in experience. But with regard to my basic views, my principles, and my beliefs, I do not ask any indulgence whatsoever. What I may say or do to offend you in this respect will not be changed. I consider it a duty and a privilege to follow the principles to which I have committed myself: a belief in the right of free inquiry and in the eventual triumph of free thought."[15]

While Ibsen paced his rooms, waiting for the revolution, Brandes stood on the firing line. He spoke his mind, declaring that Danish culture was mired in the swamp of reaction, artistically and politically, dominated by outmoded religious convictions, and out of touch with the main political and intellectual currents in Europe. The literature of Denmark toys with abstractions and ideals; the passion for thought has yielded to the passion for faith.

> Higher and higher mounts the enthusiasm for asceticism and positive religion....
>
> Where does this current finally emerge? In such figures as ... Ibsen's Brand, whose moral principles if realized would cause half of mankind to starve to death for the sake of an ideal....
>
> So strong has the current been that even a spirit as revolutionary as Ibsen's has been seized by it. Does *Brand* stand for revolution or reaction? I cannot tell, there is so much of both in it.[16]

Brandes concluded his address with a ringing cry that echoed Ibsen's extreme thoughts and boldly set generation against generation and the liberals against the conservatives.

> It is not so much our laws that need changing as it is our whole conception of society. The younger generation must plough it up and replant it before a new literature can bloom and flourish. Their chief task will be to channel into our country those currents that have their origin in the revolution and in the belief in progress, and to halt the reaction at all points where its historic mission has been fulfilled.[17]

The impact that Brandes made on the younger members of his audience is well described by one who heard him.

> His eyes flickered like those of a young panther; his supple and thin body was in continuous motion, like that of a fencing master giving lessons. From his already wrinkled brow his hair rose up like a pair of wings—or like the helmet on an unconquerable Asian warrior. And then there was his smile—trusting, nearly naive, good-natured. . . . From below the dais, the young people sat

> staring up, their eyes wide open and shining with wonder. Such a revolution was exactly what they had dreamed of. . . . The great ideals were of this earth. The preacher of the new thousand-year kingdom of beauty, the preacher of the evangel of freedom, of the emancipation of the individual from centuries of dead tradition, from the oppression of social conventions. With the book of the new covenant—the holy works of the poets—in his hand, he stood there like a Moses come down from the mountain, radiant in the light of the new revelation. . . . He was the man of the new age—the bringer of light. . . . It would not be far wrong to say that the emotions evoked in some of those young people were like those of a religious cult.[18]

The older generation, for the most part, saw this bringer of light as a Lucifer. The university council dropped all plans of giving Brandes a permanent position, if it had ever seriously considered doing so. But his incendiary words went out into the world when he published his first series of lectures under the title *Literature of the Emigrants* (*Emigrantliteraturen*) in 1872, with a second volume, *The Romantic School in Germany* (*Den romantiske Skole i Tyskland*), appearing the following year.

The outspoken critic suddenly burst upon the literary scene as a luminary of the first rank, soon exercising an influence as great as Ibsen's, as Brandes assumed the role he had asked Ibsen to fill. The irony of this furnished a motif in one of the dramatist's last plays.

The controversy surrounding Brandes turned into a violent clash between conservatives and radicals. All the leading newspapers denounced him. Even though he could not "refrain from putting the cat among the pigeons," as one of his friends said, Brandes probably had no idea that some lectures on literature could prove to be so politically inflammatory.[19] It was the specter of political revolution in Europe that made him appear as a dangerous firebrand, frightening even to many liberals. The terrors of the Paris Commune were still fresh in everyone's mind. To some it seemed that Europe had narrowly escaped the end of civilization (communists occupying Paris, the center of civilization!). So when Brandes, a Jew, launched his attack on the old values, especially those associated with the Christian church, he appeared less like a herald of new truths than the devil incarnate.

When the first volume of the lectures was published, every newspaper in Denmark expressed its disapproval. Hauch died in March 1872, leaving a written recommendation that Brandes be appointed professor of esthetics. The newspapers refused to print the letter.

Brandes sent Ibsen copies of *Literature of the Emigrants.* If Brandes had been astonished at the extent of Ibsen's radical views, now it was Ibsen's turn. Some of

Brandes's main targets were Christian teachings about sin and the life everlasting. The true fall of man, he said, was the denial of physical nature and the invention of the supernatural.

"You who are listening to me know that science has proved the revolutionary thinkers right and Schelling wrong. And we who live in the time of Charles Darwin no longer consider the possibility of an original Paradise and a fall from it. Without a doubt, Darwin's works will overthrow orthodox morality, just as Copernicus' works overthrew orthodox dogmatism. The system worked out by Copernicus deprived the orthodox heaven of a physical place, and similarly Darwin's theories will deprive the orthodox paradise of a place."[20]

The author of *Peer Gynt* was no adherent of Darwin's theories (*vide* the ape scene in act four). However, when he read Brandes, he was compelled to realize that Darwin was just the force that would bring about the collapse of the old ideas, which "will come tumbling about our ears." Losing sleep over Brandes's lectures, Ibsen wrote to him: "No more dangerous book could fall into the hands of a pregnant writer [he was struggling with the epic drama *Emperor and Galilean*]. It is one of those works that place a yawning gulf between yesterday and today. After I had been to Italy I could not understand how I had been able to exist before I had been there. In twenty years one will not be able to comprehend how a spiritual existence was possible at home before these lectures. . . . To me your revolt is a great, emancipating outbreak of genius."[21]

Bjørnson's response to Brandes's lectures was the very opposite of Ibsen's. These lectures, he said, "constitute an effort to appeal to the vanity of the people by telling them that they are not truly living if they don't live according to the latest ideas from Paris. But there is surely another kind of living than that of provocation and revolution, just as there is another literature than that which assumes as its own the revolutionary ideas of an alien people [read: the Jewish people]. . . . Where is the man who can read the same history Brandes has read but do it in the service of man's soul and spirit?"[22]

Here the liberal Bjørnson echoed the sentiments of the conservatives, while Brandes found himself alienated on both the right and the left. To gather support he tried to establish a literary society where his views might be freely expressed.

Ibsen found in all this a confirmation of his own disdain for liberal politicians. To Brandes, however, the angry man he had met in Dresden, the nihilist who wrote in his poems about torpedoing the ark of the state, had now dwindled into an apolitical poet. Though Ibsen might protest against this judgment—"I do not shrink in the least from being regarded as a partisan," he told Brandes; "I do not really understand why I am considered as belonging to no party"—the critic could now see him only as "very conservative, or rather absolutist."[23] He was the poet in an ivory tower, isolated, elitist, whose "contempt for human beings was boundless" and in whom were accumulated "forty-two years of bitterness and hatred."[24]

The disenchanted Brandes saw only the negative aspect of Ibsen, the Earl Skule in him. Actually, Ibsen was a divided soul, as the collected poems clearly spelled out. By 1871 the hate-spouting, pure-in-heart priest of *Brand* had sold out to the corruptible, self-immersed, Bøyg-haunted, uncommitted hero of *Peer Gynt.* He played the active nihilist with Brandes, the passive chiliast with the conservatives. He rejected the prospect the liberals offered, a future in which the masses thrived and the individual died. But the world of the reactionaries was not much better, offering only the faded beauty of the past. He yearned romantically for some indistinct, undefinable force that would bring spirituality back into the modern, increasingly mechanized world. In his longing, he chose to regard the German victory over France and the formation of the German Empire not as a confirmation of his worst fears but as an augury and foreshadowing of a much greater upheaval that would change the cultural and political landscape of Europe.

In the turmoil about him he saw a reflection of the conflict within himself. In his Dresden apartment, in the midst of Bismarck's empire that was hostile to beauty, Ibsen put on the mask of the conservative as a sign of that aristocracy of the spirit that he thirsted for. And daily, impatiently, hearing the tramping of the French prisoners in the street outside his window, he waited for the beginning of a new era.

In kid gloves, elegant, soigné,
I pace my room, await that day.
Till then a sanctum I require,
And on wove paper have my say.
I know the plebs will call me "snob";
They'll put me quite beyond the pale.
But I've a horror of the mob,
Can't stand the stench of reeking lips.
So I wait for the apocalypse,
Immaculate in white tie and tails.[25]

EMPEROR AND GALILEAN

While Ibsen was pacing his room in Dresden, his ears attuned to the sounds of history in the making, his mind was occupied with thoughts about his next major play. It gave him a great deal of trouble. And well it might. For what he hoped to accomplish was an epic drama that would express an all-encompassing philosophy of history, distill the essence of his own development, and reflect the contemporary state of Europe. This work was to be autobiography, world history, and universal philosophy—all in one. It was to be a summing up of his thoughts, a drama set in the distant past that was really about the nineteenth century and times to come, a drama that in depicting the psychological development of an individual provided an understanding of the major forces in human affairs. It would emulate Goethe's *Faust* as a comprehensive worldview and surpass it as drama. Above all, however, it would unite the two sides of his being, merging Brand with Gynt.

To anyone seriously interested in Ibsen, *Emperor and Galilean* provides the key to the man and his works. It reveals more about him than anything else he wrote. To the English critic Edmund Gosse he explained, "It is part of my own spiritual life that I am putting into this book. What I depict I have, under different conditions, lived through myself; and the historical subject I have chosen has a much closer connection with the movements of our own time than one might at first imagine. I regard such a connection as imperative in any modern poetic imaginative treatment of such a remote subject if it is to arouse any interest as a creative work."[1]

Ibsen regarded it as the greatest of all his plays. Just after he finished it, he called it "my chief work,"[2] an opinion he held until the end of his life. In 1898 he told the Harvard professor William Henry Schofield that it was "the best and most enduring" of all his works.[3] When his playwriting days were over, he told his masseur that it was his chief work, adding, "At any rate, without question, it was the one that cost me the most work."[4] Perhaps he held it in such high regard because he put so much of himself into it. Or perhaps it meant so much to him because it cost him years of labor. The favorite child is often the one that gives the most trouble.

It is indispensable to anyone who wishes to understand fully the plays that followed, and it contains one scene that for sheer dramatic power is unsurpassed in modern drama. Yet of the works of his maturity, it is the most neglected, seldom read by students of drama and almost never staged. This two-part work, unique in its conception, is something of a monster, both fascinating and forbidding. What Ravel said of his *Bolero* might be paraphrased for Ibsen's epic, "It's a masterpiece, but it isn't drama."

This strange double drama is like a ziggurat on the European landscape. Architecturally marvelous, with its intricate decorations, its perfect symmetry, it seems isolated and, in its isolation, forbidding. It is not like other dramas, lacking the traditional three-part structure, the buildup to a single climax. The great moment when Julian emerges from the depths of the church occurs at its midpoint, and the resolution to the conflict as presented there occupies another five acts, another whole drama. This is not theater as invented by the Greeks and as practiced by playwrights ever since.

However, what was strange to readers in the nineteenth century has its counterpart in the popular drama of a later age. It is not much different from the mini-series that attract audiences on television. In fact, it could easily be adapted into a ten-episode mini-series. It offers everything such epic tales should have: drama on both the large and small scale, set against a background of cultural conflict, a dominating hero riven with inner doubts, and a huge cast of characters, many of them offering fine acting opportunities. Much of what Ibsen relates and describes could be turned into stunning visual scenes: Julian's initiation into the Eleusinian Mysteries, his passage across the Aegean Sea, the revelatory hallucinations induced by the mystic Maximus. And the battle scenes would be perfect cinematic material, ending with the striking symbolic image of Julian being slain by his childhood friend Agathon, plunging his spear into Julian's side.

The viewer of the television series would be carried along by the power of the narrative, experiencing each incident in Julian's struggle with himself and with the times. Only later, when this viewer acquired the DVD version on two discs, would he experience it in a new way, seeing what he had overlooked before, discerning the pattern, the grand architectural design, the balancing of part against part, the subtle intricacy of the details, and, above all, viewing the ziggurat from above, comprehending it as a philosophical construct that makes *Emperor and Galilean* a unique artistic achievement.

What one reader said when the double drama was fresh off the printing presses is probably what many readers since then have thought: "I have no other overall impression than that it is a rich chaos, ending with a question mark. It is a tremendous book. But the hero is not a person; he is a system, a philosophy, or the image of a time, or a monstrous force . . . but a warm-blooded, living, suffering, feeling person he is not. The book has left a sad impression on me. But I don't understand it—not yet; and perhaps I never will. It is very strange. One never gets a strong sense of Julian. He is at once both colossal and brittle."[5]

Its seeds were sown in 1864, when Ibsen's fellow Norwegian Lorentz Dietrichson accompanied him on walks in the environs of Rome. Ibsen was newly arrived in the city, and Dietrichson was there to study Renaissance art. In August at Genzano, off the Appian Way, as they paused on one of their walks, Dietrichson read aloud a passage from Ammianus Marcellinus describing the death of the apostate Emperor Julian.[6] It was an eyewitness account by a man who had served in Julian's ill-fated Persian expedition. Seeing the ruins of ancient Rome had already stirred thoughts in Ibsen about the rise and fall of civilizations, and, as Dietrichson read aloud, these thoughts began to cluster around the figure of Julian. Ibsen felt a kinship with the emperor who had abjured Christianity and worshipped the sun god Helios. Julian had been physically unprepossessing, intellectually bright, and dedicated to sexual chastity. He had been ridiculed as a youth, had been oppressed by family circumstances, and had secretly abandoned Christianity. Much the same could be said about the young Ibsen.

Julian, who lived from c. AD 331 to 363, was caught in the epochal clash between two cultures, and Ibsen saw this as the equivalent of his own inner conflict. As part of the emperor Constantine's restructuring of the Roman Empire, the old Roman deities were replaced with the Christian God. Upon succeeding him as emperor, Julian sought a return to paganism. This swing from Roman religious tolerance to a strict Christianity and then back to paganism, all in a relatively short period, reflected the vacillation between Peer Gynt and Brand within Ibsen.

But there had to be more than just the subjective appeal of Julian's career to engage Ibsen's interest for nine years. He recognized that the central events of nineteenth-century Europe were essentially a repetition of the events of the fourth century. In the dramatic work that was fermenting in his mind, the microcosm of his inner conflict would be incorporated in the macrocosm of world history.

In his first notes, he intended to make Julian's career serve as a protest against the political and religious tyranny of the nineteenth century. Ibsen found among the members of the Scandinavian community in Rome someone in whom he could confide his radical view of the state of European civilization. This was Carl Snoilsky (1841–1903), thirteen years younger than Ibsen and from a different class. Snoilsky came from the Swedish aristocracy, while Ibsen came from a family that could not even keep its position in the middle class. Despite these distinctions of class and age, Snoilsky and Ibsen got along very well in Rome in 1864. Snoilsky, like Ibsen, was a divided personality: an esthete and an aristocrat who wanted to be directly involved in revolutionary politics. Both were distressed by the failure of the Scandinavian countries to unite against the Prussian army, a failure in their eyes amounting to treason, and both recognized the new triune despotism that was threatening Europe: the czar of Russia, the king of Prussia, and the pope in Rome constituting an unholy trinity. When the Poles had tried to throw off the Russian yoke in 1863, Snoilsky had supported the insurgents with thirteen poems, one of which, "The Polish Volunteer" ("Den polske frivillige"), ended bravely with a young soldier saying, "I could live well, but I know better how to die." Snoilsky ended another poem, ironically titled "Long Live the Czar!" ("Lefve Kejsaren!"), written immediately after the Russians put down the rebellion, with more rodomontade: "We asked for freedom—and were denied it. We ask for death—can you deny us that?" A rather delicate young man given to fits of depression, Snoilsky knew nothing about battlefields or barricades and wrote from the vantage point of an aristocrat who would never have to bear arms. His bravest deed was to come years later in the quiet of his own circle and was to provide Ibsen with material for one of his finest dramas, *Rosmersholm.*

Early in 1864 Snoilsky had published a vigorous and scornful poem about the fall of the Dannewerk, which may have led Ibsen to use that event as the climax, the madhouse scene, of the philosophical drama that informs act four of *Peer Gynt.* Certainly their conversations in Rome often centered on the Danish disaster. Years later, Snoilsky recalled in a poem his first weeks in Rome and his chats with Ibsen at their favorite café.

In eighteen hundred sixty-four
While Dybbøl's thunder
Still echoed loud
In southern groves,
In the silver glow
Of the Roman moon,
Each night we met

At Café Tritone. . . .
Your place was the middle
Of the long table,
And for us young ones
You were the chairman.
Brutal force in the north
Had maimed our race.
We shared our sorrow,
And we shared disgrace.
I can hear your voice
As late each night
Lightning flashed from neath
The big hat you wore.
That's why the Italians
At the Café Tritone
Called you "Il Capellone."[7]

Later in 1864 he wrote what was to become the best-known of his political poems, "Nero's Golden Palace" ("Neros gyllene hus"), which heralded the dawn of a new day in Italy and the end of political and religious despotism.

On the morrow St. Peter will heave a sigh
And take his leave of the Vatican;
And all nature will exult and cry,
"Awake, awake" to the great god Pan.[8]

Snoilsky dedicated this poem, certain stanzas of which were memorized by young freedom-loving Swedes, to Henrik Ibsen. The Norwegian poet's "Abraham Lincoln's Assassination," with its explicit reference to Nero's golden palace, is a commentary on it. Where Snoilsky welcomed Garibaldi's Redshirts, Ibsen looked farther ahead to the radical annihilation of the political state.

The god Pan had a special meaning for the liberals of the time. Plutarch had heard a voice from out of nowhere, commanding him to proclaim, "Pan is dead!" The early Christians made this incident, which Plutarch said occurred during the reign of Tiberius, coincide with the Crucifixion, thus marking an epoch, the end of the pagan era. Now Snoilsky saw the Christian era coming to an end with the liberal forces on the march against both the emperor and the pope. In Italy Garibaldi had defeated the king's armies in 1862. The 1863 insurrection in Poland inspired socialists with the hope that it would spread to other countries, and in that same year Ferdinand Lassalle in Germany founded the General German Workers' Association. The following year the First International convened in

London, attended by two thousand delegates. At the end of 1864, Pope Pius IX, in his Syllabus addressed to all Catholic episcopates, condemned socialism, communism, liberalism, and pantheism as among the chief errors of the age, a condemnation so sweeping that Napoleon III had to forbid its publication in France, knowing that it could only strengthen the radicals and the moderates by drawing them together.

In singling out Nero's golden palace from all the ruins in Rome, Snoilsky was following the German poet and satirist Heinrich Heine, who had referred to it in his 1843 article on communism. A band of early Christians had been tarred and set afire at Nero's palace, and Heine drew a parallel between the persecuted Galileans and the communists of his day. In prophesying the coming revolution, Heine had used "Pan is dead!" as a refrain.

At first Ibsen may have thought of Julian as a kind of Kierkegaard, waging war against the established church.[9] But there is every reason to suppose, in the light of subsequent developments, that Ibsen soon saw that the story of the apostate emperor could become something more than an antichurch tract and that it called for Heinesque treatment. Like Julian, Heine was an apostate. Jewish by birth and Christian for convenience's sake, he regarded himself as a pagan and hedonist. In his controversy with Ludwig Börne, a fellow revolutionary, Heine found a way of defining himself. The spirits of both men had been inflamed by the July Revolution of 1830, and both had exulted at the prospect of a new social order. But Heine's ardor quickly cooled as he saw that the changes would be merely political without any change in man himself. Börne, playing Robespierre to Heine's Danton, thought him an esthete without faith in the great cause. In his reply, Heine designated himself and Börne as representatives of two opposed outlooks, that of the Nazarene and that of the Hellene. The incorruptible, unwavering Börne was the Nazarene, willing to renounce personal happiness for the sake of a magnificent idea. Heine, the sensualist, regarded the flesh and the senses as having claims on the soul. "All men are either Jews or Hellenes, men ascetic in their instincts, hostile to beauty, spiritually zealous, or men of vigorous good cheer, openhearted, and practical."[10]

Heine tipped the scales in favor of the Hellene. When Matthew Arnold appropriated the dualism and relabeled it Hebraism and Hellenism, he restored the balance, and in that form it was a reflection of the conflict within Ibsen. The playwright knew that here he had the theme for a universal drama that would resonate with his own thoughts and feelings. His ultimate aim in writing this play, what kept him working at it over a period of years, was the prospect of formulating a worldview in which his own shortcomings would prove to be advantages. The inadequacies that went into the creation of Earl Skule and Peer Gynt would, when combined with the steely virtues of Brand, result in a more comprehensive grasp of the human experience through the ages. The career of the apostate ruler would serve as a template on which Ibsen's own career would take shape, and the revolutions of the nineteenth century would be seen as occurring directly above Julian's time in the spiral staircase of history.

At first this broad conception of the work must have seemed quite feasible. The problem was that he put off work on it. He was distracted by Norwegian politics and engaged in a spiteful feud with Bjørnson. And as time went by, the outline of his great drama had to undergo a radical change.

Three factors contributed to this transformation. There was, first of all, Ibsen's growing prosperity, with a concomitant abandonment of Brand's idealism. And then there was the reality of contemporary events, the slippery monster that had somehow to be grasped and held and confined in one neat concept. And finally, there was Ibsen's discovery of a philosophical school different from both Kierkegaard and Hegel.

The neatly shaved, smartly dressed Ibsen of 1870 was a far different man from the bearded and unkempt bohemian who wrote *Brand.* To the new man Julian the Apostate appeared as a worshipper of beauty who after a crushing childhood under Christianity broke free and, upon becoming emperor, restored the pagan gods. To this new Ibsen, living a comfortable, bourgeois existence, *Brand* was only an esthetic work, "an artistic work, pure and simple, and not a bit of anything else."

Yet while he was composing *Brand*, he could write to Bjørnson that estheticism was "as great a curse to poetry as theology is to religion," and take satisfaction in having "purged myself of that esthetic point of view." Near the end of act two, the hero could proudly say, "My sabbath hymn / Is sung: I ride my Pegasus no more," and resolve to devote himself to a sacred task. Yet within the next five or six years Ibsen did a complete volte-face. In 1871 he could refer to *Brand* as a "disease" that he had to drive out of his system.[11] It is hard to believe he could have undergone such a complete transformation in such a short time. In a sense, he didn't. There was no transformation; there was only a change of profiles, one side of the man turned to reveal the other side. Julian, before and after his apostasy, is a double portrait of Ibsen. He remarked to a friend, "In the character of Julian . . . there is much more of what I have lived through in spirit than I care to acknowledge to the public."[12]

Brandes experienced at first hand the two aspects of Ibsen. In July 1871 he had been warmly embraced by the talkative nihilist and political revolutionary. A little over a year later, in September 1872, Brandes paid him another visit in Dresden. He now saw Ibsen in a different light. They took strolls, had a repast at an inn, where the waiter was impressed by "the barbarian ornament [*barbariske Pragt*]" in Ibsen's buttonhole. Thence on to tea or coffee in Ibsen's apartment.

In his memoirs, Brandes gives a vivid assessment of the successful author:

> Not tall, but handsome, and with an athletic build, massive head, thick neck, powerful shoulders, he looked like a man who would have to be beaten down with clubs in a fight. He did not talk much, even though with me he was forthcoming. The strange thing about him was how quietly and slowly he spoke, and that he never smiled, not even when the other person smiled first. At times he made one feel uneasy. If one word could describe him it would be "threatening." He could seem frightening, his eyes always observant. At those moments he looked very authoritarian. He looked like a man who was accustomed in the presence of others to take the position of a schoolmaster with his boys, and accustomed to inspiring a certain apprehension.
>
> Gathered up in him were forty-two years of bitterness and hatred. His contempt for human beings was boundless. He was aristocratic in the extreme, and consistent in his position. It was an article of faith with him that all politicians, that is, men elected to parliament but not men like Bismarck, were hypocrites, liars, drivelers, dogs. They made their living off the struggle for political rights, which meant that the most ridiculous political dilettantes made themselves heard, and had to be heard, regarding the country's business. This bourgeois state and the fuss made over it should be shoved aside; it had had its day. Political organizations had rightly acquired a bad, almost ridiculous reputation throughout Europe. His hatred of the false struggle for liberties threatened to subvert his interest in the truth. He made a big speech praising the knout. "Don't ever disparage the knout," he burst out enthusiastically. "It rids the people of unhealthy fat."
>
> The decisive freedom was social freedom, spiritual freedom, freedom of thought, freedom of conscience. Working for these under a modern, sensible form of absolute monarchy was just as good as under the government of some small tyrants, even better. He despised the liberal party in Norway and regarded most of Norway's farmers as dirty, selfish riffraff.

With his unbounded belief that only a monarchy could sustain an aristocratic spirit and break the liberals, Ibsen condemned the republicanism of Bjørnson.

> The important thing was for a nation to make its contribution to world progress. A government was worth something when it drove the nation to accomplish something great and memorable. . . .
>
> At first I could not get him to read for me even a bit of [*Emperor and Galilean*]. Since he still had to make a copy to polish the prose dialogue, he didn't wish me to see the first, inferior version. He said, "I never write a line without

asking myself, what will Georg Brandes think of it? So why should I let you see the rough version?" All the same, he soon read aloud long sections for me, among them the scenes between Julian and the mystic Maximus. His voice, soft and quiet, was particularly suited to rendering the uncanny and eerie."[13]

When *Emperor* is read as autobiography, Libanius, the eloquent orator and sharp logician, is Brandes in a himation. He is Brandes in his fight against Rasmus Nielsen, and the conflict between science and religion in the nineteenth century resumes the conflict between pagans and Christians. In the early scenes Julian is positioned between Agathon, the Christian (who will suffer for his faith and be driven mad), and Libanius, just as Ibsen was positioned between the Kierkegaardian Brand and the unprincipled Peer Gynt. The tension between the sophist intellectual and the doubting Roman prince reflects the uneasy relationship of the most outspoken anti-Christian in the Nordic countries and the cautious poet who would not take a public stand against the established religion. Brandes, in his own words, fought "not only against theology, but against all so-called revealed religion. . . . I regarded the faith . . . as a harmful, destructive, disastrous power, and I thought it was meritorious to repress it."[14] Brandes wanted Ibsen to raise a banner and openly declare himself as in his camp, an anti-Christian, political liberal. But Ibsen would not. Libanius at the end of act two says of Julian, "This princely youth is a menace to enlightenment."

The meeting of Libanius and Julian in part two, after a long separation, probably carries with it Ibsen's feelings about his meeting with Brandes in Dresden. There was a warm embrace; they were friends and brothers to each other, but beneath the surface the two men were of different species. Yet Ibsen wanted Brandes in his corner. The self-centeredness and vanity in his meeting with the critic are brought out when Julian says goodbye to Libanius. "I commission you, my Libanius, to write a panegyric on me. . . . I hope you will compose something that shall do honor both to the orator and to his subject. This task, my Libanius, shall be my gift to you. I know of nothing more fitting to offer to a man like you."[15] This is probably what Ibsen was thinking when he said goodbye to Brandes in Dresden. It certainly came to pass.

Later in 1872, in the autumn, Ibsen read the first part of his double drama to Lorentz Dietrichson, the man who, years before, had read Julian's story to Ibsen. The reading took up the time from supper to midnight.

"Ibsen had no outstanding talent as a reader, but there was still an unusual and fine enjoyment in hearing him read, with his pleasant voice and his dignified presentation, clinically free from anything unnatural, and where of course everything found the right tone and emphasis."

Dietrichson was profoundly impressed. Hearing the last scene of part one,

Caesar's Apostasy, with Julian and Maximus coming up from the depths beneath the church into the light to claim the kingdom, Dietrichson felt that *Emperor* might well be the greatest literary work of the time. He went home rather shaken, confident that he had heard one of the most remarkable works in the realm of tragedy since Shakespeare.[16]

The enormous challenge facing Ibsen was to find a way of reconciling opposites. It was easy enough to see all phenomena as consisting in dyads; Brand versus Peer Gynt on the personal level; Christianity versus paganism on the historical level; thesis versus antithesis on the philosophical level. The problem lay in finding or even envisioning a level on which these opposites would coalesce and be united. Not surprisingly, he made no progress; he was unable even to draft an outline. He was confronted by the same problem that philosophers and historians have always had to contend with in one way or another, a resolution to the conflict of opposites. While Hegel's theory of sublation offered a theoretical and very abstract answer to Heine's dualism, Ibsen had to test it against the events that were taking place all around him and to examine the causes behind those events. And there sign met countersign.

During the years that Ibsen wrestled with the Julian material, Europe was struck by a series of political earthquakes that made it impossible for him to organize his thoughts. The good thing was that the turmoil within him was reflected in the turmoil without. The unfortunate thing was that the holy grail of a great synthesis kept eluding him.

For Ibsen, the path to the future was blocked by the bourgeois state, the political organization that was defined by the number of liberties it either granted or denied its different social classes. This state would be replaced by a higher concept, first by being opposed by an equally powerful force, and out of this conflict would emerge a higher order of human organization. In Heine, Ibsen could read a sketch of this mighty drama.

> Communism is the secret name of the dread antagonist setting proletarian rule with all its consequences against the present bourgeois regime. It will be a frightful duel. How will it end? No one knows but gods and goddesses acquainted with the future. We know only this much: communism, though little discussed now and loitering in hidden garrets on miserable straw pallets, is the dark hero destined for a great, if temporary, role in modern tragedy.

At the same time (Heine was writing in 1842), he foresaw

> the ghastliest war of destruction—which would unfortunately call the two noblest nations of civilization into the arena, to the ruin of both: France and Germany.... That, however, would only be the first act of the great melodrama,

> the prologue as it were. The second act is the European and the World Revolution, the great duel between the destitute and the aristocracy of wealth; and in that there will be no mention of either nationality or religion; there will be only one fatherland, the globe, and only one faith, that in happiness on earth. Will the religious doctrines of the past rise in all countries, in desperate resistance—and will perhaps this attempt constitute the third act? Will the old absolutist tradition reenter the stage, though in a new costume and with new cues and slogans? How could that drama end?[17]

In 1870, following Heine's prediction and anticipating much that was to happen in the twentieth century, France and Germany went to war. It was a war that Prince Otto von Bismarck of Prussia deliberately provoked as part of his plan to create a German confederation of states. Outside Germany, everyone expected the mighty French army under Emperor Napoleon III to deliver a sharp reminder to the aggressive Prussian that France was the ruling power in Europe. Instead the world witnessed the astonishing defeat of the French at Sedan in September 1870. The French army was thoroughly routed and 100,000 soldiers captured. Louis Napoleon was taken prisoner, and on September 4 the Third Republic was established in France. The German army then besieged Paris, which finally capitulated on January 28, 1871. Germany's defeat of France was one of the most devastating victories in military history, certainly the greatest since Napoleon defeated the German forces at Jena. Writing to his wife, Kaiser William said it was like a dream.

How had this victory against all expectations been possible? The Franco-Prussian War revealed that the power and glory of France had been an illusion. What was thought to be the strongest army in Europe was actually riddled with corruption. Louis Napoleon had thought he could put 450,000 troops in the field, but one third of these existed only on paper.

These events were devastating to Ibsen. He hated the triumph of numbers, of men and materiel, over the spirit. He had hoped for the defeat of Germany. Instead he found himself, as he put it in a poem in December 1870, standing "in the ruins of shattered dreams."[18]

Just as the Dano-Prussian War had produced the intellectual crisis in Ibsen that resulted in *Brand*, so the Franco-Prussian War produced another that spurred him to rethink his plans for his Julian play. From his apartment in Dresden, he could observe at first hand the situation in Germany. During the first weeks of the war, the country was at a standstill. So was his progress on the Julian drama.

"Current events are claiming too much of my attention. . . . No one can imagine what Germany is going through now. All industry is practically shut down. All activities have stopped. Everyone is dressed in mourning. It's all too terrible."[19]

"Dresden has fifteen thousand prisoners to provide for; and the arrival of four thousand more has been announced. Two thousand sick and wounded lie in the hospitals. Huge barracks have been built quite near our house for the Imperial Guard, and we see them pass every day, taking the walks prescribed for their health. They show no signs of having suffered any hardships at Metz. They are dressed as if for parade. The sick and wounded Saxons ordered home look as if they had gone through much more. The Frenchmen are very well treated and bear their captivity with incredible indifference."[20]

Brute force and cold calculation had won out over the immaterial, spiritual forces. Logistics won the war, not heroism. The time longs for beauty, but of this Bismarck knows nothing. Under the black and white of sorrow, the deadly colors of the Prussian clout, the bright colors of a great deed will never come forth as a butterfly from its cocoon. The victory of the German armies, under the mobilizing genius of Moltke, was the victory of numbers.

There's no feat worth celebration
Since that rising of the nation,
Splendid, beautiful and free,
Turned to staff machinery.
Pared away by calculation,—
Since von Moltke's cerebration
Murdered warfare's poesy.
(John Northam translation)

Writing this in Dresden in December 1870, Ibsen identified himself with the people in besieged Paris. Like them, he was surrounded by the enemy, the Germans, as he described himself in his "Balloon Letter to a Swedish Lady," which enraged his fellow club members.

To any thinking person the fall of Paris meant much more than a military victory. Paris was the most beautiful of capitals, the center of European culture. For Ibsen, with his Carlylean distrust of numbers, this invasion of the German army signified the calamitous triumph of machinery over art and beauty.

In a December letter to Brandes he said, "The old illusory France has been smashed to bits, and as soon as the new, de facto Prussia is smashed too, we shall enter the age of the future in one leap. How the old ideas will come tumbling about our ears."

In this new age German might and French art (as in Heine) would be subsumed. And with that thought in mind, Ibsen could write optimistically, "my new work became strikingly clear to me."[21]

While he does not provide specific information about this new era, he is quite clear as to what is wrong with the one he lives in. Fundamental to his position is opposition to the state, meaning an institution in which politicians court the voting public in order to win and hold office. The voting public wants liberties for itself, various kinds of freedoms, almost always materialistic. What was needed was a radically new vision of humanity itself. In his essay "Abydos," written in 1869 or 1870 (and unpublished in his lifetime), Ibsen wrote, "The main thing is not to introduce up-to-date improvements in what already exists. It is simply a matter of re-creating the whole spiritual environment of the individual, of tearing down prejudices a thousand years old—yes, to assail up to a point the nation itself. But anything like that could be accomplished only by a fearless and autocratic government. A democratically representative government on the European model would naturally end in some mild prating about 'the rights of man.'"[22]

While Prussia was not in fact crushed, as Ibsen had hoped, something else occurred that substantiated his view that the great conflicts repeat themselves over and over in the spiral staircase of history. The stunning defeat of the French was followed by a series of even more astonishing events that put nineteenth-century Europe directly above Julian's reign, with the same forces once again in conflict.

After the defeat of the French army, a new provisional government was set up in Paris. The German army besieged the capital, which finally yielded on January 28, 1871. Ten days earlier, William I, the king of Prussia, had been proclaimed emperor of a new confederation by the various princes of Germany in a ceremony held at the Palace of Versailles outside Paris. The Germans consummated their victory by imposing humiliating but not unbearable—conditions on the French. The politicians quickly accepted these terms, knowing that France was rich enough to pay the huge indemnities and to carry on as before, its territory virtually intact and its businesses flourishing. Only its pride had been seriously damaged.

What happened next was still more astonishing than the rout of the French army. The citizens of Paris rose up in protest against what the politicians had arranged. A bitter war ensued, more virulent than the Franco-Prussian War. This war was not a war between two political states, which shared fundamentally the same aims and purposes, but a civil war between two classes, the bourgeoisie and the proletariat.

During the siege of Paris, the Parisian proletariat, backed by the armed force of the National Guard, had formed an uneasy alliance with the Government of National Defense. The latter capitulated to the Germans in January 1871, but the National Guard refused to surrender its weapons. Two months later, Louis Adolphe Thiers, the president of the new republic, allied himself with the Germans. With the support of Prussian soldiers he tried to steal the artillery of the

National Guard. This treasonable act sparked a spontaneous uprising of the Parisian working people. The government troops were chased out; the National Guard defected, disavowing its allegiance to the official French government, and set up a committee to organize the defense of Paris. Almost spontaneously an organization of the working people arose to fill the vacuum left by the departure of Thiers and the bourgeois administration.

This new association of working people, the Paris Commune, fired Ibsen's imagination by fitting in perfectly with his theory of history. In March the Commune abolished the standing army of subscription. In April it set a ceiling of six thousand francs a year for salaries of Commune members. It decreed that all unused factories be taken over by the laborers formerly employed in them and run by a cooperative society. It was the French proletariat who had held out against the Germans, while the capitalists and the bourgeoisie in France and Germany joined forces to crush the Commune. This alignment of forces revealed the fault line beneath the political landscape.

Out of the conflict between Germany and France, a third force had emerged, a force that promised to replace the political state with a people united by a common cause. The anarchist Ibsen, who wanted to torpedo the ark of state, saw in the headlines from Paris the possible fulfillment of his cherished dreams. Here was something close to his ideal stateless society. For Ibsen as for Marx, the significance of the Commune lay in its showing pragmatically how an organization of the proletariat could take the place of the bourgeois state. "With the struggle in Paris," wrote Marx, "the struggle of the working class against the capitalist class and its state has entered upon a new phase. Whatever the immediate outcome may be, a new point of departure, of importance in world history, has been gained."[23] Marx and Ibsen were alike in their willingness to destroy the political state, though they differed about the ideal society, Marx being much more materialistic than Ibsen. Although Ibsen was far less politically engaged than Marx—to Ibsen, political involvement meant cooperating with the machinery of the state—both men saw the bourgeois state as the great impediment to progress, material progress for Marx, spiritual enhancement for Ibsen.

Moreover, there were signs that the Commune was only a foretoken of what was to come. The fires in the streets of Paris spread quickly to Germany and Scandinavia. In the spring of 1871 August Bebel addressed the German Reichstag, promising that within a few decades all of Europe would adopt the slogan of the Communards: "War against the palaces, peace with the cottages, abolition of poverty and idleness." It was this speech that brought Bismarck to recognize the danger and power of socialism.

For Ibsen's purposes the advent of the Commune could hardly have been more propitious. Not only did it suggest the real possibility of a third force, but it replayed the conflict Julian had faced in the fourth century. The Communards saw themselves as resurrected Christians. At a festival in the Tuileries, a portrait of Jesus was set up in front of the speaker's stand, as a sign of the Communards' solidarity with the early Christians in their belief in the equality of all men. Their supporters and opponents alike often referred to the Communards as apostles and prophets,[24] just as even earlier Saint-Simon had called his brand of socialism "le Nouveau Christianisme."

Even Friedrich Engels, Marx's "general," saw the similarities between the early Christians and nineteenth-century socialists. Both were heralds of the future, both made up lower-class movements, and both suffered martyrdom. "Both are persecuted and subjected to harassment," he wrote. "And in spite of all persecution, nay, even spurred on by it, they forge victoriously, irresistibly ahead."[25]

Ibsen the Mystic

In Ibsen's challenging project, the story of *Emperor and Galilean* had to play itself out on three levels simultaneously: the autobiographical, the historical-political, and the philosophical. From his very first encounter with Julian, Ibsen saw himself as his reincarnation, his divided personality a replica of Julian's. And on the historical level, the Commune provided a parallel to fourth-century Christianity. But these two levels had to have a foundation in a system of thought that was both ancient and modern.

Although Ibsen has been seen mainly as a playwright who dealt with social problems and who displayed a remarkable insight into the psychological makeup of his characters, what sustained and underlay most of his plays was a particular philosophy that embraced the leading ideas of his time. More than any other dramatist of the post-Goethe era and arguably more than any other imaginative writer of the nineteenth century, he grasped, assimilated, and expressed in artistic form all the great themes of the period. Although he minimized the extent of his reading, a study of his works reveals him to be a man who wanted to know all that was significant in science and philosophy and who kept himself well informed. In spite of his protestations to the contrary, Ibsen was a widely read man, and he knew where to find what he was looking for. When he was not reading on his own, he would be read to by his wife and son. Apparently, in a family in which there was no music, no dancing, no games, no cards, reading was the one activity apart from the partaking of meals that the three of them shared.

Brandes was well aware of the breadth of Ibsen's knowledge. "While he felt himself on a war footing with Norway, he tried to acquire . . . the cultural resources of the new Germany, as far as they were available to him and as far as he had use for them. They were seldom on his level. He was a constant attendant at the lectures given in the literary societies in Dresden."[1]

In philosophical discussions when the two found themselves at loggerheads, Ibsen could hold his own against Brandes. While Ibsen studied the German speculative philosophers, Brandes turned to the English rationalists and chided Ibsen for not adopting a "modern scientific point of view."[2] Brandes urged John Stuart Mill on Ibsen, while Ibsen found more merit in the preacher and divine Hans Lassen Martensen (1808–84). Like Ibsen in his opposition to scientific determinism and in his distrust of political institutions, Bishop Martensen believed that the looked-for end of all things was the union of body and soul, and that progress toward this goal would be made by the church as a community of spirits, under the guidance of a strong personality. In his *Christian Ethics* (*Den christelige Ethik*), published in the spring of 1871, Martensen presented Christianity as a religion that endeavored to create this paradise on earth. A year later, as if in riposte, Brandes published his translation of parts of Mill's *Utilitarianism*, setting the Englishman's practical morality against the Dane's chiliasm.

Writing to Brandes, Ibsen turned the tables, setting Martensen against Mill.

> When I remember that there are authors who write on philosophy without knowing Hegel, or without any knowledge of German scholarship in general, many things seem to me permissible. I must candidly confess that I cannot in the least conceive of any advancement or any future in the movement represented by Mill. I cannot understand your taking the trouble to translate this work, the sagelike philistinism of which reminds me of Cicero and Seneca. . . . I also believe that you do Mill a gross injustice when you doubt the truth of his assertion that he got all his ideas from his wife.—You once remarked in a conversation with me that German philosophy set itself the task of defining the meaning of things, whereas English philosophy concerned itself with showing the law of things. This remark made me want to read the English philosophers, but it does not seem to me that Mill has in the least accomplished what, according to you, was his task. "Things" are surely not all kinds of improper and fortuitous occurrences. There may be a great deal of acumen displayed in such a work; but if that passes for science, then [Martensen's] "The Ethics of Christianity" is also a scientific work.[3]

The philosophical difference between the two men is brought out in *Emperor and Galilean.* Libanius is the anti-Christian pagan, trying to convert the young Julian, still a Christian. Desiring an enlightened humanity and a world of beauty, Libanius stands opposed to the seer Maximus, calling him a juggler who enshrouds in riddles the great ideas of the past. This is Brandes's rationalism opposed to Ibsen's mysticism.

Emperor and Galilean is unique among Ibsen's works in its mysticism, so uncharacteristic of the plays on which his fame mainly rests. One reason for his rating this play as his greatest is that in it he voiced his deepest philosophical thoughts, ideas that would underlie the plays that followed, ideas that could not be fully expressed in the realistic theater. However great the impact made by contemporary events while he was writing it, the great inspiration for this unwieldy drama came when Ibsen immersed himself in the study of speculative philosophy. What his drama required was a vision or concept that would see his own inner struggles, current events, and Julian's divided career as expressions of the same great, unending conflict. Like Ibsen, the historical Julian sought for mystical knowledge to justify his revolt against Christianity. Spiritual knowledge of one sort was to contend with spiritual knowledge of another sort. The young Julian studied Neoplatonism and was familiar with Manichaeism (which blended Christianity with Persian Magism, a belief in the coming of a savior in the person of a supremely wise man). These ideas were expounded in his essays "Upon the Sovereign Sun" and "On the Mother of the Gods." In the "Sun" essay, Julian prays to be released from matter, to ascend to the heavens and find an abiding place with the sun. What Ibsen's play required was a governing idea that would accommodate both Julian's visionary dream and a more modern version of it.

He found what he was looking for in the medieval concept of the three kingdoms. The major source of this philosophical and religious idea was Joachim of Flora (c. 1132–1202), a Cistercian monk living in Calabria, who saw the story of man on earth as divided into three ages, each corresponding to a person of the Holy Trinity: a kingdom of the Father, a kingdom of the Son, and a kingdom of the Spirit. These phases overlapped. The age of the Father was initiated with Adam, but it actually came into being with Abraham. The age of the Gospel, corresponding to the modern era, is a period of striving for mystic knowledge. The age of the Spirit is yet to come. That will be an age of contemplation, an age of enlightenment, with men so wise they would no longer need a ruler or a government or any discipline except self-discipline. Therein lay part of Joachim's appeal to Ibsen, for whom the political state was anathema. Equally attractive to him was Joachim's doctrine of immanency, his conviction that the third age would not be otherworldly but would come about on this side of heaven. His three-realm concept violated orthodox Christian beliefs in promising perfection here on earth and in a period not too far in the future.

Ibsen had told his critics that his new drama would provide a positive philosophy, a brighter view of the human condition than the darkness and anguish of *Brand.* If German militarism caused him to despair, German philosophy offered hope. Nothing indicates better the change in Ibsen than his willingness to turn to Hegel for this more positive outlook. In *Peer Gynt,* he had singled out the German philosopher as the source of all that was wrong with the world. Now he saw

Hegel as offering, at least theoretically, an alternative to the seemingly irreconcilable conflict between Brand and Peer Gynt, the prospect of mediation between opposites, the conception of common ground between the ascetic and the esthete, the Nazarene and the Hellene. In the Hegelian concept of history, opposites would cancel each other out, and with this possibility in mind, Ibsen saw a new era rising out of the ruins.

The Hegelian triad, vulgarly thought of as thesis, antithesis, and synthesis, now seemed to provide a part in history for a man like himself. By looking backward, by being a political reactionary, by standing up to the mob, by worshipping beauty and disdaining the cult of numbers, he would actively further the spiritual development of the human race. Julian had tried to reestablish the pagan cult of sensual beauty and joy in the physical world but had succeeded only in strengthening Christian otherworldliness. Out of opposites came progress.

Thoughts like these renewed his interest in the Julian drama. Joachim's vision of three kingdoms would have struck Ibsen as being in perfect harmony with Hegel's triadic system, which would provide the basis for a drama now seen as being in three parts. The first two would present the conflict in its various guises; Hegelian (thesis and antithesis); Julian (Christian versus pagan); contemporary history (Germany versus France); Ibsenian (Brand versus Peer Gynt). The third part would attempt some sort of resolution, giving the whole work the structure of an Aeschylean trilogy. The unexpected emergence of the Paris Commune augured that the Third Kingdom was not entirely illusory.

This concept of a Third Kingdom, emerging out of opposites, lies at the very heart of the Julian drama. Under the guidance of Maximus, the mystic philosopher, the young prince hopes that he will be the one who inaugurates a new era, one that will supersede and change forever what had gone before. Maximus calls it the Third Empire. It is, in his words, "the empire of the great mystery; that empire which shall be founded on the tree of knowledge and the tree of the cross together, because it hates and loves them both, and because it has its living sources under Adam's grove and under Golgotha."[4]

In acquainting himself with German thought, Ibsen must have been struck by the fact that the Neoplatonic thought of Julian's time was reemerging in the idealist philosophy of Germany after 1790. Here was another confirmation of how history could be pictured as a spiral staircase, with significant events and ideas repeating themselves, only in a higher phase of development.[5]

If Ibsen did not on his own perceive the similarity between the new German philosophy and the old mysticism, he would have read about it in Heine and heard about it during the War of the Commune. Around the time of the great French Revolution there was a revival of interest in Joachim in Germany.

Lessing cites him in *Die Erziehung des Menschengeschlechts*, as does F. W. J. von Schelling in his philosophical treatises. Heine captured the essence of Joachim's millenarianism in a poem, "Auf diesem Felsen bauen wir."

> Upon these rocks we'll build a church
> To celebrate the splendid,
> The Third and Final Testament;
> Our sufferings are ended,
>
> Destroyed is the duality
> That long has bound us fast;
> The stupid torment of the flesh
> Is flung aside at last.
>
> Do you hear God's word in the darkened sea?
> Thousand-voiced He exclaims.
> And can't you see above our heads
> The thousand God-lit flames?
>
> The holy Lord is in the light
> And in the night's abysses;
> And God is everything that is:
> He throbs in our kisses.[6]

Whether or not Ibsen opened his volume of Heine for thoughts about the Third Kingdom, there was another and more immediate source—the daily newspapers. There he would learn about the death of Pierre Leroux (1798–1871). More than the poet Heine, this political activist would have appealed to Ibsen. The patron saint of socialists (he was the first to use the word "socialist," in 1838), Leroux died April 12, when the international forces were trying to destroy the Commune. The Commune accorded him full honors at his funeral, "not for the partisan philosopher of the mystical school . . . but the political man who following those days in June courageously defended the vanquished."[7] Having read Hegel, Leroux believed in triads as pervading all things. He was an ascetic in morals, like Brand, and an anarchist opposed to the state, like Ibsen. Most important for Ibsen's developing thoughts, Leroux was a mystic. Like Maximus, he was a pantheist who believed in an earthly god who would come into existence with the advent of the Third Kingdom, in which man does not need to die in order to live like a god on earth.

Leroux provided an almost perfect nineteenth-century counterpart to Maximus. Leroux's belief in a Third Kingdom amounted to a new religion uniting a rejuvenated Christianity with philosophy, a philosophy that embraced science and religion. Leroux said that philosophy "elevates both art and science . . . to an art that heeds the suggestions of the heart and by a kind of divine process creates a work that passes beyond even the known facts of science." Art is necessary because "it has as its end not merely the knowledge of and the explanation of things but the development of things, the betterment of the soul and the perfection of the world."[8] (This chimes in perfectly with Ibsen's remarks in 1887, when he declared in a public speech that it was his belief that poetry, philosophy, and religion will one day be subsumed in one new category.)[9]

Although Ibsen would have employed other terms, he saw the historical significance of the Commune, and it energized him as he worked on his "world-historical," autobiographical drama, in which the idea of a Third Kingdom would be pervasive, an eternal principle. The historical Julian would attempt to move beyond both paganism and Christianity; the present-day Communards offered the prospect of a society that would infuse the bourgeois state with a spiritual quality.

Julian as Ibsen

Julian was the nephew of Constantine the Great, the ruler who had made Christianity the official religion in the Roman Empire. After Constantine's death, and after much internecine and bloody fighting among family members, Julian became emperor and instituted the worship of the pagan gods as an alternative to Christianity. Julian's own writings suggest that this was a thinking man's decision. Having studied the Greek philosophers, he saw as much if not greater virtue, morally as well as logically, in a belief in a panoply of gods as in one.

This simple explanation for Julian's apostasy did not suit the aims of the playwright. Ibsen's hero was shunted into paganism, not by his scholarly studies but by a series of events that turned him against the faith of his childhood. When the young Julian is introduced to the idea of the Third Kingdom by Maximus, he has already passed through the first two kingdoms. In act one, set in Constantinople, Julian had experienced the repressive force of Christianity. In act two, set in Athens, he had breathed the liberating air of paganism and undergone the rite of passage for young men, initiation into the Eleusinian Mysteries. After the tyranny of the Nazarene came the freedom of the Hellene.

Recognizing now the cruelty and asceticism of the Christian regime, he succumbs to a longing for pagan sensuality. "Wasn't sin beautiful in Sodom and Gomorrah? Didn't Jehovah pour fire on what Socrates didn't shun?" Now he is torn between the two and seeks a new revelation. He imagines himself transported to a ship in a windless sea, heaving to and fro between life and death. "I feel like Daedalus, between sky and sea. A dizzying height and an abysmal depth."

"There must come a new revelation. Or a revelation of something new. It *must* come, I say. The time is ripe."

For a moment he sees himself as a martyr, with a crown of thorns. But when he tears off the crown that he is wearing, a wreath of roses, he is reminded of what he learned in pagan Athens: "The old beauty is no longer beautiful, and the new truth is no longer true."[1]

In Ephesus, against the advice of his rational friends, he consults with Maximus, who is not an invented character. Ibsen found in the historical record the man who could introduce Julian to the great all-encompassing vision. A contemporary described the seer: "The very pupils of his eyes seemed endowed with wings.... His beard was long and grey, his eyes revealed the impulses of his soul. Both to eye and ear his person had a kind of harmony." This theurgist won the respect and confidence of Julian, who praised him as "one who surpasses all men in my time."[2] Ibsen pictured Maximus as a lean man of middle height with a bronzed, hawklike face, gray hair and beard, but pitch-black eyebrows and mustache, wearing a pointed cap and a black robe.

Riven by doubts, longing for an alternative to both Christianity and paganism, Julian is extremely receptive to the esoteric teachings of Maximus, while the mystic sees in the young prince the possible embodiment of his dreams. His hope is that Julian will succeed where the other great redeemers—Moses, Alexander, Jesus—have failed. Julian is seduced by the mystic's description of the three kingdoms. Maximus prophesies that a bride shall be given to Julian, and that the marriage of body and soul will prepare for the founding of the Third Empire. Julian will succeed where the others failed because he has been promised what the others lacked—union with a pure woman.

Now the great opposites come into play. Even as Maximus expounds the doctrine of the Third Kingdom, a contradictory revelation comes to Julian. In a state of intoxication, where Pan and Logos are one and the same, where the unconscious wells up, he has another, entirely different vision of himself: not as redeemer but as denier. He sees himself building the Third Empire by being the third great betrayer, the third denier, following Cain and Judas. The mystical forces have destined him to bring about the Third Empire by acting against it, by serving as a negative force. This scene, placed by Ibsen in the center of the first part, constitutes the philosophical foundation on which the whole drama rests. The religious conflict lies on the surface; beneath it is the conflict within Julian. The vision of the Third Kingdom is Maximus's vision; the vision of Julian as denier comes from within himself.

Yet he fights against it. Young Julian naturally wants to be a positive force, a hero in the traditional vein, and he refuses the part fate or destiny or history has allotted him. "I defy necessity. I will not serve it! I am free, free, free!"[3] His protests are futile, of course. Julian fails to see that necessity, the spirit of history, has grabbed him by the scruff of the neck. He has no sooner uttered his defiance than news arrives that changes his station in life. The emperor Constantius has bestowed on Julian the purple robe of power, conferring on him the title of caesar.

He exults in the thought that now he can be what he wants to be—a positive force, not one of the great deniers. Now he need not theorize about the empire of the spirit. He feels that with the power he now possesses he can found "the great and beautiful empire."[4] He believes that he is acting freely, not accepting Judas's role, but acting on his own. A willing belief becomes a firm conviction when he learns that the emperor Constantius is offering Julian not only the mantle of power but also the pure woman, Constantius's irreproachable sister Helena. Julian takes his marriage with Helena as an augury of the new order in society and a new phase in his own life.

As a first step he thinks of breaking his covenant with Christianity, the power that has oppressed him all his life. "My whole youth has been one unending fear of the Emperor and of Christ.... When I felt the body's sweet desires, the prince of self-denial would strike terror into me with his: die in this world to live in the next."[5]

He turns his back decisively on Christianity when he learns that Helena the pure woman has been unfaithful to him. In fact, she had never loved the unprepossessing, plain-looking philosopher. She had as lovers both Julian's half brother Gallus and her Christian confessor. The truth comes out when she is poisoned by servants of Constantius, who were ordered to do so because she is pregnant and capable of producing an heir to the throne. Her mind inflamed, she raves about her lovers (in speeches "too improper to be recounted for English readers"[6]). Julian's belief in the possibility of a body-soul union is shattered.

Part one, *Caesar's Apostasy*, ends with the scene in which his denial of Christianity is acted out, one of the most powerful scenes that Ibsen ever conceived, one created wholly out of his imagination. It takes place in the catacombs in the city of Vienne in Gaul. In the nave of the church Helena lies in her coffin, surrounded by wailing women singing psalms in praise of "the pure woman." They touch the bier, expecting miracles. To Julian this worship of Helena is the embodiment of the hypocrisy, the untruth of Christianity. His guiding genius Maximus tells him, "Be a thrall under the terror, or monarch in the land of sunshine and joy.... You try to unite what cannot be united—to reconcile two irreconcilables. ... You must rise above the Galilean, if you would reach the imperial throne."[7]

Julian descends into the depths of the vault beneath the church to make a blood sacrifice to the pagan gods. In the church the choir sings, "Our Father which art in heaven!" Julian ascends from the depths, blood on his forehead, chest, and hands, having "cloven the mists of terror." Taking command of the Roman soldiers, he says, "All ways lie open before us. Up into the daylight! Through the church! The liars shall be silenced!" while the choir chants in antiphony, "Lead us not into temptation."[8]

The three-part drama that occupied Ibsen's mind for years must have ended with a vision or a sign pointing toward a realm of being, both political and spiritual, that would transcend the kingdom of the tree and the kingdom of the cross. The uplifting ending of part one, Julian emerging from the darkness of the catacombs, ready to abjure an oppressive religion, would be repeated by a scene of transcendence, something like the final moments of *Brand.* But history, neither ancient nor modern, would not allow that. Contemporary events did not behave as Ibsen wanted them to.

For a while, when Ibsen saw the Commune, unexpectedly and spontaneously, emerge out of the Franco-Prussian War, he glimpsed the possibility of a Third Kingdom. Unfortunately and inevitably, the Commune, with power invested in the people, quickly turned into its opposite. In May, Louis Charles Delescluze, the Robespierre of the Commune, assumed virtual dictatorial power and was made head of the Committee on Public Safety. The stateless Commune had become a dictatorship.

Ibsen lamented to Brandes: "Is it not shameful of the Commune in Paris to have gone and spoiled my excellent state theory—or rather non-state theory? The idea is now ruined for a long time to come. I cannot even proclaim it in verse with any decency. But there is a sound core in it. I see that very clearly. And someday it will be put into practice, without any caricature."[9]

Then in turn the Commune was smashed by the combined armies of the capitalist countries. France and Germany joined forces to destroy it in a class war that was much more ferocious that the Franco-Prussian War. Twenty thousand to thirty thousand men, women, and children were killed in one week by the Versaillais authorities. In a word, there was no sign of a third force that would subsume what had gone before. There was to be no new stateless organization, no Hegelian sublation of opposites, no Third Kingdom. What had shimmered on the horizon as a possibility suddenly vanished, leaving the hard reality of a powerful, dominant Germany in its place.

Work bogged down as Ibsen grappled with the monster play in the summer and early fall of 1871. In July he requested books and articles on Julian from his publisher, which suggests that he was recasting the original scenario. All the real work was done from June 1871 to May 1873. By August 1872 he had completed the second part of what was to be a trilogy: "Julian and the Philosophers" in three acts; "Julian the Apostate" in three acts; "Julian on the Imperial Throne" in five acts.[10]

Later in 1872 he jettisoned this three-part drama, reducing it to two. The final product is a disturbing and, to most readers, disquieting drama. The two parts are set in violent opposition to each other, as the liberating apostate turns into a willful and tyrannical emperor.

Georg Brandes spoke for many readers when he complained that Julian in the second part loses the stature of a tragic hero. "The fact is that Julian in the first drama, when he is still warm and bright and strong, captivates the reader so much more than in the second. As his vanity grows beyond all bounds, as he becomes at first repulsive, then nearly comical, and finally pathetic, the reader's interest in him receives a blow from which it cannot recover."[11]

Part two in its final version is a serious letdown to anyone hoping for something as transcendent as the ending of part one. It pictures a long decline in Julian's fate and, disappointingly, in his character as well. The young Julian, quite sympathetic, open-minded, and forthright, undergoes a complete transformation and becomes a petty tyrant, vainglorious and superstitious. Just as Ibsen manipulated the factual account in part one to make Julian more sympathetic—inventing, for example, a nymphomaniac Helena—he changed facts in part two to make Julian an unlikable despot with scarcely any of his finer qualities left over from part one. The Julian of the annals may not have been cast in the heroic mold, but he was admirable in many ways. He was broad-minded and tolerant of the Christians. He certainly was not the divided soul Ibsen wanted him to be.

The result of Ibsen's rewriting of history is an intellectual drama in which the mind is engaged but the sympathies are thwarted. Julian becomes an obsessed ruler who vigorously, even mercilessly, tries to suppress Christianity. He becomes a megalomaniac, increasingly seeing himself not merely as a caesar but as a god to be worshipped. For him, "life and blood are not enough. He who hopes to rule must rule over men's minds, over their wills."[12]

Architecturally, however, the double drama offers the dedicated Ibsenite the pleasure of a beautifully organized work. The sharp contrast between the two parts is apparent not only in the change in the hero but also in the structure of the work, the two parts perfectly balanced against each other. Part two is in direct opposition to part one: act by act, what the first part affirms, the second contradicts. For instance, in the first act of part one, Julian is a Christian; in the corresponding act of part two, he immerses himself in the pagan world. In the third act of part one, Julian learns from Maximus about the Third Kingdom; in the corresponding act of part two, he learns from Maximus that he has drawn his sword against the Third Empire. Part one ends with Julian being hailed by his troops and winning victory on the battlefield, part two with his being slain by one of his own soldiers.

As Ibsen worked and reworked the ancient accounts, the less there was of

Julian and the more of himself. Julian is a compound, an amalgam, fifty parts the historical figure and fifty parts Ibsen. What the dramatist presents is as much a picture of himself as of the apostate. He made no attempt to disguise the autobiographical elements; quite the opposite. He said, "It is part of my own spiritual life that I am putting into this book. What I depict I have, under different conditions, lived through myself."[13]

He was so determined to make Julian a replica of himself that he altered the known facts and then denied having done so. He seemed blind to what he was doing and asserted, "I have adhered strictly to the historical facts,"[14] a quite preposterous claim.

Reasonably tolerant of the Christians in part one, Julian becomes, contrary to the historical record, increasingly monomaniacal in his hatred of the Christians. Ibsen had to defend his view of Julian as a ruthless persecutor of the Christians against his old friend Jakob Løkke, a philologist, who protested Ibsen's denigrations.

"My conception of the character of Emperor Julian is, I may say, in strict accordance with historical truth. On this point the newer historians, namely the German ones, are not to be trusted. Winkelmann, Lessing, Goethe, and Schiller have warped our view of things to the advantage of Greek paganism, and moreover, Christianity is not in much favor in Germany. So one has to go back to the sources, and that is what I have done.... On the whole, all the features I have used in my play are supported by tradition; they derive from the accounts of contemporaries, and many of them not just from Christians."[15]

The Julian who figures in the first part of the double drama is much like Ibsen before his great breakthrough, which came with *Brand*. The magnificent conclusion to part one, with Julian emerging from the catacombs of the church, ascending into the blinding light, calling on his new god Helios, captures in one moment Ibsen emerging from the years of literary failure and social oppression to take on a new role as a man of renown. The second part pictures the changed Ibsen, the esthete fond of fine things, imperious in manner, intolerant of opposition. It was the Brand in him doing violence to his Gyntian self. As Shaw says, Julian is "a grotesque mixture of superstition and monstrous vanity . . . making speeches . . . worthy of Peer Gynt at his most ludicrous."[16]

Julian in part two is a fanatic bound on a crusade against the Christians and more and more removed from humanity. As he fails to suppress the Christians, he becomes increasingly nihilistic; if he cannot destroy them, he would like to see the whole world perish. In much of this we see Ibsen condemning one part of himself. Like Ibsen, this Julian is a mess of contradictions. He worships the pagan gods, especially Cybele and Dionysus, the gods of harvest and drinking, yet he is abstemious, and demands that his courtiers lead temperate lives. His hero is Diogenes, rather than Apollo. He demands honesty from others, yet surrounds himself with obvious hypocrites who sing his praises in order to stay in his good graces.

Like Ibsen, who valued nothing so much as the medals he won, and who would even at times wear them at home,[17] this Julian is vainglorious and wants statues raised to himself. Like Ibsen, who could write, "My enemies shall be made to feel that, if I am not a builder, I am at least capable of destroying,"[18] this Julian is vindictive and unforgiving. Like Ibsen, Julian toward the end of the drama is an anarchist and destroyer, who would rather see the world perish than veer from the path he had chosen for it. "The whole human race is on the wrong track."[19] Ibsen the poet said he would willingly torpedo the ark of state because he hated it so much. He would return the world to its pre-Adamic condition, uncontaminated by human life. "The whole history of the world reminds me of a sinking ship; the only thing to do is save oneself."[20] And Julian in the central scene of part two, set in the ruins of the temple of Apollo, seeks isolation, the place where it is loneliest, because the whole world is a rubbish heap. Near the end of the play, Julian, seeing how the Christians cannot be crushed, exclaims, "Oh, that I could lay waste the world, Maximus. Is there no poison, no consuming fire that could lay creation desolate, as it was on that day when the spirit moved alone over the waters?"[21] This is Ibsen in his Catiline mode.

Concordance of Opposites

Read as autobiography, *Emperor and Galilean* captures the two incompatible sides of Ibsen's personality. And while that aspect of the epic is certainly revealing, the heart of the drama lies elsewhere. Ultimately, Ibsen wanted the work to be judged as a drama of ideas, an examination of the fundamental conflicts that activate all human endeavors, whether individual or social. In 1875, two years after *Emperor* was published, he said his chief concern as a dramatist was to present "the conflict between one's aims and one's abilities, between what man proposes and what is actually possible, constituting at once both the tragedy and comedy of mankind and of the individual."[1] This applies more to *Emperor* than to any other of his plays. And never did he struggle harder to resolve the conflict than in this double drama.

On the most accessible level, *Emperor* is like an epic Hollywood film, with Christians pitted against a tyrannical ruler, ending in huge battle scenes, the cross triumphant. On the level of psychological motivation, it is a fine study of a hero at war with himself. On a deeper level it offers an explanation of the way the muse of history works. For the patient and appreciative reader, all this provides enough matter to ponder. Still, it leaves him with a nagging thought that something is missing, that there is yet another level, a subatomic level that contains the elusive force that holds everything together.

Among the works of Ibsen's predecessors, Schiller's *Wallenstein* trilogy is most like it in conception and scope, and not least in its depiction of a not very admirable hero who fights against the role he must play on the world stage. Ibsen's essential genius, like that of the ancient tragedians, lay in his ability to dramatize grand philosophical ideas, to transform abstract concepts into theatrical scenes. He assimilated them into the narrative not in soliloquies, as Schiller did, but in atmospheric scenes in which the senses are as much involved as the intellect. In

Caesar's Apostasy, the first part of the double drama, wine, dancing girls, and flute players work on Julian's mind like drugs—"I hear light and I see music"—as he listens to Maximus expound the doctrine of the three kingdoms. The mystic's voice comes to Julian from outside. But in his wine-mad state Julian hears an inner voice telling him he shall be like Judas Iscariot.

Here at the heart of the drama in the precise center of part one, the spirit of progress is seen as embodied in either a redeemer like Jesus or a denier like Judas, both of them being essential to the historical process. Although Julian wants to be a positive force, he is not constituted that way. The question then arises: how does the negative force produce a positive result? The historical answer is that Julian strengthened the resolve of the Christians by promoting the pagan gods. But for the probing mind of Ibsen, the question demanded a philosophical answer. And the doctrine of the three kingdoms did not provide it. It accounted for Jesus but not for Judas, and the *idée maîtresse* of the drama was the role of the denier in history. In this scene, Maximus comes to realize Julian's true role when he says that Julian had striven to hinder the growth of the youth. When Julian tried to restore the pagan gods, he was moving backward in time; when he tried to repress the Christians, he was inhibiting the future.

While Maximus's dream of a new era appears to provide the dynamics of the plot, there is another vision that in fact determines the outcome of Julian's struggle with his destined role in history. It is a vision of the basic structure of the world, and it is a vision that is quite different from Maximus's millenarianism. It was so vital to the unfolding drama that Ibsen violated his principle of sticking to the historical record and limiting himself to ideas that Julian might have entertained, ascribing to fourth-century Julian a revelation experienced by a fifteenth-century philosopher.

He took it from Nicolas Cusanus, or Nicholas of Cusa (c. 1401–64), German scientist, mathematician, and philosopher. This cardinal of the Roman Catholic Church believed that if contraries were pushed to their extremes, they would vanish. This fusion of opposites would occur in an exalted state in which all limitations disappeared. God transcends all opposites, and God is in fact the *coincidentia oppositorum*. This understanding of the nature of God came to Nicholas in a vision while he was, like Julian, crossing the Aegean Sea, sailing from Constantinople to Venice on a papal mission in December 1437 or January 1438. The purpose of his voyage was to unite the Greek and Roman churches. In a letter to his patron Cardinal Cesarini, he described his revelation.

"Take now, revered father, what for long I have by divers paths of learning sought to attain. Attainment, however, was denied me until I was returning by sea from Greece, when, by what I believe was a supreme gift of the Father of

Lights from Whom is every perfect gift, I was led in the learning that is ignorance to grasp the incomprehensible; and this I was able to achieve not by way of comprehension but by transcending those perennial truths that can be reached by reason."[2]

Ibsen had to find a way of transforming the abstract idea of the coincidence of opposites into a drama. In this endeavor, the ideas of the German speculative philosophers came into play, and no one was more helpful to him than Friedrich Wilhelm Joseph von Schelling (1775–1854).

Although not much read or studied now, he was a significant and influential figure in the first decades of the nineteenth century. Goethe believed that Schelling was destined "to usher in a new intellectual epoch,"[3] and Heine devoted considerable space to him. His lectures in philosophy, in which he systematically undid what Hegel had wrought, attracted such various minds as Jacob Burckhardt, Michael Bakunin, Søren Kierkegaard, and Friedrich Engels. The essence of his thought was the need to turn physical nature into mind and to make the real become the ideal, the two being united in a world soul. For him, nature and spirit were originally one and the same, and the basic thrust of human development was to reunite the two. Heine was persuaded and saw transcendental idealism and natural philosophy (that is, science) as two aspects of the same great revolution in man's intellectual development.

Julian's dream, welling up from the depths of his soul, tells him what might be. For Ibsen, it suggested that a union of opposites was possible—if not logically, then in defiance of logic, mystically. What happened at the end of *Brand,* when hate is apparently turned into love, is not what Julian is looking for. Brand was single-minded, and he was rewarded for never deviating from his goal. Julian is a divided soul whose struggle with himself makes him different from Brand and from the other great redeemers. Part of him wants to be a positive force, while another part of him compels him to be the skeptic and denier. Under the influence of Maximus, Julian can see himself as a participant in the Hegelian idea of progress, and Ibsen was drawn to the enchantments of German speculative philosophy. Kierkegaard had demolished Hegel and undermined the notion of a transition between opposites. Now Schelling offered another possibility.

All the mystical scenes in *Emperor* are dramatizations of Schelling's ideas. When Maximus urges Julian to become intoxicated, telling him that "wine is the soul of the grape. Liberated but willingly enslaved. Logos in Pan," and explains, "Intoxication is thy marriage with the soul of nature," he is speaking like Schelling. Wine contains the true secret. It "corresponds to the complete transformation, that is, the spiritualization of the primal materialist god." In Ibsen, the wine that Julian drinks contains "a spark of that fire which Prometheus stole."[4] For

Schelling, wine was the blood of the Titans, the spilled blood that represented the overcoming of the Titanic forces, the unspiritual.

While in Athens, Julian has his first intimations of the realm where opposites are united when he is initiated into the Eleusinian Mysteries. For Schelling, these rites were the condensation of man's spiritual development through the ages, that is, of his becoming conscious, of moving from the unconscious realm of nature and emerging into a state of spiritual being. The Mysteries were the repeated presentations of the past by which consciousness gained final knowledge and insight. The initiate attained momentary blessedness—*epopteia*—and was raised from the slime of matter and elevated into the sphere of the pure and immaterial.[5]

Ibsen first thought of beginning with a prologue. "The stage represents a yawning abyss. At the right, rays of light; to the left, darkness."[6] This pictured the primeval source of all being, rather like the opening of Wagner's *Das Rheingold*. Julian at his most insightful finds himself in that divided world. Ibsen wisely discarded this prologue, replacing it with a speech in act three in which Julian describes the ultimate nature of mind. This speech anticipates the end of the drama and pictures the noumenal thought behind the phenomenal events. During a night of prayer and fasting, after being initiated into the Eleusinian Mysteries, the teenage Julian found himself wafted far out into space and beyond time; he experienced a transcendent vision of a ship at sea, suspended over an abyss, and he saw how in the realm of nature opposites are united. What in Cusanus was only an abstract statement of the coincidence of opposites becomes in Ibsen's imagination an evocative instance of the thing itself happening.

> For there was broad and sun-shimmering day around me, and I stood alone on a ship, with drooping sails, in the midst of the glassy, gleaming Aegean Sea. Islands towered aloft in the distance, like dim, still banks of clouds, and the ship lay heavily, as though sleeping, upon the white-blue plain.
>
> Then behold! The plain became more and more transparent, lighter, thinner; at last it was no longer there, and my ship hung over a fearful empty abyss. No verdure down there, no sunlight, only the dead, black, slimy bottom of the sea, in all its ghastly nakedness.
>
> But high above, in the boundless dome, which before had seemed to me empty, *there* was life; there the invisible clothed itself in form, and silence became sound. It was then that I grasped the great redeeming realization . . . the realization that that which is, is not; and that which is not, is.[7]

In Julian's vision, opposites are conflated and become one. "I hang in the firmament over the yawning deep—midway between light and darkness."[8] The "slimy bottom of the sea," what the German pioneering naturalist Lorenz Oken called the *Urschleim*, is seen as dead, and the heavens, devoid of matter, are seen as full of life. Schelling speaks of the soul of Jupiter: "Under him are the shaping and the shapeless principles, which in the depths of the abyss an underground god brings together; but he dwells in the unreachable ether."[9] Schelling expressed this mystery as paradoxically as possible: "For that by which it is what is not, is just that by which it is that which it is."[10] Ibsen was more economical.

What really caught Ibsen's attention in Schelling was the necessity of negativism. Ibsen wanted to pass beyond the bleak and pessimistic insights of his two great poetic dramas and to explain how the naysayer contributes to the evolving history of humanity. To his publisher, Ibsen wrote, "That positive philosophy of life which the critics have demanded of me will finally be given to them."[11] For Schelling, "Negation is everywhere the first transition from nothing into something."[12] He employs electricity to demonstrate the difference between dualism and the union of opposites. Dualism, as in Hegel, requires two equally positive forces, but in electricity the negating fire, called –E, draws into itself +E and thus serves as the ground of the former.[13] Electricity convinced him that matter was indeed latent spirit. The opposites, matter and spirit, were actually one.

Ibsen also drew on Schelling for reinforcements in tackling the contradictions between fate and freedom. Julian says he will not serve in his destined role as a ruler and governor. "I defy necessity! . . . I am free, free!"

Yet he goes against his own will. Instead of going out into the desert, he dons the purple robe of power. Schelling's philosophy offered an insight into the paradox of willing one thing and accomplishing another, while also explaining the necessary role of the great deniers, Cain and Judas being the first two. Writing on necessity and freedom, Schelling specifically mentions Judas, the betrayer who haunts Julian's imagination. In the Ephesus scene, Julian hears the voice of Judas: "I was the twelfth wheel on the world wagon." In February or March 1871, while at work on *Emperor*, Ibsen conceived a poem about Judas.

> Among the disciples there was a strange one,
> Literally the twelfth wheel on the wagon.
>
> We know what made him commit that final act:
> It's recorded in history, a patent fact.
>
> With his conscience dulled and somewhat remiss,
> He sallied forth and gave the Savior a kiss.
>
> The result benefited both heaven and hell.
> Now, what if Judas had not had the will . . . ?[14]

Given the historical consequences, Judas's betrayal was both necessary and inevitable, but at the same time, in Schelling's view, he betrayed Christ willingly and with complete freedom. Schelling resolved the problem of free will and necessity by resorting to a distinction between the conscious being and the unconscious, the former being the sphere of the free will.

"In contrast to freedom, necessity is nothing other than the unconscious. What is unconscious in me is unarbitrary. That which is conscious in me is freely willed. To say that freedom shall again be necessary means that through freedom, by means of free action, something shall arise unconsciously and without my intercession—something I did not intend. . . . Even in the most uninhibited expressions of freedom there will arise something unarbitrary, something, perhaps, even contrary to that which is willed. And this unarbitrary realization will be something which the conscious will, by itself, could never accomplish."[15]

There is a "concealed necessity" in history "by virtue of which man through his free activity itself and ever against his will must become the cause of something that he never willed."[16]

That thought sustained Ibsen as he laid out the final general plan of *Emperor.* Here was an improvement on Greek tragedy, or at least an advance on the common understanding of it, in which the hero is seen as the plaything of indifferent gods. In Schelling, the hero is participating with a higher cause (God) even when he knowingly defies it. Ibsen conceived the Ephesus scene specifically to bring out conscious versus unconscious motivation. For the inebriated Julian, matter and spirit, nature and mind, Pan and Logos, become one, and at that moment he sees himself as Judas. He has a meaningful role to play in the ascent of the human spirit, but it is a paradoxical one.

In the final two-part version of *Emperor,* Ibsen counterpoises the vision of a Third Kingdom against the theory of opposites: Joachim of Flora and Maximus, on the one hand, and Cusanus and Schelling, on the other. In the first, progress comes about through triads, two opposed principles gradually bleeding into each other, changing both; in the latter, through ignition, two principles setting off a change but with each remaining the same. These two theories, clashing with each other, provide the bedrock of the double drama. Goethe labeled them "the concept of polarity and of enhancement" and called them "the two great drive wheels of all nature."[17]

Ibsen probably had the seminal idea of these two engines of progress in mind when he reworked his original three-part outline into a two-part drama. In the central scene of the first part the basic philosophical conflict that underlies the whole double drama is established. While Maximus conjures up the mysterious spirits and expounds the doctrine of the three kingdoms, believing Julian will be the new redeemer, a great positive force, Julian hears an inner voice telling him he is destined to be a negative force, another Judas. The idea of enhancement dominates the first part, as the young prince comes to power; the negative spirit dominates the second part. Ibsen may have been alluding to these two propelling forces when he explained to a friend, "The play deals with a struggle between two irreconcilable powers in the history of the world—a struggle that will always repeat itself, and because of this universality I call the book 'a World-History Play.'"[18] It must have given Ibsen great satisfaction to know that his singular divided personality could perfectly exemplify one of the two great wheels of history.

Cusanus described the experience of opposites becoming one, and Schelling, using the analogy of electricity, explained how it happened. Ibsen was faced with the task of dramatizing the process, of showing the moment when the opposites cross over each other. The great wheel of polarity drives the final scenes. In his war with the Persians on the outskirts of the Roman Empire, Julian commits a great military error that brings about his end: he orders the burning of his fleet. False information had persuaded him that the Persian army could be surrounded and thoroughly defeated by a land campaign. This was a perilous stratagem, exposing his defenseless ships to capture. But Julian, now quite mad, convinced of his own military genius and believing himself to be a world conqueror, stakes everything on this rash act. He sees in the flames that light up the sky the union of himself and the Galilean.

Julian exults as he sets his fleet of ships ablaze. "In the leaping flames of that red pyre the crucified Galilean is burning to ashes; and the earthly emperor is burning with him. But out of the ashes there shall arise—like the miraculous bird—the god of the earth and the emperor of the spirit *in one, in one, in one!*"[19]

What that flash of fire signifies is something quite different: the end of Julian's (and Maximus's) dream of a Third Empire. Matter and spirit, acting like positive and negative electrical charges, ignite that blaze. The Persian army attacks, confident of victory, knowing Julian has fallen into their trap. Instead they lose the battle, which would surely have been theirs but for the presence in the emperor's forces of hosts of Christians. Imbued with the spirit of sacrifice, unafraid of death, it is they who turn the tide of battle.

Christian and pagan intermingle in these last moments. The battle cry of the Christian soldiers is "With Christ for the Emperor!" Julian's fire does not herald a Third Kingdom; it only makes the Christian spirit stronger.

Julian's death is elaborately prepared for. While the burning of the fleet marks the end of a sublime vision, Julian's final moments offer a visual representation of the coincidence of opposites and a fulfillment of the vision he had crossing the Aegean Sea. The Christian soldier who impales Julian on his sword was once Julian's childhood friend, and his story is filigreed through the whole double drama. Named Agathon (*summum bonum*), he functions as the suppressed side of the emperor. He stands for the Brandian, sacrificing aspect, repressed by the

Gyntian side when Julian becomes emperor. It was the young Julian who brought Agathon into the Christian faith, and Maximus says, "How do you know, Julian, that you were not in him whom you now persecute?"[20]

In parallel developments, while Agathon goes mad because of the tortures inflicted on him as part of Julian's persecution of the Christians, Julian becomes a monomaniac bent on conquering the world. The parallel lines meet at the end. Agathon slays Julian, piercing his side with what he believes is the spear that lanced the side of Jesus at Golgotha, shouting, "With Christ for Christ!"—a striking visual representation of the coincidence of opposites. Julian dies, images of beautiful wreath-crowned youths floating through his mind. His last words concede victory to Christ: "Oh, Sun God, Sun God, why didst thou betray me?" a counterpart to the last words of Jesus.[21]

Another Triumph

Perhaps in no other play of his did Ibsen have so little regard for ordinary readers and theatergoers. Unlike Joyce and Eliot, who provided hints to the complexities and allusiveness of their masterworks, Ibsen, true to form, was close-mouthed, anticipating Nietzsche's advice, "The author must keep his mouth shut when his works start to speak." As theater in the mind, however, it offers an engrossing cerebral entertainment.

Emperor and Galilean was written to satisfy himself. It was more than a self-examination, a study of his divided nature; it was a self-justification. He knew he was not like others; he was not cast in the mold of what historians think of as great men, the magnificent doers, the positive thinkers. If Jesus was the man with the new Gospel, Ibsen was his Judas, and without Judas, Jesus might have remained an irksome rabble-rouser. He was the denier, "God's stepchild," unlike Bjørnson, God's darling.

Emperor and Galilean proved to be a great advance in his development by introducing the sense of progress in the human spirit. The prominence given in *Brand* to the sense of sin as a motivating force was replaced in the Julian drama by the evolving spirit of history. Earlier, Ibsen would have agreed with Kierkegaard that "the more developed [the individual] becomes ethically, the less will he concern himself with the world-historical."[1] That might have been true for *Brand*. Certainly, *Emperor* was a different matter.

Ibsen was gratified to see that current events were supporting his theory of history as a spiral staircase. "The trend of affairs in Europe is making this work more timely than I myself had thought possible."[2] There was a de-Christianizing in Europe, which made the apostate Julian relevant to the times.[3] There were also, however, omens of a growing religiosity. He noted "signs of something new about to break on the horizon. Or how else do you explain the craze for pilgrimages in Renan's France?"[4] Although Renan's very influential writings questioned the validity of revealed religion and reduced Jesus to an unresurrected human being, Renan's rationalism was counteracted by a growing belief in miracles.

A similar phenomenon was apparent in Germany. Bismarck sought to undermine the Catholic Church, which he saw as a threat to the state authority, by proposing laws, the Falk laws, passed in May 1873, that would in effect put many of the appointments and activities of the church under state control. In this *Kulturkampf* Bismarck sought to impose the will of Protestant Prussia on all of the German states. Many of these, particularly in the south, were largely Catholic. Angered by the strong resistance he encountered, he began to persecute the Catholic priests. In 1873–74 six bishops were imprisoned, and public worship was suspended in thirteen hundred parishes. This only made the Catholics stronger, like the Christians in Ibsen's play. In fact, they compared themselves to the persecuted Christians in Nero's reign. The growing power of the liberals and socialists compelled Bismarck to relent in his war with the church. In order to fend off the political liberals he had to find support among the conservatives, many of whom were Catholics. Some years later most of the anti-Catholic laws were repealed.

In Ibsen's battle with himself, the Nazarene had to win out eventually over the Hellene. Twist and turn as he might in his dandy's suit, with medals on his chest, glorying in his position as a significant writer, he had to acknowledge that it was the Brand in him that made him a man to be reckoned with, a herald of the future. It was *Brand* that had brought him success after many hard years, and those years of sacrifice were what made *Brand* possible. When Ibsen realized that the Galilean had to win out over the Nazarene, not only in history but in his own soul, he changed his style of dress. The outer man in 1873 was quite different from that of 1869. The dapper man who wrote *The League of Youth* sported a carefully barbered beard and wore a short, chic velvet coat; by 1873 this had been replaced by a long, black, calf-length coat of somber cut. The children in Pillnitz, Switzerland, where he was spending the summer, kissed his hand and asked for his blessing, taking him for a Catholic priest.[5]

Emperor and Galilean was published October 16, 1873, in a first printing of four thousand copies. It was a handsome book printed on superior paper. A second printing of twenty-one hundred copies was issued in December. The critics generally treated it with respect, although none of them seemed to appreciate the philosophical groundwork of the double drama. Instead they regarded it as a religious tract, with both believers and agnostics expressing their disappointment. To people like Bjørnson, it was an anti-Christian work. Christ was to be supplanted by a new messiah. There was in this play no heaven and no sin, only a man struggling against his fate. Heaven was not man's destination; man was created only to be destroyed in some endless, meaningless cycle. To Bjørnson, *Emperor* was a "big disappointment. I guess we've heard the last of Brand poetry (poetry's 'music of the future'!)—and I expect what we will now get from him—what he will be a master of—is *the play of intrigue*! We need them!"[6] A prophetic remark!

To Jens Peter Jacobsen, the disciple and translator of Darwin and future author of two of the finest psychological novels in Danish literature, *Emperor* smacked too much of mysticism, and he wrote dismissively of the drama and its characters. "There is no drive to the play, it's cold, the characters have no individuality. . . . Helena is nothing, and Julian is everything, a young Norwegian-German who has read his Søren Kierkegaard, and, depending on the occasion, acquires a touch of Hamlet, of Manfred, and of Antony in *Julius Caesar.* It's the least Ibsenian thing Ibsen has written."[7]

One of the more perceptive critiques was by a twenty-two-year-old Norwegian, Arne Garborg, whose own youth, like Julian's, was clouded by Christian gloom and doom. In his pamphlet on the play, *Henrik Ibsens Keiser og Galilæer* (1873), Garborg said no writer had ever tackled a more colossal subject. He praised the acuity in Ibsen's psychological portrait of Julian, and more than perhaps any other critic was aware of the ironies in the drama.

Many of those in Ibsen's own generation disliked him for his unsparing criticism of Norway's isolationist politics and for unpatriotically living abroad for ten years, and he had spared no words in expressing his resentment with his countrymen for sending him into exile.

Things were different when *Emperor* was published. He was now recognized as Scandinavia's greatest living writer. And so in July 1874 he returned to Norway, bringing with him his wife and son, remaining there until the end of September. On the whole, the younger generation proved surprisingly supportive. They tended to see *Emperor* as an expression of a positive philosophy, as Ibsen had hoped. The Student Association at the University of Christiania voted unanimously to hail Ibsen and offer their homage to him. They marched in procession from the university, waving their banners, to Ibsen's lodgings on Pilestredet. A deputation of students was sent up to him, and Ibsen was escorted down into the street, where the students formed a circle around him. A chorus sang a hymn composed for the occasion, and the students saluted him with cries of "Long live Henrik Ibsen." This was followed by loud hurrahs in which a large crowd of bystanders joined in.[8] At the end of *Emperor*, Julian the conqueror envies "the Galilean, the carpenter's son, [who] sits enthroned as the king of love in the warm, believing hearts of men." Now Ibsen had become, at least for the moment, the Galilean.

Ibsen, who was always uncomfortable in public fetes, responded in an artfully crafted speech, with copies being made available to the press. Uppermost in his mind were those years in which he had felt the scorn and disapprobation of many of his fellow Norwegians. An English journalist, who reported the event, gave what is probably an accurate assessment of Ibsen's standing among his countrymen.

"In spite . . . of their admiration for his great talents, the Norwegians were too good patriots to be able to pardon their master-singer for having abandoned his native land. It seemed to them as though his works lost some of their value for them by being written in a foreign country. On the other hand, they explained in some degree the satire and irony of his writings to the bitterness with which they thought he regarded his country, and took as pointed against themselves and their former blindness his sharpest and most cutting epigrams."[9]

He reached out to his countrymen by explaining that his quarrel over the years had been less with them than with himself. His speech was replete with allusions to his own works.

> Gentlemen: When during the latter years of my stay abroad it became more and more evident to me that it had *now* become a necessity for me to see my own country again, I will not deny that I felt considerable doubt and uneasiness as I prepared for my journey. To be sure, my stay here was intended to be only of short duration, but I felt that, *however short*, it might be long enough to destroy an illusion I should like to continue to live with.
>
> I asked myself: in what sort of spirit will my countrymen receive me? The favorable reception that greeted the works I sent home could not quite assure me. The question always arose: what is my *personal* relationship to my countrymen?
>
> It certainly cannot be denied that at several points there has been a feeling of animosity. So far as I have been able to understand, the complaints against me have been of a twofold nature. People have thought that I have regarded my personal and private relationship to my homeland with undue bitterness, and they have furthermore reproached me with having attacked certain events in our national life that, in the opinion of many, deserved quite a different sort of treatment than mockery.
>
> I do not think I could put this day, so honorable and joyful to me, to better use than to render an explanation and a confession.
>
> I have never made this personal relationship the direct subject of any fictional work. In my early hard times it meant much less to me than I could ever explain to myself afterwards. When the nest of the eider duck was robbed the first, second, and third times, it was robbed of illusions and great aspirations [alluding to the poem "The Eider Duck" ("Edderfuglen"), originally 1851]. At

festival gatherings when I, like a bear in the hands of its trainer [a reference to the poem "The Power of Memory" ("Mindets Magt"), 1864], reacted to little hints and reminders, it was because I knew myself to be partly responsible for those days that buried a glorious ideal beneath songs and celebrations.

Now, what does it mean to be a poet? It took a long time before I realized that to be a poet means essentially to see; but, mark well, to see in such a way that whatever is seen is perceived by his audience just as the poet saw it. But only what has been *lived through* can be seen and accepted in that way. And the secret of modern literature lies precisely in this matter of experiences that have been personally lived through. All that I have written these last ten years I have lived through in spirit. But no poet lives through anything in isolation. What he lives through, all of his countrymen live through with him. *If this were not so*, what would bridge the gap between the creating and the receiving mind?

What is it, then, that I have lived through and that has inspired me? The range has been wide. In part I have been inspired by something I felt on rare occasions and only in my best moments stirring within me, vividly alive, great and beautiful. I have been inspired by that which, so to speak, stood higher than my everyday self, and I have been inspired by this because I wanted to confront it and make it part of myself. [Obviously, Ibsen had *Brand* in mind.]

But I have also been inspired by the opposite, by what appears on introspection as the dregs and sediment of one's nature. [*Peer Gynt*.] Writing has in this case been to me like a bath from which I have risen feeling cleaner, healthier, and freer. Yes, gentlemen, no one can draw poetically anything for which he himself has not to a certain degree and at least at times served as a model. And who is the man among us who has not now and then felt and recognized within himself a contradiction between word and deed, between wish and duty, between life and doctrine in general? Or who is there among us who has not, at least at times, been egotistically, selfishly sufficient unto himself [the trolls' motto in *Peer Gynt*], and half unconsciously, half in good faith, painted a better picture of himself, both for others and for himself?

I believe that in saying this to you, to you students, my remarks have found exactly the right audience. You will understand them as they are meant to be understood. For a student has essentially the same task as the poet: to make clear to himself, and thereby to others, the temporal and eternal questions that are astir in the age and in the community to which he belongs.

In this respect I dare to say of myself that during my stay abroad I have endeavored to be a good student. A poet is by nature farsighted. Never have I seen my homeland and the true life of my homeland so completely and at such close range as I did in my absence when I was far away from it.

And now, my dear countrymen, in conclusion a few words that are also re-

> lated to something I have lived through. When Emperor Julian stands at the end of his career and everything collapses around him, there is nothing that makes him so despondent as the thought that all he has gained was *this:* to be remembered by cool and clear heads with respectful appreciation, while his opponents live on, rich in the love of warm, living hearts. [Ibsen was thinking of his friends in the Learned Dutchmen circle and contrasting them with Bjørnson's admirers.][10]
>
> This thought was the result of much that I have lived through. It had its origin in a question I had sometimes asked myself, down there in my solitude. Now the young people of Norway have come to me here tonight and given me my answer more warmly and clearly than I had ever expected to hear it. I shall take this answer with me as the richest reward of my visit with my countrymen at home; and it is my hope and my belief that what I experience tonight will be an experience to "live through," which will someday be reflected in a work of mine. If that should happen, if someday I should send such a book home, then I ask you students to accept it by way of a handshake and a thanks for this meeting. I ask you to accept it as having a share in its creation.[11]

A few days later an exuberant Ibsen wrote to his publisher, "I have been received here with the most extraordinary goodwill by everybody."[12] And true to his word, what he experienced that night did become years later the basis for one of his late plays.

Having conquered Scandinavia, the bemedaled Ibsen, honored by the monarch and now enthroned in the minds of the younger generation in Norway, was about to step onto the world stage.

Part Two

The Divided Kingdom

Changing Times

Emperor and Galilean brought Ibsen to a crossroads in his career. *Brand* and *Peer Gynt* defined the boundaries of his mental landscape, and *Emperor* filled in the territory in between. It was a summation of his beliefs and of his inner life up to the early 1870s. By then he had become the recipient of several official honors and was a prominent member of the literary establishment. He had conquered Scandinavia and was now conducting forays into Germany.

Ever since the acclamation that *Brand* brought him, he had been grooming himself as a great man, changing his costume and altering his handwriting in accordance with the different stages in his social development. The careerist in him sought to secure his position, calling in forces that lay exposed to attack and strengthening the bulwarks that had been hastily thrown up in the years of struggle. Still the doubting skeptic within him burrowed away, threatening to weaken the fortress of fame and fortune from within, undermining what the careerist had wrought.

One of his most revealing poems, one of "those little devils" that betrayed him, is "Building Plans," which alludes directly to the life he had planned for himself. It exists in two versions, written years apart. He composed the first when he was in love with Rikke Holst.

> I built a cloud castle; it rose up fast and fine.
> I set myself two goals, a small one and a great.
> The great one: I would become one of the immortals.
> The small: I would possess a little water lily.
>
> I thought there was a heavenly harmony in the plan.
> But since then, it has come to rack and ruin.
> As I grew more sensible, it all went awry:
> The great goal became so small, the small became my all.[1]

The sense of this early version, written when Ibsen was in his twenties, is that the poet in love is in danger of forgetting his true ambition. Revised in 1871, the poem carries a different import.

> I will build me a cloud castle. Two wings shall shape it forth,
> A great one and a small. It shall shine across the north.
> The greater shall shelter a singer immortal;
> The small to a maiden shall open its portal.
>
> I thought a heavenly harmony lay in this scheme,
> But since then something has wreaked havoc with the dream.
> When the builder grew wise and sensible, the castle went smash.
> The great wing proved too small, the little one collapsed.[2]

For the mature Ibsen, immortality as a poet was no longer the principal aim of his existence, while his quest for popular recognition, riches, and fame so consumed him that he could find no satisfaction in ordinary pleasures and domestic joys. Fully conscious of what he was doing and acting as if he were committed to some unalterable course of action about which it would be idle to have any regrets, he went off in pursuit of glory, while the imp of doubt rode his coattails, mocking his ambitions.

In 1873, the year in which *Emperor and Galilean* was published, *Love's Comedy* appeared in a third edition. *The Vikings at Helgeland* was issued in a new edition, with new printings called for within the next few years. *The Pretenders*, reissued in 1870, went through five printings during the following decade. In 1874 Ibsen's early play *Lady Inger of Østraat* and in 1875 his very first play, *Catiline*, were issued in new, thoroughly revised editions.

Although he had been writing primarily for the reading public since the success of *Brand*, the theaters in Scandinavia were now willing to stage the earlier dramas. The enterprising Ludvig Josephson produced *Love's Comedy* and *The Pretenders* at the Christiania Theater in 1873 and 1874. Subsequently, he staged *Lady Inger* and *Peer Gynt*, engaging the composer Edvard Grieg to provide incidental music for the latter. In Stockholm both *The Vikings* and *Lady Inger* were produced in the 1870s. In Copenhagen the Royal Theater staged *The Pretenders* in 1871 and *The Vikings* in 1876. The latter play, rejected by the Royal Theater in 1858, now proved to be such a hit that Ibsen's royalties were doubled.

In Scandinavia in Ibsen's time, the method of paying playwrights varied from theater to theater. The old system of benefit nights for the author had been superseded by a rather complicated scale of payment in which the flat fee paid for any one performance depended on the length of the play and the number of performances in an extended run. In 1876 Ibsen was irritated by the prospect that the Royal Theater in Copenhagen would drop *The Vikings* after the nineteenth performance in order to avoid paying the higher rate to which the author was entitled when his play achieved a run of twenty performances.[3]

Playwrights in Scandinavia had not yet formed an association that would protect their rights. There were no enforceable copyright laws among the Nordic countries until after 1880. The situation was exacerbated by the fact that Denmark and Sweden (including Norway) did not care to sign copyright agreements with other countries. This meant that a dramatist in Germany, for instance, could translate an Ibsen play and take all the income it generated, and into the bargain he could adapt and mutilate the play as he saw fit. In the 1870s when Germany was beginning to read and perform him, Ibsen, to protect his interests, entered into an agreement with a German translator who would prepare "original editions" of his works.[4]

In the 1870s Ibsen was seen more often in public forums than at any other time in his career. Before *Brand*, he was unknown; after *Ghosts* (1881), his public appearances were pretty much limited to special occasions in his honor. These were happy years for him. He could revel in the prospect of growing fame outside Scandinavia. He enjoyed good health, was welcomed by the intelligentsia and the aristocrats, including the king, and received a comfortable income from his publishers and the theaters, supplemented by a writer's grant from the Norwegian government. He was no longer a desperately poor poet. In 1872 his income for the year was 200 specie dollars (about 800 kronor). The following year he earned 13,303 kronor in royalties, two or three times as much as the salary of a full professor, and he was able not only to pay off all his debts but to buy stock in a streetcar company.[5]

Yet the old wounds refused to heal. The old grudges were not forgotten, and the contradictions within him were never more manifest. As we have seen, Brandes in 1872 was struck by Ibsen's bitterness and by his boundless contempt for humanity. Nothing proved more soothing to his ego than honors publicly bestowed on him. As he worked on *Emperor and Galilean*, he drew sketches in his notebook of the decorations he had received. And the honors and orders came in rapid succession.

In 1869 he had been made a Knight of the Order of Vasa, and in 1871 both the Dannebrog Order of Denmark and the Turkish Order of Medjidie with the Star of Commander had been conferred on him. In the summer of 1873, when Oscar II was crowned king of Norway, another award came his way, making him a Knight of the Order of St. Olaf. In 1875 he was awarded the king's gold medal, celebrating his twenty-five years as a creative writer. In 1876 he was decorated with the Ernestine Order by the theater-loving Duke of Saxe-Meiningen. The following year, when the University of Uppsala celebrated its four-hundredth anniversary, he was awarded an honorary doctorate. After that he always preferred to be addressed as "Doctor Ibsen."

If rumors are to be believed, Ibsen refused at first to accept the honor when he heard that Bjørnson was to receive a doctorate on the same day. Late in life, in 1903, Bjørnson said, "Ibsen once did me a great injury. . . . When Uppsala University in 1877 celebrated its quadricentennial, I learned that those in Sweden intended to award honorary degrees to both Ibsen and me. But I also know that Ibsen had explained that if I were also to get the doctorate, he would refuse and not accept the title. So I was eliminated, and Ibsen became honorary doctor."[6]

Two exceptionally fine portraits of Ibsen, one in oils, the other in prose, were rendered in that triumphal year of 1876. The twenty-six-year-old Julius Kronberg, a brilliant colorist much influenced by the Munich school, portrayed the poet as the Olympian, a medal around his neck, a scroll in his hand, an academic robe draped over his shoulder, his head thrust back, his eyes casting a suspicious gaze offstage. An admirer of Kronberg, the twenty-eight-year-old August Strindberg, librarian, journalist, and cultural critic, transformed the painting into a penetrating psychological portrait.

> One's first impression—and one's first impressions should always be considered even if they are not the whole truth—is paradoxical, intensely disquieting. Here is the quintessence of paradox. A prophet in gold-rimmed spectacles, a medal highlighted against the white shirt. The face is that of Brand, the high forehead of a fanatic, the stern mouth of a witness to the truth, but one who never actually utters the truths his hand sets down on paper, the cold, determined glance that never wavered even when it was confronted by the Spirit of Compromise—this is Ibsen, the fanatic as skeptic, the zealous doubting Thomas, standing here as the fully aware, totally self-conscious unbeliever, who awakened all that part of a nation over which Bjørnson did not hold sway. This is the great genius, wearing a white collar and clad in a poet's cape, draped to conform with the conventional statuesque pose of an author, manuscript and pen in hand as customary. Yet there is something jarring about it, something that both repels and attracts. Perhaps one has to know that Ibsen likes to obliterate his own personality, that he would prefer to cast a sheen of the ridiculous over himself than to pass as a great man. Who does not remember the appearance of the renowned poet when he visited Stockholm a few years ago? Wearing a silk jacket, a white vest with black buttons, collar of the latest fashion, an elegant stick in his hand, and a protective, ironic smile in the corner of his lips, he made his way, always avoiding profound discussions.[7]

Figure 11. Ibsen with honorary degree.
Portrait by Julius Kronberg. Munich 1877.

The outspoken young rebel who had narrowly escaped arrest in 1851, when the police rounded up the leaders of the workers, had matured into the enigmatic literary lion who prudently took advantage of his position in the establishment to await in bourgeois comfort the coming of the revolution.

It must have been Ibsen's contrariwise kind of thinking that led him to expect the advent of a new era in the 1870s, the very years that constituted the high tide of the conservative reaction in Norway and Denmark. Undoubtedly, the Paris Commune of 1871 frightened the conservatives everywhere and galvanized them into taking repressive measures. The autocratic rule of the Iron Chancellor, Bismarck, in Prussia, the replacement of Gladstone by the imperialistic Disraeli in England in 1874, and the arrest of the leaders of the labor movement in Copenhagen in 1872 all formed part of a general pattern that moved Bjørnson to say with a sigh, "The reaction is triumphant in every country. . . . I'll probably feel it here at home; my work will be endangered, since it all hangs together: the fate of one people determines that of others."[8]

In Scandinavia the swing of the political pendulum toward conservatism, after the liberating insurrections of 1848, had begun in the 1860s, which indubitably colored the reception of *Brand.* In Norway Prime Minister Frederik Stang, who in his youth had encouraged the opening up of the country by building railroads and thus stimulated the flow of new democratic ideas, rigorously opposed in the 1860s and 1870s the campaign for general suffrage and increased republicanism. In Sweden the parliamentary reforms of 1865 and 1866, which broadened the base of suffrage, resulted ironically in the accession to power of the farmers, the most conservative part of the population, who effectively stifled the progressives until 1910. Joining hands with the farmers were, of course, the clergy, whose voice grew ever more clamorous and strident in the 1870s and 1880s, as they inculcated on their parishioners the fear that the forces of irreligion were growing stronger—which they indeed were.

In 1873 the national elections in Norway, combined with a series of economic crises, divided the country into two particularly hostile camps. Bjørnson was a prominent member of the liberal group, while Ibsen was generally regarded as an adherent of the right. When his birthday was celebrated in 1875, of the groups gathered at a banquet in Christiania, only one represented the left. The principal speaker on this occasion was M. J. Monrad, a professor at the University of Christiania when Ibsen was a student there. Monrad was a Hegelian in philosophy and conservative in his religious and political views. In earlier years he had been strongly opposed to Ibsen, animadverting on the cynical and irreligious tone of *Love's Comedy* and the inhuman stance of the priest in *Brand.* Yet a decade later he was paying tribute to Ibsen.

Those years had brought a remarkable change in the Ibsen climate, and he must have been keenly aware of the ambiguity of his position. Publicly he did almost nothing before 1875 to dissociate himself from the conservatives, and in private he ardently defended Bismarck's iron rule and characterized the liberals as cowardly and compromising. Yet on other occasions he assailed the Prussian state, praised the Commune, and preached anarchy. And then he would disingenuously answer Brandes's admonitions by saying, "I do not shrink in the least from being regarded as a partisan"[9]—strange words coming from a man who had disdained all parties and advocated a Brand-like independence, "a thoroughgoing egoism."

Where in all this was the real Ibsen? A cynic might suggest that the explanation for these fluctuations lay in Ibsen's self-centeredness. He would humbly abase himself where medals were concerned, and his political compass seemed to have money as its magnetic north. His public rapprochement with the left began when he needed the support of the liberal party to augment his income from the state. In 1872 his application for a government grant was rejected by the head of the Norwegian Ecclesiastical Department. Jonas Lie, on the other hand, had had no difficulty obtaining four grants in the course of one year. Ibsen told his confidant Michael Birkeland that "Mr. Lie belongs to the party which must not be offended and I to the party which must not do anything 'in fear of stirring up trouble.'"[10] Ibsen understood that if he wanted to increase his income from the state he would have to circumvent the administration and appeal directly to parliament. This he did in 1874, when he and other writers asked for an augmentation of their grants on the ground that the failure of Norway to enter into copyright agreements with other countries reduced their potential income. The following year a proposal to raise the standard stipend for writers was defeated, with most conservatives opposing it.

It was then that Ibsen sought the support of the liberal party in parliament. In 1877 he wrote directly to the leader of the opposition, saying he had no hope of an increase in his stipend without its support. Since he regarded all political parties with disdain, these changes had little or nothing to do with his convictions. They were made because they suited his larger aims. He was a playwright before he was a politician. He changed his political affiliations as often as he changed his shoes, and for the same reason: to get where he was going. In his political beliefs he remained close to the anarchists, but in his art he underwent a transformation.

The man who was to make his mark as a realistic dramatist concerned with social problems began as a poet who wanted the stage to present an idealized vision of life. The theater reviews he wrote in the 1850s were pretty consistently opposed to the new French realist drama, which was now spreading to other European countries. The middle-class theatergoers liked it, but Ibsen didn't. He said we live in "the age of the lantern slide." People like what they recognize and consequently do not want the ideal in art. Many intelligent critics fault a play because it is not a "photographic reproduction of reality. For them realism and truth are one and the same; if the first is not copied, then, according to them, the second is not reflected in it." Ibsen found this to be a sterile approach to art: "A statue is not improved by giving it natural skin color, hair, eyes." He wanted poetry in the theater, poetry in the broad sense—an unconscious symbolism, "a spiritual majesty and calm, a recognition of mood and atmosphere." It was entirely in accord with this antirealism that he should condemn a play as being "a dissertation on social conditions—in dramatic form."[11]

The works that Ibsen wrote in the 1850s drew on history and legend and avoided the contemporary scene, and the plays he wrote in the 1890s at the end of his career were symbolist in tone and technique. The extraordinary fact is the realistic problem plays that brought him world fame were an anomaly in his career. In writing them he was working against the grain of his own nature.

He first took to capturing realistic, everyday speech in *The League of Youth*, which he wrote in response to those who thought the satiric verse of *Peer Gynt* was not poetic. If the critics thought he was no poet, he would show them what he could do as a photographer of the contemporary scene. Yet after having settled accounts with them, he did not return to verse drama. *Emperor and Galilean*, which followed, is in prose. In his "Rhymed Letter" of 1871 he said prose should be used to express concrete ideas, while verse is better for expressing visions. When Edmund Gosse suggested that *Emperor and Galilean* would have benefited from the employment of verse, Ibsen took issue with him, saying that he wanted to give the reader the impression that what was on the page was what had actually happened. Since his aim was to depict human beings, he could not let them speak the "language of the gods," as in Greek tragedy.

"As you must have observed, the play is conceived in the most realistic style. The illusion I wished to produce was that of reality. . . . If I had employed verse, I would have counteracted my intention and defeated my purpose. The many ordinary, insignificant characters whom I have intentionally introduced into the play would have become indistinct and indistinguishable from one another if I had allowed all of them to speak in the same meter. We are no longer living in the days of Shakespeare."[12]

Contradicting what he had said in the 1850s about sculpture, he now said he would "rather see the head of a Negro executed in black than in white marble."[13]

After *Peer Gynt* Ibsen wrote no more verse dramas, and after 1875 the poems he wrote would hardly fill three pages. A first-rate poet deliberately denied himself his primary means of expression in turning to the realistic drama, the medium in which his ideas would be broadcast to the world. Brandes later remarked that "at one time or other during the battle of life, a lyric Pegasus must have been killed under him," an ironic statement coming from the man whose criticism of the collected poems certainly influenced Ibsen.[14]

In a prosaic age, verse is considered confining and limiting. Strindberg in 1883 in his *Poems in Verse and Prose* (*Dikter på vers och prosa*) could declare that verse pins down the poet's thoughts "with unnecessary shackles that a new age will slough off." But it does not necessarily follow that all writers thought of rhyme and rhythm as shackles. In the romantic age, when everyone wrote verse, these were no impediment to the flow of thought, whereas good prose dialogue was difficult to write. Theatrically effective realistic dialogue was an art in itself.

The English critic William Archer, Ibsen's translator and a practicing playwright, said the custom of writing in verse "enabled and encouraged the dramatists to substitute rhetoric for human speech. It is immeasurably easier to make dramatic characters speak as men and women do not speak than to capture the true accent and the delicate interplay of actual talk, while at the same time condensing it, as drama must be condensed, and divesting it of its superfluities."[15] Testifying to this is the fact that Ibsen composed the hundreds of lines of his verse dramas, *Brand* and *Peer Gynt*, at a far faster pace than the far fewer prose lines of plays like *A Doll's House* and *Ghosts*.

Actors found it as difficult as playwrights to be simultaneously real and theatrically effective. Gradually, acting in Germany and the Nordic countries became more realistic, with some actors trying to break with the declamatory tradition, in which words were distinctly pronounced and frequently distorted to produce "stage speech," a peculiar idiom based in part on acoustical considerations and in part on a desire to separate art from life, the ideal from the real. As every actor knows, being real onstage is much more difficult than being loud, mellifluous, and extravagant. It was not until the last quarter of the nineteenth century that acting attained a uniformly realistic coloring.

To an actress at the Christiania Theater, Ibsen confessed in 1883 that during the previous seven or eight years he had written scarcely a single line of poetry, devoting himself instead exclusively "to the very much more difficult art of writing the straightforward, plain language spoken in real life. It is by means of this language that you have become the excellent artist you now are. You have never used smooth verses to delude anyone about your art. . . . Verse has been most injurious to the art of the drama. A true artist of the stage, whose repertoire is the contemporary drama, should not willingly let a single line of poetry cross her lips. It is improbable that verse will be employed to any extent worth mentioning in the drama of the immediate future and almost certain that it will be incompatible with it. Consequently, it is doomed. For art forms become extinct, just as the preposterous animal forms of prehistoric times became extinct when their days were over.

"A tragedy in iambic pentameter is already as rare as a dodo."[16]

These were hard thoughts for the man who dreamed of immortality as an artist of the sublime and whose poetic dramas had brought him extraordinary success. True to his split personality, a year after his letter to the actress he wrote to a Norwegian poet, retracting his earlier view.

"I hope that in the future you will produce much more in the field of meter and rhythm, for that is your natural realm. I have not forgotten certain disrespectful utterances of my own on the art of poetry, but they stemmed only from my own momentary attitude toward that art form."[17]

In 1899 when he was working on his last play, he wrote to another poet. "Reading your lyrics has often called forth a silent sigh over those long-ago days when I wrote poetry."[18] As a playwright in the 1870s, however, Ibsen could read the handwriting on the wall. The theater was becoming realistic, along with the novel. Twenty years earlier in France, Champfleury had asserted that verse drama was an exhausted form and that the literary genre of the future would be the novel dealing with contemporary manners and morals, not with medieval notions à la Hugo, or extravagant adventures à la Dumas *père*. Also in France at the same time Adolphe Lemoine Montigny, the great unsung hero of stage directing, was developing techniques for making salon drama seem more lifelike. He would place a table stage center, the actor's favorite spot, forcing the actor to circle around it and use furniture and props to point up the dialogue and enhance characterization.[19]

These new techniques penetrated the Scandinavian theater in the 1870s and 1880s. The pioneers were Edvard Stjernström and Ludvig Josephson, both Swedish, but the latter headed the Christiania Theater in Norway from 1873 to 1877, winning Ibsen's devotion for his productions of the playwright's work. Stjernström had acquainted himself with the new approach to directing realistic drama in Paris in the 1850s, when he had studied many of the productions staged by Montigny at the Théâtre Gymnase. In 1864 and again in 1870 he studied theater in Austria and Germany, where he was in close contact with Heinrich Laube, who had also been to school to study the Paris directors. Laube's directorial precepts were simple but innovative: careful instruction to the actors; unity of tone to be imposed by the director; close, line-by-line reading of the text; and increased number of rehearsals. Prior to the introduction of these new methods, the leading performers in Germany and Scandinavia did very much as they wished, leaving the stage manager to arbitrate traffic problems. There were, at best, perhaps ten or twelve rehearsals of a full-length play, and what artistic unity there was resulted from tradition and chance. Even in 1880 in Berlin at a major theater with a well-known actress (Hedwig Niemann-Raabe), *A Doll's House* was staged with only four rehearsals.[20] The actors learned their lines at home from parts, not from the whole script. In a letter of 1872 Ibsen insists that the actors know their lines at the first rehearsal, and that they know more than just their own parts.

> It is necessary that the actors know the whole play and not just the scenes in which they appear. If this point is not observed, then the actor cannot comprehend fully the character he is portraying.

My dialogue is full of hints, intimations, etc. They must all be understood, but they have to be given with subtlety and without such emphasis that they are torn from their organic connection with the rest of the dialogue.

Conversations must be lively, quick, and with the highest degree of naturalness in accent.

What was often lacking in my time at the Christiania Theater was the natural change from quick to slow in real speech, according to the meaning. What was lacking was the natural softness and firmness, and especially lacking was the increased speed in tempo that occurs when a person, hearing what is being said, or when he himself gets excited, feels indignant or angry or disgusted, etc. In my time they tried to register emotions by shouting louder. But that does no good. There is no other way to express rising emotion than with the rising passion with which it is expressed.

Finally, I would like to add that at all the best theaters in Europe a play is not considered properly rehearsed until it can be performed without a prompter.[21]

Laube doubled the number of rehearsals, and Stjernström did the same in Stockholm when he acquired his own theater. Unfortunately, he died in 1876 before he could accomplish all his aims.[22]

While playwrights and set designers were making giant strides in making the theater realistic, actors were very retrograde, stubbornly refusing to give up their old ways. Strindberg, in his satiric mode and still a few years away from his naturalistic dramas, *The Father* and *Miss Julie*, has given us a delectable and only slightly exaggerated description of actors in a conventional drawing-room drama.

He sets the scene. The stage is covered with an endless Brussels carpet, a couple of couches here and there, and upstage a fireplace, a clock on the mantelpiece. After the first scene in which Monsieur Anatol, carrying a walking stick, wearing pince-nez, and making a cigarette with his cigarette roller, has declared his love to the marquise, the stage is empty for a moment. The audience is still applauding the marquise after her exit. The actor playing the count is about to make his first appearance of the season. He lets the auditorium rid itself of the last vestige of the actress's applause, while poor Anatol is left hanging.

The house grows deathly quiet, and when a soft, whispered "Here he comes!" is heard, the count makes his entrance, slowly, casually. . . . Thunderous applause greets him. At first he doesn't hear it; his eyes stare out into space. Finally he comes to, looks about astonished. "What can this mean?" He had never expected anything like this! A soft smile of recognition flits across his pale lips. Touched, he moves downstage to the prompter's box and bows, hand on heart.

The audience quiets itself, and Anatol, who has been undergoing the torments of hell, seeking in vain to cut off the applause, now lunges forward.

"Jean! Is it really you, my old, loyal friend? What happy stroke of luck has brought us together?"

Deeply moved, Jean embraces Anatol, calls him his good old boy. Anatol thinks Jean looks unhappy, asks him to take a seat and unburden himself.

Jean sits down, sinking up to his shoulders in an easy chair. Anatol offers him a cigarette, which he politely declines, whereupon he begins his tale.

[A man in the audience] dozes off, waking up just in time to catch the end. Jean is ruined—down to only 6,000 francs in dividends and doesn't know what to do with himself, now that life has stripped him of all his illusions.

Anatol encourages him to seek a diplomatic position in Naples, but Jean is too proud to work.

"And now you are thinking of shooting yourself," says Anatol.

"I would regard that as a holy duty to the family whose name I have the honor to bear, but I cannot. Not now. For I—I—I—am in love."

He rises and takes a position at the fireplace.

"You are in love? With whom?"

"The Marquise de Carambole."

"The Marquise de Carambole?"

Anatol jumps up and trudges back and forth on the carpet in his patent-leather shoes.

Jean's head sinks down between his shoulders. He lifts his left downstage foot, gives the carpet a light tap with it, and with a nod of his head whispers a barely audible "Yes."

Whereupon he notices Anatol's agitation. He slowly cranks his head back up on his shoulders, rolls his eyes from stage left to stage right, and bursts out, "What is the matter with you? Why are you so perturbed?"

"Nothing. Nothing at all. An attack of vertigo. It will soon pass."

Jean leaps forward, grabs Anatol by the shoulders, looks him straight in the eye, and cries, "You love the marquise!"

Anatol squirms out of Jean's arms, collects his cigarette roller, his stick, his hat, and, as he prepares to spring offstage, cries, "Yes, I love her!"

But Jean, on to actors' deep-dyed plots, and seeking to forestall Anatol's brilliant exit, falls backward on the carpet, so that his head comes to rest on the cushion of an easy chair.

The curtain falls. Jean is called back and is given a bouquet, but Anatol doesn't dare show his face.[23]

With actors playing against one another instead of supporting each other, the overall tone of a serious play was bound to suffer. Ensemble acting with every actor subordinated to the script and to the director's interpretation of it was the goal of theater people like Montigny and Stjernström, though they made slow progress. When the latter opened his New Theater in Stockholm in 1875, he insisted on eliminating the bows and curtain calls that Strindberg satirizes (the Royal Theater did not follow suit) and allowed them only at the end of the play. At the Moscow Art Theater under Stanislavsky, actors were still taking bows at the end of each act in 1900, as they were in American comedy in the 1910s. Opera, of course, never abandoned the custom.

The Problem Play

Any playwright with something serious to say would hesitate to use the theater as a medium. Ibsen used realistic dialogue in *The League of Youth* in 1869, but that was a comedy and the characters were caricatures. He certainly hesitated to write for the new realistic theater and was impelled in that direction only because of Bjørnson, his great opposite, and Brandes, his comrade in arms. When it came to the new movements in drama and theater, both these men were ahead of Ibsen.

In his 1871 lecture Brandes had said, "What keeps a literature alive in our time is that it submits problems to debate." The old literature accepted certain moral codes and virtues without questioning them; the coming literature will put them to the test. This idea of submitting problems to debate came from Brandes's familiarity with French drama. Alexandre Dumas *fils* unwittingly introduced the problem play when he wrote *La Dame aux Camélias,* which proved to be both popular and controversial. Dumas portrayed his heroine, a demimondaine, in a favorable light, and immediately other playwrights countered him by showing how these high-class prostitutes were becoming a great danger to society by marrying into the best families. Dumas defended his kind of drama, which he called utilitarian drama (*le théâtre utile*), setting it in opposition to art-for-art's-sake drama, which had no useful purpose, being empty of meaning: "*L'art pour l'art, trois mots absolument vides de sens.*" In the preface to his play *Le Fils naturel* (*The Illegitimate Son,* 1858), he said, "The old society is falling apart at the seams; all the original, fundamental institutions, earthly and divine, are put to the question [*sont remises en question*]."[1]

Ironically, the Nordic dramatist who first responded to Brandes's call for a drama that would concern itself with current problems was Bjørnson, who detested much of what Brandes stood for. Apparently, it was Stjernström who convinced Bjørnson that realistic drama could be produced effectively on the Scandinavian stage. He abandoned the old-fashioned romantic drama he had been writing and turned to the utilitarian drama advocated by Brandes. He had two realistic plays, *A Bankruptcy* (*En fallit*) and *The Editor* (*Redaktøren*) ready in 1874, and Stjernström staged them both the following year in Stockholm. Ibsen asked for copies in March 1875, as soon as they were published.

The introduction of a new kind of drama was signaled in Stockholm by the opening of a new theater to compete with the Royal Theater. "No one doubted," said Strindberg, "that this enterprise would have consequences. There was complete surprise when a couple of weeks before the opening the papers reported that the new theater would in the near future put on two new dramas by Bjørnstjerne Bjørnson. This notice concealed two surprises: Bjørnson had broken with the Royal Theater and with the esthetic drama, which the devotees of 'art for art's sake' valued so highly."[2]

As director, Stjernström was unusually thorough in his preparation. He began his work on *A Bankruptcy* three months before the opening, spending much of the time talking to the actors on morning walks. His greatest problem was getting the actors to behave naturally while still speaking clearly and loudly enough to be heard throughout the house. To enhance the reality of the play, Bjørnson urged the director to use living models in developing the characters. (The play was not produced in Norway because Bjørnson's models were too easily recognizable.) When the logic of the scene demanded it, Stjernström encouraged the actors to turn their backs on the audience, a violation of decorum on the classic stage but one that Montigny found necessary in realistic drama. In order to make certain that the actors would feel at ease with the costumes and props, he held several dress rehearsals instead of the usual one.[3]

The opening night of *A Bankruptcy* in Stockholm was awaited with great expectations; it was the theatrical event of the season. People lined up the night before to buy tickets, some seats costing fifty kronor. As a sign of the importance of the occasion, most of the audience was in evening dress.

One need only compare the stage directions in *A Bankruptcy* with those in any earlier Scandinavian play to see the enormous strides Bjørnson took toward the thoroughly realistic and illusionistic theater. Everything that the advanced theaters in France and England had accomplished was incorporated. In the first act an actor is instructed to turn his back on the audience. For the second act, a party scene, the actors are told to improvise their chatter on the basis of some ideas suggested by Bjørnson. In the fourth act, during a moment of suppressed emotion, an actor is told to finger a chair "with which he has come into contact." Though such directions were to be found in earlier plays, notably the works of

T. W. Robertson in England in the 1860s—the "cup-and-saucer drama," as it came to be called—they were innovations in Scandinavia.

To be of a piece with the realistic acting, the sets had to be as illusionistic as possible. This meant that productions became more costly. Instead of making do with the standard painted flats stored in the scene shop, the producer had to order special ones built, as Stjernström did for Bjørnson's plays. For repertory theaters—and outside of a few theaters in the major cities, all theaters were repertory theaters—the expense could be prohibitive. Another great disadvantage to the realistic built-up set was the time and labor it took to effect scene changes. (Perhaps the most notorious example of a long scene change was the hour or so it took to replace the set of act one in *The Wild Duck* with the Ekdal quarters of act two in Paris in 1891.) Strindberg remarks on the audience's dislike of the long waits. "When one began to build onstage, the theater became a carpenter's shop, and the long intermissions were a curse and a nuisance that kept many people from the theater."[4] The box set was not introduced to the Swedish stage until 1880.

Resistance to the realistic theater came not only from impatient audience members but also from those who expected a night at the theater to be a pleasant esthetic experience. Like many people who object to vivid sexual scenes and scenes of physical violence in twenty-first-century movies and plays, there were many in the nineteenth who felt the same way about much milder depictions of real life. Such scenes undeniably mirrored the world as it was, but they had no place in a work of art. Art should be a blend of the real and the ideal. And decorum, both social and esthetic, had to be observed.

Bjørnson's two plays met with considerable resistance from the old guard, who found them too realistic. Some critics thought it unseemly that the young girl in *A Bankruptcy* should press her attentions on her young man: decorum required that the man do the wooing. They found the language too crude; words like "*skurk*" (scoundrel) were offensive. The scene in which the ruined businessman is pushed in a wheelchair by his wife was too painful to be shown onstage. In *The Editor* Bjørnson has his unjustly reviled hero suffer a violent hemorrhage, collapse, and die onstage. This was a grave esthetic error on Bjørnson's part. Scenes of bloodshed and death were accepted in the melodrama and in Shakespeare, but even in them the physical symptoms of illness were seldom shown. Camille's cough and a drunkard's delirium tremens were allowed, however; the one was fashionable and the other was morally justifiable.

In dealing with the problem of editors who wield too much power, Bjørnson overstepped the limits of what an audience would accept as a balanced view. Everyone knew that the villain of the piece, whose scurrilous accusations bring about the death of a political figure, was modeled on the editor of the conservative newspaper *Morgenbladet*, a malicious and feared man who had long personally abused Bjørnson. Yet everyone felt that Bjørnson's ad hominem polemic against him went too far. The audience at Stjernström's theater filed out without applauding. Even in Germany, where the principals were not identifiable, the play fell flat.

With *A Bankruptcy* Bjørnson equaled what the French utilitarian drama had achieved, and in some respects improved on it. André Antoine, the French theater producer, considered the fourth act (evidently act two, scene two, and act three of the Norwegian original) "the most magnificent tragedy about money that had ever been seen onstage."[5]

These two plays proved there was an alternative to standard theater fare—the French salon drama that dominated the Scandinavian stage, the drama that Strindberg described as "a bourgeois-aristocratic affair in which the leading characters have at least 12,000 francs annual income, and the events always transpire on Brussels carpets. . . . Their only occupation seems to be to keep the conversation going. Everything that ties one to life is missing. No occupation, no responsibilities, no chores, scarcely any sorrows. These people are born wearing polished shoes, sitting on sofas, with a riding whip in their hands and a revolver in the desk."[6]

Although his debt to French drama is apparent—in the case of *A Bankruptcy*, to Sardou's *La Famille Benoiton* (1865), and in the case of *The Editor*, to Augier's *Les Effrontés* (1861)—Bjørnson surpasses his teachers and goes directly to life for his material. Less shapely in form than the French "well-made" plays, Bjørnson's are also less artificial. They pulsate with real life: Bjørnson had himself gone bankrupt and had been cruelly slandered in the press.

The premiere of *A Bankruptcy* in Stockholm was an unprecedented success, thanks in large measure to Stjernström's direction. His long preparatory work with the actors paid off. "Everything seems so true to life and natural that one believes one is present in the unfortunate home," said one observer.

Ellen Key, a believer in old-fashioned values, wrote to Bjørnson of her impressions. "All around I saw sad, tearful faces and heard cries of how honest was the picture you drew and how deep your insight. Everyone recognized the characters you created, everyone remembered similar situations and a similar home. . . . You opened wide the doors of the heart and let God's true light stream in. The dark and false powers withdrew in shame, and in place of them came a host of bright and beautiful thoughts."[7]

A Bankruptcy was the first Norwegian play to achieve international success. For Ibsen, who time and again had had to follow in his rival's footsteps, the good reviews and the unprecedented number of productions in Germany must have been particularly galling. He had settled in Dresden in 1868 and moved to Munich, the literary center of the German confederation, in 1871; his eye was more and more on the German market. He had left provincial Norway behind him and assumed the airs of a cosmopolitan. He had turned from his youthful intrigue dramas modeled on the French well-made play and made his name with German philosophical drama that concerned itself with mighty issues of lasting import, promising immortality. And now Bjørnson, the plucky farm boy on whom the gods smiled, had conquered Germany with a play that featured characters from the middle class in a Norwegian backwater, concocted a plot centering on so mean a thing as a business failure, and inculcated a banal moral worthy of his clergyman father. While Ibsen was collecting medals from royalty, the republican Bjørnson was receiving kudos from the theatergoing public. All this was enough to make Ibsen recall his own theatrical triumph with *The League of Youth.*

Pillars of Society

Bjørnson's success finally led Ibsen to commit himself to the French problem play. He had already drafted some notes for a play with a contemporary setting, a drama about a ship's officer who breathes fresh life into a hidebound Norwegian town. The main theme was to be "liberation from all customs and conventions, a new beautiful life of freedom." Nothing came of this material, while Ibsen busied himself with Julian's apostasy.

It is understandable that while he was grappling with that huge double drama, he paid little heed to what Brandes was telling him, both in the "breakthrough" lectures of 1871–72 and in conversation. Brandes was publicly exhorting him to write plays that submitted social problems to debate, and in private he must have heard of Brandes's enthusiasm for the new French utilitarian drama. The critic was an expert on the subject, having delivered six lectures from April 23 to May 17, 1872, on the French drama from Beaumarchais to Dumas *fils*. His point of view was that of an out-and-out materialist and hard-line naturalist, who saw money as the basis of all morality, and who praised the new French drama for its obsession with marriage problems, sexual relations, property rights, and class differences, all the things that the middle class was talking about. Money, he said, was "the object with which morality maintains its most regular connections."[1]

Yet even after Ibsen had finished with Julian, he refused for some time to commit himself fully to *le théâtre utile*. Finally, in the summer of 1875, he overcame his inner resistance and began a play about a social problem. Undoubtedly, it was more envy of Bjørnson than advice from Brandes that made him make up his mind. Bjørnson's courage and uprightness and optimism converted Brandes's admonitions into imperatives.

A *Bankruptcy* was published in March 1875, and Ibsen read it immediately. At the end of May, when the king's medal was mailed to him in Munich, he thought about wearing it at the students' meeting in Uppsala that summer. He decided, however, not to attend, and instead sent a poem, "A Greeting in Song to Sweden" ("Sanger-hilsen til Sverige"), in which he declared that it was a poet's duty to ring in the new era. On June 2 he composed a poem, "Far Away" ("Langt borte"), printed in Brandes's journal *Det nittende Aarhundrede*, expressing his pessimistic view of the times and the hollowness of the phrases uttered at student congresses. He envisioned a threatening specter forming itself out of dead ideals at celebratory banquets and festivals.

> The ghosts of times past and dead men
> Mingle with the students once again.
>
> Out of the cigar smoke and the haze of oratory
> They come together, these spooks of history.
>
> . . .
>
> We lent our ears to scholars and others of that ilk,
> Careful ourselves to touch the world with gloves of silk.
>
> We go on dreaming, not knowing what road to take,
> Afraid of commitment to deeds that make or break.
>
> When will there come to wake us from our daze
> The spirit of the times and the augurs of our age?[2]

The poet who four years earlier had said that he would wait, elegantly attired, wearing kid gloves, for an invitation to the revolution was now reproaching himself for his isolationism.

The mood of the poem, the sense of fearful expectancy, the awareness of strong forces at work along with uneasiness about what they portended, is captured by Strindberg in an appreciation of Bjørnson's accomplishments, written for a French journal.

> Now that hypnotic trance into which "esthetic" Scandinavia had fallen began to come to an end. New winds sprang up; the thunder of 1870–71 [the Franco-Prussian War and the Paris Commune] could be heard all the way up to the Norwegian alps. The new way of seeing the world proclaimed in France by Taine and in England by Darwin, Mill, and Spencer could not help but awaken the Nordic lands, which always took note of the intellectual movements on the continent.
>
> For a while it was quiet in our tranquil countries. Bjørnson said nothing. One expected a catastrophe; but where and when it would come, no one knew.
>
> The air grew more and more stifling. Now and then one could pick up some unclear signals from the outposts, but nothing made much sense. The key to the riddle was missing.[3]

Bjørnson's realistic plays ignited this charged atmosphere. As Strindberg said, Bjørnson "had broken with . . . the esthetic drama, which the devotees of 'art for art's sake' valued so highly." He deliberately sought to awaken the public, and from then on, he was dangerous.

"Moses had come down from the mountain to talk to the people, his face bare, without the theatrical effects of clouds and thunder."[4]

A few weeks later Ibsen addressed to Brandes a rhymed letter in which he took his famous stand of noncommitment. "I prefer to ask questions; it is not my duty to answer them." The poem uses an oceangoing ship as a metaphor for modern Europe. The steamship has set its course for a new continent; he and Brandes have bought their tickets and stand on the aft deck, waving goodbye to the receding shore. The air is free and liberating. But when they have sailed far out to sea, the ship seems to slow down. Crew and passengers succumb to a feeling of indifference. What they lack is faith in the future. The poem concludes ominously, with a voice crying clearly, "I believe we are sailing with a corpse for cargo."

That powerful image was presumably suggested by the hubbub stirred up by the reformer Samuel Plimsoll in July 1875, when, in striving to protect crews who risked their lives on unsound ships, he addressed the English parliament and denounced the owners of rotten and overloaded ships as murderers and the politicians who supported them as scoundrels. The catchphrases "Plimsoll coffins" and "floating coffins" went round the world. While there was no law in England against overloading ships, seamen who refused to work on unseaworthy vessels could be punished.[5] Also, there were stories that in building the huge ship the *Great Eastern*, some workers had been trapped between its double hulls and left to die.[6]

In September 1875 Ibsen began writing a play that would feature one of these unsafe ships. Ibsen's pessimism was nothing new. In 1871 he had compared civilization to a sinking ship. Now, in 1875, his mood was actually rather optimistic. If progress cannot be made unless the people have faith, then it is incumbent on the poet to engender this faith. Adopting this attitude, Ibsen finally set to work on his first problem play, a play that he planned as counterpoint to *The League of Youth*, offering hope and encouragement in place of the cynicism and satire of the earlier play. He told his publisher he would be probing into "several of the more important questions of the day."[7]

If people like Brandes wanted him to submit problems to debate, Ibsen would provide them in abundance. *Pillars of Society* (*Samfundets støtter*) is a plum pudding of social issues: female emancipation, the workers' resistance to improved machinery, financial speculation in railroads, and marine racketeering, all of them the subjects of heated debate in the daily press. The newspapers were filled with stories about businessmen taking advantage of inside information to grow rich on the expansion of Norwegian railroads (the first was built in 1854), while the Storting considered a number of bills that would determine which parts of the country would be the first to benefit from this new mode of transportation. As the industrial age began to affect Norway, there was an enormous growth in shipping by sea, from 230,000 tons in 1850 to 1.5 million tons in 1880. In 1874 the first Marxist organization, the Norske arbeideres forening (Norwegian Workers' Union), was formed, and *Pillars of Society* marked the first time that the laboring class appeared on the Norwegian stage.

The outrage over unsafe ships being sent to sea is the basis of the melodramatic plot. When he visited Norway in 1874, Ibsen would have heard about the shipping scandals in that seafaring nation. This question, like that of unscrupulous businessmen growing rich on the rapid expansion of Norwegian railroads, is contained within the larger issue of the morality of a society that "counts human lives as so much capital investment." In accord with Brandes's materialist view, *Pillars of Society* pictures economic motives at work even in a small, undeveloped country. Laborer and capitalist are both driven solely by self-interest, the former to protect his job against the machine, the latter to secure his financial position in a world in which fortunes can be made and lost overnight.

The role of the capitalist Consul Bernick is central to the play. As an entrepreneur, he is bringing backward Norway into the modern age. Because of him the railroad will be brought to his native town and new industries will be opened. His primary interest, however, is in buying up land in order to sell it when the railroad is built. With his insider's knowledge, he can buy cheap and sell high.

When *Pillars* was produced in Germany, it was accepted as a prosocialist work, the first of that kind to win a place on the German stage. However, the major crisis in the drama is not the direct result of economic forces, nor is it resolved in economic terms. Although Consul Bernick is an enterprising capitalist, he is also a guilt-ridden sinner, a Norwegian Dimmesdale, who had let someone else take the blame for a sexual escapade in his youth. While betrothed to a young woman with the proper social connections, the twenty-three-year-old Bernick had been having an affair with an actress, whose husband returned inopportunely one night. The stepbrother of Bernick's fiancée assumed the role of the trapped lover and confirmed rumors of his guilt by taking the next boat to America. When the willing scapegoat returns after fifteen years abroad, the truth threatens to be revealed just when Bernick is preparing a financial coup that calls for the community to have absolute faith in him.

In his apprentice days Ibsen had mastered the craft of the well-made play, and *Pillars*, with its complex plot and its surprising reversals, demonstrates that he had not forgotten the tricks of the trade. And since the tricks are fairly obvious, it is hard to take the play very seriously. Compared with Bjørnson's first two realistic plays, *Pillars* seems like a clever confection, an entertainment, a melodrama in which unexpected plot twists lead to a happy ending. To save his business interests and to keep his youthful escapade a secret, Bernick intends to send his brother-in-law on a ship that has not been repaired and made seaworthy. The magnate's scandalous past will vanish in the depths of the ocean. However, the brother-in-law sails on a different ship, while aboard the doomed vessel is Bernick's own young son, an adventurous stowaway! All ends well, and grateful for the return of his son, Bernick becomes a different man.

To a Marxist, the shipowner's ruthless careerism stands for the corruption of the propertied class; to a less doctrinaire reader, Bernick stands for a male-dominated society. Ibsen defines two moral orders in terms of the sexes, the female sex being the oppressed, the exploited, and the betrayed. Women will be the bearers of a new moral standard, whose first convert is Bernick himself. The old era with "its cosmetics, with its hypocrisy and hollowness, with its ridiculous respectability and its silly proprieties, can stand," says the reformed Bernick to his fellow citizens as he is about to confess his sins, "as a kind of museum for us, open for our edification." "The new era" (the phrase is repeated several times) will begin when each individual sees deeply into himself, coming to terms with himself and not with society, for "the spirits of truth and freedom—these are the pillars of society" (the last words in the play). Everything turns out for the best in this least Ibsenish of all possible worlds.

King Oscar II asked for a copy, and Ibsen sent him an explanatory letter saying that his criticism was aimed at the individual, not at social institutions. "It is the inner being, the soul, that must be cleansed and set free; . . . it is not external liberties that should be sought after but rather the freedom of the individual, and this can be acquired and possessed by the individual himself as long as his conduct has truth as its base and origin. All this does not find direct expression in my book; however, it is my hope that the reader will see it for himself and accept it as lying at the core of the work."[8]

Pillars casts in dramatic form the main thoughts that Ibsen had expressed in his letters and poems. Society is dominated by old ideas and customs; it is like a ship with a corpse in its cargo. A new era lies on the horizon, but no one knows what it will bring. Only one thing is certain—society is built on lies, hypocrisy, deceit—and Bernick is the perfect image of this society. He is so much a part of what he himself calls "this bungled social system" that he both contributes to it and suffers from it. He tells himself that a time will come "when truth will find its way into our social order," yet when he speaks out and reveals the truth, there is no sign that things will be any different.

Pillars is an evasive and disingenuous work, with much more of Peer Gynt in it than of Brand. Like Bernick, Ibsen—who now had shares in a streetcar company in Christiania and investments in a new bank in Bergen and a steamship line in Kristiansand[9]—could admit that "a desire and a hunger for power, influence, respect, a craving for influence and for position have been the driving forces behind most of my actions."[10] And, like Bernick, he could rationalize his subterfuges by arguing that faith in man's perfectibility was needed before the new era would dawn. Worst of all, Bernick does not confess his blackest sin, his willingness to sacrifice a ship and its crew to save his reputation. His moment of truth has simply assured the continuance of the present system.

One cannot help but notice that Bernick is really not a changed man at the end. He still has control of the railroad company, and his greatest moral crime, that of sending out the leaking ship, is not acknowledged. The ending is not so much ironic as ambiguous. The citizens who gathered to cheer and applaud him as the leading pillar of their community silently drift away into the twilight, a dimming light that undercuts Bernick's words. The pillars of truth and freedom in this play form not the gateway to a new age but only the façade of an old mansion haunted by ghosts.[11]

The contrast between Bjørnson's problem play and Ibsen's is striking. Bjørnson's characters are more fully delineated, and the warmth he feels for them is evident. Ibsen's characters are essentially stick figures with labels attached to them. Caring nothing for political revolutions, only for a revolution of the human spirit, Ibsen hopes for the dawn of a new era but won't say what that entails. Bjørnson is the republican who wants to gather the people together as a political force for progress.

Ibsen was as adept at constructing clever plots as he was in knowing how far he could go without losing his largely conservative audience, the veritable pillars of society. By now, he was one of them.

Edvard Brandes, the brother of Georg, saw what a sham the play was. "What I have against *Pillars of Society* is that it is written with such extreme caution. . . . It is quite possible for the press and the public to assume that it is not a tendentious work; it can be deliberately misunderstood. And that is what has occurred here in Denmark, where its effect as opposition drama is nil. . . . Ibsen is so anxious not to offend that there is nothing BIG about this play. The big questions are there but are reduced to trivialities and are handled trivially. Technically, however, it's brilliant, and except for the fourth act produces a great effect in the theater."[12]

Strindberg pointed out the difference between Bjørnson and Ibsen. "A *Bankruptcy* and *The Editor,* the epoch-making plays by which realism may be said to have made its entrance into Sweden, convulsed society for a few moments, but the medicine was too strong. However, when Ibsen's *Pillars of Society* followed, then—yes, then our stockholders applauded it and no one seemed to mind."[13]

Pillars is a shrewd work by a man who very reluctantly tackled the problem play. He had to respond to the moral exhortations of Brandes and the artistic challenge of Bjørnson without losing his position as the Olympian poet above politics. He accomplished his aim to perfection. The play was an unprecedented success in Germany; in 1878 five theaters in Berlin were playing it simultaneously. Over the next ten years it was performed at fifty theaters in Germany for a total of one thousand performances. When it was presented at the Christiania Theater, Ibsen demanded the highest royalty that the management had ever paid to a playwright: two thousand kronor plus 2.5 percent of the gross receipts after the twenty-sixth performance.[14]

THE ROAD TO *A DOLL'S HOUSE*

Pillars of Society signaled a tentative rapprochement between Ibsen and Bjørnson. By publishing it, Ibsen adopted a political stance closer to that of his republican rival, while Bjørnson was becoming more radical in his thinking about religion. The year 1875 was crucial for both writers, with Bjørnson publishing his groundbreaking realistic plays and Ibsen finally determining to involve himself, however gingerly, on the liberal side.

An academic appointment in 1875 provided the flashpoint that brought the two writers closer together. The controversy that year over the appointment of J. Ernst Sars (1835–1917) as a professor of history at the University of Christiania brought the repressive nature of the right forcibly to Ibsen's attention. Sars was a positivist and a materialist, and one of his colleagues prophesied dire consequences if Sars were to be allowed to inculcate his irreligious views on young minds. The newspaper *Morgenbladet* took up the cudgels and editorialized against Sars, characterizing him as a "freethinker." The editor of *Morgenbladet* had frequently aspersed and calumniated Bjørnson, and Bjørnson had got his innings by portraying him in *The Editor* as a despot who wielded power with an utter disregard for the truth.

The truth was more important to Ibsen than politics. He canceled his subscription to *Morgenbladet* and began reading the liberal *Dagbladet*. In 1877 truth and freedom were the big words that ricocheted back and forth between Sweden and Norway. Bjørnson published his play *The King* (*Kongen*), an attack on the institution of the monarchy. Too controversial for its time, this play, with its call for a Norway independent of Sweden, had to wait twenty-five years for its first performance. In September Ibsen traveled to Uppsala to receive his honorary doctorate (an honor denied to Bjørnson) and spent many hours in conversation with King Oscar. While he was there, the king addressed the students, urging them to seek what is true in life. Citing the biblical commandment "Honor thy father and mother," he urged them to have respect for what had been true for centuries and consequently was true now, the status quo. This commandment, said the king, "exhorts respect for the paternal and maternal, for all that is inherent in one's native home, in state, church, the university, and many other social institutions."[1]

A month later, on October 31, Bjørnson spoke to a student association in Norway on the difference between the truth and what often passes for it. Responding to the king's rhetoric, Bjørnson said in one of his most famous speeches, "To Be with the Truth" ("Om at være i sandhed"), that there could be no honest search for the truth under those conditions. "If we can't go beyond our reverence for the existing conditions . . . we are in a sorry state. . . . We must have reverence for truth. And if we cannot begin here and now, if only modestly but honestly, then I say, the time of the visitation [alluding to Luke 19:44] has been lost. This is our opportunity. And just now a strong spirit among us—in his *Pillars of Society*, just as previously in his *League of Youth*—has suggested that we suffer from a lurking knavishness. But that is not what we suffer from, as far as I can see. No, we suffer from self-deception, we suffer from many a lie, lies that we simply don't see, as well as lies that we do see but don't know what to do about them.

"And how can it be otherwise in a time of transition such as ours? There is much of the old that is dubious, but we don't know what the coming thing is, and we are afraid of the unknown."[2]

The following year Bjørnson took the momentous step of publicly announcing that he was a freethinker who no longer believed in the divinity of Christ.

The advance copy of *Pillars* that Ibsen sent to Bjørnson contained a brief note, the first words he had addressed to the liberal leader and his literary rival in eight years. Although there was a great deal in their personalities and philosophies that would keep them from ever being close friends, the gap between them on the political and literary side was considerably narrowed in 1877, as much by Ibsen as by Bjørnson.

Anticipating what Bjørnson would say about truth and society, Ibsen in 1871 had written to Brandes, telling him not to be "frightened by the venerableness of institutions. The state has its roots in time; it will reach its height in time. Greater things than it will fall; all religion will fall. Neither standards of morality nor of art are eternal."[3]

It took some years before Ibsen could participate in the revolution and take the great leap forward. He was distracted by politics and especially by Bjørnson's progressiveness, which he neither as a public citizen nor as a dramatist could ignore. He was interested in a revolution more far-reaching than a reorganization of the political state. "Changing one form of government for another is merely a matter of toying with various degrees of the same thing—a little more or a little less. Folly, all of it."[4]

Ibsen's lifelong quarrel was with himself, and the outer scene engaged him only to the extent that it might explain or alleviate the division within himself. He was excited by Brandes's 1872 book *Emigrantlitteraturen* in that it dealt with a momentous change in the concept of the human being and came at a unique moment in his own evolution. It placed the individual in a social, not a religious, context and implied that a radical change in conventions and institutions could bring about a change in the very nature of the human being.

Just as in *Pillars of Society* women are presented as the heralds of a new era, so Brandes in *Emigrantlitteraturen* examined the relationship of the sexes as a sign of profound social changes. He used Madame de Staël's novel *Delphine*, a defense of and justification for divorce, as a springboard for his discussion of the war against society. He did not start with the French Revolution, as a thoroughly political writer would have; he quickly launched into the question of the status of women in society.

> The "war with society" which she depicts is less a conflict with the state or the law than with the jumble of conventions and beliefs, old and new, artificial and natural, reasonable and unreasonable, hurtful and beneficial, which, fused together into a cohesive and apparently homogeneous mass, constitute the stuff whereof public opinion is made. Just as so-called sound common sense, which is always ready to set itself in opposition to any new philosophy, is at any given time to a great extent simply the congealed remains of a philosophy of an earlier date, so the rules of society and the verdicts pronounced by society in accordance with these rules, verdicts always unfavorable in the case of new ideas, are to a great extent founded upon ideas which in their day had a hard struggle to assert themselves in the face of the opposition of the then prevailing public opinion. That which was once an original, living idea stiffens in time into the corpse of an idea.[5]

As we have seen, Brandes had a personal reason for beginning his survey of the main currents in contemporary literature with a discussion of novels picturing the situation of women in postrevolutionary society. *Delphine* was a herald of the many novels and plays that were to follow, works that provide the principal subject matter of the French problem play. But writers like Augier and Dumas *fils* explored the demimonde, the world of courtesans and high-class prostitutes, who were causing problems by infiltrating the best families, undermining the basic social institution, and unraveling the fabric of genteel society. In provincial Scandinavia, however, the demimondaine scarcely existed, and when writers like Ibsen tackled the woman question they followed the path taken by Madame de Staël and raised questions about women in general, not about the few who were preying on upper-class society.

This larger question about women probed more deeply into the foundations of European civilization. It went beyond social conventions and political organizations; it challenged the teachings of the Christian Church. It ventured into the realm of the spirit; hence Ibsen's interest. That woman was put on earth to be man's helpmate was a fundamental tenet of the church, and all sorts of corollaries about woman's behavior followed from that. The sermon that the archbishop of Sweden preached in 1827, appropriately on the day of the Annunciation of the Virgin Mary, clearly defined the proper role of a woman. Her place was in the home. If she attempted to invade man's world, she would become a repulsive, aggressive creature who could only be compared to a prostitute. In both cases she overstepped the bounds of feminine propriety, and the angel of innocence would blush and turn from her. A wife must always be meek and humble. She must always give in to her husband, even if he is wrong.

The stern teachings of the church blocked the attempts of liberals to improve the lot of women. Efforts to provide unmarried women with some of the civil rights that an ordinary man acquired at the age of twenty-one were consistently warded off in the Swedish parliament for nearly half a century. Part of this resistance welled up from a fear of women's sexual nature. Many men shared that ancient, deeply ingrained belief that women were creatures of irrational passion, especially at certain times in their lives, when they were possessed by insatiable sexual desire, and for that reason it would be reckless to give them the civil rights of men. Others, looking more carefully at the matter of age, thought women might attain majority at the age of thirty, when their sexual passions should have abated somewhat. However, a member of the estate of the lords spiritual avowed that all discussion was idle, since he had never heard a reasonable woman express a desire to see the laws changed. The most extreme rationalization came from the royal secretary Jonas Almströmer, who admitted that in an age of emancipation, such as this in which he found himself, it was understandable that some men should be embarrassed by the complete dependence of women on men. "But an independent woman," he reminded his hearers in the 1856–58 session of the Swedish Riksdag, "is a cipher. For she is neither man nor woman but something in between. . . . The true sense of freedom finds its expression in being dependent on another and in sacrificing for another. To the extent that the human being cuts off these bonds, she becomes of the flesh, selfish, bestial. She becomes the slave of that worst of all despots, oneself."

What does it mean to be independent? "It means to stand by oneself, to be self-sufficient [*att stå för sig själv, att vara sig själv nog*].[6] This might with some sense be said of man, since he was created first and stood by himself, the sole lord over the rest of creation." However, even this masterpiece of God could not be happy standing alone. Even he had to have a helper. "Now, then, can one conceive of woman standing independent and alone? If such a being were conceivable, she would take on the qualities of a man. Now I ask you: is it masculine women that we want? Definitely not. This devilish metamorphosis is surely something we would all wish to avoid setting our eyes on." In a similar vein, the elderly Right Honorable Vilhelm Nordenfelt waxed eloquent on the need to preserve woman's purity against the onslaughts of new ideas. "No, gentlemen, the force of knowledge, burning with the eternal flame of truth, can neither cast a shadow on, nor stain, the lily of innocence; nor does it lessen one iota that pleasant aroma emanating from the mignonette of maidenliness, since the true and the beautiful are not by any means opposed to each other; rather, they provide each other's fulfillment."[7]

In spite of such remonstrations from the forces of reaction, the majority age for unmarried women had already been fixed in 1845 at twenty-five. In the same year, women had also been given equal rights of inheritance with men, and in 1846 the right to engage in certain forms of small business on their own. Subsequently, in 1863 they were given the right to vote in local elections; in 1871 they were allowed to study for a medical degree at a university; and two years later they were admitted to any field of study.

What broadened the minds of these lawmakers was less their better understanding of woman's nature than the economic situation in Scandinavia. In the twenty-five-year period before the 1856–58 session of the Riksdag, there had been a rapid rise in population along with a decrease in the number of marriages, and the number of unwed females over fifteen had increased by 50 percent. Something had to be done to find a place in society for these women.

An English visitor to Norway found the women there well treated. "No people in the world live more happily in married life than the Norwegians. The men are kind and affectionate husbands, who never interfere in domestic concerns." He also noted that "the law of divorce is far too lax."[8]

In both Sweden and Norway a growing number of feminists were turning to the novel as a medium for voicing their demands. In Denmark the movement was distinguished by a number of sexually emancipated women, who, influenced by George Sand, adopted mannish attire, arousing the disgust of many men who might otherwise have been indifferent to the feminist movement.

Ibsen's female characters in his early plays were often of the submissive kind that would have pleased the Swedish archbishop, none more so than Agnes in *Brand*. And Ibsen was married to a woman who selflessly devoted herself to her husband's career. With *The League of Youth*, however, his treatment of women began to change. Selma Brattsberg complains to her husband that she has never been asked to make any sacrifice because she has never been considered strong enough. "How I've longed for just a bit of your worries! But if I asked, you laughed it off as a joke. You dressed me as a doll. You played with me as you play with a child."[9]

He thought about a play in which "the resounding note throughout would be women's shyness in the midst of the men, occupied with their small aims, who make themselves important in a way that both irritates and impresses."[10] Yet nothing came of this promising theme until five years later, when he set to work on *Pillars of Society*. The voices of the principal women in it form a chorus of protest against patriarchal society. Dina, the orphaned daughter of an actress, says she is terrified by all the respectability that society demands of her. Bernick's maiden sister remonstrates against the tyranny of conventions and social propriety. She tells Dina to assert herself and kick over the traces. "Rebel against it, Dina!" she says, urging her to flee from the stifling atmosphere of the small town that has starved her own spirit. Lona Hessel, the most outspoken of the women, having breathed the liberating atmosphere of America for fifteen years, vows to air out all the foul-smelling moral linen that has lain too long in the closeted minds of the town's upright citizens. She functions as the *raisonneur* of the play, doing more than anyone else to bring Bernick to his senses and bringing down the curtain with the pronouncement that truth and freedom are the pillars of society. Bernick has to acknowledge that "it is you women who are the pillars of society."

As a young girl, Lona Hessel had bobbed her hair and walked in man's boots in stormy weather. She was not entirely Ibsen's creation; she was a recognizably accurate portrait of Aasta Hansteen (1824–1908), an outspoken Norwegian feminist and an object of notoriety in 1875 when Ibsen began mulling over plans for his new play. The daughter of a professor, she studied painting in Paris in her youth, and one of her works was later purchased by Ibsen. She found her true calling as a feminist after reading J. S. Mill's *The Subjection of Women* (in Georg Brandes's translation) and dedicated herself to fighting against the tyranny of the male sex. She left the state Lutheran Church and lectured on feminism. Carrying herself like a man, clumping about in man's boots, a riding crop tucked under her arm, she cut a remarkable figure in Christiania. Although ridiculed and laughed at (for a while she took to going out only at night to avoid the heckling of young boys), she made it her special mission to carry on a campaign on behalf of a certain Swedish lady of the nobility, who had been spurned by a Norwegian student who had seduced her. She organized a public demonstration, demanding that the student either marry the lady or be dismissed from the university. In 1878 she lectured in Copenhagen and Trondhjem on "Woman Created in God's Image." She wrote a poem in which she scolded "the brave men" who provide one morality for women and another, much easier to bear, for men.[11] "This society of yours," Lona Hessel tells the men around her, "is an old bachelor's club. You never see the women."

Not quite true, of course, but it was all too true that men did tend to see women as either prostitutes or breeders of children; as either cooks and seamstresses to make men's life easier or as pretty objects for men to adore or dolls for them to play with. The image of the bourgeois wife as a doll was common in the mid-nineteenth century, prompted undoubtedly by the popularity of the toy. One of the advocates of greater rights for women spoke up in the 1856–58 session of the Swedish parliament against those men who chose to look upon a woman as "a plaything [*en rodocka*], a doll, whose purpose is to while away an idle man's time with babble and prattle."[12] In England, Bella in Dickens's *Our Mutual Friend* (1865) yearned to be "so much worthier than the doll in the doll's house." The *OED* cites the same author's phrase "a habitable doll's house" from *Bleak House* (1852). In Bjørnson's comedy *The Newly Married Couple* (*De Nygifte*, 1865), the young husband expostulates with his parents-in-law, "You allow [my wife] to treat me as the biggest doll you've ever given her. You can't afford to relinquish any more love than what she can give to a doll. . . . A child can never be a wife, and as long as she is with you, she will always be a child."[13]

William Archer in what was once the standard English translation of Ibsen's play called it *A Doll's House*, although he knew that was not quite right. *A Doll Home* would be a more accurate translation of the Norwegian *Et dukkehjem*, which, Ibsen said, was "a new word that I have coined."[14] When Strindberg countered Ibsen's play with a short story, he called it "Ett dockhem," not *ett dockskåp*, the Swedish word for the toy. Ibsen meant his title to connote a home in which both the man and the wife were little more than dolls, shielding themselves from the harsh reality outside it. In the draft of his play Ibsen has Nora say, "Our home [*hjem*] has been a dollhouse [*en dukkestue*]."[15] The title in German, said Ibsen, whose knowledge of that language was quite good, should be *Ein Puppenhaus*. There were two words in German for the toy, *Puppenhaus* and *Puppenstube* (as in Norwegian, *dukkehus* and *dukkestue*), and Ibsen preferred *Puppenhaus* because it could also mean a cocoon. In the standard German edition of Ibsen's works, published during his lifetime, the title is *Ein Puppenheim*, a coined word, like *dukkehjem*.

In English, *A Doll Home* has some of the strangeness that Ibsen's title originally had and takes advantage of the important distinction between a house and a home that exists in the Germanic languages, but for all that it is not likely to replace *A Doll's House*.

The Women Behind the Play

A *Doll's House,* a play almost as well known to the worldwide general public as *Hamlet,* did not spring forth irrepressibly from Ibsen's mind, as *Brand* and *Peer Gynt* had done. As was the case with *Pillars of Society,* he had to be nudged into writing it, yielding to pressure from a couple of woman friends, as well as from Brandes, but most of all from his wife. Ibsen's son said that the "decisive influence was certainly exerted by my mother."[1] What they all wanted from Ibsen was a social problem play about women's emancipation. With his philosophical turn of mind, however, he wanted to deal with timeless subjects. He would not have tackled the story of a married couple who did not understand each other if he had not caught a glimpse within it of a vastly greater drama, a drama not just about a change in society but about a transformation of human nature itself. His primary interest was not in feminism, and he might never have written *A Doll's House* had it not been for those women who kept bringing the movement to his attention.

Camilla Collett, sister of the eminent Norwegian poet Henrik Wergeland and an author in her own right, was a leading spokesperson for the cause in the 1870s. She exchanged many letters with Suzannah Ibsen, often touching on women's emancipation.[2] In January and February 1872, when she visited Dresden, she was a frequent guest of the Ibsens, and she spent many hours talking about women's rights with Suzannah and quarreling with her husband. About this time she read Mill's *The Subjection of Women.* She did not see eye to eye with Ibsen on matters of love and sex. She was furious when a museum displayed an instrument called "a violin," which was used to punish women who nagged and bickered. Ibsen replied that women had it better than men. When women quarreled, they got the "violin"; when men quarreled they got the ax or the sword. He also said that Collett worked not for women's rights but for ladies' rights; that is, the freedom to do whatever they felt like.[3]

In a letter to a friend she reported, "He is an egoist and a despot from top to toe, and especially so as a man to a woman. . . . I do not think anyone, certainly no man, has said to him what I was not afraid to say. . . . He listened, and read patiently my observations on the position of women, said something nice about the cleverness [*Aandrigheden*] in them—but as for the spirit [*Aanden*] in them, that he was directly opposed to. . . . I do not understand him. Or I understand him only as one of those geniuses who least of all through living have arrived at a sound view of life and who therefore in spite of their great gifts go wrong. He has always lived as a recluse."[4]

Ibsen found Collett a talented but very unhappy person, while she won the sympathy and support of both Suzannah and her sister Marie Thoresen. Suzannah had been rather conventional in her views on women until she listened to Collett. It was Collett who convinced her, a pastor's daughter from the Norwegian provinces, that women's position in society and before the law must be changed.[5]

In a series of newspaper articles printed in the Swedish paper *Aftonbladet* in 1876 (and issued in 1877 in book form as *Fra de stummes lejr* [From the camp of the voiceless]), Collett drove home the point that women were only an amusement for men, a "a culinary artwork." Man's false ideal of woman demoralized men and weakened the moral fabric of society. She singled out Ibsen as one of the worst offenders for his depiction of Agnes in *Brand* and Solveig in *Peer Gynt*, while praising him for his treatment of women in the early saga dramas.

Deeply impressed by this thin, shy, soft-spoken, and nearsighted woman, Suzannah communicated these ideas to Ibsen, probably in the hope that he would give the feminist cause a larger role in his next play. In the spring of 1877, when the Ibsens were residing in Munich, Collett was again a frequent visitor. Every night Ibsen escorted her back to her hotel. Now they got along better, being of similar temperament, if not of the same opinion. John Paulsen called her an "Ibsen in skirts."[6] He said she was so rich in ideas that out of one of her books, three average books could be made.[7] The conversations Ibsen had with the sixty-four-year-old, somewhat embittered champion of women's rights left their mark in *Pillars of Society*.

But a cause does not make a play, and what Ibsen lacked was a story, a plot. As if bidden by his genius, the woman who would provide it walked into his life. In 1870, when he drafted some notes for a modern comedy about "women's shyness in the midst of men," he received a book called *Brand's Daughters*, intended as a sequel to his epic drama and dedicated to him. Its author, Laura Petersen, was a twenty-year-old Danish woman (although born in Norway, in 1849), who like so many others had been uplifted and inspired by the pure idealism of *Brand*. After her father died, she moved to Denmark in 1872. As a woman, she felt a bit guilty

Figure 12. Suzannah Ibsen, Munich 1870s.
The only portrait of her.

for devoting herself to so unwomanly a profession as writing. Ibsen twitted her about that when he wrote to thank her for dedicating the book to him, saying that art and poetry were "not basically evil." He faulted her book for containing too much religious moralizing, which could be removed without doing any harm to the work, and he advised the young author that if she were serious about pursuing a career as a writer, she should draw on her own life.

"One must have something to create from, some real experience. The author who does not have that does not create; he only writes books."

Ibsen would not have written to this serious young woman at such length if he had not found something interesting about her. He told her that her personality, her "inner, psychological relation" to what she had written continued to occupy his mind long after he had put her book down.[8]

Petersen took this long, thoughtful letter as a personal invitation from a man she greatly admired, the man who had taught her that one's first duty was to be true to one's essential nature, regardless of society's demands or expectations. She

Figure 13. Laura Kieler (1849–1932).

had not written to Ibsen entirely out of the blue. She had grown up in Norway, and her mother had been a childhood friend of Camilla Collett. She had met Ibsen in Copenhagen in 1870, and she called on the Ibsens in Dresden in 1871 and was quickly made to feel at home. Ibsen delighted in her company and nicknamed her "the lark" (Torvald's pet name for Nora in *A Doll's House*).

Two years later this bright, blithe spirit married Victor Kieler, an *adjunct*, a teacher in a secondary school in Copenhagen. She wrote two more books, one of them about a difficult marriage, which Ibsen criticized as psychologically unsound.

Victor Kieler was his wife's antithesis. He was a rather solemn man, perpetually in poor health. He had an explosive temperament and, because his father had gone bankrupt when he stood security for a friend in need, was quite rabid on the subject of money and debts. When Laura learned that her husband's lungs were diseased and that he would have to spend time in a warmer climate, she suggested to him that he borrow from his father. He burst out in a rage: "Never!"

Then Laura, without his knowledge, borrowed money from a bank, with a friend in Norway standing as guarantor. She took Victor to Italy in 1876, letting him believe that the money had come from her writings.

On their way back to Denmark, Laura and Victor visited the Ibsens, now in Munich. Laura confided in Fru Ibsen and told her how she had saved her husband's life. Of course the story was passed on to Ibsen. Marriage had aged and dispirited Laura. Ibsen noted that she "no longer chirped her happy songs." When they parted, he said, "Don't be so afraid and despondent. You have no reason to be."

He was quite wrong. Upon her return to Copenhagen, her troubles increased. In fact, the sequence of events that followed was like a nightmare that brought her to the verge of a complete nervous collapse. She repaid her first loan by borrowing more money. This time both a distant relative and a businessman provided security for the note. Circumstances now combined against her. When the note came due, she was in bed after giving birth. The businessman asked the relative to make good his security, but the latter was himself in financial straits. Desperate, Laura sent for another relative, who never appeared.

Throughout all this she was in touch with Fru Ibsen, who told her she was keeping her husband up to date about her troubles. Laura sent Ibsen the manuscript of her latest work, "Ultima Thule," hoping he would recommend it to his publisher, who would pay an advance against royalties. In March 1878 he wrote to tell her that in his opinion the work showed every sign of being written in haste. "Not in any way could I, or would I want to, recommend this manuscript." If published, it "would ruin your literary reputation and standing." He urged her to make a clean breast of her problems to her husband. "He must take on the burden of the cares and sorrows that torture and haunt you. You have already sacrificed more than is reasonable."

Laura had not disclosed all the facts in the case, and Ibsen suspected as much. "There must be something that you hold back in your letter and that totally changes the situation."[9]

Ibsen was Laura's last hope. When her relative sent a desperate letter asking her for the sake of the children to save his reputation, Laura forged a promissory note. The bank would not accept it. She tore the note to pieces and sent them to a man who had previously refused to help her, who was enraged by her conduct. Inevitably, rumors about her financial difficulties and marital problems reached the ears of the man most responsible for them—her husband. She was now about to endure the final humiliation. At her wits' end, physically exhausted and again pregnant, she began hallucinating. She bought a set of expensive furniture for three thousand kronor because her husband had once expressed a liking for it. Her husband, outraged by the deceit and dishonesty of his sacrificing wife, initiated divorce proceedings. He insisted that the newborn, unweaned child be taken from her and that she be denied custody of their other children. On his instruction, she was placed in an asylum for the mentally disturbed.

Ibsen was promptly informed of this development. In a letter to his publisher he said, "The story of Laura Kieler, as you probably know, came to a tragic catastrophe. Her husband informed us very briefly that she had been placed in a lunatic asylum. Do you know more about the situation, and if she is still there?"[10]

The doctors soon saw that she did not belong there, and after a month she was released. Subsequently, Victor realized he had acted impetuously, and he asked her to come back. For the sake of their children, she accepted. They were reunited after two years of separation.[11]

Ibsen found in Laura Kieler's story the dramatic material he was looking for. The main subjects of the French problem play were money and women, and her experience combined the two perfectly. On October 19, 1878, a few months after hearing that Laura had been institutionalized, he jotted down some notes for "a modern tragedy."

"There are two kinds of moral law, two kinds of conscience, one in man and a completely different one in woman. They do not understand each other; but in matters of practical living the woman is judged by man's law, as if she were not a woman but a man.

"The wife in the play ends up quite bewildered about what is right and what is wrong; her natural feelings on the one hand and her faith in authority on the other leave her quite confused.... She has committed a forgery, and she is proud of it, because she did it for love of her husband and to save his life. But the husband, with his conventional sense of honor, stands on the side of the law and looks at the affair with a man's eyes."[12]

While he immersed himself in the play, Nora became a real presence in his life, an eidetic presence.

"Now I have seen Nora," he exclaimed to his wife. "She came up to me and put her hand on my shoulder."

"How was she dressed?" asked Suzannah,

"In a simple blue wool skirt."[13]

(The inexpensive dress is meant as a contrast to the well-appointed parlor; Nora has been saving on clothes while paying off her debt.)

Nora, a shortened form of Eleanora or Leonora, was not a common name in Scandinavia at the time. Ibsen explained, "Oh, her full name was Leonora; but that was shortened to Nora when she was quite a little girl. Of course, you know, she was terribly spoilt by her parents."[14]

Much of the time that Ibsen spent writing a play was devoted to familiarizing himself with his characters. A great deal of thought went into scattered notes and random jottings before he tackled the first draft. But once the action of the play had become quite clear, he spent his time getting to know the people in it.

"As a rule," he said, "I write three versions of my plays, which differ considerably from one another—in the characterizations, not in the action. When I approach the first version, it is as if I knew my characters from having met them on a train; the ice has been broken, and we have chatted about this and that with one another. With the second draft, I see everything much more clearly; I know these people as if I had been with them at a resort for a month or two. I have grasped their basic character and their idiosyncrasies; but I still might be mistaken about some essential quality in them. Finally, I reach in the last draft the limits of my knowledge of these people. I know them from my close and long study of them. They have become my intimate friends who cannot disappoint or surprise me. As I see them now I shall always see them."[15]

As a new idea for a play germinated in his mind, he would spend hours pacing back and forth, sorting out his thoughts. For most of his realistic plays, this process lasted about a year or more. His first extant note for *A Doll's House* is dated October 19, 1878, but he had been thinking about the subject of the play long before that. Seven and a half months later he sat down to write the first draft. The third and final draft was sent to the publisher in late September 1879.

Ibsen identified himself completely with Nora's point of view, so much so that on one notable occasion, he emerged from his usual shell of taciturnity to lecture the women who did not take a firm stand for women's rights. In February 1879 he fought vigorously to have a woman appointed librarian of the Scandinavian Society in Rome. When the motion was defeated, nineteen to eleven, one vote short of the two-thirds majority needed, the enraged Ibsen refused to drink with, talk to, or even nod at those who had voted against it.

Some weeks later the society held its annual spring banquet. Much to everyone's amazement, Ibsen put in an appearance. He delivered a speech, a harangue, that startled his listeners. The Danish novelist J. P. Jacobsen, who was present, wrote to a friend, "You should have seen how delightfully shameless he was against his opponents! If you see that reactionary Rosenstand, ask him about the event, and he will fly into a rage. A certain marine officer Buchwaldt almost challenged Ibsen to a duel because of this woman question."[16]

The following account of what happened, set down some thirty years later by an eyewitness, captures in spirit what it may lack in accuracy, and provides an unusually detailed description of Ibsen in his fighting mode.

> He looked resplendent in full evening dress with all his orders and decorations. He frequently ran his hand through his abundant, gray-streaked hair. He

seemed to greet no one in particular, but nodded to all. There was a vast sense of calm on his face, but his eyes, both the right one and the left, were vigilant, very vigilant. He sat down apart from the others. We all thought that he had forgiven his fellow creatures; some even said that he regretted his previous actions. That thought contributed to making the mood of the handsomely decorated Scandinavians, long deprived of a gala evening, especially hopeful and promising. Suddenly he got up and walked over to a large table, confronting the whole hall with its dancing couples.

"Ladies and gentlemen!" The moment was charged with drama. What was he about to say? Would he confess his sins? He could not possibly be proposing a simple toast! Not him! Not Ibsen! Did he perhaps wish to make some sort of offering that would transform a happy social occasion into a jubilant one that would banish past hurts in the light of present joy? Or would he—?

"Ladies and gentlemen!"

He stroked his hair calmly. He began to speak softly, but with terrible solemnity. He had recently desired to do the society a great service, even, he might say, give it great joy by channeling into it the currents of new thought. No one could avoid the important issues. Not even here. In this Scandinavian society. In this little duck pond. He did not say duck pond, but the scorn on his lips said the same thing. And how had his proffer been received? As if it were a criminal act! An assault! Voted down by a few votes. And how had the ladies responded—the ladies on whose behalf he had made his motion? They had agitated and intrigued against him. They had spurned the gift he had offered them. What sort of women were they? They were worse than—worse than the lowest, worse than trash.

He was no longer speaking quietly. He was no longer stroking his hair. He shook his head and the gray mane on top of it. He crossed his arms on his chest. His eyes blazed. His voice trembled, his lips quivered, and he thrust out his lower lip. He resembled a lion.... And he repeated again and again: what kind of ladies are these, what kind of woman, what kind of female dog—ignorant, in the deepest sense uncultured, immoral, on a level with the lowest, dirtiest, most contemptible—.

Plop! A lady, Countess B., fell to the floor. She, like the rest of us, had been expecting a terrible word. Anticipating the worst, she fainted. She was carried out. Ibsen carried on—possibly in a somewhat more restrained fashion. But eloquently, without having to grope for words. Carried away by his own magniloquence, he railed against the wretchedness of mankind, especially the female part of it, for their lack of sense, their continual resistance to the new ideas that would make people greater and wiser and in all respects richer. He appeared to be transported. As his voice thundered, he seemed to be bringing enlighten-

> ment to himself. While his tongue chastised, his spirit sorted out the stuff of his own artistic creation. It was as if he actually experienced his theories, as if he personally lived with his characters. And when he had finished, he walked out into the hall, picked up his overcoat, and went home. Calmly and peacefully.[17]

This outburst of indignation had its intended effect. Shortly after the publication of *A Doll's House* the following December, the women members of the Scandinavian Society were given the right to vote, and Miss Fanny Riis, whom Ibsen had initially proposed as librarian, was now elected. She was a Norwegian girl, an acquaintance from his Bergen days. An ostentatiously emancipated woman, she was very masculine in appearance, cut her hair short, and smoked Havana cigars.

Nora Helmer is a different sort. She has never concerned herself with women's emancipation, and there is nothing masculine in her physical makeup. She is very much like the Laura Kieler, née Petersen, who entered Ibsen's life. And her relationships with her old friend Fru Linde, in whom she confides, and with Krogstad, who holds the incriminating promissory note that imperils Nora's happiness, are taken over directly from Ibsen's life. Laura confided in Fru Ibsen, just as Nora confides in Mrs. Linde. And behind the Krogstad figure stands Ibsen himself. Krogstad, who possesses the forged note, brings Nora's marriage to a crisis. Ibsen, by rejecting Laura's manuscript, helped to bring Laura's marriage to a crisis. Krogstad, a man who has been down on his luck, is saved by the devoted Mrs. Linde, just as Ibsen, the failed playwright, drowning himself in drink, was saved by his wife, Suzannah. (Krogstad means "tavern town" in Swedish.)

The Well-Made Play Transformed

The notoriety of *A Doll's House* as a feminist document has overshadowed Ibsen's technical accomplishment, especially in his characterization of Nora. No one had created a character of such psychological complexity within the format of the well-made play or the problem play. Novelists can take their time in developing the figures in their stories, but playwrights, working within the constraints of the standard dramatic form, have to devote much of the playing time to the twists and turns of the plot, leaving little time to explore character. Furthermore, in the realistic drama, it is difficult to reveal the inner thoughts and motivations of characters without resorting to unrealistic soliloquies.

Nora gets most of the attention of Ibsen the portraitist, while her husband, Torvald, is more quickly sketched in. The patriarchal basis of nineteenth-century audiences compelled Ibsen to exaggerate Torvald's insensitivity and narrow-mindedness, reducing him to a puppet. Even the fact that Torvald and Nora are young and immature people in their late twenties does little to redeem Torvald or justify his behavior. His egocentricity ("I am saved!" not "we are saved!") assumes almost comic proportions for a modern audience, and makes him a particularly challenging character to portray convincingly by an actor. In Ibsen's time it was meant to overcome the audience's bias in favor of the man of the house, the breadwinner. Except for his self-centeredness, Torvald is an excellent husband and a caring father, a decent churchgoing citizen, upright, diligent, and a good provider. He studied law, worked himself up into a position as a bank manager, and in the process became ill from overwork. The impression we should have is that of a near-perfect marriage, a man on the rise, a comfortable, middle-class home, three children, and a maid. What more could a woman want, especially if Torvald is played by a matinee idol, as he should be? Against all this, Ibsen has

Figure 14. Dr. Rank in *A Doll's House.*

to show Torvald as a totally conventional person, unaware of Nora as an independent being and never questioning the conventions of society and the teachings of the church.

Even so, there were those who thought Ibsen had tilted the scales unfairly against Torvald. Even Camilla Collett, the ardent, outspoken feminist, complained that a man who is kind toward his wife, artistically sensitive, scrupulously honest, stern but forgiving, should be harshly judged and condemned by a woman who is actually guilty of a crime. Wasn't this too much for an audience to accept?[1]

Ibsen treated Torvald as a mere dramatic foil to Nora, but on Nora herself he lavished his genius. He introduced Dr. Rank, friend of the Helmers, not to further the plot, but to reveal aspects of her personality that she hides from both Torvald and Mrs. Linde. She knows about such forbidden topics as syphilis, from which Dr. Rank is suffering. Since her mother died when Nora was a small child, her whole life has been spent playing up to men, first her father and then her husband, both of whom spoiled her. And she is well aware of her own feminine charms and how to use them. When she takes her flesh-colored stockings out of a box and lets Dr. Rank see first the feet and then "higher up, too," she is flirting with him, seductively, mischievously, and rather cruelly. What may seem like a rather innocent episode to audiences accustomed to sexual explicitness struck pre–World War I theatergoers as highly improper or indecent. Henry James commented primly that Ibsen "actually talks of stockings and legs, in addition to other improprieties."[2] The actress Eva Le Gallienne deleted the scene from her translation of the play. The critic for the London journal *Truth* was appalled by what he saw. "The scene between the Rank Doctor and the Squirrel Nora is too dirty for discussion by decent people."[3]

If these reactions seem excessive, one must realize that before the age of sexual emancipation, a little sexuality went a long way. Audiences knew how to translate what they saw onstage into the real-life equivalent. Strindberg probably spoke for many men when he saw Nora as flirting with her eyes while working her hands into the pockets of the syphilitic doctor.[4] Dr. Rank calls her a "rascal," and not just for pretending innocence about syphilis while obviously knowing all about it and its causes. Testing her power over men, she entices him into a declaration that he would do anything for her and then upbraids him for it. She tantalizes Dr. Rank up to the moment when he says his last goodbye. He asks Torvald for a cigar, but it is Nora who is quick to strike a match. This is one of those instances in which a cigar is not just a cigar. It is a richly theatrical moment, likely to be lost on modern audiences. Lighting Rank's cigar, Nora is an *allumeuse,* a term for a flirt, a tease, one who arouses sexual passions without satisfying them. Rank's last words are "thanks for the light," thanks for all the titillating conversations. Ibsen himself said that "Nora's relationship with Dr. Rank shows her moral purity."[5]

Rank is a rich portrait in itself, drawn with a few brilliant strokes. We can piece together his past life, his upbringing, his education, and the pleasure he found in his frequent visits to the young couple, Torvald and Nora, a pleasure tempered by the melancholy thought that a family life would never be his and that even the vicarious enjoyment of it must soon come to an end. We get to know his philosophic outlook, his scientific detachment as regards his own illness, and the cruel joke that heredity has played on him, punishing him with syphilis for the enjoyment that his father got out of life. And in the silk-stocking scene, we sense the desperate longing in his aborted life to be for once something more than a bystander, for once to be accepted for more than the pleasure of his company. When Nora drops a hint that he might help her out of her dilemma, he too eagerly says he would give his life for her. She is startled; he has overstepped the rules of the game that she has been playing. In her romanticized world only her husband could make such a sacrifice. She stands up, goes into the hall, and asks the maid to bring in a lamp. This atmospheric scene in the waning light of late afternoon shows Ibsen, with his strong pictorial sense, making use of improved, more subtle stage lighting, with the intrusion of the lamp shattering the mood and revealing Nora's confused state of mind. What offends Nora is not that Rank loves her, but that he says so.

"How can I tell what I knew or didn't know? I really can't say—. How could you be so clumsy, Dr. Rank? Everything was so nice."

Dr. Rank has another, more subtle function in the play, one that is likely to escape the reader. One might say that he adds a touch of black to the color scheme of the play, a complete contrast to the brightness of the opening scene and Nora's gaiety. The actress Elizabeth Robins described how the actor playing Rank gave him "a creepy uncanniness that goes creeping over me even in memory. There was death and the grave in his long dull-coloured face. In the early part of the play Nora's warm bright confidence splintering against that tombstone of a man gave me a chill."[6]

Ingeniously, Ibsen makes the note with the forged signature serve a double function. It is not only the physical object on which the plot depends (a characteristic feature of the well-made play); it also provides insight into the workings of Nora's mind. She signed her father's name as security for the note because he was ill and dying, and she did not want to tell him about her problems. But why did she borrow the money from a stranger?

She could have turned to friends of her husband; any other woman would have done so. But Nora knew that if she turned to one of Torvald's friends for help, she would have to share her role of savior with someone else. A wife could not borrow money without her husband's consent. By borrowing from a stranger and forging her father's signature, she sees herself as sparing the sufferings of two people: her husband who is ill and her father who is dying. Thus the doll becomes the rescuer of the men who made her a doll. She revels in this role, proving herself ultimately superior to her husband, secretly enjoying the reversal of roles, and knowing that from now on Torvald will always and inescapably be in her debt. In her imagination she foresees the time when, growing old and less attractive to Torvald, she can reveal, the dated IOU in hand, how she saved him. It is her insurance policy against the future. If the forged note is removed from the picture, if Nora had secretly borrowed the money from a trusted friend, she would not have seen herself as saving her husband. The money she regularly pays Krogstad comes from the pin money and the money for clothes (remember the "simple blue wool skirt") that Torvald gives her. Torvald pays for his trip to Italy without knowing it.

The "most wonderful thing of all" of which she speaks is the gratitude that Torvald must feel when he eventually learns the truth. That moment is suddenly brought from the distant future into the present when Krogstad, from whom she borrowed the money, threatens to expose her as a criminal. Responding hysterically to this threat, she lets her thoughts rush ahead.

(If she viewed her situation calmly, she would realize that no serious crime had been committed; the only threat is to Torvald's reputation.) She imagines Torvald interceding on her behalf, taking her crime on his shoulders, behaving as the men in her life have always done, protecting her, and thereby being superior to her. But this time it will be different. She will forestall Torvald, deny his guilt to the world, and then drown herself. Dying for Torvald's sake, she will forever remain superior to him.

These thoughts fly through her overwrought mind as she dances the tarantella at the end of act two, the climactic scene. But this is not the real Nora; this is Nora in costume, still the doll dancing for her husband. The real Nora will not emerge until act three.

No one noticed what the details of the IOU tell us about Nora (those details seem there only to enable Krogstad to blackmail her) until a German psychiatrist, Erich Wulfflen, published an essay on the hysterical Nora in 1907.[7] Ibsen's English translator, reviewing Duse's performance as Nora, completely missed the significance of the forged note.[8] Duse didn't.

One of the problems with Ibsen as a dramatist, as with Chekhov, is that some information essential to an understanding of the play and the characters is presented so subtly that the playgoer can hardly grasp its significance on first hearing it. When Nora confides in Mrs. Linde in act one that she, Nora, must have something in reserve when her dancing and dressing up and acting the doll do not amuse Torvald any longer, the viewer is not likely to connect that with the details of the forged signature. The dated note in Krogstad's hands is a threat against her, but when she reclaims it, it will be evidence that she saved her husband's life. Her sacrifice was not the money she laid out; she used the household money that Torvald gave her. Her sacrifice lay in forging a name to the note, deliberately committing a serious crime. As Strindberg remarked, "That Nora forged the note in all innocence, no one believes that."[9]

Ibsen wrote the play for the sake of the last scene, the confrontation between husband and wife. He had begun with a note about two kinds of moral law, one in man and another completely different one in woman; he ended with a debate

Figure 15. The tarantella scene in *A Doll's House.*

that calls into question the position of a wife, the teachings of the church, the justice of the legal system. This was a work that carried the problem play into a new dimension. J. P. Jacobsen immediately recognized that the modernity of Ibsen's play lay in its lack of an ending. We recognize that, as in life itself, the end of one situation is the beginning of another.[10] Ibsen wrote the last scenes while staying at the Hotel Tramontane in Sorrento. He isolated himself and was rarely seen in public.[11] This was the most daring piece of writing he had ever published. This was Ibsen as he had appeared at the Scandinavian Society, denouncing its members for their moral indifference, their spiritual apathy. This was Ibsen fighting for what he most wanted, a spiritual revolution. Brandes's lectures set a gulf between yesterday and today, and now Ibsen could join with him to bridge that gap. Torvald, depicted by Ibsen as a lover of pretty things, is meant to be the typical bourgeois citizen, while Nora becomes at the end the revolutionary moralist. The new era that everyone saw looming on the horizon burst into the Helmers' parlor when Nora outfaced Torvald. Thomas Mann said that "the real dichotomy lies between ethics and aesthetics . . . and to go beyond this age [the bourgeois age] means to step out of an aesthetic age into a moral and social one."[12] Nora takes that step when she calls into question all the old values and becomes a kind of female Nietzsche. She leaves her husband and her children to forge a new conscience, which can be done only by smashing the old one. When Torvald asks her about her religion, she replies, "I don't really know what religion is."

> **Torvald.** That's unbelievable in a young woman! Well, if you have no religion to guide you, let me appeal to your conscience—your moral sense. I suppose you have one? Or, tell me—maybe you don't?
> **Nora.** Well, Torvald, that's not easy to say. I simply don't know. I'm really very confused about such things. All I know is I see things differently from you. And I've also found out that the law is different from what I thought. But I simply can't get it into my head that they are right. A woman has no right to spare her old father on his deathbed, or to save her husband's life, even. I just don't believe it.
> **Torvald.** You talk like a child. You don't understand anything about the society you live in.
> **Nora.** No, I don't. But now I'm going to find out. I have to find out who is right, society or me.[13]

Strindberg, Ibsen's most incisive critic, found Nora's actions quite incoherent. Early in the play she is afraid that because of her inheritance she may corrupt her children if she stays with them. Yet at the end she leaves them in the care of a man she now realizes is morally corrupt in the profoundest sense. For Strindberg, Nora's speechifying at the end cannot conceal the fact that the freedom she yearns for is her personal, selfish freedom to enjoy herself as she wishes. Her egoistic self-indulgence outdoes Torvald's. Nora renounces her familial duties as if they meant no more to her than the fancy dress she takes off when she prepares to leave her doll's house.[14]

To view this play as primarily a feminist tract is to ignore what it meant to Ibsen. There are only a few statements in the play that refer specifically to women's rights. Although *A Doll's House* became the "codex of the feminists," as Strindberg called it, a "gospel of the Shrieking Sisterhood," its feminism is actually quite gratuitous. At the end of his career, Ibsen, addressing the Norwegian League for Women's Rights, disclaimed the honor of having worked for the feminists. "I am not even quite clear as to just what this women's rights movement really is. To me it has seemed a problem of mankind in general. And if you read my books carefully you will understand this."[15] In August 1891 at a banquet in Christiania, he replied testily to a woman, "I write to depict people, and I am completely indifferent as to what fanatic women's rights women like or don't like."[16] On the other hand, he joined with Bjørnson in signing a petition for increasing women's property rights, sent to the Norwegian Storting in April 1884.

One of the great ironies in social history is that Ibsen, who disavowed any particular interest in women's rights, became the hero of the feminists, while Strindberg, who in the early 1880s put himself on record as advocating a number of specific rights for women, such as those for a married woman to have her own bedroom and to keep her maiden name, became known and notorious as a misogynist.

Obviously much more than feminist issues lie behind Nora's decision to leave husband and children. The anarchist Emma Goldman understood that Nora goes out into the night because she has learned that she has all along been subject to a theological myth perpetrated by patriarchal society. She has been treated as inferior to man, made out of his rib for his convenience.

Nora is a loving mother, doting on a husband who turns into an intransigent idealist. The warm and happy domesticity of the opening scene vanishes; she walks out on her husband and her children. Brand the extremist was reincarnated in Nora. At the end she becomes the religious person, in Ibsen's sense. She is willing to sacrifice everything for the sake of some inhuman, transcendent ideal.

How believable is the transformation of Nora from the doll of the first act to the iron woman of the last act? The question arises because Ibsen began with the true story of Laura Kieler, and in reality she returned to her husband. But once Ibsen identified himself with Laura's character and placed himself in her situation, she became the heroine, and there is more of Ibsen in Nora than of the woman who inspired the play. For him, the transition, or rather the abrupt change, from a high-strung, giddy young woman to an almost sexless person of iron will and resolve was perfectly understandable. It was the essence of his own divided character. The contradictions within Nora did not come from Laura; they lay within Ibsen. For some years the Gyntish aspect had been dominant in him. Now, finally, the Brand in him came to the fore.

In philosophical terms, *A Doll's House* is *Brand* all over again. Torvald, who loves pretty things—"Nobody has such perfect taste as you," says Nora—is the esthete. He likes the house to be neat; he shows Mrs. Linde how to embroider; he doesn't like to hear about unpleasant things like Dr. Rank's illness; and he choreographs Nora's dance. He is actually the doll, whereas Nora is only pretending to be one in order to please the men in her life. In reality, Nora at the beginning is already the ethical person, intent on saving her husband and afraid of corrupting her children. Her coquettishness and her cuteness are only part of an act that she has been expected to play.

The Danish actress Betty Hennings created the role at the Royal Theater in

Copenhagen on December 21, 1879, playing to a sold-out house. In what was clearly an insightful interpretation (which Ibsen never got to see), she accentuated the contrast between the real Nora and the doll Nora. She enters from her shopping spree, wearing her winter coat, her hands in a muff, and acting like a woman used to ordering servants about. She pays the porter, gives him a tip, and tells her maid to hide the Christmas tree. But as soon as she takes off her coat and hears Torvald calling from his study, "Is that my lark, singing out there?" she becomes another person. Using all her childish charms, she wheedles some money from him. "You can't imagine how many expenses we larks and squirrels have, Torvald." When she confides in Mrs. Linde, she whispers, glances around, whispers some more—with the sauciness of a pert child talking behind teacher's back. When she plays hide-and-seek with her children, she is completely at one with them, doing all their prattling for them.[17]

The difficulty in presenting Nora's apparent transformation (which is not a transformation but a revelation of the real Nora) does not lie in the scene as written. It lies in the fundamental resistance to Ibsen's kind of idealism. Who wants to abandon home and children for some directionless voyage of self-discovery? But when the part is properly acted, nearly everyone will go part of the way with Nora.

To judge from written accounts, the English actress Janet Achurch came closest to realizing Ibsen's intentions. She was memorable in both the first and last acts. She undertook the part initially in 1889, when her young years (she was twenty-five) proved an invaluable asset. Bernard Shaw recalled that her first scene with Krogstad "had a wonderful naïveté: her youthfully unsympathetic contempt for him, her certainty that his effort to make a serious business of the forgery was mere vulgarity, her utter repudiation of the notion that there could be any comparison between his case and hers, were expressed to perfection." Here she took Betty Hennings's approach to the role. The final scene was infused with the power of her intellect. As Shaw wrote, "The chill 'clearness and certainty' of the disillusion, the quite new tone of intellectual seriousness, announcing by its freshness and coolness a complete change in her as she calls her husband to account with her eyes wide open for the first time: all this, so vitally necessary to the novel truth of the scene and the convincing effect of the statement that she no longer loves him, came with lifegiving naturalness."[18]

Eleanora Duse perhaps understood better than any other actress how to make the final act emerge inevitably from the first. Unfortunately, in order to make the transformation thoroughly convincing she did great violence to Ibsen's script. She cut many lines (none in the last scene), ignored many of the master's stage directions, did away with the tarantella, and played the first two acts as if observing Nora, not being her. Not until she came to her solo scene in the second act, after Krogstad's departure, when she has to weigh the possible consequences of her action, did she reveal the depths of Nora's being and her own subtle powers as an actress. Saying no over and over again to her own thoughts, trying to drive from her mind the threats that Krogstad had just uttered, she let the audience, now deathly still, feel her anxiety. In the words of one acute observer, the writer Ola Hansson, who saw Duse's Nora in Copenhagen in the 1892–93 season, in those few moments she revealed a strange femininity, "a mixture of child and woman, the instinctive, the unconscious within this young woman. . . . She has hitherto moved through life with her eyes closed, has lived and suffered, had good times and bad, without really knowing what has been happening to her." This inner revelation came through to the audience in this scene, in which she laid the foundation for her final confrontation with Torvald.

When Torvald went into his study to read Krogstad's letter, she held his hand as if to hold him back, an automatic gesture. "Clearly, she doesn't know why she does it, whether it's worth the trouble. She does it with a lax, uncertain gesture, and then she strokes his arm delicately, as if she were begging him to be good to her." When he stormed out of his study, upbraiding and castigating her, she reacted as if he had suddenly slapped her in the face. She took her cue from Ibsen's text.

"Do you understand what you have done? Answer me! Do you understand?"

Duse's Nora looked at him fixedly, a stiffening expression on her face ("stivnede udtryk," repeated three times). The man she had loved vanished from the scene, and in the famous confrontation that follows, she was expressionless, icy-cold and determined. She had to leave this man, this stranger. In William Archer's description of this moment, "Her open-mouthed, stony astonishment . . . was as daring as it was impressive."[19]

For Duse, the scene was not an intellectual debate. It was not her reason that told her she must leave this man. Hansson said, "This Nora plays the entire part from beginning to end, driven by her womanly instincts, which do not ask why and wherefore; rather a Nora for whom feelings and deeds, impressions and decisions are all one and the same. In that way, Eleanora Duse's Nora is psychologically more unified and consistent than Ibsen's Nora. . . . I can state the difference between Ibsen's Nora and Eleanora Duse's this way: the former pictures the psychologically inadequately motivated development from a pretty doll to a pro-emancipation woman; the latter presents the development, conditioned by her nature, deep and eternally true, of a woman, who having lived for years with a man, suddenly through an unexpected catastrophe comes to realize that he was not the right man, not the one whom she must love, always and in spite of all."[20]

Duse also introduced a splendid bit of stage business. When Nora and Torvald exchange wedding rings, Nora accidentally drops hers, and Torvald has to pick it up. She thanks him with a nod and a whispered "thanks."[21]

However impressive Duse's Nora was, it was not true to Ibsen's intentions. Hers was an interpretation based on the instinctual life of woman, very solid ground for an actress to build on. Ibsen's Nora, however, was a woman who rises above her womanly nature, just as Brand rose above his human nature. Ibsen posed a difficult but not impossible task for his actress, asking her to appreciate and understand his own inner conflict. He began with a fairly typical woman, Laura Kieler, and tried to fuse her with Brand, whom she professed to admire. Laura and Nora, however, were basically different. Laura returned to her husband; Ibsen's Nora decides to ascend the heights with Brand.

Ibsen saw Duse as Nora in Vienna and was pleased (*tilfreds*) by her interpretation.[22]

With *A Doll's House* Ibsen reclaimed his true self, or at least his better self. *Pillars of Society* was a digression, a straying from the issues that mattered to him. In *Pillars,* these were kept in the background, assigned to less important characters, like Lona Hessel. *A Doll's House* provided the opportunity to reaffirm his Brandian ideals, to assert the supreme right of the individual over all prejudices and social customs, all legal codes and religious beliefs, even over natural instincts. To people like Bjørnson, the highest duty was that of being good to others. To Ibsen the highest duty was the affirmation of one's individuality.

With *Brand,* Ibsen had made himself famous throughout the Nordic countries. With *A Doll's House,* advocating the same cause, espousing the same ideals, he achieved international fame. Nora's exit became famous as "the door slam heard round the world." No play by a Scandinavian had ever scored such a popular and critical success. No other play carried so much international influence. The affirmation of his ideals in poetic form in *Brand* had brought his career to one pinnacle; the affirmation of those same ideals in the prose of everyday life brought him to an eminence (and notoriety) that few writers have ever achieved.

THE GHOSTS AT ROSENVOLD

As soon as *A Doll's House* appeared, the woman behind the play became the subject of unpleasant, unfair, even opprobrious rumors in both Denmark and Norway. It was bruited about that Laura Kieler had forged a note in order to decorate her house or pay her dressmaker. A Copenhagen newspaper published the following unsigned account on December 22, 1879.

> The closer we come to the first performance of *A Doll's House*, the more the play is discussed in many circles, and some of the circles are well informed. I am not one of the well informed, but I do listen and I can report. The story is true, perhaps not in all details, but in the main, and if not in the capital city, then in the vicinity, in such-and-such town [Frederiksborg] in Sjælland. (*Nomina sunt odiosa.*) Mrs. N.N. was married, she had some money of her own, the husband was rather sickly, income very small, the love of pretty things somewhat greater. The charming wife used her own moneys to decorate the house, but when they gave out, she took to borrowing on credit, and finally she wrote forged notes. Her husband, whether out of weakness, folly, or trust, had credited that "money of her own" with an impossible lastingness, and one fine day found out the truth. What then? Here the reports begin to diverge, like the mouth of a river forming a delta. Naturally, the husband was furious; naturally, there was talk of a divorce; but some say that the wife was forgiven, after the false notes were redeemed; others say that just like Nora in *A Doll's House*, she left her husband (and children?) in order that the two of them should find each other.[1]

The play seemed to confirm the rumors that Laura was a forger, and added a new stain to her reputation by alluding to her father as a morally degenerate man. Almost immediately after the play was published, the novelist J. P. Jacobsen was reporting (before he had read it) that it was based on the real-life problems of a certain Mrs. Kieler, "who forged her husband's name on a promissory note in order to pay her dressmaker and who was divorced by her husband on that account."[2]

Whatever the truth, her reputation had been irreparably tainted by hints that she was an unbalanced, hysterical woman and by rumors that she was a forger and thus in the eyes of the law a criminal. She spent much of the rest of her life trying to undo the harm that had been done to her. She lived under a cloud of suspicion. Everyone knew she was the woman in Ibsen's play. In a society in which borrowed money was its very lifeblood, forging a signature on a note was a serious crime. In England a woman (the mother of Sacheverell, Edith, and Osbert Sitwell) was sent to prison for three months for forging her husband's signature on a check.[3]

A *Doll's House* brought fame and fortune to Ibsen—and shame and scandal in almost equal measure to Laura Kieler. Camilla Collett asserted that Ibsen had taken "the real-life Nora as a trophy and placed her in his triumphal chariot on his ambitious march to world fame."[4] The truth of this would come to haunt Ibsen.

A *Doll's House* was published on December 4, 1879, in a first printing of eight thousand copies. A second printing of three thousand copies followed shortly thereafter, with two more printings in January and March 1880.

Bernard Shaw dated the beginning of modern drama from the last scene in the play, the discussion scene in which intelligent debate superseded melodrama. Certainly no play had ever aroused so much discussion among the broad public. In Denmark, the critics tended to defend Torvald Helmer, and some of them saw Nora as a hysterical woman. The conservative newspaper *Dagbladet* said most husbands would behave like Torvald and that Nora would soon come to her senses and return to her husband and children.

In Norway, Magdalene Thoresen reported that "the play has caused an uproar! If Ibsen had not been accepted as the great writer, he would not have gone unpunished for writing it."

She of course had a clear understanding of what the play was about: a woman who has a mission, who pursues an ideal, who agrees with the words of Jesus—you must give up all and follow me.[5]

In Germany, some actresses refused to play the last scene as written. Frau Hedwig Niemann-Raabe as Nora was drawn to the door of the nursery where her children slept and, seeing them, said, "No mother! . . . I am sinning against myself, but I cannot leave them."[6] In one version, another act was added, showing Nora a year later. She is back home, her newborn child in her lap. Helmer "steals up behind [her], puts his hands over her eyes, takes a bag of the forbidden macaroons out of his pocket and pops one in Nora's mouth. She then exclaims: 'The miracle has happened.'"[7]

Because the Nordic countries had not signed a copyright agreement with Germany, Ibsen could do little to prevent these travesties. The best he could do was to provide his own revised ending. In this version, as described by the perpetrator himself, Nora "is forced by Helmer across the door to the children's bedroom; a few lines of dialogue follow, Nora sinks down at the door, and the curtain falls."[8]

The assessment of Paul Lindau, journalist and playwright, probably represented the prevailing view of the play in Germany. He found the transformation of Nora impossible to accept, not only on dramaturgical grounds but also on moral grounds. Although Nora may think her action noble, it is atrocious and unpardonable.[9]

The dramatist who was now making his entrance on the world stage was no young man. The once fiery apostle of a new faith, the man who wrote *Brand*, was now aging into the dour, somber, rather forbidding, mutton-chop-wielding, taciturn figure the world would get to know as Ibsen. The daylong sessions at his desk, requiring enormous stamina, were now moderated into more regular working hours. His gestures became more deliberate, his features more masklike, his position more solitary. He was becoming more and more a monument to himself.

Brandes described him in 1875 as "a reserved, rather shy and silent, very unusual and bizarre Norwegian." A few years later, he filled out the portrait.

> The severe or sarcastic expression of his face conceals a delicate spirituality that only occasionally breaks through. Ibsen is short and thick-set . . . dresses with a certain style and elegance, and looks very distinguished. His walk is slow, his carriage dignified and stately. His head is large and striking, with its thick mane of grayish hair, which he wears rather long. The forehead, which dominates the face, is remarkable: abrupt, high, broad and yet perfectly formed, it bears the stamp of greatness and spiritual riches. The mouth, when in repose, is compressed, as if lipless. . . . It reveals the fact that Ibsen is a man of few words. . . . One can see in Ibsen's face that he is a satirist and thinker, not an enthusiast. . . .
>
> I know two expressions in his face. The first is that in which a smile, Ibsen's kind, beautiful smile, breaks through and animates the mask of his countenance, all the geniality and cordiality that lie deepest down in his heart coming out to meet one. Ibsen is slightly embarrassed in manner, as melancholy serious natures are apt to be. But he has this charming smile, and smile, glance, and hand-clasp say much that he neither would nor could clothe in words. Sometimes . . . with a sly laugh . . . and an expression of good-natured roguishness he will let fall some short, sharp, anything but amiable expression of dissent, which

> nevertheless reveals all that is most amiable in his character. The smile atones for the sharpness.
>
> But I also know another expression in his face, that which is called forth by impatience, wrath, righteous indignation, biting scorn: an expression of almost cruel severity. . . .
>
> It is with this expression that, as a poet, he has most frequently shown himself to the world.[10]

If Ibsen had a vice, it was a fondness for strong drink, and he often let liquor get the better of him. After a banquet with members of the Scandinavian Club in Rome in 1880, he had to be helped home from the Osteria degli Augustini, a young man on each side to keep him from falling over. He berated both with slurred insults, calling one "an awful pup" and the other "a disgusting character."[11]

Brandes's impression of Ibsen is confirmed and amplified in almost every respect by the account given by William Archer upon first meeting him at a meeting of the Scandinavian Club in Rome at the end of 1881.

> I had been about a quarter of an hour in the room, and was standing close to the door, when it opened, and in glided an undersized man with very broad shoulders and a large, leonine head, wearing a long black frock-coat with very broad lapels, on one of which a knot of red ribbon was conspicuous. I knew him at once, but was a little taken aback by his low stature. In spite of all the famous instances to the contrary, one instinctively associates greatness with size. His natural height was even somewhat diminished by a habit of bending forward slightly from the waist, begotten, no doubt, of short-sightedness, and the need to peer into things. He moved very slowly and noiselessly, with his hands behind his back—an unobtrusive personality, which would have been insignificant had the head been strictly proportionate to the rest of the frame. But there was nothing insignificant about the high and massive forehead, crowned with a mane of (then) iron-gray hair, the small and pale but piercing eyes behind the gold-rimmed spectacles, or the thin-lipped mouth, depressed at the corners into a curve indicative of iron will, and set between bushy whiskers of the same dark gray as the hair. The most cursory observer could not but recognize power and character in the head; yet one would scarcely have guessed it to be the power of a poet, the character of a prophet. Misled, perhaps, by the ribbon at the buttonhole, and by an expression of reserve, almost of secretiveness, in the lines of the tight-shut mouth, one would rather have supposed one's self face to face with an eminent statesman or diplomatist.[12]

The strict, clockwork regularity of his habits and routines dates from about 1880. While residing in Munich, he would be at his desk from nine o'clock to noon, having had a breakfast of rolls and black coffee. From twelve to one he enjoyed his morning pint, followed by a walk. In the afternoon, he would read and receive the occasional visitor. Between six thirty and seven thirty he would regularly occupy a table at the Café Maximilian. A German journalist observed him closely.

> He has a tankard of dark ale or a small cognac in front of him, and a bottle of seltzer. In his hand a newspaper, on the chair by his side a whole pile of journals. Does he read them all? I have noticed that he often holds the paper in front of himself, while his eyes, steady and keen, look over and beyond it. The people passing by, going in and out . . . provide a living chronicle. . . . Quite often he sits like a stone statue, immovable, his eyes turned inward, his lips tightly closed, his left hand on his thigh and his right hand poised as if holding a pen, as if he were sitting lost in thought at his desk, his mind totally occupied, engaged in the process of creating a new work. His mighty head exercises a magical artistic power, its sculptural lines those of a lofty, manly beauty.

At seven thirty, he would pick up his umbrella and black gloves and slowly shuffle out. He would usually retire early, about nine.

There was even a seasonal routine to his work. In the winter he would plan and outline the work; in the summer he was most productive, completing the first and second drafts of the play. He spent much time pacing his rooms as ideas came to him.[13]

With the publication of *A Doll's House* in December 1879 this uncongenial, self-important, unprepossessing figure became once again the most talked-about personage in Scandinavia. The play provoked so much furor during the Christmas season that social invitations in Copenhagen and Stockholm included an admonition not to talk about or even mention the play, lest the fellow-feeling mood of the season turn into its opposite.[14]

Most of the discussion focused on Nora's unmotherly behavior, with the unresolved ending leaving room for all sorts of interpretations. It was this lack of finality, of closure, more than Nora's accusations that fueled the controversy. The question was, where will Nora go; what will she do?

Clearly Ibsen had to respond or be accused of sensationalism, of seeking notoriety, to promote sales. He could not remain aloof and reticent. He might have appeared in the public forum with letters to newspapers, but he inevitably chose the dramatist's way: he wrote another play. He called it *Ghosts*, and its heroine, Mrs. Alving, was a mother like Nora, only considerably older.

"A writer dare not alienate himself so far from his people," he told an eminent feminist, "that there is no longer any understanding between them. . . . *Ghosts* had to be written. After Nora, Mrs. Alving had to come."[15]

The young Mrs. Alving did not leave her husband, as Nora did; nor did she question the teachings of the church or embark on a solitary quest for some higher understanding of her world. Instead she stayed home and sent her son away.

"These women of today, mistreated as daughters, as sisters, as wives, not educated according to their talents, held back from their calling in life, deprived of their share in inheritance, embittered in mood—these are the women who constitute the mothers of the new generation. What will be the consequences?"[16]

So reads an early note for *Ghosts*. The principal resistance to *A Doll's House* came from the church, and *Ghosts* begins with a scene between a clergyman and Mrs. Helen Alving, both now in their early fifties. When young, they had loved each other. But he had been poor; Helen came from a fine family, and her parents had pushed her into marrying somebody of her social stature, the dashing Lieutenant Alving. It soon became apparent that they were an ill-sorted couple. She had been drawn to Pastor Manders because she saw in him an idealist, devoted to a higher spiritual cause, while the handsome lieutenant was a pleasure-seeking, happy-go-lucky, high-spirited playboy. The marriage was doomed to fail from the start. While the personable young lieutenant rose in the social ranks, he sank deeper into a life of debauchery. And as the young wife saw the kind of man she had married, she became more desperate. Finally, she fled from his house and knocked at the door of the man she loved. Upholding rigidly the conventions of the church, he ordered her back to her husband. The link with the ending of *A Doll's House* is clearly established in act one of *Ghosts*.

MANDERS. Don't you remember that after barely being married a year, you stood at the edge of the abyss? You left your house and home, you fled from your husband, yes, Mrs. Alving, fled, fled. And you refused to go back to him, no matter how much he implored and begged you. Remember?

MRS. ALVING. And have you forgotten how utterly miserable I was that first year?

MANDERS. Yes, precisely. It's that spirit of rebellion that demands happiness in this life. What right have people to happiness? No, we have our duties, Mrs. Alving. And your duty was to remain true to the man you had chosen, the man you were bound to by sacred ties.

MRS. ALVING. You know well enough what sort of life my husband was living at that time, the excesses he was guilty of.

MANDERS. I know quite well the rumors that were being spread around. And I would be the last person to approve his behavior as a young man, assuming there was any truth to them. But a wife is not placed here to sit in judgment on her husband. Your duty was to bear with humility the cross that a higher power had in its wisdom laid upon you.[17]

A playwright as methodical in his habits as Ibsen cannot wait for inspiration, for a bright idea to strike him. He was fortunate in having Laura Kieler walk into his life just when he needed a subject for a problem play. And the furor over *A Doll's House* provided the impetus for a new play. But once the opposition between Mrs. Alving and Pastor Manders had been established, a conflict between the old values and the new, where was he to go? As always, he drew upon the subject that was always there waiting to be used—himself.

In *A Doll's House,* Nora at the end is more like Ibsen than like Laura Kieler. And in *Ghosts,* Mrs. Alving is in many ways also an incarnation of him. They are both middle-aged, about fifty, and Mrs. Alving's self-education and intellectual development are like Ibsen's. The drama is equally fascinating as a modern tragedy and as the autobiography of a man who endeavored to keep abreast of new developments.

Ibsen liked to think of himself as a lofty, independent spirit, rightly at home on Parnassus, and seldom did he admit to being influenced by anybody. But that does not mean he saw himself as spinning a cocoon from which a work of art emerged. He has often been thought of as a seismograph sensitive to all the tremors occasioned by the clash of new ideas in the nineteenth century. His genius lay in sensing what would last and in his ability to make the outer social drama his inner personal drama. Here Brandes was an excellent guide. In his letters Ibsen admits that Brandes's radicalism forced him to swim with the main currents of modern thought, but he remained his own man. To a French journalist he said, "No one is the master of my thoughts, of my philosophy, of my ideas and opinions. I have always searched within myself; everything has come from my heart. It is because life and human society have given me impressions so strong, so vivid, so demanding that I have written what I have written. . . . That has been my calling."[18] The contradictions within society mirrored the fundamental conflict within himself. That contradiction lay at the heart of Ibsen's works, and was never fully resolved because of the great psychological rift within him. *Ghosts* explores that contradiction much more deeply than *A Doll's House,* with Mrs. Alving recapitulating Ibsen's own intellectual development.

After Manders reproaches her for seeking refuge with him and exposing him to possible scandal, she tells him what her life has been like during the intervening twenty-five years. Her husband was drunken, debauched, and to keep him home as much as possible she often joined him in his drinking bouts, listening to his obscene banter, and dragging him to bed when he was stupefied with liquor. She endured all this for the sake of their son, Oswald. She reached the limit of her patience when she caught Alving carrying on with the housemaid in the conservatory of the house. Then her strength of character asserted itself. She took control of house and husband, and to ensure that young Oswald would not be tainted by his father's dissoluteness, she sent him out of the country, and for most of his adult life he has been studying art in Paris. Only on a couple of occasions, such as the funeral of his father, did he return to Norway.

For the better part of nineteen years she preserved the façade of Alving's respectability, managing the Rosenvold estate, introducing improvements and innovations for which her incompetent husband received the credit. During all these years she was denied the pleasure of her son's company. Yet all that she has done over the years was for his sake. He became her mission in life. Mrs. Alving is the kind of woman who has read *Brand* and been changed by it, convinced that life is meaningful only to the extent that one makes sacrifices for a higher cause. She was attracted to young Manders because she thought he was a dedicated Christian.

While in Paris, Oswald led a bohemian life, associating with, one may assume, the impressionist painters, and having some of his own works exhibited. Growing up away from home and enjoying the complete freedom that his mother has given him, he remembers little of his parents. The play opens shortly after his return to Rosenvold, his father having died ten years before. His return coincides with a crucial decision that Mrs. Alving has made. She is going to establish an orphanage to be named after her husband, the respected pillar of society. Pastor Manders has been called in to make the necessary arrangements. The return of Oswald and the arrival of Manders are both part of a long-planned scheme by Mrs. Alving to settle accounts with her husband's heritage and to banish the ghosts of the past.

Her marriage was one of social convenience, an arrangement made on the basis of money—"purchase money" she calls it—not of love. And she had a widowed mother and two aunts to consider. Now she wants to pay off that old debt and make a fresh start by donating the exact amount Alving was worth when she married him to the orphanage in acknowledgment of Oswald's upbringing—an orphanage rather than, say, a home for aged spinsters. None of the marriage money will be passed on to Oswald. He must be kept uncontaminated by his father's sins, and thus Helen Alving will finally free herself from the past. The sacrifices she has made over many years, none greater than that of being deprived of the company of her only child, will not have been made in vain.

"From the day after tomorrow everything shall be as if the dead man had never lived in this house. There shall be no one here but my boy and his mother."[19]

The mood of the opening scene is a mixture of hope and foreboding. The confidence Helen Alving expresses in her long chat with Manders is set against the steady rain falling outside, the sunless sky reflecting the clergyman's view of life as a vale of tears. The subtext of the long expository scenes is that the two of them had been much in love a quarter of a century earlier. After Helen's marriage, Manders would visit her occasionally, but after she came to him for help, he never called on her again as long as Captain Alving was alive. In the intervening years, he has remained the same in his views, while she, like Ibsen, has acquainted herself with the new ideas of the age. Compared with Helen, who has not only read the important books but has done a man's job in running the Rosenvold estate, Pastor Manders is an innocent child.

The mood darkens when Oswald makes his entrance. Helen Alving is proud of him for having kept "both his inner and his outer self unharmed,"[20] while Manders is astonished to see how closely Oswald resembles his father. And it is apparent from the young man's description of his carefree existence in Paris that he takes after his father in looking for what he calls *la joie de vivre*. In both looks and temperament, he is more his father's son than his mother's. His arrival at Rosenvold, promising so much to Mrs. Alving, suggests that the past is coming back.

And coming back by the very means by which she hoped to banish it. Like his father, Oswald is fond of pretty housemaids and cannot keep his hands off Regina, Mrs. Alving's housekeeper. She has employed her, out of a sense of responsibility, because she is the daughter of Captain Alving's mistress. The act one curtain provides one of Ibsen's more stunning *coups de théâtre*. Regina and Oswald are heard whispering in the dining room, making love just as years ago Alving and the housemaid (Regina's mother) were caught in the same situation when Mrs. Alving chanced to see them. As that scene is now repeated, Manders realizes that Regina is also Captain Alving's daughter and Oswald's half sister.

"Ghosts," exclaims Mrs. Alving, hoarsely. "Those two in the conservatory. They've come back."

Mrs. Alving did not encourage her son to return to the family estate after his father's death. She wanted him to be a free and uncorrupted spirit, her own kind of Siegfried, someone who could bring about a revolutionary change in the human spirit. She did not exercise any hold over him; she kept him free and under no obligation either to herself or his father. And he has had no desire to return to his childhood home. He prefers the sun of France and the *joie de vivre* of Paris to the darkness of Norway and the depressing rain of the Bergen district. He has retained no pleasant memories of his upbringing. All that he remembers, as he tells Pastor Manders, is that his father once made him sick.

"He took me on his knee and gave me his pipe. 'Smoke, my boy, smoke away!' I puffed as hard as I could, until I felt I was turning pale, and I could feel beads of sweat on my forehead. Then he laughed, laughed heartily."[21]

When Oswald makes his first entrance he is smoking that same pipe, a large meerschaum, and Manders is struck by the resemblance of son to father. From that first moment, Ibsen suggests that the sins of the father are to be visited on the son.

Because of the large part that nemesis plays in it, *Ghosts* is of all Ibsen's dramas the most like classical tragedy. One of the tenets of Ibsen's creed was the belief in retribution. The poet Falk in *Love's Comedy* says, "Nemesis runs through our lives. It strikes surely, though it may strike late, and no one can run away from it." An early note for *Ghosts* reads, "Nemesis will strike the offspring if one marries for irrelevant reasons, even if religious or moral."[22]

Fate has much crueler blows in store for Mrs. Alving than the intimation of incest that she has just witnessed. Oswald is not the rake his father was, but he is destined to pay for his father's way of life. He is prefigured in *A Doll's House*. Dr. Rank knows he must pay for his father's profligacy. "My poor innocent spine," he says wryly, "must do penance for the gay lieutenant's life my father led."

There is a world of difference between the workings of nemesis in *Brand* and in *Ghosts*. Brand's whole life was a struggle against the inherited sense of guilt. Just before the avalanche overwhelms him, he says, "Condemned is every son of man / To die the death for mankind's sins." And his final words are: "Answer me, God, here in the grip of death, does a measure of human will not count toward salvation?" The entire argument is couched in theological terms. That is what bothered Brandes when he remarked in his 1871 lecture that the work was as reactionary as it was revolutionary.

In the 1870s Ibsen had to come to terms with the new ideas that were changing the cultural landscape of Europe, and no idea made a greater impact than Darwin's theory of evolution. It was first presented in Scandinavia by the Danish writer J. P. Jacobsen, who translated *On the Origin of Species* in 1872 and *The Descent of Man* in 1875. Ibsen may not have read these works, but he certainly read about them. Jacobsen incorporated Darwin's ideas in his novels, notably in *Niels Lyhne*, an atheistic work which so impressed Ibsen that he read parts of it aloud to visitors during the Christmas season of 1880–81, a few months before he began to write *Ghosts*.

His alter ego Mrs. Alving has made the same passage from the old to the new. If it was no longer possible to bring God into his family drama, the new ideas offered a perfect substitute. Instead of a supreme being lording over the world, there was Darwin, and in place of nemesis and fate there was scientific determinism. An impalpable God hovering over the action was much less effective and believable than a physical force visibly striking its victims.

Darwin's theory of evolution made it possible to conceive of a world without a creative or interfering God. To many, the slipping away of God revealed not an abyss of nothingness but a world of marvels, the world Darwin described in restrained but glowing prose on the last page of *On the Origin of Species.* "Thus, from the war of nature, from famine and death, the most exalted object which we are capable of conceiving, namely, the production of the higher animals, directly follows. There is grandeur in this view of life, with its several powers, having been originally breathed by the Creator into a few forms or into one; and that, whilst this planet has gone cycling on according to the fixed law of gravity, from so simple a beginning endless forms most beautiful and most wonderful have been, and are being evolved."

The optimists welcomed Darwin's theory, seeing in it the improvement of man's lot; pessimists saw in it a war of nature, the struggle for survival. In England, Tennyson saw "nature red in tooth and claw." Matthew Arnold imagined a meaningless world where "ignorant armies clash by night." To many, Darwin's "descent of man" meant a descent from a godlike being to a lower species, a descent from angel to ape.

At first Ibsen was opposed to Darwin, and in *Peer Gynt* he ridiculed the idea that man and ape were closely akin. And, like Helen Alving, he accepted the new ideas rather slowly. What troubled him about the new positivistic theories was that they were completely materialistic. Darwinism and determinism were inimical to his whole philosophical project. In his philosophy there had to be a place for man's indomitable will, a place for a creature like Brand. In the spiritual realm of *Brand* it was possible to speculate on the victory of man's will over inherited sin. *Brand* is an optimistic tragedy. Ibsen found it hard to surrender to Darwin his conviction that man's will determined man's destiny, just as his own inner determination had given him the strength to write *Brand* and *Peer Gynt.* But in the 1870s he had to face the fact that his epic dramas were situated in an ideal world, where abstractions like sin and inherited guilt and conscience were palpable forces, while the realistic drama that he was now committed to had to picture a world in which physical nature determined what was to come. God, the ultimate spiritual being, which had provided the fundamental basis of his metaphysical drama, had to yield to Nature, and Brand's struggle, which was essentially a struggle within himself, became a war against physical inheritance and against one's environment.

Yet when he was compelled to deal with scientific determinism, he found that his fatalistic philosophy could easily accommodate it. The world of ideas was governed by the same ineluctable force as the Darwinian world of matter: the Juggernaut of past ages bearing down on the individual.

"When I heard Regina and Oswald in there," says Mrs. Alving, "it was as if I saw ghosts from the past. I almost think we are all ghosts, all of us, Pastor Manders. It is not only what we have inherited from father and mother that comes back. It is all kinds of dead ideas and all sorts of old, dead beliefs, things like that. They are not alive in us, but they stick to us, and they won't let go. I only have to pick up a newspaper and read, and it's as if I saw ghosts stealing between the lines. There must be ghosts haunting the whole land. They must be like the sands of the sea, so many, I think. And we are all, all of us, so pitifully afraid of the light."[23]

Pastor Manders tells her that thinking like that is the result of reading "those disgusting, revolutionary, atheistic books," the books that he saw lying on the table when he entered, the sort of books that Ibsen himself had been reading in the 1870s.

Syphilis, the Unmentionable Disease

Mrs. Alving had sent her son away when he was a mere boy as a way of eluding the particular ghost that haunts the Rosenvold estate, the ghost of her husband. (There is no mention of where Oswald spent his boyhood. His stay in Paris was later, when he aspired to become an artist.) At the end of the play she realizes her efforts have been in vain: Oswald is dying from a disease passed on to him from his pleasure-loving father.

Everyone who read the play (very few saw it onstage since every theater company in the Nordic countries, except one, refused to produce it) knew that Oswald was afflicted with syphilis. Yet Ibsen never mentions the disease by name. In those days it could not be mentioned in print in any journal that a woman might read or in any play that a woman might see. The word was banned even from a learned journal like *Ny svensk tidskrift* (Uppsala), in which Professor Seved Ribbing wrote extensively about Oswald's illness ("Om den samtida dikten och dess förkärlek för sjukdomsskildring," 1885) without once mentioning syphilis. Not only in Scandinavia but throughout Europe, syphilis was a verboten subject. The first time the word appeared in a French newspaper was in October 1901, twenty years after Ibsen's play, in an article on Brieux's play *Les Avariés* (The Damaged Ones, a euphemism for syphilitics). Writing to a woman in 1895, Anton Chekhov, a licensed doctor, referred to the disease by the letter S, "out of modesty." It was the sexual disease that dared not speak its name.

Yet everyone was aware of syphilis since it had assumed almost epidemic proportions. Nora in *A Doll's House* teasingly hints to her friend Dr. Rank that she knows what lies behind his remarks about suffering the consequences of his father's high living. In *Ghosts* there are hints aplenty that Oswald is suffering from syphilis. When he speaks of the disease that he had acquired in Paris and that was now softening his brain, any lingering question in the minds of the audience would have been answered.

Syphilis was rampant in Scandinavia in the 1880s. According to Iwan Bloch, in Copenhagen during the period 1876 to 1895, 16 to 20 percent of men in their twenties were infected with venereal disease, one in eight with gonorrhea, one in fifty-five with syphilis.[1] The writer Victoria Benedictsson, who resided in southern Sweden and consorted with the Scandinavian literati in Copenhagen, estimated that 50 percent of the men she knew were infected with venereal disease. It was common for bachelors to compare notes on syphilis when they withdrew from the ladies to have after-dinner drinks and cigars in the library. The discussions also invaded the legislative chambers when certain proposals put forth by the medical profession urged the separation of married couples if one of them had the disease. The clergy opposed these measures, and the lawmakers hesitated to act. However, some legal reforms were passed in 1878.

Ibsen intended *Ghosts* to serve as a reply to critics of *A Doll's House*. Using syphilis, he could continue to examine the whole question of marriage and make a case—admittedly, a very special case—for a wife who left her husband. But the insidious disease soon became in his mind a symbol of the dark side of modern society. It was its very pervasiveness that made syphilis a fitting representative of Mrs. Alving's ghosts, the old traditions, the hidebound conventions, transmitted from one generation to the next, which held society in their sinister grip. As the instrument that dooms a young and innocent man, it imbued the whole drama with despair at the ineluctability of fate or something like it, the injustice of its blows, and the awful fascination of things that are not to be talked about. To represent the power of convention and received ideas by ghosts creeping out from between the lines of the newspapers and haunting Mrs. Alving's mind is a fine poetic device, but for theatrical effectiveness it cannot compare with the physical collapse of Oswald, the decline from *joie de vivre* in Paris to madness at Rosenvold.

By taking up this forbidden subject Ibsen was venturing into dangerous territory, more dangerous than he at first realized. In *A Doll's House* he had been discreet, keeping the subject very much in the background and letting it serve as a dark shadow cast by parents on their children. In *Ghosts* the disease spreads through the whole drama from the moment Oswald enters smoking his father's pipe until the very last moment when his mind collapses in front of his horrified mother.

The idea of employing syphilis as a central metaphor may have come from Georg Brandes, to whom Ibsen owed so much. After being denied the chair of esthetics at the University of Copenhagen, Brandes left Denmark to make a career

Figure 16. Georg Brandes 1879.
Portrait by Christian Krogh.

as a writer and critic in Germany. In need of a translator, he arranged to meet Adolf Strodtmann, who had rendered some Byron and some Tennyson and two of Ibsen's plays into German. He had a very high opinion of Ibsen's *Pretenders*, which he praised as "by far the most significant work not only of Norwegian literature but . . . perhaps the greatest drama the theater has seen since Shakespeare's day."[2] Within a short while Brandes fell in love with Strodtmann's wife, Henriette. Remembering the adverse publicity he had received in Denmark for his affair with a much older married woman, publicity that quite likely was a factor in his losing the professorship, Brandes kept his relationship with Henriette Strodtmann as secret as possible. But he may have told Ibsen about it on one of those occasions when they met and unburdened their souls to each other. It is unlikely that all their talk was about literature and revolutions, political and spiritual.

Brandes's story might have piqued the interest of any writer. He had learned that Adolf Strodtmann was suffering from syphilis, having picked up the disease as a young man in Paris. (Oswald blames his bohemian existence in Paris for his illness.) As a consequence, he had lost the sight of one eye. When he married

Henriette, he said nothing about his disease, but out of consideration for her he never consummated the marriage. Having had a very strict upbringing in an era when modern sexual hygiene was hardly talked about or practiced, she knew nothing about her husband's disease until after the marriage and perhaps not until after she met Brandes. He noticed certain sores on Strodtmann's tongue, consulted a doctor about them, and learned that they were common symptoms of syphilis—and only of syphilis. About 1873 Brandes wrote to Henriette, informing her of the true facts of her marriage. Four years later, he married her.[3]

In the third volume of his *Main Currents in Nineteenth-Century Literature,* printed in 1874, Brandes had censured society for forcing women to give birth to a child who would inherit its father's corrupt tendencies. The rhymed letter that Ibsen wrote to Brandes in 1875 gives a despairing view of progress in which the ship of civilization carries "a corpse in the cargo," reeking of superstition and hidebound traditions, a preliminary study for Mrs. Alving's "ghosts" speech. All of this was material that occupied Ibsen when he drafted his new play.

When he mentioned Dr. Rank's illness, he did not have to explain how the good doctor came to have his father's illness. Was it congenital? Or was it a question of the same lifestyle—like father, like son? But in *Ghosts,* a true-to-life play in which scientific determinism informs the action, Ibsen had to get his facts straight.

By putting syphilis at the center of his drama, Ibsen was venturing into a field where medical authorities could challenge him and question the whole foundation of his play. Consequently, he was very painstaking and meticulous in his research. This was before the syphilis spirochete had been isolated and described (in 1905) and before Paul Ehrlich's "magic bullet," neosalvarsan, provided a cure of sorts; Ibsen had to rely on the best authorities available at the time.

Oswald says he consulted "one of the leading doctors" (*en af de første læger*)[4] in Paris, and it is reasonable to think that Ibsen did the same. In 1880–81 the leading authority on syphilis was Dr. Alfred Fournier, for whom a special chair had just been created in the Faculty of Medicine of Paris. In Fournier's works Ibsen could have found all he needed for his depiction of Oswald's illness. In Fournier's *Syphilis and Marriage: Lectures Delivered at the St. Louis Hospital, Paris,*[5] which Ibsen may have read in the original French edition or in a German translation, the chapter on paternal heredity ("A man with syphilitic antecedents who contracts marriage may become dangerous to his children") would certainly have caught his eye.[6] In Fournier's *La Syphilis du cerveau,* published in Paris in 1879, Ibsen would have found a description of a patient in the last or tertiary stage of syphilis, a young man close to Oswald in age. "He is today only a big child, a 'grand enfant,' docile, inoffensive, who has to be dressed and undressed, led by the hand in the street. . . . He passes the day in a chair, not saying a word. He does nothing, he reads nothing." Another patient in the last phase of the disease is a *gateux*, an idiot who has lost control of his excretory organs.[7] Oswald fears that moment when he will be "turned into a helpless child again. To have to be fed—to have to be . . ." (*at bli' ligesom forvandlet til et spædt barn igen; at måtte mades, at matte*—), "incurably ruined for the rest of my life" (*uhelbredelig ødelagt for hele livet*).[8]

There is one small detail in Oswald's description of his illness that pretty much confirms that Ibsen relied on Fournier for his medical facts. The doctor told Oswald that he might live in that childlike state for a long time. "He called it," Oswald tells his mother, "a softening of the brain—or something like that" (*et slags blødhet i hjernen—eller noget sligt*).[9] Now, Fournier writes at some length about *ramollissement*, softening of the brain, characterized by lesions, which occur most often in the second stage of syphilis (as is the case with Oswald at the beginning of the play). Fournier describes two kinds of softening, *ramollissement chronique* and *ramollissement aiguë*. This second type, also called *ramollissement rouge*, is comparatively rare. Ibsen gave Oswald the second, the rare type, and Fournier provided him with a macabre detail concerning the redness of the lesions. Oswald says, "It always makes me think of cherry-colored velvet drapes—something soft and delicate to stroke" (*Jeg kommer altid til at tænke på kirsebærrøde silkefløjels drapperier,—noget, som er delikat at stryge nedad*). Fournier was the first specialist to specify this rare type of syphilis, convincing evidence that Ibsen did in fact consult his works.

Elsewhere in Fournier Ibsen would have read about the pain in the back of the head "as though a tight ring was being screwed round my neck" (*Det var som en trang jernring blev skruet om nakken og opover*). Fournier mentions "a feeling of pressure, as if the brain were held in a vice," along with terrible fatigue, an inability to concentrate on one's work.[10]

As for Oswald's seemingly normal appearance in the first part of the drama, Fournier remarks that in the middle stage of syphilis the disease is hard to diagnose. For every case with obvious external signs there are ten without.[11]

The sudden collapse of Oswald's mind at the end of the play struck many critics as not in accord with what was known about syphilis. Even if allowance is made for the need to concentrate time in a play, Oswald's deterioration from the normal-seeming young man of act one to the helpless *gateux* at the very end seemed too abrupt and precipitous to be convincing. But those critics should have turned to Dr. Fournier before faulting Ibsen. The medical facts and actual cases supported Ibsen's depiction. In the first place, a great change takes place in Oswald after the fire breaks out in the orphanage at the end of act two. From the moment the curtain rises on act three, he is a different person. In the terrifying scene in which he demands that his mother kill him, he seems deranged. As for the last moment when he sits quietly, mumbling and calling for the sun, that sudden breakdown is exactly like one described by Fournier, the condition of a patient immediately after an acute attack (ictus). The patient did not lose consciousness; he felt as if struck by a club. The doctor arrived to find him stretched out on the sofa, so weak he could scarcely move his head. Fournier describes one patient who lapsed into a coma, the face becoming expressionless, stupefied—exactly like Oswald.[12]

Moreover, Oswald's abrupt transition in the very last moments of the play from a thinking and speaking person to an incoherent idiot has its parallel in some famous cases. The mind of the French writer Jules Goncourt suddenly collapsed in January 1870, reducing him to a childlike state. A closer parallel to Oswald is the case of Friedrich Nietzsche, a classic instance of the sudden outbreak of madness due to tertiary syphilis. In December 1888 the sight of seeing a horse maltreated caused his mind to snap. Brought home, he slept for two days and awoke a madman. At the clinic in Basel he was diagnosed as being in the final stage of syphilis, "terminal lues" or "general paralysis of the insane." As with Oswald, there were few noticeable symptoms of the illness before his breakdown, apart from a recurring inflammation of the retina. Nietzsche perhaps acquired the disease in 1870 or 1871, when he became very ill with a jaw infection; as with Oswald, it lay dormant for many years, eighteen in Nietzsche's case. Again like Oswald, he was left in the care of his mother.[13]

Although Ibsen refrains from saying anything about it, the actor playing Oswald can suggest by the way he places his feet on the ground early in act three that the disease has reached a new stage. Even before the symptoms of paralysis are detected, "there may be something stiff, proud, abrupt about it; the steps shorter and quicker, and the foot being set down more sharply."[14] The actor who created the part of Oswald in Scandinavia simulated the shambling walk of *tabes dorsalis* in the last scenes of the drama.

Most important for a proper understanding of Ibsen's tragedy is the way in which Oswald was infected. It was assumed, even by some of the medical experts, that the father's syphilis was transmitted to him at birth, an assumption that has led some commentators to ask unnecessary questions such as "Why wasn't Mrs. Alving infected?" and has led some translators into errors. When, near the end of the drama, Oswald says that he got the disease from his father, he calls it his legacy (*arvelod*), a point lost when *arvelod* is translated as "birthright" (William Archer) or "the disease I have inherited" (J. W. McFarlane). Fournier takes pains to disabuse his readers of the idea "that syphilitic contagion can only be transmitted by the genital organs... This is an error which it is important to correct on every occasion."[15]

Oswald was not born with the disease; it was passed on to him when he smoked his father's pipe, a fact that Ibsen makes abundantly clear (and specifies a large meerschaum, to make the point visually). Oswald twice remarks on it. He says all he remembers about his father is that he made him sick when he smoked the pipe. In Scandinavia it was assumed the disease could be transmitted through oral contact, a drinking glass or a pipe. Strindberg in a letter could refer casually, with *Ghosts* in mind, to the "smoking pipe with hard chancre."[16]

Still, some medical authorities questioned Ibsen's knowledge of syphilis. Dr. J. Bang, in a letter to *Aftensposten* in Christiania in 1882, wrote that "[not] in all of medical literature can there be found a case like that of Oswald." But Brandes defended Ibsen and said that Oswald unquestionably suffers from and goes insane because of inherited syphilis. On March 16, 1882, he wrote to the English critic Edmund Gosse, "A doctor recently declared that the case was so strikingly depicted that one would believe that Ibsen had observed exactly this case in the hospital."[17]

When William Archer, who was to become Ibsen's chief advocate in England, questioned him in 1882 about the transmission of syphilis through a pipe, Ibsen was evasive.[18] Archer thought the disease was congenital, and Ibsen did not want to enter into a dispute with his English translator. The English disagreed with the French experts on such things as the manner of transmission and its connection with general paralysis of the insane. Fournier, on whom Ibsen relied for his "facts," turned out to be the best authority.

To sum up: although various medical authorities questioned the correctness of Ibsen's depiction of syphilis, it appears in the light of more recent research that he was essentially right in every respect—in the manner of transmission, in the long period of dormancy, in the progress of the disease through the three stages, and in the suddenness of the final mental collapse. Fournier proved to be a very reliable guide.

Fournier also proves to be invaluable for anyone who wants to have a complete understanding of the play. He provides a timetable for certain not atypical cases of syphilis of the brain (tertiary syphilis) in which the inception commonly occurs between ages three and ten and the tertiary stage manifests itself often twenty to twenty-six years after infection. This would appear to be the pattern that fits Oswald's case.[19]

Now, if one reads *Ghosts* attentively with Fournier's timetable in mind, it is possible to reconstruct the principal events out of the past that lead up to Oswald's return to Rosenvold, the point at which the play begins. For the sake of argument one can assume this is the date of the play, 1881.

Before 1852, the bon vivant Lieutenant Alving, scion of a fine family, was already a womanizer. In 1852 he settles down, like a typical young man who has sown his wild oats, and marries Helen. She is a young woman who, unlike her husband, wants to devote herself to some worthy cause.

With Helen and her husband having such totally different temperaments and aspirations, the marriage begins to fall apart. Lieutenant Alving quickly returns to his old ways. Disgusted by his behavior, Helen leaves him and runs to Pastor Manders, the man she had always been fond of. They are both idealistic and share a religious view of life, and Helen would certainly have married him but for her parents, who wanted her to marry into one of the finest families in the district. Afraid of what a scandal might do to him in his new position in the church, Manders sends her back to her husband.

She tries to make the best of her situation, and she and Alving come to some sort of understanding that involves their moving from the city and the temptations it offers the handsome officer to Rosenvold, the Alving family estate in the country.

In 1854 Helen becomes the mother of a boy, Oswald. The happy father leads a proper life—for a while. Helen describes him as improved. It is about this time that he is promoted to captain.

In 1857 a young woman, Johanna, is hired as a maid and proves to be an in-house temptation to Captain Alving. Helen refuses to have sex with Alving, whom she has never loved. He begins having affairs with the women in the neighborhood of the estate or with prostitutes in the town. In the nineteenth century, when many, if not most, middle-class marriages were arranged by the parents, it was common for men to preserve the appearance of a satisfactory marriage while they satisfied themselves in brothels. Emma Goldman said that "fully 50 percent of married men are patrons of brothels."[20]

As a result of his philandering, he is infected with syphilis, and shortly thereafter mucous patches containing the germs of the disease form on his lips and inside his mouth. These are symptoms that develop in the secondary period of syphilis, six months to three years after the initial infection.[21]

In 1858 little Oswald is forced to smoke his father's pipe, and the disease is transmitted to him through his lips. Ibsen provides a broad hint of this when Pastor Manders comments on how much Oswald resembles his father: "Something about the corners of the mouth, something about the lips, that reminds one exactly of Alving . . . at least when he is smoking."[22] The greatest likelihood of transmitting syphilis is in the first year or so after infection. Oswald is so young at the time that Helen is later surprised he remembers the incident at all. Alving is in a good mood, which suggests that the incident occurs before the crisis brought on by his affair with the maid Johanna. Or he may be in a good mood because of his promotion to chamberlain, which occurs between 1857 and 1860.

In 1860 Helen catches her husband in a compromising situation with Johanna. This is the last straw. She dismisses Johanna and takes full charge of the estate. The tone of Johanna's protests to Alving suggests that they are not old lovers at the time.

The following year Johanna gives birth to Regina. Johanna did not contract syphilis from Alving because her affair with him began more than three years after he had been infected. According to Fournier, the chances of infecting one's sexual partner are greatly reduced after the secondary phase, that is, after three years normally.

About this time Helen determines that Oswald must be brought up away from his father, and she may place him in the care of her relations. He is nearly seven when he leaves.

From 1861 to 1871 Helen manages the estate while her husband declines, sinking more and more often into a drunken stupor. His efforts to reform are inevitably followed by relapses and days of moaning and self-pity. His lucid intervals grow less and less frequent.

He dies in 1871, a diseased and broken man. Oswald comes home for the funeral, his first visit to Rosenvold since he left in 1861.

When he returns to Paris, Oswald, now seventeen, begins getting violent headaches. Some years later, in 1880, he develops definite symptoms of tertiary syphilis.

In 1881, knowing he will soon need to be cared for, he returns to Rosenvold. His mother plans on celebrating his return by shutting out the past. The tainted Alving money will go toward the establishment of a home for foundlings. Such homes were desperately needed in Scandinavia because of the blight of syphilis. Thousands of children, abandoned by their syphilitic mothers, needed to be placed in foster homes.

At this point the play begins, an excellent example of what is known in playwriting as a late point of attack, a technique brought to the height of perfection by Ibsen. The background story that unfolds through the three acts is as rich in incident as a long novel, and if Ibsen had been a novelist, he might have begun his tale on a dark and stormy night when the recently married Helen Alving seeks refuge from her drunken husband and comes knocking on the door of her idealistic and naive friend Pastor Manders, only to be turned away.

Many in the younger generation saw in the doomed Oswald the embodiment of their own plight. The painter Edvard Munch considered himself afflicted with the curse of a diseased heredity. In one of his poems the young Strindberg chastises the older generation for feasting at the banquet table and leaving nothing for their offspring. "We inherited your debts and your syphilis / And the ideals you dreamed of in the '40s. / You gobbled up all the choice bits / And left us to gnaw on forgotten promises."[23]

In the 1880s there were many young men of Strindberg's age who felt themselves the unwilling inheritors of problems and attitudes they wanted no part of, ghosts like those haunting Mrs. Alving. These feelings were crystallized in the scene in which Oswald, knowing he may collapse into insanity at any moment, asks his mother to help him by killing him.

Mrs. Alving screams, "Me!"

"Who has a better right than you?"

"Me! Your mother!"

"All the more reason."

"Me! Who gave you life!"

"I never asked you for life. And what kind of life have you given me? I don't want it! You have to take it back!"[24]

She rushes out into the hall, shouting for help. Oswald pursues her and locks the door so she cannot get out and no one can get in. Steadying herself, she comes back into the garden room.

"If you love me, Mother," says Oswald, "how can you let me suffer all this unspeakable terror?" and he extracts a promise from her that she will administer the fatal overdose of morphine.

This magnificently melodramatic scene gripped the younger generation as much as it revolted the older. The first Scandinavian actor who dared to portray Oswald was August Lindberg, who became a kind of James Dean hero to the young rebels. Lindberg's slightly rustic accent and his highly personal style of acting deprived him of a place in the Royal Theater in Stockholm and made it difficult for him to win more than a grudging nod of approval from the critics. However, in his portrayal of Oswald his unschooled naturalism proved to be an asset, and he created a clinically accurate portrait of a syphilitic patient that was the absolute center of attention.

The English theater critic William Archer described Lindberg's performance.

> At first I thought Lindberg's make-up was wrong—you couldn't look at him without seeing that he was more than slightly damaged inside. It was a masterly make-up as far as illusion went—short curling black hair, and a small black moustache, a very pale face, and those blinking, uneven, sort of light-shy eyes one so often sees in broken-down debauchees, one or other of the eye-

Figure 17. Scenes from *Ghosts*. August Lindberg as Oswald, Hedwig Winterhjelm as Mrs. Alving.

> brows having a tendency to rise now and then, without any apparent cause, and seemingly involuntarily. Altogether he was uncanny to look at—too much so, I thought at first, and I'm not sure but what I was right; but before he had been three minutes on stage I knew it was going to be a masterly piece of playing. The mere time that he took it in was admirably conceived—slow, deliberate, dreamy, the manner of a man to whom the world has become unreal. I never saw a part better filled out, as it were—it deserved to be called a creation, because Lindberg had actually invented and worked out in its smallest details the *manner* of the man, which, though it harmonized entirely with Ibsen's indications, was by no means to be found ready-made in them. He spoke his lines perfectly, but it was the business and in fact the mimik of the performance as a whole which specially struck me.[25]

To many, Oswald became the chief character, the tragic hero, of the play. He was the subject of most of the discussions, resulting in a slanted view of the drama in which the physical agony of Oswald outweighed the mental anguish of Mrs. Alving. But Ibsen clearly meant her to be the central character, a woman who sacrificed her own happiness for the sake of her son, sending him away from Rosenvold, only to find when he returns to her that he is a dying man. She is faced with the terrible alternative: kill the one person who gave meaning to her life of sacrifice or keep alive a horrible reminder of the pointlessness of her life. Her morally impossible situation made her a representative, however extreme, of the crisis of conscience afflicting Scandinavia in the 1870s and 1880s.

Mrs. Alving has spent her life doing her duty as she sees it and making sacrifices, none greater than sending her son away from the baleful influence of Rosenvold. But when Oswald returns he brings with him a new outlook, an alien philosophy acquired in the liberated world of bohemian Paris—that one should place happiness above duty, the instincts above social codes, the indulgence of the senses above regard for crusty, age-old inhibitions, the sheer joy of living above the painful satisfaction of having done one's duty. By the time Oswald reenters her life, she has advanced far beyond Pastor Manders's "What right have people to happiness?" But Oswald's defense of a life in the sun, away from the gloom of a life of duty, comes to her as a revelation. "Joy of life" (*livsglæde*) is Oswald's phrase, and when she hears it, she is startled.

"Can there be salvation [*redning*] in that?" she exclaims. "Salvation" puts more stress on the religious aspect than the Norwegian word *redning*, which carries the sense of hope and escape, deliverance rather than salvation. Brand sought "salvation" for his soul; Helen Alving thinks of an alternative existence. She has advanced a long way from her religious youth; she has read, we may assume, Mill, Taine, some Darwin, and Georg Brandes, the books that Pastor Manders to his dismay finds lying about, and her mind is open to new ideas. But to hear of the joy of life breaks the final barrier between the conventional thoughts that had been instilled in her mind and a whole world of experience that has so far been denied to her. To her, *redning* means escape, an opening to a different life. The phrase startles her like the sudden revelation of an undiscovered world.

"The joy of life" is Oswald's slogan, diametrically opposed to Manders's view of life as a vale of tears, and also far removed from his mother's belief in the necessity of sacrifice, the need to give oneself to a higher cause. Although by no means a neologism when *Ghosts* appeared (Ibsen had used the word *livsglæden* in 1851 in a review of a play, *Asylet paa Grönland*), it became a part of the language through the discussions aroused by Ibsen's play.

For the young rebels who adopted Oswald's manner of dress and smoked meerschaum pipes, it was a cry of liberation; for the defenders of inherited ideas and the status quo it was an invocation to the devil, the *evoe* of the modern worshippers of Dionysus.

The case for those who saw the dangers in the joy of life, Oswald's carpe diem philosophy, was forcefully put in a leading article early in 1882.

> Hitherto the fulfillment of one's duties, the keeping of one's promises, the love of one's children have been regarded as the serious considerations in a moral system. Ibsen and the chief person in his drama find all this to be nothing but empty platitudes of no significance, ghosts of some lost and innocent time when people didn't know any better. One can only laugh at a priest who instead of taking advantage of a runaway wife's love for him, tells her to return to her abandoned husband.... For Ibsen's characters the joy of life is the highest guide to life. And what sort of joyful life follows? Not the quiet, serene joy that comes with the satisfaction of having done one's duty, not the peace of one's home and the love of one's cherished children—but the noisy, clamorous joy of life that finds no outlet in a medium-size town, that must have the whole world in which to express its happiness, a *joie de vivre* that finds in Paris the realization of its dreams. Stripped of its fancy trimmings, it says that the purpose of living is pleasure, fun and games. Oh, my native land is too confining for my joy of life—so shake the dust from your feet, and hurry off to the big city of pleasure and get your fill of it. Cast off all the bonds of family life! A union based on mutual need and desire—what a silly, old-fashioned idea. No, enjoy a casual pairing-off, united today, separated tomorrow. And if the sorrows and tribulations are part of marriage—what of it—break the bonds. It is only life's delights, not its trials, that give meaning to life.

This is Ibsen's teaching in all its utter repulsiveness.[26]

Public Enemy

The controversial nature of *A Doll's House* only added to Ibsen's fame and renown, and he may have thought that *Ghosts*, which was certainly artistically superior, would be another controversial and much-talked-about best seller. Since *Brand* and *Peer Gynt* he had enjoyed nothing but success, and even when he ventured into the unfamiliar territory of the realistic problem play, following the advice of Brandes and the example of Bjørnson, he found his popularity spreading from Scandinavia to Germany. But with *Ghosts* he miscalculated greatly.

The public debates that surrounded Nora's late-night abandonment of husband and children were conducted in a spirit of social goodwill. Everyone, of whatever age or social class, agreed that Ibsen had a perfect right to raise questions about the place of women in nineteenth-century society. And if he left important issues unresolved at the end of the play, that was only a sign of his open-mindedness. There was room for good people to disagree. They might raise their voices, but they remained civilized.

Ghosts was different. When he made the scabrous subject of syphilis central to the drama, he overstepped the bounds of decency. He may not have mentioned the disease, but he pictured the effects of it, the general paresis of the insane, in a graphic scene. And to what end? Apparently, to stir up controversy about such forbidden subjects as incest and euthanasia. Mrs. Alving contemplates without horror the possible union of Oswald and Regina, his half sister, and she promises to kill Oswald when he declines into the final stage of dementia.

There were two serious consequences to Ibsen's use of syphilis as a metaphor for the power of the past. The focus of attention was shifted from Mrs. Alving, the true protagonist of the drama, to Oswald, and this led to a profound misunderstanding of Ibsen's intentions. The other consequence was that his string of successes was snapped. *Ghosts* turned out to be a very bad career move.

The strongest opposition to this family tragedy was raised by the subventioned theaters and the state church, the two most conservative social institutions at that time. All the state-supported theaters in Scandinavia rejected it as an immoral, antisocial work.

The censor at the Royal Theater in Copenhagen, a former songwriter and lyricist, found that Ibsen's reputation as a master dramatist could not put him above the accepted standards of morality; in fact, his fame would only heighten the danger in presenting this play, which has a "disgusting pathological phenomenon as its main theme, while it undermines the moral system that provides the foundation of an orderly society."[1]

"This alone, that the play attracts the theatergoer's interest in the development of and consequences of a syphilitic infection which Oswald has either inherited along with his father's blood or else sucked in through his tobacco pipe, and which brings about the catastrophe by striking his brain and causing a paresis, this by itself provides sufficient reason for rejecting the play."[2]

In Norway, the play reader at the Christiania Theater would not even allow that Ibsen was a craftsman and a master of his art.

"This play is not an effective drama, and it tries to make up for this by the use of dramatic stimulants. The theater cannot possibly concede that such means can serve as a substitute for true dramatic effectiveness; such a concession would be tantamount to pronouncing a death sentence on itself. The consequences of such an attitude would be that one closed the theater and opened a state hospital with an entrance fee."[3] This censorship dominated the established theaters in Norway, and the play was not performed in one of them until 1890.

Outside Scandinavia, theaters responded in much the same way, and the authorities wanted nothing to do with it. America was more daring than Europe. The world premiere of *Ghosts* took place in Chicago, May 20, 1882, performed by a troupe of Scandinavian actors. The European premiere was August Lindberg's staging of the play in Helsingfors, Sweden, on August 22, 1883. In Germany it was banned by the police, and performed there for the first time, privately, in Augsburg in April 1886. Another members-only performance took place in Berlin in January 1887. And when the enlightened Duke of Saxe-Meiningen staged it at his own court theater in December 1886, his subjects protested, even though they had not had the opportunity of reading the play. They refused to purchase tickets, and the duke, having invited Ibsen to the performance, gave tickets away free of charge and, anticipating trouble, had policemen stationed in the house. Ibsen probably never knew that the house had been papered.[4]

The reluctance of theaters to stage *Ghosts* was one thing; much more serious to Ibsen was the loss of his reading public. Since there were few theaters in the Nordic countries, and there was no organization that would ensure standard royalty payments, the sale of the printed play became more important to Ibsen than theater productions.[5] His experience with *Pillars of Society* brought this home to him. The Danish Royal Theater requested that the publication of the book be delayed in order to heighten interest in the premiere of the play. Since the theater would not increase his royalty, Ibsen refused this request, saying he now felt "compelled to make the sale of the book my chief source of income."[6]

Beginning with this play, Ibsen made every effort to get his plays published in time for the Christmas season, but he also circulated copies of *Pillars of Society* and *A Doll's House* among theater managers before the publication date. When the theaters rejected *Ghosts*, Ibsen gave up this practice and concentrated on his potential readership.

The anomaly of a playwright writing mainly for readers is virtually without precedent in the history of the theater. Playwrights in the past wrote for the stage, hoping that success in the theater would stimulate sales of the published script. In fact, dramatists were as a rule reluctant to publish because their plays could then be pirated and acted without payment of royalties. The situation was better in Germany and France, where there were many theaters, and the most popular playwrights kept their eyes on both markets, the theater and the bookstall. But it was Ibsen who more than anyone else made the reading of plays a necessity for the intellectual who wanted to keep abreast of the times. To make his scripts as readable as possible, he, like Bjørnson, avoided the technical jargon of scripts intended for the theater, and stage directions right and left were from the audience's point of view, not the actors'.

Ibsen and his publisher, Hegel, were confident that *Ghosts* would attract an enormous number of readers, and an unprecedented first printing of ten thousand copies was ordered to be ready for the Christmas season. *A Doll's House*, with its Yuletide setting and a final scene that allowed for some hope—"the miracle of miracles" are Torvald's last words—was an appropriate gift for that time of year. *Ghosts* was not, and Ibsen and Hegel displayed great insensitivity in thinking that ordinary people would consider this drama with its syphilis and euthanasia a proper gift. The public spurned it; bookstores returned hundreds of copies, and it took thirteen years to sell out the first printing.

"If there are still people who celebrate the New Year with Saturnalia like the ancient Romans," wrote one reviewer, "then Ibsen's *Ghosts* should make an appropriate present. But in a Christian home on a table with Christmas decorations the book has absolutely no place."[7]

Anticipating the screeds and diatribes that would appear in the English press when the play was translated, some Norwegian reviewers outdid themselves in berating both the play and its author. Wrote one: "The whole thing is a confused collection of immoral, scoundrel-like, old-womanish people, who live in perverse relationships amid decayed institutions. . . . The only thing that offers one comfort, when one has read the book to the end, is that it is much more poorly written than the author's other works, which means, first, that it will cause less harm, and, second, that this shabby piece of writing will demonstrate that belles-lettres [literature] will not let itself be used for the purposes intended by the author."[8]

The center of opposition was the religious establishment. Ibsen had been carrying on a war with the church ever since his youth. Though the conservative politicians could at times embrace him, the clergy always knew that between them and the dramatist lay an unbridgeable gulf. *Love's Comedy* had been assailed by the churchmen as an attack on the institution of marriage, and when Ibsen had applied to the state for a poet's stipend, the strongest protest had come from Chamberlain Riddervold, the head of the Norwegian Ecclesiastical Department. Some years later, in 1872, when Ibsen, now the decorated author of *Brand*, applied for a travel stipend, it was Riddervold again who vetoed it.

"I don't feel my reputation," commented Ibsen, "is affected in the least. It is not within the power of the Norwegian Ecclesiastical Department to affect my reputation."[9]

In 1880, when that department through its supervision of education refused to admit Ibsen's son, Sigurd, to the University of Christiania, Ibsen promised that "that black gang of theologians who now run the Norwegian Ecclesiastical Department shall receive a fitting literary memorial as soon as I can get around to it."[10] True to his word, he drew the inept and naive Pastor Manders as typical of religious reactionaries.

As a caricature, Manders is etched with more malice than Pastor Strawman in *Love's Comedy*, as befits the dark and desolate mood of Ibsen's naturalistic tragedy. Where the comedy, in the eyes of the clergy, undermined the institution of marriage, *Ghosts* challenged the very existence of family, state, and church. Ibsen himself called it a representation of the nihilism inherent in the times.[11] Behind this questioning of all values loomed Darwin and his theory of evolution. The Lutheran Church was feeling the pressure brought to bear on it by modern science and historical research, which put into doubt much of what was written in the Bible. Widespread acceptance of Darwinism would topple the pillars on which the institutions of state and family reposed. Ibsen was leaning hard on those pillars, and if they fell, God would fall too. The church was fighting to keep the human being at the center of the universe as God's special creation. By espousing Darwinism and naturalism, Ibsen was reducing man to the level of a savage animal, straining at the bars of his cage. If he broke out, if everything was permitted, would he revel in the joy of life, without concern for spiritual values?

While the clergy could only pray that this vision of the state of affairs in the nineteenth century was utterly mistaken, the bleak honesty of the work won the admiration of an enlightened few. Bjørnson, Jonas Lie, and Brandes were the most notable defenders of Ibsen's play. Bjørnson was one of the first to speak out. And Ibsen was very grateful. "He is the only man in Norway," he said, "who has stood up frankly, boldly, and courageously on my behalf. That is characteristic of him. He has indeed a great and noble soul; and I shall never forget what he has done just now."[12]

Bjørnson thought *Ghosts* was Ibsen's best work, the one in which "his creative talents reveal themselves most fully and in which he plumbs his material most deeply."[13] It was an opinion that Bjørnson retained. When news of Ibsen's death reached him and he was asked what was Ibsen's most important play, he replied, "*Ghosts.*"[14]

Bjørnson had recently left the church, and his public utterances were in harmony with what Ibsen was implying in *Ghosts.* In January 1880, right after the publication of *A Doll's House*, he said his fellow countrymen were divorced from reality. "Between us and reality are hazy dreams, old half-realized ideals, resurrected memories.... We are impotent where we should be strongest, in our will. Life is falling to pieces for us, because our connection with it is broken in two ways. We have broken with our ideals, because we cannot live up to them or because we no longer believe in them; and we have broken with the others, the thousand-voiced laboring force, because our intellectuals are not here with us. They are not here to answer our crying need—they are up in the skies—or traveling abroad."[15]

Writing to Brandes, Bjørnson remarked that Ibsen "must have developed significantly since—well, in just three or four years. Devil knows what happened to him, but this is a real piece of work. I take my hat off to him."[16]

For Lie, *Ghosts* was a "major surgical operation right into what people don't talk about—it puts to shame the hundreds of moralistic, dirty books."[17]

For Brandes, Ibsen's tragedy ripped away the last veil of hypocrisy that shrouded marriage. "For centuries society had through its priests and poets extolled marriage ... as a haven. [In *A Doll's House*] it was seen to be a bay full of reefs and shoals. And it was Ibsen who had extinguished the warning fires.... [With *Ghosts*] it was as if he had extinguished the stars themselves.... Not a bit of light."[18]

Andreas Munch, esteemed Norwegian lyric poet, son of a clergyman, put the darkness of Ibsen's play in a religious context. His poem "A Fallen Star" describes Ibsen in its first stanza as a rising star, greeted by all as a sign of hope and progress. In the second stanza the star changes course, plunges toward earth, caught by its gravitational pull. Worms crawl around it, making it stink like a carcass. Munch concludes his poem with a prediction that heaven will punish him who has sinned against the Holy Ghost.

The rest of the literary world also turned against Ibsen, with both the liberals and the conservatives anathematizing him, denouncing his drama as "the shameless manifesto of modern abominations" and "a piling up of dirty language, a cloaca of fashionable repulsiveness."[19]

The tone of the play, said one critic, "brings it far down, down to the level of Zola. . . . The overall impression left by the book is one of utter disgust. It is as if Ibsen took delight in saying the ugliest things that could possibly be said and saying them with as much exaggeration as possible."[20]

The novelist Alexander Kielland said the same thing but with a touch of humor, comparing Ibsen to Nora, who got a thrill out of saying forbidden words.

Emile Zola, the most talked-about writer on the continent because of his notorious novels depicting the seamier side of life, had just published his essays on Naturalism in the theater (1878–79). The Swedish painter Georg Pauli thought he was complimenting Ibsen when he compared him to Zola. "With just this difference," Ibsen sharply interrupted him, "that Zola climbs down into the sewers to take a bath, I to clean them."[21]

Even the freethinker Arne Garborg found *Ghosts* "positively ghastly. After reading it, the good old writings seem to deserve unqualified praise. At least one could read them without doing damage to one's nerves."[22]

It was obvious that the controversy had little to do with literature and everything to do with religion. In 1880 Brandes in a speech declared that underlying all the main issues of the time, whether literary or moral or political, was the confrontation of the liberals and the clergy, with the clergy using their political clout to inhibit free thought. "The breach between the naturalists and the churchmen is the one that is incurable, but it is political, not literary."[23] Ibsen blamed the misleading and perverse interpretation of his drama on the theologians and the so-called liberal press. "A great many of the professional reviewers are theologians, more or less disguised, and these gentlemen are as a rule quite unable to write about literature in a rational way. That enfeeblement of the judgment which . . . is an inevitable consequence of protracted occupation with theological studies betrays itself in judging human character, human actions, and human motives. Practical business judgment, on the other hand, does not suffer so much from theological studies. Hence the reverend gentlemen are often excellent members of local boards, but they are, unquestionably, our worst critics."[24]

Ibsen's initial response to the uproar was to cloak himself in the mantle of imperturbability. Being savaged by the critics was not a new experience for him, as he reminded his publisher.

"I am not in the least disturbed by the violence of the reviewers and all the crazy nonsense written about *Ghosts*; I was prepared for it. When *Love's Comedy* appeared, there was just as great an outcry in Norway as there is now. *Peer Gynt*, too, was reviled. So was *Pillars of Society.* So was *A Doll's House*. The cry will die away this time just as it did before...

"There is one thing that does worry me, however, when I think of the size of the first printing. Has all this uproar hurt the sales of the book?"[25]

Realizing that sales were indeed being hurt by the controversy instead of being helped by it, as was the case with *A Doll's House*, Ibsen tried to salvage the unsold copies by resorting to equivocation. In a letter that he wanted made public, he denied that there was a single opinion expressed by the characters in *Ghosts* that could be laid to the account of the author and protested that in none of his other works was he such an outsider, so entirely absent, as in this one.[26] But since the choice of subject and the shape and tone of the play were Ibsen's own, everyone saw through the transparent subterfuge. The outspoken Strindberg, young and brash, said that Ibsen was behaving like a coward. Judged by Strindberg's own incautious and reckless behavior, Ibsen was. When communing with himself, he must have often accused himself of cowardice, just as Mrs. Alving repeatedly arraigns herself for not having spoken out clearly and forcefully years ago.

In a private letter he took a different position. "I myself am responsible for what I write, I and no one else. I cannot possibly embarrass any party, for I do not belong to any. I shall stand like a solitary franc-tireur at the outpost, acting entirely on my own."[27]

That image of himself at a solitary outpost was to dominate his thinking as he prepared to reply to his critics. He stood now as one of a small band fighting against the solid citizenry. He was Brand again, opposed by the mayor and the sheriff, and abandoned by the public that had followed him halfway up the mountain.

He knew he was in league with the future. "All the decrepit old fossils who jumped in to attack my play will have a shattering sentence pronounced on them in future histories of literature. And the anonymous poachers and highwaymen who have showered me with abuse from their ambushes . . . will sooner or later be forced out into the open. My book belongs to the future. Those fellows who have bellowed so much about it do not have any real contact with the living spirit of their own times."[28]

Ibsen's greatest disappointment was with the behavior of the liberals, although it confirmed his views on the shabbiness of politics. "I was quite prepared that my new play would provoke a howl from the camp of the stand-patters; and that bothers me about as much as a pack of chained dogs barking at my heels. But the alarm I have observed among the so-called liberals has given me cause for reflection."

Returning to his old theme of political versus spiritual liberty, he remarked on the champions of liberty who had been frightened out of their wits by *Ghosts*. "Is it only in the field of politics that the work of emancipation shall go on? Must not men's minds be emancipated first of all? Men with such slavish souls as ours cannot make use even of the liberties they already possess. Norway is a free country peopled by unfree men and women."[29]

The behavior of friend and foe during the uproar over *Ghosts* provided this keen observer of human nature with a wealth of material for a new play. "I have made many studies and observations during the storm," he wrote to his publisher, "which I shall find very useful in my future works."[30]

The bitter experience yielded a surprisingly sweet fruit, after only a year: a play called *An Enemy of the People*. It was a comedy with a serious theme, and he did not know whether to call it a comedy or a drama.[31] It was the distillate of his observations of the public and the press, heated by his wrath and then cooled by being filtered through his recollections of small-town politics. Like a revival of a successful television series, it takes some of his favorite characters and puts them in a new situation. Adjunct Rörlund from *Pillars of Society* is still teaching school, and Stensgaard from *The League of Youth* is now a governor, after having been a newspaper editor. Neither actually appears in the play. But Aslaksen, who was running a newspaper when Stensgaard was roiling the political waters, is still doing business at the same old stand. For a play that deals with the independence of the press, it was natural that Ibsen would bring back Aslaksen, who was modeled on N. F. Axelsen, the printer of the satiric, short-lived journal *Andhrimmer*, to which Ibsen contributed in his youth.

The center of the drama is the outspoken Dr. Stockmann, who refuses to yield to pressures brought to bear on him when he insists on speaking the unpleasant truth. No weathervane like Stensgaard, he has convictions and stands by them whatever they may cost him. He is one of Ibsen's most appealing characters because he is a compound of real people whom Ibsen liked. The play is a counterpart to *The League of Youth*, in which Ibsen had caricatured Bjørnson and Lie as a response to their shabby treatment of him. Now, after they had come to his defense over *Ghosts*, he owed them a debt of gratitude. His reconciliation with Bjørnson at this time brought him closer to the man than he would ever be again. When he was working on the final draft of *An Enemy of the People*, he wrote Bjørnson to praise him for his greatness of soul and for practicing what he preached, quite the opposite of what he had thought about him thirteen years earlier.

"To me the greatest and most important thing is that you put into the field the whole of your strong and truthful personality. That is poetry put into practice. Your work has a primary place in our literature, and this it will always have. But should I have to decide what to inscribe on a monument to your memory, I would choose these words: 'His life was his greatest poem.'"[32]

Similarly, Lie, who had earned Ibsen's contempt in 1869, was rehabilitated in *Enemy of the People.* Previously caricatured as one of Bjørnson's hypocritical henchmen, he was now seen as a man of upright character and strong principles.

Both Bjørnson and Lie went into the creation of Dr. Stockmann. He was endowed with Lie's irresistible charm and rather cuddly lovableness and equipped with Bjørnson's powerful orator's voice and his fiery tongue. (Even as late as the mid-twentieth century, Stockmann's language had to be bowdlerized for Norwegian radio.)[33]

Lie came to spend a holiday at Berchtesgaden at Ibsen's suggestion, and the two saw quite a lot of each other. Lie has given us a vivid impression of the idiosyncratic dramatist. Ibsen was in good humor, often laughing and revealing two prominent front teeth with a large space between them. He took his constitutional alone, stopping whenever he heard the sound of an approaching carriage in the far distance. He would carefully prepare for the passing of the wagon, taking a silk handkerchief from his left breast pocket, wiping his glasses, and neatly folding and replacing it. When the wagon had passed by, he would "walk on, taking small, quick steps, precise and looking elegant, in spite of the green Tyrolean hat, which he had purchased soon after his arrival, and to which he had added a huge cock's feather that flopped with each step he took."[34]

But the spine of the character, the willingness to stand alone, is Ibsen's, and Ibsen gave him the name Stockmann because Ibsen was born in the Stockman house in Skien. The ideas he expresses and the situation he finds himself in are unmistakably Ibsen's own.

He told his publisher, "Dr. Stockmann and I . . . agree on so many subjects. But the doctor is more muddle-headed than I am, and moreover he has other idiosyncrasies that permit him to say things that would not be taken so well if I myself said them."[35] He probably had in mind Lie's disarming and ingratiating manner.

From the beginning, Ibsen as the franc-tireur at his outpost was to be the leading figure in the drama. But what would be the central situation? What could he find that would be roughly analogous to the *Ghosts* controversy, in which he had been accused by so many good citizens of wallowing in filth? Again, as in the case of *A Doll's House,* he was lucky.

In 1874, shortly after Ibsen had paid a brief visit to his native country, an apothecary named Harald Thaulow took to making public speeches about corruption in high places. Finally, in 1880, he took to print and published a pamphlet called *The Pillars of Society in Prose,* a title that must have caught Ibsen's attention. Thaulow singled out the Christiania Steam Kitchens, ostensibly a charitable organization to feed the impoverished, as a cover for graft. At a public meeting in February 1881, when he was to make good his charges that the steam kitchens were a profit-making scheme, he was prevented from speaking. Pandemonium broke loose. Leaving the meeting, he shouted, "No one can stand up against the brute mob. I want nothing more to do with you. I will not cast pearls before swine. This is a diabolical misuse of a free people in a free society. I shall go now. Do me the favor of hiding your heads in shame. Shame on all of you!"[36]

Suddenly, two weeks later, he died.

The mob at that meeting was the compact majority that Ibsen always contemned. It was the Great Bøyg that drove Peer Gynt away from the straight and narrow, away from his true self. It was what made Ibsen distrust democracy and republicanism.

For the corruption and graft in a charity that incensed the muckraking Thaulow, Ibsen substituted the polluted waters at a Norwegian spa. He may have heard or read about a doctor at the spa in Teplitz in Bohemia, who in 1831 ordered the baths closed when a cholera epidemic broke out.[37] Like that German doctor, Stockmann knows that to prevent an epidemic the baths must be shut down. At first the townsmen, who have no direct interest in the spa business, which has been financed by the town's leading citizens, the pillars of society, side with the good doctor. They form a compact majority, ready to stand solid as a wall against the vested interests. But the wall crumbles at the mere mention of the tax increase that will be imposed to bear the cost of rechanneling the waters for the baths.

The ever-optimistic and irrepressible Stockmann believes he can make himself heard through the independent press. But how independent is it? When the mayor paints the bleak future of a town that will be known as a pesthole throughout the country, the editor is sufficiently intimidated to close his paper to Stockmann.

Now Stockmann must turn directly to the townspeople in order to get a hearing. The climactic fourth act of the play, the scene of the public meeting, is a farce about parliamentarism. Stockmann has called the meeting, but before he can speak, his enemies insist that the meeting be conducted along democratic lines. First a chairman must be elected. Once in place, the chairman entertains a motion that Stockmann not be allowed to make irresponsible statements about the baths without presenting verification of his findings.

Effectively gagged on the main question, Stockmann demands the right to speak on another matter. Enraged by the way he has been treated when all he has tried to do is speak the truth, Stockmann becomes Ibsen's mouthpiece, and the baths become a symbol of a wider and more pervasive infection. He arraigns the whole social community, charging it with moral stultification. The democratic notion that the majority is always right is a delusion. The compact majority is always wrong because it always feeds on the moldy truths of the past. Democracy only succeeds in making the wise subject to fools, for they are always in the majority.

After this impassioned onslaught on mob mentality, Stockmann is publicly branded as an enemy of the people and treated accordingly. The mob smashes the windows in his house; his daughter is dismissed from the school where she has been teaching; and the man who had provided the hall for the public meeting is fired from his job. Indomitable and irrepressible up to this point, Stockmann finally gives up. He decides to sail to America with his family.

Now comes the clever twist in the plot. The leading citizens of the town cannot believe that anyone can be as idealistic and truth-loving as Dr. Stockmann. No reasonable man would sacrifice his good position and the happiness of his family simply to shut down the pestilential baths. He must have a hidden agenda. Imparting to Stockmann the same self-interest that drives them, they can only suppose that his exposé is part of a collusion, that he has entered into a conspiracy to drive down the value of the shares in the spa corporation so that he can buy a major interest for a mere pittance.

When Stockmann realizes that the people fear that his cunning may be greater than theirs, he sees how the compact majority feeds on itself. By standing above and apart from them, he scores the final triumph. His recognition of this provides the ringing conclusion to the play: "the strongest man in the world is he who stands most alone." He resolves to stay in Norway and fight for the truth.

Dr. Thomas Stockmann's main opponent in the town is his brother Peter, who is the mayor. Their Christian names point to their different philosophies. Peter stands rock solid for the status quo and believes that "the mass is best served by the good old recognized ideas that they already have." The skeptical Thomas, on the other hand, is constantly questioning the received ideas, and though, like his brother, he has contempt for the people as a mass, he believes in educating them. His next step in the fight for the truth is to open a school in the very room where he was branded an enemy of the people.

The upbeat ending, combined with the Dickensian characters and the buoyant spirit of Dr. Stockmann in particular, made it impossible for anyone to be deeply offended by the play. Ibsen had astutely tempered his spleen with humor to make this one of his most successful works. The theaters that had rejected *Ghosts* clamored for *Enemy of the People*. The Christiania Theater, which had found the previous play too depressing for its public, was forced by Ibsen to pay double the usual royalties for *Enemy of the People*.[38]

Ibsen insisted on complete realism in the staging of *An Enemy of the People*, both in the sets and in the acting. He wanted "the illusion that everything is real and that one is looking at something that is happening in real life."[39] "The spectator must feel that he is an unseen guest in Dr. Stockmann's rooms."[40]

He wanted to break away from the standard practice of casting according to "lines of business": Character Comedy, Old Man, Walking Gentleman, Juvenile Comedy Lead, and so on. Already in 1869 in London the pioneer of stage realism, T. W. Robertson, both an actor and a director, while listing the parts according to lines of business, was also supplying his actors with detailed descriptions. The "character comedy" in *School* was meticulously described in the acting edition as "a man of about sixty, aged more than his years by fast life. . . . Nervous twitchings in his hands; inability to walk steadily . . . very near-sighted, yet hesitating to betray this effect by using his eye-glass, often dropping it after he has taken hold of it for use."[41]

Perhaps out of respect for professional actors, Ibsen hesitated to play their parts for them. But he might point them in the right direction, which he did when he objected to a well-known, solidly built actor being cast as Dr. Stockmann. Ibsen reminded the theater producer that "hot-headed people are generally slender-limbed. . . . [The actor] should make himself as short and thin as possible."[42]

To invest themselves thoroughly in a part, actors often create biographies of their characters. Ibsen helpfully does that for Hovstad, the liberal newspaper editor who yields to political pressure and refuses to print Dr. Stockmann's exposure of the contaminated baths. Hovstad, said Ibsen, should not be physically impressive. He "comes from a peasant family, grew up in an unhealthy home, poorly and insufficiently nourished, was cold and worked hard as a child, and later as a young man endured many a loss. A life like that sets its mark not only on the inner man but also on the outer person. Heroic figures from the common people are really exceptions. Above all, Hovstad must have something somber about him, somewhat shrunken, stooped in his posture, hesitant in his movements, all this, rendered, of course, completely true to life."[43]

Ibsen protested strongly against the conventional casting of two young girls, with wigs and corsets, to play Stockmann's sons, ages ten and thirteen. He insisted the parts be acted by boys, who should, moreover, "be rehearsed to the point of exhaustion until the difference in their personalities becomes clear."[44]

All this information, so helpful to actors and readers, does not appear in his printed plays. Bernard Shaw, years later, had sense enough to include lengthy descriptions of his characters and their ambiance. It is a considerable loss to a full understanding and appreciation of Ibsen's plays that he was so old-fashioned, so far behind T. W. Robertson's comedies of the 1860s, in not giving actors and readers more information about his characters, especially since we know that they all existed so fully in his mind as he wrote.

The broad success of *An Enemy of the People* could not undo in Ibsen's mind the harm done to his career and reputation by *Ghosts*. He had wanted to stand alone, apart from the crowd, and, like Brand, to shape his own conscience in defiance of taboos and conventions, and without the help of sects or tribes or parties. His loyalty had to be entirely to himself.

Writing to Brandes, he said, "There is something demoralizing in engaging in politics and in joining parties. It will never be possible for me to join a party that has the majority on its side. Bjørnson says, 'The majority is always right,' and as a practicing politician, he is bound, I suppose, to say so. [This was written before Ibsen learned of Bjørnson's defense of *Ghosts*.] I, on the contrary, must of necessity say, 'The minority is always right.' Of course, I am not thinking of that minority of stand-patters who are left behind by the great middle party that we call liberal. I mean that minority that leads the vanguard and pushes on to the point the majority has not yet reached. I mean that man is right who has allied himself most closely with the future."[45]

In the abstract, or in the ideal, poetic world of *Brand*, Ibsen could safely argue for the complete independent spirit of the individual without arousing the opposition or the fury of the guardians of the social and moral order. But the grim words uttered by Mrs. Alving, a woman caught up in the currents of radically changing thought and drifting toward an indistinct future, deeply upset most ordinary people as well as most of the intellectual elite. Ibsen, however, was in the paradoxical position of wanting to be both a path breaker and a conservative member of the establishment. And he knew that whatever greatness he might achieve, it would come to him because he forged ahead into new territory.

"It may well be that this play [*Ghosts*] is in several respects rather daring," he admitted. "But it seemed to me that now was the time when some boundary posts had to be moved."[46]

And again: "In these times every piece of creative writing should attempt to move the frontier markers."[47]

Georg Brandes, who had first pointed him down the path that led to *Ghosts*, said that when Ibsen wrote it he wagered his long-fought-for social reputation, his favor with the public, and his eminence as a writer. "This book may not be his most nearly perfect drama . . . but it is the noblest deed of his literary life."[48]

In his provocative foreword to *Married* (*Giftas*, 1884), the young Strindberg saw the ironies in Ibsen's relationship with the public. Ibsen wrote *Brand* as a protest against watered-down Christianity, but the pietists took it as Scripture.

He wrote *Ghosts* against immorality, but the prigs called it immoral. He wrote *An Enemy of the People* about himself, but the true enemies of society stoned him.

Ibsen's entire career up to this point, measured in terms of his success with the public, was a series of rapprochements and fallings out, at best an uneasy alliance with those he looked down on. For *Love's Comedy,* he was ostracized from the better homes in Christiania. For *Brand,* in which he expressed the same philosophy, he was eulogized throughout the Nordic countries. For *The League of Youth,* the anarchist was crowned poet laureate of the conservatives. For *A Doll's House,* he was hailed as a master of the problem play and embraced by the liberals. For *Ghosts,* a much more controversial and hard-hitting drama, he was shunned by nearly all the liberals.

The deepest irony was that this rebel wanted to be esteemed by the very people he reproved and denounced. He sought a secure position in the society that his plays undermined. He doodled sketches of medals and insignia as he drew up notes for his next nihilistic work.

Only now the longed-for honors stopped coming his way. Between 1869 and 1876 he had collected six orders, which he proudly displayed. After *Ghosts,* no such honor would come to him in Scandinavia for more than ten years.

The Slain Pegasus

Writing at the end of the 1870s, Emile Zola, the chief literary exponent of naturalism, condemned the frivolous theatrical entertainments of Eugène Scribe and his followers and called for a dramatist with "the cleverness or the might to impose himself and to remain so close to truth that his cleverness would not lead him into lies.

"And what an immense place this innovation would occupy in our dramatic literature! He would be at the peak. He would build his monuments on the desert of mediocrity. . . . He would put everything in question and remake everything, scour the boards, create a world whose elements he would lift from life, from outside our traditions. Surely there is no more ambitious dream that a writer from our time can fulfill. The domain of the novel is crowded; the domain of the theater is free."

Right on cue, Ibsen made his entrance. His eyes focused on the French theater, Zola scarcely noticed his coming. Yet all that he advocated Ibsen accomplished.

"The formula will be found; it will be proved that there is more poetry in the little apartment of a bourgeois than in all the empty, worm-eaten palaces of history. . . . [W]e must go back to [neoclassic] tragedy," urged Zola, "to its simplicity of action and its unique psychological and physiological study of the characters. . . . One deed unwinds in all its reality and moves the characters to passions and feelings the exact analysis of which constitute the sole interest of the play—and in a contemporary environment with the people who surround us."[1]

Ibsen could not have created a character as complex as Nora or plumbed the depths of Mrs. Alving's anguish without inventing new dramatic techniques. Caught in the irresistible currents of popular culture, he had to use the format of the French well-made play if he wanted to hold an audience in the theater. Its emphasis on plot twists and surprises, however, made it intractable to detailed character portrayal or subtlety of thought. Dumas *fils* enriched the well-made play by making it deal with social problems. Ibsen followed in his footsteps by writing *Pillars of Society.* There his social conscience made the play seem more significant than Scribe's cleverly contrived dramas. As a display of his mastery of the nuts and bolts of dramatic craftsmanship, however, it did not differ significantly from them.[2]

In the next two years, however, as he worked on *A Doll's House,* he reinvented the well-made play, overlaying its skilled carpentry with the poetic genius of a true artist, and changing it almost beyond recognition. Under Ibsen's genius, theater, the art of the obvious, was transformed into the art of the super-subtle. His accomplishment was the equivalent of making B movies into vehicles for advanced thought and novel-like richness of plot and characterization. The result confounded both audiences and critics.

The well-made play was based on the classical three-part structure: an exposition setting forth the principal conflict, followed by the rising action, in which the conflict is intensified until it reaches a climax, and this in turn is followed by the falling action (dénouement), concluding with a resolution of the initial conflict. Practitioners of the well-made play inevitably relied on a secret, its revelation held back until the right moment, to make the action engrossing and full of suspense. The secret was usually associated with a physical object, such as a letter, as in Victorien Sardou's *A Scrap of Paper* (1860), or in something more substantial, as in Scribe's aptly named *A Glass of Water* (1840). In *A Doll's House,* Nora's secret—that she saved her husband's life without his knowing—reposes in a promissory note and Krogstad's letter.

Now consider the plight of the audiences who first saw *A Doll's House.* Where they expected the revelation of the secret, they got a tarantella, danced by Nora when she tries to prevent her husband from opening his mail (which would have revealed the secret). Where they expected a resolution, in the last act, they got the revelation of the secret. Totally confusing was the exposition of the principal conflict. Instead of coming at the beginning, it came at the end, in the discussion between husband and wife, the scene that Bernard Shaw denominated as the beginning of modern drama. It might be argued that the play was such a shocker to audiences because it delivered a jolt to their esthetic sensibilities as well as to their moral sense.

William Archer, Ibsen's English translator, described how the stage manager responded to the last scene when he saw it in a dress rehearsal, with the splendid Janet Achurch as Nora.

"'You'll excuse me, Miss Achurch, it's no business of mine, but I can't help saying that that scene's splendid—most interesting—certain to go.' She rushed across the stage and almost embraced him, and we were all delighted to have conquered the doughty [Mr.] Y. But next day he came to me and said, 'It was rather good, my going into raptures over that last scene. *I* had no idea it was the last act. *I* thought it was the first act, and it was all going to be cleared up.'"[3]

Although Ibsen may have turned the well-made play inside out, it becomes clear, once one lets the play speak for itself, that a sensitive artist is at work. For this artist something besides the story line holds the play together. For him, the beginning, middle, and end of the narrative are part of a larger scheme. Ibsen's great love was painting, and he used his instincts as a visual artist to organize the story and the characters as elements on a large canvas. The ideal spectator at an Ibsen play would look at it as he might study a painting, appreciating the unity of the design, seeing how part relates to part, and coming to the realization that within or behind the design lies the full meaning of the work.

Imagine the story of Nora and Torvald told without the Christmas setting, without the tarantella, or without the presence of Dr. Rank. None of these is essential to the well-made aspects of the play. Eleanora Duse, who was no dancer, eliminated the tarantella but retained the costume, and made an unforgettable impression in the last scene.

Some of the visual effects in *A Doll's House* are obviously suggestive. The Christmas tree is decorated in the first act, but at the rise of the curtain for the second act it is stripped, its candles burned out. Nora wears a brightly colored shawl when she dances and a black shawl when she contemplates suicide. Black becomes dominant in the last act. Dr. Rank leaves his calling card, a black cross above his name. Torvald enters, a black cloak over his evening dress. When Nora contemplates suicide, she wraps this cloak about herself and throws the black shawl over her head. An attentive and imaginative designer or director might have thought of these symbolic touches if Ibsen had not put them in his script.

But what about the tarantella and Dr. Rank? At first glance, they appear to be widely separated elements on the broad canvas. In fact, they are connected by the design that slowly reveals itself, as one steps back to contemplate the canvas in its entirety.

Coming at the end of the second act, the tarantella scene is the structural center of the play, and all that is significant radiates out from it. Nora's dance costume was bought in Italy. She was in Italy with her husband because of his ill health. She had paid for most of the expenses by borrowing money and has had to scrimp and save in order to pay back the debt. This has been her secret, and she dances knowing that Torvald will soon learn of her sacrifice. "Then the tarantella will be over," she says.

The tarantella was supposedly danced to rid the system of the poison from the bite of the tarantula. Nora's marriage has been infected by the poison of Krogstad's threat to reveal her secret, and she dances to delay the moment of truth. The question in her mind is, will Torvald embrace her for what she has done? Up to now, he has loved her primarily as a sexual object, a mother and a mistress. Her wild dance sets his blood on fire, and he cannot wait to have sex with her. So the dance becomes an erotically charged reenactment of their married life, as she sees it. For her, it unites sex and sacrifice. Now that the dance is over, she wants to see the other side of her husband: the man who, once he learns the truth, will make a sacrifice for the sake of the woman who has given him so much pleasure. It does not happen, and the true nature of their marriage stands exposed.

For Ibsen, the dance was a distillation of the conflict that obsessed him: the conflict between Brand and Peer Gynt. The pleasure-loving Torvald is another Peer, and Nora, renouncing domestic happiness, will become a follower of Brand.

The other characters, while functioning as cogs in the machinery of the well-made play, are caught in the web that has Nora at its center. The union of Krogstad and Christine Linde, based on sacrifice, is counterpoised to Nora's marriage. Dr. Rank's syphilis represents sex in its most destructive aspect. When Torvald empties the mailbox immediately before the final scene, he holds in his hand the letter from Krogstad and Dr. Rank's calling card with the black cross. Here, as a shadowy hint of what is to come, the two contradictory motifs of sex and sacrifice are presented together, as they were in Nora's dance.

If one studies the canvas as a whole, Christian elements force themselves on one's attention. They seem to function as a frame of reference that includes everything else. Christ is the ultimate representative of the spirit of sacrifice, and his birth ushered in a new era in Western history. *A Doll's House* is set at Christmastime; Christine (n.b.) and Nora serve as vicarious agents of Christ; and the talk about miracles, which seems out of tune with the realistic characters, strikes the right chord in this larger drama. At the end of act two, Nora says she is waiting for a miracle, and the very last lines of the play have both Nora and Torvald wishing for "the miracle of miracles." For Nora, the miracle would be a true marriage with Torvald, a union of sex and sacrifice. For Ibsen, that miracle would be the advent of the Third Kingdom, and as the curtain falls on his play, he seems to allow Nora and Torvald a dim glimpse of that impossible place.

The most influential commentators on Ibsen's work appeared to have no idea that beneath the story line there existed a whole world of meaning that sustained the life of the play. The subterranean symbols and intimations were like the roots of a great tree that is praised for its beauty and magnificence, while the source of that beauty is barely mentioned. Georg Brandes in Denmark and William Archer in England preferred realistic drama to poetic drama, and they saw only what they wanted to see in plays like *A Doll's House* and *Ghosts*. Apart from an exception like Jennette Lee's *The Ibsen Secret: A Key to the Prose Dramas of Henrik Ibsen* (1907), a free-association analysis of some of the plays, there was no understanding of the rich symbolism in them until after the Second World War, when John Northam in England, Francis Fergusson in America, Else Høst in Norway, and others, all probably influenced by the New Criticism, chose to study the plays more as poems than as social commentary and psychological investigations.

Ibsen himself can be blamed for this delayed appreciation of the poetic values in his realistic plays. He usually fended off any discussion of symbolism by admitting its universality while questioning the ability of critics to deal with it properly. To Archer in 1887 he explained that since life is full of symbolism, "his plays are full of it, though critics insist on discovering all sorts of esoteric meanings in his work of which he is entirely innocent. He was particularly amused by a sapient person in *Aftenposten* who had discovered that Manders in *Ghosts* was a symbol for mankind in general or the average man, and, therefore, called Manders."[4]

In the 1890s, when the French symbolist movement was in full swing, Ibsen told his French translator Moritz Prozor, "We are all living symbols. Everything that happens in life follows certain laws that one makes perceptible by presenting them faithfully. In that sense I am a symbolist. Not otherwise."[5] On another occasion, he complained about the ineptitude and insensitivity of the critics. "They don't always do their job very well. They love to symbolize because they have no respect for reality. But if you really give them a symbol to deal with, they turn it into something trivial and become insulting."[6]

Ibsen's evasiveness in discussing the symbols in his own plays is consistent with his view of their purpose in creative writing, a view that he held all through his life. As a young man, he admired the "unconscious symbolism" in folktales and ballads and decried the heavy-handed use of obvious symbols. "Bad writers, misconstruing the theory that the significant phenomena of life must be intensified, make this symbolism conscious. . . . Instead of it existing hidden in the work, like a vein of silver ore in a mountain, it is continually being dragged into the light of day."[7]

The lyrical Ibsen was always a symbolist whose poems held concealed messages. In "Till de Medskyldige," he hinted at his method: "Deep inside, a poem within the poem is hidden, and if you grasp that, my people, you grasp the song."[8]

Reflecting on the difference between the lyric Ibsen and the realistic dramatist, Brandes said that "at one time or another in the battles of life a lyric Pegasus had been slain under him."[9] Ibsen agreed with Clemens Petersen, who had told him that "verse with symbolism behind it was my natural bent."[10] Anyone familiar with Ibsen's best poems can appreciate the great effort involved in giving up verse and becoming a "photographer," capturing life realistically.

However, his poetic genius did not leave him when he turned to the realistic drama. It expressed itself not lyrically but in images, which can often be more evocative onstage than mere words: they could distill the essence of the work, hidden deep inside, like that vein of silver ore in a mountain. What Shakespeare did with "To be or not to be," Ibsen accomplished with the tarantella—the heart of the play with the life of the play flowing forth from it.

Ibsen was right to be noncommittal and tantalizing about symbols. When he refused to offer any interpretation of his plays and when he discountenanced those critics who tried to bring light into their murky depths, he was being consistent with his purpose as an artist. He accepted the idea that a true symbol concealed meaning while at the same time revealing it. As Carlyle wrote in *Sartor Resartus*, "In a Symbol there is concealment and yet revelation: here, therefore, by Silence and by Speech acting together, comes a doubled significance."[11]

This double function of a symbol suited Ibsen's purposes. By containing so much more than a few words could express, the symbol served to concentrate meaning, and for a dramatist, unlike a novelist, concentration is necessary. This was the practical purpose of a symbol. There was another purpose in Ibsen's case. He wanted to communicate on two levels. The philosophical Ibsen shared with Hazlitt the view that "the highest efforts of genius, in every walk of art, can never be properly understood by the generality of mankind."[12] The dramatic Ibsen knew, however, that the outer parts of a work had to appeal to a larger public. Since his deepest convictions and beliefs would alienate and offend the generality, he constructed his plays on two levels. Always on a war footing with society, he learned how to create these magical plays with double bottoms, in which he could be true to his own philosophy while winning the attention and often the admiration of the public, which understood only half of what he was saying.

He once broke his silence on his own use of symbols when a French journalist, Maurice Bigeon, brought up Zola's name. Commenting on the naturalist novels *Germinal* and *La Terre*, Ibsen referred to them as "two symbols of a depth that makes one dizzy, the like of which I know not. . . . But the symbols of Zola are the result of the general action, they are the conclusion of the drama. My symbols are the beginning, the premises. They are the *raison d'être* of things. They contain reality, while those of Zola are explained by reality."[13]

The distinction that Ibsen draws is made clearer by comparing his method with that of Zola. *Germinal* is a powerful socialist arraignment of capitalism, set in a miners' community. The mine itself becomes a potent, ever-present symbol of the life of the laborers, the underclass. In his notes for the novel, Zola said the collier must be shown suffering, "sunk in a veritable inferno." Everything must follow logically "from the original unhappiness and suffering, the cause of which is universal, and traceable to the unknown social factor, the god Capital." Everything takes place "not by the desires of the masters . . . but arising from a state of affairs beyond their control and determined by the age."[14]

The mine may seem at first glance as equally comprehensive a symbol as the tarantella. The difference is that Zola stops short of explaining the cause of this miserable state of affairs. It is simply "determined by the age." Zola does not give the *raison d'être* of things. The symbol of the mine is "explained by reality." The mine stands for what the workers endure, whereas the symbol of the tarantella contains the reality of Nora's life, both her sexuality and her sacrificial spirit, which together are the driving forces of the drama.

Ghosts offers perhaps the most nearly perfect example of Ibsen's method. With *A Doll's House* in mind, one notices that in *Ghosts* the fire that breaks out at the end of act two corresponds structurally to the tarantella. Now, as far as the plot is concerned, this fire seems a distraction. Critics as varied as Georg Brandes, a naturalist, and Francis Fergusson, a symbolist, found fault with it. Brandes in 1882 called it "the unsatisfactory episode of the fire at the asylum." Fergusson could not reconcile the fire with the symbolic significance of the orphanage, which represented the Alving heritage, and said Ibsen put it in only because he needed a strong theatrical effect at this point.[15]

If Fergusson had pursued the matter further, he would have been led to a strange conclusion. If the orphanage represents the Alving heritage, the ghosts of the past, its destruction would seem to run counter to what the play is supposed to be about. Helen Alving should be happy to see the flames destroy the orphanage, and we should have the sense of a cleansing, a small-scale Ragnarök. But it strikes neither her nor us that way. The fire is an ominous portent of worse things to come.

To understand what that fire means, it has to be put in its proper context. At this point in the play, Mrs. Alving has just learned from her son that life can have meaning only if there is joy in it, sheer physical joy. Startled, she exclaims, "The joy of life? Can there be salvation in that?" To her, whose life has been one of duty and sacrifice, Oswald's hedonism comes as a revelation. But she senses that he may be right. After all, what have been the consequences of her dedication to higher principles? She realizes that she brought no joyousness to her own marriage, that her puritanism drove her virile young husband to the taverns and brothels. She had been a female Brand chastising by word and deed her Peer Gynt of a husband. Her part in the broad scheme of things becomes clear to her.

"Now I see how it all fits together. . . . Now for the first time I see it. And now I can speak out."[16]

A few moments later, as if in response to her, the fire breaks out, linking what has come before to what is about to happen.

In the last act Oswald says that he too is burning. His brain is on fire; he is about to enter the last stage of syphilis, general paralysis. Although his collapse is precipitated by the nervous excitement and physical strain caused by the fire, the anterior and original cause is his father's way of life. As he says, "Everything will burn. Everything that recalls Father's memory is doomed. Here I am, I'm burning down, too." The desire for a life of joy, of sensual pleasure, the kind of life that destroyed Captain Alving, has now led to his son's mental collapse.

The fire represents the destructive aspect of *joie de vivre.* Its positive side was pictured by Oswald when he described his artist's life in Paris as a life in the sun. He says he cannot live without the sun. Regina, the maid in the house and his half sister, is a sensual young woman, full of the joy of life and eager to be his sexual partner. But not his solace in a time of need. When he succumbs to the last stage of his illness, she abandons him. She goes off with Engstrand. She will become the chief attraction in a sailor's refuge that will be nothing more than a brothel, a brothel set up by Engstrand in connivance with Pastor Manders as a result of the fire in the orphanage. The joy of life degenerates into prostitution; the Alving orphanage, intended to house the offspring of syphilitic mothers, turns into a whorehouse, managed by Engstrand, who, with his deformed *left* leg, is the devil's vicar. What Oswald feared—"I'm afraid that what I want in life would degenerate into something ugly here"—actually happens.[17]

Her son's eloquent defense of a *carpe diem* philosophy triggers Mrs. Alving's outburst, "Can there be salvation in that?" However, for some time her thoughts have been moving in that direction. She has been reading up on the advanced thought of the period—those books that horrify Manders—and they have replaced Holy Scripture as a guide to living. But the answer to her question comes not from Oswald but from the subtext. The fire breaks out, providing a sharp visual response to her question.

Here at the technical climax of the play, the fire becomes the nexus connecting Oswald's story with Mrs. Alving's. When she recognizes the possible error of her beliefs, when she sees suddenly and clearly how all things fit together and realizes that the sensual life might offer a viable alternative, the fire breaks out in the orphanage, the Alving fire that she, because of her puritanical upbringing, had suppressed. And when this fire—the symbol of the sensual life that Oswald, the son of his father in more ways than one, espoused—erupts, it overexcites his diseased brain and brings about his final collapse. The fire in his brain is fused with the fire in the orphanage, that is, his syphilis is equated with the Alving heritage; and the motivation for the fire is consistent on both the naturalistic and the symbolic levels.

As an answer to Mrs. Alving's question, the fire simultaneously condemns her for having denied *joie de vivre* and Oswald for having lived it. As an example of what in playwriting used to be called tying the knot, there are few that can match this fire in the orphanage, which even the best-intentioned critics dismissed as merely a melodramatic *coup de théâtre*. At the end Oswald is seen calling for the sun. The disease has now entered its last stage. He wants to die. He calls for the fatal dose of morphine tablets. But he now suffers from paraphasia, a common symptom of general paralysis. He says one thing and means another. He is asking for the pills, but in his deranged mind those white pills become the white sun, the symbol of all that he has wanted from life. What he wants now is death. Using medical fact, Ibsen achieves a chilling poetic effect when Oswald, with his back to the rising sun, calls for the tablets and repeats in a toneless voice, "The sun. . . . The sun. . . ."

Brandes and the French critic Emile Faguet sparred over the nature of Ibsen's symbolism, with Brandes taking the extreme position that Ibsen did not use symbols at all. What about the sun rising at the end of *Ghosts*, asked Faguet. That is not a symbol, said Brandes. In Oswald's diseased mind, the sun is the deadly medicine he wants his mother to give him. "Oswald asks for the poison and for nothing but the poison; but, as he becomes crazy, he employs one word for another, and he says *sun* for *poison*, and there is nothing more to it, and one must have the subtlety of insanity to see anything else in it."

Faguet responded to Brandes's jeers. "If Oswald had said to his mother, 'Give me the poison. Give me the tongs. The tongs! The tongs!' we could indeed see in his words only the incoherency of a poor lunatic. But the author takes the trouble to make the sun rise. He takes the trouble to put into his text the words, 'The sun is rising. On the horizon the mountains and the plain are resplendent with the morning rays.' Therefore, unless he himself has something of the mental aberration of Oswald, we may believe that he attributes a certain importance to the sudden intervention of so considerable a character as the sun, and that, consequently, when he makes Oswald exclaim, 'The Sun! Give me the Sun!' it is not at all as though he made him say, 'Give me the ladle,' or 'Give me the sugar-grater.' Evidently there is something more present. It is not any chance word that Oswald utters as a result of his delirium, after having asked for poison. It is a word corresponding to the appearance of the sun on the horizon."

Faguet provided a limited explanation of the sun symbolism. It must symbolize, he said, "the end of suffering, deliverance, emancipation for a being who is at the bottom of that dark and hideous gulf called neurasthenia."[18] This mention of neurasthenia keeps the symbol still within the range of naturalism. But Ibsen intends much more than that—the sun stands for a whole way of life, the way that Oswald had chosen, the way of his carousing father. In so doing it affords a fine example of what Ibsen was talking about in setting himself apart from Zola. Faguet is talking about Zola's kind of symbolism, which, in Ibsen's words, is the result of the general action, whereas his symbols form the premises of the action. They constitute reality; Zola's symbols explain reality.

To some commentators the rising sun creates a final moment that is either too theatrical or too ironic to be meaningful. The attentive reader or spectator, however, would have noticed that the sun is only another form of the fire symbol. Imagine a perfect production of *Ghosts* and consider what we would see at the end of it: the mists dispersing and the sun rising, lighting up the back part of the stage. Keep in mind the end of the second act: the mist in the background giving way suddenly to the glow of the fire in the orphanage. Now, where does this fire begin? Where does the fire symbol first appear? With Oswald's entrance in act one, when he comes onstage smoking a large meerschaum pipe, his father's pipe, the pipe that made him ill. From that moment the fire burns its way through the play, bursting forth finally in a blaze of sunshine. There we see the end of Oswald's pursuit of pleasure. The fire symbolism mimics the course of Oswald's disease from beginning to end.

But what about Mrs. Alving? As soon as she hears Oswald talk about the joy of life, she comprehends the powerful truth in it. For years she had thought that the great error of her life was returning to her husband (and critics have mistakenly assumed that *Ghosts* is a thesis play arguing that "conventional marriage is . . . an evil tyranny").[19] Now, at the turning point of the play, she realizes that she may have committed an even greater error when she treated her ardent husband as if he were some disgusting animal. She drove him back to the tavern. Now, some twenty-eight years later, she admits her error to Oswald in order that he shall know the full truth. In fairness to him she must disabuse him of the idea that his bohemian life in Paris was the source of his illness.

In the last act she is a woman torn between two mutually exclusive philosophies: her old one of sacrifice and the new one of *joie de vivre.* She is now not engaged in a struggle with social conventions nor with church dogma nor with established beliefs. She had fought and, at least in her own mind, won that battle before the play begins. It is true that the ghosts she speaks of to Manders, the ghosts of old beliefs, old theories, and things like that, still remain oppressive forces, hostile to both philosophies and obscuring the main issue. However, when Manders and Engstrand leave, when the mists clear and the rains cease, we see that the contention all along has been between duty and inclination, between virtue and pleasure, between Brand's way and Gynt's. Here, at the very end of the play, the choice between the two is forced upon her in the cruelest way. If she commits herself to Oswald's philosophy, she will give him the pills and destroy all that makes life dear to her. If she remains faithful to her old ideal of sacrifice and duty, she will devote herself to caring for him even though he is nothing more than a living corpse. In the first alternative the joy of life proves to be the death of life. In the second alternative the life of sacrifice also proves to be the death of life.

Downstage, Mrs. Alving stands undecided, fumbling for the pills. Behind her the sun rises, but it is not the sun of enlightenment, as some critics have thought. It is the pagan sun of pleasure, of *joie de vivre*. And it rises on the white mountain peaks, the peaks of sacrifice that Brand climbed. The final image is of the clash of irreconcilable opposites, the visual counterpart of the conflict in Mrs. Alving's mind.

Mrs. Alving's dilemma was also Ibsen's. In *Ghosts* he faced the fact that the conflict between Brand and Peer Gynt that shaped all his important work could find no resolution under the conditions of naturalism. He could honestly protest, in response to critics who were accusing him of tolerating euthanasia and incest, that nothing was said by the characters in the play that expressed his own thoughts.[20] But he could hardly deny that on the deep symbolic level he was revealing the essential Ibsen.

In *Ghosts* he achieved a nearly perfect fusion of symbol and plot. The impact that the drama made on readers and playgoers was caused as much by its form as by its subject matter. From the first moment to the last, the intensity builds unrelentingly. Unquestionably, *Ghosts* offered an emotional experience unique not only in the drama but in nineteenth-century literature as a whole. Edmund Gosse called it "one of the most thrilling and amazing works in modern literature."[21] James Huneker designated it "the strongest play of the nineteenth century, and also the most harrowing. Its intensity borders on the hallucinatory."[22] Arthur Symons wrote, "I know nothing in any play so complete in its mastery over the springs of horror and sympathetic suffering as the last scene, the expected and dreaded climax—the final flowering of the latent germ of madness in the innocent Oswald."[23] The novelist George Moore said that in the half hour of the last act, "I lived through a year's emotion. . . . [M]ost assuredly nothing finer was ever written by man or god. Its blank simplicity strikes upon the brain, until the brain reels, even as poor Osvalt's [*sic*] brain is reeling."[24]

Ibsen never attempted anything quite like it again. His next play, *An Enemy of the People*, was comparatively lighthearted in tone, open in form, and untroubled by his obsessions. Two years later, with *The Wild Duck*, he once again set about resolving the conflict in Mrs. Alving's mind, in a work totally different from *Ghosts*, half comedy and half tragedy, and employing yet another new dramatic technique.

THE WILD DUCK

In *A Doll's House* and *Ghosts* Ibsen reenacted the struggle within himself between Brand and Peer Gynt. He sent Nora out into the night to become a disciple of Brand, leaving her husband, Torvald, to hope for the most wonderful thing of all, a union of husband and wife on some higher plane. Ibsen's thoughts were always directed at that point where opposites meet. But what was left open as a possibility in *A Doll's House* ended in a clash of irreconcilable opposites in *Ghosts*, his darkest and most pessimistic work. "The whole of mankind is on the wrong track," reads one of his notes for the play.[1]

This bitter truth was borne home to him by the unexpected harshness of the criticism heaped on his tragedy. The animadversions of the conservative party meant little to him, but when the progressive forces joined the chorus in abusing him, he realized that there was no solid front pushing forward into a new era. The fact was that the radicals who had been united in 1879 were breaking up and losing ground, and, as in the case of all movements fed in large part by artistic egos, the radicals began to fight among themselves, as they became aware of how little they actually had in common. Brandes was deserted by many of his followers when he vigorously espoused greater sexual freedom. The poet Holger Drachmann, who had been a supporter of the literary left, now aligned himself with the Danish nationalists and the anti-French school, spurning Brandes and all that he stood for. In 1883 Carl Ploug, the editor of the far-right newspaper *Fædrelandet*, gloated in a poem, "To My Contemporaries," over the setback of the literary left. "You submitted problems to debate," he said, "but where are the results? You certainly stirred up a fuss in confused and unstable minds. But where is the victorious army, and where the conquered forts?"[2]

Edvard Brandes told Strindberg, whose satiric stories about married life had gotten him into hot water, "You seem to think that we [in Denmark] form a party.

Lord help us! No, we are only three or four who barely manage to stay afloat. There was once a literary left that was anti-romantic and anti-religious, but that is past. We are only the remnants."[3]

As Ibsen became aware of the animosity he had aroused with *Ghosts*, his first response was to reaffirm in *An Enemy of the People* his position as upholder of the truth and to declare that his strength lay in his independence from those who temporized with their avowed principles: Brand's message repeated after eighteen years. If he was to be shunned by the public, very well, he would proudly claim the title of public enemy. Since the masses were always wrong with regard to the future, it was necessary for the prophet to league himself with the small minority. Eventually the crowd in the street would march down the path blazed by the pioneers and accept the ideas they had once rejected as radical and intolerable. That a truth lasts only about seventeen or eighteen years, at most twenty, was Dr. Stockmann's discovery as he faced the compact majority.

For Ibsen, this relativism had a double edge. After he had vented his spleen in *Enemy of the People*, he reexamined his own progress. The absolute truths of *Brand* were now eighteen years old, and, though they were of a different order than the truths Stockmann had in mind, might they not be subject to the same law of change? In *Ghosts* he had depicted the ambivalence of his own position, somewhere between the life-denying inflexibility of Brand and the *joie de vivre* of Oswald. Half a year after the publication of *Enemy of the People* he wrote to Brandes of his own unceasing progress. "At the point where I stood when I wrote each of my books there now stands a tolerably compact crowd; but I myself am no longer there. I am elsewhere; farther ahead, I hope."[4]

This was written as the plot of his new play was taking shape in his mind. After completing the first draft, he reassured his publisher that the play did not deal with political or social questions. "The action takes place in the area of family life. It will certainly provoke discussion, but it cannot possibly give offense to anyone."[5]

He was half right. *The Wild Duck* did provoke discussion, but it also offended finer sensibilities, and in the Victorian era there were many of those.

Just as *Ghosts* had developed out of *A Doll's House*, so *The Wild Duck* continued Ibsen's progress after *Enemy of the People*. Nora Helmer had been happy in her doll home, but viewed from Brand's lofty position, it was a false happiness. The pleasures of eating macaroons, playing games with the children, and making love to her husband stifled the development of the essential Nora, the woman who made sacrifices to save her husband's life. Helen Alving carried on where Nora left off. Being older than Nora, she sought to fulfill herself through her son. Instead she learned that there was perhaps more value in the sensual happiness he experienced than in the spiritual ideal she pursued. For Oswald, as for Julian, the driving force in history was the collision between repression and liberation. For Helen Alving, as for Brand, the driving force was the collision between sacrifice and self-indulgence.

In *The Wild Duck*, Brand in the guise of Gregers Werle invades the happy home of the Ekdal family and very nearly destroys it. He knows that the Ekdal marriage is based on a lie, and he believes fervently that the truth shall provide a firm foundation for a lasting union. As obsessed as Brand, Gregers misjudges Hjalmar Ekdal, having once admired him and looked up to him. But Hjalmar is just an ordinary man, and to him a happy lie is better than the dreadful, bitter truth.

From the hostile reception of *Ghosts* Ibsen had learned that the average man is too weak a vessel to withstand the shock of unpleasant facts, which usually entails the loss of some ideal or other. There was at this time much controversy about Darwin's theories and the impact they had on the old ideals. Here again Bjørnson was in the forefront, announcing his apostasy. Disillusioned with Grundtvigianism, he came to see that Christianity, with its fear of God and the devil and its subservience to the Bible, made man weak, not strong.[6] In 1883 he published *Beyond Human Power* (*Over ævne*), a drama that had been fermenting in his mind since 1878, when he lost his Christian faith and accepted Darwin's theory of evolution. The point he made in his play was that religious doctrines, especially the belief in miracles, seduce human beings into going beyond their capabilities. Brandes praised it, saying, "Bjørnson has never written a better play—nor has Ibsen," while Christopher Bruun, a priest and one of Ibsen's models for Brand, scorned it. Bjørnson informed him that there are no miracles and that those who try to achieve the heavenly ideal on earth, like Kierkegaard and Brand, are doomed to fail. What pass for miracles nowadays are nothing but hypnotic experiences.

This exchange between Bjørnson and Bruun was aired in the newspapers from February through May 1884, when Ibsen, after some months away from his desk—an absence he blamed on his agitation over political developments in Norway—began the first draft of *The Wild Duck*. After finishing it, he told a friend that he had long ago given up "making universal demands of everybody . . . because I no longer believe that they can be applied with any inherent right. I mean that the best and only thing that any one of us can do is realize oneself in spirit and in truth. In my view, this constitutes true broad-mindedness, and that is why I am so deeply opposed in many ways to the so-called liberals."[7]

Gregers Werle, the idealist in *The Wild Duck*, is a grotesque caricature of Brand. Like Brand, he is driven by a sense of guilt to reform the world, but there is a difference. Whereas Brand's feelings of guilt derive from the fall of man, Gregers's are very personal. He hates his father, whose philandering drove his mother to drink, and he hates himself for not having exposed his father's business chicanery. His silence allowed his father to become rich and put Hjalmar's father in prison. Although he knows that revealing the truth will rid him of his feelings of guilt, he makes the idealist's mistake of believing that what works for him will work for others. Hjalmar and Gina Ekdal are a perfectly contented couple, for whom the truth can only bring unhappiness. Gregers, on the other hand, believes in the necessity of truth. He believes that Gregory the Great, from whom he takes his name, was right: "But if the truth causes scandal, then it is better a scandal arise than that the truth be abandoned."

Ibsen goes out of his way to demean Gregers, making this idealist a rather pathetic figure. He gives him an ugly-sounding name, makes him unprepossessing in appearance, inept and clumsy physically, and sexually suspect. That there is some aberration in Gregers's psyche is suggested not only by his Oedipus complex but also by the fire symbolism in the play. When he tried to light a fire in his room, he kept the damper shut, filling the room with smoke, and then tried to put out the flame by pouring a pitcher of water into the stove. It is absurd that a man who has lived by himself for years in a small mining settlement would not know how to light a stove.[8] Given the conventions of the realistic drama and the inhibitions of nineteenth-century society, Ibsen had to resort to symbolism in order to give us a glimpse of Gregers's inner nature.

Not only does Ibsen depict Gregers as sexually inexperienced, he also implies that Gregers has homosexual inclinations.[9] He idolizes the good-looking Hjalmar and has done so ever since their schooldays. Even face to face with the shiftless Hjalmar, Gregers still sees him as "a strong character" and a "shining light."

One of the most extraordinary features of Ibsen's works is the way in which, after his apprenticeship, each play grows out of its predecessor. Together they form chapters in a magnificent narrative that cannot be properly understood unless they are read in the order in which they were written. In *The Wild Duck* what the absorbed and attentive Ibsenite has been waiting for happens: Brand and Peer Gynt finally confront each other. Ibsen brings them down from their poetic heights and places them in the prosaic world of ordinary people. When Gregers complains that where he had expected to see the light of transfiguration shining from both husband and wife, he sees instead nothing but gloom and depression, Gina's reply is to take the shade off the lamp: "Will that help?" And when Hjalmar confronts her with the newly acquired information that she had been old Werle's mistress and wonders why she hasn't been writhing with penitence and remorse all the years of their marriage, she explains that she has all she can do just to take care of the house and get through a day's work.

Peer Gynt fares less badly than Brand in the descent from the heights. Hjalmar, Ibsen's most richly detailed comic character, is a man whose company one can enjoy. His faults and foibles are part of his charm. He may be self-centered and self-deluded, but he is never false or hypocritical. He is accustomed since childhood to being admired, coddled, and cared for. He dresses like an artist, plays the flute, collects notes for his memoirs, and indulges himself in every way possible. When he decides to leave the house after learning about Gina's relationship with old Werle, all that Gina has to do to make him change his mind is to place before him a tray with coffee and rolls.

> HJALMAR. Some arrangement must be made. I don't exactly intend to throw away my life, either.
> (*Looks for something on the tray.*)
> GINA. What are you looking for?
> HJALMAR. Butter.
> GINA. Coming right up.
> (*She goes into the kitchen.*)
> HJALMAR (*calling after her*). Oh, it doesn't matter. A dry crust is good enough for me.
> GINA (*bringing a dish of butter*). Look here. Freshly churned.
> (*She pours him another cup of coffee. He seats himself on the sofa, spreads more butter on the already buttered bread, and eats and drinks awhile in silence.*)
> HJALMAR. Do you think I could—without being subject to intrusion—intrusion of any sort—do you think I could stay in the sitting room there for a day or two?[10]

Read as self-analysis, *The Wild Duck* shows Ibsen attributing his idealistic, uncompromising self to his break with his family. Brand was born when the teenage Ibsen left home, although the seeds were planted earlier, when the boy fell under the spell of his pietistic mother. Gregers, like Brand, has a tender conscience, which, as Håkon Werle reminds him, was a legacy from his mother. Hjalmar, on the other hand, was reared by two maiden aunts who adored and spoiled him. For Ibsen, Hjalmar is an imaginary alter ego, the dreamer and teller of tales, like Peer Gynt. As autobiography, the Ekdal story is fiction; the Gregers story is true.

Hjalmar's role in life is to be the center of attention. A monument of egotism, he lets Gina work her fingers to the bone for him; refuses to acknowledge his broken and alcoholic father in public; even allows his daughter, Hedwig, to strain her weak eyes retouching photographs rather than give up the pleasure he gets from puttering around in the garret. He basks in the love of those around him. He is king in his home, and his home is a very happy one. Old Ekdal is grateful to him for free room and board. For Gina, a former housemaid, marriage to Hjal-

Figure 18. Emil Poulsen as Hjalmar Ekdahl. Royal Theater, Copenhagen.

mar was a step upward in the social scale. For Hedwig, only fourteen, Hjalmar is the dearest person in the world. And for just that reason no one can be so unkind to her as Hjalmar.

When he returns from the Werle dinner party, having forgotten to bring something back to her as he had promised, he offers instead the dinner menu and tells her to read it while he describes how each dish tasted. This Barmecidal feast only makes her cry.

"It's monstrous," exclaims Hjalmar, pacing up and down, "what absurd things a father is expected to think of! If he forgets the smallest trifle, he's greeted with sour faces. Well, well, one has to get used to everything."

Gina and Hedwig know that he is upset with himself, and all it takes to offer a reconciliation is Hedwig's suggestion that she bring in a bottle of beer for him. As she runs toward the kitchen, Hjalmar stops her and hugs her.

"Hedwig, Hedwig!"

Her tears of disappointment turn to tears of joy. "You're the dearest, kindest father in all—"

"No, don't call me that. Here I've been feasting at the rich man's table—battening at the groaning board—! And I couldn't even—!"

Gina says, "Oh, nonsense, nonsense, Hjalmar!"

"It's not nonsense. But you mustn't be too hard on me. You know I love you for all that."

Hedwig throws her arms around him. "And we love you, oh, so dearly, Father!"

"And if I am unreasonable once in a while—why then—just remember that I am a man beset by a host of cares. There, there."

Drying his eyes, he declares, "No beer at such a moment as this. Give me my flute.... With my flute in my hand and you two at my side—ah—!"

Ibsen insisted that the part be played without "any touch of parody, nor with the faintest suggestion that the actor is aware there is anything funny about his remarks. He has a warm and sympathetic voice, as Relling says, and that should be maintained above all else. His sentimentality is genuine, his melancholy charming in its way—not a bit of affectation."[11] As a model for the actor, he suggested Kristofer Janson, the Unitarian minister who inspired Bjørnson in creating the pastor in *Beyond Human Power.* (An advocate of Norwegian Landsmål, Janson was one of those whom Ibsen had caricatured as Huhu in *Peer Gynt.*)

Capable of touching the heartstrings, Hjalmar's warm and sonorous voice invests even his most pathetic scenes with a theatrical aura. Over Hedwig's dead body he can sob, "I hunted her from me like an animal! And she crept terrified into the attic and died for love of me! I can never make it up to her! Never tell her—! Oh, God in heaven—if thou art in heaven—if thou art at all!—wherefore has thou done this to me?"

Even in this, the most tragic moment in the play, his thoughts are about his own sufferings. His life is essentially a performance. As long as he is with people who flatter him with attention, he can survive all the disasters that life has to offer. His self-love gives him a resilience that the self-loathing Gregers lacks, and when Gregers's ideals are smashed, his world is shattered. He seeks only to die.

The Wild Duck is a new kind of tragicomedy. The older kind centered on a plot that brought the good hero close to tragedy, with his death being averted at the last moment. Ibsen created a form of drama in which the tragic and the comic are interfused, tears and laughter intermingled. Listening to Hjalmar at his most self-indulgent, one doesn't know whether to laugh or cry. Most audiences, accustomed to conventional drama, would not know how to respond to Ibsen's humor, and the first performances of the play were poorly received. Typical of the quandary that many playgoers found themselves in was the bewilderment of a London critic in 1898. "No one was able to decide if *The Wild Duck* is the very funniest play ever written, or a desperately serious problem. Has Ibsen any sense of humour at all, or is he the funniest fellow who ever put pen to paper? . . . For our own part, since Mr. W. S. Gilbert wrote *Engaged* and *Tom Cobb*, no play was ever written so exquisitely ludicrous as *The Wild Duck*. We shrewdly suspect that Mr. Laurence Irving shares our opinion, for he played Hjalmar Ekdal, the sublime egoist, so magnificently that the house pealed with laughter."[12]

Most non-Nordic readers and playgoers did not (and still do not) realize how funny a play it is, while Scandinavian actors sometimes couldn't resist playing for laughs. Some of the humor doesn't translate well, especially Gina's malapropisms (e.g., "divide oneself" for "divert oneself"). *Mandfolk . . . skal altid ha' noget at dividere sig med* might be rendered, aiming more for the spirit than the sense, as "Men always have to have something to abuse themselves with." Ibsen found the Danish production too farcical and insisted that "it must be played as tragicomedy, otherwise Hedwig's death will be incomprehensible."[13]

Ibsen's primary purpose in writing *The Wild Duck* was to bring Brand and Peer Gynt into a confrontation with each other. The bifurcation in his personality had to be reexamined in the light of changing times and a changed man. When Gregers enters Hjalmar's home, the two of them had not seen each other for eighteen years, and 1884, the year of the play, is approximately eighteen years after Ibsen published *Brand* and *Peer Gynt* (1865 and 1867). What changes the new era had brought about in Ibsen's thinking is immediately apparent in his treatment of Gregers, about whom little good can be said. He is unattractive physically and awkward socially, and he possesses a sick conscience. Hjalmar, on the other hand, is a Peer Gynt stripped of that rascal's ruthless business enterprises and Kierkegaardian angst, leaving only the romantic, childlike, innocent dreamer. Eighteen years earlier, Ibsen had seen Peer as representing the dregs of his own nature, and Brand as representing the best in him. Now in 1884 his position seems to be almost the reverse of that, an extraordinary shift brought about by the Modern Breakthrough and the introduction of radically new ideas, religious and scientific, into the cultural life of Scandinavia.

Dr. Relling appears at first glance as Ibsen's spokesman, the *raisonneur* in the play. His prescription for a reasonably pain-free existence is the life-lie, a dream or illusion that gives one a sense of purpose. He offers amelioration, not a cure. Hjalmar's life-lie is his belief that he will restore the family honor by making a remarkable invention, although he knows, as he says, that everything has already been invented. Relling sustains him in this belief, nourishing Hjalmar's vain hopes.

Dr. Relling is a proto-Freud. His remedy for the ordinary man's discontents is precisely what the Viennese doctor prescribed in his *Civilization and Its Discontents*. "Life as we find it is too hard for us; it entails too much pain, too many disappointments. We cannot do without palliative remedies. . . . There are perhaps three of these means: powerful diversions of interest, which lead us to care little about our misery; substitutive gratifications, which lessen it; and intoxicating substances, which make us insensitive to it. Something of this kind is indispensable."[14] His three means correspond to Gregers's mission, Hjalmar's appetite, and the alcoholism of Molvik, the would-be theologian.

Directly opposed to Relling is Gregers, who sincerely believes that Hjalmar will be transformed by knowledge of the truth about his marriage, making him the man Gregers idolized when they were both young. Gregers tells Relling, "I shall not give up until I have rescued Hjalmar from your clutches." The drama lies in these two encountering each other, the idealist and the pragmatist, the destroyer of lies and the keeper of illusions. To Dr. Relling, Gregers is a high-strung, disturbed personality, driven by a mania for righteousness. Given the unpleasant nature of Gregers, Ibsen seems to have made the conflict a one-sided affair, the Gyntish man with all his faults seen as preferable to the heaven-storming Brand. But it turns out that Gregers does not stand alone. High ideals might at this point have lost their appeal to Ibsen, but their fascination had not. He could no more leave Gregers isolated and ineffective than he could eliminate half of his psychic being.

To his father, Gregers is neurotic (*overspændt*). To Dr. Relling, Gregers is "mad, crazy, cracked." The doctor may be more than half right. The Gregers that Ibsen depicts is certainly neurotic—fashionably so, since *la névrose* was "*la maladie du XIXe siècle.*"[15] Gregers's particular type of neurosis is well described by the eminent alienist Henry Maudsley in his influential work *The Physiology and Pathology of Mind,* in which he discusses a mild form of insanity "characterized by singularities or eccentricities of thought, feeling, and action. It cannot truly be said of any one so constituted that he is mad, but he is certainly strange, or 'queer,' or, as it is said, 'not quite right.'"

Maudsley also makes the point that these neurotics are often ugly, and Ibsen goes out of his way to make Gregers physically unattractive.[16]

To some of his acquaintances, Ibsen himself seemed neurotic; there was much more of Gregers than Hjalmar in him. Bjørnson said there is "something hysterical in his writings."[17] The art historian Julius Lange, who conversed with Ibsen in 1868, found that works like *Brand* and *Peer Gynt* betrayed a "psychic overexertion" (*sjælelige Overanspændelse*).[18]

In some cases, this "peculiarity of temperament," says Maudsley, borders

> very closely upon genius. . . . The novel mode of thinking at things may be an actual advance upon the accepted system of thought; the individual may be in a minority of one, not because he sees less than, or not so well as, all the world,

> but because he happens to see deeper.... He may differ from all the world, not because he is wrong, and all the world is right, but because he is right, and all the world is wrong. Of necessity every new truth is at first in a minority of one; it is a rebellion against the existing system of belief; accordingly the existing system, ever thinking itself a finality, strives with all the weight of its established organization to crush it out.... The genius is always recognized to be in the van of his age; in that wherein he is in advance, he necessarily differs from his age, and is often enough therefore pronounced mistaken, unpractical, or mad.[19]

If Ibsen read Maudsley (Strindberg read him in the French edition of 1883 and called him "perhaps the most intelligent of all the madhouse doctors"[20]), he would surely have been struck by his close resemblance to these neurotic geniuses. There was no novelty in thinking of genius and madness as being near allied; Maudsley's contribution was to define this particular type of eccentricity as a neurosis, *neurosis spasmodica,* and to set it in the evolutionary development of the human species. He also carefully distinguished this kind of insane temperament from true genius. Lacking "by reason of his great sensibility, the power of calm, steady, and complete mental assimilation, [he] must fall short of the highest intellectual development."[21] And yet it is often upon people of this sort that progress depends.

It was only after the major characters had established themselves in Ibsen's scenario that he introduced young Hedwig, who would find inspiration and even a tantalizing exaltation in Gregers's belief in higher ideals. And it was only after Hedwig's appearance in his notes that Ibsen brought in the wild duck, recognizing the need for some symbol or focus of interest that would unite the many elements in an increasingly complicated story. "Similarity to a wild duck when it is wounded—goes to the bottom, these intractable devils—bite themselves fast.... Hedwig as wild duck."[22] The behavior of the wild duck was already part of Norwegian legend in 1836 when J. S. Welhaven published his poem "The Sea Bird" ("Søfuglen"), in which a wild duck is shot for the mere sport of it and dives into the dark waters of the fjord, preferring death to capture. As with Ibsen, Welhaven had in mind a human parallel: he was inspired by the sight in a Paris morgue of a young girl who had drowned herself.[23] What attracted Ibsen to the legend was its anti-Darwinistic aspect. It went against the idea of a struggle for existence and posited an ideal higher than life itself.

Hedwig becomes the center of events past and present. Her story is inextricably involved with the story of the wild duck, which is kept as a pet in the storage room of the Ekdal apartment. Old Werle shot the duck, but because of his poor and failing eyesight, he succeeded only in wounding it. The duck dove into the depths, clutching onto the weeds. But Werle's retriever brought the duck back into the light. It ended up in the Ekdal home and became Hedwig's dearest possession. It is halt, it has a broken wing, but it is fat and contented.

This straightforward story of the duck turns into something else when Gregers hears it. He reads deep significance into it. He sees Hjalmar as the duck, complacent and happy in his innocence, and the Ekdal home as the equivalent of the murky depths, a place where the light of the truth cannot penetrate, and he pictures himself as the clever dog who will bring the duck back to its natural state, that is, bring his hero, Hjalmar, to see the truth.

For the audience the story of the duck acquires a wider meaning as the plot unfolds. It becomes a kind of guide to the way the past has determined the present. Werle's failing eyesight caused the duck to be wounded; the duck becomes Hedwig's possession; now Hedwig's eyesight is failing. When Werle confers a deed of gift on Hedwig, Hjalmar realizes, beyond a doubt, that Hedwig is Werle's illegitimate daughter. Egged on by Gregers, Hjalmar wants some proof that Hedwig will still love him. Gregers has instilled in the receptive mind of the young girl the importance of sacrifice, and suggests she give up the duck as a sign of her devotion to Hjalmar. What promises to be a sentimental ending, with the wild duck offered to Hjalmar, turns cruel and tragic when Hedwig, holding the duck, pistol in hand, overhears Hjalmar wonder aloud to Gregers whether she would be willing to give up life for his sake. Overwrought and oversensitive, she goes Gregers one better, and turns the pistol against herself.

For Ibsen, her death brings Hjalmar (Gynt) and Gregers (Brand) together on the transcendental plane. Hjalmar wanted Hedwig to prove she loved him; Gregers wanted Hedwig to understand the need for sacrifice. In her action, opposites are joined together as in the last moments of *Brand*. But what was deliberate and miraculous and sublime on the black peak seems here impulsive and absurd.

What, exactly, was Gregers's motivation in asking Hedwig to sacrifice her beloved duck? After he hears the shot, he says, using his customary overblown, rather biblical language, "I knew it, I knew it, through the child, restitution [*oprettelsen*]."[24] Gregers has to force himself to believe that Hedwig's death will bring out the noblest aspect of Hjalmar, while Relling knows that it will soon be the occasion for one of Hjalmar's sentimental, self-pitying speeches. What distresses Gregers is not the suicide ("Hedwig has not died in vain," he says) but the possibility that Relling may be right. Hedwig's death will not change anything.

GREGERS. If you are right and I am wrong, life isn't worth living.
RELLING. Oh, life wouldn't be so bad if only we could be left in peace by these blasted idealists, demanding perfection of us poor souls.
GREGERS (*staring into space*). In that case, I'm glad my destiny is what it is.
RELLING. And what, may I ask, is your destiny?

GREGERS (*turning to go*). To be thirteenth at table.
RELLING. Oh, like hell it is.

Gregers's speeches in the play often echo biblical language: "great sacrificial offering of forgiveness" (*den store tilgivelsens offerstemning*);[25] "it is not finished" (*det ikke er fuldbragt*),[26] alluding to Jesus's last words on the cross (John 19:30); "have to bear the cross of being named Gregers" (*har det kors på sig, at hede Gregers*).[27] Since he firmly believes that without self-sacrifice nothing significant can be accomplished, he tends to identify himself with Jesus. All of that changes in an instant at the end, when he sees Hedwig's dead body. As he suddenly realizes the enormity of what he has done, his whole body twitches convulsively. When he says his destiny is to be thirteenth at table, he is alluding to an old folk saying that that unlucky person will die within a year.[28] In the life of Jesus, Judas was the thirteenth at the table. In that last scene of the play, Gregers not only feels that his life will be short but also knows that he has been Judas to Hedvig's Christ figure.

Maudsley has considerable sympathy for these neurotic, original thinkers who, dissatisfied with the existing state of things, drag the world forward at the cost of their individual comfort.

> Consider what an amount of innate power a man must have in order to do that, without himself sinking under the huge weight of the opposition! Many earnest and intense reformers, whose vital energies have been absorbed in the promulgation of one truth, which was perhaps an important one, have notoriously broken down in the face of the crushing force of the organized opposition. They have been so abandoned to their idea, so carried away by it, so blind to the force of the circumstances with which they have had to contend, so one-sided and fanatical, as to be almost as inconsiderate of the manifold relations of their surroundings as actual madmen are; and accordingly they have often been called, and sometimes perhaps were, mad.[29]

"By his acts, as well as by his speech, does man utter himself," writes Maudsley,[30] and Gregers's intimation that he will kill himself, preceded by his convulsive twitchings, tells Ibsen's Dr. Relling what agony Gregers is suffering. Maudsley says of those who suffer from "impulsive insanity" that they "may at any moment be excited into a convulsive activity" as the result of "some great moral shock."[31] Instead of condemning him for Hedwig's suicide, the good doctor offers what consolation he can.

The fine Swedish character actor Gustaf Fredrikson, who usually played elegant leading men, seems to have struck the right note in his portrayal of Relling. His characterization was that of a shipwrecked soul, only of a superior sort. The doctor's disappointment in life, his failure to marry Mrs. Sørby, has made him a nonjudgmental and sympathetic observer of the lives of others. Fredrikson's Relling was relaxed, good-natured, easygoing, *gemütlich*. An unkempt, scraggly beard, spectacles, a stooped posture with hands in pockets, added to the characterization. In his interpretation of the part, this last scene with Gregers was greeted with sympathetic mirth, and Relling's last remark, "Oh, like hell it is" (Å, *fan' tro det*), became in altered form "Like hell, said Relling" (*Fan tro't, sa Relling*)—a catchphrase for good-natured doubt or skepticism.[32] That Fredrikson could bring the curtain down on an upbeat note testifies to a tremendous and insightful feat of acting as well as to the sustained comic obbligato of Ibsen's play.

However much one tries to regard Gregers with sympathy, in the final analysis he is the destructive force in the play. For all his talk about ideals and setting things to rights, his basic motivation is very selfish. All his anger and hatred is directed at his father, who was unfaithful to his wife, driving her to drink, and unscrupulous in business, bringing about the ruin of old Ekdal, and cowardly in his treatment of Hedwig, fobbing her off on Hjalmar. Gregers is hardly exaggerating when he tells his father in parting from him, "When I look back upon your past, it's like looking at a battlefield with shattered lives in every direction."[33] But when he looks back upon his own life, he sees that he himself, through his silence, is largely to blame for the misfortunes of the Ekdals. His main concern is to give some relief to his aching conscience, and there is only one place where restitution might be made: in the Ekdal home. He will tell the truth to Hjalmar; Hjalmar will forgive Gina; and Gregers can then take credit for putting the Ekdal marriage on a sound basis. But he naively misjudges Hjalmar, who disowns Hedwig. Then Gregers has to implant in the child the idea of proving her love by making a great sacrifice. Hjalmar will then take her back as his own child and embrace Gina as his true wife. By killing the duck, Hedwig will expunge the lies of the past and relieve Gregers's conscience, all in one bold gesture. These must be his thoughts when he hears the shot and says, "Through the child, restitution."

With such expectations, Gregers understandably goes into shock when he sees Hedwig's body. Nothing has changed for the better, only for the worse. Not even his childhood hero, Hjalmar, has emerged a better man. No wonder Gregers resolves to die.

As in *Ghosts*, heredity plays a decisive part in the tragic events. Oswald's insanity and Hedwig's impending blindness are both manifestations of the inescapable past, and both are caused by sexual disease. Avoiding the blunt methods that offended the public in *Ghosts*, Ibsen kept the disease in the background, where only the more sophisticated members of the audience would notice its presence. They would understand the unintended implication in Hjalmar's remark that there is retribution in old Werle's blindness. Werle is paying not only for his shady business practices but also for his sexual escapades. "He was a wild buck in his day," we are told. Audiences of the time would have been inclined to attribute Håkon Werle's blindness to gonorrhea, and they would have believed that it was transmitted from parent to child.[34] In the year that *The Wild Duck* was written, a committee of the Ophthalmological Society of England "investigated four lunatic asylums, and they found that up to 41 per cent of the blind patients were blind because of gonorrhea."[35]

The blindness motif insinuates itself into the first act of the play through the subdued light of Werle's study, contrasting sharply with the bright light of the music room upstage. When Werle is first seen, he is being led into the library by his companion Mrs. Sørby.

"You mustn't remain there any longer, staring at all the lights," she says. "It's very bad for you."

Werle lets go her arm and passes his hand over his eyes. In the next act, set in the Ekdal home, we see Hedwig shading her eyes with her hand as she reads and draws. In the last two acts all the references to blindness have a single purpose: to confirm that Werle is Hedwig's father and the cause of her failing eyesight.

The Past Recaptured

Ibsen gave *Ghosts* the cruelly ironic subtitle "A Family Drama." It would have been more appropriate for *The Wild Duck*. The play is the story of two families, and both of them are recognizably like the family of Ibsen's childhood and adolescence. In 1881 he had sketched out the first pages of an autobiography, but his publisher dissuaded him from continuing with it, rightly believing that the market for Ibsen's life story would increase with each passing year. The uproar over *Ghosts* led Hegel to caution Ibsen against making any public statements about his plays. He even hoped that no revealing notes about the plays would survive Ibsen's death. He said, "Your works are like a row of statues in a gallery and, like such statues, keep the viewer at a certain distance. If the statues stepped down from their pedestals, they would engage with the public, for the public is insolent and seldom greets with clean hands. Each of your works speaks for itself and says as clearly and earnestly as possible what it has to say." In his reply, Ibsen said he agreed but noted that many of his friends thought he was too secretive and guarded.[1] Abandoning the autobiography, he incorporated the essential part of it in *The Wild Duck*.

The earliest notes for the play refer to memories of childhood. "Gregers' experience of a child's first and deepest sorrows. They are not sorrows over love; no, they are the pains of family life, the distressing in the home situation."[2]

A radical change occurred in the Ibsen home in the mid-1830s, and it might be fair to say it was then that Ibsen became a divided personality. The move from Skien to the farm at Venstøp meant an end to the congenial social life the prosperous Ibsens had led in town. Mother and father drew apart from each other, and no more children were born to them. All this had a profound effect on the future playwright. During the years the family lived at Venstøp, the young Ibsen grew more introspective, became absorbed in his marionette theater and in painting, while subjected to the teasing of children his own age. At the end of this period, the Ibsens moved back into town, and not long thereafter Henrik was cast out into the world to fend for himself.

If we study the plays in the order in which they were written, as Ibsen wanted us to, then we can see how *The Wild Duck* continues some of the main themes from *Ghosts* and *An Enemy of the People.* In the latter play the truth is worth fighting for, even if it makes the compact majority unhappy. In *The Wild Duck* an insubstantial hope or a fond dream serves humanity much better than a bitter truth. Within a few years Ibsen's outlook changed radically from the firm stand he took at the end of *A Doll's House,* when he sent a firmly committed Nora out into the world, to the end of *The Wild Duck,* in which a shattered Gregers prepares to leave a world that has no place for idealists.

What remains consistent in these works is Ibsen's compulsive need to bring the two sides of his nature into some kind of harmony. In *The Wild Duck* he tried a new approach to his problem by tracing the division within himself back to its origins. In this self-analysis Ibsen sees the source of his peculiar kind of bipolarity as lying not in his blood but in social circumstances.

The traumatic experience of his early days was the sudden decline of the family fortunes. In *The Wild Duck* the fall from fortune is transformed into an elaborate tale involving two families: the Werles representing the prelapsarian Ibsens, and the Ekdals, the Ibsens fallen upon hard times. This dramatic strategy was necessary for the playwright, who wanted to show how irreconcilable were the two sides of his nature.

This meant inventing two separate family histories, each worthy of novel-length treatment, and each built up on the basis of relatively few facts. Neither Gregers nor Hjalmar is Ibsen, but both are believable might-have-beens.

The break between the two families occurred about seventeen or eighteen years before the play begins. At that time Ekdal, a forester, entered into a business deal with Werle, who owned mining interests in a place called High Valley (Høidal). A perennial problem was getting enough wood to fire the furnaces in the ironworks, and also to provide for the houses of the workers. Gradually, the business shifted from iron production to lumbering. If the ironworks were operated under the king's patent or license, wood from the king's forests could be used; otherwise, the forests available to the lumber business were circumscribed to a certain area. In Ibsen's play, trees on royal land near the mine were cut down. Charges were brought against Ekdal and Werle; the latter was able to avoid trial, while Ekdal was found guilty, sentenced to prison, and deprived of certain civil rights. While the investigation was being conducted, Ekdal felt the shame of it so keenly that he contemplated suicide. His son Hjalmar, who was about twenty at the time, was forced to leave university because the family's assets had been wiped out. In fact, Ekdal was left owing money to Werle. Hjalmar, too, thought of killing himself.

In the meantime, Gregers, about the same age as his admired school chum, the handsome Hjalmar, was going through a crisis of his own. His hatred of his father deepened when he discovered how Werle had deceived Ekdal and escaped the clutches of the law. Fearing the wrath of his father, Gregers did not speak out at the Ekdal trial. Despising himself for his cowardice, he left school, shunned his father, and went to work as an ordinary office clerk in the mining settlement in High Valley. There he went from cabin to cabin urging the workingmen to raise themselves above their station by pursuing some high ideal, whatever it might be. Dr. Relling, the medical officer in the settlement, counteracted Gregers's preaching and proselytizing by recommending the life-lie, a supportable dream rather than an ideal impossible of realization.

Shortly after Gregers left home for High Valley, his mother died. She had been an alcoholic for some years, suffering fits of jealousy, certain that her husband was carrying on an affair with the housemaid Gina Hansen. Once in an ungovernable rage she had slapped Gina, who thereupon left the Werles' employment. After his wife's death, Werle forced his attentions on Gina and got her pregnant.

Mrs. Werle's jealousy, her alcoholism and insane rages, could have been lifted from the pages of medical books of the time. What Gregers hints at is spelled out in Maudsley's description of climacteric insanity.

> An insane jealousy, having its roots in the apprehension of the extinction of the power to provoke desire, sometimes shows itself in an extremely exacting form, in unfounded suspicion of a husband, in gross accusations of unchastity, in much violence of passion and conduct; and a habitually indulged propensity to alcoholic stimulants, which may have been taken in the first instance to relieve the feelings of mental depression and bodily sinking, makes more frantic the paroxysms of jealous fury. This sort of insane jealousy is certainly not special to the climacteric period; it may be met with before that change in women who have lived the sort of life of self-indulgence to evoke and foster it; but is most likely to break out or to be greatly exaggerated then.[3]

The embarrassment of an illegitimate child had to be avoided, and Werle found a way around this difficulty that would not only give the child a proper home but would also enable him to pay off an old debt. Hjalmar Ekdal, out of college, with no means of support, was the man the situation called for. After leaving Werle's employment, Gina went to live with her mother, who owned a small café and let out rooms. Håkon Werle told Hjalmar that a room was available to him there. Gina and Hjalmar became lovers, so while Gina was learning the craft of retouching photographs, she was sexually involved with both Werle and Ekdal. By setting up Ekdal as a professional photographer and seeing to it that he married Gina, Werle avoided a parental suit while simultaneously easing his conscience a bit for the deceit he had practiced on Ekdal when trees were felled on government land. A new deceit would heal the old one. Thus, about two years after Ekdal's trial, Hjalmar and Gina were married, and a few months later Hedwig was born.

In depicting the home life of the Werle and Ekdal families, Ibsen drew on memories from his childhood, especially in contrasting the wealthy Werle with the destitute Ekdal. Ibsen left his parents in 1843, and he was not in Skien to see at first hand the sad decline of the family and to witness his father's fall from respectable citizen to eccentric town character. Nor did he exchange letters with his parents. Nevertheless, he would have learned one way or another about his parents' fate. In the years after 1848, Knud Ibsen was called seventeen times to appear before the Court of Conciliation in the matter of his unpaid debts. He began to drink heavily, and his relatives hesitated to give him money, knowing he would squander it on liquor. In 1865 he was separated from his wife, who died four years later. He tried his hand at raising chickens, failed, and was listed in the census as indigent. He could often be seen wandering in the streets wearing his old peaked volunteer soldier's cap. He died in 1877.

Old Ekdal, putting on his uniform and reliving happy days, is a remarkable likeness of Knud Ibsen. (It should be compared with the sketch of Daniel Hejre in *The League of Youth*, which captures the sharp-tongued and spirited Knud before his pathetic decline.) Ekdal is a social outcast who drinks on the sly, wears a scratch wig, and does copy work for Werle's office. (The hot water that he says he needs to thin ink is really for his hot toddy.) Unlike Ibsen's father, Ekdal cannot wear his soldier's uniform in public, having lost his right to do so when he was convicted of illegal lumbering and sent to prison. Ekdal's crime has no precise equivalent in Knud's life; Knud's offenses were comparatively minor.

There were several instances of illegal lumbering in the 1860s in Scandinavia, and one of them was certainly familiar to Ibsen through the daily papers.[4] He found forest exploitation a more dramatic subject than the minor fault that brought some shame on his father. The playwright compressed his father's various business failures into one rash, ill-considered act and all the public humiliation into a prison sentence.

From the Ibsen home in Venstøp, one could see the Fossum ironworks, owned by Chamberlain Løvenskiold. His manor house provides the setting for the first act of *The Wild Duck*, and, much like old Ekdal, Ibsen's father was employed irregularly, doing odd jobs.[5] Looking back, the successful middle-aged dramatist knew that those years at Venstøp had given birth to the dreamer and fantast in him. Scattered throughout *The Wild Duck* are clues identifying Hjalmar with Ibsen. Hjalmar's smoking jacket, his talk of the need for a great sorrow, his plan to achieve greatness in life and then to die, remind one of the Ibsen of the 1850s and 1860s. Hjalmar's concern with the reputation of the family is the same as Ibsen's throughout his life.

Hjalmar is the dreamer that Ibsen might have become but for the Gregers in him. The fact that Hjalmar takes up photography calls to mind Ibsen's decision to give up poetry for "photography," to venture into the realistic drama after his great achievements *Brand* and *Peer Gynt.* Like Hjalmar, who is taking notes for the story of his life, Ibsen had written the first few pages of his autobiography in 1881.

If Hjalmar is Ibsen as he might have been had he never left home and country, then Gregers is the Ibsen who by sheer force of will (and with the indispensable support of his wife) created *The Pretenders* and *Brand.* Gregers is the Ibsen who quarreled with his family, who but for a brief visit to Skien in 1850 never saw his parents again, and who never returned to the scenes of his childhood. "I have entirely separated myself forever from my own parents, from my whole family," he told Bjørnson, "because being only half understood was unendurable to me."[6] It was this Ibsen who, even when he was growing prosperous and buying stocks, never sent his impecunious father a dollar or two. It was this Ibsen who, though he took several sojourns in Norway, never called on him. Even in his late years, Ibsen declined an invitation to be honored in Skien as its most famous citizen. As his daughter-in-law said, "Ibsen's sore point was Skien."[7] Yet on one occasion he did write to his father. This was in 1875, when Knud was seventy-six. It was the first contact between them in twenty-five years. Hjalmar's refusal to recognize his father at the party in Werle's house distilled into one moment the many years in which Ibsen turned his back on his father. In contrast to that moment are the many warm and tender scenes between old Ekdal and Hjalmar when in the comfort of their own home. Were those scenes wrested from Ibsen by his guilty conscience? Or were they re-creations of happy experiences, those times when father and son went hunting together?

In 1877, in response to the news of his father's death, Ibsen sought to excuse himself for neglecting his parents. Writing to his half uncle Christopher Blom Paus, who had loaned him money in 1850 to prepare for entrance to the university in Christiania, he acknowledged that

> in the eyes of the world it may indeed seem as if I had deliberately made myself a stranger to my family, or at least completely separated myself from them. But I believe I may honestly say that it was mainly unalterable circumstances and conditions that separated us from the beginning. . . .
>
> From my fourteenth year I was thrown upon my own resources. It has been

> a long, hard struggle to reach my present position. I seldom wrote home during those years of struggle because I could offer no assistance of any kind to my parents. It seemed useless to write when I could not be of any real and practical use. I went on hoping that my circumstances would improve. But the improvement was very long in coming, and did not come until fairly recently. . . .
>
> I want you to know, and I wish you in turn to tell the others, that taking upon yourselves, out of affection for my parents, the duties and obligations that I myself should have borne was a great help during my years of struggle and hardship, and furthered the accomplishment of what I have been able to achieve in this world.[8]

The equivocations in this letter betray his bad conscience. It is true that the difficult years from 1850 to 1867 had made it impossible for him to provide substantial assistance to his parents. But he could have written a letter or two; he might have called on them to see for himself how they were faring. And after 1867 the author who was fêted in Stockholm and whose royalties allowed him to invest in stocks could certainly have sent some money home. It may have been necessary for Ibsen, humiliated as he had been for years by his father's social decline and repelled by his mother's religiosity, to make a clean break in order to fulfill himself as Brand, the incorruptible idealist. Yet by the time he wrote *The Wild Duck* the grudge he had held against his parents for so many years must have struck him as quite unconscionable. His quest for fame and fortune had alienated him from the most basic human relationships. To see life whole, a reconciliation had to be effected between what he now was and what he had once been. Accordingly, Brand's longing for the unpeopled heights dwindled into the mania of a neurotic son who hated his father.

Ibsen gave Gregers the prosperous, aggressive father who from the perspective of a seven-year-old child might have loomed as a cruel tyrant who changed his wife into a melancholy, brooding, pietistic woman. As father to Hjalmar, Ibsen summoned up from the reports that reached him the eccentric, broken man who lived on memories of the past. For the Ekdal home, the playwright drew on his recollections of the farm at Venstøp. The cluttered garret in which the duck thrives is Ibsen's evocation of the attic in which he played and conjured up tales for his miniature theater.

Other minor details can also be traced back to the Skien district. The guests at the Werle dinner party have names suggestive of families well known in that area. Mrs. Sørby gets her name from a lady who ran an inn in the town. Old Ekdal's speech is flavored with some words peculiar to the Skien dialect.[9] The only family member with whom Ibsen was in touch, though sporadically, was his sister, Hedvig. His closeness to her must have been the inspiration for those mystical scenes in *The Wild Duck* in which Gregers and his half sister, Hedwig, commune with each other. The suggestion that Ibsen identified himself with Hedwig seems very plausible, since it is in her mind that the opposing forces represented by Hjalmar and Gregers meet, clash, and resolve themselves. She is devoted to her father (Peer Gynt), but she is also mysteriously drawn to Gregers (Brand).

Her suicide is a crushing blow to everyone, and it left audiences in the nineteenth century stunned not only because it seemed unprepared for by the tone of the drama but because it violated esthetic principles. It took years for the play to be properly appreciated. Although the 1885 production in Copenhagen had a strong cast and was expertly directed by William Bloch, who followed Ibsen's stage directions faithfully, neither the critics nor the audiences were much impressed. There was only a small audience at the second night. The political conservatives hissed the play.[10] The sensibilities of one reviewer were ruffled by hearing Hjalmar speak words "that no one, whether sane or mad, would use nowadays."[11] Fru Wolf, who created the part of Gina in the Christiania production, couldn't bring herself to utter the simple, uncouth language that Ibsen wanted.[12] The Christiania production was not sold out, either on the first night or afterward. The scheduled last performance had to be canceled when the box office took in only one krone, twenty øre. Ibsen had demanded twenty-five hundred kroner in royalties.[13]

Perhaps the most scathing criticism came from the poet and novelist Helena Nyblom, writing shortly after the publication of the play. She found all the characters in it to be rascals, idiots, or whores. Mrs. Sørby is a whore who makes good; Gina is a whore with less luck. The only bright spot in the play occurs when the young girl has sense enough to shoot herself, to escape from this pack of good-for-nothings.[14]

In 1887 the Freie Bühne in Berlin, an experimental theater, thought it advisable to present it at a single matinee performance, fearing that most people would find it offensive. Most critics did; their censure, however, was directed primarily at the graphic reality of the scenes in the Ekdal home, where Ibsen spared no grubby detail of life among the lower orders. There was sexual immorality, with Gina casually admitting that she had had two lovers at the same time. And there was the gratuitous vulgarity of the breakfast scene in which the crapulent clergyman manqué Molvik becomes nauseous and has to rush from the table. A German critic singled out the scene for disapprobation, finding the language of "absolutely unpoetic coarseness," in which Ibsen allows "corned beef and pickled herring to be mentioned"[15] (actually, salted freshly killed rabbit).

Literary critics saw that the play broke more than the rules of social decorum. The poet Theodore Fontane felt that "the structure of traditional esthetics had collapsed completely." Certainly, the area between tragedy and comedy had turned into a no-man's-land.

It took a decade or so for *The Wild Duck* to be widely accepted as a masterpiece. What the impact of the play was like on audiences fortunate enough to see it well done is best described by Bernard Shaw, reviewing the 1897 London production.

"To sit there getting deeper and deeper into that Ekdal home, and getting deeper and deeper into your own life all the time, until you forget you are in a theatre; to look on with horror and pity at a profound tragedy, shaking with laughter all the time at an irresistible comedy; to go out, not from a diversion, but from an experience deeper than real life ever brings to most men, or often brings to any man: that is what *The Wild Duck* was like."[16]

In Scandinavia, the play represented another milestone in the development of realistic theater. The proper effect of *The Wild Duck* depended on a casual naturalness that is one of the most difficult things to achieve onstage. If it had not been for a quite sudden advance in stage realism in the Nordic countries, Ibsen might not have attempted such a play. *The Wild Duck* lacked set speeches and clever repartee; it required a nonstandard and elaborate set and special lighting; and, above all, it had to have ensemble acting to make the proper impression.

To impose a unity of tone on such a play and to marshal the various elements of acting and set design, the director had to assume almost dictatorial powers. The standard German system of having in effect two directors, neither one of whom had much authority over the leading actors, the system that Ibsen had been trained in while in Bergen, was gradually being abandoned. In the 1880s directors like August Lindberg in Sweden and William Bloch in Denmark were overseeing every aspect of a stage production. When Bloch directed *An Enemy of the People* at the Royal Theater in Copenhagen, the scene of the public meeting in act four required a separate promptbook of 111 pages in which Bloch assigned movements and responses to each of the fifty-three members of the crowd.

The same sort of care and attention to detail went into Lindberg's staging of *The Wild Duck* at the Royal Dramatic Theater in Stockholm. There were real doors, not ones of flapping canvas; the doors had knobs; there was even a commode with washbasin and chamber pot (not mentioned by Ibsen). The actors were instructed to move about as if they were in a real room; unfortunately, in this regard the acting did not match the other elements in the production. Actors, the most conservative of artists, held on to the old ways, presenting their best features to the audience, claiming center stage as their entitlement, and speaking as if they were at a public meeting. Lindberg was the radical exception. His voice and manner did not fit him for the conventional stage roles, and he saw the great potentiality in Ibsen's plays for a new school of acting. After reading *The Wild Duck*, he said, "I get dizzy thinking about it. Such great opportunities for the actor! Never before have we been faced with such possibilities." He told

Ibsen that the play was an incursion into virgin territory, "where we have to make our way with pick and shovel. . . . The people in the play are completely new, and where would we get by relying on the old theatrical clichés?"[17]

Generally hailed as the father of modern drama, Ibsen was also, though to a lesser degree, the father of modern realistic acting. Although the story of the rise of the modern realistic actor usually begins with Stanislavsky and his exploration of Chekhov's plays, most of what he accomplished after 1896 was already under way in Scandinavia and Germany in the 1880s. But neither Lindberg nor Bloch had Stanislavsky's expository skills, nor did they form schools of acting, with specific exercises set down and disciples trained to teach them. Nevertheless, their contributions are a matter of record that deserve to be better known to students of theater history.

In 1876 Ibsen admonished the stage managers at the Christiania Theater for their unimaginative stage-center grouping of actors. The arrangement of the characters onstage, he said, should be broken up and changed as often as would seem natural. "Each scene and each stage picture should be an image of reality, as far as that is possible. . . . Complete naturalness is what I would hope for." He also protested against the stylized gestures and the slow, declamatory delivery of Norwegian actors, who were still holding on to the old style of romantic acting.[18]

In creating his plays, he saw in his mind every detail of the staging. When Lindberg asked him for suggestions about the business in *The Wild Duck*, Ibsen gave him a detailed description of the final scene.

"After Hedwig has shot herself, she should be placed on the sofa so that her feet are in the foreground, so that her right hand with the pistol can hang down. When she is carried out through the kitchen door, I have imagined that Hjalmar holds her under her arms, with Gina carrying her feet."[19]

Ibsen also helped to advance the art of stage design by calling for subtle lighting effects that were now possible thanks to gas jets that could be easily adjusted. As a would-be painter, he knew how effectively light and color could be used to convey a mood or psychological state. He could hardly have been unaware of the impressionists' experiments in capturing light on canvas, often painting the same scene again and again as the light shifted. He might even have read—or read about—Zola's 1878 novel *Une Page d'amour*. Zola, ardent promoter of the impressionists, described the same view of Paris as seen under different conditions, each one a reflection of the state of mind of the main character: Paris in the bright morning light, Paris under a cover of lowering clouds, Paris at night cloaked in rain and mist.

Ibsen does something similar in *The Wild Duck*. Calling the Norwegian producer's attention to the significance of the lighting, he said, "It is different for

Figure 19. Hedwig's death.

each act, and it is calculated to correspond to the fundamental tone that stamps each of the five acts with a distinct character."[20] In the first act, set in Werle's library, the dim light cast by oil lamps with green shades suffuses the downstage area, while the brightly lit party room upstage provides a sharp contrast. In the second act, set in Hjalmar's studio, a lamp on a table affords the only light at the rise of the curtain. Gina and Hedwig sit at the table, Gina sewing, Hedwig reading. Later in the act we catch the first glimpse of the loft, moonbeams spilling through the skylight and barely illumining some parts of the mysterious room, while other parts remain in deep shadow. In the next act, morning sunlight floods the studio, and when the double door to the loft is opened, we can see the doves and hens that inhabit the space, while a makeshift curtain of fishnets and sailcloth conceals the floor of the loft from our view. In the fourth act, after the true nature of Hjalmar's marriage has been revealed to him, the sun is setting, and Gina lights the lamp. In the last act, the morning light is cold and gray, and "wet snow lies upon the large panes of the skylight."

In Ibsen's symbolic language, that wet snow underscores Hedwig's suicide. At the end of *Ghosts*, the snow on the mountains clashes with the bright sun. For Mrs. Alving there could be no resolution of her inner conflict. By contrast, Hedwig's suicide suggests a fusion of opposites. The snow melts, the sunlight is gray.

The Depths of the Sea

The Ekdals occupy the top floor of a building, and the main room serves as both living room and photographer's studio. A large slanting skylight allows the maximum of sunlight to enter. At the back of this space is a wide double sliding door. We do not get to see what lies behind it until the middle of the second act, and then we get only a tantalizing glimpse into a loft, partly in the dark, partly lit by moonbeams. Bit by bit we learn what that loft contains: pigeons, rabbits, the wild duck, a few withered pine trees. These four or five discarded Christmas trees that old Ekdal has collected and placed there are for him the great forest in High Valley. The cock and hens are big game birds, and the rabbits that go hopping about are the bears that the mighty hunter once shot and killed. For him and Hjalmar the loft restores the past, the life they lived before the trial broke them. In there old Ekdal can wear his soldier's uniform and imagine himself the man he once was, and Hjalmar can avoid the present. It is a place of refuge for those who have retreated from the battles of life.

But the loft contains much more: books, bureaus, cupboards, pictures, and a clock that stopped running long ago. Here we have the junkyard of humanity, a jumbled record of man's past. Most of the objects were left there by an old sea captain, nicknamed the Flying Dutchman, who was claimed by the sea on his last voyage. What all these things have in common, the books and the trees, the cabinets and the rabbits, is that they are all associated with time gone by.

As an image of what once was, it is also a place of death. Hedwig shoots herself there. After her death, old Ekdal, muttering that he is not afraid, slips unnoticed by the others into the garret, closing the door.

Ibsen begins his play in Werle's library, a richly furnished room, representing the physical comforts and intellectual attainments of modern society, a place where culture and power are united. Behind is the party room in which the cream of society is gathered. We leave that setting and find ourselves in the comfortable but plain home of the Ekdals, considerably lower on the social scale than the Werles' manor house. Behind their studio room in a sharply narrowing perspective we are meant to see the early phases of man's social development. To move (in the reverse direction) from the cluttered loft to the elegant home of Håkon Werle is to traverse history from the earliest signs of civilization to the nineteenth century.

In the garret Hjalmar and his father relive the happy days when they hunted real bears, not rabbits; in that sense, it suggests their past lives. In a broader sense, however, it is a domesticated version of nature, tamed and reduced to manageable proportions. "Nature red in tooth and claw" exists outside this space. Torn and bleeding from the struggle for survival, the Ekdals have retired to their lair to lick their wounds and to console themselves with dreams, like old dogs before the warm hearth, their paws twitching in pursuit of phantom prey. The wounded duck, snug and comfortable in its basket, is the very image of the Ekdals.

Håkon Werle, who carved out his empire from the woods and mines in High Valley, is now aged beyond passion and battle, and with blindness encroaching upon him, he wants to retire, letting Gregers take over the business. In his heyday Håkon was the ruthless entrepreneur, a firm believer in the survival of the fittest, a man whose sharp practices and shady dealings, both commercial and sexual, put old Ekdal in prison and drove his wife to drink.

Gregers is different from both his father and Hjalmar. He wants to be fully involved in changing the world. Although he may talk of his own early demise, he is more actively engaged in the life around him than anyone else, except Gina. In the limited circle that Ibsen draws, Gregers represents the type that reshapes the world for better or worse. He sees immediately that the loft exercises a seductive power, a pull backward into the past that must be overcome. More than anyone else, he understands the symbolic richness of the garret. He is spellbound by it. He sees that it is not only a retreat into the good old days; he sees that it is the stored-up experience of all living things.

In fact, Gregers is our best guide to what Ibsen was trying to express through the elaborate symbolism of the loft. He is not only the first person to grasp the significance of the domesticated duck; he is the one who sees into the hidden depths of the loft. Talking of the duck, he says it has been "down in the briny depths of the sea," using an old-fashioned expression (*havsens bund* rather than *havets bund* or *havbund*) that catches Hedwig's attention. In sympathetic response, she says that "the whole room and everything in it should be called 'the briny depths of the sea.'" Hjalmar and his father seem to have had the same insight. Their curtain is made of fishnets and old sailcloth, and when it is slipped into place, the floor of the garret is concealed and the mysterious space becomes, in effect, the bottomless depths of the sea.

In *Ghosts,* Ibsen found in syphilis a strikingly dramatic representation of the unremitting force of the past. In *The Wild Duck,* physical inheritance is gathered together in a larger symbol, the garret through which the whole of man's history and evolution is extruded. In this storage room, the boldest and richest of Ibsen's inventions, he created a more comprehensive symbol, one that encompassed the newest ideas about mankind's history. He had been slow in accepting the grand theories that were quickly coming to the fore in the nineteenth century as they found support among scientists and researchers. Even in the 1870s, when many of his contemporaries were responding to them, Ibsen remained aloof. There was not only Darwin's shattering theory of evolution; there were new theories about man's prehistory (that is, before recorded history), as well as new insights into the subconscious or unconscious life of human beings. In *Peer Gynt,* Ibsen the idealist ridiculed Darwinism, recognizing in it a threat to man's will. In *Emperor and Galilean,* Maximus propounded the old idea that with man, will arose upon the earth, "and man, and beasts, and trees, and herbs re-created themselves, each in its own image, according to eternal laws."[1] As his vision broadened, as it did in *Emperor and Galilean,* it brought man's will into harmony with the will of the universe. German speculative philosophy provided the basis for a sweeping worldview that, at least in Ibsen's mind, answered all the important questions. Then, quite suddenly, in his daily reading of journals, newspapers, and books, he saw that German metaphysics had evaporated under the bright glare of the new sciences.

Above all, it was Darwin's theory of evolution that vaporized the old philosophy, that virtually eliminated spirit, replacing it with flesh and blood. The chief spokesman among the literati for the new view was Zola. He named the new movement Naturalism, meaning the scientific study of the world of physical matter.

"I have called naturalism the return to nature, the scientific movement of the century; I have shown the experimental method brought to bear upon and applied to all the manifestations of human intelligence; I have tried to explain the evident evolution which is being produced in our literature by establishing the proposition that the former subject of study, the metaphysical man, is being replaced by the physiological man."[2]

Immanuel Kant had declared that there were certain questions that lay beyond the power of the human mind to answer. In his *Critique of Judgment* (1790), Kant found it impossible to account for the orderly processes of nature without postulating supernatural final causes. "It is quite certain that we cannot even satisfactorily understand, much less elucidate, the nature of an organism . . . on purely mechanical natural principles. . . . We may confidently say, 'It is absurd for a man to conceive the idea even that some day a Newton will arise who can explain the origin of a single blade of grass by natural laws which are uncontrolled by design'—such a hope is entirely forbidden to us."[3] Yet within the span of two generations, as the German scientist Ernst Haeckel (1834–1919) triumphantly remarked, this impossible Newton appeared in the person of Darwin. In place of God calling Adam to life, as on the Sistine ceiling, Haeckel offered a picture of a one-celled animal that initiated life on this planet.

Championing the experimental methods of the scientists, Zola ridiculed the philosophers, who, "left to themselves, will sing forever and never discover a single truth."[4]

In place of Schelling's mystical fusion of opposites, biology showed life emerging from matter. It was a revolutionary thought that impressed Ibsen. In one of his jottings from about 1880 (a note for *Ghosts*?), he wrote, "The inorganic comes first, thereupon the organic. First dead nature, then the living."[5]

In *Emperor and Galilean*, in the mystical scenes with Maximus, Ibsen postulated a universe in a fixed state with the individual human being caught between eternal opposites, taking, in the case of Julian, the form of the pagan and the Christian. In the naturalistic world, however, there was no fixed state: everything was changing, evolving from one state into another. Julian-Ibsen was suspended between the deep sea and the boundless heavens; Gregers-Ibsen was transfixed by the measureless depths from which all things had developed. Maximus's chamber of spirits, mysterious because supernatural, was replaced by the Ekdal storeroom, mysterious because of its unfathomable richness. Julian's vision of himself at sea, when he experienced the great revelation, represented an effort to preserve spirit in a world of matter. He saw his ship as hanging over an empty abyss. "No verdure down there, no sunlight, only the dead black, slimy bottom of the sea [*den døde, slimede, sorte havbund*] in all its ghastly nakedness.

"But high above, in the boundless dome, which before had seemed to me empty, *there* was life; there the invisible clothed itself in form, and silence became sound."[6]

In *The Wild Duck*, the images are reversed. The sea is the source of life, and when Gregers talks about it, he uses a different term, not *havbund* but *havsens bund*, which sounds more mysterious. This surprises Hedwig, and pleases her, because to her the loft is a place of life, not Julian's black and lifeless *havbund*.[7]

Ironically, just after the publication of *Emperor and Galilean* in 1873, the *Challenger* expedition (1873–76) under the direction of Sir Wyville Thompson and Dr. John Murray revealed the extent of life in the deep oceans. As Haeckel said, "The depths of the ocean, and particularly the immense deep-sea basin from 6000 to 9000 metres in depth, were, thirty years ago, considered to be lifeless deserts, not inhabited by any living creature. . . . These ocean-depths are now known to be inhabited by many thousand varieties of wonderful Protista, which, by the incredible beauty and variety of their one-celled structure of body, surpass everything of the kind hitherto known. This discovery has opened up to us a new world for investigation and study, and has extended our knowledge of the biological domain in a way which would formerly have been considered inconceivable."[8]

Darwin's theories were quickly disseminated throughout the Nordic countries, beginning with J. P. Jacobsen's explanatory articles in *Nyt dansk Maanedsskrift* in 1871. His translations of *On the Origin of Species* and *The Descent of Man* followed in 1872 and 1875. There is good evidence that Ibsen read Darwin in Jacobsen's translations.[9] In the winter of 1878–79, while residing in Rome, Ibsen had many conversations with Jacobsen, and what impressed him appeared in an early draft of *A Doll's House,* in which a doctor expounds the law of the survival of the fittest. "Follow the natural sciences, ladies, and you'll see how there is a universal law in all things. The stronger tree takes nourishment from the weaker and uses it for its own purposes. The same with animals. The weaker ones in a herd have to yield to the stronger ones. And that's why nature advances. It's only we human beings who deliberately hold progress back by taking care of weaker individuals."[10]

Ibsen did not enlarge on these Darwinian ideas in *A Doll's House,* but he made up for their absence there by putting them all into *The Wild Duck.* He may have been encouraged to do so by reading Zola. In 1880, in calling for a reform of the theater, Zola said, "I am waiting for a dramatic work which, purged of declamation and free of fine language and pretty sentiments, has the high morality of truth and the terrible lesson of sincere inquiry." And by sincere inquiry he meant, of course, the naturalistic, scientific approach, which would not allow any supernatural agent to interfere in the action.[11]

Everything that Zola advocated in his reform of the theater is to be found in *The Wild Duck:* the unconventional plotting, with the great secret being revealed offstage; the characters and their environment firmly integrated; the crude speech of real people; and an inquiry into the lives of these people that shuns metaphysics. That is not to say that Ibsen read Zola and was persuaded to change his outlook; rather, he found confirmation for what he himself was hoping to achieve, for what he had been working toward, ever since *A Doll's House.*

More than any novel or play by Zola, *The Wild Duck* is permeated with Darwinism. The extent to which Ibsen emphasizes the "depths of the sea" suggests that he read up on the subject of evolution by studying the writings of Haeckel,

Darwin's chief disciple in Germany. More than his master, Haeckel discussed how life originated from single-celled creatures in the sea. As a biologist and field naturalist, he made significant contributions in the area of primitive forms of life, beginning with his paper on Monera in 1864. The German naturalist Lorenz Oken had postulated in 1805 the existence of an infusorial mass or protoplasm, the *Urschleim*, from which all the larger organisms evolved. But he could produce no physical evidence to support his theory. Haeckel was the first to describe these shapeless bits of matter that contained the elements of life, little lumps of slime, consisting of an albuminous combination of carbon. A couple of years later the English naturalist Thomas Henry Huxley found deep in the ocean what he thought was an example of this earliest form of living matter, a bit of protoplasm that he named after Haeckel (*Bathybius haeckelii*). The German biologist congratulated Huxley on the discovery of this remarkable specimen, a wonderful organism living in the immense depths of the ocean, twelve thousand, even twenty-four thousand feet below the surface.

The startling revelation that Haeckel conveyed to his readers was that life originated in lifeless matter. "There exist no complete differences between organic and inorganic natural bodies, neither in respect to form and structure, nor in respect to matter and force. . . . The actually existing differences are dependent upon the peculiar nature of the *carbon*. . . . There exists no insurmountable chasm between organic and inorganic nature."[12]

This scientific miracle, the reduction of life to a chemical formula, with the implication that man's spirit arose out of matter and was not mysteriously injected from above, was more astonishing than the biblical creation. It had what the other lacked: hard evidence.

Haeckel was an unabashedly atheistic proponent of Darwin's theories and repeatedly emphasized, as Darwin did not, the purely materialistic, nonmiraculous history of creation. Although the idea that life originated in some moist substance and then evolved into complicated forms was as old as the ancient Greeks, Haeckel defined the substance and located its position, even drew pictures of it in its one-celled form. To minds receptive to new ideas, the revelation that life grew out of inorganic matter was the intellectual equivalent of the discovery of America. It opened up extraordinary vistas in which man appeared both smaller than ever before (because only a complicated, nonangelic piece of matter) and larger than ever before (he was the Promethean discoverer of the ultimate mystery).

Haeckel's *History of Creation,* first published in 1873, won a wide readership, and soon every educated person was aware of his theory of the origin of life from simple one-celled bits of slime. Strindberg wrote a satiric poem about it.

The cell, already installed
as the highest being in the new faith.
Oh, cell (also known as *Urschleim*
and as protoplasm in learned jargon),
oh, cell, captain of my fate, and everyone's,
come free us from life's miseries![13]

As Strindberg composed this poem, Ibsen was at work on *The Wild Duck*. The one-cell theory of the origin of life captured his imagination and compelled him to reexamine the basis of his philosophy. In fact, the whole conceptual scheme of *Emperor and Galilean* was turned upside down. The great synthesis formulated in it rested on German speculative metaphysics in which it was possible to entertain the notion of the coincidence of opposites, of the negative and the positive being two aspects of the same thing. Now, faced with the discoveries of science, he had to reconstruct his worldview, with Darwin and Haeckel replacing Maximus the mystic. *The Wild Duck* was meant to match *Emperor and Galilean* as a universal history, in keeping with Ibsen's compulsive desire, like Wagner's, to make drama into philosophy and philosophy into drama. *The Wild Duck* was to be the new dispensation, and just as comprehensive as the old one.

In Ibsen's former Weltanschauung, man's will had to be taken as a given, requiring little explanation. In the new view, man was driven by natural forces, and his wishes, or rather his compulsions had to be explained in physical terms. Just as the progress of Oswald's illness had to follow known medical facts, so the behavior of the characters in *The Wild Duck* had to be seen as the focus of several factors. While Brand's striving for spiritual perfection was motivated by his hatred of his materialistic mother, Gregers's idealism is seen as the convergence of several vectors: a grasping, hypocritical father, a mistreated mother, and a freak of nature. While Agnes's willingness to sacrifice appears as the necessary anticipation of Brand's final moments, Hedwig's sacrificial act occurs because of her physical condition, the onset of puberty.

Ibsen had to accommodate his vision of the human being in a struggle with himself, Brand versus Peer Gynt, by setting it in the large framework of man's evolutionary history. His fascination with this new conception inspires the dialogue between Hedwig and Gregers about the depths of the sea. These two have an instinctive understanding of each other and of the ultimate nature of things. There is something perennially immature about Gregers that adds to his freakishness. It is what brings him close to Hedwig. His idealistic innocence finds a rapport with Hedwig's physical and mental immaturity. They see more deeply into things than the others, and together they stand for what was most important to Ibsen. To him, Gregers was the more advanced being on the evolutionary scale. Loyal to the Brand within him, Ibsen had to elevate the man who believes in self-sacrifice and in the need for ideals above the run of mankind.[14]

Considering that Gregers is filled with self-loathing and sees himself as doomed to an early death, that he is neurotic and inept physically, it may seem wrong to regard him as a higher form of human being. In the struggle for existence, he is a loser. As a physical specimen, he is ill favored. If the principle of the survival of the fittest is invoked, he should be least likely to survive. Yet Ibsen could extract from his reading of Haeckel an explanation for Gregers's special place in the evolutionary scheme.

The new varieties and species that emerged were often odd and freakish compared with their ancestors. What could be odder than the first creatures that crawled out of the water to find a home on land? Or the first vertebrate? A small lanceolate fish, said Haeckel, "stands at the lowest stage of organization of all the Vertebrate animals known to us" and lives widely distributed in different seas, often found buried in the sand on flat shores. "It has no legs, and neither head, skull, nor brain." Yet, "in its internal structure [it] possesses those most important features which distinguish all Vertebrate animals from all Invertebrate animals, namely, the spinal rod and spinal marrow."[15] Haeckel called this lowly creature "next to Man . . . the most interesting of all Vertebrates."[16]

The idea that this strange creature could lead eventually to the highest form of life impressed Ibsen. In a draft for a later play, *The Lady from the Sea,* he wrote, "A kind of fish forms an early link in evolutionary development."[17] At the end of act three of *The Wild Duck* he suggests that Gregers, with his sick conscience and his idealism, is a strange species who should be considered as the beginning of a higher, further evolved human being.

After Dr. Relling tells Gina that Gregers is suffering from "acute rectitudinitis" (*akut retskaffenhedsfeberen*),[18] an excessive obsession with justice, she paces back and forth, upset and disturbed. "Ugh, that Gregers Werle! That man was always a disgusting fish [*det har altid vær't en fæl fisk*]."[19] The epithet that Gina uses, *en fæl fisk,* was not a common expression and calls attention to itself, as Ibsen intended. Uttered along with the ugly-sounding "Gregers Werle," it reinforces our impression of him as unpleasant and strange. Gregers himself says, "'Gregers—and then 'Werle' after it! Have you heard anything so disgusting, have you [*har du hørt noget så fælt, du*]?"[20]

Neurotic, as his father sees him, a crackpot in Relling's eyes, and to Gina a "disgusting fish," Gregers is set apart, an object more of scorn than of pity. But there is in him, as there must have been in that first vertebrate, an intimation of a higher existence. He represents the type that reshapes the world. Opposed to the Darwinian principle of survival of the fittest is the idea of self-sacrifice, and

Gregers is meant to stand for that radical, Christian idea. It is the idea that he inculcates in Hedwig. And she would have sacrificed the wild duck she loves had it not been for other factors.

Ibsen projects the story of the Ekdals and the Werles against the backdrop of mankind's emergence from the first beginnings of life. In the jumble of the loft all of history, or rather prehistory, is compressed. What we as spectators should sense is vividly described by Thomas Hardy in his 1873 novel *A Pair of Blue Eyes*. His hero, Henry Knight, hanging on the edge of a cliff near Land's End, sees an embedded fossil.

"Time closed like a fan before him. He saw himself at one extremity of the years face to face with the beginning and all the intermediate centuries simultaneously.... Savage man, mastodons, the megatherium, all in juxtaposition." Further back, huge-billed birds, colossal lizards, and, folded behind, dragon forms, flying reptiles. "Still underneath were fishy beings of lower development; and so on till the lifetime scenes of the period confronting him were a present and modern condition of things."[21]

Gregers and Hedwig, more than the others, feel the pull of the past and recognize subconsciously, when they speak of the depths of the sea, how the eons of the past impinge on the present moment. The access to this vast history is made through the unconscious, and the loft filled with the detritus of many yesterdays is Ibsen's representation of that obscure part of the mind. That there was a connection between the unconscious and the evolutionary history of the human being was one of those revelations that stirred the imagination of writers in the latter half of the nineteenth century. Before Darwin, irrational thoughts and actions were attributed to agencies lurking in what was popularly called the night side of existence. It is the phrase Hjalmar uses when he contemplates the connection between Werle's oncoming blindness and Werle's hoodwinking old Ekdal. "It is profitable," he tells Gina, "to plunge into the night side of existence once in a while."[22] The romantic poets and thinkers, knowing that drastic actions often erupted from the night side, explored this dark realm as best they could. "The forces of desire remain hidden away from light," said Schiller.[23] Thomas Carlyle commented on how little was known about the hidden life of the mind. "The uttered part of a man's life bears to the unuttered, unconscious part a small, unknown proportion. He himself never knows it, much less do others."[24] Coleridge remarked on "that state of nascent existence in the twilight of imagination and just on the vestibule of consciousness."[25] One of the most influential works on the subject was G. H. von Schubert's *Ansichten von der Nachseite der Naturwissenschaft* (*The Night Side in the Natural Sciences*, 1808), a treatment of mystic forces, spells, sleepwalking, oracles, split personalities, second sight, and whatever else that could not be easily explained. Brandes called it "one of the most perverse [*forskruede*] works of its time,"[26] but it appealed to writers like Heinrich von Kleist, who based his fascinating play *The Prince of Homburg* on what Schubert had to say about somnambulism.

"The unconscious" was the term used by German writers like Schelling and Schiller to designate the obscured side of the psyche. The poet Jean Paul Friedrich Richter described "the kingdom of the *Unconscious*" as "at once a kingdom of the unfathomable and the immeasurable, which possesses and rules every human mind, makes the barren rich and pushes back their boundaries into the invisible."[27]

Sooner or later the time would come, as Joseph Weber said in 1816, when "the true night-side of nature would be illuminated, and the most inexplicable would be explained."[28] In 1869 a bright young philosopher, Eduard von Hartmann, argued that the unconscious was nothing but Hegel's absolute idea and Schopenhauer's world will in a more recognizable form. This study of what Hartmann called the metaphysic of the unconscious proved to be incredibly popular and inevitably controversial. In the six years after its publication there appeared fifty-eight works either opposing or supporting him.[29] As a cultural force in Germany, he was mentioned in the same breath as Bismarck and Wagner.[30] Thanks in large part to Hartmann, the concept of the unconscious was as familiar and as much discussed as the theory of evolution.

While Hartmann in Germany was treating the unconscious as essentially immaterial, Hippolyte Taine in France was arguing that the mind emerged along the path of zoological evolution.

"Beneath the ordinary sensations which we know by consciousness, there descends an indefinite series of analogous mental events. . . . This successive lowering which has its counterpart in the attenuation of the nervous system, leads us to the foot of the zoological scale, while connecting together, by a continuous sequence of intermediate links, the most rudimentary outlines and the highest combinations of the nervous system and the mental world."[31]

Haeckel saw that the evolutionary development of an animal tribe or phylum was repeated, roughly, in the development of any individual of that phylum. He called this the "fundamental law of organic revolution" and beginning in 1868 in his *History of Creation* made it central to his study of evolution. (It was first formulated by Fritz Müller in *Für Darwin*, 1864.) "The series of forms through which the individual Organism passes during its progress from the egg cell to its fully developed state is a brief, compressed reproduction of the long series of forms through which the animal ancestors of that organism . . . have passed from the earliest periods of so-called organic creation down to the present time."[32] Concisely formulated, ontogeny, the history of the development of the individual, recapitulates phylogeny. What transpired over thousands of years in the Darwinian scheme flashed by in the first ten or twenty years in the life of the individual.

Others quickly seized upon the fundamental law of organic evolution and applied it to the evolution of the individual as a social creature. The popular writer John Lubbock, after noting that the law of organic evolution was rapidly gaining ground among naturalists, compared the development of society from savagery to civilization to the development of a child into maturity. "The close resemblance in ideas, language, habits and character between savages and children," which has been regarded as a curious accident, is now recognized as an important truth.[33]

The substructure of *The Wild Duck* suggests that Ibsen was keeping up with these new ideas. In one of his preparatory notes for the play he wrote, "In becoming civilized, man undergoes the same changes as when a child grows up. Instinct weakens, but logical thought develops."[34] Hedwig, about to celebrate her fourteenth birthday, becomes the chief bearer of these ideas. She is on the threshold between childhood and adulthood. When she thinks about sacrificing the duck, she is standing just behind the door to the loft. That places her on the threshold between past and present, between primitive and civilized society, and between the conscious and the unconscious. Having invested so much symbolic meaning in the loft, Ibsen clearly wanted it to convey the complexity of motives that floated through Hedwig's mind. There could be no verbal expression, since the motives are half conscious, half instinctive, largely irrational, and all in a tumult.

Ibsen need not have read widely or deeply in the literature of the unconscious to cram so much meaning into that storage room or to bring himself up to date on the latest theories about the mind. A few standard works would have provided all he needed. Especially helpful would have been a work by his fellow Scandinavian Harald Høffding. Called *Psykologi i omrids* (*An Outline of Psychology*), published in 1882, it surveyed all the significant theories concerning the mind and gave a lot of space to theories about the unconscious. The image of the boundary between the conscious and the unconscious as a threshold is used repeatedly by Høffding. At one point he compares the unconscious mind to "a warehouse or storehouse where ideas are hidden until needed again,"[35] an analogy that would have caught Ibsen's eye. It was probably this image that transformed the storage room at Venstøp into a symbol of mankind's past. More significantly, Høffding adapts Haeckel's law of ontogeny, the recapitulation in the individual of the physical evolution of the race, to the evolution and development of ideas and feelings.

Figure 20. The loft in *The Wild Duck*. Design by Valdemar Gyllich, Copenhagen 1885.

"The fundamental forms and powers of the conscious mind have evolved from the use of them by the primal race under certain conditions. The thoughts and feelings that are typical for the human race are therefore a priori for the individual; that is, they cannot be fully explained by his or her experiences; these are conditioned in reverse by their basic origin. On the other hand, these feelings and emotions can be accounted for if one considers the whole race and the endless line of experiences that occurred in the course of evolution. What is a priori for the individual is a posteriori for the race."[36]

Dr. Relling understands that Hedvig is at a critical age, undergoing the onset of menstruation, and counsels Hjalmar and Gina against doing anything that might upset the child: "She may be getting all sorts of mischief into her head." Gina has already noticed that Hedwig is acting strangely, playing with fire in the kitchen. As a medical man, Relling would know about the dangers inherent in puberty. Maudsley said, "The great internal commotion produced in young girls at the time of puberty is well known to be an occasional cause of strange morbid feelings and extraordinary acts. . . . [The] irregularities of menstruation, always apt enough to disturb the mental equilibrium, may give rise to an outbreak of mania, or to extreme moral perversion, more afflicting to the patient's friends than mania, because seemingly willful. The stress of a great disappointment, or any other of the recognized causes of mental disease, will meet with a powerful co-operating cause in the constitutional predisposition."[37] Maudsley also noted the impulse to "set fire to property [that is] sometimes manifested by young women of average understanding at or after puberty, when they are undergoing the mental revolution which accompanies sexual evolution."[38]

Maudsley's concern is with girls who have inherited a predisposition to mental imbalance. That does not appear to be the case with Hedwig. However, being placed in Hedwig's position, hearing both her sympathetic and understanding friend Gregers and her adored father ask her to make a great sacrifice, would be enough to cause her to lose her mental equilibrium and to surrender to a wild impulse.

A Visit to Norway

After being denied a position at the University of Copenhagen, and faced with the hostility of the Danish press, Georg Brandes exiled himself to Germany, where he quickly established a reputation as a significant cultural critic. On July 3, 1882, he received an invitation from an anonymous association of men and women to deliver public lectures at the University of Copenhagen over a period of ten years, with an honorarium of four thousand kronor a year. (He was making more than this in Berlin; a skilled worker in Denmark made about one thousand kronor a year.) This reaching out to Brandes was a sign that the political winds were blowing in a different direction. Donations for the Brandes fund came from both liberals and conservatives.

Another sign of changing times was the establishment of the liberal Student Association (Studentersamfundet) in Copenhagen. Many members, perhaps as many as two hundred or three hundred, of the conservative Student Union (Studenterforening) indicated their willingness to join the new organization.[1] The two groups (these "student" groups were really alumni associations) welcomed Brandes's return to Denmark on February 20, 1883. Three days later he delivered his first lecture at the University of Copenhagen in a hall that seated two hundred (the largest lecture hall at the university). Those who got seats had to wait an hour for the doors to open. Some people in the crowd fainted. Brandes obligingly repeated the lecture a few days later.[2]

His triumphant return to Copenhagen and the university that had rejected him a dozen years earlier seemed at first to indicate not just a change in the wind but a shift in the political climate. However, the events that followed made Brandes's return to Denmark seem a bit like Napoleon's return from Elba. It only took a hundred days or so to reveal that the triumph of the liberals was more show than substance. Coming events cast their shadow before them, and in this instance it was the shadow of the Danish poet Holger Drachmann (1846–1908). In the autumn of 1882, in a lyrical piece, "To Something in Norway" ("Til Noget in Norge"), he in effect announced his abandonment of the liberal cause. A year later he denounced Brandes for introducing the new trends in literature to Denmark and especially for his advocacy of naturalism. Having rediscovered religion, he followed this up with a book-length broadside against the demoralization of modern culture, *Silhouettes from Travels at Home and Abroad* (*Skyggebilleder fra Rejser i Indland og Udland*). Brandes replied, commenting on the apostasy of his former comrade in arms by ridiculing the thirty-seven-year-old Drachmann as an old fogey. "He's got gout, he's all bald, he's his own grandfather."[3]

Ibsen agreed. In his notebook he jotted down, "Many doctrinaires little by little become their own grandfathers—Drachmann, e.g."[4]

In the January 1883 elections in Norway, 83 newly elected members of the Storting organized themselves as a union of the left. In the 1884 elections the left gained a number of seats in both the Danish and Norwegian parliaments. Brandes put his faith in an alliance of the workers and the students. His optimism was "naive," as he later put it.[5] What at first appeared to be a consolidation of liberal forces, both in politics and literature, soon turned into its opposite: a split in the ranks of the liberal forces. Their victory at the polls prompted the conservatives to regroup and reorganize. The number of conservative political associations grew from 100 in 1883 to 174 by the spring of 1884.[6] Brandes found the situation deplorable. The conservatives stuck together, while the left was divided, and consequently the right was always able to swing part of the left to its side.[7]

Brandes himself may have contributed to the disarray. In June 1884, at a meeting of liberal voters and politicians, he delivered an extemporaneous speech in which he declared that he was not a liberal, and not broad-minded, and not truly a democrat. Democracy, he said, was only a means to an end, and the end should be the enrichment of the cultural and intellectual life of Denmark, whether the source of this enrichment was native or foreign. An insular Denmark was like an old maid, infertile. These remarks were greeted with consternation; from then on many felt that Brandes really belonged to the right.[8]

True to his spontaneously expressed thoughts on that evening, Brandes developed in the following years into an "aristocratic radical," a term he applied to Ibsen. But 1884 and that particular audience were the wrong time and place to reveal his true position.

Ibsen's ambiguous position on matters political was similar to that of Brandes. "Zola is a democrat," he remarked in 1882, "but I'm an aristocrat."[9] He saw politics as class warfare, with those in power, a minority, very reluctant to cede many of their rights to the underprivileged majority. In Norway, the farmers were now in control, and the low opinion of them that informed the troll scenes in *Peer Gynt* had hardened with time into absolute conviction. He told Bjørnson that he could not find among Norwegian peasants "an atom more of real liberalism than is to be found among the ultramontane peasantry of the Tyrol.... No doubt the politically privileged class may acquire some new rights, some new advantages, but I cannot see that the nation, as a whole, or that the individual, gains very much by this. I admit, however, that in politics, too, I am a heathen. I do not believe in the emancipatory power of political measures; nor have I much confidence in the altruism and goodwill of those in power."

He then proceeded to spell out what he would advocate. "If I could have my way at home, then all the unprivileged should unite and form a strong, resolute, progressive party, whose program would include nothing but practical and productive reforms—a very wide extension of the suffrage, the statutory improvement of the position of women, the emancipation of national education from all kinds of medievalism, etc. I would give theoretical political questions a long rest; they are not of much consequence. If such a party were formed, the present party of the left would soon be seen for what it really is, and what it must be from its makeup—a center party of moderates."[10]

Ibsen's dim view of the liberalism of the left was confirmed in 1885 by the Kielland affair. The novelist Alexander Kielland applied for a government stipend, and though he was an established writer, his application became the subject of a serious debate in the Storting on June 10, 1885. Ibsen, accompanied by Bjørnson's son, attended the session, commenting, "Both sides defend their narrow views with great skill. Both sides have good speakers. But Norway is still a small country."[11] Although the Storting was dominated by liberals, the application was voted down, fifty-six to fifty-three, with Kielland's agnosticism alienating the farmers. This enraged Ibsen, who told Bjørnson's son that he wanted to stand with the young generation in Norway and to serve "as the pivot man on the left."[12]

Ibsen had just returned to Norway after having been away for eleven years, and he found the political climate very chilly. He found as many backs turned on him as arms opened to him. He had been forewarned by his wife, who had said in a letter that she was astonished by the degree to which he stood in bad odor with the party of the right.[13]

The liberals and radicals, however, were eager to welcome him. In Trondheim, the ancient capital of Norway, the workers' union (Arbeiderforening) organized an elaborate reception for him. He arrived on June 11. On June 14, at seven thirty, a large crowd gathered and, with a band and a men's chorus leading the way, marched to the hotel where Ibsen and his wife were staying. None of the pillars of society were in attendance. H. S. Kjaer, the union leader, spoke for his fellow workingmen.

"You have pictured the world in its naked reality, and society has learned from that that it has not treated as it should the little people, the unfortunate ones. The light that these times demand in order that the truth shall prevail has been spread by you over the nation, Herr Ibsen, as by no other person."

This welcoming speech was followed by hurrahs and the singing of a song composed for the occasion. Ibsen replied in a carefully prepared speech that, more than his other public utterances, revealed both how much he differed from and how much he agreed with the political left. He found that individual rights were not being safeguarded, and he feared that the attainment of real liberty was beyond the power of the present democratic government. "A ruling majority," he said, with a pointed reference to the Kielland affair, "does not grant the individual either freedom of belief or freedom of expression beyond a certain arbitrarily fixed limit."

The perplexing aspect of his political views lay in his distrust of democracy and majority rule. His position could be seen as elitist or monarchic.

> An element of *nobility* must enter into our national life, our administration, our representative bodies, and our press.
>
> Of course I am not thinking of a nobility of *birth*, nor of that of *wealth*, nor that of *knowledge*, nor even of *power* or talent. I am thinking of a nobility of *character*, of a nobility of will and spirit.
>
> Nothing else can make us free.
>
> This nobility that I hope will be granted to our nation will come to us from two sources. It will come to us from two groups that have not as yet been irreparably harmed by party pressure. It will come to us from our women and our workingmen.[14]

The full disclosure in this speech put him firmly, in the eyes of the conservatives, on the left, while the socialists embraced him as one of their own by playing down the aristocratic and elitist overtones of his antidemocratic utterances.

The Trondheim speech is the clearest expression of Ibsen's political views, which have often disappointed those who believe that democracy is self-evidently the best form of government. Consistently, throughout his career (at least after his flirtation with the workers' movement in 1849), he distrusted majority opinion, the great Bøyg of politics. He disdained freedom-mongering liberals, each of whom wanted his own special freedom while denying freedoms to others, as in the Kielland affair. On the other hand, Ibsen's elitism alienated Marxists and communists, who saw the nihilistic writer as a "petty bourgeois revolutionist," taking refuge behind vague concepts such as "the nobility of will and spirit" and preaching a moral law that is both inhuman and unrealizable, as in *Brand*.[15] To many students of Ibsen there is a feeling that in his pursuit of fame and honor, in his passion for knighthoods, he compromised himself seriously, turning himself into a Janus-faced, bemedaled Great Man. There is unquestionably some truth in this, but there is perhaps more truth in his assertion that he was always consistent in his political views. His spontaneous remarks in conversations are all of a piece and all in accord with what he told the workingmen in Trondheim.

"The worst thing one can do is become a member of a party."

"The people on the Norwegian left say they crave freedom—no, they crave only certain freedoms."

The freest people in the world were the Romans under the papacy, "because then each person could do exactly what he wanted." The peasants were "the least artificial, most natural people in the world."

The artist Marcus Grønvold jotted down these remarks,[16] and in 1888 Ibsen bought Grønvold's oil painting *Out of Work,* which pictured the miseries of the proletariat.[17]

To his biographer Henrik Jæger he said in 1887 that he shared the principles of the extreme left but could not join a party because in party politics friendship became more important than truth.[18] "The only natural society is one in which individuals gather together through their own inclinations."[19]

In 1880, upon hearing that in France the monks were being driven out of the monasteries: "Haven't I always said it?—the republicans are the most tyrannical of all. They have no respect for individual freedom. A republic is the state in which individual freedoms are least respected."

"The only ones who have my sympathy are nihilists and socialists. They want the whole thing, and are consistent."[20]

If the men of the left "don't make the workers' cause their own, they have betrayed their purpose."[21]

Years after the Trondheim speech he was still repeating its main theme. "Our purpose and our goal is not to celebrate triumphs but to ennoble the human mind through visions of beauty and revelations of the truth."[22]

"Norway is not the home of two million people but two million cats and dogs."[23]

In a dinner-table conversation in Sæby, Denmark, in the summer of 1886, Ibsen explained himself most clearly.

"I want nothing at all to do with politics!"

His wife exclaimed, "How can you say that, Henrik. Hardly a day goes by without you talking about politics."

"No. I want nothing to do with politics! I can't stand politicians. They are all so busy trying to seize power. But it is justice they should be working for, and for that I place my hopes in the workingmen and in the women, ahead of politicians."

His host interjected, "Yes, yes, but do you think, Herr Ibsen, that one can accomplish justice without having power?"

"No. But it is the natural power that the workers and the women possess that shall give society an equitable and just organization."[24]

The author Kristian Gloersen recorded some remarks that Ibsen made in 1882 in Rome, not direct quotations but paraphrases.

> The most essential thing was for each country quite rightly to provide everyone with a good breakfast. At home Captain Henry Heyerdahl was laughed at when he said this. They should not have; they revealed their own stupidity. . . .
>
> One should chop the heads off the bourgeoisie, just as a hundred years ago in France they chopped the heads off the aristocracy. No one in Norway who calls himself a liberal or a republican will offer anything he owns; he will sacrifice nothing in order for the lowest to be made equal to himself. When things get serious, he won't risk his life on the barricades.
>
> And there must be a revolution; all that we have now must go down, down, down! All that petty stuff they putter with has no meaning—lies and humbug, all of it!
>
> The right, you say—dear friend, I have nothing to do with people of that sort. They no longer count. They play no part in the story of what's to come. The only good they do is this: in the most fundamental way they undermine their own position and point out the easiest way through the ruins.
>
> That's why the reactionaries are our best comrades.[25]

In 1886 he spoke in a conversation of his contempt for majority rule and the tyranny of political parties in such sharp tones that the person recording the remarks felt obliged to paraphrase them rather than quote Ibsen's exact words.

> It will be a great misfortune for us if this confluence of parties and party leaders becomes a chronic illness in our country. The best thing in a nation is its personalities, personal experiences and personal convictions. What happens to these forces in the long run under the tyranny of parties? And it is only these forces that are capable of representing the nation and carrying it forward. It has nearly reached the point where many of our best men let themselves be hog-tied by the party commandos. Those who know best and are most capable of being leaders are under the whip of those who know least and are the least capable. This is an unhealthy situation, and it cannot possibly continue.[26]

Ibsen's visit to his homeland united the family. Sigurd Ibsen, now serving as Norwegian attaché in Stockholm, joined his mother and father for a journey down the Norwegian coast. Leaving Trondheim, they traveled a few miles south, passing through numerous fjords, to Molde, a town on the Romsdal fjord, the high mountains protecting the town from the cold northern winds. Its spectacular scenery, moderate climate, and colorful flowers, especially roses, had recently made it a popular resort, even attracting tourists from abroad. The Prince of Wales and William Gladstone came for a brief visit on August 26 and 27. The Ibsen family arrived there on July 7 for an extended stay, checking in at the fashionable Hotel Alexandra. Lorentz Dietrichson arrived at about the same time. There was a large reception for Ibsen on July 24 in the Grand Hotel. Among the first to greet him was Ludvig Daae, once a member of the Dutchmen circle, now a professor of history and a member of the editorial staff of the right-wing paper *Morgenbladet.* Daae was at Molde not to enjoy the scenery but to stump for the conservative cause. Knowing that Ibsen would be there, Carl Snoilsky and his wife came to see him, and stayed at the Alexandra Hotel from August 11 to 15.

It might have been the occasion for a sentimental reunion, Ibsen, Snoilsky, and Dietrichson meeting for drinks and pleasant conversation as they had done in 1864 and 1865 in Rome, when Ibsen had been writing *Brand.* But much had happened since then, and the three men never met together in Molde. Dietrichson, ultraconservative, had parted company with Ibsen over politics and art.

He avoided him as much as possible, claiming he did not wish to disturb the great man pondering his next play. Inevitably, in the small resort town, they could not avoid seeing each other on social occasions. Ibsen found in Dietrichson "a smallness of mind, a weakness of character, a cringing respect for other people's ideas and opinions, all of which could not help but affect me adversely."[27] Dietrichson's opinion of Ibsen was no higher. Now a professor of art history at the University of Christiania, Dietrichson was a deep-dyed conservative in both esthetics and politics. In 1882 he had delivered a lecture to the Student Association condemning naturalism as contributing to decadence in modern culture. In it he singled out *Ghosts* as a vivid example of the great falling-off of Ibsen's artistry. And Ibsen's speech in Trondheim would have further alienated Dietrichson.

Snoilsky and Ibsen, on the other hand, spent many pleasant hours together in Molde. They had met at least twice in the intervening years, but since their last meeting, in 1877, Snoilsky had become a changed man. The story of what had happened to him provided excellent dramatic material, and Ibsen soon made use of it.

Although Snoilsky came from a distinguished Swedish family, he felt he was a weak representative of its heroic traditions. He grew into a shy young man, careful not to offend by revealing his antipathies. Kristoffer Manderström, the minister of foreign affairs (ridiculed by Ibsen in *Peer Gynt*), found a place for the tactful youth in the diplomatic corps. At twenty-six he married a rich heiress, Countess Hedvig Piper, and from that point on he was a divided man—like Ibsen. He had

Figure 21. Carl Snoilsky, 1887.

a fine talent as a lyrical poet and published his first volume of lyrics when he was twenty. His wife, a socialite, took no interest in his poetry. For some years he pursued a double career as poet and diplomat. He moved upward from one office to another, while his volumes of poetry consistently won the praise of the critics. In 1876 the young poet was elected to the Swedish Academy.

But he was a man fighting against himself, and the struggle was taking its toll. His life as a refined aristocrat, going to social gatherings, poring over his collections of fine books and rare stamps and coins, not only bored him but plagued him. To judge from portraits, his physical appearance changed remarkably from 1869 to 1875. In 1879 the volcanic forces that had been building up deep within him erupted. He confessed to his friend Gustaf Klemming, chief clerk at the national library in Stockholm, that he

> could no longer endure a shadowy life of lies—a cowardly, miserable life a thousand times worse than death, and I had already some years ago decided to make a change, one way or another. Of weakness and vacillation I have had enough in my time. Now I hungered to redeem myself in my own eyes in a way *I* could understand. I knew that a great crisis was brewing in my life. . . . From the beginning it was absurd to suppose that I could always live a routine life in

> our hidebound and prejudiced society. Every day I felt it slipping off me more and more, this mask of indifference and materiality that I had carefully applied to my real face. The storm came, and the mask crumbled. But believe me, the price is high. I know how it feels to end a life, a wasted one. I have heard the funeral bells tolling—and seen the grass grow on my own grave.[28]

His divorce from his wife was finalized November 18, 1879. He returned her dowry of 180,000 kronor, resigned his position in the Department of Foreign Affairs, and exiled himself to France and Italy. In Marseilles, on February 5, 1880, he married a Norwegian woman, Countess Ebba Ruuth, a widow, who dabbled in writing, A son was born to the couple in November. (The family relationships behind this marriage are rather complicated: Snoilsky married his father-in-law's widow.)

Snoilsky and Ebba often visited the Ibsens in Rome in the early 1880s. Encouraged by his wife, he mined a new vein of poetry. His social conscience found expression in poems like "The Servant Brother" ("Den tjenanden brodern," 1883), which addressed those who live in comfort and do little to help the lower classes. This and some other poems, such as "Aphrodite and the Grinder" ("Afrodite och Sliparen"), with the same tendency may have been written in response to Georg Brandes, who chided Snoilsky for standing aloof from the important issues of the day. In that same year he abjured his earlier work and dismissed poetry that exists for itself, advocating a poetry that does not disdain to live the life of our time, a poetry "that above all has a word for the weak and the unfortunate in this world, which is *not* the best of all worlds, however pleasant it may seem to many."[29]

But his sincere desire to advance the cause of the working class was thwarted by his heritage, his life of privilege, and his cultural background. He had friends in both camps, King Oscar among the conservatives and Georg Brandes among the radicals. Incapable of speaking the language of the proletariat and distrusted by his own class, he had no firm base in either camp. His refined upbringing and his naturally mild disposition made him wish for a reconciliation of the warring parties, while all the time fearing that the world as he knew it was coming to an end. However much he admired Ibsen, he was deeply disturbed by *Ghosts*, which offered no hope for Christian charity and human love. "Truly, it's a pity that such a genius should only tear down, never build up."[30] For the same reason, he could not appreciate Strindberg's genius.

When he met Ibsen in Molde, Snoilsky was a controversial figure and had been for some time. His divorce from his first wife was in itself cause for scandal, but when she died of consumption three years after their separation, he was accused by his enemies of hastening her death. A poem he wrote in 1885 based on Swedish history, "The White Lady" ("Hvita frun"), reveals that his tender conscience suffered from the knowledge that he had caused her grief in seeking his own happiness.

At Molde, Ibsen and Snoilsky clearly enjoyed each other's company. Ibsen once said that no one had ever charmed him as much as Snoilsky.[31] A woman who was part of his circle described him as having "aristocratically lofty and melancholy features. But when he relaxed, his smile was enchanting, his eyes sparkled, and a jest played about his lips."[32]

Snoilsky and his wife, whom Ibsen praised as a broad-minded woman, spent most of the day with the Ibsens. He found the usually gruff playwright warm, communicative, smiling, and wrote a fine poem, "A Memory From Molde" ("Ett mine från Molde"), giving his impression of the man.

> I remember him well, the enigmatic brooder
> Midst the mountains and the lowering sky.
> Nor can I forget how warmly he smiled
> Midst the roses in the city of flowers.[33]

Although Ibsen, the closet radical, insisted that he belonged to no political party, the liberal forces felt, rightly, that he was closer to them than to the conservatives. On September 26 the naturalist painter Fritz Thaulow (Paul Gauguin's brother-in-law) proposed to the Student Association of the University of Christiania that its members should honor the writer with a torch-lit parade to the Grand Hotel before he left Norway. The proposal was well timed. Many of the radical members were present for the discussion and on this occasion outnumbered the conservatives. Lorentz Dietrichson, who had been elected president of the organization the previous spring and who had done his best to avoid Ibsen in Molde, had to convey the invitation to Ibsen, which he did on September 28. Well aware that the officers of the association did not hold him in high esteem, Ibsen took the invitation to be merely a courteous gesture. He said he did not want a public demonstration and that he had already declined a similar invitation from the workers' union in Bergen.

Dietrichson could have let the matter end there. But, speaking for the members of the Student Association, he said they would be sorely disappointed and chagrined by Ibsen's refusal. In response Ibsen said something—exactly what cannot be retrieved—that would turn a minor social contretemps into a political controversy. The gist of it was that he did not care to hear the students of this conservative association shouting hurrahs at his departure from Norway.

Dietrichson immediately notified the Student Association of Ibsen's response by posting it on the bulletin board. At about the same time, Ibsen sat down and wrote a letter to the Christiania Labor Union, declining its request to honor him with a public demonstration. "It has been a necessity in my life's work," he said, "to be independent and not to partake of events that seem like celebrations."[34] On September 30 he left Christiania for Copenhagen.

In the meantime one of the students, Ove Rode, had called on him, seeking an explanation for Ibsen's regret. At the next scheduled meeting of the association, on October 3, Dietrichson formally reported on his meeting with Ibsen. Then Rode rose to speak, saying he had been authorized to explain Ibsen's response. Ibsen felt that, coming from the governing board of the association, the invitation was hardly an honor. If this body truly wanted to honor him, it would dismiss the board and elect a liberal group of officers in its place. If that happened, Ibsen would gladly accept the homage of the students.

Furious, Dietrichson sent Ibsen a telegram on October 5, accusing the playwright of duplicity. He had told Dietrichson that he did not want a torch-lit parade in Christiania any more than he had wanted one in Bergen, while telling Rode that he rejected the invitation because the board of officers was conservative. Ibsen fired back with a telegram the next day. "Your account of my refusal has been incomplete. What I said in part was: I don't wish to hear students hurrahing me because I was leaving the country. My real meaning [*Hjertensmening*] was: I have nothing in common with the association under your leadership. Tell the students that."[35]

What had been seething but suppressed in Molde now burst out into public view. When the association met the following Saturday, October 10, Dietrichson gave his version of events. He said he had not reported Ibsen's words about cheering students because they were uttered in passing and with a smile. Then he went on to accuse Ibsen of evasiveness, of lacking the courage of his convictions, of failing to live up to the ideals of Brand. He accused him of being a little man in his behavior, narrow-minded in his views, and tyrannical in disposition.

"No, my friends, a thousand times no! This is not the voice of Henrik Ibsen. Don't we recognize it? It is the spirit of compromise that speaks to us, disguised as the voice of Ibsen."[36]

The sense of the meeting was to approve Dietrichson's speech, after which the members gathered around the punch bowl, as was customary. There Dietrichson put his stamp on the evening by reciting a poem he had composed for the occasion. Without mentioning Ibsen, the poem accused him of betraying his own principles and ended: "The Norwegian student feels both anger and sadness / Whenever he sees a star fall." The clear allusion was to the poem in which Andreas Munch had compared the author of *Ghosts* to a fallen star.

On October 12 Dietrichson wrote a long letter to Ibsen, thoughtfully phrased, as gracious as possible, expressing his regret that a long friendship had come to such a sad end, but leaving no room for a rapprochement. He remarked that

Ibsen had insulted the students and that as head of the organization, he—Dietrichson—had to defend them.[37]

Dietrichson's speech and Munch's poem were published, and the newspapers reported on the events. Dietrichson had hit Ibsen where he was most vulnerable. Ibsen had to defend his integrity both as a person and as an artist. On October 23 he composed a very long letter, one of the longest in his collected correspondence, in which he set forth his version of all that had happened. First, he had to explain that he had been misunderstood by the young student who interviewed him. He did not tell him that he hoped the party of the right, which constituted the majority in the student league, would unseat Dietrichson and elect a liberal central committee. What he had actually said was that it would please him to see the minority grow strong enough to unseat the conservatives.

Then he had to respond to Dietrichson's slur on his character.

> It is . . . quite understandable that Mr. Lorentz Dietrichson should at this particular time have seized on an opportunity to make a speech against me, especially since I was absent. And I consider that his introducing into the speech all kinds of low innuendos and charges was particularly well timed and opportune. It seems to have pleased the Student Union so much that the speech is recognized by it as an expression of the feelings of the union in this matter. . . .
>
> Neither the union nor its president will succeed in doing me any enduring harm, except that this episode will leave behind a certain feeling that will remain with me for the rest of my life. I shall be the same man I was the day before Mr. Lorentz Dietrichson's assault. During the whole course of this torchlight-procession affair, I have had no opportunity of proving myself either "small" or "great," either "narrow-minded" or "broad-minded." The "spiritual tyranny" which has been imputed to me is an empty phrase, and my behavior during the whole affair has not been at any point (nor could it have been) a contradiction of my "theory" or my writings. . . .
>
> I demand that on the first Saturday after its arrival—previous announcement having been made—this whole letter shall be read from the same place in the hall of the union from which I was insulted, without any provocation on my part, by the president of the union and with the approbation of the majority of its members.[38]

In the meantime, the liberal members, incensed by Dietrichson's behavior, proposed sending a letter to Ibsen, expressing their admiration for the poet and their solidarity with his views. The proposal was resoundingly approved on October 16, with only 50 nays being recorded in the assemblage of 850.

The radical members of the association drafted the message to the great man, stressing the support he had among the younger generation, and the draft was approved by a vote of 650 to 50. On November 12 the liberal members seceded from the association and formed the Liberal Student Union (Den frisinnede Studenterforening), electing as its officers Fritz Thaulow and Christian Krohg, both painters, and the historian Ernst Sars. Elected as honorary members were Ibsen, Jonas Lie, and the feminist Camilla Collett.

Although the episode may seem like a tempest in a teapot, more than sensitive egos were involved. Ever since the publication of *Ghosts*, Dietrichson had been actively engaged in a campaign against naturalism in the arts, and Thaulow and Krohg were the leading naturalist painters in Norway. For the conservative forces, naturalism was almost as alarming a specter as atheism.

On October 3, in Copenhagen, at the same time that the student league in Christiania was meeting to discuss the Ibsen affair, Brandes invited Ibsen and his wife to dinner, and then persuaded Ibsen to attend a banquet for freshmen given by the Student Association. His surprise visit delighted the students, and Ibsen enjoyed himself, staying until one in the morning. Harald Høffding, the philosopher, toasted him in a warm speech. The fifty-seven-year-old Ibsen, his face already blotchy and florid,[39] responded, saying, "I hope to be a freshman all my life. The day when I am not, I would not consider life worth living."[40]

Brandes picked up on the theme. "It is comforting to see that this man . . . doesn't go backward. The other evening, when I left Ibsen, I thought, what if he died? It struck me that Scandinavian literature, yes, all Nordic culture, would be decapitated in one stroke. So let us hope that he will live on and remain what he is: the great threat and the great benefactor to the Nordic countries."[41]

ROSMERSHOLM

Ibsen and his wife had ventured to spend the summer in Norway to determine whether or not they should resettle there. His experiences disappointed him. He said, "I always felt that when someone was walking behind me, he wanted to stick a knife in my back."[1] "Never have I felt myself further from understanding and sympathizing with the way my Norwegians carry on [the *Thun und Treiben* of my Norway]," he told Brandes. "Never have I been more repelled. Never more disgusted."[2] Two years later he still felt alienated from his homeland. "It would be quite impossible for me to settle for good in Norway. Nowhere would I feel less at home than there. A man of some intellectual development can no longer be satisfied with the old conception of nationality."[3]

The political strife and the hostile reception given him by the conservatives made him appreciate Germany all the more; there he was widely recognized and admired as a writer with strong socialist sympathies. He returned to Munich, one of Europe's principal cultural centers, where he could be kept abreast of the latest ideas and enjoy the company of notable writers spanning the literary spectrum: at one end the idealist Paul Heyse, at that time one of Germany's most highly esteemed poets and novelists; and at the other the disputatious Georg Conrad, who in 1885 had just founded the journal *Die Gesellschaft,* which became the chief forum for naturalism. For the first time Ibsen bought furniture for his apartment; up to now he had lived abroad in furnished flats.

He did not, however, return from Norway empty-handed. When he bade farewell to Molde, he told the local choral society that he intended to write a play based on his days in their charming town. The following February he told Snoilsky that he was "engrossed in writing a new play that I have been thinking about for a long time, and for which I made careful studies during my visit to Norway last summer."[4] By June 1886 he had the first draft ready.

He had left Munich with ideas for a quite different play germinating in his mind, a play that would have the sea, the source of life, as a central motif. As in so many of Ibsen's works, this one would continue ideas that had been broached in the immediately preceding work. Central to *The Wild Duck* was the loft that held relics, both real and symbolic, of humanity's past, a past that extended into the depths of the sea. In his new play Ibsen intended to venture into those depths once again. While in Molde he spent many hours gazing into the waters.

The present, however, overwhelmed the past, and his involvement in Norwegian politics, especially the unpleasantness with Dietrichson and his meetings with Count and Countess Snoilsky, drove from his mind the play he had been contemplating. Instead, as with *A Doll's House,* a superb subject was handed to him as he sat conversing with the Snoilskys. Here was a drama ready for the taking. All he had to do was Ibsenize it. The hero of this drama would be an aristocrat with a social conscience. Like Ibsen, Snoilsky wanted to raise up the laborer, make an aristocrat of him. But by betraying his class, he would be snubbed by old friends. Those who knew Snoilsky recognized him immediately in Ibsen's portrait of Johannes Rosmer, a striking likeness not only in personality but also in political stance. Like Rosmer, Snoilsky was a man of quiet charm and gentility, and an aristocrat with a delicate social conscience.

In writing *Rosmersholm,* Ibsen could invest much of himself in Snoilsky because their political beliefs were strikingly similar. Ibsen shared with him a longing for a revolution within the human being, a spiritual change that would be the foundation of social change. What Snoilsky wrote in a letter to a close friend in 1883 was completely in harmony with Ibsen's thoughts in 1885 and 1886, though Snoilsky struck a more optimistic tone.

> I truly believe that whatever in our heritage holds a germ of new life, of renewal, will not die, no matter how violent the deluge.... The best, the eternal—I'm thinking first of all of Christianity—shall rise up, cleansed, from the new Flood. The churchly forms of belief, for example, may die, but not the divine element. The same is true in politics. There too shall a new and more just order gradually develop from all the strife, which may be coming. Still, it is not blind chance that governs. Even when it seems as if the world has gone mad, there is cast abroad that seed which future generations will be thankful for. Take the French Revolution of 1789. Out of its orgies there did arise a truer, nobler, freer, and more fortunate world, even in those countries that seem to keep their distance from the great movements. All the advances of humankind, both spiritual and material, can, as far as our century is concerned, trace their lineage back to those principles of 1789, which got rid of so much tyranny, cliquishness, and rigid thinking.[5]

In *Rosmersholm,* all the talk about the ennoblement of mankind, which is a recurrent theme, is a shorthand expression of the fundamental beliefs of Snoilsky as voiced in letters such as this and by Ibsen in his speech to the workers in Trondheim.[6]

Anyone familiar with Ibsen's experiences in Norway in the summer of 1885 can see how he made use of them in his new play. In *Rosmersholm,* Rector Kroll, headmaster of a boys' school, finds to his dismay that some of the advanced students have organized themselves into a club of radicals. Dietrichson faced a similar situation when part of the Student Association broke ranks and sent a welcoming delegation to Ibsen.

Ibsen quickly saw that the political drama would amount only to another *Enemy of the People,* and that the ideas stirred up in his mind by meeting the Snoilskys centered on the personal, psychological drama. What could have caused Snoilsky to make the final, decisive break with his past, to divorce his wife and publicly align himself with the workingman? It surely must have been Ebba Ruuth, the other woman, the one Ibsen chatted with at Molde, and whom he found engagingly broad-minded. Once she became the driving force in the emerging drama, Ibsen saw that his thoughts about the unconscious and the depths of the sea would allow him to make the Snoilsky story, which on the surface was a simple social scandal, into a profound study of human motivations. In other plays, he had absorbed the great ideas of the philosophers and scientists, adapting them to suit his purposes. In *Rosmersholm,* however, he seems—knowingly—to have gone beyond the latest ideas in the field of psychology and to have given dramatic form to a theory that would not be formulated by psychologists until some years later. Looked upon as a thought experiment, and as a layman's investigation of areas reserved for specialists, *Rosmersholm* is perhaps Ibsen's most stunning achievement.

It is also perhaps his murkiest work, with one mystery encoiled in another. The immediately accessible story is a melodrama in which Rebecca West, a strong-willed woman, finds herself deeply drawn to Johannes Rosmer, an older married man. He is youthful in looks, delicate and charming, while she is a modern emancipated woman, who is infatuated with him at first sight. Determined to have what she desires, she gets rid of his wife and takes her place as manager of the Rosmer estate. How she accomplishes this is the first mystery, which is solved in the third act of this four-act play. Yet when Rosmer proposes to take her as his second wife, she rejects the offer. Therein lies the second and far more puzzling mystery. Why would this ambitious woman, who had few scruples about removing Rosmer's wife from the scene, refuse to marry the man whom she loves passionately, and for whom she committed a murder, or something like it?

A guilty conscience—that would appear to be the answer, and in the hands of a lesser dramatist, nothing more would need to be said. But Ibsen insists on examining the very concept of conscience and in the process proposes a theory about its origin. In conventional melodrama, the villainess would simply and inexplicably suffer qualms of conscience, and her inner torments would require no more explanation than her willingness to murder would. Ibsen, instead, shows how a strongly motivated woman like Rebecca can be conscienceless in furthering her own selfish aims and conscience-stricken once she has gained them.

Emile Zola in his *Thérèse Raquin*, first a novel in 1868, then a play in 1873, had offered a naturalist explanation for what good Christians thought was a God-given conscience. Thérèse and her lover drown her husband and appear to have committed a perfect crime. The police cannot possibly make a case against them. Eventually, however, they punish themselves, not because their consciences give them no peace of mind, but out of fear that one will betray the other to the police. They are afraid of each other, not of some supernatural agency. The play was soon recognized as a landmark in naturalist drama and subjected to a rigorous critique by Louis Desprez in his fine survey of the serious contemporary French drama, *L'Evolution naturaliste*, published in 1884 (and immediately snapped up by Strindberg).

Although Ibsen's approach is equally naturalistic in denying the influence of a heavenly power implanting a conscience in the unborn child, it does not attribute Rebecca's actions to the possibility of being caught. She has committed a truly perfect crime and has no fear of either God or the law; yet she kills herself. Her suicide is not an act of expiation, at least not in the ordinary sense. She kills herself not out of remorse for what she has done; her suicide is a sacrifice and an immolation.

The path to the waterfall in which she drowns herself is like a labyrinth, extremely difficult to follow, yet it forms the main plot of the drama. Ibsen places extraordinary demands on his audience, with the result that on the whole the play did not fare well in the theater, where audiences could not take time to ponder the subtleties of the story, although it was well received in Berlin. Even a dedicated and insightful actress like Eleanora Duse failed to discern the principal through-line in the complicated plot. At the end of act one, Rosmer and Rebecca, obviously in love with each other, bid each other good night. She asks, "Are you going upstairs so early tonight?" He replies, "Tonight as usual." And she says, "Good night, and sleep well."

"At these words," said Duse, "the whole house broke out in a storm of laughter. This emotional coolness struck the audiences in Rome as so funny that I did not dare to perform the play very often."[7]

As an Italian, Duse attributed the response to the differences between southern and Nordic temperaments. But the Italian audiences may not have been at fault. Duse probably failed to set up the scene properly. Writing in 1905, James Huneker observed that "not a half-dozen actresses on the globe have grasped the complex skeins of Rebecca West's character, and grasping them have been able to send across the footlights the shimmering music of her soul. Thus far Scandinavian women have best interpreted her to the satisfaction of the poet. The Italians are too tragic, the French too histrionically brilliant; it is a new virtuosity, a new fingering of the dramatic keyboard, that is demanded."[8]

If the groundwork is laid properly, the audience response at the end of act one should be one of curiosity: what is the barrier between Rebecca and Rosmer that keeps them from going to bed together? Even greater curiosity should be aroused at the end of act two, when Rebecca rejects Rosmer's marriage proposal. The audience should react as Rosmer himself does. Thunderstruck, he says to himself, "What—is—this?"

A year rich in incident has preceded this moment, and what happened in that year, and the years before that, has to be pieced together from scattered remarks in all the conversations that follow. Here Ibsen employs what is often called the retrospective technique. He was the unquestioned master of it, the greatest since Sophocles, and in *Rosmersholm* he stretched the technique to its breaking point, exceeding the bounds of theatrical propriety, and placing excessive demands on audiences.

He begins the action very late in the long series of events, filling in the past bit by bit. The information that the audience hears moves on two tracks simultaneously, one carrying the story forward in the present, the other bringing the past to light. It was a technique perfectly suited to his purposes. He wanted to make Rebecca, and the audience with her, become gradually aware of memories from her early years, memories that she has repressed, images and impressions that are forced from her unconscious under the pressure of Rosmer's changing relationship with her. From the theatrical point of view, however, the problem with this *dévoilement,* this dredging up of the past, is that it is almost as difficult for the audience to follow as it is painful for Rebecca to experience. As theatrical fare, *Rosmersholm* is too rich to be digested without some preliminary commentary. Reading the play affords a different kind of experience, surely one of the most fascinating in the annals of creative writing. By turning the pages back and forth to see hidden connections, the reader can function like a psychoanalyst reviewing his notes. The most helpful suggestion for a reader is the one Ibsen gave to the actress who created the part of Rebecca in Christiania. "The only piece of advice I can give you is to read closely the whole play over and over again and carefully observe what the other persons say about Rebecca."[9]

Hermann J. Weigand in his *The Modern Ibsen,* a commentary that occupies the same place in Ibsen criticism as A. C. Bradley's in Shakespeare studies—both being consummate psychological investigations—says of Rebecca that "no other character of Ibsen's creation ... puts such obstacles in the way of vivid intuition. Time and again, after one has fairly caught the elusive meaning of one of her cryptic phrases, the situation yet fails to be lighted up so brightly that one can see her every contour.... From act to act our conception of her requires revising, as she removes one veil after another from her past. Even her confessions, themselves but further manifestations of her complex self, do not provide us with a ready-made synthetic picture of her personality; it is we who must ourselves create this synthesis by balancing her every word and her every act against one another, making allowance, moreover, for the subjective bias which attaches to every individual's interpretation of his own actions."[10] In his preface, Weigand says that "a more fascinating or grateful task than the analytical recreation of the situations of these dramas and the characters that live in them can not be imagined.... I had the feeling of being embarked on a voyage of discovery; again and again I experienced the thrill of discovering psychological relationships and subtle workings of subconscious impulses that at first I had not even suspected."[11]

Rebecca West came from a remote town in northern Norway. When her mother died, she was adopted and raised by Dr. West, a ship's doctor and a radical thinker. When he moved south, he brought Rebecca with him. She had heard that Johannes Rosmer had in his youth come under the influence of Ulrick Brendel, a freelance expounder of highly original ideas, just as she herself had. She imagined meeting Rosmer and working with him, and through Rector Kroll, the headmaster of a boys' school and once Johannes's tutor, she found a position at Rosmersholm. An ambitious and intelligent woman, she soon became virtually the manager of the estate.

Johannes Rosmer was the scion of the most distinguished family in the district, whose portraits adorn the set in act one. Reared by a tyrannical father, a major in the army and a severe and intimidating disciplinarian, Johannes was a quiet, unsmiling, obedient child. After finishing his schooling, he became a clergyman and married Beata, Rector Kroll's sister.

As in so many of Ibsen's plays, the two principal characters are depicted as opposites. Rebecca is a morally uninhibited woman, beyond good and evil, a Nietzschean before Nietzsche. She was raised in the heathen north, a place supposedly on the frontier of civilized standards. "When I came down here from Finmark—along with Dr. West—it was as if a great, wide new world was opening up before me. The doctor had taught me all sorts of things. All the scraps of knowledge about life that I knew in those days."[12] In contrast, Rosmer's father would not hear of any new ideas in his house, and he repressed any independence of spirit that might have existed in his son.

That was the situation when Rebecca met Rector Kroll and his sister Beata. Her youth and vigor enchanted them both, and she was welcomed at Rosmersholm. There she quickly fell under the spell of Rosmer's quiet charm, and before long she saw herself as forming a partnership with him, in which her political ambitions and his social position would make an effective combination. She began to imagine a Rosmersholm without a Beata. Lacking moral scruples and possessing a strong will to power, Rebecca let her desires become a reality.

If Rosmer and Beata had been a happily married couple, nothing would have come of Rebecca's dreams. But the marriage had been a failure from the beginning, and when Beata proved infertile, all that kept the couple together was custom and tradition. The presence of Rebecca, young, lively, and energetic, shattered the bonds of the marriage. Beata saw that her husband was attracted to Rebecca, as she herself had been at first, and she noticed how he was increasingly influenced by her radical views. Desperately seeking to hold on to him by conceiving a child, Beata became insatiable in her sexual demands. She displayed all the symptoms, the wild, aberrant behavior described by the eminent Dr. Maudsley as characteristic of the insanity attendant upon the cessation of menstruation.[13] Johannes turned in revulsion from her. In a further attempt to hold on to him, she sought to provoke a scandal by putting in the hands of Peter Mortensgård, the opportunistic editor of a liberal newspaper, a letter in which she hints at Rosmer's infatuation with Rebecca. When she came to believe that Rebecca was pregnant with Rosmer's child, she resolved to sacrifice herself for her husband's sake and, in a nearly demented state, threw herself into the waterfall on the grounds of Rosmersholm.

Rosmer knew why she had killed herself, and at the beginning of the play he cannot shake off the thought that he was indirectly responsible for her death. (Those in the know would see the similarity to Snoilsky.) During the past year, he has avoided the bridge over the rapids. His guilty conscience is for Rebecca an unexpected consequence of her plans, in which she saw Rosmer marching into the political arena to take an active part there. When he hesitates, she compels him in the presence of Kroll to declare that he has joined the liberal forces.

To save Rosmer from himself, to rid him of his guilt, Rebecca confesses that it was she who drove Beata to her death. In an extraordinary scene, the technical climax of the drama (the end of act three in a four-act play), Rebecca relates how through insinuations and half-formed thoughts, she made Beata believe that she was pregnant with Rosmer's child. She calmly tells Rosmer that she had to choose between his life and Beata's. Without laying any plans, she proceeded in a half-conscious state, taking advantage of circumstances as they arose.

"Do you think I acted cold-bloodedly, calculatingly? I wasn't then the person I am now, telling you this. And, anyway, there are two kinds of will in us, I mean that. I wanted Beata out of the way. One way or another. But I didn't believe that it would really happen. With each step that I dared to take, it was as if something within me cried out: No further! Not a step more! And yet I *could not* let it be. I had to, had to go just a little bit further. Just one little bit! And then one more—always just one more. And then it happened. That's how such things come about."[14]

Strindberg, who kept abreast of all the new developments in psychology, added the suicide of Beata to his list of what he labeled "soul-murders," in which mind and spirit are fatally destroyed through the power of suggestion.[15] Audiences found it the more comprehensible part of the play, and most of the critics and commentators focused their attention on it. Typical is Julius Brand, who in the German journal for naturalism, *Die Gesellschaft,* called *Rosmersholm* "a drama of suggestion."[16] Rebecca's confession leads directly to the final scene, in which she must atone for her crime by hurling herself into the torrent as Beata did. It provides the essential link in the chain of events that culminates in the double suicide of Rosmer and Rebecca.

And yet its easy comprehensibility diverted attention from a more extraordinary revelation in the play, a revelation that comes slowly and only with a very close reading of the text.

Just as Rebecca fell under Rosmer's spell, so he came under hers. At first she was his comrade, a source of comfort as his wife's mental condition worsened. She brightened his days, and he took a new lease on life. Still, he could not overcome his guilt feelings, and Rebecca was compelled to reveal her part in Beata's death. The result of this confession was cruelly ironic: instead of dispersing the doubts in Rosmer's mind, she destroyed his dream of ennobling human society. It became a broken dream when he saw that passion and the aggressive instincts were operative. They brought about action, true, but it was a damaging and malignant action, while the civilizing force, with conscience a crucial part of it, represented by the Rosmersholm tradition inhibited action. Rebecca eliminated Beata out of her passion for Rosmer, her desire to possess him, whereas Beata sacrificed herself for the sake of Rosmer's happiness. Rebecca now sees that her efforts to radicalize him were misdirected and counterproductive. After hearing her confession, Rosmer joins forces with the conservative Rector Kroll.

"The Rosmer philosophy of life," she says, "ennobles. But . . . it kills happiness." Here she anticipates Freud and his view of the dilemma of modern man. In his *Civilization and Its Discontents,* he said his intention was "to represent the sense of guilt as the most important problem in the evolution of culture, and to convey that the price of progress is paid for by forfeiting happiness through the heightening of the sense of guilt."[17] That statement might serve as epigraph to Ibsen's play.

Figure 22. Sophie Reimers as Rebecca West. Christiania Theater, 1887.

What was going on in Rosmer's mind during the year before the play begins must have been very similar to Snoilsky's experience when he resolved to be true to himself and divorced his first wife. But no more than Snoilsky did Rosmer know his true self. He was not made for the rough give-and-take of politics; he can be no more than a figurehead, a front man, as Kroll well knows.

After talking to Kroll and his friends, Rosmer realizes that "the work of ennobling the minds of men is not for me."[18] His collapse under a little social pressure could scarcely come as a surprise to Rebecca. From the beginning she would have seen this gentle soul as her cat's-paw. But her sense of him changed as she gradually succumbed to his refinement and graciousness. She now saw their relationship as that of two equal comrades, her ruthlessness complementing his gentleness.

The idea that a man and a woman might live together as comrades, as true partners, rather than as husband and wife—with the implication that in marriage woman served man's needs—was a hotly debated subject when Ibsen wrote *Rosmersholm.* It had flared up after *A Doll's House:* the final scene there suggested that the very basis of marriage had to be changed in order for women to find their own true nature. The so-called morality controversy (*Sædelighedsfejde*) was reaching the boiling point in 1886. Strindberg had argued for women's rights in some short stories in 1884 and would satirize the whole notion of comradeship in his 1887 comedy *Comrades.* Brandes and Bjørnson bombarded each other with plays and articles that would end in a rupture between them that was never to be healed.[19]

In *Rosmersholm* comradeship proves to be only a phase in a quickly changing relationship. While Rebecca comes to believe that she and Johannes can join together as equal partners in their great work, he begins to feel increasingly attracted to Rebecca as a woman, not merely as a fellow worker and comrade in arms. Finally he proposes marriage to her in a scene that is as startling to her as it should be to the audience. Speechless for a moment, she cries out with joy, but after this impulsive outburst she gains control of herself and says, coldly, "Don't bring that up again. I will never be your wife."[20] This strange volte-face received little attention from the commentators until Freud discussed it. W. Berteval (*Le Théâtre d'Ibsen*) makes no mention of it. Hjalmar Hjorth Boyesen (*A Commentary on the Works of Henrik Ibsen*) does not appear to understand it. Henry Rose (*Henrik Ibsen: Poet, Mystic and Moralist* [New York, 1913], 67) reads the play as about a bad strain of character in Rebecca without any further explanation. Bernard Shaw (*The Quintessence of Ibsenism* [London, 1891]) ignores it. Even the usually astute Huneker (*Iconoclasts*) is silent on the subject.

Yet without that scene the transition in Rebecca from the aggressive and amoral Valkyrie who first entered the Rosmer household to the spiritually crippled woman who is willing to pay for her deeds by committing suicide is incomprehensible. One of the extraordinary tasks that Ibsen set for himself in *Rosmersholm* was to show or describe step by step a profound metamorphosis of character. Drama is not the best medium for doing this. The conventions of melodrama may allow for instant conversions, but serious drama does not, unless through the artifice of a *deus ex machina*. Transformations take time, and drama is short of that. Even Shakespeare in the four thousand lines of *Hamlet* lets the great change in his hero take place offstage. By contrast, Ibsen provides his audience—an extremely attentive audience, it must be said—with what it needs to account for the change in Rebecca from amoral adventuress to self-sacrificing expiator.

The benign influence of Johannes Rosmer goes only a short way toward accounting for the emergence of something like a conscience in Rebecca. Finding in him a complement to her own nature actually led to her crime: she had to have him to herself. Furthermore, her bold, almost brazen confession in act three might be seen as having a selfish motive: by freeing Rosmer from his sense that he was responsible for Beata's suicide, she thinks he will become her partner in carrying on the great work of reforming society. Neither of these explanations can carry any weight. She tells Rosmer in act two that she can never be his wife, and in admitting in the presence of Rector Kroll that she was responsible for Beata's death, she has effectively closed off any possibility of a career for herself. It is clear that her confession is not made with any ulterior motives. It is a sacrificial act: she gives up everything she has attained at Rosmersholm in order to give Rosmer his "happy innocence back again."

With a less profound dramatist the matter might end there, with the audience left to assume that Rebecca does have a conscience, after all. However, Ibsen was aware of the new directions being taken by the naturalist writers and post-Darwinian philosophers in exploring the human psyche and in seeking non-Christian explanations for the origin of the conscience. Zola's *Thérèse Raquin* would have been familiar to him, and he may have encountered Paul Rée's *Der Ursprung der moralischen Empfindungen* (*Sources of the Moral Sense*, 1877), which Brandes certainly read. But, as Brandes remarked, it contained nothing that would have been new to any student of English empirical philosophy.[21] On the other hand, Rée's more significant work, *Die Entstehung des Gewissens* (*The Origins of Conscience*, 1885), would have given Ibsen, just as it gave Nietzsche, something to think about. Rée proposed to treat the origin of the conscience by giving an entirely natural explanation for it, using the historical approach and applying the principles of evolution. There is no evidence, however, that Ibsen read the work, which did not attract much attention. But Nietzsche read it, and it inspired his rejoinder, *On the Genealogy of Morals*.

Ibsen was pursuing his own thoughts, and in *The Wild Duck* he had explored depths that no dramatist had previously ventured into (except, possibly, Shakespeare in *Macbeth*). In *Rosmersholm*, what his narrative required was something in the past, some physical event, that would rise up and change the direction of Rebecca's life.

The revelation of this past event comes slowly because Rebecca has repressed it. It lies coiled in her unconscious and does not strike until Rosmer and Kroll inadvertently disturb it. First Rosmer, by asking Rebecca to be his wife, his companion in bed; then Kroll, who corrects Rebecca as to the time during which her father practiced medicine in Finmark. Once Kroll confronts her with that information, Rebecca's conscious mind has to accept what has been kept hidden ever since her childhood. The irrefutable facts are that she was Dr. West's mistress and that Dr. West was her father.

(Was Rebecca indeed the natural daughter of Dr. West? Emil Reich put the question to Ibsen in 1896. He smiled craftily. "It is at least very likely."[22])

The significant aspect of Rebecca's incest is that it has been repressed. This is what is novel about Ibsen's treatment of it. Hitherto discussions of the unconscious pictured its contents as a jumble of ideas, any one of which might suddenly come to the fore. Ibsen's image of the unconscious as the loft in *The Wild Duck* fit this conception perfectly. Everything in that storage room is accessible. Rebecca's memory of incest is different; it is not accessible, because she has repressed it. This idea of repression is, according to historians, what distinguishes Freud's understanding of the unconscious from that of his predecessors; it is the key to psychoanalysis. When, for example, Hippolyte Taine and Friedrich Nietzsche discussed the unconscious, they did not suggest that something had been repressed. The unconscious was for them only an undercurrent of ideas, images, and feelings. The idea that something once conscious has been driven into the unconscious was missing. That idea was Freud's contribution. Yet it would seem that Ibsen anticipated him by a few years.[23]

The monstrous sin of incest is the crime that even the freethinking and emancipated Rebecca cannot bear. When Rosmer, fifteen years older than she, suggests a change in their relationship, with the comrades becoming lovers, the adventuress in Rebecca utters an exclamation of joy, which is immediately and involuntarily suppressed by the dark side of Rebecca. Subsequently, after hearing Kroll, she cannot hide the truth from herself. She paces back and forth, wringing her hands.

"That's impossible. You're just trying to make me believe it. It's not true, not for all the world. Can't be true! Not for all the world—."[24]

Once she has faced the truth about her past, she finds it easy to tell Rosmer how she managed to drive Beata to suicide. What is that crime compared with incest? What troubles her inwardly is not the crime of getting rid of Beata, but her knowledge, albeit only half conscious, of having been the sexual partner of her father. When that knowledge breaks to the surface, the other crime is easy to acknowledge, especially since, in committing it, she was partly motivated by the desire to give Rosmer peace of mind. In other words, the incest taboo gives rise to what might be called a conscience. What before had been a necessary step in the great work of raising mankind to a higher level, ennobling it, now appears in a different light. With the incest taboo comes a sense of sin, of wrongdoing, even in the hardened amoral adventuress.

Ignoring the hints pointing to incest, the literary critics failed to understand what drove Rebecca to confess to the murder of Beata. Yet this is where Ibsen made a striking contribution to the study of conscience. It took a psychoanalyst, Sigmund Freud, in a brilliant essay published in 1915, to explain what was going on in Rebecca's mind—and to appreciate Ibsen's genius in revealing it in dramatic form. Freud explains convincingly that it is only after Rebecca learns of her incestuous union that she surrenders herself "wholly to her now overmastering sense of guilt. She confesses to Rosmer and Kroll that she was a murderess; she rejects forever the happiness to which she has paved the way by crime; and prepares for departure. But the true origin of her sense of guilt, which wrecks her at the moment of attainment, remains a secret. We have seen that it is something quite other than the atmosphere of Rosmersholm and the refining influence of Rosmer."[25]

Freud invoked the Oedipus complex to explain the main events in Rebecca's life. "Everything that befell her at Rosmersholm, the passion for Rosmer and the enmity towards his wife, was from the first a consequence of the Oedipus-complex—a compulsive replica of her relations with her mother and Dr. West."[26] And for Freud, the conscience or the superego derived from the Oedipus complex. A decade or so before Freud, Ibsen ventured a similar explanation in dramatic form. Both rejected the supernatural explanation for the emergence of conscience and saw its origin as lying in the prehistoric, primitive human being. Freud said, "The past, the tradition of the race and of the people, lives on in the ideologies of the super-ego, and yields only slowly to the influences of the present and to new changes."[27]

Ibsen said much the same thing in 1887 when he replied to a young man who had inquired about the meaning of the play. Ibsen focused on Rebecca and said the play "deals with the struggle that all serious-minded human beings have to wage with themselves in order to bring their lives into harmony with their convictions. For the different spiritual functions do not develop evenly and abreast of each other in any one human being. The acquisitive instinct hurries on from gain to gain. The moral consciousness—what we call conscience—is, on the other hand, very conservative. It has its roots deep in traditions and in the past generally. Hence the conflict within the individual."[28]

Freud made the Oedipus legend basic to his psychoanalytic theories, and there are signs that Ibsen borrowed from it to tell Rebecca's story. While Rosmer is unquestionably modeled to a large extent on Snoilsky, Rebecca seems to be Ibsen's creation, and she quickly became the driving force in the drama, as Ibsen submerged himself in the depths of her psyche.[29]

The events at Rosmersholm bear more than a passing resemblance to those in ancient Thebes, although the similarity is obscured by Ibsen's changing Oedipus into a woman. Rebecca-Oedipus slays the monster Sphinx (the nymphomaniac Beata), a deed that clears the way for Rebecca-Oedipus to cohabit with Rosmer-Jocasta. Thus Rebecca-Oedipus is united sexually with the parent figure. The narrative begins, as in Sophocles, with a plague, here the spirit of radicalism that Kroll (Creon) must deal with. The parallels cannot be extended very far, but it is conceivable that when Ibsen set up the opposition between a man of conscience and an amoral woman, that is, an opposition between the moral consciousness and the acquisitive instinct, his inquiring mind would ask at what point the two would certainly clash. In the prehistory of mankind, a subject that was preoccupying Ibsen in 1885 and 1886 (of which more later), there came a time when primitive man developed an aversion to incest, even a horror of it, ranking it as a worse crime than murder. In Sophocles's *Oedipus Rex* that is clearly the case, and the sequence of events in *Rosmersholm* points in the same direction.

The disclosure of Oedipus's incest came about because of a plague sent by the gods. In Ibsen, Kroll investigates Rebecca's shady past in order to defame her. What would have happened if Kroll had done nothing? Probably the main events would have been the same. Rebecca would have rejected Rosmer's proposal, and she would have confessed to her crime. The difference would have been that we would not have learned why she reacted as she did.

The motivation behind Rebecca's confession is both too clear and too obscure. Looking into it raises a troubling question. The dedicated Ibsenite, coming to *Rosmersholm* with a knowledge of the previous works, would quickly see that the dramatist has set up Rebecca and Rosmer as opposites at the beginning of his play only in order to have them joined together at the end. That is the basic thrust of most of his plays: the need to find the means by which the two warring sides of his being can be brought into harmony. The novelty in this play is that they change sides and cross over. The arc of Rosmer's progress takes him from inhibited man, corseted by tradition and custom, to breaker of class and social taboos, tolerant of the extremes in human behavior. This arc intersects with Rebecca's progress, which takes her from being an emancipated, aggressive woman, above society's laws, a murderess, to being spiritually broken, a woman burdened with a conscience. Sharing life with Rosmer, Rebecca finds that the "sense-intoxicated desire" that had once possessed her has passed away.

"All the pent-up passions settled down quietly into stillness. There came over me a peace of mind like that of a bird cliff under the midnight sun up north."[30] The heart of the play lies in these transformations, and the fascination lies in how Ibsen makes them credible. Mrs. Alving in *Ghosts* was depicted in the process of learning that there was as little to be said for her self-sacrificing idealism as for her son's self-indulgence and *joie de vivre*. Ibsen could find no way out of her dilemma. In *Rosmersholm* he sought a resolution by having two characters represent the division in her mind and bringing them together in a mystic union.

The agent instrumental in forming this union is Ulrik Brendel, the bankrupt philosopher, once an inspiring teacher, now an indigent lecturer. He was once an influence on both Rosmer and Rebecca, serving as tutor to the young Johannes and filling the mind of young Rebecca with radical ideas. His works were in Dr. West's library. When Rosmer's father heard what Brendel was teaching Johannes, he whipped him out of the house. And Rector Kroll got Brendel turned out of the university debating club. In act one he shows up at Rosmersholm to ask for a small loan, and he returns in act four to resolve the dilemma in which Rebecca and Rosmer find themselves.

Brendel is the former, idealistic Ibsen, now a bit careworn and shabby but still expounding the philosophy of Brand. The name Brendel sounds like a diminutive of Brand and suggests a burned-out ember. (Ibsen did not coin the name; there was a Brendel family in Skien.) This is the Ibsen who returned to Norway and found that he had little to offer. Brendel wants to put his ideals into practice, to descend from the philosophical heights to the level of the public arena. The result is disastrous, just as Ibsen's involvement in Norwegian politics left him disgusted. He has learned that the politicians, the compromisers, who are capable of living a life without ideals, inherit the world. They possess the secret of omnipotence because they never will more than they are capable of. The newspaper editor Mortensgård and Rector Kroll come under this indictment. (Kroll managed to have Brendel blackballed by the debating society; Lorentz Dietrichson tried to keep Ibsen from appearing as honored guest of the Student Association in Christiania.)[31] True to his old ideals, Brendel says that if Rosmer has a great cause to fight for, he can achieve victory only if he demands a sacrifice. The indispensable condition is that the woman who loves him should hack off her little finger and "slice off her incomparably molded left ear."[32] Here Ibsen is alluding to a passage in the last act of *Emperor and Galilean*. The apostate Julian, recognizing that the Christians have survived in spite of all his efforts to suppress them, scorns his own followers for lacking the spirit of sacrifice that imbues the Galileans.

"These Galileans, I tell you, have something in their hearts that I would greatly wish might stir up yours. You call yourselves followers of Socrates, of Plato, of

Diogenes. But is there one among you who would die in ecstasy for Plato's sake? Would our Priscos sacrifice his left hand for Socrates? Would Kryton, for Diogenes' sake, let his ear be cut off? And surely you would not! I know you—whited sepulchers. Get out of my sight."[33]

Unless sacrifice was involved, the matter was of no great significance. It was an essential element in Christianity, and it was equally essential to Brand's philosophy. Although Ibsen by this time had abandoned much of what he had put into *Brand* (when a certain woman praised it, he replied gruffly, "That was something I wrote in my younger days"),[34] the old idea of sacrifice remained intact, and the burned-out Brendel is its representative. At the end of *Rosmersholm*, Rosmer and Rebecca sacrifice themselves in a double suicide.

When she asks what she can do to give him back his belief that mankind can be ennobled, raised to a higher, more spiritual level, he immediately thinks of the sacrifice that Beata made for his sake. He finds "an alluring horror" in the very thought.[35] The last scene between Rosmer and Rebecca is a *folie à deux* in the making. Knowing that her life is really over, that she can be no more than "a sea troll dragging down the ship that is to carry you forward," she says she is willing to throw herself into the torrents where Beata died. For her, it will be a positive deed: it will convince Rosmer that she, for one, has been ennobled. The Rebecca who first came to Rosmersholm has been transformed into a Brand-like figure.

However, her commitment to this ideal can have no practical consequences. It may be intended to prove to Rosmer that she has changed and that it was he who changed her, but Rosmer has also changed. What there was in him that might have contributed to the work of ennoblement was due to Rebecca's power over him. Without her by his side, he is only one of the old Rosmers, of the same party as Rector Kroll. "There is," as he says, "nothing left to save in me."[36]

That seems too harsh a judgment. There is in the new Johannes Rosmer a pagan spirit and a sexual drive. He can even guess at and accept Rebecca's incest, and doing so, he smiles—for the first time. In the double suicide the apostate Rosmer embraces the Galilean Rebecca. To call the play *Emperor and Galilean* in modern dress, as one critic did, is not far off the mark.[37]

At the end Rosmer speaks of his emancipated view of life. He says, "There is no judge over us. And therefore we must do justice upon ourselves." He has, thanks mainly to Rebecca, become emancipated from his heritage, just as she was early in her life emancipated from Christianity. Then what will serve as instruments of justice? Apparently, the teachings of Ulrik Brendel. The crime that must be atoned for is Beata's suicide, for which both Rosmer and Rebecca feel responsible. Rebecca's suicide will compensate for Beata's; both women kill themselves for Rosmer's sake. Rosmer's suicide is more problematic. He dies because as the new, emancipated Rosmer, he wants Rebecca sexually. Since he cannot have her in this life, he unites with her in death. "The husband shall go with his wife, as the wife with her husband."

The last moments of *Ghosts* afford a contrast. Mrs. Alving is not sufficiently emancipated to kill her son. Ibsen told his English translator that but for the ghosts that still haunt her, she would have given him the fatal pills. There is, of course, a ghost that haunts Rosmer and Rebecca, the ghost of Beata. But the dead Beata represents not so much the past as the spirit of sacrifice.

After *Rosmersholm*

Rosmersholm did not fare well with either the literary critics or theater audiences. The ideas in it were scandalous, and the motives of the principal characters were extremely difficult to follow. It was a work of such disturbing originality that it could be appreciated only by the cognoscenti, and by them only after some time.

Bjørnson opined that Ibsen had constructed a poor play. In his rewriting of it, the nobility of Rosmer would have forced Rebecca to confess her crime. After that, Rosmer would not have felt the need to press the matter further; he would have escaped the spell of the monstrous woman and certainly not thrown himself into the cascade with her. This version would have given humanity increased courage and faith. "But this business of being a real devil and doing all sorts of tricks that everyone admires has seduced Ibsen, and the whole play is as if written with a wet phosphorous match in the dark."[1]

This was written in 1886. A few years later, a French critic gave an assessment that might be said to represent the consensus of later generations.

"It is a marvel of psychological thought, a feast to which one can invite only the most fastidious. In part, a conflict between honor and duty, happiness and crime, liberty of action and determinism; and in part, as a substratum to all this, a conflict between new ideas (Rebecca, Brendel) and the old ideas transmitted through heredity (Rosmer, Rector Kroll)."[2]

In Germany, where Ibsen had been finding his most appreciative audiences, there was no rush to stage the work. Its premiere there took place not in one of the major cities, but in Augsburg. Ibsen, who was living in Munich, only thirty miles away, was invited by the director, Felix Philippi, to the third rehearsal, by which time the actors were off book. He arrived punctually at ten, neither a minute earlier nor a second later. At first he sat with Philippi at the director's table in the auditorium. But he quickly grew uneasy, and his mood affected the actors, who blew their lines and messed up their speeches. Clutching the orchestra rail, he kept moaning, "Oh, my God, oh, my God." Philippi apologized to Ibsen, who went up onstage, greeted each actor, smiled, shook hands, and then withdrew to the auditorium.

To Philippi he said, "What excellent, dear, talented people! Please don't forget to tell them that."

He paced up and down the aisles, tapping himself on his chest. Asked if anything was wrong, he said, laughing, "Oh, no! It is just a habit with me. I had it already when I directed plays in Bergen. You must not let it bother you and the actors."

When Rosmer entered in the third act wearing *piqué* spats over polished boots, Ibsen staggered and exclaimed, "Look at that, look at that!"

However great his disappointment, he had to be grateful to this company for daring to stage his difficult play, in which nuances and intimations are the lifeblood of the dialogue. (The theaters in Munich would not produce it.) There came a moment in the fourth act when he stopped and rapped hard on the prompter's box. This was the point when Brendel suggests that Rebecca cut off her finger—"... sich ihren seiner kleinen, rosenroten Finger abhackt."

Philippi asked the actor to repeat the line. Again the sharp rapping.

"It's false," said Ibsen in his light voice.

The line was repeated a third time, and again Ibsen said it did not ring true.

Later at dinner Philippi asked Ibsen what was wrong.

"It's false, my friend. One doesn't say to a lady that she has rosy-red [*rosenrote*] fingers; one says rosy [*rosige*] fingers."[3]

Here is an example of the care Ibsen lavished on the dialogue, with much of the real import lying in subtle nuances, often difficult to convey in translation. The original has: "sin fine rosenhvide lillefinger." The 1898 German translation reads: "seiner rosenweissen, kleinen Finger." The Archer translation: "her tender, rosy-white little finger." *The Oxford Ibsen:* "her dainty, pink and white little finger." Ibsen's "rosenhvide" is unusual; "rosen-fingret" is conventional Dano-Norwegian.

There were only three performances of the play in Augsburg, intended mainly for the local subscription audience. The audiences, however, consisted mostly of visitors from Munich, the intelligentsia, eager to see Ibsen's latest creation. The production was deemed an artistic success, and though it could not have lived up to Ibsen's high expectations, he certainly appreciated Philippi's efforts and followed his subsequent career with interest.

Rosmersholm was hardly the play for those seeking entertainment in the theater. But even for those who were ready to dedicate themselves to serious drama and who welcomed the intellectual challenges Ibsen offered, the play posed a number of artistic and philosophical problems. The first challenge the actors faced was that of making the story line as clear as possible. Apparently, even the incomparable Duse did not succeed in conveying to her audiences what was going on in the depths of Rebecca's mind. But the task was not impossible.

Minnie Maddern Fiske, probably the finest American actor of her generation, ventured to act the part in 1907, but only after having studied the play for years. She knew, as her biographer relates, that "Rebecca's confession was precipitated by something like an algebraic equation completing itself in her mind and giving an answer of incest—something never put into words in the course of the play, or guessed by the other characters. Her confession and the final disaster followed inevitably for those who could 'hear Mrs. Fiske think.' . . . For those who got the full meaning and those who did not, Mrs. Fiske made Rebecca's scene with Kroll one of the most powerful they had witnessed on any stage, and she achieved it with the greatest economy of means, never rising from her chair, and almost without gesture."[4]

As formidable as the acting problem was the director's problem of dealing with the disjuncture between the psychological drama and the political drama, the latter calling for a cool cynicism, the former for extraordinary passion, rising to a kind of exaltation at the end. The two levels called for two different moods. It would seem that Ibsen intended that the high-flown talk about ennoblement would connect with the political drama, the one serving as a contrast to the other.

When Ibsen wrote the play, phrases about ennobling mankind and aristocratizing the masses were not empty blather; they resonated with a guarded optimism about the direction that society would take in the next few years. Those who had soured on politics and saw democratic government as an impediment to the development of the best minds placed their hopes in a cultural aristocracy. Already in 1880, Georg Brandes, having had bitter personal experience of the pernicious power of popular opinion, dreamed of an entente between the intelligentsia and the masses. Writing to Paul Heyse he said, "My desire is to civilize the farmers, to make them receptive to modern ideas, and to humanize the intelligentsia, to deprive them of their foolish class prejudices."[5]

An aristocracy of the spirit was a slogan that gained currency in Germany in the 1880s. When Ibsen in his speech to the workers in Trondheim in 1885 expressed his hope for a new aristocracy, a nobility of character, will, and spirit, he was not launching a new idea. It was very much in the air. Two years later in Stockholm, in a speech at a banquet given by the Heimdall Society with 250 persons attending, he elaborated on the idea of an aristocracy of the spirit and made it his own by uniting it with his conception of a Third Kingdom.

I believe that the teaching of natural science about evolution is also valid as regards the spiritual aspects of life. I believe that the time is not far off when political and social conceptions will cease to exist in their present forms, and that from them there will arise a unity, which for a while will contain within itself the conditions for the happiness of mankind. I believe that poetry, philosophy, and religion will be merged in a new category and become a new vital force, of which we who are living now can have no clear conception.

It has been said of me on different occasions that I am a pessimist. And so I am insofar as I do not believe in the everlastingness of human ideals. But I am also an optimist insofar as I believe in the capacity for the propagation and development of ideals. Especially, to be more definite, I believe that the ideals of our time, while disintegrating, are tending toward what in my play *Emperor and Galilean* I designated the Third Kingdom.[6]

The master of ceremonies, Adolf Hedin, a member of the Swedish parliament to whom Ibsen had, in 1869, addressed his poem "To My Friend Who Talks of Revolution," thanked him in a particularly warm speech for using his genius as a dramatist to further the development of society.

From the stage he reached out his hand to the lawmakers in parliament in the collaborative work of getting rid of the injustices of our time, the abolition of class differences. In his merciless depiction of the faults and failures of our time, its sins and crimes, he seems to have had in mind what the ancient thinkers set as the aim of tragedy: the cleansing of human passions through pity and fear.

He is not like certain other writers [meaning naturalists like Zola], who call themselves realists, apparently because their works are a shameful parody of real life, in which they seek the meaning of life in its ugliness, and seem to think that the gift of language has been granted mankind in order to degrade human beings, and have lost sight of the true reality. For to this reality Ibsen assigned those ideals without which this life would be worthless and death a meaningless annihilation. Above all, the ideal of working for and offering oneself to others, for society, for the future, in order that the generations to come will be better off and more fortunate than we. He has been the poet of duty, who has never flattered the masses or the minorities, neither individuals nor nations.[7]

Snoilsky, who was there, reported, "There was an unusual conciliatory mood in [Ibsen's] words, although the basic thought—about the Third Kingdom—was very obscure and ambiguous. Hedin's speech was exceptional."[8]

The younger generation responded more warmly than Snoilsky. The writer Gustaf af Geijerstam, twenty-nine years old at the time, thought Hedin's speech was empty rhetoric. But Ibsen's speech, delivered slowly and with great inner force, impressed him deeply. Years later he would write that no speech before or since had left such a mark on him. He approached the great man, who was surrounded by friends and admirers, but was too timid to say anything. However, in the jostling of bodies Geijerstam found himself face to face with Ibsen, who looked him in the eye, clinked glasses with him, and asked, "Don't you agree?"[9]

A couple of weeks later, in Copenhagen, Ibsen declined to speak to the union of radical students at the University of Copenhagen that he had addressed previously, while accepting an invitation from the more conservative Student Society.

The notion of an aristocracy of the spirit was to culminate in the writings of Nietzsche, whose philosophy was, as we shall see, first broadcast to a wider public by Brandes, his sympathetic but somewhat unreliable interpreter. He made no connection between Nietzsche and Ibsen.

However, the Swedish poet and essayist Ola Hansson did. In an 1891 article in *Die Gegenwart*, the journal for naturalism, he became perhaps the first critic to see that the dramatist and the philosopher had similar visions of a world to come. *Thus Spake Zarathustra* had only recently been published (the first three parts), and Nietzsche's superman was in many respects an exemplar of Ibsen's nobility of the spirit. A very perceptive cultural critic, Hansson saw the connection between the new ideas in science and philosophy, and understood that the visionary dreams of both Ibsen and Nietzsche originated in the theory of evolution.

"The conflict between power culture and spiritual culture, which Ibsen brings to the fore, examining their contradictions, belongs to the miniature forms of 'burning issues' and contemporary problems—this is unmistakably clear when he, as in *Rosmersholm*, treats the same problem that Nietzsche does: aristocratic individualism. Nietzsche's genealogy of morals is new, just as any organism is new, and the conflict between hostile cultural currents that he presents spans the evolutionary history of humanity. Zarathustra stands with one foot far in the bestial past and with the other far in a superhuman future."[10]

To readers of *Rosmersholm* a century or more later, the ennoblement of mankind may sound like an empty phrase, too idealistic to have any practical meaning and too antidemocratic to have a wide appeal. That certainly was not true in the 1880s. Those words carried with them a host of ideas that called for serious discussion. A century later, in a more cynical age, the phrase could easily seem inauthentic, and one scholar could argue that Ibsen meant it to ring hollow and that he used it to conceal, not reveal, the true human relationship of Rosmer and Rebecca.[11] That is to trivialize the play and to take Ibsen's public pronouncements about a nobility of spirit as equally inauthentic.

The next play that Ibsen wrote, *The Lady from the Sea*, provides an extraordinary contrast to *Rosmersholm* in almost every respect. When he spoke of himself as an optimist, he could not have been thinking of *Rosmersholm,* in which the idealists hurl themselves into the torrent, leaving the world in the hands of practical politicians. But he might have had in mind the ending of *The Lady from the Sea.*

Having suffered a loss of income from *Rosmersholm,* Ibsen seems to have resolved to compose a work that would not end in suicide, that would not deal with politics, that would have a plot that the tired businessman could follow, and that would make utterly palpable the hidden life of the soul. Instead of teasing out a meaning from the densely woven text, the reader or viewer of *Lady from the Sea* would have the meaning thrust upon him.

Before he and his wife visited Scandinavia, Ibsen had been developing ideas for a play about the allure of the sea. While at Molde in 1885 and again in Denmark in the summer of 1887 he spent many hours communing with the ocean. At first he and Suzannah stayed at Fredrikshavn on the Kattegat bay, renting rooms in the Hoffman Hotel in the center of town. He mixed freely with guests at mealtimes and enjoyed talking about his travels. When Suzannah complained that there were no pleasant woodsy walks nearby, they moved on to the small town of Sæby, a few miles away, occupying a large, sparsely furnished main room, with two adjoining bedrooms, in the only hotel in town, Hotel Harmonien. On his matutinal walks he would wear his frock coat, even on the hottest days, protecting his head from the sun with a broad-brimmed hat. He made a point of talking to the fishermen and would spend hours looking down into the water. At lunch with his fellow Norwegian Henrik Jæger, he would "suddenly and spontaneously start to talk about all he had seen down there in the depths, talk about the wonderful life that existed down there, about crabs and starfish and a hermit crab that had put its unprotected backside into an empty snail. . . . And all the life down there that was only a strange variation of life on earth among human beings."[12] William Archer visited him in Sæby in July and found him to be relaxed and without affectation or stiffness of any sort. Although he found Ibsen to be "a paradoxist" like Bernard Shaw (Archer's good friend) and much more a poet than a philosopher, he admitted that, except for Shakespeare, there was no one "in all literature whom I would care so much to know as Ibsen. Of course one would like to have seen Goethe or Thackeray or George Eliot, but they have not the enigmatic attraction of Ibsen."[13]

On August 29 the couple returned to Fredrikshavn, and from there, on September 8, they proceeded to Sweden for a series of receptions in his honor. In Stockholm, on September 24, he gave his "Third Kingdom" speech.

Back in Denmark, as the guest of honor at a party given by his publisher (October 5, 1887), he spoke of his attraction to the calm Danish sea, which gave his soul peace and quiet, and said the impressions left on him would figure in his writings. It was not, however, the coast of Denmark that provided the setting for his next play. For *Lady from the Sea* he had in mind the scenery of Molde and the Romsdal fjord, the same as for *Rosmersholm*.[14]

The Lady from the Sea would have followed immediately after *The Wild Duck* if *Rosmersholm* had not intervened. The mysterious loft that comprehended the past, not only the youthful days of the Ekdals and the prehistory of man but all the eons since the emergence of life itself, continued to exert a spell on Ibsen, and in *Lady from the Sea* he clearly hoped to find a direct link between the depths of the sea and the depths of the human mind.

In his exploration of the subterranean realms, both physical and psychological, he employed both the latest scientific theories and his own intuition. As he said in his 1887 speech in Stockholm, "I believe that the teachings of natural science about evolution are also valid as regards the spiritual aspects of life." He was embarked on a journey that Freud would take a few years later.

In Ernst Haeckel, that popular German expositor of the theory of evolution, he might have read about the origin and development of the human mind from base matter.

> [It is] the history of the evolution of the central nervous system which for the first time enables us to understand the origin of life of the human mind from natural causes, and the gradual historical development of the psychic activities of man. . . . The history of the evolution of the spinal marrow and the brain of the human embryo at the same time directly leads us to understand the Phylogeny of the human mind, that most sublime activity of life which in the developed human being we are accustomed to regard as something wonderful and supernatural. . . .
>
> Happily, our knowledge of the Ontogeny of the central nervous system of man is so satisfactory, and agrees so perfectly with the supplementary results of Comparative Anatomy and Physiology, that it affords us a perfectly clear insight into one of the highest problems of philosophy, namely, the Phylogeny of the *psyche*, the mind, or the history of the ancestral lineage of man's psychic activities, and leads us into the only path by which we shall ever be able to solve this highest of all problems.[15]

It is obvious from Ibsen's letters, his conversational remarks, and the notes to his plays that he was well acquainted with the latest scientific theories concerning evolution, especially the emergence of the human mind as the repository of ancient ideas, superstitions, and traditions, a hotly debated issue in the 1870s and

1880s. It would lead to Théodule Ribot's theories about racial reminiscences lying buried in the unconscious and to Freud's theory of the collective mind.

In his *Die conventionellen Lügen der Kulturmenschheit,* which went through several editions in the 1880s, the journalist Max Nordau popularized Ribot's conviction that it is through the unconscious that age-old beliefs and superstitions continue to exercise the power of a law. Inheritance, according to Ribot, is to the species what memory is to the individual. The past continues to exist in the individual in the form of frequent, unconscious, obscure, yet ever-present reminiscences that require only an outer hint to light up and irradiate the whole life of the soul.[16] When subsequently Freud wrote about what he called the collective mind, and when he described tradition as "equivalent to the repressed material in the mental life of an individual," he was building on fairly well-founded ideas.[17]

Much of what psychologists were saying about the unconscious workings of the mind would have occurred to Ibsen on his own. Only now, in his naturalist mode, he wanted scientific backing for his ideas. He told a reporter who interviewed him, "Sometimes I have to dive deeply into a scientific work to collect psychological and physiological facts for my plays; but [and?] I seldom read nowadays without some such object."[18]

Some of his notes from 1888 connect the symbol-laden loft of *The Wild Duck* with the setting of *The Lady from the Sea* and reveal his awareness of the new ideas about racial memory, about the emergence of life from the sea and of the mind from matter.

"The sea's power of attraction. The longing for the sea. Mankind in relation to the sea. Captured by the sea. Dependent on the sea. Must return to it. A species of fish forms a new link in evolutionary development. Do rudiments of it still exist in the human mind? In the mind of some individuals? . . .

"The sea exerts a power of suggestion that works like one's will. The sea can hypnotize. Nature on the whole can do this. The great secret is the dependence of man's will on the 'will-less.'"[19]

In *The Lady from the Sea*, Ibsen set himself the task of dramatizing these ideas, believing that a true poet had an obligation to transmit the best thoughts of the best minds. "To popularize philosophy," he said, "is the poet's duty. Most people are born, live and die without knowing what has happened to them."[20]

This longing for the sea is embodied in Ellida Wangel, a high-strung woman, considerably younger than her husband. She is obsessed with the sea, and we are meant to think of her as a mermaid stranded on a beach. Her life has been bound up with the sea ever since her birth. Her father was a lighthouse keeper who died when she was a child. She was reared by her mother, a lonely, melancholy woman, who died insane. As a young woman, she found companionship with her tutor, Arnholm, who offered to marry her. When she rejected him, he understood it was because she looked upon him as a trusted friend, not as a lover.

She married Dr. Wangel, a middle-aged man, a couple of years after his first wife died. He has two daughters who have never quite accepted Ellida as one of the family. Wangel, a doctor of medicine with an extensive practice, is a kind, considerate husband, easygoing, and given to drink. He found Ellida physically attractive and "took a fancy" to her. She married him because she was lonely and uncared for, and he promised to keep her comfortable and well provided for all her life.

About three years before the play begins a child was born to the couple. Its death when it was only five or six months old produced a crisis in the marriage. From then on Ellida has refused to have sex with her husband. Although he has respected her wishes, he has sought to overcome her fear of sex and her lassitude and what he calls her nervous condition by giving her morphine. This is barely hinted at in the dialogue, but apparently (to judge from an 1888 interpretive essay on the play, which Ibsen approved), readers back then would have understood. Wangel's elder daughter says that "he often gives her medication that can't be good for her in the long run"; it brightens her spirits for a while.[21]

Although Ibsen knew his characters thoroughly—how they looked, what they wore—he was irritatingly frugal in sharing this information, except when specifically asked for advice, or when he saw from reviews that an actor had misrepresented the character he was portraying. He corrected the actor playing Rector Kroll with a letter that shows how fully he imagined and visualized his characters.

> Rector Kroll has a domineering nature with a highly developed authoritarian streak, such as one usually finds in schoolmasters. He comes of course from a good family. Major Rosmer's son married Kroll's sister. The rector behaves like a well-born government official. In spite of a certain asperity that sometimes breaks forth, his manner is friendly and pleasant. He can be charming when he sets his mind to it or when he is with people he likes. But one sees that he likes only those who share his views. The others irritate him, and with them he easily becomes reckless and a bit malicious. His appearance is distinguished. He is handsomely dressed, in black. His coat reaches to his knees, but no further. He wears a white cravat, long and old-fashioned in style, one that goes twice around his neck. Hence no tie. His clothes explain why Ulrik Brendel at first mistakes him for pastor Rosmer and then for "a brother of the cloth."[22]

The actor playing Arnholm, the teacher, in *Lady from the Sea* might easily give a wrong interpretation of the character if he relied on what is said about him in the text. The two young daughters of Dr. Wangel think of him as old and decrepit.

But Ibsen warned the actor against taking seriously what they say. "It is only to young girls that he looks like that. His hair has thinned out, and he's tired from his teaching—but that's all."[23]

Our initial impression of Ibsen's characters would be quite different in many instances if they were described with a Shavian amplitude. As it is, one must consider what little Ibsen gives us as being significant.

Wangel knows that Arnholm had once, ten years ago, been in love with Ellida. Proceeding like an amateur psychologist, Wangel wonders if an old flame can be reignited, and he invites Arnholm to his home. Although nothing comes of that, he is right in believing there is something in Ellida's past that is the cause of her present condition.

The door to the past is opened when Mr. Lyngstrand, an aspiring sculptor, tells Ellida of an experience he had when he was on the crew of a sailing ship. The boatswain on the ship, laid up because of a sprained ankle, was going through a pile of old newspapers when he read that the woman he had been engaged to had married another man. He vowed to find her and claim her as his own.

The boatswain's passion so impressed Lyngstrand that he has planned a large sculpture depicting two figures: a woman, lying half asleep, and her husband, a drowned man, standing at her bedside.

Lyngstrand's tale stirs up old memories in Ellida. Ten years ago while she was living at the lighthouse, she met a sailor who entranced her. They met frequently until he got into trouble. In a scuffle aboard his ship, he killed the captain. Forced to flee the country, he met Ellida for the last time. They vowed eternal love; he swore to come back and claim her; they plighted their troth by exchanging rings.

Hearing Lyngstrand's story, she believes that the boatswain is her former lover. Moreover, she imagines that the moment her former lover learned by chance of her marriage was the very moment when she had a vision of him, a vision both fascinating and frightening. What haunts her imagination is the tie pin that he wore when they parted, a tie pin with a pearl like the eye of a dead fish. This image flashed into her mind while she was making love to her husband. From that moment she could no longer sleep with him.

When her child was born, she saw in its eyes the pearl of her lover's pin, and when it died, only a few months old, her troubled mind associated its death with her broken promise.

On someone else the spell cast by the sailor would probably not have been so intense. But in Ellida's case there were predisposing factors. Her childhood was spent close to the sea; her father was a lighthouse keeper, and her mother was mentally unstable. She was baptized Ellida, the name of a ship in heroic legend.

It would have been odd if her romance as an impressionable teenager with a reckless adventurer had *not* haunted her imagination. Her marriage with Dr. Wangel was the complete opposite of her affair with her romantic hero, its calm domesticity contrasting with the images conjured up by those unforgettable moments in the arms of her lover, images that she probably admitted into her mind as the middle-aged, gentle and caring Dr. Wangel made love to her. In his early notes for the play, Ibsen wrote, "The secret in her marriage—what she hardly dares acknowledge to herself, hardly dares think about, the power of the imagination to draw her back to the former. Toward the lost one. At bottom—in the spontaneous images, it is *him* with whom she lives her married life."[24]

The Lady from the Sea

Rosmersholm delved into man's conscience, which in a secular age is seen as a product of man's social development. In *The Lady from the Sea* Ibsen continued his exploration of the unconscious, the dark side of the mind, and went beyond what was hinted at in *The Wild Duck*. Ellida's mental journey takes her further back in the evolutionary chain of being, back into the depths of the sea, where the sexual drive is as primary as hunger. In this exploration of the still-dark continent of the human psyche, there was a person among his acquaintances who could serve as a guide. This was Magdalene Thoresen, the stepmother of Ibsen's wife, Suzannah, and sometime lover of Bjørnson. According to Suzannah herself, Magdalene was "the real model for 'the Lady from the Sea.'"[1] Magdalene recognized in Ellida a woman after her own heart. Ellida, she told Suzannah, "is in complete accord with my own fantasies and innermost nature."[2]

Although *The Lady from the Sea* may not be Ibsen at his best, all its faults are redeemed by its portrait of the enigmatic Ellida, one of the most complicated women in dramatic literature. Critics and psychoanalysts have studied her as if she were a real person. Because we know so much about the lady who sat for the portrait, it is possible to see genius at work, to note what it keeps and what it adds in creating an enduring work of art.

When Ibsen wrote *The Lady from the Sea*, Magdalene was a minor celebrity in Danish and Norwegian social and literary circles, as well known for her rather scandalous personal life as for her writings. Her affair with Bjørnson was hardly a secret, a situation that Ibsen exploited in the Anitra scenes in *Peer Gynt*. She was not conventionally beautiful. As Peer says of Anitra, "Her shape and form are, well, extraordinary / Not your normal beauty, quite the contrary."[3] Her dark hue made her seem a child of nature, of the earth, earthy. But her element was the sea.

She described herself as being born and bred by the sea. All her lasting childhood impressions were of the sea.

"Of course I had received an education in general culture," she said, "but the great works of civilization never inspired me to the extent the sea did when I looked out over it, sitting on a naked stone."[4] In the Anitra scenes, Peer (Bjørnson) tries to educate her and to give her a soul—without success. She thought Nora in *A Doll's House* was a Jesus in a skirt.

Born in 1819 in Fredericia, Denmark, a small but cosmopolitan town, shielded from the storms of the Kattegat, she was the daughter of Niels Kragh, a seafaring man, a ship's carpenter and occasional pilot. When his ship collided with another vessel, he lost his license. He took to drink and died at sea in 1846. The young Magdalene grew up a tomboy, dressing as a sailor as a prank, and running wild with the boys along the shore, smoking a cigar (or chomping on it). Her native intelligence and her strong personality caught the attention of a businessman, who sent her to Copenhagen to study to be a teacher. There she met an Icelandic student, Grímur Thorgrimsson Thomsen, who was writing his doctoral dissertation on Lord Byron (and borrowing some ideas from Søren Kierkegaard without acknowledging their source). Grímur was of as romantic a nature as the English poet, just as temperamental, as consummately fascinating, and as egotistical. Magadalene herself described the effect this magnetic personality had on her.

"While studying in Copenhagen, I met a young man, a wild, extraordinary creature, a force of nature. We studied together, and I knelt down before his gigantic, demonic will." She said, "He could have claimed me for his own in a fierce and consuming love."

After a two-year affair with him, she found a position as governess in the home of Hans Conrad Thoresen, a clergyman, and a recent widower with five children who needed looking after. One of them was Suzannah, who was to become Ibsen's wife. His parish was in the province of Sunnmøre, on the Norwegian Sea, north of Bergen. When she arrived there in the autumn of 1842, she was pregnant with Thomsen's child. In June she was back in Copenhagen to give birth to a boy, who was placed in an orphanage. Evidently there were rumors about who the real father was, the clergyman or the wild lover.

Thoresen married Magdalene in 1843. But some years later, about 1851, the marriage foundered. She grew increasingly concerned about the child she had abandoned in Copenhagen, and she wrote to her former lover, begging him to adopt the child. He agreed to do so, and Hans Thoresen traveled to the Danish capital to make the necessary arrangements.

Although Grímur abandoned her, Magdalene never reproached him. She said she met a better man and found a better life with him. She gave birth to four children in her marriage with Hans Thoresen. Yet the life that might have been always obsessed her. "I have always known that the love that was in me *could* have been nurtured and made to bloom. So I have gone on, feeling the desire and the loss, reaching high, reaching low, reaching for shadows always. And the longing for love did not disappear with the years, only grew stronger."[5]

She was frank and forthright about her marriage. "Thoresen was my friend, my father, my brother, and I was his friend, his child. . . . He was the sort of man to whom I could tell everything and be understood." She had from the beginning confessed to him her affair with Thomsen, that "tragic episode in my restless life. . . . But the past, those events in which I was an unwitting wretch, and uncared for, things that I could not possibly deal with, not for my own sake or that of others, all that I begged him to treat as a closed book and to consider me as I was, the result of a long struggle, and—if he found me worthy—to let everything else be put aside. He agreed to that."[6]

Dean Thoresen was transferred to nearby Bergen, and it was there in the Thoresen house that Ibsen first met Magdalene. Over the years they met on many occasions. She spent most of 1879 and 1880 in Italy, where she frequently called on the Ibsens, then residing on the Via Capo le Case in Rome, and she visited them several times after they had settled in Munich. Ibsen had many opportunities to observe this lady of the sea at close range, and through Suzannah he would have learned all about her adventurous life.

As luck would have it, he encountered her again in Trondheim in 1885, when he was hatching plans for a new drama. The basic idea concerned the effect that the unconscious has on our lives. However, as a result of his experiences in Norway, particularly his renewed friendship with Snoilsky, those first plans bifurcated, one set leading to *Rosmersholm,* the other to *The Lady from the Sea.* Magdalene Thoresen the governess to an older clergyman metamorphosed into Rebecca West; Magdalene the passionate lover of a romantic poet was transmuted into Ellida. (In the early notes, the Ellida character is named Thora.) Together, the two plays provide a remarkable study in the workings of the unconscious and the subconscious. In the first case, what was in the unconscious was repressed; in the second it could not be suppressed.

Freud said that the finest creative artists had an intuitive knowledge of the human psyche that psychologists had to labor to obtain. What Ibsen discovered in these two plays about the dark side of the mind was subsequently confirmed by professional experts. He brought himself up to date on what the scientific specialists had revealed about evolution and then in the laboratory of his mind went a giant step further by uniting the theories of Darwin, Haeckel, Taine, Maudsley, Ribot, and Herbert Spencer with his own insight into human nature. Literature offers few examples of comparable inventiveness. Magdalene Thoresen's remarkable life was a romance, the stuff of a four-decker Victorian novel. In Ibsen's hands it was transmuted into a pathbreaking inquiry into the deeper recesses of the mind. Where others would be content to say that Magdalene was obsessed by the sea, Ibsen's critical concern was with the source of that obsession.

Some of the early commentators recognized his accomplishment. Henrik Jæger, his early biographer, saw Ellida as a mentally disturbed woman, whom Ibsen examined in the light of the latest psychological theories. Her illness, said Jæger, "is a pathological nervous phenomenon, one of the inexplicable phenomena that science only recently has taken from the quacks practicing magnetism and spiritualism and made the subject of systematic study."[7] Subsequently, most of the interpreters of the play have taken much the same approach, reading it as a remarkable anticipation of a Freudian analysis. In fact, Gunnar Brandell argues that *The Lady from the Sea* was a formative influence on the young Freud, who read it at the time when he was about to choose psychotherapy as his profession.[8] In 1907 Carl Gustav Jung described one of his patients as being very much like Ellida. "Every properly analyzable case has something aesthetically beautiful about it, particularly this one, which is an exact copy of Ibsen's *The Lady from the Sea*. The build-up of the drama and the thickening of the plot are identical with Ibsen's."[9]

The psychological interpretation of *The Lady from the Sea* is appealing because it makes the drama seem contemporary and provides a story line that is easy to follow. Ibsen, however, had a deeper purpose in mind than a psychological exploration, and the pattern he wove is broader and more comprehensive than the Freudian one. The play is first of all a study in how human beings have acclimatized themselves over the course of millennia—the word "acclimatize" is repeated four times during the span of the play. In that respect it continues the ideas about evolution broached in *The Wild Duck*. With her longing for the sea, from which all life emerged, Ellida is a study in atavism, and her progress in the play brings her from a primitive state in which the passions rule to a modern, civilized condition. The conflict is between nature and culture, as Jonas Lie observed, a conflict incarnated in the sailor and Wangel and brought to a head in the last scene. "At that point," Lie told Ibsen, "my nerves tightened up. The unconscious mermaid's life seethes in the blood, while step by step we are brought to see into a human being, to see that we are at a border crossing, with a choice between Nature and Culture. . . . It's all done in a properly terrifying way."[10]

The play is clearly meant to be a companion piece to *Rosmersholm*. In that play the moral consciousness was seen as a conservative force, inhibiting progress. In the following play it is Nature and the primitive instincts that inhibit the development of human society.

The seafaring adventurer, whom Ibsen calls A Stranger (*En fremmed mand* or *Den fremmede*), is a brutal man, driven almost entirely by his instincts, a savage who ruthlessly takes what he wants and who can kill a man without feeling any remorse. Such men have always exerted a powerful attraction, dreadful and fascinating, an attraction that Ibsen attributes to those basic instincts that are part of our heritage. They can never be entirely sloughed off, being too deeply ingrained in us; they can only be held in check by an act of will. This is the point that Ibsen wishes to make.

His principal objection to naturalism, however, was not its indecency, its coarseness, or its frank depiction of sex. His quarrel was philosophical. What troubled him about this scientific movement was its determinism, its thoroughly materialistic explanation of human behavior. Naturalism in the arts was part of natural philosophy, with human behavior explained in terms of material causes, allowing little room for free will. What fate was to the ancients, determinism was to the naturalist. The author of *Brand* never quite lost his belief in the power of man's will as the true force of progress. Determination would in the long run override determinism.

In May 1888, when he was preparing the working draft of *Lady from the Sea*, he read a critique of naturalism, *Den nyere Naturanskuelse* (*The New Scientific View*), sent to him by its author, Ernst Ferdinand Lochmann, a doctor of medicine, an epidemiologist, and a professor at the University of Christiania. Lochmann surveyed all the new theories stemming from Darwin and noted how they had penetrated all modern thought, not just science but literature and politics as well. The result was that the boundary between the living and the lifeless was being erased, with conscience and morality being treated accordingly as malleable concepts. Heredity had replaced ancient fate as the governing force in man's existence, as can be seen in a contemporaneous literary work of great formal perfection, an obvious allusion to *Ghosts*. However, there were signs of change. Haeckel's theories about ontogeny had come under attack; the missing link between ape and man had not been found; Hippolyte Taine, advocate of a scientific approach to literature, in his latest book accepted conscience as bestowed on man by God; and the old vitalism was now emerging with renewed strength. There was, in fact, no reason to believe that science would make any further advances in the area of evolutionary theory. The process of adaptation had now reached an end.

Thanking Lochmann, Ibsen replied, "I have read your book with great interest, all the more so since I have for a long time busied myself with the subjects you discuss. But none of the conclusions that science seems to have reached have been able to satisfy me. Consequently, I have formed my own personal and independent view of nature. I believe that both the theologians and the scientists lose themselves in one-sidedness. 'Nature' is not as material as many want to make it. But exactly *what* it is that lies behind—that is the great mystery, the temporary secret.

"Temporary, I say. For I live in the hope that future developments will manage little by little to replace that great secret with a completely liberating revelation."[11]

His thoughts here are in keeping with the grand vision of a "Third Kingdom"—so obscure and oracular to Snoilsky, so inspiring and revelatory to Geijerstam—that he had sketched out in his speech in Stockholm a few months earlier, in September 1887. When he had said that the present time might "[with] good reason be described as a conclusion, and that something new is about to be born from it," he was anticipating Lochmann. What he added to Lochmann, who appealed to the old customs and standards as having continuing validity, was the vision of a new "vital force," creating a new category uniting poetry, philosophy, and religion.

Ibsen believed that the intuitive poet could complement the work of the investigative natural philosopher. In *Lady from the Sea,* which was to be his last naturalist work, he depicted in the case history of a neurotic woman the advance of humankind through acclimatization. In his speech he had said that what science tells us about evolution also applies to "the spiritual aspects of life." In the works of Herbert Spencer, a philosopher whom Ibsen evidently admired (he expressed a desire to meet him), he would have found passages that could well serve as background matter for his play. Discussing how life has to adapt to surrounding conditions in order to survive, Spencer said, "Whatever possesses vitality obeys this law. We see it illustrated in the acclimatization of plants, in the altered habits of domestic animals, in the varying characteristics of our own race.... *Such changes are towards fitness for surrounding conditions.* ... Civilization instead of being artificial is a part of nature; all of a piece with the development of the embryo or the unfolding of a flower.... Man needed one moral constitution to fit him for his original state; he needs another to fit him for his present state; and he has been, is, and will long continue to be, in process of adaptation. By *civilization* we signify the adaptation that has already taken place. In virtue of this process man will eventually become completely suited to his mode of life."[12]

The idea of acclimatization was a part of scientific knowledge even before Darwin published his major works on evolution (the passages from Spencer are from 1850), but the emphasis was on physical development and adjustment to the material environment. Following Ribot and others, Ibsen wanted to apply the same principle of acclimatization to the mental development of the human being. As he said in his 1887 speech: "The teaching of natural science about evolution is also valid as regards the spiritual aspects of life." What was unique about *Lady from the Sea* was the method Ibsen devised for dramatizing the development, re-

Figure 23. The last scene in *The Lady from the Sea*. Berlin 1889.

capitulating in Ellida the emergence of civilization from man's primitive state. Perhaps he was referring to this technique when he told his publisher that "in many respects it [*Lady*] marks a new direction for me."[13]

He took the bold step of bringing the Stranger, her demon lover, onstage. Audience expectations probably required a direct confrontation between Wangel and the Stranger, with Ellida torn between the two. But the figure of the Stranger presents a problem. Given the realism of the play, he cannot come onstage as a specter-like figure, a phantasm of Ellida's imagination, the man she has slept with in her dreams. However, as a solid, palpable character, with bushy, reddish hair, a Scotch tam-o'-shanter on his head, a pack slung across his shoulder, he is bound to disappoint expectations, both the audience's and Ellida's. She first recognizes his voice, then turns around and, seeing him, is disappointed and confused. Only when she looks into his eyes does she recognize him. At that moment, she staggers backward and cries, "The eyes, the eyes!"

Her odd, ambivalent response is like Rebecca West's when Rosmer proposes taking her as his wife. The first, immediate reaction is contradicted by what follows. In both instances there is a conflict between the conscious and the unconscious mind, a sudden sharp clash between the two revealed in the physical action. Fear and attraction fight against each other.

Ibsen wanted to show Ellida overcoming her primitive passions and, as a representative of the human race, rising to a higher level of development through the force of reason. But he made it rather easy for himself and Ellida by letting us see in the flesh the romantic Heathcliff of her imagination.

Obviously, the reality doesn't conform with her romantically enhanced memory of him. Consequently, the alternatives that confront her *before* the arrival of the Stranger, the dull husband of her present life or the passionate demon of her adolescence, are totally different from the alternatives offered her *after* the arrival of the Stranger, a choice between a caring husband and a somewhat deflated lover. Seen in that light, her decision does not seem to be one requiring enormous strength of will or reason. What continues to draw her to the Stranger is not the man himself but what he represents to her: freedom, or what Wangel calls her "craving for the limitless and the infinite." Knowing this, Wangel counters the Stranger's offer. He annuls his marriage to her. Once Ellida recognizes Wangel's sincerity, once she is set free from her marriage, the Stranger's spell over her vanishes.

The moment when Wangel gives Ellida her complete freedom cannot have the impact now that it was meant to have in 1888. In the patriarchal society of the nineteenth century, Wangel's emancipatory act was astonishing. It leaves Ellida literally speechless. It deeply offended the censor at the Royal Theater in Copenhagen, who would not approve a drama in which a husband releases his wife from the responsibilities of caring for the home and children just because a criminal type has exercised her imagination. He was overruled.[14]

Dr. Wangel does, however, add a clause to his release of her. He tells her she can choose in freedom but with responsibility. In practice, this means she must be a mother to Wangel's two children.

Freedom with responsibility is an innocuous motto, unlike the challenging principles or idealistic watchwords found in other Ibsen plays: "all or nothing," "the miracle of miracles," "the strongest man in the world is he who stands alone." In *Lady from the Sea* Ibsen seems to have abandoned the old ideals of perfection and descended far down into the valley of ordinariness. The concept of a Third Kingdom, the union of opposites, has turned into a compromise between the ungoverned passions and social conformity, a compromise effected by acclimatization, with Wangel an agent in the process.

Ellida is both frightened and fascinated by the Stranger and what he stands for. But what she calls "the terrible" (*det grufulde*) is only the stuff of a schoolgirl's imagination. There is a world of difference between Ellida's listless mopings and Miss Julie's sexual frenzy in Strindberg's drama, which was written at the same time. Shying away from the brutal naturalism of Hans Jæger and Emile Zola, and uncomfortable with the depiction of raw sexual passion, Ibsen produced a kind of domesticated naturalism, its teeth pulled, its Darwinism blunted.

In *Rosmersholm,* Rebecca West is haunted by dim, repressed memories of an ogre, forbidding sex. Ellida is spellbound by memories of sexual fulfillment, irrepressible memories. Both plays had the same starting point, the mermaid out of its element, but the one is a tragedy, the other is an entertainment, with Ballested, painter, tourist guide, dancing master, barber, and president of the local music society, serving as master of ceremonies. Before the play has barely started, he tells us he is working on a painting that will show a mermaid who has strayed in from the open sea, has been stranded on the beach, and is slowly dying in the brackish waters. This factotum, obviously Ibsen himself, painter manqué, sets a lighthearted mood for the play, and the bright music of wind instruments underscores the mood of the last scene. He also serves as *raisonneur* and states the theme of the play: human beings "can ac-cli-matize themselves." (He is not stammering; he is having difficulty with a foreign word.)[15]

Ibsen did not think the Stranger presented a problem in the acting of the play. He saw it as staged in Weimar in 1889 and praised the actor who played the part: "a long, slender figure, hawk-faced, with black, piercing eyes, and a splendidly deep and hushed voice."[16] He knew that the Stranger must retain an aura of mystery and must not be too clearly defined. He goes by various names and appears to have no trade, other than that of a sailor. Ibsen strongly objected to the Stranger being listed in the cast as a sailor or pilot or anything equally precise.

"He is in fact none of these. When Ellida met him ten years ago he was a second mate. Seven years later he signed on as a simple boatswain, that is, as something considerably less. And now he arrives as a passenger on a tourist ship. He is not part of the ship's crew. He is dressed for a short tour, not for a long journey. No one should know what he is, any more than they should know *who* he is, or what his name really is. This uncertainty is precisely the point of the method I have chosen for the occasion."[17]

Moreover, Ibsen wanted the Stranger's physical appearance to be as vague as his profession. After the dress rehearsal of the play in Berlin, he said that the Stranger should stand upstage, half hidden by the bushes, only his upper body visible, lit by moonlight. His standing there in the light, with darkness all around him, with his features not clearly visible, will add to the uncertainty as to who he is, giving an impression of something both unfamiliar and human.

The reporter who recorded Ibsen's comments also remarked on the difficulty of acting the part of the Stranger. In the Copenhagen production, he said, the appearance of the Stranger gave at first the impression of something eerie, but the moment he stepped forward, all the magic vanished. The same was true in the Berlin production. The reporter (Ove Rode, who a few years before had spoken for the radical students) faults Ibsen for creating a figure whose power might be imagined by the reader but cannot be transmitted from the stage to the audience. "In the theater we cannot be entranced by the Stranger's eyes, as we may be in the reading with the aid of one's imagination.

"Ibsen has placed some surprisingly cold words in the Stranger's mouth. It is the actor's job to put passion into them and carry us with them. So far, the actors have deliberately let the audience remain indifferent and skeptical."[18]

However impressive the actor playing the Stranger might be, he cannot resolve the esthetic contradictions in the play itself. The work is overloaded with ham-handed symbolism: the open waters, the carp pond, the promontory high above the sea, Ballested's painting of a mermaid dying slowly in brackish waters, Lyngstrand's sculpture of a drowned man, and the Stranger himself. Although they were supposed to encapsulate the central mystery, in fact they play against the subtle inner drama. The Stranger is a figure out of early nineteenth-century romanticism crudely inserted into a realistic play brimming with modern ideas. There was general agreement that in the theater the apparition of the Stranger, half real, half symbolic, could not bridge the gap, nor could it give a sense of what it was that fascinated Ellida.

In essence, he stands for raw, brutal male aggressiveness. Writing in the summer of 1888, Strindberg depicted the type straightforwardly in Jean, the servant in *Miss Julie.* Strindberg did not make Jean carry a heavy symbolic burden, whereas Ibsen, hard at work on *Lady* at the same time, wanted the Stranger to be a natural force in Darwin's evolutionary scheme. It would seem that here Ibsen's theatrical instincts failed him. Certainly, if he had emphasized the sheer physicality of the Stranger, the aura of male sexuality, the play would have worked better in the theater. When the Stranger hints to Ellida (in act two) that he stabbed the ship's captain who attempted to sodomize him, he is not the vaguely symbolic figure we see onstage.[19] That crucial incident reveals both his sexual allure and his savagery, and he becomes a human being rather than a link in the evolutionary scheme. The Copenhagen production in February 1889 was not a success in spite of twenty-three rehearsals, an exceptional number at that time. Even a symbolist production by Lugné-Poe in Paris in 1892 did not solve the esthetic problems epitomized by the physical presence of the Stranger.

To reinforce the moral of his tale, Ibsen presents a parallel case. Wangel's elder daughter, Bolette, rather lightheartedly promises to marry Lyngstrand, a sailor (at least for a while) like the Stranger. He is a frail, tubercular artist, doomed to die young. Bolette's former teacher Arnholm appears on the scene and promises to show her the great world, without any obligation to him. However, when he hints that they might eventually marry, she feels she cannot accept his generosity. He reminds her of the alternatives, a quiet life in a small town or a life of travel and expanding intellectual horizons. Then, like Ellida, being free to choose and to weigh her options, she decides upon a decent and comfortable life with an older man. Culture trumps Nature.

Contemporary criticism focused on the reconciliation of Wangel and Ellida and ranged from the cynical to the rapturous. Ola Hansson in a letter to Strindberg said, "Because of the ending the book will naturally be greeted with cheers from the sheep and rabbits. It can be read as the apotheosis of the sanctity of marriage."[20]

Georg Brandes, not one of the sheep, thought the ending was meretricious. Referring to "the magic words, 'Liberty, with responsibility,'" he commented, "There are few things less capable of calming a woman who is longing for a free, adventurous life with all its mysteries, than the offer of such moral advantages as free choice with responsibility."[21]

Lou Andreas-Salomé, Nietzsche's companion, delighted in the ending. She wrote that when Wangel gave Ellida her freedom, "Nora's dream of the 'most wonderful thing of all' became a reality."[22] Typical of the negative critics was Erik Skram, who objected to both the symbolism and the lack of psychological truth in the relationship of Wangel and Ellida. He found it hard to believe that they could have been married so long without knowing each other better. More disturbing to him was the figure of the Stranger, whose unreality was not in harmony with the rest of the play. Skram also found the concluding moral, "freedom with responsibility," as banal as a politician's slogan.[23] The Swedish critic Urban von Feilitzen was much more severe. Putting freedom ahead of responsibility, he said, marked a reversion to barbarism.[24]

Whether the ending was meant to be a happy one has been endlessly discussed. Ibsen's own comments suggest it was left deliberately ambiguous. To someone who, after the Berlin premiere, expressed some slight doubts about the ending, Ibsen replied, "Well, whether my Ellida and Dr. Wangel can now live together, that the future must tell us."[25] On another occasion, when asked if it was true that his new play ended happily, Ibsen cunningly and with a smirk answered, after a pause, "Oja, aber ganz ohne Teufelei geht es doch wieder nicht ab" ("Oh, yes, but it won't happen without some devilry").[26]

These equivocal remarks are in keeping with the final scene of the play, which could be read as striking a positive note. Ellida resolves to stay with Wangel and to become a mother to his daughters. She recognizes that there is "work for me to do here," and she accepts the fact that she can never find her way back to the sea. The band plays brightly, while the last tourist ship of the season sails away.

Although *The Lady from the Sea* met with a mixed reception in Germany, the author himself was hailed there as the greatest living writer. In March 1889 three of his plays were running simultaneously in Berlin: *The Lady from the Sea, A Doll's House,* and *The Wild Duck.* Ibsen was there for a weeklong tribute, appearing in theaters thirty times in response to plaudits. He was, second to Bismarck, the most-talked-about man in Germany. Oscar Blumenthal, manager of the Lessing Theater, who seven years before had dismissed *A Doll's House* as a boring and meaningless piece, now, after his fine production of it, handed Ibsen a laurel wreath. *The Wild Duck*, which a few years before had bewildered critics, was now hailed as the play of plays, the *crème de la crème* of dramatic art.

Five theaters in Berlin competed to premiere *Lady from the Sea*, with the Königliches Schauspielhaus winning out—rather surprisingly, since it was noted for lighter entertainment. On opening night, Ibsen was called forth time and again, although the applause was more for the man and his previous accomplishments than for his play. At the end of the week, on the day before he returned to Munich, the journalist and future play director Paul Lindau gave a luncheon for Ibsen, attended by notables in various fields: government officials, professors, authors, and composers, Johannes Brahms among them.

Although *Lady from the Sea* has never been ranked among Ibsen's finest dramas, it does contain the portrait of a woman who merits a place alongside Nora Helmer, Rebecca West, and Hedda Gabler in the gallery of remarkable women's roles. In its subtlety and depth it poses the ultimate challenge to actresses. The critic who compared Ellida to Hamlet, as someone who "loses the sense of life's laws and realities in the inward ocean of timeless, endless contemplation," may have sensed the source of its appeal to actors.[27]

It was the favorite role of Duse, the supreme tragedienne of her time. She closed her 1909 season with the play when she retired (temporarily) from the stage, and it was one of the first she performed when she returned to the stage in 1921. She began her final American tour with *The Lady from the Sea*, presenting the play in the cavernous Metropolitan Opera House in 1923 to a sold-out house, with scalpers charging as much as two hundred dollars for a ticket.[28] She was then in her early sixties, and her hair was graying. But her voice was still a magnificent instrument, capable of being heard in the remotest corners of the house even when she spoke in conversational tones. Her nervous intensity and her expressive gestures, sometimes languorous, sometimes spasmodic, suited the part of Ellida perfectly. Her Ellida in the first act was happy and carefree until Lyngstrand tells the story about the American sailor.

Some intimations of what made Duse the perfect Ellida may be gleaned from the account of a journalist in Turin in the spring of 1921 who managed to slip into a rehearsal. His notes offer a rare opportunity to observe how the dramatist's genius infuses that of the actress and give a sense of the potential theatrical greatness that lies at the heart of the role.

The rehearsal has reached act two, the scene that usually proves to be the most effective onstage. Duse is leaning against a chair, and Ermete Zacconi, playing Dr. Wangel, is upstage. He says, "Ellida, we are alone."

Figure 24. Eleanora Duse as Ellida
in *The Lady from the Sea*, 1890.

The voice of Duse marks a momentary pause. Her eyes take on an expression both sweet and slightly nervous, and she utters these simple words, "Come sit next to me," with such an inflexion of the voice that it enchants and enthralls.

The characters study each other, having opened up themselves to each other.

Duse is not satisfied and does it again. Ermete Zacconi, who has come near her, consults briefly with her, a brief, quiet exchange of words, and the two artists start again. The right expression is found and Duse can be heard saying, "This is fine." The scene continues. The two artists proceed expertly with the nervous, lean, deliberately spare Ibsenian dialogue. The long work of the rehearsals . . . has made them the unquestioned masters of their parts. Ermete

Zacconi, the calm, debonair, inquisitive but sweet-mannered Wangel... insists on unveiling the soul of Ellida.... Eleanora Duse, the dreamy, ardent Ellida, who is still trying to keep her secret, yet feels certain that it will be torn from her bit by bit by the person who will help her win the battle for her liberation, is a whole mystery of gesture and words. Her face conveys only one impression: that of a faraway dream, a painful torture that holds her in the spell of its charm, but is no longer urgent and imperative. Her voice is at times low, at other times nervous.

[He tells her,] "You cannot live here. Our mountains are oppressing you, there is not enough light for you here, the horizon is not wide enough for you, the wind is not blowing strongly enough."

The actor pauses. There is a flash in the eyes of the great actress. Zacconi understands that he must do it again, that the tone is wrong. He repeats the passage twice, until Ellida stops him with a smile and says, "It is true, day or night, winter or summer, I always feel attracted by the sea."

It is said that many "Ibsenian" actresses speak this sentence with a halting or excessively declamatory tone of voice, making a state of mind sound artificial, when the voice should convey it simply as it is. There is nothing of the sort in the voice of Duse. A great, painful calm, an almost melancholy certainty, a regretting that she is not able to love what her devoted husband loves, and a desire she tries to defend herself against... all expressed with the most effective and simplest voice one can imagine.

...

[Ellida tells Wangel what she and the Stranger talked about.] "We talked about tempests and days of calm, about dark nights and days full of sun. We talked about whales and about seals dragging themselves on the rocks in the sunlight, and of the winds and sirens. Then it seemed to me that all of them had to belong to the same race, and it seemed to me that I myself had to belong to the ocean."

How can one render this brief passage in which all the life of a Nordic sea is made to live again in the reality of all its aspects and in the dream of a soul inebriated by the spell of that reality?

"He took from off his finger a ring that he always had with him, and made me give him a ring I had, and putting them together he said that from that moment we were married to the sea, and then threw far away, far away into the waves the two little circles of gold."

Far away, far away. And the gesture that Eleanora made, and her look, accompanied the simple words with such expressiveness that it raised a murmur of admiration....

"Those eyes I saw once again!"

The pause that follows is entirely filled with a worried silence. Is this one of those famous silences of Duse? Now I understand why they have been so much discussed. I understand why her marvellous, clear, firm, never shaky voice is equaled in one's memory only by her silences.

"When? Where?"

"At Brathammaren. . . . Ten years ago."

"What are you saying?"

"The boy had the eyes of the stranger."

Her voice has started to tremble. One realizes that this woman, with those words, is revealing her mystery, that her entire life and its sufferings are pent up in that sentence, locked in her heart for ten years, and that the moment of truth cannot bear a scream of either repugnance or boldness.

"Ellida."

"Now you must understand why I do not want, why I cannot live with you—as your wife."

The anguished cry bursts out; Ellida cries out, raises her hands towards her judge, looks at him, and flees while throwing her very soul at him, with a desperate look in her eyes, before disappearing from sight.

Eleanora has disappeared, and I too tear myself away from my hiding place and return to life, to reality. I cast a glance at the audience. Strong emotions can be seen on everyone's face. And above all I see Ermete Zacconi exclaim, his eyes sparkling with emotion and joy: "What a perfect Ellida!"[29]

The English critic James Agate, who saw Duse in 1923, conveyed some sense of her genius in bringing Ellida's haunted past into the present.

The long second act was a symphony for the voice, but to me the scene of greatest marvel was the third act. In this Duse scaled incredible heights. There was one moment when, drawn by every fibre of her being to the unknown irresistible of the Stranger and the sea, she blotted herself behind her husband and took comfort and courage from his hand. Here terror and ecstasy sweep over her face with that curious effect which this actress alone knows—as though this were not present stress, but havoc remembered of past time. Her features have the placidity of long grief; so many storms have broken over them that nothing can disturb again this sea of calm distress. If there be in acting such a thing as pure passion divorced from the body yet expressed in terms of the body, it is here. Now and again in this strange play Duse would seem to pass beyond our ken.[30]

THE IMMORALISTS

In 1883 Bjørnstjerne Bjørnson celebrated his silver wedding anniversary by publishing a play called *A Glove* (*En hanske*). Scandinavian plays written shortly before this, such as *A Doll's House* in 1879, *Ghosts* in 1881, and Edvard Brandes's *A Visit* in 1882, had advocated a more liberal attitude on the question of the double standard for men and women. In *A Glove*, however, Bjørnson, the recognized leader of Norwegian liberalism, took the extreme position that men should be as restricted in their sexual activities as they expected women good enough to marry them to be. In his play, the heroine throws her glove in the face of her fiancé when she learns that he is not without sexual experience. Although no one at first took Bjørnson very seriously, a fire had been lit that would rage for years. Strindberg responded to Bjørnson in a satiric short story, "The Wages of Virtue," challenging the Norwegian's preachments by showing the disaster that befalls a young man who rigidly abstains from sexual intercourse. Strindberg's publisher was summarily brought to trial, officially for a blasphemous reference to the Lord's Supper but obviously for Strindberg's indecent sexual posture. At about the same time, the fire was fed by Arne Garborg in his lighthearted, sensual short novel *Youth*. Georg Brandes said that the sense of the story was that the sexual drive, if repressed, would cause irreparable harm to the human being.

No one better represented aggressive naturalism in the arts than Hans Jæger (1854–1910). A young, hotheaded intellectual, schooled in German philosophy, a rebel against bourgeois society and its institutions—especially that of marriage, which he argued was a major cause of immorality—he deliberately provoked a confrontation with men like Lorentz Dietrichson, the guardians of the established order.

So far the fictional treatment of sexual mores had featured middle-class citizens. Then suddenly artists and prostitutes appeared on the scene. In December

1885 Jæger's brutal novel about brothel life, *From Christiania's Bohemia* (*Fra Kristiania-Bohêmen*), was published in Norway—and immediately confiscated. Jæger was fined six hundred kronor and sentenced to a sixty-day term in prison for "blasphemy and offenses against public decency and morality." The publisher saved what copies he could and transported three hundred of them to Sweden to sell under the title "Christmas Tales" (*Julefortælling*).[1]

The event, symptomatic of the issues seething beneath the surface of Norwegian life, polarized the artistic community. The confrontation between Ibsen and Dietrichson was part of the same scene. Under it lay a seismic cultural shift, in art, politics, religion; and Ibsen, like no one else in Scandinavia, pictured it with a fullness and faithfulness that seemed to betoken its inevitability. For the old guard, Ibsen was anathema.

A year later the artist Christian Krohg published his novel *Albertine*, about the making of a prostitute. It too was confiscated. But Krohg was not to be silenced. The book was read aloud at meetings of the workers' union in Christiania, and Krohg put Albertine on canvas in a striking naturalistic painting: "Albertine in the Waiting Room of the Police Doctor." Shortly afterward, the Norwegian government annulled the law legalizing prostitution.

Ibsen was offended by the frank description of the seamier side of the artist's life in these works.

"What a fine literature is being established in Christiania! Hans Jæger's vulgar book was sent to me and I glanced through it. I don't know *Albertine*, and I don't care to get acquainted with it. Anyway, it's only possible to see this rabble mentality as a temporary madness. But in any case it shows clearly enough that our nation is not nearly ready for the principles of freedom."[2]

This moral debate provided the background to the disagreements within the Norwegian Student Association that led in 1885 to the formation of the more liberal Student Union. As we have seen, Ibsen was caught up in the controversy when the liberal members chose to regard him as one of themselves. Consequently, the presiding officer of the conservative association, Dietrichson, could not avoid locking horns with Ibsen.

The animosity had been brewing for some time, ever since Dietrichson in 1882 condemned *Ghosts* as an inferior work, revealing a falling-off of Ibsen's creative powers. What he really meant was that *Ghosts* was naturalism at its worst. To him the downward course of naturalism bottomed out in the sheer depravity of a play that dealt with syphilis, incest, and euthanasia.

He had a clear idea of the implications of the naturalist philosophy, which he saw as the basis of a world without a moral center. He regarded the breakup of the Student Association not as a minor skirmish over political differences but as a sign of a new era in which the old moral values would be cast aside. He was stunned by the sexual cynicism of many of the young men. In his memoirs he described the impact it had on him in 1885.

"When I saw around me all those grinning, laughing, jeering young faces—they were like a pack of satyrs—and noticed how all their remarks about woman's animal nature were greeted with thunderous applause, while remarks, or even so much as a word, that suggested something beyond the worship of the flesh were greeted with hisses or scornful laughter, I thought: what will become of these young men; how can there develop any character in this generation that sneers and sniggers when it hears such words as Ideals, Idealism, Spirituality, Soulfulness? And my impressions turned out to be right. Many unfortunate young people were badly harmed in this period of the apotheosis of the flesh."[3]

According to Dietrichson, many liberal writers were reluctant to dissociate themselves from these worshippers of the sensual. Even Ibsen's name was used as a shield by them. "Could they not hope, precisely because he was not present, to use his great name and his broad-minded views to decorate this filth, certain that he would not climb down from his poet's heights—now any more than in the past—to disavow any such misuse of his name? This quiet hope became the basis of the tactics used against the association [in 1885]."[4]

In the 1885–90 period, literary Scandinavia was aflame with the controversy. In the center of it stood Georg Brandes. Spokesman for the godless naturalists, he praised Garborg, sided with Strindberg, and defended Jæger and Krohg. He even took to using the nom de plume Lucifer to bait and ridicule those angelic ladies who proclaimed the virtue of "conventional married life in which half the ladies produce children while living together with a husband for whom they feel nothing at all and in which consequently the sexual urge . . . becomes the only factor."[5]

No one was more furious than Bjørnson, who railed against "that impotent little Brandes, who sits there and talks about us as if we were like him! Damn it, I'd like to call up a hundred Hungarians with saddles and sabers to attack all the Jew goats in literature."[6]

The morality feud, as it came to be known, reached its highest pitch of virulence in 1887. A league of women under the leadership of Elisabeth Grundtvig held public discussions on the role of sex in women's lives. One point that she made particularly rankled Brandes. She argued that it was obvious from the writings of men like Schopenhauer, Strindberg, and Garborg that greater sexual freedom only led to greater unhappiness. Brandes replied that he was not advocating total sexual license; he was urging a higher form of sexual morality. One member of the women's league answered him in reasonable tones, concluding, "We are not angels." For some unfathomable reason, this unleashed a virulent response from Brandes, who accused Grundtvig of violating the biblical commandment against bearing false witness, of perfidy, of defamation of character. The woman sued for libel and brought to court the newspaper that had published Brandes's article. She won, and the paper was fined one hundred kronor plus legal expenses. (Brandes was not charged because he had signed the article "Lucifer," not with his name.)[7]

Bjørnson protested in print against Brandes's "brutal assault" on the lady, and toured Norway and Sweden to lecture on polygamy and monogamy, thereby confirming Brandes's observation that the main concern of Scandinavians was to watch over each other's sexual drives. "Our main occupation is anxiously to see to it that others aren't satisfying that urge." Bjørnson's lecture tour took him to more than a hundred towns, and everywhere the natives welcomed him as a hero. The year ended with a clear defeat for the sexual liberators, with Sweden in particular being described as "terrorized by the moralists."[8]

In December, Brandes wrote to a German friend:

> I do not know . . . if you have followed the bizarre moralizing plague that in the past few years has spread from Bjørnson's *Glove* and infected the Nordic countries. All the old syphilitics beaming with joy at the thought of male virginity! All the old maids ranting about equality. And Bjørnson, that old goat, who seems to have entered into the equivalent of woman's change of life, delivering exactly the same lecture day in, day out, in eighty different towns in Scandinavia, preaching the new gospel that one mustn't kiss the girls. And three nations are by this moved to tears, while the only tangible result of the business is the thousands and thousands of coins that go to line Bjørnson's pockets.[9]

A caricature of the time pictured Bjørnson in the guise of Venus, his left hand on his breast, his other hand, gloved, demurely hiding his sex; around his head the glory of a saint with angelic faces peeping out everywhere; by his feet a bag labeled "60,000 kronor," the income from his lecture tours.[10]

In that same letter Brandes went on, "There is something senile in this chastity madness. And alas, alas, I find traces of the same in Ibsen. What else is that impossible doctrine of a cleansing, purifying influence that flows from the sexless Rosmer. There is something totally seminarian in taking sexlessness for purity."[11]

In 1883 when the morality feud erupted, Brandes, having resettled in Denmark after some years in Germany, was having an affair with a well-to-do Copenhagen girl, Bertha Knudtzon. Brandes's wife, assiduous in her spying, removed the travel stickers on her husband's luggage and had Bertha's mother do the same to the girl's luggage in order to prove that the lovers had been staying in the same towns.[12]

Brandes by this time was a different man from the youth who championed women's rights, translated Mill, and took as a lover a married woman whom he saw as stultified by marriage. She was his first love. But when she abandoned him for another, he became cynical about love and marriage. "The first love of my young years," he said, "left me for an Italian donkey driver who could neither read nor write, and this after she had lived with me for years and assured me again and again that she could never love anyone else."[13] (Brandes once remarked that Danes had uttered their only witticism about marriage when they coined the word *gift*, which means both married and poison.)[14]

Harassed at home, badgered in public, always the center of the turbulent intellectual life of the 1870s and 1880s, Brandes in that crucial year 1887 looked older than his forty-four years. His tribulations had etched deeply the lines that time had penciled on his face. There were heavy bags under his gray eyes, and gray strands in his thick, lusterless hair. But his sexual potency was not appreciably diminished, and his soft voice, his homely but expressive face, and his unquestioned genius exercised a compelling attraction for many women, even those, especially those, who learned to despise him. Such a one was Victoria Benedictsson.

She grew up in southern Sweden in the fertile province of Skåne. Her tyrannical father, Thure Bruzelius, brought her up as a boy, perhaps because of his disdain for women but more probably because he had lost, a year after Victoria was born, a twelve-year-old son whom he mourned profoundly. In order to escape from her dour, pietistic mother, she rashly married in 1871, when she was twenty-one, Christian Benedictsson, the forty-eight-year-old postmaster in Hörby, in southern Sweden. He was a widower with five children. She gave him two more, one of whom died in infancy. When married life began to pall, she sought further liberation by writing stories, under the nom de plume Ernst Ahlgren. The many months she had to spend in bed as the result of a knee injury (*periostitis con fistula*), which evidently never did heal properly, gave her ample opportunity to exercise her pen. Her first published works, *From Skåne* (1884) and the long short story "Money" (1885), brought her immediate recognition as a social realist and a temperate feminist, defending divorce but censuring free love. Her idol was Georg Brandes, the spearhead of the new breakthrough in literature, the early champion of feminism, the dauntless fighter against the religious doctrines and the bourgeois codes that had stunted her own spiritual growth. She dreamed of meeting him and becoming part of his cosmopolitan world.

In 1886 her dream came true. She threw herself at him, unaware at first that her idea of the relationship between man and woman was different from Brandes's. Developments in the morality controversy had made it clear that his kind of feminism aimed at lowering sexual barriers for women, not raising them for men. The feminists sided with the retired "old goat" Bjørnson and reprobated the immoralist Brandes, for whom, they said, free thought meant free love. Benedictsson was averse to sex, either because of her strange upbringing or because of some physical hindrance that prohibited sexual fulfillment.[15] She wanted to be a mother to Brandes, the breast on which her hero would recline his head after his battles in the political arena, the soulmate who would inspire him and who would be inspired in turn. What she found instead was a child who hungered for esteem and admiration. He was vain and deceitful. She winced at his Don Juan complex, his pride in relating his sexual conquests to her. She quarreled with him over his advocacy of free love. To Benedictsson, if love was free, it was worthless; it had to be coined by the intellect, not wasted in physical orgasms. To her diary she confided, "As a person you are so much less than I, but as a writer so much more."[16] Yet she had no high opinion of herself as a person. She feared she was plain, and she recognized that hers was a man's mind in a woman's body.

She and Brandes would meet in Copenhagen in her room in the Hotel Leopold, the habitat of the Swedish colony there. He would talk; she would record much of what he said in shorthand; he would attempt to seduce her; she would rebuff him; he would leave.

Brandes thought her another of those hysterical women who had been created by morbid sexual conventions and was confident that if he once possessed her she would be set free. It was not that simple. She felt that if she gave herself to him, he would discard her like an old glove. And she was neurotic, a woman who wanted to succeed as a man. "Damned to be a woman, but with a man's energy and drive," she complained.[17] But when she was asked by the feminists to write on the subject, she contributed an ambivalent piece that caused her to lose the support of some of her literary friends in Sweden. This was typical of her affair with Brandes, which brought to the surface the deep division in her soul.

In her diary, she wrote on April 21, 1886, "I will certainly show my personal liking for him, but I won't stand behind his view that nature desires polygamy and that monogamy is an artificial construct. I am convinced of the opposite: that monogamy is natural for the human being, like walking on two feet, even if he once walked on four." And later, on June 17, "I don't see anything harmful in a person being in love, if it's only natural. But if a woman married to a man falls in love with another, that's against nature, that's disgusting."[18] Yet she had also, earlier, confided in her diary, "In everything that involves being with other people I've loved lawlessness. . . . In reality, ever since my childhood I've sought for this one thing: a lawless person—someone for whom conventionality is only proper attire, which he wears casually, but which he can throw aside when he wants to feel free.

"Oh, how I hate conventionality! Why have I never met a really hot-blooded, deliberate lawlessness? Why always this inhibited, detestable philistinism?"[19] When her novel *Fru Marianne* appeared in 1887, Georg Brandes's brother Edvard dismissed it in a sarcastic review, and Georg in a letter to Victoria wrote that even with the best will in the world he could see in it nothing more than a romance for a lady's magazine. Doubtless, Georg's opinion was colored by his part in the morality feud, for in that context the novel seemed reactionary. He did not appreciate Victoria's acute psychological insight into the lives of ordinary people. She thought alternately of killing herself and shooting Brandes. In her diary she wrote, "The death sentence was passed on my writing, perhaps on myself."[20]

Sexual intercourse, which Brandes regarded as a casual physical function but which she invested with her own kind of mystique, only emphasized the differences between them. She knew she was only an interlude in his life. She knew she could never truly be a part of his world, the world she had dreamed of for years. She was, as she herself put it, "a little planet that had come too close to a bigger one."[21]

Her desire to ingratiate herself with a man who was for her the incarnation of lawlessness, says one critic, can be traced back to her being raised by diametrically opposed parents. "It can well seem paradoxical, but one can neither simplify it nor explain it away. It is evident throughout her life, and it is what proved her undoing."[22]

In January 1888 she determined to kill herself by taking an overdose of morphine. She confided her plans to her comrade Axel Lundegård, a man with whom she shared all intimacies except physical ones. An enlightened, freethinking respecter of the rights of the individual, Lundegård sat at her bedside as her life began to ebb away. She grew restless and told him to leave, to ensure that he would not be implicated legally in her death. As he walked down the hall, he heard her bolt the door.

Staying at the Hotel Leopold at this time was Strindberg, who had been virtually ostracized by his countrymen. Lundegård had furnished the Danish translation of Strindberg's *The Father*, which had just recently been staged in Copenhagen, with Georg Brandes as consultant (who toned down some of the dialogue); and Lundegård had collaborated with Strindberg on a sprightly satire on the new woman, an antifeminist, anti-Ibsen comedy known in its various stages as "Female Slaves," "Duel," "Fads and Fancies," "Marauders," and finally *Comrades*. With the last title Strindberg was alluding to the friendship between Victoria Benedictsson and Lundegård.

When Lundegård knocked on his door, Strindberg was sound asleep. With astonishing naiveté, Lundegård confided the details of Benedictsson's plight to Strindberg, expecting him to keep them secret. "He listened," said Lundegård, "with an expression that will always remain seared in my memory, an expression of implacable, cannibal-like interest without the slightest trace of human compassion."[23] In the morning Strindberg left the hotel to betray Lundegård's confidence to Brandes.

In the meantime Victoria Benedictsson vomited up much of the morphine, but she remained affected by the drug for the next few days. She remembered through the haze that Brandes had come to see her twice. Three days after her attempted suicide she and Brandes had another brief conversation, the gist of which she recorded in her diary.

> It's nauseating to commit suicide; he has no sympathy for me—less than ever now. Says we should stop *tutoyering* each other.
>
> Thrown away like an old glove.
>
> A sullen indignation begins to seethe in me—the first sign of life perhaps.
>
> And . . . Axel said to me, "You are a sentimental fool!" Said it so gently and affectionately.[24]

Her compulsion to suicide was not to be easily thwarted, however. Six months later the sentimental fool, drawn to the millrace, as she put it, glancing at the double suicide in *Rosmersholm,* attempted once again to kill herself. On July 18, 1888, she wrote a long letter to be delivered to Brandes after her death. The last lines read, "There is no hope left. Down into the black depths. How happy is he who can die among loved ones, holding someone's hand. Be happy. Dearest! Dearest! Dearest! Your friend, Ernst."

Three days later she lay down in her room in the Hotel Leopold and, sometime after the clock struck midnight, holding a mirror in one hand and a straight-edge razor in the other, hacked away at her throat, the first three times rather tentatively. On the fourth stroke, however, she cut deep, and blood and life spurted from her.

The Scandinavian literary world had long buzzed with rumors of the affair between Victoria Benedictsson and Georg Brandes, and her death was not unexpected. Strindberg immediately capitalized on it. His play *Miss Julie* needed a resolution, and he found one in Victoria's suicide.[25] Miss Julie's recital of her upbringing as a boy almost certainly derives from Strindberg's knowledge of Benedictsson's life. The newspapers of course carried the story of the suicide and implicated Brandes, while Lundegård, faithful to the memory of comrade Victoria, did all he could to blacken Brandes's already tarnished reputation. More than almost anyone else, Brandes represented the immoral and superior being who put himself above laws and conventions. His increasing alienation from society coincided with his involvement with Benedictsson, but she scarcely offered the refuge and support he needed. That came unexpectedly from another source, from a man who was equally alienated, virtually unknown, however, and quite untouched by scandal.

As early as 1883 Brandes had evinced some interest in the German philosopher and classicist Friedrich Nietzsche. But it was not until 1887 that the German Antichrist and the Danish Lucifer could meet on somewhat the same footing. Brandes was being assailed by old enemies and former friends for his stand in the morality feud when there arrived in the mail a copy of Nietzsche's *On the Genealogy of Morals.* To a German friend Brandes expressed his delight: "You have in Germany a philosopher whom I value very highly and who has recently written wisely and well about ascetic ideals. I refer to Friedrich Nietzsche in his book *On the Genealogy of Morals.* He seems to me the most brilliant of Germany's thinkers."[26]

To Nietzsche himself he wrote:

> For the last four years I have been the most detested man in Scandinavia. Every day the papers rage against me, especially since my last long quarrel with Bjørnson, in which the moral German papers all took part against me. I dare say you know his absurd play A *Glove,* his propaganda for male virginity and his covenant with the spokeswomen of "the demand for equality in morals." Anything like it was certainly unheard of until now. In Sweden these insane women have formed great leagues in which they vow "only to marry virgin men." I suppose they get a guarantee with them, like watches, only the guarantee for the future is not likely to be forthcoming....
>
> You speak somewhere with a certain reverence for marriage.... Why not for once say the full truth of it? I am of opinion that the institution of marriage, which may have been very useful in taming brutes, causes more misery to mankind than even the church has done. Church, monarchy, marriage, property, these are to my mind four old venerable institutions which mankind will have to reform from the *foundations up* in order to be able to breathe freely. And of these, marriage alone *kills* the individuality, paralyzes liberty and is the embodiment of paradox. But the shocking thing about it is that humanity is still too coarse to be able to shake it off....
>
> In these realms [Scandinavia] I am even more hated now than I was seventeen years ago. This is not pleasant in itself, though it is gratifying insofar as it proves to me that I have not yet lost my vigor nor come to terms on any point with all-pervasive mediocrity.[27]

Although there was much in the German's philosophy that Brandes thought forced and strange, especially in *Thus Spake Zarathustra,* which he found came perilously close to madness, on salient points there was agreement. He fully approved Nietzsche's theory of the origin of the tender conscience, according to which the repressed classes made a virtue out of their weaknesses and turned their aggressive instincts against themselves, labeling as sins what the rulers regarded as virtues: pride, physical strength, cruelty. Ascetic morality, Christian morality, was a slave morality that had to be eradicated. A moral revolution was in the offing, and to bring it about the great man, not the common man, had to be cultivated.

So impressed was he by Nietzsche that early in the spring of 1888 he decided to expound Nietzsche's teachings in a series of five public lectures to be given on Tuesday of each week. On April 3 Brandes sent word of his intentions to Nietzsche and asked him for a photograph and a vita. Since no one had heard of Nietzsche, the first lecture on April 10 was attended by only one hundred fifty or so, a poor number for Brandes. But publicity was given to the series by résumés in the newspaper *Politiken* and by an article that Brandes wrote, with the result that three hundred people filled the hall to overflowing at subsequent lectures. "What makes this so interesting," said one young listener, "is that it has not to do with books but with life." The awkward lecturer who in 1871 had to apologize for his lack of experience on the platform was now a spellbinding orator who carefully planned his rhetorical effects. The last lecture of the series was greeted with a thunderous ovation.

Victoria Benedictsson had attended at least two of these lectures and on May 2 heard her difficult hero describe guilt feelings as a sign of illness, while exalting strong-willed, noble Caesar over narrow-minded, mean, uxorious Brutus. She heard him proclaim that although the ascetic ideals, so long triumphant, still had no real assailants, the prophets of a new order were about to appear. Superseding the martyr with the crown of thorns and the hair-shirt prophets who dig their nails into their own flesh, who flagellate themselves and turn society into an immense hospital, would be the prophets who would contemn weakness, humility, asceticism, and above all guilt. "In our day a new ideal is in the process of formation, which sees in suffering a condition of life, a condition of happiness, and which in the name of a new culture combats all that we have hitherto called culture."[28]

In effect Brandes, who had in his youth translated Mill's *Utilitarianism*, repudiated the dominant ideas of the 1880s that he had helped advance. He declared that he was bringing Nietzsche to the attention of Scandinavia because people continued to busy themselves with the same old doctrines: certain theories of heredity, a little Darwinism, a little female emancipation, a little utilitarianism, a little freethinking, a little lip service paid to democracy.[29] In the peroration of his last lecture he lashed out at the mediocrity into which Scandinavian culture was sinking and asserted that the creation of art demands intellects that are distinguished by their independence, their defiance of popular thought, their aristocratic self-supremacy. The object of Brandes's attack was what Nietzsche termed cultural philistinism, a phenomenon new to the nineteenth century: a poverty of culture accompanied by a perverse belief in its ubiquity.[30] For Brandes, the genius could not be a product of the mass. He would have to be an outsider, who would appear like a mutation, a leap made by nature. Estranged from society, such a man, said Brandes, cannot be happy. His destiny is to be heroic, than which there can be no greater destiny.

Such was the substance of the new philosophy that Brandes championed and to which he gave the name aristocratic radicalism. "Quite the cleverest thing I have yet read about myself," said Nietzsche, who had been calling himself a radical nihilist.[31]

While Brandes was doing all he could to proselytize for Nietzsche, the philosopher went mad, in the final phase of syphilis, collapsing on January 3, 1889. A letter on the last day of the old year, signed "Nietzsche Caesar," embarrassed Strindberg. In Latin he warned Nietzsche not to go to extremes, and, going Nietzsche one better, signed his reply "Strindberg (Deus, optimus maximus)." He forwarded Nietzsche's letter to Brandes and asked whether the sly Pole (Nietzsche was then thought to be of Polish heritage) was really mad or deliberately seeking to compromise him and Brandes. The latter, who twelve months before had been warned by Paul Heyse of signs of madness in Nietzsche's writings, recognized that Nietzsche was utterly insane. "A great, a profound misfortune," he wrote to Strindberg on January 4. "Such a superb mind, so rare, so rich—struck by megalomania."

On the same day that Brandes wrote to Strindberg, Nietzsche wrote to Brandes. "Once you had discovered me it was no trick to find me. The problem now is to get rid of me. The Crucified One." A prophetic remark. Though Nietzsche, incurably mad, was confined to his mother's care, his thoughts began to spread throughout the world, thanks first of all to Brandes. From the speaker's platform he had been the first to call attention to him. His revised lectures were printed in a Danish magazine in August 1889. This article was translated into German and appeared in the April 1890 issue of *Die Deutsche Rundschau*. After that it was impossible to make Nietzsche disappear. He became the center of a cult, and the intellectual world was divided over him.

The controversy over Nietzsche began, as might be expected, in Denmark. Brandes's aristocratic radicalism was impugned by Harald Høffding in an article titled "Democratic Radicalism." In the polemics that followed, with Brandes advocating the great-man theory of civilization and Høffding arguing for egalitarianism, the issues were more sharply defined than they afterward became when the tides of war blurred the battle lines. In retrospect the contenders may appear grotesquely unmatched: Høffding against Brandes and Nietzsche. But it must be borne in mind that Brandes was still smarting from the morality feud in which he had lost the support of many liberals and that Nietzsche was known only through Brandes's lectures and articles. The best-known fact about Nietzsche was that he was mad, and Brandes was compelled to strengthen his forces by invoking Flaubert and Renan, who had by this time been canonized by free-thinking spirits.

Høffding, on the other hand, was the most highly esteemed philosopher in Denmark and would become internationally known during the next decade. He was the quiet voice of reason and moderation; Brandes and Nietzsche were the clamor of the demon in man. Høffding was a man of deep humanitarian instincts, a student of the English school of Mill, Darwin, and Spencer, and politically aligned with the social democrats. His chief work, *Ethics*, published in 1887 (again that crucial year), contended that social morality could not be predicated on any religious imperative but that it was the product of historical conditions and man's nature. The individual learns he can develop most freely when he joins forces with all or part of society in seeking the truth. It was a work that pleased the liberal Bjørnson as much as it irked Brandes, who had learned from bitter experience the emptiness of Høffding's ideas, some of which he had helped advance in his youth but had since put behind him as childish things. What deeply offended Høffding was Nietzsche's exaltation of egoism, that "unshakable faith that to a being such as 'we are' other beings must be subordinate by nature and have to sacrifice themselves."[32] On that salient he launched his attack.

For nine months the public debate continued. In his second article, with the challenging title "The Great Man, Source of Culture," Brandes noted that he had had the same opponents for twenty-four years, among them Høffding and Bjørnson, and that Høffding always cast himself as the angel of light and Brandes as the demon of darkness. Now once again Høffding was taking the safe popular side. As for Høffding's democratic radicalism, that was a gross misnomer. There was nothing at all radical about it. Høffding "always pitches his tent where gentle reason, calm respectability, honest industry, prudent tentativeness, and cautious noncommitment reign supreme."[33] The point, said Brandes, is that great culture is produced by great men, and that the cultural life of a people is deficient when great spirits are not allowed to develop, when everything that smacks of genius is put down. And then, seeking to turn the tables on Høffding, Brandes asked how that general welfare which is man's goal can be attained without great men.

Høffding seized on this by remarking that Brandes was now backsliding in endeavoring to accommodate the superman to the general welfare. This is not Nietzsche's thought, and it destroys the basis of aristocratic radicalism. Brandes regards himself, insinuated Høffding, as the stifled genius. "He has now come to the superman. It makes me dizzy to think," he added, glancing at Brandes's atheism, "what heights he will attain on his next swing." As for himself, he will stick to the people of the earth.[34]

In defending Nietzsche's *On the Genealogy of Morals,* Brandes took aim at Høffding's *Ethics* and asserted that moral laws are only rough guidelines that have become bonds on the human spirit. Høffding replied that the world was not the unlivable, nauseating place that Nietzsche described, and that Nietzsche was not a philosopher but a frenzied poet, fighting phantoms in his own mind. The cultural disharmonies that ring through Nietzsche's work and that he raged against really owe their existence to the fact that he himself was a cracked bell.[35] Brandes retorted that the German philosopher passed beyond Høffding's understanding because Nietzsche was unique and mysterious, a demon whose thoughts moved in great leaps, whereas he, Brandes, could understand, for he was a bohemian and Høffding was a *citoyen.*[36]

Ibsen certainly followed the morality controversy of the late 1880s, and it gave him the basic material for *Hedda Gabler,* both for its plot and for its theme. With that drama he looked to the future, whereas in the preceding plays he had let the evolutionary past provide the groundwork for what happened in the present. In 1887, when the controversy was at its height, Ibsen delivered his most optimistic speech. Toasting the future, he declared that something new was about to arise, what he called the "Third Kingdom." Only a few months later, Brandes was agreeing with Nietzsche on the need to reform all social and cultural institutions from their foundations.

The newspaper résumés of Brandes's lectures appeared during April and May 1889.[37] Brandes's essay "Aristocratic Radicalism," the distillation of his lectures, was published in the August 1889 issue of the journal *Tilskueren.* Ibsen began sketching a new play the following month. One of his early notes reads, "The play shall deal with the 'impossible,' that is, to aspire to and strive for something that is against all the conventions, against what is acceptable to the conscious mind—also in Hedda's."[38] The debate between Brandes and Høffding occupied the pages of *Tilskueren* from August 1889 to May 1890. Ibsen worked intensively on *Hedda Gabler* from July to November 1890, completing the first draft on October 7.

Ibsen's quintessential genius for distilling the major issues of his time into drawing-room dramas is never in more brilliant display than in this play.

If we cast onto *Hedda Gabler* the light of our knowledge about the morality controversy and the subsequent debate over Nietzsche, we can see projected behind the plodding scholar Tesman the shadow of Høffding, and behind the libertine genius Løvborg the double shadow of Brandes and Nietzsche. The divergent careers of Høffding and Brandes almost certainly provided Ibsen with the backgrounds for diligent, prudent, respectable Tesman and erratic, rash, immoral Løvborg. In 1871, when Brandes was lecturing himself out of a professorship, Høffding was appointed a *Privatdocent* at the university. In 1880 he was promoted to docent and in 1883 to professor, taking Rasmus Nielsen's chair. At the same time, a group of anonymous donors, recognizing the injustice that had been done to Brandes, invited him to return to Denmark to give public lectures. In 1885 Ibsen was actually present with both Høffding and Brandes for a brief moment at a Student Association meeting in Copenhagen.[39] Shortly after that Brandes became the central figure in the morality feud. In 1887 Høffding was the author of *Ethics*, while Brandes in that year was the author of any number of scandals. Two years later Høffding and Brandes confronted one another in the pages of *Tilskueren*. All this Ibsen has concentrated into the competition between Tesman and Løvborg for a professorship, a position that the latter actually scorns.

Many of Ibsen's preliminary notes for *Hedda Gabler* betray the kinship between the immoralists Brandes and Løvborg:

> If society won't let us live morally with them (women), then we'll have to live immorally with them.
>
> Why should I conform to social morals that I know won't last more than half a generation.
>
> Great prejudice this: that one loves only one.
>
> Ejlert Løvborg has a double nature. It is a fiction that one loves only one person. He loves two—or many—alternately, to put it frivolously.[40]

The last couple of notes recall the opinions of Hans Jæger, who felt that the average man should have twenty mistresses in the course of his life. "Under present social conditions," said he, "I am cheated of nineteen-twentieths of my share of life."

From the notes we also learn that Tesman, like Høffding, is a meliorist who believes that the future is directed to the great, the good, the beautiful.

> Yes! But the great, the good, the beautiful of the future won't be the same as it is for us.
>
> Tesman is on the verge of losing his head. All his work meaningless. New thoughts! New visions! A whole new world![41]

The fact that Ibsen has Tesman (whose name means thesis-man) doing research on medieval Brabant is probably due to a rubric that Brandes put at the head of one of his rebuttals to Høffding: "*Auf die mittelalterliche oder Ritterzeit ist die neuere oder Professorenzeit gefolgt; jetzt wird die neueste oder Menschenzeit kommen* (Anon.)."

The relationship of Thea Elvsted and Løvborg mirrors that of Victoria Benedictsson and Brandes. In his notes Ibsen describes Thea as "the type of conventional, sentimental, hysterical philistine"[42] and "the nervous-hysterical, modern individual."[43] The irony is that this conventional woman behaves unconventionally. She "who forces [Løvborg] into respectability runs away from her husband."[44] Benedictsson, basically a conventional woman, firmly opposed to free love, left her postmaster husband and her stepchildren and tried to reform Brandes. Similarly, Thea left her sheriff husband and stepchildren to reform Løvborg. (However, Benedictsson had two children of her own; not so, Thea.)

Ellen Key, who wrote the first biography of Benedictsson, published in 1889, described her as a goddess, "a being from the ancient world" (probably with Hera or Demeter in mind, not Aphrodite); this may account for the name Thea.[45]

Ibsen had met Victoria Benedictsson in Stockholm on September 22, 1887, at a supper party given by the feminist writer Anne Charlotte Edgren (née Leffler). He told the young littérateur Gustaf af Geijerstam that the meeting had been too brief for him to get to know Benedictsson's inner nature very well. However, after her death, Geijerstam sent Ibsen a "sympathetic account of her life" that left a lasting impression on Ibsen.[46] And the first biography of Benedictsson, Ellen Key's *Ernst Ahlgren*, appeared later that year.

Present at Fru Edgren's soirée were some of Stockholm's most prominent Ibsenites. The morality controversy naturally came up in the conversation, and Geijerstam courageously defended Brandes. (Benedictsson was the butt of gossip because she was staying in Geijerstam's house in Stockholm.) Both in her diary and in a lengthy letter to Brandes, Benedictsson described what happened when Ibsen joined in the talk.

> Ibsen was in an expansive mood, chatting up the ladies, patting them on the shoulder, and was worshipped like a god. I was disgusted by this adoration and with a kind of perversity kept my distance the whole evening, telling myself it made no difference whether or not I spoke to him. But however it happened, he came and stood in the doorway where a group of ladies stood, I among them. Naturally the group opened up, with the guest of honor at the center.
>
> "Have any of you been following the quarrel between Georg Brandes and Bjørnson?" said the old one, quite unexpectedly.
>
> Some said yes, some said no.
>
> You can imagine how my eyes widened and my ears took it all in. There were these sanctimonious hypocrites all around!

> Someone remarked that [Brandes] had been unfair to Miss G. [Elisabeth Grundtvig] and bitter in attacking her—personally.
>
> And then those small, gray Ibsen eyes glinted.
>
> "It may be that he was bitter," he said, "and it may be that he behaved outrageously, but you have to bear in mind how he has been attacked and how he has been treated. And Denmark should appreciate what a man they have in him."
>
> There got to be some cackling about propriety and morality, and even I could not keep quiet.—It got to be rather lively. Then he smiled that calm, wise smile.
>
> "I shall tell you all something," he said, "something you should take note of. What one should insist on, insist on and defend, is the moral sense that one has inside, within oneself—just what social morality calls devilishness—because that is what is new, what is germinating, what is going to grow."[47]

Two nights later there was a gala banquet for Ibsen, the culmination of his visit to Sweden. He used the occasion to deliver his remarkable speech about the Third Kingdom.

A new era in man's history: this is of course the subject of Løvborg's manuscript, the one that Hedda destroys, the very fulcrum of the play. As in a typical well-made play, it is the physical object on which the plot depends. It is here that the influence of Nietzsche directly manifests itself. Løvborg had written one book that had won the acclaim of the critics and brought him into prominence, making him a contender for a professorship at the university. But his real task was to adumbrate the future development of society, and that he had done in the work that is still in manuscript. Ibsen's notes inform us that Løvborg's first book dealt with the historical development of social doctrines and that the new volume will deal with the ethics of the society of the future, its principal theme being the comradeship of men and women.

Nietzsche had also written works that concerned themselves with the evolution of social doctrines: *Beyond Good and Evil*, with the subtitle "Prelude to a Philosophy of the Future," and *On the Genealogy of Morals*. It was these works that won the admiration of Brandes and thereby brought Nietzsche fame. Moreover, Nietzsche's new work, his work in progress, was to be "The Will to Power: A Revaluation of All Values," in which he intended to set down "the history of the next two centuries." He foresaw the "advent of nihilism" and recognized that "for some time now our whole European culture has been moving toward a catastrophe." It was on this work that he was occupied when he went insane.

Now, who is this Hedda who destroys this vision of the future? Who is this Hedda who burns Løvborg's manuscript? Although she certainly represents the new woman, that third sex, that half man, half woman who, as Strindberg said in 1888 in his preface to *Miss Julie*, was stepping forward to be recognized, she is, more than anyone else, Ibsen himself. What Ibsen said of his heroine he could have said of himself. "Hedda feels herself demonically attracted by the tendencies of the times. But she lacks courage. Her thoughts remain theories, ineffective dreams."[48]

"Løvborg has turned toward the bohemian life. Hedda is drawn in the same direction, but she does not dare to take the leap."[49] The rebellious young Ibsen had suffered as a bohemian and social outcast. With the success of *Brand* he resolved to be an outwardly respectable member of a society that he regarded with considerable disdain. Inwardly, he remained an anarchist, stunning the young Brandes in 1871 with the extremity of his thoughts. But it was Brandes, not Ibsen, who stepped into the arena to battle for the new causes against the philistines, while Ibsen played an ambivalent role, hiding his nihilistic lights under a bushel, collecting medals while disavowing the radical notions his dramatic characters expressed. The mature Brandes found Ibsen reactionary and priggish. Introducing him to Nietzsche, Brandes wrote that as a man Ibsen did not "stand on the same level he reaches as a poet. Intellectually he owes much to Kierkegaard, and he is still strongly permeated by theology."[50] He was distressed to find Ibsen contributing to the "chastity madness" in the morality feud. Nietzsche, writing in 1888, also saw in Ibsen "the typical old maid," afflicted with an idealism that has "the aim of poisoning the good conscience, that which is natural in sexual love."[51]

While Ibsen dreamed of liberation, he leagued himself with the moralists, like Hedda who marries Tesman, although her imagination is with Løvborg. Ibsen envisioned a new world where he need have no fear of scandal or sex. Although his ideas of the manner in which this new world would come into being wavered, generally he put his faith, like Nietzsche and Brandes, in superior individuals: the "nobility of character, of will and spirit," as he phrased it in his 1885 speech. In many respects Ibsen's thoughts were strikingly like Nietzsche's. But like Hedda, he was afraid. "I want to know everything," she says in one of Ibsen's jottings, "but keep myself clean."[52] The result of her endeavors to avoid ridiculous scandal was that she would be trapped in a ménage à trois with Judge Brack, "the representative of the personal bourgeois attitude." Similarly, Ibsen's deepest drives and thoughts were traversed by the "cultural philistines" without whose support he could not have had the security and social position that one aspect of his divided psyche demanded.

Like Nietzsche, Ibsen knew that when the instincts are turned inward, they become destructive. He also understood the need for a tension to exist between the Apollonian and Dionysian aspects of man. This tension kept him productive and sane. In Nietzsche the bond between the two snapped. Ibsen could hardly have known that Nietzsche's mental illness was due to syphilis, but that knowledge would only have confirmed him in his fear of the Dionysian. Løvborg, whom Hedda pictures in her reveries with Bacchic vine leaves in his hair, dies in a brothel, a bullet in his groin (unlike Hedda's carefully aimed bullet to her brain).

Ibsen's play is not about the future development of mankind but about those who inhibit it through their fear of scandal and their trepidations about sex. Thwarted by her role in society and envious of the conventional Thea, Hedda burns Løvborg's manuscript, leaving those philistines Thea and Tesman to reconstruct from his notes a work they cannot possibly comprehend. "Tesman reads in the manuscript," says one of Ibsen's notes, "about 'the two ideals.' Mrs. E. cannot explain what Løvborg meant. Then comes the burlesque note: both Tesman and Mrs. E. are going to devote their lives to interpreting the mystery."[53]

Knowing the real people behind the fictional characters makes the irony even more pungent, and also makes one wonder at Ibsen's powers as a clairvoyant. Nietzsche's philistine sister, under the influence of the teachings of her anti-Semitic husband, pieced up from Nietzsche's notes an incoherent version of "The Will to Power: An Attempt at a Revaluation of All Values," which led to much misunderstanding of Nietzsche. In 1911, when the Danish translation of *Thus Spake Zarathustra* appeared, it was Høffding who wrote the introduction. And when Brandes came to write about Ibsen's play, he chided the author for making Løvborg desire to read his manuscript to Tesman, for whose opinions Løvborg supposedly had nothing but contempt. Brandes found this as "great a disfigurement of [Løvborg's] character as his having misconducted himself toward Hedda," and added in apostrophe, "You are no gentleman, Mr. Løvborg."[54]

In typical fashion the great playwright disavowed being influenced by Nietzsche. After the philosopher's death a reporter asked Ibsen what he thought of Nietzsche. "I wasn't well acquainted with his work. . . . His was a peculiar talent, but because of his philosophy he could not become popular in our democratic age."[55]

Was this more irony, or the straightforward opinion of the man who believed in the "nobility of character, of will and spirit," and whose whole career was a demonstration of the triumph of the will to power?[56]

The Unspoken *Hedda*

In *Hedda Gabler*, the last of his social dramas, Ibsen painted one of his finest portraits, a woman as compelling as Medea, Electra, or Lady Macbeth. Her character is so contradictory in its details that it defies classification and makes us wonder where in all this is the core of her being, admiring her, in spite of ourselves, for being so much more interesting than all those who surround her. She has the best mind of them all, and yet she is the most destructive.

That estimable French Ibsenite Auguste Ehrhard described Hedda as "a sick woman, suffering from a nervous condition. Her mood, usually delicate, is complicated by the particular vexation brought on by her pregnancy. Her nerves are stretched to the breaking point. . . . She is given to acts of cruelty for which she is not responsible. . . . Ibsen softens her wrongful acts. He knows that in these times in order to respond to certain evil influences, a strength of character that does not exist in the ordinary person is necessary. The intransigent moralist of the past shows signs of pity for the guilty ones. The spectator shares this indulgence with him. Hedda is not a completely hateful person. Her story interests us and her unhappiness moves us."[1] Ibsen approved this description of Hedda and praised Ehrhard's book as not likely to be soon surpassed.[2]

As with Nora, Mrs. Alving, and Rebecca West, Ibsen faced the challenge of depicting the inner life of a very complicated woman. The essential drama of *Hedda Gabler* is played out within the heroine. In a note for the play, Ibsen jotted, "It's about 'subterranean powers and forces.'"[3] Once again he had to devise a method for revealing this inner life on the realistic stage.

Before the advent of realistic drama, a playwright found no difficulty in having his characters express their inmost thoughts. Shakespeare could write soliloquies for the introspective Hamlet, and Racine could let the spectators in on Phèdre's smoldering jealousy by letting her speak directly to them. But the nineteenth-century dramatist who wanted to present a photographic semblance of actual human beings onstage had to avoid the soliloquy and the aside. If the rules of the fully developed realistic drama were faithfully adhered to, the spectators had to be thought of as unseen guests, observing what happens onstage but ignored by the people up there. Since the characters onstage could not break through the fourth wall of the set, the viewer had to figure out what was going on in their minds by watching them as they engaged in the ordinary business of daily life, chatted with friends, poured tea, arranged flowers, and passed the time of day.

One of Ibsen's more remarkable achievements was to find ways of revealing the unspoken thoughts of his characters without violating the conventions of realistic theater. Often there are overtones in his dialogue that hint at things not actually said. Just as often, the stage properties and the costumes silently but eloquently comment on the spoken words and the physical action.[4]

There is, however, yet another method that Ibsen used to express what his characters cannot say directly if they are to behave like real people and what he as author could not verbalize for the audience without breaking through the fourth wall and turning himself into a novelist. In *Hedda Gabler,* Ibsen made the stage itself speak. He divided the stage into distinct areas that have special significance, especially when they are considered in relation to one another. A crude form of this technique was employed in the medieval drama, in which heaven and hell were sometimes set up at opposite ends of the playing area, and in the Elizabethan theater, where in *Antony and Cleopatra,* for example, profligate Egypt was opposed to stolid and proper Rome by means of signs over the stage doors. This method is almost uniquely theatrical. It does not work for novelists and lyric poets and nonoperatic composers, though painters have certainly made use of it. Ibsen, who had once set his heart on being a painter, may have been the first realistic dramatist to employ it rigorously throughout a whole play. (In *The Lady from the Sea*, Ibsen made use of a divided set, but not consistently throughout the action.)[5] Although it could be used effectively in earlier times, a great drawback to its use in the realistic theater of the nineteenth century was that explanatory signs could not be hung about the stage. Given the conventions of the peephole stage, what could not be blatantly labeled had to accrue meaning gradually through associations as the play progressed. The hidden drama had to come to light slowly, as in real life.

Ibsen helps the spectator as much as he legitimately can by calling attention in the first moments of the play to the significance of certain visual elements on the stage. When Hedda first appears, she objects to the sunlight flooding the room and asks that the curtain be drawn over the glass doors opening onto the veranda. Her husband's aunt had opened the doors wide to let in the air and the sun. Hedda does not want nature to intrude that much into her life. On the other hand, she does not want the doors closed. She only wants the curtains drawn over the opening. Her husband, George Tesman, does her bidding, saying, "There you are, Hedda. Now you've got both shade and fresh air."

A minute later she crosses the room to the side opposite to the glass doors and stands at the tile stove. She makes this cross when Tesman asks her to look at the old slippers that Aunt Juliane has brought him. Hedda is irritated. "I'm really not interested," she says, coldly.

Her husband follows her across the stage, insisting that she show some interest for his sake; after all, the slippers call up so many pleasant memories for him. Hedda turns from him, moves to the table that occupies the center of the room, and from that point makes her devastating remark about Aunt Juliane's new hat, spitefully and deliberately mistaking it for the maid's. "We shall never manage with that new maid. . . . Look, she's left her old hat lying on that chair." This is her spontaneous retort to Tesman: the hat against the slippers, tit for tat.

Observing this little scene, the audience can see battle lines being drawn up in this quiet domestic setting: Hedda against the Tesman clan, those boring, well-intentioned, ever-so-good denizens of the middle class, who, in Ibsen's words, "stand as a hostile and alien power opposed to [Hedda's] fundamental nature."[6] Moreover, the stage has become a divided room. At the left (from the audience's point of view, as are all the stage directions in the play) the sun enters the room, while toward the right the room is comparatively dark. Dominating that side of the room is a large stove, faced with dark tiles. Hedda launches her sally on the Tesmans from the stove, moving from there to the table in the center to point at the hat.

Each movement by itself seems insignificant, but, lingering in our minds, these movements acquire meaning and become signs in a theatrical language that is not difficult to read. Thea Elvsted is seated in the easy chair next to the porcelain stove as she tells Hedda of her unhappy marriage and of having left her husband. When Hedda expresses surprise at this defiance of social morality—"I don't see how you dared!"—Thea rises from the chair, crosses the room, and sits in the sofa near that glass door. "I simply had to do what I did," she says.

These episodes point to the tensions and conflicts that will dominate the drama: the aristocratic Hedda against the middle-class Tesmans, social propriety against natural instincts. When Judge Brack and Hedda have their tête-à-tête hinting at a ménage à trois, notoriously Norwegianized by Ibsen as *trekant* (triangle), they are seated on the sofa at the right, near the stove. In act two, however, when Hedda reminisces with Løvborg as he recounts his sexual escapades, they are seated on the sofa at the left, near the garden. Judge Brack, the embodiment of sexual and social hypocrisy, never sits on the sofa at the left. Similarly, when Thea, that seemingly proper woman who has flouted social convention by walking out on her husband, says, "People can say what they want," she sits down on the sofa at the left. In contrast, when Brack utters his famous last line, "Such things just aren't done!" he is ensconced in the armchair near the stove on the side of the stage that connotes propriety and the repression of the instinctual life.

Going through the play scene by scene, one can find example after example supporting this interpretation of the division of the stage, left and right. However, Ibsen's characters do not confine themselves to horizontal movements across the stage. They also move up and down it. In fact, the most obvious aspect of the set is the division of the playing space into a downstage area, the drawing room, and an upstage area, the inner room where Hedda will shoot herself. This room is definitely Hedda's domain. She claims it by hanging the portrait of her father there and by having her piano moved into it. This room is her refuge. When Tesman wants her to show her friendliness by addressing his aunt with the familiar *du*, Hedda declines and goes toward the inner room as if to escape from the insufferably sweet Tesmans.

Yet it is obvious that the playgoer cannot identify the inner room exclusively with Hedda. Other people use it. In one of the central scenes in the play, Tesman and Brack sit there while Hedda and Løvborg are seated downstage pretending to be looking at pictures in a photograph album while actually reviving their old relationship as trusting comrades. In those days when they were seeing a lot of each other, Løvborg whispered his secrets to Hedda while General Gabler sat nearby, reading a newspaper. The tolerant father sat near the window in the light, while the two young people sat on the darker side of the room. Now, in the play as we see it, we are in another house and the past is imposed on the present. General Gabler's portrait in the inner room looks down on Hedda and Løvborg, while Judge Brack sits under the portrait, keeping a jealous eye on them. The inference to be drawn from this is that the inner room is not so much Hedda's refuge as it is a link to the past. Ibsen has divided upstage from downstage, inner room from living room, to suggest that the past is ever present in the lives of these people. This is a variation on a technique he had employed in earlier realistic plays. In *Ghosts* he had brought the past to bear on the present by having Oswald make love to Regina, just as years before Oswald's father had made love to Regina's mother. And in *The Wild Duck* he had made the loft at the rear of the stage a repository of things past, imbuing it with an atmosphere that affects the living characters.

Behind the inner room are more rooms, yet even back there, where the bedrooms are located, a symbolic division exists between right and left. Tesman enters from the right when he first appears onstage, and Hedda from the left. Hedda's ancestors were Viking barbarians; George Tesman's were tillers of the soil (their first names—Hedda, a form of Hedvig, meaning battle, and George, meaning husbandman—point to this difference in their lineages). Even in representing the past, Ibsen remains consistent in having the left side stand for the free and untamed human being, and the right stand for the domesticated home dweller. Hedda wants to act like her barbarian ancestors by exerting her power over others, while Tesman, living up to his name, is writing his doctoral dissertation on the domestic industries of Brabant.

Here Ibsen is adopting the ideas of Brandes and Nietzsche, seeing in the Vikings the true origin of the noble, the daring, the beautiful, the warlike. When these savage instincts were suppressed, they turned inward, creating a thwarted Løvborg and a conflicted Hedda.

If the rear area of the stage opens up a vista on the past, and if the main part of the stage where most of the action takes place represents the present, then the extension of the timeline implies that the area farthest downstage might contain glimmerings of the future. It is hardly a matter of chance that in act one Judge Brack and Tesman discuss the latter's hopes for the future while they are seated at the oval table that is closest to the apron of the stage. Again, in act three, when Brack, with barely concealed relish, informs Hedda that Løvborg is a ruined man who will be shunned by every decent person after the brawl in a madam's house, and insinuates that from now on he will take Løvborg's place in Hedda's life, he is seated at this same table at the longer and dominant upstage side, while Hedda is at the left side of it.

The end of act two also connects the downstage table with future events. As Løvborg leaves for Brack's bachelor party, the maid enters with a lighted lamp that she places on this table. Thea says uneasily, "Hedda, Hedda, how is this all going to end?" There is really no need to bring on the lamp shortly before the curtain is to come down on the act except to emphasize Thea's words—and to call our attention to the table.

The table is not empty. The flowers that Thea brought to the Tesman house in the first act were moved from the piano (at the left, on the side of nature) and placed on that table. More to the point, the manuscript of Løvborg's revolutionary work, the book about the future course of civilization, lies on the table as Brack, Tesman, and its author discuss it (while the appurtenances of Tesman and Brack—books, hat, and coat—are grouped together upstage right). During a large part of the act the manuscript and the flowers are displayed together on the table, a weighty image, considering that it was only through Thea's loving care that Løvborg was able to write the book.

At the end of the act, the stage grows dark as the sun sets. Løvborg puts the manuscript in his pocket as the maid brings in the lamp that casts its light on the flowers. The connection between the flowers and the manuscript is now severed, and the viewer is left to wonder what indeed will happen to Løvborg's vision of the future.

Hedda herself is thinking about the immediate future. "At ten o'clock, Løvborg will be back," she says, "with vine leaves in his hair." The phrase is disconcerting and was greeted with derisive laughter when the play was first produced in Munich and Copenhagen.[7] It comes without any preparation; up to this point no one has mentioned vine leaves. Now we both hear about Hedda's vine leaves and see Thea's flowers. Then, at the very end of the act, while Hedda repeats the phrase about vine leaves, she threatens to burn Thea's hair. She virtually drags her into the inner room, behaving like a ravaging Viking, while downstage the light falls on Thea's flowers. There is flow and counterflow to the action. The lamp, brought in from the rear room, comes in from out of the past, as it were, while Hedda hauls Thea back into the past, treating her as she did when they were schoolgirls and Hedda used to bully and torment her by pulling her hair.

Naturally, most of what we see and hear concerns the present, the 1890s, and takes place on the main part of the stage. Behind the middle-class world of the late nineteenth century, spatially and chronologically, lies the world of the barbarians, the Vikings, the precursors of the aristocratic class that has been pretty much replaced by the bourgeoisie, leaving behind only a few relics like Hedda. But this middle class, although it has superseded the aristocracy, is divided against itself. Within it there has sprung up a group, the bohemians, that spurns the values of the tradesmen and has formulated its own code of ethics. These bohemians see the upholders of middle-class values as hypocrites. In Hedda's drawing room the philistines and the bohemians collide. "I only wanted to show," said Ibsen, "what results from the contact between two social classes that do not understand each other."[8]

The Tesman family exemplifies the middle class at its best: gentle, considerate of one another, and self-sacrificing, whereas Judge Brack is the exemplary philistine, the bourgeoisie at its worst, pharisaical, self-serving, and pretentious. His very name was the slangy Swedish contemptuous term for a philistine (*bracka*). What made the philistine so unpleasant was that he harbored petit bourgeois values while entertaining aristocratic pretensions. Brandes in his lectures on Nietzsche in 1888 declared that the assault on the culture-philistine mentality was a phenomenon of the nineteenth century.

The repartee between Judge Brack and Hedda is a fencing match between one who is truly cultured and one who is not. Brack wants to acquire status by possessing Hedda, while she can have a better time dueling with Brack, with whom she has much in common, than prating with her husband. What she has, Brack wants.

What Hedda wants is quite another matter. Like Brack, she would like to be a free spirit, rising above the conventions and prejudices of a society that bores and frustrates her; but, also like Brack, she wants a secure position in that society. The result is hypocrisy in Brack and fretfulness, restiveness, malice, and resentment in Hedda. The child in her womb, now six months after conception beginning to stir noticeably, only exacerbates her nervousness. It will commit her to all that she despises—domesticity, the isolation of motherhood—while Løvborg offers the possibility of at least a momentary escape. She is a woman not only in conflict with the society in which she lives; she is also in conflict with herself. There are demons within Hedda that she cannot control, imps engendered by the intermingling of the Viking spirit with middle-class propriety and restraint. The aggressive barbarian will has been stifled and, finding no outlet in a social environment that confines women to the home, has turned against Hedda herself. Nietzsche in one of his prophetically Freudian remarks said that "all instincts that do not discharge themselves outwardly turn inward," and Ibsen's drama affords a vivid demonstration of those words.[9]

Why did Hedda, an intelligent, sophisticated, stylishly handsome woman from a good family, one of the most admired women in town, accept in marriage the hand of George Tesman, a man she cannot help but ridicule in her chat with Judge Brack? She says it all happened because of an impulse of the moment. Walking home from a party one evening, Hedda, who was only trying to make conversation with Tesman, tongue-tied in the presence of this awesome woman, happened to remark as they passed a handsome town house that she would like to live there. That "brought on the engagement, and the marriage, and the honeymoon, and the whole lot." The cruel irony is that she did not even like the house.

We can guess why she yielded to the impulse, and the stage arrangement provides a visual confirmation of our thoughts. The picture provides the subtext for the scene. During their conversation, Hedda sits in the armchair next to the tile stove, and Judge Brack stands behind the chair. The chairs represent middle-class conventionality and comfort, and the stove is the home of the imps and demons bred by repressed instincts and desires. When Hedda says that "these impulses come over me all of a sudden, and I just can't resist them," she "throws herself down in the easy chair by the stove." Although the stove suggests domesticity and protection against the elements, the man-made fire in it can be as destructive as any natural force, and more pernicious. Hedda's desire to be assured of the comforts of life and a good place in society led her to marry Tesman. Now she is bored and looking for some kind of excitement that will relieve the tensions within her. In the next act the demons will break loose, and the fire will blaze in the stove.

Hedda grows increasingly enraged and destructive as the drama unfolds. In fact, the plot forms a crescendo of malignity, and each one of her wicked acts makes use of a different part of the stage. In act one she makes fun of Aunt Juliane's bonnet, moving from the stove to the table at stage center to do so. In act two she induces Løvborg, the reformed alcoholic, to drink. This happens at the sofa on the left, the garden side, which suggests that Hedda regards it as a creative gesture: she hopes to transform Løvborg into Bacchus. In the third act she burns his manuscript in the stove, killing the "child" of Thea and Løvborg. In the final act she kills herself—and the child within her—in the room at the back of the stage.

The burning of the manuscript constitutes the climax of the drama, and in order to leave no doubts in the viewer's mind about Hedda's reasons, Ibsen for once resorts to the soliloquy, realistically motivated by the circumstances. Since Hedda's mind is exposed here, the scene provides the perfect occasion for a confirmation of the symbolic significance of the division of the stage space. The fire in the stove dominates the scene visually, emphasizing the right-hand side of the stage. The left side, however, is not dark. Earlier, Hedda had gone to the glass door and opened the drapes, letting the bright morning sun pour into the room. Her behavior here contrasts with her dislike of the sun in act one. Furthermore, the stove was not lit in the two previous acts. Although it would seem more true to life to have a fire in the afternoon of act two, when guests were entertained, Ibsen has artfully saved the lighting of the fire for the third act in order to call attention to it. He has also arranged for the curtain covering the opening to the inner room to be drawn shut. The viewer's eye, then, is caught by the shafts of sunlight to the left and the reddish light from the stove on the right. Pictorially, the stage presents a conflict between the sunlight and the firelight, between nature's light and man-made light, between nature and civilization or, more specifically, bearing in mind the time axis of the stage, society at the end of the nineteenth century.

At the beginning of the act there are only a few embers glowing in the stove, and, in keeping with this, Hedda is asleep on the sofa at the left, the side of the natural instincts. The fire will grow brighter throughout the act, and Hedda will be feeding it with the manuscript at the end, burning the "child" of curly-haired Thea. Taking the scene in through our eyes, reading the ideograms of the stage, we see the natural emotions being stifled and perverted, becoming destructive rather than creative. Hedda burns the manuscript out of spite and jealousy. Resentful of Thea (Thea = Dorothea, "the gift of the god"), and envying her abundant hair, her life-giving spirit, and her caring nature, Hedda would rather kill new life and close off the future than see her rival accomplish what she herself could not. The image is that of a pregnant woman throwing the newborn babe of another mother into the fire. And in his inimitable fashion Ibsen combines the intellectual motive with the emotional. Unlike Thea, Hedda understands the significance of the manuscript; hence the destructive act, an infanticide, is raised in our minds above the merely psychological. "Her act," as the French critic Ehrhard wrote, "is not one of simple female vengeance; it is an act of vandalism, a crime against humanity. In committing it, Hedda becomes something other than a mentally disturbed person [*une simple détraquée*]. She assumes in our eyes a superhuman stature; her role takes on a metaphysical aspect. Hedda is the genius of evil fighting against progress."[10]

The Ibsen-hating London critic who called Hedda "a fiend in human form" was not entirely wrong. "She is a revolting, abominable, heartless woman. See her acted by Miss Elizabeth Robins! Do we hate her, do we despise her, do we condemn her? No; we admire her for her very wickedness."[11]

Seen in the perspective of history, the Viking despoiler has degenerated into the Victorian spoiler. Just how true this is may be seen by comparing the early Ibsen play *The Vikings at Helgeland* with *Hedda Gabler.*[12] In the former the heroine, Hjørdis (who is equivalent to Brünnhilde in Wagner's *Der Ring des Nibelungen*), prefers to slay herself and her love rather than to live on in a Christian world in which the Viking qualities of pride and self-assertion would be regarded as moral defects.

"The white god heads north," she laments. "I do not wish to meet him. The old gods are no longer strong. They sleep. They are but shadows, half-alive. With them shall we fight! Out of this life, Sigurd! I will set you on the throne of heaven, and I shall sit at your side."[13] She kills Sigurd with an arrow from her bow, only to learn that he had become a convert to Christianity and that consequently they will not meet in the afterlife. Hedda's destruction of Løvborg contains a much greater irony, for Hedda at that moment is no Hjørdis. She burns the manuscript in resentment against the good Christian Thea, whereas Hjørdis acts out of regret, maintaining her nobility of character. But, like her Viking forebear, Hedda must face death alone, knowing that Thea and Løvborg will exist together in the future through the salvaging and reconstruction of the manuscript.

When Hedda burns the manuscript, exulting in this surrogate infanticide, she is at her worst. The admirable Viking attributes, the willingness to face a challenge unflinchingly and the ability to bear defeat without rancor, have deserted her. The stage picture tells as much. The rear room, the area representing her ancestral past, is closed off throughout the act so that we may see her as trapped in a middle-class Victorian parlor and motivated largely by middle-class standards of respectability, seeking an outlet for her energies not through brave deeds but through a cowardly, selfish, dog-in-the-manger act.

In the last part of the play Ibsen attempts to redeem his heroine. Visually, the opening of the fourth act serves as a sharp contrast to the ending of the third. There the inner room was concealed; the sunlight entered from the left; the fire burned in the stove at the right. As the curtain rises on the fourth act, the drawing room is in darkness, and the inner room is lit by a lamp hanging over the table. The arrangement of light and dark is the reverse of what it was. The implication is that Hedda's Viking spirit is asserting itself. Having carried on like a hysterical, neurotic woman in the previous act, she will now perform with the pride and self-esteem of the barbarian and the hauteur of the aristocrat. Matthew Arnold's designation of the aristocratic class as barbarians applies here: "The Barbarians, to whom we all owe so much, and who reinvigorated and renewed our worn-out Europe . . . The Barbarians brought with them that staunch individualism . . . and that passion for doing as one likes, for the assertion of personal liberty."[14]

In the last act, Hedda the barbarian asserts her personal freedom in the most extreme manner. When Judge Brack, the consummate philistine, insinuates that he, knowing who owns the pistol that killed Løvborg, will blackmail Hedda, she realizes that she must either be forever sullied by public scandal or embraced by the unctuous Brack as his mistress. Either way, she loses her independence and purity. She takes the only way out—for a barbarian. She retreats into the inner room, goes back to her ancestral origins, sits at the piano, the family heirloom, and under the eyes of her father, whose portrait hangs in that room, blows her brains out with her father's pistol. Like Hjørdis, she vehemently rejects a world that does not measure up to her standards, preferring to join the shades of her ancestors.

The painter's eye and the psychologist's insight are at work in the scene in which Brack exerts his power over Hedda. Talking of her fear of scandal, he leans on the back of the armchair at the right, while Hedda, sitting on the ottoman belonging to the chair, is conspicuously at his feet. But she is near the stove in which the demons dwell. When Brack bends over her and whispers his threats, she says, "I'd rather die." The fact that the fire is out implies that she is no longer in the grip of her emotions, no longer *détraquée*. She is thinking clearly. Here the stage picture speaks more eloquently than the words because the properties, the chair, the stool, and the stove, have gradually been accumulating symbolic weight during the first three acts.

There are, however, other symbols in the play that weave through the dialogue to create patterns of meaning. The most obvious of these, the one that stridently calls attention to itself, is the image of Løvborg as a Bacchic or Dionysian figure. Hedda visualizes him returning from Brack's bachelor party with vine leaves in his hair.[15] When that vision is shattered, she imagines him dying "in beauty," that is, by shooting himself in the temple.

Although men in those days did sometimes go to parties at which they wore wreaths of vine leaves on their heads, Hedda certainly does not have in mind one of those staid affairs, such as the Christmas banquet of the Scandinavian Society in Rome, with women wearing wreaths of roses accompanying the men. She is conjuring up an image of Dionysus as Nietzsche pictured him. In *The Twilight of the Idols* (*Götzen-Dämmerung*), which appeared in print only a year before *Hedda Gabler*, the German philosopher described his Goethean superman as a "highly cultured human being who keeping himself in check and having reverence for himself, dares to allow himself the whole compass and wealth of natural being—a man to whom nothing is forbidden, except weakness. . . . He no longer denies. . . . Such faith is the highest of all possible faiths; I have baptized it with the name Dionysus."[16]

Løvborg's work on the history of social and cultural forces and what they portend sounds very much like Nietzsche's *Beyond Good and Evil*, which has the subtitle "Prelude to a Philosophy of the Future." Løvborg's manuscript is in two parts, the first on cultural forces in the past, the second on the future course of civilization.[17]

With Nietzsche's name on the lips of every literate person, contemporary critics immediately saw Hedda as a kind of superwoman, a higher being who places herself above society's moral standards, a woman liberated from conventional attitudes toward motherhood and family life. Not long after Ibsen's play was published, E. F. Lochmann, the doctor who had earlier warned Ibsen against the destructive tendencies of modern science, expressed his view of its heroine: "Hedda Gabler corresponds to Nietzsche's man of the future. She belongs to the supermen, a coming higher stage in evolution. She has emerged a little too early, however, and goes down to defeat in that petty and confining modern society that has no place for these higher existences. . . . Her death is, take note, a "death in beauty"; in actuality, a death without solace and without hope, a complete annihilation."[18]

For Lochmann, who was a political conservative, an antifeminist, anti-Semitic, Christian believer, Hedda was a destructive and cruel human being and her creator the incarnation of a maleficent force.

Nietzsche himself understood the double nature of his higher form of humanity. In a passage that reads like a commentary on *Hedda Gabler*, he said: "Superior spirits run no small danger of learning, one day or another, to look out for the terrible joy that is to be found in destruction . . . in the event of creative activity being absolutely denied them. . . . For such spirits there then remains no other alternative; they may feel themselves constrained to destroy, gradually, insidiously, and with diabolical delight, just what they have loved most."[19]

Like one of these superior spirits, Hedda brings to ruin the one person she admires when he fails to live up to her ideal. When she challenges Løvborg to drink in act two, she wants him to conform to her image of the strong man to whom nothing is forbidden, the superman who is able to retain control of himself while experiencing all that nature offers. She sends him off to Judge Brack's bacchanal for the same reason, convinced that he will return as master of himself—in her words, "a free man for the rest of his life." Seeing herself as a kind of goddess, above and apart from other mortals, she is the uncompromising esthete, and when her lost comrade falls short of her image of him as Nietzsche's Dionysus, she asks him to regain some of his lost glory by making his suicide a beautiful gesture, an esthetic feat beyond the comprehension of shallow souls—"a bullet in the head, it can't get much better than that, *le vrai chic!*" as Ehrhard put it.[20] Like Nietzsche, she believes that only as a work of art and not as a moral product can the world be justified, and only as transmuted into music and not as reduced to reality can the world be redeemed.

At the beginning of the last act, she is waiting for the news that Løvborg has died "in beauty." The idea of dying in beauty would have resounded with echoes of recent sensational events. Only the year before, in 1889, the circus performer Elvira Madigan and her married lover, Count Sixten Sparre of Sweden, had killed themselves in an idyllic setting in Denmark, preferring to die in beauty rather than to live a life that could never be free of scandal. Their tragic fate was the subject of newspaper stories and a popular ballad. Their decision to put their love above and beyond the reach of social convention was inspired by the Mayerling tragedy. Only six months earlier, Archduke Rupert, the crown prince of Austria, had killed the woman he loved, Marie Vetsera, and then shot himself, when the emperor had ordered him to end his liaison with her. An early commentator on *Hedda Gabler* remarked that the audience, upon hearing "die in beauty," would recall all the "theatrical death arrangements" of recent years.[21]

Understandably tense, Hedda paces the darkened room; then moves up into the inner room, which is lit; strikes a few chords on her piano; and comes back into the living room. She crosses to the glass door and looks out into the garden, which lies in darkness. Although she has received word that Tesman's aunt Rina has died, her mind is occupied by other matters: Løvborg's suicide and her pregnancy. She must reconcile herself to a life with the most un-Dionysian of men. Yet her mood is not one of complete frustration. True, she will give birth to a child she does not want, but she is also about to enjoy the thrill of exerting her power over someone else's destiny. The child should have been Løvborg's. Now she must be content with Løvborg's poetic death—an esthetic and sublime deed that she can savor again and again in the tiresome days and years that lie ahead.

Figure 25. Elizabeth Robins as Hedda Gabler, London, 1891.

To Judge Brack she expresses the sense of release and freedom she feels, believing that Løvborg died following her wishes. "I feel liberated, set free, knowing that a bold, gratuitous act is still possible in this world. An instinctive act, shimmering with pure beauty." She utters these Dionysian thoughts while seated in the easy chair near the stove.

Now, it would seem that the more appropriate place for these thoughts would be on the garden side of the stage. Why does Ibsen have Hedda cross the stage and sit down at the stove when her mind is preoccupied by a bold, defiant, unconventional deed, completely in contrast to what the right-hand side has come to represent? If she is imagining her Dionysian Løvborg dying in beauty, why does she take her place with the Pharisees who do not appreciate true beauty and have no conception of the higher man?

Here the stage picture speaks more profoundly than the words. Hedda's physical movement exposes the substratum of her emotional life and betrays what has stirred her more deeply than Dionysian beauty. She returns to the place where she burned Løvborg's manuscript, and she burned the manuscript out of jealousy of Thea. Although she speaks to her confidant of a beautiful, audacious, convention-defying death, her inner being wants Løvborg dead because she cannot have him, because he belongs to someone else. She acts out of resentment, the most un-Nietzschean and un-Dionysian of sentiments. It was the one response to an unpleasant and demeaning world absolutely denied the superman. Carelessly destructive he might be, but never resentful. By putting Hedda in the armchair, Ibsen is pronouncing a Nietzschean judgment on her.

At that moment she is as mean in spirit as she was at the end of act three when she bade goodbye to Løvborg. "I want you to take something to remember me by," she had said, moving upstage. It is a wonderfully revealing moment, its impact often lost in performance because it happens so quickly. Both the manuscript and the pistols are in the desk upstage, and when Hedda takes the one and not the other, the attentive viewer will understand exactly what it is that motivates Hedda and what underlies the talk about dying beautifully.

Equally revealing is her stage cross in the last act when she realizes she is in Brack's power. She rises from the easy chair and crosses to the writing desk, moving into the light, toward the garden of nature, and preparing through her suicide to rejoin the nobler races, who, as Nietzsche described them,

> savor a freedom from all social restraints, they compensate themselves in the wilderness for the tension engendered by protracted confinement and enclosure within the peace of society, they go back to the innocent conscience of the beast of prey, as triumphant monsters who perhaps emerge from a disgusting procession of murder, arson, rape, and torture, exhilarated and undisturbed of soul . . . convinced they have provided the poets with a lot more material for song and praise. One cannot fail to see at the bottom of all these noble races the beast of prey, the splendid blond beast prowling about avidly in search of spoil and victory; this hidden core needs to erupt from time to time, the animal has to get out again and go back to the wilderness.[22]

Hedda takes the other of the two dueling pistols that belonged to her father and retreats into the inner room (off left), where she shoots herself after playing the piano.

The final stage picture sums up the play. The characters onstage are clad in black in mourning for Tesman's aunt. The downstage table, pointing to the future, stands empty. The advance of culture envisioned by Løvborg and understood intuitively by Hedda seems doomed. The manuscript that would have adumbrated the future course of civilization has been destroyed by an undisciplined Løvborg and a spiteful Hedda. Judge Brack is in the armchair at the right, exclaiming, "Such things just aren't done!" That side of the stage was made relatively dark when Tesman moved the lamp from the table above the easy chair to Hedda's desk on the other side of the room. The light is on the left where Thea and Tesman sit, piecing together Løvborg's manuscript, which is entirely beyond their comprehension. Yet they are on the side of life: Tesman, a good man devoted to his aunt; Thea, with her round, watery blue eyes, nervous gestures, and abundant hair that Hedda has always envied. They belong among those who affirm human existence, regardless of its quality, often by sacrificing themselves for the sake of others. And ultimately, even for Ibsen, life itself is more decisive for the progress of humanity than are ideas about life.

For Ibsen, but not for Hedda. When she takes her own life, she escapes from the slave morality of those who surround her and becomes the magnificent barbarian. She takes time to play the Dionysian music for her own death, and she dies beneath her father's portrait. She asserts her Viking heritage while at the same time fulfilling her dream of an exalted life. When she shoots herself, she acts destructively and wantonly but without meanness or rancor. By her own standards and Nietzsche's, she dies in beauty.

Part Three

The Lost Kingdom

World Fame

Ibsen's growing international renown meant more to him than the wealth that came with it. The humiliations he had endured because of his father's business failure would never be completely banished from his thoughts, the mortification never forgotten. However old he grew, he was always quick to take offense at even the slightest slur on his reputation or social rank. It was never a joking matter with him. In 1866, at a feast held by the Scandinavian Society in Rome, toast followed toast as the evening wore on. When to the horror of the imbibers there seemed to be no one left to toast, someone thought of thanking Ibsen for his help in arranging the dinner. Ibsen jumped up, stamped the floor, and burst out angrily, "No one is going to toast me as a member of the committee on FOOD!"

True, he had been drinking too much on that occasion. But he was sober enough at his seventieth-birthday banquet when he was presented with the Great Cross of the Dannebrog Order and, one would have thought, sufficiently secure in his position as an eminent man. Yet when he opened the case and saw the imitation medal—which it was customary to present, since the recipient was expected to pay for the real decoration—Ibsen thought he was the butt of a demeaning prank. The incident was not smoothed over until the minister of culture personally called on him the next morning to hand him the jeweled star as a gift from the king.

Bjørnson, who was equally famous in Norway and more liked (the heart of the nation, as opposed to Ibsen, the mind of Norway), was a republican who disdained awards from the monarch and urged Ibsen to do the same. Ibsen would have none of that. "I am not partial to a republic," he responded. "We [poets] accept money from the government in the form of grants; royalty gives us decorations because it respects popular sentiment and acknowledges its existence. Why reject the one when both are expressions of the same thing?"[1] As one of his countrymen said of him: "Norway has had the honor of producing the most extreme anarchist of the nineteenth century, who could also at times be the most respectable of citizens."[2]

His regard for the monarchy and the pride he took in his medals bordered on the absurd. When he worked on his plays, his doodles often took the form of the orders he had won.[3] When he was in his fifties, famous as Scandinavia's greatest dramatist, and already the recipient of six honors, he could on occasion be seen in public dressed formally in top hat, long black frock coat, the revers of the lapel glittering with medals, not the ribbons, as would be proper, but with the stars themselves—the gaucherie of an upstart bourgeois. When a coach emblazoned with the coat of arms of a noble family passed by, Ibsen took off his hat and bowed—even when the coach was empty.[4]

He put on his medals and decorations at every possible opportunity, often improperly, violating custom and decorum. Attending the performance of *Ghosts* in Saxe-Meiningen, he wore the Knight's Cross along with the insignia of a higher degree of the same order. Ibsen explained that the earlier award had meant so much to him, he could not bear to be parted from it.[5]

The reception of *Ghosts* demonstrates both the obstacles Ibsen had to overcome and the success he achieved, and also how much his fame was due to the controversial nature of his work. He must have felt that the play could hold its own with Greek tragedy, a true tragedy for the modern age in which scientific determinism replaced the ancient gods. Ibsen had been riding the crest of fame, with *Brand, Peer Gynt, The League of Youth, Pillars of Society,* and *A Doll's House* establishing him as a major writer in Northern Europe, with France waiting to be conquered. *Ghosts* proved to be an unexpected and stunning setback. The first printing, in 1881, of ten thousand did not sell out for several years; there was no second printing until 1894. The major theaters in Denmark and Norway rejected it, and the world premiere took place in Chicago. The first performances in Scandinavia, in August 1883, were given, as we have seen, by a troupe of players touring northern Sweden under the leadership of the young actor August Lindberg, itching to play the part of the syphilitic Oswald.

An account of the progress of this play across the stages of Scandinavia and Germany from 1883 to 1887, from the brink of failure to the height of success, epitomizes a career in which censure and disapprobation contributed as much to Ibsen's growing fame as did his artistic genius.

The hostile reception of *Ghosts* was a setback not only to his professional career but equally to his artistic aspirations. He knew he had created a masterpiece, not only a perfect union of realism and symbolism, but a structure in which philosophic thought and dramatic plotting were in lockstep with each other. The failure of this play called into question both his method and his intellect. When the play finally reached Germany, it was at a private performance in Augsburg, April 14, 1886, with Ibsen present. In December it was staged by the Duke of Saxe-Meiningen at his court theater before an invited audience, again with Ibsen in attendance. It was performed in Dresden in December 1887, then banned for a while.

The defining moment came when the drama was staged at the Residenz Theater in Berlin. Again this was a private performance, on a Sunday, January 9, 1887. The great actor Josef Kainz, sometime favorite and intimate companion of King Ludwig II of Bavaria, had refused the part of Oswald, convinced that the end of act one would be greeted with peals of laughter.[6] Stepping in to take his place was a young actor, Franz Wallner, a light comedian.

The dress rehearsal, with Ibsen on hand, came off very well, and there was a strong sense that this special single performance would be a major cultural event. The director, Anton Anno, had skillfully created a strong ensemble, the actors well aware of the importance of the performance. Wallner said much later that the intimate effect of the ensemble playing was unique. After the rehearsal the producer, Otto Brahm, asked Ibsen if he would be willing to take a curtain call at the premiere. Ibsen paced up and down the hotel room, muttering, "If only it might happen, if only it might happen."[7]

The leading literary lights of Berlin were in attendance, including the young Gerhart Hauptmann. The theater seated one thousand, and fourteen thousand people had sought tickets. Five thousand copies of the play were rushed from the publisher in Leipzig.

According to Wallner's account, "As the curtain fell on act one, silence reigned for several seconds, so spellbound was the audience by the powerful drama. Then a storm of applause burst forth, the like of which I had never heard in a theater. As with one voice, the audience called for the author, and willingly, drunk with victory, he took bow after bow, while glistening tears of joy ran down his cheeks. An unforgettable moment."

The second act went equally well, although a few voices of dissent were heard at the end. The same thing happened at the final curtain, a few hisses mingling with cheers for the author.[8] Surely, the success of *Ghosts* on this particular night must have been one of the most satisfying moments in Ibsen's life.

Otto Brahm, a noted critic devoted to furthering the cause of naturalism, reported, "Here and today begins a new era in literary history."[9] With the collapse of the old and decaying fashionable plays came the recognition that drama could take its place as an art on the level of painting and music.[10] Commenting on the lasting impact of *Ghosts*, Brahm said, "I have read the play again and again; I saw the dress rehearsal and the performance; and each time I encountered more deep connections, true-to-life symbols, powerful and insightful; this work, a true work of art, is as inexhaustible as life itself, like the world."[11]

During the next few years, between 1887 and 1892, there were productions in Berlin of twelve different plays by Ibsen, among them *The Lady from the Sea* at Königliches Schauspielhaus, *The Wild Duck* at the Rezidenz-Theater, and *A Doll's House* at the Lessing Theater. The series of productions of his plays at the principal theaters in Germany in February and March 1889 constituted what Ibsen called "the most brilliant time in my life."[12] He was acclaimed above all for bringing to the stage, as Otto Brahm put it, "the unvarnished truth, the merciless, melancholy truth."[13]

The Prussian capital was caught up in what a songwriter called Ibsen fever.

Ibsen, Ibsen überall!
Da geht nichts mehr drüber!
Auf den ganzen Erdenball
Herrscht das Ibsen-Fieber!
Ibsen, Ibsen everywhere!
All the wide world over
There is nothing can compare—
All have Ibsen fever.[14]

The hostile reception to *Ghosts* in 1881 and 1882 had been a terrible blow to Ibsen; now what had seemed like the one great miscalculation of his career had been corrected.

A couple of years later, on February 10, 1891, when he attended the performance of *Hedda Gabler* at the Lessing Theater, he was inured to success and applause. He took his seat in the stage box left, sat throughout the performance like a statue, imperturbable, bedecked in all his medals, his copper-red face glowing. Called after each act, he acknowledged the applause without any sign of emotion.[15]

The mature plays of Ibsen required a new acting technique, and most actors were incapable of learning it. He said it was difficult to cast his plays because most actors habitually declaimed their lines instead of speaking naturally.[16] The leading roles were unusually complicated, and to present them required not only an understanding of the character but the means to express this complexity. Stanislavsky in Russia had not yet developed his method of training actors, while in France actors had not yet mastered naturalistic acting, although they were moving rapidly in that direction.

Although it might seem that acting in a realistic play would be easier than acting in high-flown poetic drama, the reverse is true, as Ibsen well knew. For him, the real test for an actor was the delivery of everyday dialogue in a totally convincing manner. When he heard that a young actress had made her stage debut as Svanhild in his verse drama *Love's Comedy*, he remarked that the part offered no reliable test of her talent. He said, "She floats along on declaimed lines, on the verses. She may perhaps be a success, but to judge whether she is really talented, a part of this sort won't do. How much more challenging it is to make one's debut in a prose play! Try saying in a natural way an everyday remark such as 'Good morning, how are you?' Or 'Please, do sit down.' That's where one is not deceived by declamation, and it's comparatively easier to tell whether or not she has talent."[17]

The wonder is that Ibsen's demanding plays succeeded as well as they did. In nearly all instances it was the power of the material itself, not the acting, that carried the play. An actor of the conventional school complained, "This crazy apothecary will ruin our whole theater." The actress Louise Dumont, writing in 1909, said the old theater world had to collapse in order for a new one to arise. The actor had to express the deepest emotions without resorting to flowery language and tempestuous speeches that might transport the audience; he had to use the plain, simple language of ordinary speech. Dumont put the actor's problem very succinctly: Ibsen "demands the greatest self-denial on the part of the actor, the profoundest grasp of the poet's intentions along with the abandonment of all of the actor's freedom. Therein lies the conflict that will not easily nor quickly be resolved."[18]

Eleanora Duse had said much the same thing a few years earlier, in 1901. "To save the theatre, the theatre must be destroyed, the actors and the actresses must all die of the plague. They poison the air, they make art impossible. It is not drama that they play, but pieces for the theatre. . . . We must bow before the poet, even when it seems to us that he does wrong. He is a poet, he has seen something, he has seen it in that way; we must accept his vision, because it is vision."[19]

Not only did actors have to rid themselves of the old declamatory techniques and the compartmentalization of roles, but directors, who were often the leading men in theatrical companies, had to learn how to deal with the subtleties of Ibsen's plays in which plots or story lines could not easily be reduced to simple statements. In a conventional melodrama, the main plot might be quite simple: for example, A must take revenge against *B*. But what would be the comparable line of action in *The Wild Duck* or *Rosmersholm*? Ibsen's plays were staged and directed without any deep understanding of what lay at the core of them. Even as late as 1897 in Sweden at the principal theater in Stockholm there was little effort made to impose a unifying vision on a play. A leading critic wrote that the most serious fault of the contemporary theater was that it "all too seldom and often not at all takes into consideration the overall effect of a play, its character as a unified work of art with its specific qualities, its specific tone and atmosphere. A dramatic work is regarded by our actors as a rather arbitrary conglomeration of roles, some big, some small, some rewarding, others not."[20] The theater was still dominated by the conventions of the conversation pieces that Strindberg had satirized fifteen years earlier.

Change was in the air, a change associated primarily with Antoine in Paris and Stanislavsky in Moscow. The latter, especially in working with Chekhov's plays, emphasized the importance of finding the unifying thematic line in a play, what he called the through-line. The significance he gave to that was, in his own view, his most important contribution to dramatic art.

Said one writer, "One can consider Ibsen a classic of the same rank as Shakespeare and the three great Greek tragedians."[21] Another said that "in the realm of thought and ideas Ibsen attained those peaks of eternal snow where no one had gone before."[22] That strange, neurotic genius Otto Weininger praised *Peer Gynt* as superior to Shakespeare, better than *Faust* and equal to *Tristan* and *Parsifal.*[23]

Making his success all the more remarkable was the fact that Ibsen won this fame not by pleasing the multitude (like Dickens) nor by expressing the views of the moral majority, nor by portraying mankind at its best. His plays, most of them best sellers, presented a bleak picture of human lives falling short of their aims.

Along with the fame came the protests. He was ridiculed by the Italians for his sexual coldness, classed among the degenerates in Germany, dismissed by the French as illogical and obscure, and abhorred by the English as nasty and obscene. Even his fellow Scandinavians found him too unremittingly severe.

As Edmund Gosse wrote, "There was no other writer of genius in the nineteenth century who was so bitter in dealing with human frailty as Ibsen was."[24] The American critic James Huneker noted that the most famous writer was the least loved: "Henrik Ibsen was the best-hated artist of the nineteenth century. The reason is simple: he was, himself, the arch-hater of his age."[25]

Perhaps the longest sustained attack came from Max Nordau, described by Bernard Shaw as "one of those remarkable cosmopolitan Jews who go forth against modern civilization as David went against the Philistines . . . smiting it hip and thigh without any sense of common humanity with it,"[26] who accused Ibsen of spinning out stories that were not true to life and for creating pathological characters outside the bounds of normal behavior, egomaniacs responsible to no one but themselves. His obsessions "have existed in his own diseased mind, and have not sprung from observation of the world's drama. The pretended 'realist' knows nothing of real life." The principal characters in the plays of this immoralist are obsessively of two basic kinds, "the avowed and violent anarchist and . . . the crafty and timorously deceitful anarchist." Nordau ranted on like this in *Degeneration*, his lengthy depiction of the *Götterdämmerung* of Europe in the latter half of the nineteenth century, indirectly paying Ibsen, the archfiend, the great compliment of giving him more space in his diatribe than any other of the "decadents," who included Tolstoy, Wagner, Zola, and Nietzsche.[27]

On the other side of the controversy were those who admired him for his probity, his willingness to tackle the most serious subjects without flinching, and his exposure of the hollowness of bourgeois existence. Undermining the middle class and its politics, he seemed to point to the future, and many of his most ardent admirers were political radicals—especially odd since Ibsen was very evasive about his political beliefs. But the anarchists sensed the anarchist in him. Among his strongest supporters, whether in politics or in art, were the young. To them he was the great innovator, always renewing himself.

By the 1890s Germany had come to accept Ibsen's plays as worthy of serious discussion, however controversial the subject matter. Not so in England and America, where the puritanical element denounced them as morally deficient and sexually perverse, and therefore unfit for public discussion. In 1892 Mr. Pigott, the English examiner of stage plays, handed down his opinion.

"I have studied Ibsen's plays pretty carefully, and all the characters in Ibsen's plays appear to me morally deranged. All the heroines are dissatisfied spinsters who look on marriage as a monopoly, or dissatisfied married women in a chronic state of rebellion against not only the conditions which nature has imposed on their sex, but against all the duties of mothers and wives; and as for the men, they are all rascals or imbeciles."[28]

In America in 1894 the highbrow theater critic and Shakespeare enthusiast William Winter predicted a quick end to any interest in Ibsen. "Mr. Ibsen's abominable stuff, which is both dull and dirty, will never prosper in this capital [New York City]. It may obtain, here and there in a corner, the attention of those uneasy persons, of no sex in particular, who hang limp upon the fringes of nastiness and think that everything is bold and strong ('virile,' they commonly call it) which happens to be shameless and impudent; but the health and good sense of the American audience will never accept the nauseous offal of Mr. Ibsen's dissecting table as either literature or drama."[29]

In England, Ibsen had two redoubtable champions: William Archer, who with his firsthand knowledge of Norwegian translated many of the plays, and Bernard Shaw, who gave Ibsen the same status in the arts as Wagner. The production in 1889 of *A Doll's House* with Janet Achurch as Nora aroused the cultural world as much as Wagner had a decade earlier. The turning point in the Ibsen controversy came in the first months of 1891 when in a ten-week period *Rosmersholm*,

Ghosts, *Hedda Gabler*, and *The Lady from the Sea* were staged in London. Critics and audiences found themselves in a quandary. Confronting them on the one hand were realistic, three-dimensional characters, up-to-date social problems, and entrancing stories; on the other hand, there was Nora's teasing in the "stocking scene," Oswald's syphilis, the bullet in Løvborg's groin, and Ellida's sexual frigidity. Tipping the scale in Ibsen's favor was his mastery of his art. Said one critic, "The plain truth is that Ibsen writes for the stage as no modern English author knows how to write or could write if he took fifty years to learn his business." And another critic for the daily papers said that in *Hedda Gabler* Ibsen "presents one of the most wonderful and subtle conceptions of woman in the whole range of dramatic literature."[30]

Less influential but probably more typical of the response of the intellectual elite to Ibsen was Henry James. Stimulated by that most Jamesian of the Norwegian master's dramas, *Hedda Gabler*, James remarked, "Whether or no Henrik Ibsen be a master of his art, he has had a fortune that, in the English-speaking world, falls not always even to the masters—the fortune not only of finding himself the theme of many pens and tongues, but the rarer privilege and humour of acting as a sort of register of the critical atmosphere, a barometer of our intellectual weather. . . . [Ibsen's] remarkable art, his admirable talent for producing an intensity of interest by means incorruptibly quiet, by that almost demure preservation of the appearance of the usual in which we see him juggle with difficulty and danger and which constitutes, as it were, his only coquetry. . . . Ibsen is massively common and 'middle-class,' but neither his spirit nor his manner is small."[31]

In London from May 29 to June 3, 1893, Ibsen was accorded the unique honor of a mini-festival at the Opéra Comique, with performances of *Rosmersholm*, *Hedda Gabler*, *The Master Builder*, and act four of *Brand*.

As play after play appeared, the one thing his detractors had to admit was that no dramatist since Shakespeare had brought onstage characters of such complexity and vivid presence or dealt so compellingly with the major issues of the time. His works united the skill of the trained craftsman with the insight of a practicing psychologist and the intellect of a far-seeing philosopher. As in no other writer since Goethe, whatever was significant in religion, politics, sexual relations, science, and history, whether it be the decline of Christianity or the rise of democracy, the advent of Darwinism, feminism, and Nietzscheanism, all found a place in Ibsen's dramas. Almost single-handedly he restored drama to the place it had held in ancient Greece as a forum for public debate.

Hedda Gabler, published in 1890, put an end to the magnificent series of realistic dramas that gave him international fame. It must have been apparent to Ibsen himself that he had exhausted that vein. And yet he was only in his early sixties, and his creative powers were as strong as ever. His audience would, as usual, be expecting another troubling play from the master's hand. Every two years, beginning with *The Pillars of Society*, and excepting only *An Enemy of the People*, he had not disappointed his readers.

Nor himself. He had committed himself to the daunting task of turning out a masterwork every two years. With that kind of commitment, he could not rely simply on inspiration. He was a creature of habits, a man of strict routines and Kantian scrupulousness, both at his desk and in his daily routines, which he adhered to with clocklike regularity.

In the early 1890s, when he had resettled in Christiania, he would rise at seven o'clock in the warmer months, later in the winter. Morning ablutions took one and a half hours. After a light breakfast at nine, with black coffee, he worked until noon, pacing his rooms much of the time. An American journalist who gained access to him in his study noticed odd toylike figures in a tray on his desk. There was "one of those small wooden carved bears so common in Switzerland. Beside it was a little black devil for holding a match, and two or three little cats and rabbits in copper, one of the former of which was playing a violin."

Said Ibsen, "I never write a single line of any of my dramas without having that tray and its occupants before me on the table. I cannot write without them. It may seem strange—perhaps it is, but I cannot write without them . . . but why I use them is my own secret."[32]

Bernard Shaw used a chessboard to work out the stage directions in his plays, and Ibsen probably did much the same using his special objects, each one distinct, so the whole set could represent the cast of players.

His daily routine in Christiania did not differ significantly from what it had been in Munich in the 1880s. A typical day: He is in his study most of the morning. At noon he leaves his desk and heads for the café at the Grand Hotel. He walks slowly and carefully, carrying an umbrella, taking small steps, in his elevator shoes. He is usually dressed in a black broadcloth coat that reaches below his knees, black stockings, stiff white collar, cylinder hat, with coat buttoned across his chest, his hands gloved. He is much respected by his fellow citizens, who make way for him, doffing their hats and often turning around to stare at him.[33] He looks at shop windows, some of which display portraits and caricatures of himself. Well aware that he is a tourist attraction, an ambulatory statue, he does not shun attention. In fact, he obviously enjoys being gawked at. He has a habit of standing and looking about, one hand behind his back. To those who approach him at the right moment, he is courteous and cordial, even indulgent to those who know nothing about him except that he is world-famous. He often enters the Grand Hotel through the back door and sits in the reading room, looking at newspapers. In the café, he installs himself at his *Stammtisch* and sips whisky and seltzer.

He is usually stared at by curious visitors and tourists. Conservative in dress and severe in expression and demeanor, he can seem formidable. A French journalist said that one would not think of addressing him as "Cher maître," only as "Monsieur le Docteur." He is as "vibrant" as a woman. Like Zola's, his hands are nervous and fretful, white like a woman's. One senses in him a man who suffers from feeling too intensely.[34]

In conversation, he can be very charming, speaking in a soft voice, almost chanting. He can also be very abrupt. When his niece commented, "You have given us so many unattractive characters in your plays. Can't you just once set up an ideal for us?" he snapped back, "There aren't any."[35]

The present writer can add to this picture of Ibsen as tourist attraction. Some time ago, in the 1960s, when I was teaching a course in nineteenth-century drama, I put *Brand* on the reading list. I spent an hour talking about the epic. At the end of the class, one of the students came to me and told me that her grandmother had once met Ibsen. This was about as close as I could possibly come to the physical presence of the man—only three degrees of separation—and I listened attentively to the story she told. It was a mere anecdote but one that had the ring of authenticity and captured the aura of a vanished age. Her grandmother had graduated from Vassar in the 1890s, and she and two or three of her classmates had set off on the customary Grand Tour of continental Europe. They expanded it, however, to include Norway with the express purpose of meeting Ibsen. In their German classes they had read *Brand* and *A Doll's House*, which gives some idea what an advanced school for women Vassar was. They knew where to seek him out. Being brash American women, they did not hesitate to approach the stern figure, sitting by himself. They came armed with copies of *Brand*, in German, which they asked him to inscribe. They addressed him respectfully as "Herr Doktor Ibsen," and they conversed in German, Ibsen's second language. By now the author of *The Master Builder*, a play about his fear of the upcoming generation, was flattered by the attention of young people, especially young women, and he chatted amiably with these intelligent, well-informed college graduates, who must have impressed him with their knowledge of *Brand*, which was not then well known in the English-speaking world. Finally, the grandmother of my student had to put the question that was uppermost in her mind.

"Herr Doktor," she asked, "your plays are so filled with life. They have so much to tell us. But so many of them end with death. Why are they so tragic?"

And the great man replied, "Oh, my dear children, it's not death that's so tragic; it's living."

Figure 26. Ibsen, 1891.

At about two thirty he leaves the Grand Hotel and catches the streetcar that takes him back to his second-floor apartment at Victoria Terrace, appropriately near the Royal Palace. He has dinner at three o'clock and spends the rest of the afternoon reading. He has an agent who handles his business affairs. But he has no private secretary and handles his own correspondence. He retires early to bed, at about seven o'clock.[36] This was not a rigid schedule. On at least one occasion in 1893 he arranged to meet someone at the Grand Hotel between six thirty and seven thirty.[37]

One of the best descriptions of the man and his physical presence is that of the French journalist Maurice Bigeon, who interviewed him late in 1892 in the Grand Hotel.

> He has a large nose, his cheeks are red and puffy, a prominent chin. Wears large spectacles with bows of gold. His beard, thick and white, frames his face and gives him the air of a good, honest soul, like a provincial judge. The poetry hidden in his soul and the splendor of his intelligence are revealed in his lips, long and delicate, somewhat sensual, often curling into an expression of haughty irony. At times he appears gentle and melancholy, at times sharp and aggressive. He has the look of a mystic and of a fighter, troubling, disturbing, as tormented as the Norwegian soul itself [!]. Most impressive is his forehead, magnificent, square and solid, the forehead of a hero and a genius, as vast as the world of ideas that it contains. And dominating the whole visage and accentuating the spiritual vitality that imbues his physiognomy is a white mane of hair, fiery, untamable.[38]

The inner contradictions manifested themselves in the whole man. The German writer Paul Lindau was struck by the incongruity of Ibsen's head and his whole figure. "His head has something of the wild genius, of a great revolutionary. His body is sturdy and broad-shouldered, but small, while the clothes give the impression of something pedantic and proper. In all, the head of the pathbreaking poet and the figure of a punctilious public official."[39]

New Directions

By 1891 Ibsen had achieved as much fame, and as much money and as many medals, as any artist could reasonably hope for. They must have provided a soothing balm for the wounds inflicted on him in his early years. However, along with a sense of triumph came the feeling that his career had reached its acme. As a master dramatist he could hardly go any further technically than he had in *The Wild Duck*, as a psychologist he could not surpass the insights of *Rosmersholm*, as a portraitist he could not expect to match the brilliance of *Hedda Gabler*.

In his next work, *The Master Builder* (*Byggmester Solness*), Ibsen veered away from realism and naturalism into a world of might-be and might-have-been. It begins the last series of plays, four of them, that are highly retrospective and very subjective, really self-portraits. *The Master Builder* is about an artist who seeks a new beginning, and in the act of writing it, Ibsen reinvigorated his creative spirit and reached out to new forms of dramatic expression.

This search for the new in the arts was accompanied by a return to the old in his personal life. After having lived in self-imposed exile for many years, with only infrequent visits to his native country, he now considered the possibility of spending more time there. At first he probably had no intention of moving from cosmopolitan Germany, where he was now a writer of the first rank, with much of his income deriving from productions of his plays. He was well off financially, with a number of investments, including a steamship company. And compared with Munich, Christiania, though it was the capital of Norway, was still a very provincial city. Ibsen complained in 1891 of its narrow-mindedness and provincialism.[1] Although its population had grown by almost 50 percent in the 1880s, the average income for a well-placed person was between three thousand and four thousand kronor a year, which in Germany and France was the income of a common laborer.[2]

However, it was not the fact that his royalties and dividends would go further in Norway than in Germany that caused him to resettle in his homeland. Nor was it his wife. Suzannah suffered from rheumatism and sought warmer climes, Italy rather than Norway. Ibsen changed his mind about Christiania for two reasons. He was very cordially received there by parties both left and right, much more warmly than he had anticipated. His change of attitude is reflected in his inscription, dated January 21, 1892, in a copy of *Catiline*. He quoted the last stanza of his poem "Burnt Ships" ("Brændte Skibe"), the bitter lines he had pointedly placed at the end of the original edition of his collected poems, and then he added a new stanza.

> He alighted from his steed,
> Found all doors opened to him.
> Perhaps the homeless one
> Has tarried too long.[3]

However gratifying his warm reception in Norway may have been, it was only the silver lining to a dark cloud. He could not help but feel that he, now in his early sixties, was being treated as an elder statesman, honored for what he had accomplished, not for any controversial works he might still have in him. His return to Norway could be seen as a sensible withdrawal from the front line of controversy or as a well-earned rest after the steady labors of the previous fifteen years.

Whatever his reasons, his return to Norway was a wise career move. His fame in Germany had peaked. *Hedda Gabler* received a poor reception in Munich and Berlin, with audiences laughing at Hedda's exit line at the end of act two: "And then—at ten o'clock—he'll come, Ejlert Løvborg—with vine leaves in his hair."[4] Suzannah went public to defend it, saying it usually took critics several years to understand her husband's plays: "[He] figures on about ten years for the public to arrive at an understanding of his dramas."[5] In Norway, on the other hand, the play was a great success. Moreover, the theater in Christiania announced plans to stage a cycle of Ibsen plays in the 1891–92 season.

It was obvious that his career was at a critical juncture. He saw himself compared to the great giants of literature, past and present, while at the same time he heard that the plays that had made his international reputation, plays that were masterpieces of psychological insight, were now faulted for lacking real depth. Already in the 1890s there were rumblings about his outmoded technique. Writing on *A Doll's House,* one critic commented on "the factitiousness of the plot, the quaintness of the characters' comings and goings, and the programmatic last-act resolution."[6]

Throughout Europe the intellectual climate was undergoing a rapid change. In France, naturalism suddenly became passé, as the symbolists rose up against

Zola. In Austria, the journalist and theater critic Hermann Bahr proclaimed that "the synthesis of naturalism and romanticism is the present task of literature."[7] In Sweden, the poet Verner von Heidenstam in his *Renaissance* (1888) assailed the pessimism and somberness of naturalism and urged a return to gaiety and joyfulness. He refused to believe that the artist should be "a two-legged camera" and called for an embrace of fantasy and imagination, the natural realm for a creative artist.

In Denmark, Georg Brandes, having discovered Nietzsche, spearheaded the attack against the naturalism of the 1880s, dismissing it in 1889 as "a little Darwinism, a little female emancipation, a little utilitarianism, a little populism," all of which he himself had helped to promote.[8] Now he urged the cult of the individual, unique, independent, defiant, nobly stubborn. Two years later, in the final chapter of *Young Germany* (*Det unga Tyskland*), he proclaimed himself a nihilist and confessed his disillusionment with progress. Abandoning his youthful search for truth and freedom, he adopted the aristocratic position of being above the fray.

All of this, but especially Brandes's new position, would have given Ibsen much to think about and encouraged him to turn from his realistic plays in search of some new approach. With his extraordinary feeling for the coming thing, he may have decided quite deliberately to depart from the realism of *Hedda Gabler*. Unlike others of his generation, he was not afraid to venture into new areas. He wanted to be accepted by the younger writers. They, however, wanted to escape from his spell, that huge shadow looming over them. Leading them was the upstart Norwegian novelist Knut Hamsun, who belittled Ibsen and other writers of his generation in sardonic language for never having probed deeply into the nature of human existence. To him, the characters that Ibsen had created were psychological constructs, not real human beings.

On October 7, 1891, Ibsen paid one krone to hear Hamsun lecture on Norwegian literature in Hals's Recital Hall in Christiania. Hamsun, only thirty-one years old, the author of a novel, *Hunger* (*Sult*), that explored the irrational side of man, singled out Ibsen for his attack on the literature of the 1880s. Hamsun had already the year before declared his opposition to the psychological school in an article, "From the Unconscious Life of the Soul" ("Fra det ubevidste Sjæleliv"), in the journal *Samtiden*.

"What if literature ... now began to concern itself a little more with psychic conditions.... We might learn a little about the secret movements at work in the remote parts of the soul, the unpredictable disorder of the senses, the delicate life of the imagination ... the whisperings of the blood and the entreaties of the bone."[9]

Addressing the Norwegian intellectual elite and the students from the university, Hamsun at the lectern, tall, erect, with flaming red hair, was the embodiment of the young radical, determined to shock. "The point is this," he said, "Ibsen's characters have all too often been only instruments that represent and stand for concepts and ideas. And about concepts and ideas one can talk an awful lot of twaddle." This must have been especially painful for Ibsen to hear, since he always insisted that his aim first and foremost was to portray living human beings.

Surprised to see the object of his attack sitting in the front row and caught in the glare of Ibsen's skewed eyes, Hamsun became increasingly nervous, and more violent in his attack.[10] "What is this *Lady from the Sea*? I don't know, I really don't know. Because she talks divine nonsense.—No, it's a book for the Germans. It's a book for people who are prepared to and are used to reading profound works. Ibsen has written a book, that's all that matters. All his followers prepare themselves to probe his words superstitiously and to find them superbly obscure. And the Germans hug themselves and rub their hands—*ach, wunderschön!*"[11]

Ibsen was furious. To a journalist attending the lecture he said, "If we were living in a civilized country, the students would have knocked the block off that fellow."[12]

While the public Ibsen was being challenged, the private Ibsen was undergoing a late midlife crisis. He was world-famous, still a master craftsman, yet he was not at peace with himself. Although he was warmly welcomed by his countrymen, his home was cold, his wife distant and difficult, in constant pain from gout and rheumatism. Inevitably, after the exaltation of success came the reckoning. Success came with a price.

"It doesn't bring with it any sense of joy," he wrote in a letter. "So what is it all worth, at bottom?"[13] At a dinner party he remarked, "What's so great about fame? In a few years the younger generation takes it away. And no one knows how many have been crushed under the wheels of good fortune."[14]

Solness, the protagonist of *The Master Builder*, is at the beginning of the play a man in that pessimistic frame of mind. In fact, Solness is a superb self-portrait. Ibsen considered *The Master Builder* the play into which he had put more of himself than he had into any other,[15] and to a group of students in 1898 at his seventieth-birthday celebrations, he said of Solness, "There was a man who had something in common with me."[16]

In the realistic plays Ibsen could say that no one of them stood for himself or his own views. But there can be no doubt that Solness is the man himself. He has made himself younger by about eight years, but apart from that Solness is a striking likeness as regards Ibsen the self-made man who had risen from a poverty-stricken family to international eminence. His alter ego is a poor boy from a country village who rose to fame. He is a self-educated building contractor, not an architect with a degree. It is an important distinction insisted upon by Ibsen.[17] His lack of genteel culture is betrayed in his speech. He calls his demons *dævler,* whereas in literary language it would be *djævler;* he uses the colloquial *klejn* (sickly) instead of the more proper *dårlig.*

The similarities between Ibsen and his protagonist extend to their domestic situations. The picture of the home life of Solness and his wife, Aline, confirms what is known about the home life of the Ibsens and offers a chillingly accurate portrayal. One can only wonder what Suzannah thought of it. Visitors were struck by the lack of warmth and affection in the marriage.[18] Suzannah was often away from home, traveling with Sigurd. Bjørnson told his wife, "Ibsen is deeply distressed that his wife and Sigurd never come to see him. Whenever I see him in a social gathering . . . he sits himself down and complains to me. He says, you [Bjørnson] of course will soon win Sigurd's confidence, I know that. I have never had it, and I never will have it. I go about, he says, I warm up the rooms for them, and they disappoint me every time."[19]

In October 1892 Sigurd married Bjørnson's daughter Bergliot. Sigurd had been the emotional link between his parents, and for Ibsen a pleasant evening at home would consist in having his wife and son reading aloud to him. Now those days were past. Magdalene Thoresen, Ibsen's mother-in-law, after remarking to a friend on how well-off the Ibsens were, how elegantly they lived, added, "For all that, [they live] in middle-class stillness; these are two lonely people, each for himself—each absolutely for himself."[20]

The wife of the mayor of Christiania noticed how lonely Ibsen was and how much he liked social gatherings. "He entered, quietly and a bit awkwardly, but after a few banal words, and overcoming his timidity, he became very animated and was interested in everything." She also sensed that he had an inexpressible need for a warm friendship.[21]

When there were visitors, Ibsen referred to Suzannah not by her name or by some nickname, only as "my wife." The strong bond between the two of them was his career. She had sensed the genius in him from the beginning, and she had cared for him during those desperate years when nothing went right. She remained dedicated to Ibsen, but more to the career, in which she had invested her whole life, than the man. There was no strong emotional bond between them. They formed a partnership rather than a marriage, and they had no children after the birth of Sigurd. All the strong emotions that were suppressed in his marriage went into his plays. Once in a while they broke out in real life. When Frederick Hegel, the son of his publisher, unexpectedly called on Ibsen, awakening him from his nap, the writer was noticeably irritated at being disturbed. But as they talked, he began to recall the past. He spoke softly, very emotionally, and ended by putting his head on Hegel's shoulder and crying.[22]

Who Is Hilda?

Though Ibsen was venturing into new territory and changing the direction of his work, there is no sign of hesitation or self-doubt in the creation of *The Master Builder.* It is a remarkably self-assured work. This self-confidence was the result of the entrance into his life of a young woman, who surely inspired Ibsen as much as Hilda Wangel gave new life to Solness.

There is little talk of or evidence for any women in Ibsen's life until 1888. Suddenly the sixty-year-old man was involved in relationships with young women, much younger, by thirty or forty years. He loved their company and, on occasion, carried on flirtations with them, albeit of a literary kind.

These affairs, four in particular, aroused a great deal of curiosity while he was alive and even more after his death. Scandalmongers, psychologists, biographers, and literary critics all wanted to know why the sexagenarian dramatist began to encourage the attentions of young women and what impact they made on his work. Did they sit as models to the creative artist, or were they the objects of his sexual passion? Or both?

It is no coincidence that these young women entered Ibsen's life when he had become a celebrity. Fame can be an aphrodisiac and a sexual lure. The first of the four was Emilie Bardach, whom Ibsen encountered in the summer of 1889 in the small resort town of Gossensass in the Tirol, near the Brenner Pass and not far from Munich. Beginning in 1876, the Ibsens had spent many summers there. From the village one could ascend the nine-thousand-foot Hühnerspiel in four and a half hours along a footpath. Ibsen never attempted it. But he found the mountain climate conducive to work, and, departing from his routine in Munich, he would write late into the night. He took in the Alpine scenery by viewing it from a clearing in the woods just above the village. As his fame grew, his presence in Gossensass became an added tourist attraction. The innkeeper

Ludwig Gröbner had the bright idea of designating this spot "Ibsen-platz." At the dedication ceremonies on July 21, 1889, Ibsen remarked that much of his artistic development and growing fame was associated with Gossensass and noted that some of his works had originated there and others had been completed there, in the midst of nature's beauty.[1]

After this thank-you speech, Emilie and Ibsen exchanged glances and then words. Her family was Jewish, well connected socially, and she was an intriguing youngster, only eighteen, well aware of her charm, which was not lost on the Ibsens. Suzannah called her "princess,"[2] and his pet name for her was "princess of Orangia [Apfelsinia]."

In the following years, Ibsen wrote several letters to her. Soon after his death and while his wife was still alive, Emilie offered the letters to Georg Brandes, who, reliably indiscreet, published them.[3] This was the first time that the broader public became aware of Ibsen's fascination with young women. Years later, first in 1923 and again in 1928, the comparatively staid sentiments expressed in the letters were revealed to be only a feeble expression of his true feelings when excerpts from Emilie's journal, those describing the summer in Gossensass, were published.[4]

The diary entries present an Ibsen who is swept off his feet by the enchanting Emilie, an Ibsen who even talks of leaving his wife. If they were reliable, they would picture an Ibsen we have not seen before. "He means to possess me," says the diarist. "This is his absolute will. He intends to overcome all obstacles. I do what I can to keep him from feeling this, and yet I listen as he describes what is to lie before us—going from one country to another—I with him—enjoying his triumphs together."[5] In the most thorough account of the diary, Joan Templeton concludes: "The question of the authenticity of Bardach's reminiscences is a mare's nest of such a rare order that it is impossible to unravel it unless an original diary is found."[6]

In Gossensass another young woman, Helene Raff, had noticed with jealous eyes the chatty conversations that Ibsen and Emilie Bardach were having. In her diary (all young girls kept diaries), Helene jotted down her observations: "The B completely mad about I" and "B heartbroken."[7]

This is probably true; Emilie was enamored of the famous dramatist, while he enjoyed basking in her admiration. But Ibsen kept her at arm's length. He knew that the relationship had to remain on the level of fantasy. He and Suzannah looked upon her as the daughter they had never had, while Emilie liked to think that the great man was passionately in love with her. She was the importunate one; she sent letters which he answered without making any commitments.

"Do you recall our conversation about stupidity and craziness? . . . You took the part of the teacher and remarked in your soft, melodic way, and with your faraway look, that there is always a difference between stupidity and craziness. Now, of course, I've always been aware of that. But this episode—like all the rest, nonetheless sticks in my memory. I continually brood over this: was our meeting stupidity or was it craziness? Or was it stupidity as well as craziness? Or was it neither?"[8]

In the fourteen letters that he wrote to her, all but one dated between September 20, 1889, and December 30, 1890, he let her know that she was more an object of contemplation for him than one to be possessed.

"Frankly speaking, dear princess—in many definite respects we are strangers to each other.

"In one of your earlier letters you have said almost the same thing in regard to my writings since they are not accessible to you in the original language."[9]

Two months later, in a delayed response to her latest letter, he wrote: "From now on, until we see each other in person again, you will hear from me only a little, and indeed very seldom. Believe me, it is better so. It is the only right thing. I feel it is a matter of conscience to break off my correspondence with you, or at least limit it. You must, for the present, have as little to do with me as possible."[10]

Months later, when she sent him a picture she had painted, his reply was: "My wife thinks the picture very pretty. But I beg you: for the time being, please do not write me."[11]

After that, the correspondence was broken off until March 1898, on the occasion of Ibsen's seventieth-birthday celebrations, when Emilie sent her congratulations. He replied briefly, "The summer in Gossensass was the happiest, the most beautiful of my whole life."[12] Reading between the lines, one might infer that what she wrote in her diary about Ibsen's passion for her may have been true. But for Ibsen, what made him happiest was success and fame as an artist. In March 1889 he had been hailed in Germany and Austria as one of the greatest living writers, and he had five plays running simultaneously in Berlin. This is what made 1889 so special to him. He told his friend Julius Hoffory that the week in Berlin was "the high point of my life. When I think back on it, it all seems like a dream. It almost frightens me."[13] A few months later he sat in the scenic spot in Gossensass that had just been named Ibsen-platz in his honor, and an attractive young woman boldly offered herself to him. But she was not what made the summer of 1889 the most beautiful of his life. She was only the icing on the cake of fame and fortune.

Emilie admitted in her diary that Ibsen never kissed her,[14] and Suzannah never felt jealous of her. In fact, Suzannah liked Emilie, "a very quiet, fine, pretty girl with an engaging—charming—personality."[15]

Her name usually arises in discussions of *Hedda Gabler* on the mistaken assumption that she was a model for Hedda. But the very young and flirtatious Emilie had little in common with the ten-years-older and coolly detached Hedda. If Ibsen did draw on an Austrian woman for some traits that would fill out his image of Hedda, it was Frau Alberg, a Munich actress with a reputation as a seductress, "a bird of prey," as Ibsen called her. He said she was one of "those common and obliging women who harbor an irresistible urge to steal a husband or lover."[16]

Helene Raff (1865–1942), who resided in Munich, took Emilie Bardach's place as an object of study for the playwright, whose thoughts by now were circling around the idea of a play about the challenge of the young generation. After the summer season in Gossensass in 1889, Ibsen and Raff both returned to Munich, and she reintroduced herself by waiting for him on his street. The daughter of a composer, Helene was part of Ibsen's social set. Moreover, she was a painter, and Ibsen always took an interest in painting. He frequently called on her in her atelier during the period from the autumn of 1889 until the summer of 1891, when the Ibsens moved to Norway. Ibsen's chats with Emilie Bardach were only poetic ramblings, but his conversations with Raff covered a wide range of subjects—hypnotism, the latest novels, the art of acting, the future society—and she took notes on their chats. She also took a genuine interest in his works and taught herself Norwegian in order to fully appreciate them. She also got along with Suzannah. Like Emilie, Helene was the daughter she never had. Ibsen told Helene, "My wife is so truly, cordially fond of you. And I, too. As you sat there in the twilight and told us various things so thoughtfully and with such understanding, do you know what I thought then, what I wished? No, you do not know. I wished—alas, if I only had such a dear and lovely daughter."[17] A couple of years later, at the end of 1892, Ibsen sent her a copy of *Master Builder,* inscribed, "A voice from within me cries out to you."[18]

Upon settling in Norway, Ibsen and Suzannah grew even more distant from each other. Often separated from her, Ibsen began to spend time with youngish women. In the summer of 1891 Suzannah and Sigurd went on vacation in the mountains of Jotunheimen in central Norway while Ibsen sailed to the North Cape. In August he returned to Christiania, where he was seen at cultural and artistic events in the company of the Swedish singer Sigrid Arnoldson. She had recently married the theatrical impresario Alfred Fischhof. By this time she was an international star, a success in Moscow in *Lakmé* and *La Traviata,* in Paris as Mignon, and praised as much for her charming stage presence as for her coloratura. She was thirty when Ibsen met her. In 1891 she was a sensation in Scandinavia. Although Ibsen had no ear for music and took little interest in it, he attended all of her performances.[19]

These women offered Ibsen a pleasant evening's company and gave him a chance to bridge the generation gap. They could not have meant very much to him other than as social companions and as objects onto which he could project some of his fancies. The woman who was to provide him with genuine inspiration now when he desperately needed it was a fellow Norwegian, Hildur Andersen, a highly gifted pianist and a devotee of Richard Wagner. Like Hilda in the play, she had once crossed his path years ago. Now he encountered her again in Christiania, and not by chance, for they had been in indirect contact with each other for some years. Hildur's reentrance into his life came at just the moment when he sought contact with the younger generation. Her providential reappearance when he was contemplating a work about an aging artist seeking rejuvenation provided the basic situation for *The Master Builder*, as well as for the crucial events ten years before when Hilda first met Solness.

While the apprentice playwright was living in Bergen in 1851, he boarded with Madam Helene Sontum, who took a motherly interest in the young man. He let a room in her house for a while and took his meals there for six years. While he resided there, one of the Sontum daughters married Oluf Martin Andersen, and in 1864 they became the parents of Hildur Andersen. Oluf Martin Andersen resettled in Christiania, and when Ibsen visited the capital in 1874 he would have met him and his daughter, then ten years old and considered a musical prodigy. The child must have made a deep and lasting impression on him. The brash and bold Hilda Wangel in *The Lady from the Sea* seems like a forestudy of Hilda in *The Master Builder.* Memories of the child Hildur may have resurfaced in the late 1880s. Sigurd Ibsen, serving as attaché with the Swedish-Norwegian legation in Vienna, might have looked her up when she was studying piano there in 1887, and he would certainly have written to his father about her.[20] Did Ibsen remember her as she had been in 1874 and portray her accordingly in *The Lady from the Sea?*

Upon moving to Christiania in 1891, Ibsen renewed old acquaintances and became very friendly with Oluf Andersen, now a civil engineer (under the professional name of Aksel Arstal), and his relations. The grandson of Madam Sontum became Ibsen's doctor in 1891, and Ibsen was a fairly frequent guest in the doctor's summer place in Grefsen, famous for its tonic air. Dr. Sontum's daughter remembered Ibsen's deep bass voice, his treating children as adults, not condescending to them, not even addressing them informally or *tutoyering* them. He carried a gold-headed walking stick, which was necessary because of his nearsightedness. "His gold spectacles hung at an angle, emphasizing one eye. The left eye always appeared larger and more drooping than the right and exaggerated the severity of his piercing gaze."[21]

Figure 27. Hildur Andersen.

When Hildur Andersen reentered Ibsen's life in September 1891, he was living alone at Victoria Terrace, no. 7B, his wife and son having returned to Munich. Like Hilda in the play, Hildur had been backpacking in the fjelds.[22] On September 24 he accompanied her to a piano recital given by Martin Kautzon, who, like Hildur, was a student of the renowned Polish pianist and teacher Theodor Leschetizky. She returned to Vienna to continue her music studies in February 1892 and was there for several months. Ibsen kept track of her travels through the Sontums, often dropping in on them at five in the afternoon. A month later, Ibsen destroyed the notes for the play he had been working on and turned his thoughts to a new work. While working on it, he wrote a poem, "They Sat There, the Two of Them—" ("De satt der, de to—"), dated March 1892, which is a distillation of the mood of the play.

> There in the cozy house, the twain, they dwell
> Through the long autumns and the wild Decembers—
> The house burnt down. All to sheer rubbish fell.
> The twain must grope, must grope among the embers.
>
> For in the embers is a jewel lying
> Hidden, a jewel fire can never hurt.
> If each searches faithfully, there's no denying
> That he or she may find it 'mid the dirt.
>
> But if they find it, if—those burnt-out twain,—
> This precious jewel fire cannot destroy.
> Never shall she find her burnt faith again;
> Never will he discover his burnt joy.[23]

The couple in the poem seem very like Solness and Aline in the drama—and also very like Ibsen and Suzannah at this time. What the poem omits is the young woman. Hilda in the play brings joy to Solness, and Hildur gave a new lease on life to Ibsen.

In May 1892 there was a severe crisis in the Ibsen marriage, and two months later Suzannah and Sigurd returned to Christiania. She was very unhappy with the apartment at Victoria Terrace, and a year later the couple moved to Arbins Gate (street). By then Hildur was so much a part of Ibsen's life that she helped arrange the furnishings.

The Master Builder was finished in September, and the date September 19 had special significance. On that date ten years earlier Hilda saw Solness climb the church tower. On that date Hilda shows up to claim her kingdom from Solness. Ibsen gave Hildur a ring inscribed September 19. He also gave her a manuscript of the play, dated September 19 on the last page.

A few weeks after the publication of the play, he sent a letter to Hildur in Vienna, where she was seeking out Johannes Brahms. "To my wild bird of the woods!" he wrote at the end of it. "Oh, how I long for my princess. A longing from the heights of dreamland. Long to descend to the earth again, and do what I've told you, so very, very often.... Your very own master builder."[24] During the 1890s they exchanged numerous notes, delivered not by the postman but by special messenger. "I don't dare express myself as I would like. The post is so unsafe."[25] According to Hildur, he returned her letters to him, advising her to keep the whole correspondence. "Take good care of them," he said. "They have a higher destiny."[26] This could only mean that Ibsen believed they should eventually be published. Yet, except for a very few, they were destroyed by Hildur.

Among those that survived was one from October 22, 1893, just after Hildur had received a rave review for her piano recital in Bergen. Her family had moved to a new apartment.

> Well, that must have been a wonderful time for you in Bergen, I just hope you haven't been plagued by too many visitors in these busy times—people dropping in can after a while be quite inconvenient when what one wants most of all is some peace. I have thought so much about you, my sweet Hildur!
>
> Believe me, I feel so melancholy walking past no. 35. The windows are so big and cold and empty. No curtains and no flowers. And no princess coming into view behind the windowpane. No lovely *Kopf* peering out. No little white hand waving to me from the distance. Yes, everything is completely empty now!
>
> I had a chance to look into your new apartment yesterday. Of course, everything was still in disorder. But it can be beautiful when everything is arranged after your taste. Oh, Hildur, let me meet you there again, unchanged, just as you were when you left me! I have this feeling that I have loaned you out to many, many strangers. I want you back again just as you were. Do you hear me, Hildur? Will you promise me? A thousand greetings fly out to you from your devoted H.I.[27]

In 1894 he gave her a copy of the new printing of *Ghosts*, inscribed with two lines from the last act of *Peer Gynt*: "Oh, awful truth, the game cannot be played again! / Oh, my heart's anguish, here was my kingdom!"[28] Strongly suggesting that the bond between them was artistic were other gifts to her in 1894 and 1895: drafts of *Hedda Gabler* and *Rosmersholm*.

Hildur functioned as a creative muse for Ibsen, whereas Helene Raff and Emilie Bardach only provided pleasure, flattering him with their interest in him. Emilie was hardly more than a bauble for him, someone whose beauty and guilelessness could stir his senses. Helene, a painter and would-be novelist, probably meant more to him. With her he could converse about serious subjects. Hildur, however, existed on a different plane. She was an exceptionally talented pianist and a dedicated Wagnerite. They were both committed artists, whose fields complemented each other. She would attend lectures and theatrical performances with him; he would go to recitals and concerts with her. Ibsen told Helene Raff that "music makes me nervous."[29] (Christopher Due, his friend from the Grimstad days, said Ibsen had no ear for music.)[30] But he liked the music Hildur played for him: Grieg's "Solveig's Song," excerpts from Wagner, "Connais-tu le pays" from Ambroise Thomas's *Mignon*, which he could hear over and over again, and especially music from Viktor Nessler's popular *Der Trompeter von Säkkingen* (1884).[31]

Suzannah was never bothered by the presence of Emilie Bardach and Helene

Raff and rather welcomed them as youthful and refreshing spirits. Hildur was a different matter. In 1895 the marriage threatened to come apart when rumors reached her that Ibsen and Hildur Andersen were behaving like an engaged couple and that he wanted to be a free man. Much of the time Suzannah lived apart from him, preferring the warm climate of Italy, where she and Sigurd lived very comfortably. Suzannah sent him a letter telling him that if the rumors were true, she wanted to hear it from him. His reply placed all the blame for this painful situation on Magdalene Thoresen.

> It has hurt me deeply to read your latest letter, dated May 1. And I hope that you now, after more careful consideration, regret that you sent it. It is your stepmother, that damned old sinner, who now once again has gone out of her way to stir up trouble by setting us against each other. . . .
>
> I don't understand your stepmother's screwed-up way of talking and her second-rate insights. Have never in all the world understood them. But when she writes something like that I "want to be free whatever the cost," let me assure you and tell you loud and clear that I have never seriously imagined or intended anything of the sort and that I never will imagine or intend it. What I may have in sudden anger blurted out to you when outbreaks of your temper and your state of mind at times drove me momentarily crazy, that is another matter and nothing to be concerned about. Now my earnest advice is that if you want to have any peace of mind, which is necessary for your health, break off any correspondence with that addle-headed stepmother of yours. It's quite possible that she means the best for you. But that woman's interference in any matter or situation has always proved to be fatal. If you want me to tell her that, I will. But first I must have your consent.[32]

Still, he could not let Hildur go; she became something like the unobtainable maiden of a medieval romance. A few years later, on September 19, 1899, he gave her a bouquet of nine roses, one rose for each year since their first meeting in Christiania. "9 red roses for you, 9 rose-red years for me. Take these roses as thanks for the years." He also presented her with a set of his collected works, twenty-five slim volumes. "These 25 twins belong to us together. Before I found you, I wrote looking for you, seeking you. I knew you existed somewhere in the wide world, and once I found you, from then on I wrote only about the princess in various guises."[33] At about the same time, riding in a sleigh on a winter's day, Ibsen saw Hildur, perhaps for the last time. He stopped, lifted his arms, stretched them out, and exclaimed, "Bless you! Bless you!"[34]

These expressions of love were genuine, unlike the flattering and blandishing notes he had sent to Fräulein Bardach and Raff. To a young Norwegian Ibsen said, "Oh, you can always love, but I am happier than the happiest, for I am beloved."[35] That Ibsen's affection for Hildur was profound and long-lasting is beyond doubt; how much she cared for him is difficult to say. How much was love and how much selfish pleasure in being loved by one of Norway's most famous citizens? She is not on record as having declared her love for him, though she lived on long after both Ibsen and his wife were dead. (She died in 1956.) Unquestionably, the strong feelings came from him, not from her, although his passion was one of Kierkegaardian longing, not of consummation.

Hildur Andersen also differed from Emilie Bardach and Helene Raff in that she had been part of Ibsen's youth. The young prodigy had left a strong impression on him, and when they met again in 1891, he would have recalled those earlier times, and much that he had forgotten would have come back into the light. The long passages in which Hilda stirs Solness's memories, re-creating the past, constitute the finest writing in the play and ring completely true.

They also provide a fascinating parallel to the aging Goethe's affair with Bettina Brentano. Goethe had loved her mother and to her had confided many secrets of his youth, which she had passed on to Bettina. Years later Bettina developed an ardent interest in the great poet, and finally met him in 1807, when he was fifty-eight and she was twenty-two, much like Hilda and Solness. He was fascinated, mainly because she could tell him details about his youth that he had quite forgotten.[36]

Ibsen himself was struck by how much his relationship with Hildur resembled that of Goethe and another young woman, Marianne von Willemer, with over thirty years' difference in their ages, as with Ibsen and Hildur. When Brandes wrote an article in January 1895 about Goethe's affair,[37] Ibsen promptly thanked him for it. "When I think of the character of Goethe's works during those years, the rebirth of his youth, it seems to me I should have known that he must have been blessed with something as wonderful for him as meeting this Marianne von Willemer. Now and then, fate, chance, providence can indeed be rather kind and well disposed toward one."[38] On the other hand, Ibsen could dismiss the aging Goethe as "that old he-goat," reinforcing one's impression that Ibsen's "affair" with Hildur was not sexually charged.[39]

The Master Builder is less about love than about artistic creativity. Unlike Emilie Bardach and also unlike Suzannah, Hildur was an artist. That was the strong bond between them. Ibsen seems never to have held her in his arms. Theirs was a romance without physical passion. He got enormous pleasure from looking at her from a distance without rushing up to embrace her. It was she, not Suzannah, who sat next to Ibsen when Hamsun, speaking for the younger generation, castigated the playwright. The two of them also attended Hamsun's second lecture, two days later. Said Ibsen to Hildur, "You must realize that we have to go so we can learn how to write."[40]

The real passion was the artist's interest in his work and his need to re-create himself. This portrait of the artist as an aging man had to be a dramatic one. His career, like his carefully constructed dramas, had to have a beginning, a middle, and an end; and, now that he had returned to his homeland after years of exile, the middle was probably over. He knew that this was the point at which he must evaluate what he had accomplished and ask, "Whither now?" *The Master Builder* turned out to be a play about how the master builder came to write *The Master Builder*. The play reflects the life, distorting it like a funhouse mirror, but keeping all the essential features.

The Story of Solness

After Solness married the well-to-do Aline, they settled into the family mansion, an unattractive, dark barn of a place, but cozy enough and comfortable. They became the parents of twins, two boys. Young and ambitious, the building contractor Solness found himself wishing that a fire would destroy the house and make it possible for him to construct a housing development on the land.

Sure enough, a fire did break out, as if in fulfillment of his wishes. But in accordance with the adage "Be careful what you wish for, for surely you will have it," the twins, only two weeks old, died, not in the fire itself but as an indirect result of it. A couple of years later, Solness built a church tower at Lysanger, which he promised himself would be his last. As part of the customary topping-off ceremony, he climbed the tower, and there at the top he broke his compact with God and resolved to build "houses for human beings." At a celebration afterward, he met Hilda Wangel, only twelve or thirteen years old at the time.

As the play begins, he is completing his new house, which occupies the site of the old mansion. It is a large house with a tower, like many Victorian houses. Now Hilda Wangel shows up, exactly ten years after the episode at Lysanger. She has come to claim her kingdom, once promised to her by Solness.

Meeting with Hilda gives him new inspiration. He now determines to repeat what had happened ten years before. He will climb another tower and renew his career. He will stop building homes for human beings; he will build "castles in the air."

However, the man who intends to change the direction of his life is not the man who climbed the tower at Lysanger. Not only is he older, but he now has dizzy spells, the manifestation of a guilty conscience. Aline, his unhappy wife, is a constant reminder of the cost of his success. She too had a talent for building, but hers was a mother's talent for nurturing souls. She lost the opportunity for doing that when the twins died, and along with them she lost her family house, the old portraits, the jewels and dresses handed down from one generation to another. To build castles in the air, to follow where Hilda leads, Solness will have to subdue his conscience, become like the Vikings of old, as Hilda urges him to do, and climb to the top of the tower.

Formulated this way, the plot sounds like a standard psychological drama with motives and actions explained in terms of cause and effect. But the play takes us in a different direction when Solness begins talking about the trolls that seem to govern his life. In his previous drama, *Hedda Gabler*, Ibsen portrayed a woman who was driven by certain dark desires, and the playwright could show their direct connection with such factors as her upbringing and her social background. This was the kind of psychological drama that in Hamsun's opinion had exhausted itself.

What happens in *The Master Builder* occurs in a largely unexplored subcontinent of the mind. As Hilda draws out his innermost thoughts, the landscape of the drama changes. In willing success for himself he in effect signed a document without reading the small print. He understands now that there were little demons, blond ones and dark ones, that were ultimately responsible. These imps and devils push the drama out of the strictly psychological into the realm of the irrational. The trolls make one do things that are illogical, "impossible," with little concern about consequences. That there is something strange and demonic about him is suggested by his dark mustache and thick, dark eyebrows, setting him apart from others.

Solness's dreamlike memories of the episode at Lysanger reflect Ibsen's own vagueness as he attempted to make sense of his extraordinary success. In January 1887, at a grand banquet in his honor, he had said that his life seemed like "a fairy tale" in which wishes come true. Now it is how and why they came true that intrigues him. Solness tells Hilda, "The more I think of it now, the more it seems to me as though I have gone about all these years torturing myself . . . trying to get at something—some actual experience, which I seem to have forgotten. But I could never lay my hands on it, whatever it was."[1]

In talking to Hilda, Solness realizes that his extraordinary success has been due as much to inexplicable factors—call them what you will, helpers and servers or trolls and devils—as to his own conscious decisions. When he determined to cease building churches and to turn to the building of homes for human beings, his efforts were successful because of a mysterious fire. Although he had wished for it, he had not planned it. And when he wished for it, he thought it might break out where there was a flaw in the chimney. He did nothing to repair it, hoping the old house would be destroyed. And indeed the house was burned to the ground.

But—and here he realizes that trolls and devils were at work—the fire was not caused by the faulty chimney. It broke out in another part of the house. His wish was fulfilled, but not in accordance with his plans.[2]

The new phase in his career will be devoted to building "castles in the air." These insubstantial structures suggest a life lived in harmony with the irrational or the subconscious, an acceptance of the demonic, rather than a repression of it. Since those airy castles are meant to be built on "a firm foundation," reason is not excluded. Instead there will be a fusion of the conscious and the unconscious, the rational and the irrational. It is Hilda who brings out the irrational in him. She is the one who tells him to climb the tower; he merely accedes to her wish. And why does she reenter his life? She came as if he had called her. It is impossible in this irrational world to distinguish cause from effect. As at Lysanger, the helpers are helping him, the servants are waiting on him.

Two things about Solness's career are clear: he does climb to the top of the tower, and he does fall from it. This ending may be less ambiguous than it seems at first. He succeeds in overcoming his vertigo (his guilty conscience) because of his need to create. For the true artist, the imperative drive to surpass himself cannot end until he is defeated. In a sense, a certain kind of defeat defines the artist's victory. This paradox seems to be implicit in Ibsen's explanation to his French translator of Hilda's function in the play. As the incarnation of the creative spirit, she survives her work of destruction. "May all the Solnesses go down in defeat as long as Hilda may continue her mission until she meets the man strong enough to overcome his dizziness."[3]

In the self-referential, autobiographical narrative, the artist Solness-Ibsen does write the pathbreaking drama, launching a new phase in his career. The immediate cause of his fall is left ambiguous, in keeping with the tone of the play as a whole. In typical Ibsen fashion, the ending is a web of motives. He may have fallen because Hilda distracted him when she took Aline's shawl, a symbol of Solness's troubled conscience, and waved it at him. Or he may have fallen because the scaffolding collapsed under him. Planks and fragments of wood are seen falling with him, in which case his death is merely an accidental one that could have happened to any workman.

The mysterious forces that brought him success in the past now bring both success and death. Read as autobiography, the ending appears to say that in finishing this new play, climbing another tower, Ibsen can go no further as an artist. Read as tragedy, the play says that any great achievement has its price. Building houses cost Aline her happiness. Building castles in the air brings about Solness's death.

Once, in a conversation, Ibsen offered his own commentary. The crisis for Solness occurs when he sees that he "still has a desire for life, a longing for happiness, and can't imagine living a joyless life, in dark resignation. And so they decide to build castles in the air and to live together in spirit. This lifts him up, higher than before, to the point where he can do things that for a long time were impossible (symbolically). But he risks his life in doing so, and more than life. Now, what's crazy about risking one's life if one can win happiness for the first time?"[4]

The key to the play in performance is this sense of being uplifted, transported to some higher, more sublime level of existence. The long dialogues between Solness and Hilda are intended to be like operatic duets in their emotional intensity. In the exchanges between the two of them, Ibsen wrote some of his finest dialogue. As one Norwegian said of it, "The dialogue flows so easily and naturally from one's lips. The pauses and punctuation marks are always right . . . and every nuance is so clearly marked that one doesn't have to think about it."[5] The audience should feel what Hilda feels when she, in an exalted state, talks of "impossibly high towers" and finds her meeting with Solness "wonderfully exciting." When she sees Solness reach the top of the tower, she hears "harps in the air," and she echoes Jesus's last words, "Now it is finished!"

The Man Behind the Mask

To the experienced eyes of practicing dramatists like Hugo von Hofmannsthal and Frank Wedekind, it was obvious that the whole play was an autobiographical allegory. Hofmannsthal described it as "a curious mixture of allegory and real life . . . with hollow, humanlike puppets."[1]

This was just the sort of criticism that Ibsen dreaded. Protesting against "the profundities and symbols" ascribed to him, he declared, "I only write about people. I don't write symbolically. Just about people's inner life as I know it—psychology, if you like."[2] He was thinking of *The Master Builder* in particular when he said this and trying to divert attention from the hidden secrets in his play.

Wedekind, hostile to both French symbolist drama and Ibsen's bourgeois puritanism, felt a need to "unmask the old magician." He faulted Ibsen's characters for lacking an "intimate connection with nature," for being only "arbitrarily imagined abstract ideas." Hilda Wangel is "a superficial allegory masked as an individual." Once started on this path, Wedekind quickly deciphered the meaning of the other characters. Solness is of course Ibsen himself. Aline represents the older school of drama; Knut Brovik stands for the older generation; Ragnar Brovik, his son, for the younger generation. Kaja Fosli, the secretary employed by Solness, represents Ibsen's domestic dramas, and Hilda is the incarnation of Ibsen's youthful idealism.

Further, the twins who died as a result of the fire that destroyed the old house are identified as *Brand* and *Peer Gynt*, and the nine dolls that Aline cherished and lost are the nine muses. To Wedekind, *The Master Builder* when measured against serious art is only "deliberate counterfeiting."[3]

Georg Brandes took issue with Wedekind's allegorical interpretation. Consistent with his emphasis on the material and the sexual, he said that what Wedekind saw as the bloodlessness of Ibsen's characters should be attributed to the playwright's characteristic inability to depict erotic passion. Ibsen's upbringing in Protestant Norway resulted in his picturing sexual passion in the worst possible light.[4]

Just how right Wedekind's allegorical interpretation is becomes apparent when one refines it, refurbishes it, and adds a few more details. Crucial to the effectiveness of an allegory is its consistency, how well the "real" events and the parallel story keep in step with each other. The great weakness in Wedekind's interpretation is that it says nothing about the significance of the central event in Solness's past, the climbing of the tower at Lysanger, and little about the peculiar fire that determines the course of Solness's career. Finding the equivalents in real life to these events will tell us a lot about Ibsen's own thoughts. As in all of his best works, the subtext is extraordinarily rich.

At Lysanger, Solness at the top of the tower saw the schoolgirls below, and after the topping-off he was greeted by students who honored him with songs. The corresponding event in Ibsen's life was the celebration in his honor in September 1874 when he was hailed by the students in Christiania.

Ibsen responded to their songs by delivering that moving and carefully crafted speech, summing up his career. He had feared that as one of his country's severest critics, he might receive a cool welcome after many years abroad. Instead he received acclamation from these young students. He had ended his speech: "Now the young people of Norway have come to me here tonight and given me my answer more warmly and clearly than I had ever expected to hear it. I shall take this answer with me as the richest reward of my visit with my countrymen at home; and it is my hope and my belief that what I experience tonight will be an experience to 'live through,' which will someday be reflected in a work of mine. If that should happen, if someday I should send such a book home, then I ask you students to accept it by way of a handshake and a thanks for this meeting. I ask you to accept it as having a share in its creation."

It was a glorious moment for Ibsen, and it turned out that after it he had to move on to another kind of drama. As Solness vows to stop building churches, so Ibsen abandoned epic drama. Solness turned to building homes for human beings; Ibsen turned to writing the great realistic problem plays.

Now, what was it that made it possible for Solness to become a builder of houses? It was the fire, a fire that was not exactly the one he had imagined. Ibsen dwells on this strange turn of events, which seems unnecessary to the main plot. "It sounds like such a ludicrous little thing," says Solness. "You see, the whole business turns upon nothing but a crack in a chimney."[5] Why did Ibsen concoct such a strange story?

Here he continues the allegorical line by playing on the similarity between the Norwegian word for fire (*Brand*) and the name of the great influence on his life, Brandes. Ibsen hoped that a work like *Brand* might lead to a great reformation of society. It did not turn out that way; it was dramas like *A Doll's House* that over time made the greater impact. And what led him to pursue realistic drama? It was mainly the impact of Georg Brandes, who chided him in 1871 for not having "adopted the modern scientific point of view."[6] Consequently Ibsen shunted aside idealism and metaphysical drama for naturalism and the drama of social problems.

The controversial Danish critic was associated with fire both by those who hated him and by those who admired him. In 1874 Jakob Løkke, Ibsen's friend and Brandes's enemy, described Brandes as "an arsonist [*Brandstifter*] in moral society."[7] He was praised by his friend Julius Lange as "a natural element—fire itself" at a banquet honoring Brandes in 1877.[8] Lange's whole speech was built around the fire metaphor. This provided Ibsen with that realistic detail concerning the crack in the chimney. Lange said that there were those who wanted a fire to warm up the University of Copenhagen, but they were voted down by the sensible majority who feared that "so much fire would cause a fire [*Brand*] in the chimney pipe, which undeniably did not draw especially well and had not been properly cleaned."[9]

Interpreting Ibsen's hieroglyphics, we see that the fire caused by the faulty pipe is Georg Brandes's fire; the fire that actually occurred is Ibsen's *Brand.* Solness never repaired the crack, because through Brandes (the eventual fire) he would become a force in Denmark. "Through that little black crack in the chimney, I might, possibly, make my way upwards." That was his intention. To repair the crack would mean rejecting Brandes, when he was hoping he could advance his career through Brandes's influence.

Thoughts about Brandes would have been in Ibsen's mind when he was planning and writing *The Master Builder.* In 1891 Brandes was honored for twenty-five years of writing. On October 25 Ibsen sent him a telegram congratulating him for a quarter century of "pioneering work in the cause of man's spiritual freedom." When the Norwegians honored Brandes at a banquet in Christiania in April 1892, Ibsen was one of the hosts.

The literal-minded Brandes had no idea what lay behind the fire symbolism. He thought it might refer to Ibsen's years of exile.[10] The great irony is that Ibsen sought the support of a man who never really understood him.[11]

The Return of Nora

It is characteristic of Ibsen's artistry that he is very meticulous about details and consistent in his handling of them. The fire in the house and the episode at Lysanger are the two main incidents in Solness's past, and once they are linked to Ibsen's own life, the other pieces in the parable fall neatly into place.

In this autobiographical drama, he could hardly ignore the crucial part that Laura Kieler, the model for Nora, had played in his career. Like Hildur Andersen, she had entered Ibsen's life just when he needed inspiration. Much of the first act sketches out that background story. The story of Kaja and the Broviks, father and son, serves as a prologue, in which we learn about Solness's rise to fame as a self-made building contractor.

Old Brovik, a skilled architect of the old school, once employed Solness. Solness branched out on his own and destroyed old Brovik's business. Subsequently he hired Brovik and his son, because they were licensed architects, which he was not. Kaja Fosli became engaged to Ragnar some four or five years before the play begins. When she calls on Ragnar at the office, she meets Solness and becomes infatuated with him. She enters Solness's life just when he needed her, as if she were answering his unspoken wish.

These puppets act out Ibsen's progress as a dramatist. At first he wrote old-fashioned plays (old Brovik); but he soon became a master of his trade, expertly using the clever devices associated with Scribe and the well-made play. Young Ragnar represents the new and innovative ideas that Solness must make use of. The results of this fruitful collaboration were the works that brought Solness financial prosperity (for Ibsen, *The League of Youth* and *Pillars of Society*).

At this point Kaja entered his life. With Kaja (as material) and Ragnar (as the innovator), Solness could create homes for human beings (A *Doll's House* and the realistic masterpieces that followed). Solness has no love for her. He employs her in order to keep Ragnar under his thumb. With the arrival of Hilda, all this changes; Solness is willing to let Ragnar go off on his own, and he dismisses Kaja. (Read: Ibsen has finished writing realistic problem plays and is about to embark on something new.)

A whole story lies behind Solness's brusque dismissal of Kaja Fosli, a backstory that could find no place in the drama itself. Kaja is a hasty sketch of Laura Kieler, who had reentered Ibsen's life ten years after *A Doll's House*. She spent those years trying by every possible means to redeem her reputation. All those whose ears were attuned to rumor and speculation knew her as the woman who had, like Nora, forged a promissory note, deeply embarrassing her husband. Since the publication of the play, she had sought to remove the stigma attached to her name as a hysterical and irresponsible woman. In 1888 she wrote a play, *Men of Honor* (*Mænd af Ære*), a polemic against Georg Brandes.

Brandes heard about the play before it was published, and in the August 6, 1889, issue of *Verdens Gang*, in his review of the latest fascicule of Halvorsen's *Dictionary of Norwegian Authors* (*Norsk Forfatterleksikon*), which revived the old rumors, he went to unwarranted lengths to gibe at Kieler without mentioning her name, which was hardly necessary. Instead of sticking to the events in the play, Brandes accepted the ten-year-old gossip as true and denigrated Laura Kieler as having forged a note not in order to save her husband but to prettify her house. On November 29 the same journal printed her reply, "A Protest." The editor apologized for having printed Brandes's article.[1]

Kieler managed to get a hearing in Copenhagen in the spring of 1890. Some scenes from her play were printed in the newspaper *Venstrebladet*. The next month, May 21, 1890, the play was produced at the Casino Theater in Copenhagen.

The reviewer for *Dagens Nyheder* labeled the play "a complete joke" without a single honest line or believable character. After acknowledging that Ibsen had praised it, the reviewer admitted that as propaganda the work was not without interest. It displayed a stunning coarseness of thought and expression that one would not expect from an author who liked to present herself as a lady above reproach. Moreover, although the play was hailed as a powerful attack on Brandes's philosophy, it was nothing of the kind, being too tainted in its source and too imbecilic in its development.

Calling the play a "fiasco," the critic said the actors shamed themselves by appearing in it. The spectators in the higher-priced seats, the parquet and the loges, restrained themselves from showing their scorn, while no honest person had any doubts that the noisemakers who occupied the cheaper seats in the gallery and parterre were hired demonstrators.[2]

The same newspaper reported that the last performance, on May 23, was attended by a large audience, who greeted the cheap effects in the play with rounds of applause.[3]

Why such a fuss over this play? Why would Ibsen praise a drama that actors considered not stageworthy? Why would Brandes go out of his way to revive all the worst rumors about Kieler? Why would his brother, the aggressive Edvard Brandes, intervene personally to see to it that the Royal Theater in Copenhagen rejected the script? Why would her usual publisher tell her that he did not dare to print it out of fear of being boycotted by Brandes and his party?

The conflict between Kieler and Brandes was deeply personal. Laura Kieler was a religious woman (she had read *Brand* as a drama about the need for faith) who abhorred the atheism and sexual license of Brandes. Her three-act play centered on a talented young writer who succumbs to the enticements of a Brandes-like liberation, only to see the error of his ways when he causes the death of the woman he loves. To everyone in the Nordic literary world, the allusion to Brandes and Victoria Benedictsson was unmistakable. Her suicide in 1888 hovers in the background of *Men of Honor* and Strindberg's *Miss Julie*, both written in 1888, as well as in 1890 in Benedictsson's own play *The Enchanted* (*Den bergtagna*), a loose transcription of her affair with Brandes, which she finished shortly before taking her own life. Brandes could no more shake off Victoria Benedictsson's suicide than Laura Kieler could rid herself of the forged notes. His response to Kieler's play was his resurrection of her scandal.

This literary skirmish sent the old rumors and ugly gossip back into circulation. Kieler considered suing Brandes but wisely decided that such action would only upset her husband and his relations. She appealed to Fredrika Limnell, the Madame Récamier of Stockholm, who had welcomed Ibsen into her literary salon in 1869. She took up Kieler's cause and sent a letter to Ibsen, enclosing all the relevant articles, asking him to intervene in the controversy on Kieler's behalf. Specifically, she asked Ibsen to dispel the rumors by denying publicly that Laura had served as his model for Nora.

This put Ibsen in a difficult position: between Brandes, with whom he never quarreled in public, and Laura Kieler, to whom he owed so much. His reply to Limnell on July 1, 1890, when he was deeply absorbed in writing *The Master Builder*, reveals the Peer Gynt side of Ibsen, frightened by the Bøyg and going round about.

> It isn't at all clear to me what Laura Kieler wants to accomplish by trying to involve me in these disputes. An explanation from me, of the kind that she wants, namely, that "she is not Nora," would be both meaningless and ridiculous, since I have never suggested that she was. If in Copenhagen there were

> untrue rumors being broadcast that she at an earlier point in her life did something that bears a likeness to the forged note business in *A Doll's House*, then she herself or her husband, preferably both together, are the only ones who with an open and emphatic denial can squash these false rumors. I do not understand why Mr. Kieler has not long ago taken this course of action, which would soon put an end to the gossip.
>
> I am truly sorry that I cannot comply with your request to intervene. But I believe that you will, after weighing the matter more carefully and with an eye to all its aspects, as far as they are known to you, agree that I can best serve our mutual friend by remaining silent and not involving myself.
>
> Right now I am hard at work on my new play [*The Master Builder*], which has to be ready by autumn.[4]

To his credit, Ibsen did try to support Kieler's cause. He had read *Men of Honor* in manuscript and praised it.

"I have read [it] with intense interest, and I think all our theaters should hasten to stage it."[5]

He pressured the Christiania Theater into staging *Men of Honor*, although the actors and the director thought the script was irredeemably untheatrical. It received three performances, and on the last night, before a very small audience, the actors walked through their parts, cutting most of the scenes.[6]

The whole episode places Ibsen in a particularly unflattering light. He made Laura Kieler notorious, and he should have acknowledged this. Without *A Doll's House*, her family problems would have been known only to her acquaintances. She never committed a crime that would have brought her into court or into the public eye. As far as the facts allow, all one can accuse her of is borrowing money without telling her husband. She may, in her desperation, have contemplated forging a note to secure a loan, but there is no hard evidence that she actually did so. This means that the forgery that lies at the heart of Ibsen's drama was the immediate cause of the scandal that consumed Laura Kieler's life. What Ibsen required to build up the plot was what made her situation the talk of the town. As a man of honor, he should have admitted that he had met her on a few occasions and then declared that the forgery was his invention.

People like Georg Brandes, with access to thousands of readers, spread the rumors that Kieler was a flighty, irresponsible creature. He persisted in maliciously traducing her, and as late as 1906, in his obituary of Ibsen, he repeated the story that "the lady (later Nora) borrowed money by forging a signature, indeed for a less than ideal purpose—not to save her husband's life but to decorate her house."[7]

Lying beneath this quarrel between Kieler and Brandes was of course something more fundamental than her notoriety. There was in the tenor of the times a kind of thinking that she had to contend with in seeking rehabilitation. A letter to *Dagens Nyheder*, published before *Men of Honor* was staged and printed under the title "The Concept of Honor and Women's Emancipation," brought out a point of view probably shared by most of the male population.

The writer says that women were in former times allowed to gossip and spread rumors as a way of compensating for their physical inferiority. It was their way of defending themselves. Now, however, when women have claimed equality with men, they must accept man's moral code. Consider a case in which a woman publicly denigrates a person, drawing a recognizable portrait and holding him up to suspicion and ridicule. Is this consistent with the code of honor?

Let us take another example, says the writer. A woman commits an illegal act, falsifies a bank draft, in order to save her nearest and dearest from ruin. She acts out of love and a warm heart. Can this be reconciled with the code of honor? If she were a man, she would have no right to be called a person of honor.

But in the case of women, the letter writer continues, the matter has taken on a different aspect ever since Ibsen with his Nora messed up the concept of honor as shared by man and woman. Now that the women's movement has gained force, it might be hoped that another view of Nora might get a hearing and that she might be placed where she belongs. The writer does not doubt that after having forged a note in order to send her father [*sic*] to a health spa, and after having fled from husband and children in order to save her better self—a pretty expression, that—she has kept her honor completely intact. Nor does the writer doubt that society will not be too hard on her for her earlier indiscretions, on condition that she live quietly and modestly, all the while seeking to save herself.

"On the other hand, should she start to sound off and to tell us what man's concept of honor is, then she might have to be reminded of the old saying, '*Sic tacuisses* . . .' ['If you had been silent . . .']

"Unfortunately, women find it difficult to be silent."

The letter was signed "Helmer," the name of Nora's husband.[8]

A second letter from "Helmer" followed three days later. He writes that, from what he has read in the other Copenhagen papers, Laura Kieler has used his first letter as an excuse to present herself "as the innocent victim of a secret scandal." Why does she intrude in his (that is, Helmer's) affairs? "If she intends to liken herself with my runaway wife in one way or another, that is entirely her business."

The editor of the newspaper added his comments. He said *Dagens Nyheder* did not print Kieler's letters of protest because she did not specify the exact nature of the calumny that Dr. Georg Brandes supposedly uttered against her. Nor did she explain why the letter from "Hellmer" is defamatory.

"In any event we have it from an absolutely reliable source that Fru Kieler herself has described *Men of Honor* as a *pièce à clef* directed against two living men. It is a lampoon, and lampoons are the stuff of scandal, inevitably giving rise to defamation. So Laura Kieler has no cause to complain about being paid back in the same coin."[9]

In writing *The Master Builder* Ibsen relegated Laura Kieler to the past. The woman he had studied so carefully and who, incarnated as Nora, became one of the best known of all female characters in drama, was dismissed in order to make room for a new muse, Hildur Andersen.

The nine dolls whose loss Aline laments—very weirdly—are not the nine muses, as Wedekind thought, but Ibsen's first nine plays, those he allowed to be reissued and made part of the official canon. These plays were based not on contemporary subjects but on the old sagas and Norwegian history. But Wedekind was right in assuming that the twins, the "two little boys" who died as a consequence of the fire, are *Brand* and *Peer Gynt*.

Together they would have formed the foundation for the Third Kingdom. That dream became an illusive mirage when Ibsen turned to writing realistic dramas. In the parable, the fire that destroyed her family home plunged Aline into a deep depression that seriously affected her health. As a mother, she lacked the milk to nourish her two small boys. For Ibsen, the idealistic spirit that infused his early works withered when he followed the path chosen for him by Brandes.

The fact that the fire breaks out not where Solness thought it would but somewhere else illustrates the great irony of Ibsen's artistic career. He consciously chose to follow Brandes (a planned fire, not the real fire), only to realize that there was another force at work. There were devils and trolls at work all the time. When the fire broke out, he seemed to be the man with all the luck. But these helpers and servers have their own code, it seems. Though they bring luck, they make one pay a terrible price for it. Solness, like Ibsen, is burdened with a great sense of guilt, and Aline is the ever-present embodiment of it.

"Well, let me tell you," he confesses to Hilda, "what this good luck—to me—feels like. It feels like a huge, raw sore on my chest. And the helpers and servers, they flay off pieces of flesh from other people to patch up *my* sores."[10]

In the final analysis, then, Ibsen is saying it was not Brandes that ultimately determined the course of his career, but *Brand*. This was the fire set by the helpers. The basic motivation in the epic drama was the necessity of overcoming inherited guilt. The connection between great achievements and the sacrifice they entail on the one hand and the concomitant bad conscience on the other provided the foundation of Ibsen's dramas.

Solness as Superman

In *The Master Builder* Ibsen challenged himself to do the impossible: to cast off, as if it were an old coat, the ingrained conceptions and beliefs of Christianity. The castles in the air would replace the city of God, and Hilda, the conscienceless bird of prey, espousing the old Viking ways, would make it possible.

This aspect of the drama, the attempt to move beyond Christian notions of sin and guilt, surely owes something to Nietzsche. Perhaps even Solness's dizziness at the top of the tower as the physical symptom of spiritual qualms can be traced to the philosopher who viewed the man of great achievements as standing without fear or giddiness. In *The Birth of Tragedy,* Nietzsche compared conscience-stricken man to "a man who throws himself from a tower in order to put an end to the unbearable sensation of vertigo."[1] Also in Nietzsche—or in Brandes's essay on the philosopher—Ibsen would have read that "the aspiring mind creates the helpers it requires."[2]

Solness is most Nietzschean when he creates his own moral code by virtue of his strong personality, which sets him apart from others. This emphasis on the unique and powerful individual lay at the heart of Brandes's interpretation of Nietzsche. Whereas Aline is obsessed by her sense of duty to others, Solness feels that his highest obligation is to himself. In a conversation with Ellen Key, Ibsen sounded like Nietzsche himself.

"Those who have not been able to create for themselves an idea of justice in each special case will have to follow the general sense of justice. But a strong personality will create his own idea of justice. And then for him there will not be any 'duties,' only his duty."[3]

Solness does reach the top—a triumph. He is seen "striving" with someone, which must be seen as Solness striving with his god—not the Christian one, clearly, but rather like the god in *Brand,* the god of achievement through sacrifice. The end reads like a repetition of that central artistic and philosophical achievement, the tower replacing the Ice Peak, with Hilda as a bird of prey replacing Gerd and the falcon of compromise. In both instances, Ibsen attempts to unite irreconcilable opposites.

The last moments are like the final scene in *Brand*. The great difference between the endings is the replacement of a supreme ideal, a *deus caritatis*, by castles in the air. The one definite thing that can be said about them is that in the mind of Ibsen-Solness they were to succeed the homes for human beings to which he had devoted so much of his life and work. The house with the tower was to be the last of these. He reaches the top because of Hilda's confidence in him. When he gets to the top, he sings a song of triumph, signifying another radical break in his career. After *Emperor and Galilean*, Ibsen looked down on the young students who cheered him and gave up writing epic dramas. Nevertheless, his dream of a Third Empire still inspired him. At Lysanger, Solness looked down on the young people who hailed him and vowed to build no more churches. Yet, in a significant way, Solness's break with the past at the top of the tower is even more radical. The newly finished house has three nurseries in it—for a couple that has no children! And Hilda sleeps in it. In Ibsen's coded language, this means that with the completion of this house, Ibsen will no longer search for the Third Kingdom. A castle in the air will supplant it.

When Hilda claps her hands and joyfully exclaims, "My lovely, lovely castle. Our castle in the air!" Solness adds, "On a firm foundation." For Ibsen that firm foundation lay in his romance with Hildur Andersen, not something he imagined or dreamed of, and not an "affair" or a liaison but a union of kindred spirits. Not since *Brand* had he attained such heights of exaltation. He had found his Beatrice. The sixty-four-year-old poet seemed rejuvenated. Brandes said he had never before seen Ibsen in such high spirits. "He seemed positively glad to be alive; he was bursting with energy."[4]

Conquering France

Ibsen's reception in France was of a different nature than in Germany. In Germany it was the naturalist Ibsen who was embraced and admired. This was also true at first in France, with the naturalist Zola being quick to encourage the production of *Ghosts*. However, *A Doll's House* was not staged in France by a professional company until 1894, fifteen years after its world premiere in Copenhagen. Gabrielle-Charlotte Réjane, the reigning star of the Parisian theater, admired for the realism of her acting and expertly coached by the Danish writer Herman Bang, played Nora.[1] Ibsen sent her a telegram on April 20, 1894, thanking her for having "made my fondest dream a reality."[2]

Hedda Gabler is the most French of the master's plays, and its tone, its sophistication, and its cynicism suggest that Ibsen hoped to break the Parisian barrier with it, just as *Pillars of Society* with its political overtones had made him a popular and respected playwright in Berlin. *Hedda* bears all the earmarks of what the French called *comédie rosse*, hard-boiled, cruel drama, the characters depicted with an unsympathetic and unflinching eye and from an amoral, nonjudgmental point of view. The genre was initiated by Henri Becque's *Les Corbeaux*, produced in Paris in 1882. From all the contemporaneous French plays, Ibsen singled that one out for special praise.[3] *Les Corbeaux* was about greed. Becque's next play, *La Parisienne* (1885), was about sex and featured a ménage à trois. Just as eager as Ibsen to conquer Paris, Strindberg in 1888, right after finishing *Miss Julie*, wrote his brilliant three-character play *Creditors* (*Fordringsägare*), featuring a woman, her former husband, and her lover. He called it a tragicomedy, but it might more accurately be labeled a comédie rosse. Two years later Ibsen produced *Hedda*, with its teasing allusions to a triangle (*trekant*) and its derisive tone, as if challenging the audience to make up its mind about the play. Are we supposed to congratulate Hedda on her doing beautifully what Løvborg bungled, a bullet in the head versus a bullet in the groin? Should we, like one German critic, find some delicious humor in Løvborg's accidental death in "*ein lustiges Haus*"?[4]

If Ibsen intended to make his mark in France with a sophisticated, amoral drama, something like a comédie rosse, it was not to be. He entered Paris not through the boulevard theater but through the avant-garde. It was the anarchist Ibsen and the symbolist Ibsen who fired the imagination of the younger writers and critics in France. The ground had been prepared by the introduction of the great Russian novelists Tolstoy and Dostoyevsky. Compared with the cynical, world-weary French, these writers—and Ibsen—seemed spontaneous, naive, idealistic.

He quickly gained notoriety in France not for his views on women, as Strindberg did, but for his politics. When *An Enemy of the People* was staged by Lugné-Poe in November 1893, it was treated as anarchist propaganda, and the speeches attacking the "compact majority" were censored. For the crowd scenes a number of young anarchists offered their services. A month later the anarchist Vaillant threw a bomb into the Palais Bourbon, where the French deputies were gathered. At his trial he declared that his goal was to realize the ideas of justice and freedom expressed by writers like Ibsen.[5] There was a different Ibsen for each country he invaded. "Nothing testifies better to Ibsen's greatness," said Brandes, "than the fact that in Norway he was regarded first as a conservative, later as a radical; in Germany hailed as a naturalist and a socialist, in France as a symbolist and anarchist."[6]

Ibsen was nervously attentive to the reception of *The Master Builder* in France. He welcomed journalists during the time when the play was about to be issued and in the weeks thereafter, willing to "hype" the play for a French audience. Early in 1893, shortly after the publication of the play in Christiania on December 12, 1892, in a printing of ten thousand copies, he chatted at length with Maurice Bigeon, a French correspondent, who called on the great man in Christiania. Ibsen was in an usually expansive mood, giving freely of himself, aligning himself with the symbolists among the literati and with the young radicals in politics.

Although Ibsen was not reticent, the interview does not ever suggest that he was caught off guard. Quite the opposite. Like a good politician who comes to an interview carefully briefed, he was ready to talk about France's most famous and most controversial author, Zola, and about the latest developments in art and politics.

Zola and he "don't take the same path," he said, "and we don't hold the same views. He is a socialist and a collectivist. I am an anarchist and an individualist. The difference is crucial. It results from philosophical outlooks that are completely opposed to each other."

For once he acknowledged his indebtedness to the French masters of the well-made play. "I have studied the dramatic technique of your great playwrights. But none of them has governed my thoughts, my philosophy, my ideas, and my opinions. I have found everything within myself; everything has come from my heart. It is because I have had very vivid and strong impressions of life and society, overpowering ones, that I have written what I have written. . . . It has been my vocation."

He reached out to the next generation. "Yes, these young people are my children. They share my aims. They seek to liberate the individual and to improve society. They have only begun, but they shall go farther and faster than I. They will head the movement of human renewal that I had dreamed of accomplishing, but which is beyond the power of one man. . . . I don't know them well, unfortunately. They are young, and I am very old. But I like them because they feel the frisson of the future; they sing the hymn of a new day dawning. . . . I've just finished a play in five [!] acts, a symbolist play."[7]

Ibsen came to regret his candor and outspokenness. A couple of years later he told another interviewer, an American, that his remarks had been misinterpreted. He explained that he was an anarchist only with regard to modern French drama, whatever that might mean. Misinterpreted, he said he was "assailed on all sides."[8]

In writing *The Master Builder*, Ibsen may have been responding to Hamsun's stinging remarks about the bankruptcy of naturalistic, psychological drama. Clearly, he felt he could hardly add anything new to what he had accomplished in *Hedda Gabler* and *The Wild Duck*, and *The Master Builder* is in some respects in line with Hamsun's ideas. The play does give us "the secret movements at work in the remote parts of the soul" and "the delicate life of the imagination." Yet Ibsen's examination of these subtleties is more in tune with what the French symbolists hoped to express. Hamsun wanted to capture the irrational, the impulsive, whereas Ibsen wanted to bring to the surface the hidden promptings of the soul. Hamsun heroes respond to the moment and react spontaneously; Ibsen's master builder is delving into something that is present and has been present for a long time, not something fugitive or of the moment.

Ibsen's comments about symbolism in his plays were always ambivalent. Although he would admit that his late plays were symbolist, he did not under any circumstances want them to be produced in a nonrealistic, "symbolist" manner, which is what happened in France when the Théâtre de l'Œuvre staged *The Master Builder* in 1894, with Lugné-Poe playing the lead. Touring Europe, the company performed the play in Christiania in October 1895, with Ibsen seated in a loge. According to Herman Bang, the Danish writer who had been Lugné-Poe's adviser on the production, Ibsen sat quite unmoved during most of the first act.

But during the second act he got to his feet. "At the back of the loge, he leaned against the wall and followed every gesture of the actors. And as if the watchful eyes of the master increased the power and capabilities of the actors, the love song onstage rushed forward like a storm—until the fall of the curtain. Later, at the Grand Hotel, Ibsen came up to me. Only once have I seen him deeply moved, and that was at this moment. He stretched out both hands to me—they were ice cold from the emotional experience—and said, 'This was the resurrection of my play.'"[9]

Yet in 1897 Ibsen told the French journalist Jules Claretie that Lugné-Poe had introduced too much symbolism into his plays, using mysterious lighting, hanging a scrim in front of the stage, and having the actors deliver their lines in an artificial way, half-chanting them. Ibsen objected. "I don't create symbols; I portray human beings."[10] He did not want his characters to appear suspended between the world of matter and the world of spirit. When he told a correspondent in 1900 that "symbolism is something that well-wishing and profound readers find in my uniformly realistic representations," he probably had in mind French symbolism.[11] And perhaps what others might call symbolism he called poetry, as in his formula for his kind of playwriting. "I take an incident from life within my own experience or knowledge; I throw in a little poetry, and that's how it's done."[12]

It may have been Lugné-Poe's portrayal of Solness that won Ibsen's approbation. Bernard Shaw praised it as strikingly realistic. In vulgar trousers, his face red and blotchy (like Ibsen's?), Lugné-Poe gave "life to that portrait which, in every stroke, from its domineering energy, talent, and covetousness, to its half witted egotism and crazy philandering sentiment, is so amazingly true to life. . . . He recognized Solness as a person he had met a dozen times in ordinary life, and just reddened his nose and played him without preoccupation."[13]

In an interview in January 1894, Ibsen cautioned the artists working on *The Master Builder* against looking for symbols. "The characters that I created resemble real people that I wanted to portray after having actually met them. Otherwise they would make my work incomprehensible."[14] And again in 1900, he said that symbolism "is something that well-intentioned and profound readers imagine as being in my consistently realistic portrayals."[15]

In Sweden the part was taken by August Lindberg, the unconventional actor who staged *Ghosts* when no other theater in the Nordic countries would touch it. He built the part along tragic lines, and his Solness was no ordinary person. He was a charismatic hero from his first entrance, an imposing sporting type, self-assured and intimidating, with nothing in his outward appearance suggesting what is to come. Then Hilda appears. As the voice of the younger generation that he is beginning to fear, she fascinates him, and as scene follows scene, he undergoes a metamorphosis. In quietly spoken conversations he reveals his inner turmoil, his guilty conscience. Simultaneously, his need for her grows ever greater until finally he is completely under her spell, and nothing else matters.[16]

The perceptive Maurice Maeterlinck, a Belgian poet and adherent of the new symbolist school in France, captured as well as anyone the elusive atmosphere of Ibsen's new play, and he was among the first to appreciate its significance as innovating a new kind of drama. He saw that *The Master Builder* was essentially an antidramatic drama. It begins conventionally enough, with a solid set, the quick development of an intrigue, and confrontations between characters. Then, with the entrance of Hilda Wangel, it shifts into something different. It becomes a story in which little devils and trolls, mysterious fires, cherished dolls and castles in the air play major parts. Action stops, nothing much seems to happen, until the very end. Objective reality dissolves, the world of appearances gives way to a world of memories and dreams and imaginings, revealed gradually through long conversations. In a landmark essay inspired by the play, Maeterlinck called it "a transposition of life." His point was that conventional plays, filled with violent action, murders, and suicides, have by their very exceptional nature very little to do with the life of ordinary mortals. But action isn't necessary for a tragedy; there should be a sense of the tragic in daily life. An old man sitting in an armchair, "submitting to the presences of his soul and his destiny," may have "actually lived a more profound and typical life than the lover who strangles his mistress, the captain who comes home victorious, or the husband who avenges his honor."

Drama without action seemed to be a contradiction in terms, but Maeterlinck believed a "static theater" was possible, and he found it in Ibsen's play. The conversations of Hilda and Solness "resemble nothing we have heard before, because the poet has tried to mingle internal with external dialogue in the same passage. There reigns in this somnambulistic drama some inexpressible new power. Everything spoken hides and, at the same time, uncovers the sources of a life unknown. And if we are sometimes astonished, we must not lose sight of the fact that our soul often appears to our impoverished eyes as an irrational power, and that there are in man many regions more fecund, more profound, and more interesting than those of reason or intelligence."[17]

Maeterlinck called the long arias between Solness and Hilda "dialogue of the second degree." The words build up a world of feeling and ideas that somehow runs parallel to the physical world, a world where longings might become realities, where the past might be reshaped if only by being reinterpreted and revisited.

This 1894 essay became an important contribution to the controversy surrounding symbolism in the 1890s. Although symbolism in a broad sense is as old as art itself, beginning in the late 1880s in Paris it took on a more specialized meaning as the young generation of poets rebelled against Zola as Hamsun had turned against Ibsen. In France the movement was primarily an effort to restore the spiritual element to a world that was becoming scientific and materialistic. In the visual arts, the postimpressionists, like Gauguin and van Gogh, were putting on canvas figures and images that were imbued with some otherworldly significance. Where the impressionists (whom Zola preferred to call naturalists) tried to catch the play of light and ascertain the laws governing color, the new school sought to deal with feelings rather than facts and to capture the tremors within the human soul rather than the forces impinging on it from outside. This meant plunging into a world where the laws of physical causality gave way to a world of feelings, hard to represent or draw except in a roundabout way. Basically, it was an antiscientific, antirational, antideterministic view of human existence.

In *Hedda Gabler* a number of forces, social, historical, psychological, combine to produce the events in the drama, and the symbols in the play—the pistol, the portrait, the manuscript—represent those forces. In *The Master Builder* the symbols are harder to define. The tower, the dolls, the trolls exist mainly as images in the mind, together forming another reality, one created by the human mind rather than by the hard facts of science and physical nature.

It was typical of Ibsen that he wanted to have it both ways—to be a symbolist with the symbolists and an antisymbolist with the naturalists.

He feared that his characters might seem less than real if they were shrouded in some symbolist aura. He was right to be concerned. For Ibsen concealed as much as he revealed in his story of the master builder, and what he concealed lurked behind the symbols. As a dramatist he prided himself on creating believable characters, but in this highly personal, autobiographical play he wanted to be ruthlessly honest with himself while being discreet with the public. The result was the half world of the play. Lugné-Poe wanted to shadow it forth by means of a scrim between actors and audience; Ibsen wanted it to emerge directly and simply from everyday dialogue, a point that Maeterlinck understood and appreciated.

Still, Maeterlinck misunderstood Ibsen's play, not in emphasizing the importance of the inner life but in believing that the forces at work there were too mysterious and elusive to be pinned down: they could only be hinted at or suggested. That was not Ibsen's view. He looked for specific causes, with a sense of mystery arising from the very complexity of life. The fire that broke out in Solness's house is a fine example of this. For the symbolists, there was something unfathomable about existence; for Ibsen, the truth was deep but not beyond reach.

LITTLE EYOLF

In his next play, *Little Eyolf,* Ibsen appeared to have abandoned the symbolic technique of *The Master Builder* and returned to the psychologically probing of the plays of the 1880s. However, this first impression is misleading.

The play was published in December 1894, two years after his previous play, as was customary with the methodical Ibsen. Once again, he produced a phenomenal best seller. Ten thousand copies came off the presses, with another printing called for within ten days. The first three printings netted Ibsen ninety-three hundred kronor. On top of that were the theater royalties; in German theaters it proved to be a considerably greater success than either *Hedda Gabler* or *The Master Builder.*[1]

In Norway and Denmark the phrase "the crutch is floating," a repeated motif in the play, became, like "castles in the air" and "harps in the air," a popular saying. It was a catchphrase even before the book went on sale, provoking a contretemps between Ibsen and his publisher. Ibsen insisted on absolute secrecy surrounding his play, in part because, for copyright reasons, a new work had to appear in England and Germany at the same time it was published in Copenhagen. The Danish newspaper *Politiken* in its November 14 issue published an account revealing some details of the plot. Investigations revealed that a young Norwegian author with access to the printing room had appropriated about sixteen pages of the book.[2] A new work by the dramatist stirred up enormous interest, especially in Norway. The publisher, Gyldendal, was located in Denmark, and the books had to be shipped to Christiania. As soon as the steamship was sighted, plowing its way through the icy December seas, the book dealers, some of whom had ordered a thousand copies, showed up at the docks, waiting for the crates to clear customs. The process was slowed down because the invoices, which the dealers had to present, were not mailed ahead of time, as was customary, but came with the ship. These invoices contained the name of the play, and both Ibsen and his publisher wanted that withheld until the last possible moment. In the printing shop the title page was the last off the presses.

In the case of *The Lady from the Sea*, one newspaper scooped its rivals by being in telegraphic communication with Copenhagen.[3] Usually, the distribution of the books at the dock took about two hours, from noon to two o'clock. Yet by evening the daily papers contained a summary of the play.

Little Eyolf is a deeply flawed work, its first two acts promising much more than the third provides. Henry James's response to the play was probably typical: an initial enthusiasm engendered by the first two acts, followed by a great disappointment. In a letter to his publisher, who had supplied him with an advance copy of the English translation, he said *Little Eyolf* "takes hold as nothing else of his has as yet done—it appeals with an immoderate intensity and goes straight as a dose of castor oil!

"It is of a rare perfection—and if it keeps up the tremendous pitch of 1 and 2 it will distinctly stand at the tiptop of his achievement. It's a masterpiece and a marvel."

But, as James soon found out, there was a tremendous falling off in the third act. "It seems to me a singular and almost inexplicable drop ... in short strangely and painfully meager. It has beauty ... but only as far as anything so meager *can* have it. The worst of it is that it goes back, as it were, on what precedes, and gives a meagerness to that too—makes it less interesting and less significant."[4]

The English critic W. L. Courtney, while praising the first act, found the end of the play psychologically improbable. "The figures of the drama are ineffectual shadows, mere sketches and outlines which we know not how to fill in, skeletons which it is more difficult to cloak with human flesh and blood."[5] To Ibsen, who prided himself on creating flesh-and-blood characters, this was damning criticism.

Yet there is no escaping the feeling that the figures in the drama, except for Rita and the Rat Wife, have no life of their own. Working our way through the last act, we can see they are being manipulated to fit in with the pattern in the carpet. It is easy to see that the motif dominating the action is the change and transformation in outlook that accompany the aging process. The three major characters undergo a radical transvaluation of values in the third act, a development that should in theory provide a satisfactory denouement to the drama.

It is a theme that makes *Little Eyolf* serve as a counterpart to *The Master Builder.* In that play Ibsen tried to reinvent himself by renouncing realistic, socially oriented drama for a more esthetically pure art form; in *Eyolf* he seems to backtrack, returning to the idea of social responsibility. The egocentric ascent that culminated in "castles in the air" is now replaced with a humanistic earthboundness that involves caring for the less fortunate. Hilda's ecstatic cry, "Now it is finished," is hardly matched by Rita's calm hope that "a Sabbath peace will descend on us once in a while."[6] Where Solness tried (and perhaps successfully, at least for a moment) to repress the urgings of a guilty conscience, Alfred Allmers and Rita come to recognize its implacable demands.

In the first act of the play they lose their only son, Eyolf, nine years old, who is lured away from home by the Rat Wife, falls off a nearby pier, and drowns, even as some young boys look on. A momentary inattentiveness by his parents allowed the boy to slip out of the house unnoticed. That in itself would make the parents feel guilty in his death. But their guilt has deeper roots. Eyolf as a baby was crippled when he fell off a table while his parents were absorbed in their lovemaking. His crutch is a constant reminder of their negligence, and his drowning brings back the past in all its horror. The image of the floating crutch haunts them. (Ibsen's brother while an infant was dropped by his nurse and crippled for life.)[7]

So far the story Ibsen tells is fairly straightforward. It becomes more complicated with the introduction of Asta, Alfred's younger half sister. He took care of her and served as her guardian. One of his reasons for marrying Rita was to enjoy the benefits of her wealth; as a mere tutor, he would have found it difficult to support both himself and Asta. The bond between the two was exceptionally strong and somewhat peculiar. Alfred treated her as a younger brother, sometimes dressed her as a boy, and called her Eyolf. Soon after marrying Rita, Alfred tells her about this cross-dressing game. He chooses an odd moment to do so. He tells her when embracing her, at or near the moment of orgasm. And it was at that moment, when Alfred told Rita about his imaginary Eyolf, that the real Eyolf was injured. This revelation provides the knot of the drama, the point at which the main threads of the story are woven together. It is hard to imagine a more complicated knot than the one Ibsen fashioned here. It is because of this scene that the play has proved so refractory to interpretation. It is Ibsen's most hermetic work, which he himself called a "hellbroth" (*djäfvulstyg*), a recipe for black magic.[8]

The main concern of the drama is with change and maturation. The principal characters undergo transformations, changes in what they see as their purpose in life. At the beginning of the play, Alfred Allmers has already decided to give his life a new direction. During his wanderings in northern Norway, living in solitude there, he resolved to abandon the work that had occupied him for years, a philosophical study of social responsibility. He has determined to devote himself to the much more practical aim of making "a regular fresh-air boy" of Eyolf. The arrival of the Rat Wife and the drowning of Eyolf put an end to that plan.

The last act of the play is mainly devoted to the great change in Rita from the passionate, sexually demanding woman of the first act to a humanitarian do-gooder who will devote herself to improving the lot of those poor, underprivileged children who watched little Eyolf die. In broad outline the play makes sense as the story of how two married people respond to the tragic loss of their only child. The problem with this view is that the most intriguing scene in the play, Alfred's confession that he played transvestite games with his half sister, appears to have no connection with the main theme.

Little Eyolf presents the same kind of dramaturgical problem that we faced in *Ghosts*. The outbreak of the fire in the orphanage seemed at first glance to have little relevance to the developing story of Oswald and his caring mother. Yet that fire, on the symbolic level, gathered together and intertwined the main strands of the plot. Knowing Ibsen's methods, we can assume that the confession scene serves a similar purpose.

Unlike *Ghosts*, however, *Little Eyolf* won't yield its secrets unless one recognizes that here, as in *The Master Builder*, Ibsen is writing autobiographical drama. Under Hilda's influence, Solness stopped building homes for human beings and dreamed of building castles in the air, and Ibsen as the master-builder dramatist made a similar change. Allmers continues the story of Ibsen the artist. Allmers has decided to give up his major work, the book on one's obligations to society, and turn to something perhaps less ambitious but more satisfactory. And like Ibsen, Allmers spent some time in northern Norway, apart from his wife.

The resemblances end there. The passionate Rita bears little resemblance to Suzannah; the boy who drowns is not a counterpart to Ibsen's son, Sigurd. And Asta appears to have no connection with the young women in Ibsen's life. And, for that matter, Allmers himself, a slim man in his midthirties, is an unlikely representative of the stout, aging author. If one is looking for parallels between the outward circumstances of Ibsen's life and the Allmers family's story, one won't find them. This is because *Little Eyolf* conceals the inner story of Ibsen the artist, and, as a German critic said, Ibsen resorted to "sibylline symbols" ("*sibyllinische Sinnbilder*") in order to conceal his own soul.[9]

Entrance into Ibsen's hidden life comes through the most memorable character in the play, the Rat Wife, who is indirectly responsible for Eyolf's death. The ordinary reader will think of her as a female version of the Pied Piper of German legend, while the Ibsen aficionado will recall what Ibsen told his French translator: "The Rat Wife was a little old lady in Skien who came to our school to exterminate the rats. She carried a little dog in a sack, and it was said that the children who followed her were drowned."[10] Here the wily Ibsen was luring the reader away from the real identification of this singular figure.

In 1893, when Ibsen set to work on *Little Eyolf*, Camilla Collett, the writer and women's rights advocate, celebrated her eightieth birthday and was honored with banquets in both Christiania and Copenhagen. On January 23 women paraded in front of her house before the banquet, hosted by the Norwegian Student Association. The students entered with torches and sang to her. Ibsen was her escort and presented her with a bouquet of flowers, while Lorentz Dietrichson gave the main speech, hailing her as one of Scandinavia's greatest authors.[11] Later, at the banquet in Copenhagen, Magdalene Thoresen extolled Collett's accomplishments in a moving tribute.

Ibsen's friendship with Collett went back to 1871, when she often called on him and Suzannah in Dresden, and she was also a frequent visitor in the spring of 1877, when the Ibsen family resided in Munich. Ibsen walked her to her hotel every night. As we have seen, she probably pressed him into emphasizing the feminist component in *Pillars of Society,* while to some *A Doll's House* was "but a dramatic adaptation of Mrs. Collett's feminist ideas."[12]

She liked to think of herself as playing a significant part in Ibsen's writings, not only prodding him into introducing feminism into his plays but also serving as model for Ellida in *The Lady from the Sea.* Although she could be severe with Ibsen for using Laura Kieler as his model for Nora, she remained his staunch ally and was one of the few who strongly defended *Ghosts* in 1884.[13] She also supported him when he refused to become a member of the conservative Student Society in Copenhagen.[14]

Ibsen acknowledged his indebtedness to her, writing in 1889, "It is now a good many years since you through your intellectual career [*åndelige livsgang*] in one form or another began to play a role in my works."[15] After he resettled in Norway he saw her quite often, and in 1892 he pressured her publisher into issuing her collected works.[16] When she was buried in 1895, Ibsen was conspicuously present, looking "sphinxlike," in high hat and black gloves and carrying his indispensable umbrella. Fru Ibsen was too ill to attend.[17]

The Rat Wife is Camilla Collett only slightly disguised. She appears in *Little Eyolf* just after the celebrations in her honor, when Ibsen would have had occasion to reflect on the part she had played in his writings. The similarities between her and the Rat Wife are unmistakable, made all the more noticeable because both are such odd characters.

Collett was already an eccentric in middle age, looking like a specter from some old family history. Her usual topics of conversation were stories about her own past and women's emancipation. She had a great gift and penchant for revivifying her memories. She was very nearsighted, and perhaps because of this, her favorite color was red. She always carried an umbrella, shading her weak eyes with it on sunny days.

Her thoughts dwelled so much on the past because of the great tragedy of her life, which probably aged her prematurely. As a shy seventeen-year-old girl she had fallen in love with the poet Johan Welhaven, who refused to marry her, preferring to see her as his heavenly muse. She could never forgive him for turning what should have been the happiest days of her life, when she was filled with passionate longings, into the saddest ones. When at age seventy she reminisced about her love for Welhaven, it was as if all the intervening years were wiped out by this painful memory of her youth.[18]

The Rat Wife is Collett as Ibsen would have seen her in the early 1890s, "a thin little shrunken figure, old and gray-haired."[19] She enters carrying a large red umbrella. She tells Eyolf that in the old days she used to lure men, one in particular, her own sweetheart, who is now down where all the drowned rats are. (Welhaven died in 1873.)

In an early draft of the play, Ibsen provided another clue pointing to Camilla Collett. Her maiden name was Wergeland (wolf land); in the draft the Rat Wife is called Miss Wolf (*frøken Varg*). In the finished play, Ibsen does not let the name go unnoticed.

EYOLF. Auntie Asta, isn't it strange, having a name like Rat Wife?
ASTA. She's called that because she goes up and down the country driving away rats.
ALLMERS. Her real name is Varg, so I've heard.
EYOLF. Varg? That means "wolf," doesn't it?
ALLMERS [*patting him on the head*]. So you know that, do you?[20]

(Collett read *Little Eyolf* in 1895, shortly before she died. She was deeply moved by it, saying it brought back memories. Did she recognize herself?)[21]

Once the Rat Wife is unmasked as Camilla Collett, this play, the most impenetrable of the master's puzzles, begins to yield its secrets. Here, as in *The Master Builder*, Ibsen is viewing his career through a prism that distorts and compresses the past. Alfred Allmers must be the author's alter ego. Like him, Ibsen had spent his solitary time in northern Norway meditating on the direction his life should take. The first product of this pilgrimage was *The Master Builder*. When he revisited the past again in *Little Eyolf*, he seems at first to have picked up where the master builder left off: he had abandoned his work on human responsibility, just as Solness decided to stop building homes for human beings. But it soon becomes apparent that Allmers is altogether a different being from Solness. Where Solness began to think of reaching new heights and of building castles in the air, Allmers finds himself drawn downward into the depths where his son lies. Hilda inspired Solness by bringing him back to his moment of greatest triumph, climbing the church tower, whereas the Rat Wife, in luring Eyolf to his death, brings Allmers back to a time when everything went wrong.

Ibsen compresses that time into the dreadful moment when the infant Eyolf was crippled through the negligence of his parents, the moment when Rita was lost in sexual passion, while Alfred was reliving in his imagination his cross-dressing games with his half sister, Asta. If the ascent of the church tower at Lysanger represented a unique and worthy achievement, the laming of Eyolf, in this retelling of the author's career, must stand for a work or an action that Ibsen regrets. Eyolf must in some way or other represent a goal or an ideal that was never fully realized, compromised at first (the crippling) and then lost altogether (the drowning).

Allmers is thirty-six or thirty-seven at the beginning of the play, and he has just returned from that solitary visit to the mountains. If we seek a connection between Ibsen and Allmers, we see that Allmers must have been born about 1853–55; it was then that Ibsen in the poem "Building Plans" dreamed of the promises or possibilities that life held for him. In the dream castle of his imagination, one wing, the larger one, would house the immortal poet; the other wing would shelter a lily. In this house of the soul his two great desires, everlasting fame and domestic happiness, would coexist.

If this was indeed Ibsen's starting point, then Allmers represents not the poet himself but something more abstract: the poet's career. In *The Master Builder* Ibsen found one way of transforming his autobiography into drama. In *Little Eyolf* he took the method a step forward: he made the principal events in his artistic career into puppets and then fleshed them out as characters. With the information supplied in the play, one can build a chronology in which, as we shall see, significant dates in Allmers's life correspond to equally significant dates in Ibsen's progress as a writer, with Rita, Asta, and Eyolf serving as milestones.

Although the appearance of Camilla Collett as the Rat Wife was an inspired bit of dramatic inventiveness, her part is comparatively small. The key to an understanding of the play lies in Eyolf, whose presence is felt from the beginning to the end. He owes his existence to a controversy between Christen Collin and Georg Brandes that erupted early in 1894. In a series of ten articles published in *Verdens Gang,* beginning in February, Collin assailed the naturalism of the 1880s and the cult of the superman that Brandes expounded. He called upon writers to identify themselves with their fellow human beings and to develop a moral philosophy that would provide a meaningful life for the many. He pointed out that a moral system does not consist simply of prohibitions but should also provide imperatives for the improvement of human conditions. As an example, he argued that monogamy is more likely to promote the welfare of the race than polygamy.

Much of this would have struck a responsive chord in the young Brandes, who had been a strong advocate of English utilitarianism. But to the Nietzschean Brandes of 1894, Collin's moralizing was humdrum philistinism. Collin allied Ibsen with Brandes and called into question the whole naturalist movement and the Modern Breakthrough, to which the dramatist had committed himself in the 1880s. When he published his essays in book form with the title *Art and Morality: A Critique of Realism, Its Writers and Critics* (*Kunsten og moralen: Bidrag til kritik af realismens digtere og kritikere*), he recapitulated Ibsen's career from *Pillars of Society* to *The Master Builder* and found in this body of work "a *lack of courage* to live" and a fear that the individual would lose himself by enlarging his life to include others.

Here Collin was following in the footsteps of Max Nordau, whose massive study of modern literature, *Degeneration* (1893), reduced nearly all the great creative artists of the latter half of the nineteenth century to unhealthy, sickly creatures suffering from various forms of neuroses and egomanias. As we have seen, Ibsen was allotted even more space than Nietzsche, since Nordau felt compelled to respond to those "voices [that] have been heard in all countries claiming for Henrik Ibsen the highest intellectual honours at the disposal of mankind."[22] Nordau dedicated his book to Cesare Lombroso, Italian criminologist and professor of psychiatry at the University of Turin, whose studies had convinced him that genius was a degenerative condition, akin to insanity.

Collin was much more moderate in his assessment of modern Nordic literature, but he found, as Nordau did, a disquieting egomania in Ibsen. He called upon Norwegian writers to look beyond themselves and take responsibility for the damaging effect their works might have upon the next generation, not only the young in Norway but the young throughout the educated world. Norway was no longer a negligible cultural outpost. "Now is the time for our writers to show their power. *Now is the time to remind them of their responsibility.*"[23]

> It would be a crying shame if our sense of power did not awaken a corresponding sense of responsibility. It is especially through our art that we Norwegians have influence in the world. Finally we have it. For the first time in many, many years. Now we too can help mankind move forward. And it is precisely now that help is *needed.* . . . And should not critics have the right to consider whether our writers are pushing mankind forward or backward? Whether they are seers or deceivers? Whether they—consciously or unconsciously—strengthen or weaken us in the struggle for existence. . . .
>
> Now, when Henrik Ibsen stands perhaps at the height of his powers, now is the time to speak frankly about that bitter satisfaction felt at the self-destruction and self-doubts infecting part of his works.[24]

This was what Bjørnson liked to hear, and he called Collin "a pioneer in a new method of criticism. He takes moral questions into consideration, and denounces what is not calculated to do good. What we want in the future is a literature which will make men better."[25]

When these essays were published in book form, Collin expanded his treatment of Ibsen, emphasizing in the dramatist's works the drift toward individualism, and in Ibsen himself the reluctance to associate himself with any party. Nowhere was this clearer than in the master's latest play, *The Master Builder.*

> At bottom, individualism consists in a *lack of courage* to live; within it is a fear that we shall lose ourselves if we enlarge our lives by including others. The free love of individualism is afraid of "binding itself" with the bonds of family life. Every development in life brings with it new responsibilities, greater demands on our strength. Solness was afraid of making room for the young with their abilities and desires; that would involve a dangerous competition. "That's why I have locked myself in," he says. It is out of a fear of life itself that he undermines others, *binding* their talents, instead of helping them. Individualism is like a monstrous damming up or closing in of power; in order to grow, we think we have to stunt the growth of others, and the consequence is that we only half develop ourselves. There is something insecure and anxious in this egotistic craving for power; having suppressed others, one is always afraid of retribution; one feels that those bound-up forces are waiting....
>
> We must give up the cowardly, the fearful that is part of self-assertiveness. Not be afraid of joining with others and finding strength in all quarters. Not be like Ibsen's Rosmer or Stockmann or Ibsen himself, afraid of being a member of a party; not fear the influence of the will of the people.[26]

In rebutting Collin, Brandes said that moral standards have nothing to do with art and poetry; art is sovereign to morality. He took Nordau's assessment of the major creative artists as a given and blamed critics for confusing two separate entities: art and morality.

"It is an obvious fact that all the great poets and writers in our century from Byron to Swinburne, from Musset to Maupassant, from Goethe to Heine, have appeared to their philistine contemporaries and to the polemical critics bothered by philistine morality as monsters of immorality."[27] This was in harmony with Brandes's aristocratic radicalism.

Collin now brought up his major argument. What was at stake, he said, was not art or morality but life itself. "Even artists, who have been thought of as a natural aristocracy, because they are *born* as artists, do not have the right to harm life itself. Art exists for the sake of people, not people for the sake of art. Any art that in the main does not strengthen but weakens us—it would be cowardly if we let it flourish. It is a critic's duty to object if he believes that a great part of poetic works, which should train and develop the higher humanity in us, is on the contrary inhibiting us in our growth."[28]

"The moral law comprises the laws of life's growth. . . . They are present even in the imaginative, fantasy work of the artist. Knowledge of our inner life and experience in general shows that the imagination plays a major part in our moral development, in the building of our character. It is outmoded scholasticism to have art say to morality, 'I'm superior; your laws don't concern me.' Art and practical life or the art of living [*livskunsten*] *both* must derive the laws of their advance and perfection from the general laws of life itself."[29]

It was the word *livskunsten*, a neologism coined by Collin, that caught Ibsen's attention.[30] He used it in an early draft of *Little Eyolf*, where the following exchange between Allmer [*sic*] and his wife takes place.

> ALLMER. I don't want to cram him [his son] with book learning. It's the very art of living [*livskunsten*] that I want him to understand. Make the art of living part of his nature.
> MRS. ALLMER. Oh, my dear, what on earth is "the art of living"? I don't see that there's any art to it—living.
> ALLMER. You don't see that?
> MRS. ALLMER. No, it's the simplest thing in the world—living. When we have all that we need for living, as we do. When we can live just as we want. When we don't have to do anything but what's right and proper.
> ALLMER. Ah, yes, you have a light and happy spirit.[31]

Ibsen soon found that this concept was so essential to his drama that it acquired a life of its own. He expunged it and to take its place he created the character of Eyolf.

At some point fairly early on in the writing of *Little Eyolf*, the play took on the qualities of a medieval morality play in which abstractions like Good Deeds and Avarice could be represented by actors. Alfred Allmers was now seen as the Poet's Career; Rita stood for Fame and Fortune; Asta as Artistic Perfection; and the Rat Wife as the Women's Movement. This may seem totally foreign to Ibsen's usual method. But the play has never made any sense as psychological drama and for that reason has been considered his most obscure work. As a parable of the dramatist's career, however, all the pieces of the play fit together neatly.

The first two acts serve as a response to Collin's recapitulation of Ibsen's development. Whereas Collin regarded the dramatist as an amoral, self-centered naturalist and assigned him a place in Brandes's camp, Ibsen in this autobiographical parable drew a much more complicated picture of himself. What Collin did not grasp was that the driving force in Ibsen was not naturalism or Nietzscheanism, but what Yeats would call the perfection of the life and the work, symbolized by the dream castle in "Building Plans."

Equating that poem (circa 1853–54) with Allmers's birth provides the base for a sketch of Ibsen's development as he now saw it. The birth of Asta, when Alfred was eleven or twelve, corresponds to the writing of *Brand* (1865). The fanciful games that Alfred played with Asta, dressing her up as a boy whom he called Eyolf, recall the great achievement of *Emperor and Galilean* (1873), in which opposites were united and the Third Empire represented the "art of living." The marriage with Rita alludes to *Pillars of Society* (1877), the play that made Ibsen a fortune. Allmers married her for her "gold and green forests," proverbial in Norwegian (and Swedish) for great riches.[32] Shortly after that, Allmers set to work on his book, which would occupy him for years. This work on human responsibility, equivalent to the realistic social plays of 1879 to 1890, was made possible because Rita could support him. He says, "When I look back over my life—and my fortunes—for the past ten or eleven years, it seems to me almost like a fairy tale or a dream."[33] That does not make much sense when applied to Allmers, who has been plugging away at his magnum opus, but it is a fitting description of the triumphal 1880s in Ibsen's career. The birth of Eyolf (the art of living)—the real Eyolf, not the imaginary one of *Emperor*—should be assigned to about 1880–81.

In 1891 Allmers went soul-searching in Norway's fjelds and, upon returning to Rita, announced that he had given up his great work. A changed man after his lonely vigil in the north, when he saw the "sunrise gleaming on the mountain peaks," he now believed that responsibility begins at home and that his first concern should be not with his highly personal investigation of moral problems but with Eyolf. His purpose now is to bring Eyolf's "desires into harmony with what lies attainable before him. . . . All his longings are for things that he can never have in this life. But I will create a sense of happiness in his mind."[34]

Read metaphorically, this means that Ibsen is abandoning his search for the Third Kingdom as an unrealizable ideal. The art of living (Eyolf) must have a more practical goal. But at this point the Rat Wife lures Eyolf to his death. Read as autobiography, this means that Camilla Collett, as the embodiment of women's emancipation, lured Ibsen into writing the great series of social plays, which are now seen as Collin saw them, the works of a man obsessed with his personal philosophical and psychological problems and reluctant to take a firm public stand on the great issues of the time: women's emancipation and the rise of the labor movement.

This is an extraordinary self-indictment. Looking back, Ibsen can see where things went wrong. In the parable this has to be the moment when Eyolf was permanently crippled. This was the moment when Rita and Allmers were making love; this was the time when he told Rita about dressing up Asta as a boy and calling him Eyolf. If one transposes the play into the life, the time is 1881–82, when *Ghosts* was written and produced such a furor. After the unprecedented success of A *Doll's House,* Ibsen hoped to further his career in two ways: developing his philosophy of the Third Kingdom and attaining even greater fame as a dramatist. Rita, embracing Allmers, pictures the latter aim. The cross-dressing of Asta stands for the Third Kingdom. Conjuring up the scene in his imagination—that is, Ibsen recalling his accomplishment in *Emperor*—Allmers intensifies his erotic experience (read: Ibsen dreaming of attaining greater fame while revealing the Third Kingdom in dramatic form). But it was sex itself that upset Ibsen's plans. Syphilis and incest, which figured so prominently in *Ghosts,* gave Ibsen's career (= Allmers) a severe setback. On the philosophical level, *Ghosts* suggested that the Third Kingdom was an unrealizable ideal; in the parable, Eyolf (the art of living) is badly harmed.

Allmers and Rita blame each other for what happened to Eyolf. Allmers says, "I forgot the child—in your arms! . . . At that moment you condemned little Eyolf to death."[35] (Read: Ibsen neglected the higher purposes of his art in his infatuation with fame and immortality.) Rita says she is equally guilty, and both agree that while he lived, they let themselves shrink away from him in secret, abject remorse. This is Ibsen's way of saying that in the masterpieces of 1879 to 1890 he made the great error of trying to attain the ideal, the Third Kingdom, through the anti-idealism of naturalism. This was to be his life's philosophy, what Collin called "*det praktiske Liv eller Livskunsten*" ("the practical life or the art of living").[36] This project was compromised early on in *Ghosts,* symbolized by the floating crutch that haunts Allmers and Rita.

Like a guilty parishioner, Ibsen took Collin's sermon to heart, admitting to himself that he had put his own inner struggles above the problems faced by the majority of mankind. In that sense he was, as charged, an egotist and an immoralist. He answered Collin's accusations by writing the third act, which is all about change and transformation. Here we see that the essence of the whole play is the abandonment of the Third Kingdom. Asta, who stands for the Ideal, reveals that she was actually never related to Allmers, and makes a new life by marrying an engineer. And with "a melancholy smile," Rita says, "You see, I want to ingratiate myself with those great, open eyes," by caring for the poor neglected children in town, even though they had done nothing to prevent Eyolf from drowning.[37] For Allmers those children will take Eyolf's place (a new philosophy of life).

One of the paintings hanging in Ibsen's study was Marcus Grønvold's picture of a proletarian family being evicted from their home.[38] As might be expected, Ibsen denied that he had a political purpose in mind. Asked if *Little Eyolf* might be viewed as an instructive drama, he replied, "In this play I had in mind no pedagogical or utilitarian aim. With such purposes I don't concern myself. My aim is always strictly artistic."[39]

Ironically, in this third act, in which Rita and Allmers recognize that they are "creatures of the earth," the play becomes less real. In place of the passionate figures of the first two acts, we see two shadows talking largely in abstractions. Although *Little Eyolf* shows Ibsen turning his back on the striving idealism of *Brand* and confessing that in his elitism and search for superhuman qualities he has neglected the common man, the transformation of Allmers and Rita lacks conviction. Even Ibsen had doubts. He wanted Allmers to be played by an actor with a soulful voice, as if the faults of the play could be overcome by mesmerizing the audience. "There are places in Allmers's role," he said, "where a lyrical temperament bursts forth, places where what lies behind the words can only be understood through the tenor of the voice."[40]

After the premiere of the play in Christiania, he joined the Sontum family for a supper at the Grand Hotel. Mrs. Sontum opined, "Poor Rita, now she has to go to work with all those mischievous boys."

Looking doubtful, Ibsen replied, "Do you really believe so? Don't you rather think it was more of a Sunday mood with her?"[41]

John Gabriel Borkman

Ibsen obviously had serious doubts about his play. He was extremely nervous at the premiere and kept saying, "Let us get out of here before the curtain comes down." He refused to respond to calls for the author.[1] This was not typical of him. Seeing the play performed, he may have realized that it was not one of his best efforts.

In his next play he made up for the weaknesses in *Little Eyolf*. *John Gabriel Borkman*, the play that the ever-methodical Ibsen had ready for his publisher precisely two years after *Little Eyolf*, revealed the dramatist at or near the top of his form, his playwriting skills undiminished, and this time the passions would be real to the very end. Eyolf had turned out to be a broken-backed play, its spine twisted by a last act that did not answer the questions raised in the brilliantly titillating first part. The sentimental ending, meant to provide some spiritual uplift, was unconvincing, in spite of the author's best efforts to bring about a transformation in Rita's character. *John Gabriel Borkman*, in contrast, is a tightly constructed work, in which the past lives of the characters, gradually revealed through their conversations, functioned like the Greek gods of ancient tragedy to bring about the inevitable end.

It was obvious that the play, like *Little Eyolf*, was to some extent autobiographical. Borkman, the great entrepreneur and financier, was clearly Ibsen's alter ego, each a giant in his own realm. The fact that the empire builder had fallen far from the heights of his greatest achievements while Ibsen was still an enormous cultural force did not detract from the resemblance. As was clear from the previous two plays and from Ibsen's personal remarks, he felt that his works had, judged as expressions of his deepest thoughts, proved disappointing, and that fame had not brought happiness. Endlessly pacing his room, Borkman thought he knew where things had gone wrong. So did Ibsen as he paced back and forth in his study, bringing the past back to life. Now he saw that the narrative he had constructed in *Little Eyolf* was unsatisfactory; the emphasis he had given to the women's emancipation, making the Rat Wife so crucial to the play, had been misplaced. By being so plausible, one cause had drawn attention away from a deeper cause.

Outwardly, Ibsen was now more successful than ever. His name was known throughout the world; as an intellectual force, he ranked with Nietzsche and Tolstoy; as a commercial product, he was a best seller. His latest plays had been issued in first printings (in the original language) of ten thousand copies. Now Hegel ordered a first printing of thirteen thousand. Copies disappeared from the counters so quickly on the day of publication, December 15 (many of them surely intended as Christmas presents for one's intellectual friends), that Hegel immediately had three thousand more printed. Translations into English, French, German, and Russian appeared within the next few months. (Ibsen's son, Sigurd, made the first German translation.) All the major European theaters vied to be the first to stage the play, with the Frankfurter Schauspielhaus presenting the world premiere on January 16, 1897.

The critical response must have been very gratifying to Ibsen. He was still seen as the unequaled master of dramatic technique, still the profound analyst of the human soul, still the insightful interpreter of the zeitgeist. The *Frankfurter Journal* called the hero of the play "one of the greatest characters that world literature has brought forth."[2] Certainly, Borkman is one of Ibsen's most vivid, most richly nuanced portraits. In Berlin, Ibsen was hailed in a socialist journal as the creator of a modern symbolism that succeeds in elevating the present workaday world to the level of universal significance, without recourse to past ages and archaic heroes. Reading the play as a political critique, the Marxist reviewer found that capitalist anarchy became a living entity in the superman (übermensch) Borkman. He went on to compare Ibsen with Zola. In the Frenchman's novel about stock market speculation, *L'Argent* (1891), the hero is an unsavory beast, representing one aspect of the demon of capitalism, whereas Borkman is the demon itself. "In Zola, common, grubby little people carry on in a heroic symbolic landscape; in Ibsen, heroic symbolic people sit on ordinary sofas."[3] Here the critic noted the source of much of Ibsen's unique power: a genius for endowing the ordinary with symbolic significance.

In France, the critic for *Le Figaro* stressed this aspect of *John Gabriel Borkman.*

> One finds here, indeed, deep philosophy, a moral concern, an understanding of life and "the sublime," which one expects in an Ibsen drama. But one finds something more. And this something is what the French spirit, fostered by the

classics and the modern dramatists, has regrettably not found in Ibsen more often: brilliant clarity, startling drama, logical thought, not purely speculative (*A Doll's House*) but real logic, such as we see in ordinary life. *Borkman* is a philosophical drama, like all those that have issued from this powerful mind. But it is also a drama of living reality, accessible to the nonintellectual and the casual reader.

And what one must admire above all, I believe, is the reconciliation achieved fundamentally, without those mysteries that perplex the larger public, this fusion of philosophy and action. With *Borkman* Ibsen reaches the summit of his art and of rigorous dramatic technique.[4]

The reception in England was decidedly mixed. The influential Clement Scott, always hostile to Ibsen, declared it a total failure as a play. "As such we have no hesitation in saying that it is perfectly useless, perhaps the worst possible specimen of the master's theory, the greatest 'swashing' blow to the disciple's faith. It fails in that important essential which the drama, viewed in any light, imperatively demands—contrast."[5]

Scott, writing for a daily newspaper, spoke for the ordinary theatergoer. The anonymous critic for the highbrow *Saturday Review* had a different opinion. He lauded the undiminished powers of the dramatist, finding *Borkman* "every whit as powerful a piece of composition as any one of its predecessors." Further, he found the play "a vivid and almost entertaining drama. . . . There is less [in it] than in most of Ibsen's later works to distract the public and give his disciples mysterious airs."[6]

Of the English and American commentators, Henry James had perhaps the most perceptive understanding of Ibsen's accomplishment.

> [Ibsen] arrives at the dramatist's great goal—he arrives for all his meagerness at intensity. The meagerness, which is after all but an unconscious, an admirable economy, never interferes with that; it plays straight into the hands of his rare mastery of form. The contrast between this form—so difficult to have reached, so civilized, so "evolved,"—and the bareness and bleakness of his little northern democracy is the source of half the hard frugal charm that he puts forth. . . .
>
> Never has he juggled more gallantly with difficulty and danger than in this really prodigious John Gabriel, in which a great span of tragedy is taken between three or four persons—a trio of the grim and grizzled—in the two or three hours of a winter's evening; in which the whole thing throbs with an actability that fairly shakes us as we read; and in which, as the very flower of his artistic triumph, he has given us for the most beautiful and touching of his heroines a sad old maid of sixty. Such "parts," even from the vulgarest point of view, are Borkman and Ella Rentheim![7]

For all its lack of physical action, *John Gabriel Borkman* is an eminently theatrical work. In fact, it is the lack of physical action, of a chance for some relief from intense emotions, that makes the play so effective in the theater. The critic reviewing the play for the *Frankfurter Zeitung* in January 1897 noted that the full impact of the tragedy could be experienced only in the theater, where phrases that seem insignificant on the page become startlingly effective. "From the first words heard in the darkened house, one senses the fervid spirit of this mighty work, gripping one, growing ever stronger and more intense until one feels that here is one of the greatest emotional experiences that the theater is capable of offering."[8]

Purely as drama, *Borkman* is one of the craftsman's most impressive works. Not only does it contain three great roles, it is also a masterpiece of construction. The four acts flow from one to the next without any interruption in the time scheme; the time of performance coincides with the time of the narrative. There is a relentless drive toward the tragic end, with the accumulated facts serving as the equivalent of Greek gods. And Ibsen builds suspense by keeping the main character offstage until the second act, emulating Molière's *Tartuffe*. Marring, perhaps, the perfection of the work are the scenes in which Borkman's son Erhart proclaims his independence from his father. Making up for this blemish is the magnificent final scene, set in a snowfield, in which the twin sisters, Ella and Gunhild, are united over the body of Borkman. Harking back to the end of *Brand*, this last image could properly serve as Ibsen's epitaph.

After the initial flurry of interest, *Borkman* proved to be one of Ibsen's neglected masterpieces. To a connoisseur, like James, the play cast a unique and powerful spell; to others, to those less familiar with Ibsen's oeuvre, it seemed unrelievedly somber, portentous without being enlightening. To those, however, who traveled with Ibsen over the years and who read the plays in the order in which they were written, *Borkman* is unquestionably the capstone of his life and works. It is a self-portrait of Rembrandtesque authority and honesty, in which he proves to be his own harshest critic. In *The Master Builder* he luxuriated in dreams; in *Little Eyolf* he indulged himself with a tacked-on false and specious upbeat ending; but in *Borkman* he was almost masochistically faithful to reality. This tragedy about a man who has deceived others with his conviction that he is a man of genius and love is a work of self-condemnation, the portrait of a man of cold-blooded egotism, interested only in himself.[9]

Very few in Ibsen's audience would have seen the play as autobiography. Borkman would have struck them as an imaginative representative of unbridled capitalism. This was the era of those giants of acquisitiveness, those Vanderbilts, Carnegies, and Rockefellers, who amassed huge fortunes, destroying many lives in the process. Most like Borkman was Cecil Rhodes (1853–1902), the "colossus of

Africa." Like Borkman, Rhodes was a miner with great ambitions, one of which was to corner the diamond market of the world. Supported by the Rothschilds, Rhodes had by 1888 won control of 90 percent of the world's diamond production. Along with this wealth came political power. In 1890 he became prime minister of the Cape Colony. Then in 1896 (when Ibsen was immersed in his play) came the downfall. The year before, he had authorized a military raid into the Transvaal, and the consequence of this was his resignation as prime minister in January 1896; in 1897 he was found guilty by the House of Commons of dereliction of duty. His disgrace was so complete that he thought of killing himself. The parallels with Borkman are so striking that one might be tempted to say that Borkman is a composite of Ibsen and Rhodes.

Whether or not he had Rhodes in mind, Ibsen wanted his drama to be viewed as a probing psychological drama about a ruthless empire builder. On that level, it could be—and was often enough—appreciated as effective theater. His primary purpose, however, was to reveal to the discerning few, the very few—and perhaps only to himself—the drama of his own life. Studying the play carefully, taking note of all the specific details about Borkman's career, and there are many of them, one sees that they all relate to Ibsen. Like *Little Eyolf*, *Borkman* is a cryptogram. Within the poem another poem is hidden.

Borkman, like Ibsen, is a deeply conflicted man. He can find no peace until he can bring into harmony his two warring selves. His full name, John Gabriel Borkman, hints at the inner conflict. John stands for the public man, the great entrepreneur; Gabriel (the hero of God) is that part of him that wants to create a spiritual kingdom on earth; Borkman suggests a hardened miner (*bergman*).[10] When he talks in exalted tones of what he wants to accomplish, his vision takes him alternately into the empyrean and into the depths. His dreams of great projects are sometimes like perilous balloon trips; at other times he sees himself as a miner, extracting the wealth of the earth for the benefit of mankind. From his youth Ibsen identified himself with the mine worker; his early poem "Bergmanden" (circa 1850–51) pictures a man who shuns the light of day and seeks treasure in the dark depths of the mountains, which are likened to the chambers of the heart. To bring these two selves into harmony would be the equivalent of attaining the Third Kingdom.

Projected outward, these two selves appear as the twin sisters Ella Rentheim and Gunhild Borkman. The main plotline raises the question of which of the two shall possess Borkman's son Erhart, who is in his early twenties. The two sisters had both loved Borkman, and to get ahead in the financial world he had chosen to marry Gunhild. Subsequently, because of the collapse of Borkman's fortunes, Erhart was for a period of about ten years in the care of Ella. After Borkman had

Figure 28. August Lindberg as John Gabriel Borkman.

served his time in prison, Erhart came to live for a while with his parents in a large house that belongs to Ella. When he became a student, he found separate quarters in the nearby town. As the play begins, Ella, who is mortally ill with only a few more months to live, comes to call on her sister for the first time in eight years. She wants to reclaim Erhart by offering him the prospect of a well-to-do existence. Gunhild has a different aim: she wants Erhart to redeem the name of Borkman. The two sisters, physically similar, are opposites in spirit. Gunhild obsesses about fame, reputation, and money; Ella considers a loving relationship to be the highest prospect in life. She believed that Borkman's great error lay not in his financial speculations but in denying his love for her and marrying Gunhild. She accuses him of having committed "the great, unpardonable sin" of having murdered "the love life in a human soul."[11] The possibility of a reconciliation is represented by young Erhart. Borkman explicitly says his wife and Erhart "are included in what I mean when I say myself." In his earlier plays Ibsen saw this inner conflict as equivalent to a struggle between Brand and Peer Gynt. In *Borkman* he takes a different view: Gunhild and Ella cannot be aligned with those two epic figures. Instead Gunhild stands for Ibsen's passion for fame and fortune, the obliteration of all the humiliations he suffered in his childhood and youth, while Ella stands for the artist's philosophical ideal. Ibsen describes Ella as dying from an illness caused years ago by an extreme emotional disturbance. This is the dramatist's way of saying that his search for the Third Kingdom had been undermined by his ventures into naturalism and contemporary social problems.

Erhart is about twenty-three as the play begins, and Borkman is in his sixties. If we take 1896 (the year Ibsen wrote the play) as the time of action, Ibsen/Borkman would have been sixty-eight, and Erhart would have been born in 1873—the date of *Emperor and Galilean*. Given these dates as a starting point, the crucial periods in Borkman's life can be assigned specific years. It is in the exactness of the dates, which is not essential to the story line, that Ibsen encourages the inquisitive reader to see what lies beneath the surface.

Borkman spent four years under investigation, 1879–83, and endured five years in prison, 1883–88.[12] In Ibsen's life, the first period covers the years from *A Doll's House* to *An Enemy of the People*; the second, from *Enemy* to *Lady from the Sea*. These were the years in which Ibsen produced the works that brought him international renown. From his point of view, however, these were the years in which his ideal, the Third Kingdom, slipped from his grasp, because of his struggles with naturalism, the latest scientific theories, and the rapidly changing political scene. In *Little Eyolf* he had seen his artistic development from the same perspective, but now he found that his failure as poet of the ideal had deeper roots than his promotion of women's rights. In place of the Rat Wife stood Hinkel, the lawyer, who had been instrumental in Borkman's downfall.

Although Hinkel never appears, he inhabits the drama like an offstage actor waiting to make his entrance. He figures in Ella's life, and young Erhart spends much of his time in his house, located not far from the house that harbors the broken Borkman. Just who he is in the real-life story becomes apparent when we consider what happened to Ibsen in 1883, the year Borkman was sent to prison.

Betraying the trust placed in him, Hinkel published some of Borkman's letters that proved incriminating. He ruined Borkman not out of a sense of duty but out of jealousy. He had loved Ella, who had spurned him because she loved Borkman. And Borkman had loved her, but in order to promote his career by securing for himself a position as a bank director through Hinkel's influence, he had not married her. Instead he had married Gunhild, choosing worldly success rather than the Ideal. He had deluded himself with the thought that by creating a kingdom of riches for himself he would also be improving the well-being of mankind. Ella saw things differently. To her, he had committed the unpardonable sin of killing love, that is, abandoning the Ideal.

In 1882 Georg Brandes had written some articles about Ibsen in which he quoted extensively from letters, written in 1870 and 1871, in which Ibsen had expressed his anarchistic views, railing against the political state and debunking democracy. Never before and never after did Ibsen write such frank and revealing letters. Brandes selected the choicest passages.

"Of course it is a benefit to possess the right to vote, the right of self-taxation, etc. But who benefits? The citizen, not the individual. Now, there is absolutely no logical necessity for the individual to be a citizen. On the contrary—the state is the curse of the individual.

"The state has its roots in time; it will reach its height in time. Greater things than it will fall; all religion will fall. Neither standards of morality nor of art are eternal. What is there that we are really obliged to hold on to?" This from a letter dated February 17, 1871.[13]

At the time that Ibsen confessed these private thoughts he was outwardly the most upright and conservative of men, a pillar of society. When Brandes published them (first in the Danish weekly *Ude og Hjemme* in August and September 1882 and then, somewhat revised, in the German journal *Nord und Süd,* November 1883), Ibsen had become the controversial author of *A Doll's House* and *Ghosts* and was concerned about the damage done to his reputation. After the stunning success of *Pillars of Society* in Berlin, Ibsen hoped to secure his place on the German stage. Brandes undermined Ibsen's reputation by exposing him as a political radical at a critical juncture in German history, a time of political reaction. As part of it, the German emperor was involved in a campaign against liberal antistate writers. Brandes stepped in to present Ibsen as an author hostile to the state while he himself was playing up to Chancellor Bismarck, the epitome of state authoritarianism. A critic has called Brandes's articles a deliberate sabotage of Ibsen, presenting Ibsen to German readers as hostile to the state, not stopping short of accusing Ibsen of "a capital offense" (*Todesverbrechen*). Borkman's crime was meant to be of an equally serious nature.[14]

Borkman says, "There wasn't a corner of my life that I didn't dare lay open to him. Not a nook or cranny of my life that I hesitated to lay open to him. And then, when the moment came, he turned against me the weapons I myself had placed in his hands."[15]

Brandes sent Ibsen the German version of the articles, accompanied by a letter (now lost). Ibsen waited until June 1884 to reply. In an artfully crafted letter, he neatly skirted the subject of anarchy and the "capital offense." Instead he parried Brandes's allegations by noting that the two of them now stood in closer rapport than ever before. "I believe the reason is that we have been moving toward each other in our paths of development."[16] Supporting Bismarck, Brandes had shifted away from his former democratic principles, while Ibsen had ventured into the treacherous seas of Brandes's naturalism.

Why would Brandes go to such lengths to impugn Ibsen? The play, read as autobiography, provides the answer. As we have seen, in the early 1870s Ibsen and Brandes saw themselves as comrades in arms in the coming revolution. Back then Ibsen's radical ideas had astonished the young Brandes. But astonishment turned to disappointment. For the dramatist, this revolution would bring about a transformation of the human spirit, the high ideal represented by Ella. Brandes, however, thought in terms of a political revolution and felt betrayed when Ibsen backed off. In the play Hinkel wants to marry Ella (read: Brandes wants to be part of Ibsen's revolution). This marriage cannot come to pass because Ella stands for spiritual transformation: as the metaphysical ideal, she cannot be allied with naturalism. What set an unbridgeable gap between the critic and the poet was the Brandian ideal, which for Brandes smacked too much of the Christian religion.

The letter that Ibsen sent to Brandes was composed by the Gunhild in him. More important than a frank discussion of their respective positions was the dramatist's growing fame. Renouncing Ella, Borkman married Gunhild and through Hinkel's influence became director of the bank in Denmark. Ibsen joined the naturalist movement, whose strongest proponent was the Dane Brandes, and in so doing became the enormously successful and famous dramatist. As an influential cultural critic, Brandes served as a publicist for Ibsen in Germany, and for that Ibsen was deeply grateful. As Borkman says, "Without his [Hinkel's] support, I couldn't have done anything."[17] Handling the funds of the bank, Borkman believed he could use these resources for enterprises that would benefit mankind. "Everything in the earth, in the mountains, in the forests, in the seas, all the riches they contained, I wanted to rule over it all and create a kingdom for myself, and in that way provide for the well-being of thousands and thousands more."[18] In the collateral autobiography Ibsen used naturalism in the hope of uniting it with his dream of a Third Empire. This appropriation of naturalism to further a metaphysical ideal was an "embezzlement."

"My God, Ella, it's not easy to recall what motivated me twenty years ago. I only remember that back then, alone and in the silence, I would toy with all the great enterprises that I would set up. It was as if I saw myself as an astronaut. In those sleepless nights, I saw myself inflating a giant balloon, getting ready to sail out over an unknown, perilous sea, big as the whole world."[19]

He knew the risk involved, and for that reason he set aside some funds, reserved exclusively for Ella, that could not be affected by his speculations. Yet all went wrong. He misused his genius for a lost cause, and his ideal suffered (Ella's illness). And ironically, it was his dreams as an entrepreneur that proved his undoing when it became apparent that he was using naturalism to further his own interests, soaring into unknown regions, seeking the Third Empire.

Autobiography and drama are much more successfully interwoven here than in *Eyolf*, and the correlation between the hieroglyphics of the play and the crucial events in the life are astonishingly detailed and consistent. The parts played by the sisters Ella and Gunhild and by Borkman's friend Foldal are like separate chapters in Ibsen's secret confession.

Consider Ella as the Ideal. She was not affected by the collapse of Borkman's fortune because he had set aside a sizable amount for her that he did not touch in his financial schemes. The parallel in the confession is that Ibsen never abandoned the Brandian ideal in his naturalist plays (consider Gregers). However, this ideal is only a pale shadow of what it had once been (Ella is terminally ill).

Gunhild represents the longing for fame and fortune. Released from prison in 1888, Borkman came to live with Gunhild in a house that was actually owned by Ella. In 1888 Ibsen, with the publication of *The Lady from the Sea*, began to win back his early supporters. The Danish novelist Erik Skram registered the change in the Ibsen climate.

"Among Scandinavian writers Ibsen was certainly the one who for a long time would have easily collected the most votes as chief priest in the temple of modern religion. But he hazarded a part of his reputation with *An Enemy of the People*, did not win it back with *The Wild Duck*, and when he published *Rosmersholm*, he was definitely no longer a candidate for this position. Now with *The Lady from the Sea* the old poet has again made contact with his former friends."[20]

In writing *The Lady from the Sea*, Ibsen had tempered his naturalist and deterministic outlook with a strong suggestion that the human being had free will. This was in keeping with the New Romanticism, which harked back to the time before Brandes's Modern Breakthrough. Official recognition of the retrograde Ibsen took some time. After *Ghosts* he was awarded no medals of honor until 1892. In waiting for them, he was rather like Borkman, self-deluded into thinking that the princes of the world would come knocking on his door.

Foldal and Hinkel

In the great summing-up that *John Gabriel Borkman* was meant to be, both Bjørnson and Brandes had to play significant roles. In Ibsen's development as an artist, Bjørnson was just as influential as Brandes, not so much for his ideas but as a literary rival. Ibsen had no doubts about his own superiority as a poet and thinker, yet it was Bjørnson, the younger of the two, who served as his mentor, who gave him a helping hand in his time of need, and who preceded him in bringing the new social drama to the Nordic countries. It was galling to the splenetic and envious Ibsen, who let his true feelings emerge in *Peer Gynt*, secretly there, and openly in *The League of Youth*. But the Bjørnson sketched in those plays is an amiable fool compared with the rather invidious caricature Ibsen drew in *Borkman*.

It may seem at first that Vilhelm Foldal, a "bent and worn man" with unkempt hair, could hardly be meant to portray the imposing and physically vigorous Bjørnson. However, in the kind of game that Ibsen was playing, concealment was as necessary as revelation. He had to be honest with himself while avoiding any direct confrontation with his perpetual rival and antithesis.

The scene between Foldal and Borkman in act two is a masterpiece of mordant comedy. While Ibsen built himself up as a half-mad egomaniac, striking Napoleonic poses, he diminished Bjørnstjerne Bjørnson into Foldal, a meek, mild-mannered amateur poet. The more injurious the portraiture, the more obscure the clues. Bjørnstjerne means bear-star; Foldal means colt-dale, the cosmic opposite. (In *drames à clef*, opposites are often at work. Hinkel in German was an affectionate name for a close friend, which Brandes wasn't.) Foldal has five children, as did Bjørnson. Foldal's daughter Frida will run off with Borkman's son; Bjørnson's daughter had married Ibsen's son in 1892.

Borkman and Foldal have been feeding each other's hopes and illusions for years, much like Ibsen and Bjørnson, whose careers were inextricably linked, although the two writers had little in common. Even physically they were opposites, the tall, well-formed Bjørnson looming over the squat and stocky Ibsen. For years Ibsen had stood in his shadow, waiting for the success that seemed to elude him while the younger Bjørnson was fortune's darling. Eventually, their roles were almost reversed. Ibsen became world famous, while Bjørnson remained on the international scene a provincial writer. Yet Ibsen could never forget what he owed the generous, good-hearted Bjørnson, not only for jump-starting his career in the 1860s but also for lending him support when *Ghosts* brought him into disrepute. Bjørnson, for his part, never truly appreciated Ibsen's works. Of *John Gabriel Borkman* he remarked, "Oh, that is a piece I can't stand . . . entirely pessimistic and useless; not the kind of thing we want at all."[1]

The unmasking scene between Borkman and Foldal is splendid drama just as it stands, but it becomes doubly ironic when the pentimento beneath it is revealed.

BORKMAN. I no longer have any use for you.

FOLDAL (*softly, taking his portfolio [of poems]*). No, no, no: I dare say not.

BORKMAN. So you have been lying to me all the time.

FOLDAL (*shaking his head*). Never lying, John Gabriel.

BORKMAN. Haven't you sat there building up my hopes and faith and confidence with lies?

FOLDAL. They weren't lies as long as *you* believed in *my* vocation. As long as you believed in me, I believed in you.

BORKMAN. So we have been deceiving each other the whole time. And perhaps deceiving ourselves—both of us.

FOLDAL. But isn't that just the essence of friendship, John Gabriel?

BORKMAN (*smiling bitterly*). Yes, to deceive—that's friendship. You are right about that. I have learned that once before.[2]

This is part of what Borkman calls the comedy of his life, and properly acted the scenes with Foldal should make the audience (granted, a sophisticated one) savor what Archer rightly called its "exquisite humor" and shake with inward laughter, as Borkman must when he sees how things are turning out: two old acquaintances acting out Lewis Carroll's advice, "If you'll believe in me, I'll believe in you."

The intrusion of the younger generation—Borkman's son Erhart, Foldal's daughter Frida, and the worldly-wise Mrs. Wilton—seems strident, and although the three of them were clearly meant to serve as a contrast to Borkman, Gunhild, and Ella, their noisy clamor disrupts the somber music of the drama as a whole. Erhart's petulant cry for happiness, "I am young! I want to live, live, live," could have been toned down, and in a more economically constructed play, Mrs. Wilton could have been dispensed with.

For Ibsen, however, assessing his place in the grand scheme of things, the presence of the younger generation was imperative. These three represent what comes after Borkman and the dissolution of his great dream. They have been partying at Hinkel's house, and their outlook on life is pretty much like Brandes's. By this time (1896), Brandes was the chief Nordic exponent of sexual freedom and the brightest disciple of Nietzsche, the loudest advocate of Nietzsche's amoralism. Borkman describes Hinkel as "completely plagued and poisoned by the morals of a super-rascal" (*"helt igennem forgiftet og forpestet af overskurkens moral"*).[3] William Archer noted, as many others must have, that Borkman is parodying Nietzsche's Übermensch (*"overskurk"* = super-rascal). When Archer suggested this to Ibsen, "he neither affirmed nor denied it. I understood him to say, however, that in speaking of 'overskurken' he had a particular man in view."[4]

When Ibsen was at work on *John Gabriel Borkman*, Brandes was recognized as the spokesman for a modern paganism, the idea, as one commentator put it, "that obedience to law is degrading; that conformity to traditional morals is soul-crippling and unworthy of a free spirit; that only by giving sway to passion will the individual attain that joy which is his right."[5] In 1896 Ibsen read Brandes's monumental study of Shakespeare, a work that is filled with Nietzschean thinking.[6]

Like *The Master Builder*, *John Gabriel Borkman* raises questions about the influence of Nietzsche on Ibsen. More than one critic has read the play as a portrayal of the superman as capitalist. Shortly after the play was published, Leo Berg described Borkman as "a Napoleon of money, who in his greatest battle was crippled—the hero on the borderline between genius and rascality. The sense of Ibsen's poem is of the higher humanity, the modern individual, the royal thought of the future—the superman."[7]

Although Suzannah Ibsen said her husband had not read a word of Nietzsche and that the German philosopher was "only a name in the papers to him," he was certainly familiar with his teachings.[8] Through Brandes, Ibsen early on acquired a knowledge of Nietzsche's attacks on Christian morality and his anti-democratic promotion of the superior individual, a set of tenets that, as we have seen, Brandes labeled aristocratic radicalism. These ideas would have resonated with Ibsen, since they had been present in his own work from his early formative years. In *The Pretenders*, Bishop Nicholas stands beyond good and evil and is part of the will to power. Brand might fairly be described as a superman, one who envisions—and foreshadows—a new god.[9] But there are crucial differences. The bishop is a perfect Nietzschean hero except for the fact that he loses out to the non-Nietzschean Håkon. And Brand's will is fueled by his conscience, the Christian integument that the superman has sloughed off.

Anyone traversing the broad swaths of the cultural history of the nineteenth century will see that Ibsen anticipates the essential Nietzsche in many respects. His works fill in the decades between Goethe's superman and Nietzsche's. A French commentator saw Ibsen's whole oeuvre as an attack on Christianity.[10] And the insightful German critic Roman Woerner said, "We find Ibsen everywhere on Nietzsche's mountain path"—the blond beast in *The Vikings at Helgeland,* the hatred of the herd mentality and the will to succeed in *Brand,* the opposition of the Apollonian and Dionysian in *Emperor and Galilean.*[11]

The similarities in thought between the dramatist and the philosopher conceal the great rift that had opened up between them. It was what separated Ibsen from Brandes, and the twin sisters Ella Rentheim and Gunhild from each other. For Borkman and Ibsen, the will to power could have no justifiable existence without a higher spiritual purpose. Ella was a necessary part of the equation.

Emil Reich in his lectures on Ibsen expressed the fundamental difference between Nietzsche and Ibsen aphoristically. The finest attribute for the former was "the will to power"; for the latter it was "the power to will."[12] Willing without a higher humanitarian ideal was anathema to Ibsen. In 1902 he warned a young poet about Nietzsche: "That crazy man! You should have nothing to do with him."[13]

Fanny is a divorced and experienced woman who takes the considerably younger (by as much as eight or nine years) Erhart as her lover. She invites the teenage Frida, who is staying with her, to come along so that when she and Erhart have tired of each other, he will have Frida as a sexual partner.

True to form, Brandes found Fanny Wilton an admirable character with a practical philosophy of life. To him, she was

> the personification of a not particularly high-flying type of the joy of life.
>
> In what a masterly way is this lady painted, and in how few strokes of the brush; she who "is quite used to saying both yes and no on her own account." And what a delicate little touch it is that whereas Ibsen introduces her to us as a lady "in her thirties"—over thirty therefore—she herself, on the one occasion on which she mentions her age, says to Erhart's mother, "I'm always reminding him that I am seven years older than he"—that is to say, than the youth of twenty-three. She forgets a few years. Finally we have all her practical wisdom in the speech in which she explains to Erhart's mother, half in jest, that she is taking little Frida Foldal with her in case of changing circumstances: "When Erhart is done with *me*—and *I* with *him*—then it will be well for us both that he, poor fellow, should have someone to fall back on. . . . *I* shall manage well

enough for myself, rest assured." It would be impossible to portray a character more fully in a whole novel than is done here in half a score of short speeches.[14]

Brandes was right to praise Ibsen's dramaturgical efficiency in depicting Fanny Wilton. Her name and some of her turns of speech suggest an international background—English, French, and Norwegian—and an ease of manner that cuts through social pretensions. Cosmopolitan, full of life, and remarkably self-possessed, she provides a jarring contrast to Mrs. Borkman and Ella Rentheim. In the pattern of the play, she heads a trinity of young free spirits counterpoised to the trinity of Borkman and the twin sisters. Dashing off in a sleigh, the young people herald a new age in which living and loving are ends in themselves, a new pagan era in which sacrifice and higher purpose count for nothing. Borkman and the twin sisters were dedicated to their respective missions, represented by Erhart. But Erhart will have none of it. His departure signals the final collapse of Borkman's world—and of Ibsen's.

Borkman. ... Come, we two, out into life, working together!
Erhart (*passionately*). But I don't *want* to work! Not now—I'm *young!* I never thought about it before. But now I feel it, warm and gushing through me! I don't want to *work!* I want to live, live, live!
Mrs. Borkman (*breaking in, apprehensive*). But, Erhart, what will you live for?
Erhart (*his eyes shining*). For happiness, mother!
Mrs. Borkman. And where do you think you will find *that?*
Erhart. I've *already* found it![15]

With his uncanny sensitivity to the coming thing, Ibsen hints at a new society in which women will set the standards. Following Strindberg, whose tragedy *The Father* (1887) presaged a matriarchal society, Ibsen places Mrs. Wilton at the head of the new triumvirate. She treats Erhart like a puppy dog, calls him "good boy," and the young man enjoys being under her spell. Having spent his childhood and adolescence being indoctrinated with the idea that he has a mission, a duty, to fulfill in life, he is ushered by Hinkel and Mrs. Wilton into a new world where the senses rule. It is the world of the lusty Peer Gynt and the pagan Julian. And in *Borkman* there is no Strange Passenger and no Maximus to evoke otherworldly spirits. Ibsen does nothing to darken his portrait of Mrs. Wilton; he offers no explicit criticism of her and her laissez-faire sexuality.

Those who were familiar with Ibsen's work found his depiction of Fanny Wilton baffling; some found it indecent and insulting. The French critic Francisque Sarcey called Fanny's cynicism appalling and was offended that Ibsen would put such language in the mouth of a woman who was supposed to be

French![16] Another French critic, Jules Lemaître, expressed the confusion that many readers must have felt. There is much talk about love and the sanctity of love, he said, and Borkman's crime was that he sacrificed love for the sake of his ambitions. Yet the future belongs to Erhart, who runs off with Mrs. Wilton as his paramour, and he is a silly, vain youth who ignores his duty to his parents. Hence the play appears obscure because we assume in advance that it contains serious, high-minded ideas, and we find at the end that it contains an immoral idea. "When these puritans try to be pagan, they are awful."[17]

The critic mistakenly assumed that Ibsen was advocating this new paganism. He wasn't. He was only predicting that the amorality of Brandes would take hold among the young generation. In this he was quite right. In the early years of the new century there was in the Nordic countries a signal shift toward greater sexual openness, especially among women, who felt increasingly free to take the sexual initiative, with many of them brazenly taking young men as lovers.[18]

Foldal is also left behind as his daughter joins Erhart and Fanny. Worse, he is knocked down and nearly run over by Fanny Wilton's sleigh as it carries the young people off to foreign parts. When he makes his final exit, Borkman comments: "It's not the first time in your life that you've been run over, old friend." In the so-called morality controversy of 1887 Brandes had ridiculed Bjørnson's old-fashioned views on sex and marriage, and in the changed moral climate of the 1890s Brandes spoke for the young generation. The sleigh incident is a not-too-cryptic allusion to the chastity feud in which Brandes rode roughshod over Bjørnson.

The drama could not end with the sound of sleigh bells ringing in a new era. The substance of the play concerns the failure of Borkman to fulfill his own aspirations. Through him Ibsen provides a chilling self-indictment in which he reproaches himself both for pursuing an impossible dream and for having betrayed it.

The speech Ibsen made in Stockholm in 1887 expressed as clearly as he could his vision of the future and its connection with his works. "I believe that the ideals of our time, while disintegrating, are tending toward what in my play *Emperor and Galilean* I designated 'the Third Kingdom.'"[19] Borkman recalls the great projects he had in mind twenty years ago (that is, shortly after *Emperor and Galilean*), when he was preparing "to soar away into perilous, unknown regions." But the balloon that was to carry him into the empyrean came crashing down. The philosophic ideal was supposed to add the spiritual element to the materialism of the naturalistic philosophy. Instead the reverse happened. In retrospect, Ibsen could see that Brandes had led him down the wrong path.

However, in this many-layered ransacking of motives and causes, Brandes could not bear the ultimate blame. Ibsen had always known that he and Brandes belonged to different schools. He had made a point of this in 1883 in the preface to the second edition of *The Feast at Solhoug.* By that time, Brandes had published two influential assessments of Ibsen in which he deplored the dramatist's aloofness from the real world. Ibsen's philosophy of life was one in which "a man may think and may write poetry, but he cannot act; nay, in the present state of society, he is hardly even justified in speaking out plainly, because he thereby in a manner calls on others to act, which in this case is equivalent to rushing on their own ruin."

Here was a stinging allusion to Ibsen's refusal to join Brandes on the revolutionary ramparts.

> He who, from the height of his aspiration after great, decisive, sweeping revolutions, looks down indifferently or contemptuously on the slow, petty changes of ordinary progress, on the politician's gradual, dilatory, small improvements, on the compromises to which the practical reformer must consent in order to attain even the partial realization of his idea, and on those associations without the help of which it is impossible for any but an autocrat to carry a single scheme into practical execution—the man, I say, who looks with contempt on all these things, must give up all thought of moving a finger in practical matters. Like Søren Kierkegaard and like Brand, he can do nothing but point to the yawning chasm that separates existing from ideal conditions. If such a man were to take, or induce others to take, active measures to realize his aspirations, he would simply lead his followers headlong over the brink of the dizzy abyss that separates the actual from the desired state of things, and run the risk of being promptly arrested. Even the poet can only express such extremely ideal views indirectly, suggestively, ambiguously, through the mouths of independent dramatic characters who relieve the author of all responsibility. Only vulgar adversaries could take the grim jest about the torpedo under the ark to be literal, bloodthirsty earnest.
>
> Such a philosophy entails a separation of the theoretical from the practical, of the individual from the citizen, of intellectual liberty from that practical liberty which means responsibility—a dualism which can be carried into practice only by a dramatic poet living in exile, who need have nothing whatever to do with state, society, politics, parties, or reforms.

This strong language revealed how much Ibsen's political apostasy in the 1870s still rankled in Brandes's mind. The critic's very personal final paragraph made the difference between the two men all too clear.

> Nor does the ideal of spiritual nobility inherent in this philosophy seem to me a very high one. It is quite true that a great author best maintains his personal dignity by never being seen in the thick of the fray; it is true that it gives an im-

> pression of distinction to hold back, never to interfere in the disputes of the day, never to write a newspaper article. But it seems to me that there is more distinction still in the action of the legitimist generals who enlisted as common soldiers in Condé's army and fought on foot in the foremost ranks. By so doing they lost not a whit of their inner, essential dignity.[20]

These well-aimed barbs should have provoked a stinging rebuke from the hypersensitive and irascible Ibsen. They didn't. In his preface to *The Feast at Solhoug* he merely expressed a regard for the "friendly spirit" with which "Brandes invariably criticizes my work." However, he adverted the reader, i.e., Brandes, to two works by a young Swedish scholar, Valfrid Vasenius (supplying the full bibliographical data for them), in which could be found a true understanding of the poet's principles. In his doctoral dissertation Vasenius had explicitly faulted Brandes for failing to appreciate Ibsen's approach to ancient history as dramatic material. After pointing out the inconsistencies in Brandes's remarks on the early heroic plays, Vasenius concluded, "What an extraordinary misadventure it was for the great critic to attempt to fathom Ibsen's innermost thoughts."[21]

Ibsen himself could not have said it better. He let the brash academic, writing in an antagonistic spirit, be his spokesman. Of course, the always aggressive Brandes would not let the matter rest. His riposte was to revise his 1882 Danish essay and publish it in German with the remarks about Ibsen's "capital offense." This was his way of saying that he was the one who truly understood Ibsen, the closet radical who concealed his deepest thoughts behind the façade of bourgeois respectability.

Ibsen could never forgive Brandes for betraying him by publishing the contents of personal letters. He undoubtedly felt justified in calling Brandes-Hinkel a "super-rascal." The inability of the two men, the critic and the dramatist, to see eye to eye on what mattered most to them provides a vein of irony running through *John Gabriel Borkman*. The man who more than anyone else steered the dramatist into the plays that brought him world fame was the man who had no understanding of the metaphysical Ibsen—and little liking for Ibsen the human being. Writing to Nietzsche, he characterized Ibsen: "This oddball is great and strong and unlovable but worthy of love."[22] In old age, Ibsen remarked to Christopher Bruun, the minister who had served as a model for Brand, "I think I may say that what lay deepest in my writings Brandes never understood."[23] What lay deepest was the conception of the Third Kingdom, and Brandes never appreciated how essential it was to Ibsen's worldview.

Although the future belonged to Brandes (at least, as Ibsen saw it), the play could not end with the departure of Mrs. Wilton and her young charges. If act three points to the future, the fourth and last act contains a judgment on the life

Figure 29. *John Gabriel Borkman*, last scene, designed by Thorolf Pedersen. Royal Theater, Copenhagen 1897.

and works of Borkman. In the great reckoning, after having settled accounts with Brandes and Bjørnson, Ibsen had to deal with himself, with what he had accomplished, and, more pointedly, with what he had failed to accomplish.

The very last scene takes place on a snow-covered outlook point, with mountain peaks visible in one direction and a deep fjord below. The aging Ibsen sometimes visited the Sontum family, whom he had known since his days in Bergen. Dr. Sontum ran a sanatorium at Grefsen, where there was an outlook with a panoramic view that Ibsen enjoyed, even though the climb up to it tired him. There he found his inspiration for the last scene of *John Gabriel Borkman.*[24] We follow Borkman and Ella Rentheim as they leave the house and trudge through the snow, a transition scene that required elaborate stage machinery, a *Wandeldekoration*, a painted scene moving behind the actors. The scene designer at the Christiania Theater cautioned Ibsen against using it, saying (rightly) that theater critics would ridicule its use. Yet Ibsen insisted—either the scene as written or no play—even though, as he admitted to the director at the Bergen National Theater, the play "poses rather unusually difficult problems with regard to both casting and set design and stage machinery."[25] As predicted, at least one critic recommended the transition scene for children's theater.[26]

Now, it is understandable that Ibsen would want this autobiographical work to end in an all-encompassing symbolic landscape, the peaks and the fjord suggesting the division, the irreparable breach within the hero, a harking back to the world of *Brand* and *Peer Gynt,* a perfect backdrop for the final reckoning. But why not an old-fashioned change of scene, instead of the cumbersome and unreliable *vandreteppe* (the Norwegian term)? Why was it necessary for Ibsen to show Borkman and Ella climbing slowly upward?

One possible answer is that he was set on demonstrating that he had lost none of his dramaturgical skills and was still the master of his craft. (And he had to make up for the bungled ending of *Little Eyolf.*) The structure of the play is a technical marvel. The action of the drama is an almost seamless succession of scenes: the downstairs drawing room, followed by, with no break in time, the upstairs lair of Borkman, and then the climb to the outlook, with the time of action from act one to the end corresponding to performance time (if there are no intermissions), a rare feat in drama. And there was another notable effect: the delayed entrance of the hero, the best instance of it since Molière's *Tartuffe.*

The purpose of the transition is mainly symbolic, with the visual images, as so often in the works of a dramatist who wanted to be a painter, establishing, moment by moment, a solid background. As Borkman leaves the house in which he has lived in virtual isolation for years and steps out into the dark night, the moon only faintly gleaming, he moves backward in time to the point at which his great life-changing decision was made. The ascent in space is a descent in time. The setting is the world of *Brand* and *Peer Gynt,* only now the mountains are in the distance. The fjord lies dark, and the outlook point is far below the mountain peaks; it represents the halfway point both in Borkman's life and in his psychic being, space and time commingled.

There was a precedent in the theater for this visible merging of two realms, time and space interwoven. In Richard Wagner's *Parsifal,* the young hero is transported in act one from the forest to the temple of the Holy Grail, a journey that is an ascent to Montsalvat. According to Wagner's libretto, "Gradually, while Parsifal and Gurnemanz appear to walk, the scene changes imperceptibly from L. to R. The forest disappears; a door opens in rocky cliffs and conceals the two; they are then seen—again in sloping passages which they appear to ascend." Parsifal says, "I scarcely move,— / Yet swiftly seem to run," and Gurnemanz replies, "My son, thou seest / Here Space and Time are one [*zum Raum wird hier die Zeit*]."[27] To accomplish this, Wagner's stage technicians devised the Wandeldekoration, which consisted of three tall canvas rolls, the changing scenery painted on them, which, when rolled (by hand) horizontally, created the sensation of movement. It was deemed "hugely effective by most who saw it."[28] The effect was greatly enhanced by Wagner's transition music, a resource denied to Ibsen.

The premiere of Wagner's music drama in 1883 was a major cultural event, which Ibsen would certainly have been aware of. But the idea of using the Wandeldekoration in *John Gabriel Borkman*, which he was working on thirteen years later, probably came to him from Hildur Andersen, his soulmate, and now on her way to becoming the leading authority in Norway on Wagner. With her he could discuss artistic matters, impossible with his wife and son. And when his Norwegian stage technicians advised against the vandreteppe, he could insist on its use, knowing of its success in *Parsifal*.

At the end of the transition scene and having reached the overlook, Borkman tells Ella about the kingdom he once dreamed of conquering, a kingdom that is represented both by the mountains in the distance and the precious metals hidden deep in the earth. Achieving the Third Kingdom meant uniting these opposites. He thought he could reach the mountaintops, "my vast, my infinite, inexhaustible kingdom," by releasing the wealth buried in them.

Ella says that an icy blast comes from that kingdom. Borkman replies in a speech that, in the coded language of the play, constitutes Ibsen's harsh self-judgment. Nothing that he ever wrote reveals more of the man.

"That blast is the breath of life to me. That blast comes to me like a greeting from subject spirits. I seem to touch them, the prisoned millions; I can see the veins of metal stretch out their winding, branching, luring arms to me. I saw them before my eyes like living shapes, that night when I stood in the strong room with the candle in my hand. You begged to be liberated, and I tried to free you. But my strength failed me; and the treasure sank back into the deep again."

Behind Borkman in the vaults of the bank, where Hinkel is a powerful figure, stands Ibsen deciding to commit himself to the naturalist philosophy of Brandes. The treasure is of course the Third Kingdom, the new higher stage of human development that Ibsen aspired to achieve.

And he failed because he lost sight of the ideal. He teamed up with Brandes-Hinkel because more than anything else he wanted fame and honor, power and glory.

With outstretched arms he says, "I will whisper it to you here in the stillness of the night: I love you, you lying there, seeming dead, in the depths, in the darkness. I love you, you treasures craving life, you and your shining train of power and glory! I love you, love you, love you!"

Ella replies, "Yes, down there is where you still have your love, John. It's always been down there. But up here in the daylight, you see, here there was a warm, living human heart, that throbbed and beat for you. And it was that heart that you crushed. No, worse than that! Ten times worse! You *sold* it for—for—"

Borkman trembles and a cold shudder goes through him. "For the kingdom—and the power—and the glory—you mean?"[29] A few moments later he dies, a hand of ice clutching at his heart. The twin sisters, Gunhild and Ella, clasp hands over his body. The three figures form an image of the Third Kingdom gone wrong, subverted by Borkman's overriding desire for fame and honor. Instead of Brand set against Peer Gynt or the pagan counterpoised to the Christian, we see the Ideal (Ella) set against Reputation and Fame (Gunhild). In this final reckoning Ibsen confessed that the Third Kingdom had eluded him. He had to blame himself for succumbing to the temptations of the Modern Breakthrough, which gave him international recognition. In joining forces with Brandes, he corrupted the high ideals expressed in the visionary *Brand*, a work for which the advocate of political revolution had little appreciation. The great tragedy for Ibsen was that there was too much Peer Gynt in him and not enough Brand. Or, more precisely, the mentality of Catiline, the hero of his first play, who desired immortality no matter what the cost, proved to be the driving force throughout his life. Compared with the torch of fame and renown, the Third Kingdom was an ignis fatuus.

What Borkman says earlier in the play could have been said by Ibsen himself: "I have been my own accuser, my own defender, and my own judge. More impartial than anyone else—that I may venture to say."[30]

Seventieth-Birthday Celebrations

In his next—and last—play, Ibsen continued to ransack his past life and to pass judgment on himself. This time he reincarnated himself as a sculptor, whose lifelong work was to be called *Resurrection Day. When We Dead Awaken*—Ibsen wanted the "we" stressed—is a play about a life gone wrong, a remorseful summing up of his career. *John Gabriel Borkman,* if it had been his last work, would have provided a perfect capstone to all that had gone before, an objective view of his extraordinary success and the price he paid for it. Yet something was missing in that ruthless self-analysis, and his conscience would not let him finish his life's work until he had supplied it.

When We Dead Awaken did not appear punctually two years after his previous play. For the first time in twenty years he spent three years writing a play. The delay might be attributed to a decline in the creative powers of the aging dramatist. More likely, the extraordinary series of events celebrating his seventieth birthday in 1898 kept him from his desk.

They began with the presentation on the day itself, March 20, of a three-piece silver service, a gift representing the contributions of forty of his English admirers, headed by his English translators William Archer and Edmund Gosse, and including the novelists Henry James and Thomas Hardy, the actors Herbert Beerbohm Tree and Elizabeth Robins, the playwrights J. M. Barrie and A. W. Pinero, the classicists Gilbert Murray and Jane Harrison, the Shakespeare scholar A. C. Bradley, the critic Bernard Shaw, and the politician Henry Herbert Asquith, the future prime minister of England. Many who wished to contribute were excluded because of the need to send the gift in time for Ibsen's birthday.[1]

On that day, two theaters in Copenhagen, three in Stockholm, six in Berlin, and four in Vienna were presenting works by him. In Christiania the Central

Theater staged *Ghosts*, while the Christiania Theater produced *The Feast at Solhoug*, along with some scenes from *Peer Gynt*. The next evening Ibsen attended the production of *The Master Builder* at the Christiania Theater. The following day the university students honored him with a procession, and on March 23 an official banquet brought the Norwegian festivities to a close.

The theme of his speech at the banquet was his relationship with his countrymen, always a sore point with him. Having spent most of his productive years abroad, he admitted that it would take time for him to feel truly at home in his native land. He referred to the possible misconception that his success abroad, his "rare fairy-tale fate" of "gaining fame and fortune yonder in foreign lands," had given him true happiness. That kind of success came with a price, however. "He who wins a home for himself in foreign lands—in his inmost soul he scarcely feels at home anywhere—even in the country of his birth.

"But perhaps that may yet come. And I shall regard this evening as a starting point."[2]

A week later he was in Copenhagen, where King Christian IX decorated him with the Grand Cross of the Dannebrog Order, making him the first Norwegian writer to be so honored. On the following days he was the guest of honor at the Women's Literary Society and the Student Society of the University of Copenhagen. On March 31 he attended a performance of *The Wild Duck* at the Royal Theater. At a grand banquet on April 1 he reminisced about that April of 1864, when he passed through Copenhagen on his way to Italy and the making of *Brand*. And on Sunday, April 3, he attended a performance of *Brand* at the Dagmar Theater.

An odd nonevent occurred in the university town of Lund in southern Sweden, where Ibsen and Strindberg did not meet. The already notorious Swede was in Copenhagen on his way home from Paris while Ibsen was in the capital city being honored by the Danish king, and the whole town knew of his presence. On April 6 both men crossed the Öresund by ferry to Malmö; Strindberg proceeded by train to Lund, his final destination, arriving there at 3:31. Ibsen, after making his way through the toll station, boarded the express train to Stockholm. The train stopped at Lund forty minutes later, at 4:10, and stayed there longer than usual to allow the dignitary to receive the cheers and songs of a huge crowd, estimated to be one thousand strong, mostly students (with only a sprinkling of academics), who had gathered there on a blustery and rainy day.[3] Now, Strindberg would surely have known about Ibsen's movements, and he obviously avoided meeting him, although he had just sent him a copy of *Inferno*, the work that signaled a new phase in Strindberg's artistic development and in Nordic literature.

Since Norway was nominally still under the Swedish flag, the most brilliant events took place in Stockholm, with royalty present. On Saturday morning, April 9, Ibsen had a five-minute audience with King Oscar, who placed around his neck the Order of the North Star (*kommendörstecknet med stora korset av nordstjärne order*). No Scandinavian writer had ever received such a high honor. That evening he had dinner at the Royal Palace, with thirty people attending. At a reception for him given by King Oscar and Queen Sophia at the Royal Palace, the king rather ungraciously remarked, "You really should not have written *Ghosts*, Ibsen. That is not a good play, no. Now, *Lady Inger of Østraat*, that's a fine play." Ibsen held his tongue, while the queen tried to smooth things over by changing the topic of conversation. After a long pause Ibsen burst out, "But, Your Majesty, I *had* to write *Ghosts*!"[4]

On April 11 the Swedish Society of Authors hosted a banquet for him at the Hasselbacken restaurant. Here Ibsen spoke informally about the need for better translations of literary works. Sixty persons attended, including Snoilsky, seated at Ibsen's left, and across the table, facing him, the aristocratic poet Verner von Heidenstam and Axel Lundegård, Strindberg's coauthor of *Comrades*. Strindberg had sent word, along with a copy of *Inferno*, via Gustaf af Geijerstam that he could not attend. "Strindberg is ashamed that he as a prominent Swedish author could not take part in the celebrations for the Master, from whom he has learned so much. But he was depressed and did not feel that his homage could either honor or please anyone here on earth."[5]

Interviewed in Stockholm, Ibsen called Strindberg "a very great talent. I don't know him personally—our paths have never crossed—but I have read his works with *great* interest. Especially his latest book, *Inferno*, which has made a deep impression on me."[6]

Ibsen replied to Geijerstam a few months later. "Convey to him [Strindberg] my warmest and most sincere thanks and tell him I am overjoyed that he has thought so kindly of me. As you know, I have his portrait always before my eyes in my study, and he lives in my thoughts through his books, which I always buy and read as soon as they are published. I do not wish to write directly to him. I would prefer to find a reason to meet him in person."[7]

The Swedish cartoonist, satirist, and journalist Albert Engström was also present at the authors' banquet and could hardly refrain from laughing at Ibsen's pomposity. "Was this little black-clad, infinitely spruced-up, spectacle-adorned, bureaucratic figure, with mutton chops, pot belly, and fantastically high heels, really the author of *Brand* and *Peer Gynt*?"[8]

As president of the society, Snoilsky gave the principal speech. At one point his voice broke as he recalled the memories of 1864, when all the dreams and promises of a common Scandinavian resistance to the German invasion of Denmark were broken. While others abandoned their ideals, only Ibsen remained true to them and wrote *Brand.*[9]

On April 12, 1898, *The Pretenders* was presented at the Vasa Theater. The audience applauded Ibsen as he entered his loge and sang, "Yes, We Love You" ("*Ja vi elsker*"), the unofficial Norwegian national anthem, which was followed by fanfares from the orchestra, as Ibsen bowed repeatedly. He was handed a laurel wreath as the audience shouted "Hurrah!" The next morning he received at the Hotel Rydberg a deputation of students from Uppsala University. The spokesman for the student association thanked the dramatist for what he had given the young generation. Ibsen kept up a lively conversation with the students for a couple of hours and then invited them all to a "*déjeuner*" at the hotel.

The celebrations culminated in a gala on the evening of April 13, held at the Grand Hotel, with 250 persons attending, including government officials, military and civilian officers, members of the Supreme Court, representatives of the artistic and literary worlds, and not a woman among them. As he entered the hotel, Ibsen was greeted by a song from the famed Bellman Chorus. The banquet hall was decorated with Swedish and Norwegian flags. At the main table, seated to Ibsen's left were Prince Eugen, heir to the throne, and Minister of State Erik Boström, a key figure in the negotiations concerning Norway's desire for complete independence. To Ibsen's right was Foreign Minister Count Ludvig Douglas, also involved in the union question. The official toast to Ibsen was entrusted to Prince Eugen; it was followed by a keynote speech, delivered by Ibsen's old friend Count Snoilsky. The Stockholm newspapers all printed editorials hailing Ibsen not only as a poet but as a Norwegian. Even those like Carl David af Wirsén, the doyen of Swedish literary critics, who disliked Ibsen for his naturalistic works, went along with the king in doing public honor to him.

It must have pleased Ibsen to see himself as a major player, at least for one night, in the field of national politics, an ambassador of goodwill. But the finest tribute of the evening came from the world of theater. August Lindberg, the Swedish actor who had dared to stage *Ghosts* in Scandinavia when all the regular theaters had rejected it, praised Ibsen in an informal but obviously well-crafted speech for re-creating the theater.

"They said of one or another of his dramas that this cannot be played; it goes beyond all the usual rules. So I say to you, when didn't Ibsen go beyond all the usual rules? . . . We offer him our heartfelt thanks for the shining clarity of his works, for the objective reality of his characters. We have felt that we stood so close to them that we could touch them with our hands. We praise him for his majestic austerity and his superhuman seriousness, which has given us a joy that has affected our very lives. We thank him for his writings, which are as rich as nature itself and which enwrap us in an illusion that borders on bewitchment. And now when an actor in this brilliant gathering is allowed to pay him tribute, then it is a sign of the times that, thanks to Ibsen, it can happen."[10]

Ibsen's relatively brief response to all the praise was to view his unexampled success as a miracle, a fairy tale. "It seems like a dream, my visit here in Stockholm. And indeed it is a dream. The first figure that met me in the dream was His Majesty the King. He bestowed upon me the greatest honor that could have been accorded me. I was astonished. I who came here to express my gratitude was given still more to be grateful for. And then I was invited to this splendid and brilliant gathering, so representative in every way. When His Majesty the King did me such a great honor, it all seemed like an ingenious royal eccentricity."

Then, alluding to the time of year, Easter, he ended his remarks: "My life has been like a long, long Holy Week, and now, in the real Passion Week, my life is transformed into a fairy play. I, the old dramatist, see my life re-created as a poem, a fairy tale. It has been transformed into a midsummer night's dream. Thank you, thank you for the transformation!"[11]

The following night Ibsen attended a performance of *Lady Inger* (undoubtedly chosen because it was set in the sixteenth century when Norway was under Danish dominance). King Oscar himself was present for the occasion and joined in the applause when Ibsen bowed to the cheers and hurrahs.[12]

Ibsen stayed in Stockholm longer than he had intended when the feminists insisted that he speak to them. Since there were many women who had not been invited to the king's banquet, two women's societies, the Frederika Bremer League and the New Idun, organized a separate event on April 16 at the Hasselbacken restaurant. Seated beside him were the two most prominent feminists, Fru Ellen Anckarsvärd and Ellen Key. Ibsen was obviously displeased when he was asked to escort to the table the elderly Fru Anckarsvärd, only sixty-five but quite ill. He glowered, and his lower lip protruded. And when Ellen Key, in delivering the encomium, addressed him with the intimate form "du," his lips expressed disapproval. His mood brightened noticeably when nine young girls from "The Friends of Folk Dance" appeared in native costumes and twirled around the floor. One girl in particular caught Ibsen's eye.

Ellen Key's address disturbed many in the audience. She said that men as well as women were denied opportunities to develop as free individuals. With its references to the Third Kingdom, this speech was probably meant to counteract the tributes of the previous days in which Ibsen was treated and described as a conservative. But in the days to come, many women protested against the tenor of Key's remarks, which they felt carried an implicit encouragement to free, illicit love. Some of them appealed to Ibsen, asking whether Key had represented his views correctly.[13] Key defended herself by claiming that her speech was based point by point on Ibsen's own utterances.[14]

Back in Christiania, he followed up the birthday celebrations by accepting an invitation to address the Norwegian League for Women's Rights on May 26. He must have disconcerted its members by disclaiming "the honor of having consciously worked for the women's rights movement. I am not even quite clear as to just what this women's rights movement really is. To me it has seemed a problem of mankind in general. . . . True enough, it is desirable to solve the woman problem, along with all the others; but that has not been the whole purpose. My task has been the *description of humanity.*"[15]

He concluded by proposing that women might help to solve the problems of mankind in general by being good mothers, hardly acceptable advice to women who sought to be liberated from their conventional roles. Certainly, Nora in *A Doll's House* acted in defiance of such advice.

Publishers were quick to exploit the seventieth-birthday festivities by issuing the dramatist's collected works. The handsome German edition (1898–1904) was overseen by Georg Brandes, Julius Elias, and Paul Schlenther, with forty thousand copies printed.[16] The Dano-Norwegian edition (1898–1902) included a facsimile of Ibsen's handwritten note in which he urged readers to explore his works in the order in which they were written; otherwise they would be misunderstood.

Ibsen entertained plans for guiding prospective readers through his fifty-year career. Interviewed at the time of his seventieth birthday, he said he planned to write "*an analytic study of his collected works* and a biography—a presentation of what had happened to him and what he had gone through [*gjennemlevet og oplevet*]. A book in which he will show how the plays hang together, and how they all arose according to a definite plan."[17]

It is difficult to imagine him writing an exegesis of his works. It would violate a basic principle of his creative technique, which was to conceal while revealing. The artist in him sought a full explanation; the public figure wanted to keep his reputation intact. "Deep inside, a poem within the poem is hidden, and if you grasp that, my people, you grasp the song."[18] He quickly abandoned any plans for an explanatory autobiography and turned to his natural realm: a drama in which the events reveal in a distorted but recognizable way what the outer man had experienced, while the true meaning, the reason for writing the play, lies in what the inner man had suffered through. As soon as the birthday celebrations were over, he told his English translator that he had put aside the plans for an autobiography and "was now [1898] maturing the scheme of a new drama."[19]

Ibsen agreed with his French translator in placing it in the context of the earlier plays. "You are basically right when you say that the series which ends with the epilogue really began with *The Master Builder.*"[20]

To a journalist he explained, "[What I] meant by epilogue was simply that the play forms an epilogue to the series of my dramatic works that began with *A Doll's House* and now concludes with *When We Dead Awaken*. This last work belongs with the experiences I wanted to depict in the whole series. It makes for a wholeness, a oneness, and now I am done with it."[21]

There is no contradiction in these two statements. The series that begins with *The Master Builder* forms a backward-looking assessment of his career, while the series that begins with *A Doll's House* is the career itself.

A Dramatic Epilogue

The probing self-autopsy of *John Gabriel Borkman* should have provided a fitting conclusion to Ibsen's lifework. Coming after *The Master Builder* and *Little Eyolf,* it provided a corrective to them, and its last scene, in contrast with the final moments of those plays, was an act of self-interment. *The Master Builder* suggested the possibility of a new beginning, with the artist reaffirming his supremacy as an artist. But the ambiguity of the final scene intimated that the artist's position was a shaky one. In *Little Eyolf* the artist recognized his responsibility to his people. Still, the division within Ibsen's soul remained as great as ever, and the ending of the play, the hoisting of the flag and the hymn-like language, lacked conviction and weakened what was otherwise a strikingly original drama. Finally, in *John Gabriel Borkman,* Ibsen saw what the ending to his life and work had to be. He viewed his career with merciless honesty and produced a play that ranks among his very best. Ibsen's autobiography is contained in *John Gabriel Borkman,* and its last scene should have ended the long saga.

There seemed to be nothing more to say. Yet playmaking filled so much of his existence that he could not lay down his pen and retire. What followed *Borkman* was a work that he knew was not on a par with his best. It was a mere appendix, almost an afterthought, to what had gone before. Attaching another episode to it threatened to destroy the near perfection of the entire oeuvre. In calling it *When We Dead Awaken,* he seemed to be bringing Borkman back to life.

In retrospect, the play did in fact provide the epilogue to Ibsen's entire work. At the time of publication, however, he preferred to regard it as an epilogue to only a part of his work. When the press interpreted "epilogue" to mean that the sixty-eight-year-old dramatist would not be writing any more plays, Ibsen replied that he meant nothing of the sort: he meant that "the play forms an epilogue to the series of my dramatic works that began with *A Doll's House* and now concludes with *When We Dead Awaken.*"[1]

He was right to emphasize the connection with *A Doll's House.* The play cannot be understood and properly appreciated without seeing that the very substance of the play derives from the earlier work. But this last play has an even more obvious connection with *Brand.* The avalanche at the end brings the reader back to the final, unforgettable scene in that epic drama. In *When We Dead Awaken* Ibsen ties together *Brand,* his unsurpassable breakthrough idealistic poem, and *A Doll's House,* his breakthrough realistic drama. Seen in this connection, his very last play is an epilogue not just to the series of realistic plays but an afterpiece to his entire body of work and a concise summing-up of the themes that had obsessed and driven him as an artist.

Two specific events provided the dramatic material for the play: the production of *Brand* that he saw at the Dagmar Theater in Copenhagen and a face-to-face meeting with Laura Kieler. As both a tribute to Ibsen on his seventieth birthday and a showcase for his own towering talents, the actor-director Martinius Nielsen, a tall man with a stentorian voice, chose this epic work. During the performance, Ibsen whispered to a woman in his party, "This gets to me! It's my whole youth. I haven't thought about *Brand* for thirty years." During the fourth act, he broke down and cried. "Don't blubber," he said to himself.[2]

Of course, he had thought about *Brand* often enough in those thirty years. Only a few years before, in 1895, he had proved to be a sharp businessman in negotiating with the Swedish actor August Lindberg over royalties for *Brand,* demanding as much for it as for *Little Eyolf,* three thousand kronor.

Astonished, Lindberg said,

> "Doctor Ibsen! When you ask 3,000 kronor for an old work like *Brand* and compare its monetary value with a new work, as new as *Little Eyolf,* let me tell you that *Brand* can't be compared with any other work, least of all with *Little Eyolf,* as regards royalties."
>
> "Why not?"
>
> "Because what happened to *Brand* isn't what happened to *Little Eyolf.* All the first sheets were nearly stolen from the printing room in Copenhagen."
>
> While I had been talking, he had taken his glass and was about to bring it to his lips, when he leaned back and looked at me. It was the look that frightened Sinding when Ibsen posed for him. Slowly and as if he were weighing them came his next words. "So you think it was *that* that explains the success of *Little Eyolf?*"
>
> I was still furious, and I answered with a shrug. He continued slowly and with imperturbable calm. "I thought it was my writing."

> In response I could only say, "I'm sitting here with my hat in my lap, but if I were wearing it, it would be raised for something as great as Henrik Ibsen's writing. But that's not what's at issue here; it's the royalties, which are much too high. I came here to agree on terms. People know that in Christiania. But now I say goodbye to you and take my leave. It will get out that I wasn't successful, because I will never pay 3,000 for *Brand,* and I am amazed that you, sir, could ever suggest anything like that."
>
> "No, no. Oh, for God's sake, don't leave," he exclaimed. "We have to take the lead in bringing Norway and Sweden together. Can you pay me 2,000 for *Brand?*"[3]

They finally settled on one thousand. And so on October 21, 1895, *Brand* was staged for the first time in Norway, ironically by a Swedish company. It was a considerable commercial success, running for nine performances before going on tour. The Ibsen biographer Halvdan Koht says it was an artistic failure, with Lindberg resorting to empty declamation. Lindberg's account intimates that the playwright never came to see it.[4]

So it is likely that Ibsen saw *Brand* onstage for the first time when he was seventy years old. The uniqueness of this experience may account for his highly excitable mood on that occasion. At the cast party after the performance he praised Nielsen's interpretation of the part. "It's *my* Brand, just as I've seen him."

Unusually talkative and in an expansive mood, he stayed at the party until three in the morning.

"I have to leave now," he said. "I have to be at my desk at 7 a.m."

"Surely not this morning," said one of the party.

"Oh, yes," he answered, "come and see. I'll be there at 7."

Nielsen said, "But then, sir, you won't have gotten a good night's sleep."

"Oh, yes," replied Ibsen serenely, "I'll sleep so much harder."[5]

But he didn't. He spent a sleepless night, during which the idea for a new and necessary play began to stir his imagination.[6]

In *When We Dead Awaken* Ibsen incarnates himself as a sculptor, inspired perhaps, as Bernard Shaw speculated, by the extraordinary, worldwide fame of Auguste Rodin.[7] The play pictures Professor Arnold Rubek, renowned for his realistic busts, married to a much younger woman, less than half his age. Rubek's masterpiece, the work of a lifetime, is an elaborate composition known as "Resurrection Day," which began with the statue of a nude woman, standing alone, an image of the Ideal. This ambitious piece underwent a number of radical changes since he began work on it. Around the original nude figure he placed a number of sculpted heads, amazingly realistic. In a confidential mood, he reveals their true nature.

> There is something concealed, something lurking within and behind these busts that people can't see.... Only *I* can see it. And it amuses me so unspeakably. On the surface is this "striking likeness," as they call it, that makes them stop and stare in astonishment (*lowering his voice*), but at bottom they are all respectable, honorable ugly horseheads and opinionated ass snouts and low-browed, lop-eared dog skulls and fattened-up pig faces, along with some dull and brutal bull facsimiles ... in a word, all the dear domestic animals. All the animals that man has botched up by making them in his image, and in return that have botched up him. (*Emptying his champagne glass and laughing*) And it is these cunning works of art that prosperous people come and order from me. And pay for in good faith—and in goodly sums, almost their weight in gold, as the saying goes.[8]

For Rubek, as for Ibsen, fame and fortune came at a price: the abandonment of youthful ideals.

"When we dead awaken ... we see that we have never lived." These words, spoken by Irene, contradict the spirit that Rubek thought he was instilling in his masterpiece. The truth is that everything that was added to the original single figure was a falling-off from the ideal. All those efforts to bring about the Third Kingdom served only to diminish what Brand struggled to achieve. All those domestic animals—the desperate Mrs. Alving, the neurotic Gregers, the burned-out Brendel, the cowardly Hedda—marked the failure of the great enterprise.[9]

Rubek is vacationing with his wife, Maia, at a health resort when he encounters Irene, the woman who posed for the initial statue. That nude figure made her famous and notorious. Abandoned by Rubek, she became a star of the variety stage, displaying herself virtually naked on a turntable. She suffered a mental collapse and is now attended by a nurse, who watches over her.

In this, the thinnest of all the plots devised by the master of complexity, these two women stand for the two irreconcilable sides of Ibsen. Usually, the end of his narratives has brought the two sides into an approximate union, as in *Rosmersholm* and *Little Eyolf* and *John Gabriel Borkman.* Not this time, however. The last scene of *When We Dead Awaken* harks back to *A Doll's House*, when Nora chose to follow Brand's example.

Irene is Laura Kieler come back to haunt Ibsen. They had met again in 1885, when as a correspondent for the Danish newspaper *Morgenbladet* she interviewed him. They spoke to each other as strangers. After the fracas caused by her play *Men of Honor*, she had appealed directly to Ibsen in 1890, asking him to deny publicly that she had been the model for Nora. As we have seen, he had then told her that there was nothing to deny, since he had never stated or even implied that she was the inspiration for Nora. In November 1891, although her husband had forbidden her to contact Ibsen, Laura wrote to him, asking to meet with him in private. She finally managed to beard the lion in his den. He invited her to lunch at his new apartment on fashionable Victoria Terrace in Christiania.[10]

The scenes between Rubek and Irene are a nightmarish reimagining of that afternoon, when Kieler pleaded with Ibsen to announce publicly that she was not the model for Nora. She had been placed in a sanatorium, like Irene, and virtually banned from good society in Copenhagen, branded as a giddy wife who forged promissory notes to buy expensive dresses or, as Brandes said, to beautify her house. She resurrected the past, reminding Ibsen of her youthful admiration for *Brand*. She had praised the work and had written her own sequel to it. And she told him how he had disappointed her when in 1870 he had told her that her book smacked too much of a religious tract and that his epic poem was an "esthetic" work and nothing else. She quoted *Brand* at him and reproached him with moral cowardice. Confronting Ibsen over the lunch table, she in so many words accused him of cowardly equivocation and moral irresponsibility. Their conversation lasted four hours, and at parting all he could say, with tears in his eyes, was, "Oh, Laura, Laura! It seems that I can never separate myself from you. But you must not come again tomorrow. No, no, it cannot be. It cannot. It is impossible."[11]

When We Dead Awaken is in essence a continuation of Ibsen's last meeting with Laura Kieler. When he drafted the scenes with Irene, he clearly had in mind the four-hour-long, soul-searching confrontation with Kieler in his apartment on Victoria Terrace.

A few years later he invited her to the gala banquet on the occasion of his seventieth birthday. She declined.[12]

Irene's age is not mentioned, but when the play was staged in Christiania she was portrayed, with Ibsen's approval, as being quite young. His fellow playwright Gunnar Heiberg noticed that a young Irene was inconsistent with the experiences that Irene has gone through. He stopped Ibsen on his daily walk and pointed out the discrepancy.

> He answered, "Irene should be twenty-eight years old."
>
> I said that was impossible.
>
> He looked at me, looked me up and down, and replied quietly and crushingly, "So you know better than I do, do you?"
>
> "Yes," I answered, "I guess I do."
>
> And I went on to explain why Irene had to be at least forty years old. Many years must have gone by since she and Rubek last met. It was precisely the *many* years that had passed that made the breakup *now*, once again, so decisive and significant for the two of them. Small things were forgotten. That they had once loved and meant everything to each other was all that they remembered. The

many intervening years lay like a mist between then and now, and out of that mist they had emerged into light and a quiet and peaceful recollection of the past, which allowed their words to fall so clearly and expressively.

Ibsen interrupted: "Irene should be twenty-eight. And why do you ask, if you know it all?"

And he turned away brusquely.

The next day I got a letter from him. It read: "You are right. I was wrong. I have consulted my notes. Irene is about forty years old."[13]

How could Ibsen have made such a mistake? Re-creating the past, he collapsed two crucial incidents concerning Laura Kieler into one. In 1879, when she was twenty-eight, her husband had her placed in a sanatorium to recover from her nervous breakdown. This was the Laura who appears as the disturbed Irene. However, the substance of the conversation between Irene and Rubek comes from that afternoon in 1891 when Kieler called Ibsen to account, when she confronted him and upbraided him for being a mere poet and not a man with convictions. She would then have been forty-one.

Laura Kieler recognized herself in Irene; and the costume Irene wears—a long dress reaching down to her feet and a large shawl of white crepe—was what Kieler wore when she met with Ibsen.[14] Ibsen gave Irene an excellent Norwegian accent, devoting several lines of dialogue, unnecessary for the plot, to make the point. Laura Kieler (née Petersen) had spent her childhood years in Norway.

Irene's opposite is Maia. Having achieved world fame, Rubek married this much younger woman. Having little in common with him, she is hardly more than a trophy that comes with success and fame. After four or five years together, they have grown bored with each other, and at the health resort they come to realize how incompatible they are. We see them first on a lovely summer morning, drinking champagne, each absorbed in a newspaper. Some of the best talk in the play—Ibsen in a new vein—reveals the emptiness of their life together.

While Rubek meets the woman who truly inspired him, Maia takes up with Ulfheim, a prosperous sportsman. The action of the play shows Rubek and Maia going their separate ways, she descending into the valley with her man of the flesh and Rubek ascending the heights with his creature of the spirit. While Maia rejoices in being set free, singing ecstatically, "I am free as a bird," Rubek and Irene are whirled to their deaths in an avalanche. To audiences of the time, "free as a bird" was an allusion to the bohemian way of life. Henri Murger's *Scènes de la Vie de Bohème* was called *De frie Fugle* (*Wild Birds*) in Denmark at this time.[15]

The young lady's name is doubly significant, suggesting Maytime, springtime, and youth, and also Maya, the Sanskrit term for illusion, given wide currency by Schopenhauer. In the first pages of his *The World as Will and Representation*, he defined "Mâyâ" as "the veil of deception, which covers the eyes of mortals, and causes them to see a world of which one cannot say either that it is or that it is not; for it is like a dream, like the sunshine on the sand which the traveler from a distance takes to be water, or like the piece of rope on the ground which he regards as a snake."[16]

Unlike the scenes with Irene, which are based on reality, the scenes with Maia are imaginary, Ibsen fantasizing, seeing himself after five years of marriage to a once seductively attractive young woman. He had a particular one in mind, a girl who at their last meeting aroused his passion to an ungentlemanly degree.

One of the nine young women performing in the folk dances at the Hasselbacken restaurant in Stockholm on April 16, 1898, was Rosa Fitinghoff. Her striking good looks, her sparkling gray eyes, her luxuriant hair, and her high spirits made her the center of any social gathering. In his brief description of Maia, Ibsen singles out her lively, teasing eyes as a special characteristic. Rosa was used to attention and did not shun it. Born in Norrland, Sweden, in 1872, she came from a highly respected family, her father a member of the Baltic nobility. He died when Rosa was only eight, and she and her mother moved to Stockholm, where they could rely on the kindness of friends and distant relations to see them through hard times.

Like Emilie Bardach and Helene Raff and all young women of those times, Rosa kept a diary. Her entry for Saturday, April 16, 1898, tells of her first meeting with Ibsen.

> After the dance, Ibsen came over, stroked my hair and said hair so rich and beautiful was not to be found in Norway. When I smiled and said surely it did, he said definitely not—not even in Germany had he seen anything like it. A little later he came over and handed me a large bouquet of roses that he had been given, and said that they were the very image of me. We stood there alone and chatted for a while and he kissed me on my hand. After that at least twenty people kissed me on the same place, and everyone asked me how much I charged.—Ten kroner, I laughed, happily. Ibsen delivered his speech and after it came back to me, tugged at my apron, and begged me to follow him to Christiania the next day.—His eyes were sharp and piercing, and he begged me to come to the station the next morning to say goodbye.
>
> At the station Ibsen was surrounded by cabinet ministers and other dignitaries. I didn't think he would remember me, but he right away came to Mamma and me. We were alone for a moment, and he begged me earnestly to write.—I thought I would die, I was so proud.

Back in Christiania, Ibsen sent her his portrait, and later, on May 25, a short letter.

Figure 30. Rosa Fitinghoff, February 1903.

"The Swedish folk dances that I saw at Hasselbacken made an unforgettable impression on me, and my thoughts often return to those shining hours I spent there surrounded by intelligence, youth, beauty, and grace. And now I sit here and watch the spring turn green and think about my dear friends in Stockholm."

A year later, when he was hard at work on *When We Dead Awaken*, he sent her a thank-you note. He was now immersed in writing the first draft of the play, with the working title "Resurrection Day" ("Opstandelsens dag").

"You are more than kind to send me the little blue flower—*die blaue Blume* that is so full of significance and so seldom found or earned.—And many thanks for giving me a thought or two for April 11 [*sic*] last year. That day will always remain in my memory. Be assured of that.—Your letters live in their own little room in my desk, and when I set to work in the morning, I always look in on them and say, 'Hello, Rosa.'"[17]

In German myth, finding the *blaue Blume* opened the way to hidden treasure.

In July Rosa and her mother journeyed to Christiania and arranged to see Ibsen. Rosa in her diary:

> We were to meet at the Grand Hotel. I was very nervous about approaching him, but he came to me, and said—So here you are finally, I've so longed for

you. We chatted quite a while, and then agreed that Mamma and I would come to his place [on Arbins Gate] the next day at 11:00. Then I handed him a red rose and he kissed my hand three times. We sat first in his library, and then he showed us all the rooms and all his paintings, saying that if I knew how things were when he wrote, it would make writing easier for him. We were there for a whole hour and agreed to meet at the Grand Hotel at 18:00 that evening.

Ibsen began by saying how wonderfully well his writing had gone after we had visited him. He ordered two bottles of champagne and wanted to order a third, and offered us ice cream and pastries.—I never thought you would recognize me yesterday, I said.—Ah, answered Ibsen, how could you possibly think that. After all, I'm not a polar bear. Yes, this is where I usually sit, gathering my thoughts, and pretend that I'm reading, he said.

We could have spent the whole evening, but in all conscience we could not stay longer with him in spite of all he said. There were groups of people all around us, gaping and curious. In the windows and everywhere where we stood, there were people staring at us. After we had said our goodbyes, Mamma and I walked around a while to calm our nerves.

Another entry:

Terrible weather, high winds and rain in Christiania. At 11:00 [on July 26] I went to Ibsen's home, as he had asked. He opened the door and led me into the library and said—With all my heart I want to have you here, sitting here every day while I write, it would be so much easier to write. All the while he kissed my hand, held me, and petted me. He would not let me go, but Mamma was waiting for me, and so he let go of me.

He gave me a photograph of himself, the one of him at his desk. He said all sorts of warm and wonderful things to me, but I don't dare to write them down. When I said goodbye, he kissed first my cheek and then my mouth several times, *long* and *hard,* and he had tears in his eyes, *full* of tears, as he thanked me. He was so excited that he began to tremble, followed me out to the hallway without bothering a bit about a man who was waiting and who looked completely flustered when he saw us.[18]

Whoever the man in the hallway was, one can understand that he might have been bewildered and bemused at the sight of a radiantly attractive young woman being kissed by Ibsen, "this old man with the head and hair of an electrified Schopenhauer and the torso of a giant," in James Huneker's evocative description.[19]

He sent her a signed photograph of himself at his desk, inscribed, "In memory of our summer meeting in Christiania 1899, 26 July,"[20] and he sent her a signed copy of *When We Dead Awaken* as soon as it was published.

Hildur Andersen was a different sort, "an intimate friend of mine—a good, wise, and faithful friend."[21] She could, like Laura Kieler, encourage him to ascend to the heights. Although Rosa might seduce him with images of sexual passion, she belonged to the lower regions, which were not the artist's true realm. Rubek says, "I don't believe I have ever seen a sunrise," meaning he has never experienced a night of unrestrained lovemaking. Maia stands for a world that could never be part of reality for Ibsen. It meant the veil of deception or illusion. For Ibsen, the world of art was the reality, while sexual passion was a distraction, an enticement, and a threat.

Rubek says, "I have come to realize that I am not the sort who looks for happiness in idle pleasure. . . . I must go on working—producing one work after another—right up to my dying day."[22]

For him the only possible sunrise was the one that might greet him at the top of the peak after he had ascended "through all the mists, and then right up to the summit of the tower that shines in the sunrise." This was the only reality for the creative artist. It was the only way in which he could find some kind of peace.

When We Dead Awaken pronounces the severest judgment on the artist's work. In the previous autobiographical dramas, the attempt to realize the Third Kingdom was seen as the driving force behind the creation of a notable oeuvre. If the great ideal remained ultimately beyond the artist's grasp, the masterpieces justified the attempt. In this last work, however, in this epilogue to the whole series of realistic plays, Ibsen says clearly enough that the entire endeavor was misguided. The Third Kingdom was a chimera, a will-o'-the-wisp, that lured him from the great work.

What did exist was the dualism, the unbridgeable separation of Brand and Peer Gynt. In *When We Dead Awaken* Maia and Ulfheim represent the Gyntian element. But Ibsen-Rubek could never give himself over to that side of things. Those dalliances with young girls à la Peer Gynt were only fantasies, illusions.

Rubek's marriage with Maia obviously has no real counterpart in Ibsen's life. But his flights of fancy involving young women did form part of the landscape of his imagination. However, in this epilogue to his main work he wanted to show that for the artist in him these romances of the mind meant very little; that in fact they stifled his creative genius.

Here, as always, sexual passion is seen as a diversion from the artist's work. And here, as almost always, Ibsen is Strindberg's direct opposite. Rubek tells Maia that within him is a casket of artistic visions, and Maia does not have the key to it. "So all that's in it lies unused. And the years pass! No way for me to get at the treasure."[23] Irene held the key to the treasure, and when she posed for Rubek, and they played their little games, she was the swan that drew Lohengrin's boat, and he was the knight of the Holy Grail.

In this, the last scene that the dramatist ever wrote, Ibsen admits that his search for the Third Kingdom ended in failure. Maia is a female version of Peer Gynt; Irene is another Agnes, willing to be sacrificed to Brand's idealism. But Ibsen allows no possibility, even a symbolic one, of a union of Maia and Irene.

When We Dead Awaken is both an attempt to set things right with Laura Kieler and another recapitulation of his artistic career. He had first of all to atone—esthetically, in a play—for his dismissive treatment of Kieler as Kaja Fosli in *The Master Builder*, written within a year after his four-hour lunch with her. Kaja had served Solness well but had to be dismissed to make room for Hilda Wangel: the old source of inspiration had to give way to a new one. Some years later, however, in 1898 and 1899, his perspective changed. The cloud castles of the master builder had proved to be no more than that. What followed in *Little Eyolf* and *John Gabriel Borkman* was not a truly new Ibsen, only an Ibsen feeding his genius on his past. The same is true of *When We Dead Awaken*, with the crucial difference that here the career of the artist is subjected to a further distillation.

For Ibsen, the only true freedom could come by reaffirming the Brandian ideal. In *When We Dead Awaken* he returned to the source of his creative genius, the decision to choose all or nothing, not to compromise. Rubek had to part from Maia and be reunited with Irene for peace of mind ("Irene" = "peace"), admitting that his success as an artist could not compensate for his failure as a human being. Ibsen wrote his last play to atone for his abandonment of what Brand stood for and his callous treatment of Laura Kieler. Actually, these two cardinal sins were one and the same.[24]

THE LAST YEARS

After *The Master Builder* Ibsen thought more and more about how to bring his creative life to an end. To a foreign visitor in 1894 he said, "I have never given up the hope of writing another drama in verse. I have often made beginnings, but never carried them out. I should like my last drama to be in verse—if only one knew beforehand which was going to be the last!"[1]

One of his growing concerns was the way in which his plays were being misinterpreted. In March 1898 he penned a special note that introduced his collected works.

"Simultaneously with the production of my works another generation of readers has grown up, and I have often noticed with regret that their knowledge of my more recent works was considerably more detailed than of my earlier ones. Consequently, these readers lack an awareness of the mutual connections between the plays, and I attribute a not insignificant part of the strange, imperfect, and misleading interpretations that my later works have been subjected to in so many quarters to this lack of awareness.

"Only by grasping and comprehending my entire production as a continuous and coherent whole will the reader be able to receive the precise impression I sought to convey in the individual parts of it."[2]

At the same time in a speech in Christiania he said he intended to write a book "that will link my life and my works together in an explanatory whole."[3]

While he was finishing the final draft of *When We Dead Awaken*, the new National Theater opened in Christiania on September 1, 1899, and the two founding fathers of Norwegian drama, Ibsen and Bjørnson, were honored with productions of their plays and the unveiling of statues. On that date, *An Enemy of the People* was performed as a tribute to Ibsen. He sat alone in the manager's box, responding to repeated shouts of "Long live Ibsen" with tears in his eyes. When the audience finally allowed him to leave the theater, he walked with some difficulty.

A year earlier, on March 19, 1898, he had claimed proudly that he was in good health. He told a journalist, "I have never been sick, not a single day of my life. I've never called for a doctor. I have never taken prescription drugs."[4] This was an exaggeration. In the winter of 1889–90 he had been seriously ill with influenza.[5]

He exerted himself greatly in writing *When We Dead Awaken*, and the play shows signs that his powers of concentration were not what they had been a year earlier. On March 12, 1900, after attending a ball at the Royal Palace, he had a slight stroke. That summer another stroke affected his leg, and an outbreak of erysipelas added to his physical decline. He spent most of the summer of 1900 recuperating at Dr. Sontum's sanatorium. In January 1901 he complained to Rosa Fitinghoff that he was ill for the first time, with a bad foot causing him pain.[6] In the spring he was ill for five weeks. After an apoplectic seizure he gave up his daily walk to the Grand Hotel, and from then on he let the citizens of Christiania view him as he passed by in a horse-drawn carriage. In an interview on November 25, 1901, he said he felt better than he had for a long time, but walking caused problems. "I cannot complain about my head. That is in full vigor. But I tire easily, and my doctor has ordered me not to work too hard."[7] Another stroke in March 1903 affected his mind, causing amnesia, loss of memory, mixed-up words. In 1904 he suffered yet another stroke, after which he was no longer able to write. He said to his son, "See what I am doing! I am sitting here, learning to make my letters—my *letters!* I who was once an author!"[8] On November 23, 1905, he had a relapse after his son unexpectedly called on him. His personal physician, Dr. Bull, father of the eminent Ibsen scholar Francis Bull, prescribed iodine and potassium carbonate for arteriosclerosis. In 1906 he was completely immobile. He died at two thirty in the afternoon on May 23, 1906. Arteriosclerosis was listed as the official cause of death. His last words, uttered the day before, were "Thank goodness" ("*Gudskelov*").[9]

Suzannah was always present. He had once told her, "If you die before me, I'll die five minutes later." After May 16 he was virtually comatose, with only brief moments of awareness. According to Suzannah, Ibsen's last words were spoken to her the night before he died: "My sweet, sweet wife, how kind and good you have been to me."[10]

Or so Suzannah told her daughter-in-law. But considering how comatose Ibsen was during his last days, quite incapable of forming complete sentences or even short phrases, it seems likely that Suzannah may have been recalling what he had said to her long before.

During those last nonproductive years, figures from the past came calling. On the occasion of Ibsen's seventy-fifth birthday in 1903, Bjørnson was the first to pay his respects. Suzannah saw to it that they would not be disturbed, and they spent two hours together. According to Bjørnson, when they parted, "Ibsen told me, word for word, 'Among my memories and of all the people I've known, it is you whom I think of most often.' He clasped my hand and added, 'It is you whom I hold most dear.' We were both deeply moved."[11]

Jonas Lie, now a successful novelist and recipient of the Great Cross of St. Olaf, arrived a little later. He thanked Ibsen for what he had done for the Norwegian people.

Ibsen replied, "You have done just as much."

"No, you know perfectly well that no one has done as much for our country as you."[12]

Christopher Bruun, the pastor whose strong convictions and idealism had helped Ibsen in creating *Brand*, called on him more than once, not merely to chat but to counsel a dying man. When Bruun brought up the question of Ibsen's religious beliefs, Ibsen burst out, his face red with rage, "Let me worry about that!"[13]

He liked to hear his works read to him. Listening intently, he would correct mispronunciations or wrong intonations.

His sister, Hedvig Stousland, came to see him on several occasions, bringing honey cakes.

In February 1906 Eleanora Duse, on tour in Christiania, telephoned Suzannah, asking to see Ibsen. By that time he could receive no visitors. Duse stood in the snow outside Ibsen's apartment house, hoping to catch a glimpse of him.[14]

Georg Brandes and Bjørnstjerne Bjørnson, the two men who had sent him sailing through the intellectual currents of the nineteenth century, both called on him for the last time in 1903. Brandes saw Ibsen early in the year, when Ibsen was very weak. "It was a pleasure to see him once again, but a melancholy one. After a stroke, work became impossible for him. His mind was still clear; a striking mildness had taken the place of the former severity; he was more cordial than before, as refined as ever, but the whole impression was one of weakness."[15] Bjørnson visited him for the last time in the autumn just after he, Bjørnson, had been awarded the Nobel Prize, which was denied Ibsen.[16]

Ibsen had had to steer a perilous course between the two, keeping a little to the right of one, a little to the left of the other, always knowing that they did not truly appreciate his work. Bjørnson found his plays too pessimistic and called them "coffins," and Brandes never understood the mysticism inherent even in the master's most realistic plays.[17]

Bjørnson did not attend the elaborate funeral services, nor did Suzannah. Bjørnson excused himself, saying Ibsen had been dead for six years, having in mind Ibsen's last play, which appeared in 1900. Suzannah, as her biographer remarks, knew she had already done all she could to honor him.[18]

She outlived him by eight years, dying April 3, 1914. She stayed on in the Arbins Gate apartment, receiving visitors occasionally.

In his first drama, Ibsen had set up the positive and negative poles that would energize all his subsequent work. Looking at that work years later, he said its concern was "the conflict between one's aims and one's abilities, between what man proposes and what is actually possible, constituting at once both the tragedy and comedy of mankind and of the individual."[19]

Near the end of his career he expressed the same thought more lyrically: "Like a perfect poem, may your life express / The reconciliation of duty with happiness." This was inscribed in a copy of *Brand*, given to Hildur Andersen's year-old niece in 1896.

Perhaps his life and works did not add up to a perfect poem. But they came close. His oeuvre, certainly, taken in its entirety, achieves an extraordinary artistic unity, with the great work closing in on itself, subsuming itself. As an artist, seeking the perfection of the work and not the life, he could hardly have done more. As a human being, however, he could accuse himself of moral cowardice. Yet without that accusation always in play, without Brand always challenging Peer Gynt, there would not have been that strange phenomenon known as Ibsen.

An anecdote related by Gustaf af Geijerstam sums up what lies at the heart of Ibsen's works, the spirit that animates the whole career. In the Ibsen obituary for a German journal, Geijerstam recounted that the dramatist "once mentioned that his works were only a preparation for the coming thing, the Third Kingdom, that shimmers in the distance. He once said to me, in an unforgettable moment, that in his works there were these that for him had a deeper personal meaning than all the others: 'Only what has been lost remains eternal.' ['*Nur Verlorenes bleibt dir ewig.*'] With his strong and mild voice he spoke these words and repeated them once again with a special emphasis: 'Only what has been lost.'"[20] Ibsen must have had in mind Svanhild's transfiguring cry near the end of *Love's Comedy*, "I have renounced you for this life, but I have found you for eternity."[21] It was Ibsen's early recognition of that paradox that lured him on, that drove him on toward the heights. At the end of act four of *Brand*, when the hero knows his wife is dying, he cries out, his hands pressed against his chest,

> Soul, be patient in thy pain!
> Triumph in its bitter cost.
> All to lose was all to gain;
> Nought abideth but the Lost![22]

Although Kierkegaardian in spirit, this paradox lay not only at the core of Ibsen's philosophy, it also lay at the heart of his emotional life, shaped by his early years. It provided the psychic energy in his search for the Third Kingdom, the ideal that would compensate for the great loss.

Surely there were times in the last years when the two incompatible, warring sides of his psyche slipped unforcedly into a kind of equilibrium, moments when the life may have seemed like a perfect poem. An anecdote related by Brandes captures a moment like that. He and the elderly Ibsen had dinner on a summer evening on the terrace outside a restaurant overlooking a fjord in Norway.

> There was a lamp on the table, which was removed, since the sky was still bright. Ibsen's form, his majestic forehead and the flowing hair, merged with the haunting natural scene and its magical light. It grew darker and finally all one could see of him was the reflection of his spectacles and the movements of his lips. He spoke in his quiet voice, sipping now and then from his glass, telling stories and joking.
>
> We had dined on lamb, and I remarked, "Lamb is really the best meat."
>
> "Absolutely," said Ibsen. "I once thought of writing a play about a lamb. A man is deathly ill. He can't possibly recover unless he has a complete transfusion of blood. So fresh blood is taken from a lamb and given to him, and he regains his health. After that, he can't stop thinking about seeing that lamb again. He owes his life to it. Finally he finds the lamb in the shape of a woman. He loves her. Why shouldn't he love her?"
>
> "Oh, absolutely. Only it doesn't happen very often that one meets a woman who is a lamb."
>
> "Oh, it happens, it happens."
>
> And in the silence, he smiled, and the dim night sky and the distant, dim fjord, smooth as a mirror, blended in with that smile.[23]

In the 1898 celebrations he said his life had been transformed into a fairy tale. In the gathering twilight of his life he must have entertained images of the wretched apothecary's assistant in dismal Grimstad transformed into a citizen of the world, his chest laden with medals, one of the immortals, his lifework shaped into a nearly perfect whole, the plays being consubstantial with the man himself.

It happened.

NOTES

The following abbreviations are used in the notes for collections of Ibsen's writings:

HI skrifter	*Henrik Ibsens skrifter.* 17 vols. Oslo, 2005–10.
HU	*Samlede Verker: Hundreårsutgave.* Edited by Francis Bull, Halvdan Koht, and Didrik Arup Seip. 21 vols. Oslo, 1928–57.
OC	Œuvres complètes. Edited and translated by P[ierre] G[eorget] La Chesnais. 16 vols. Paris, 1930–45.

INTRODUCTION

1. Dutton Cook, *On the Stage* (London, 1883), 1:117.
2. Arthur Symons, *Studies in Seven Arts* (London, 1906), 336.
3. *Iconoclasts: A Book of Dramatists* (New York, 1905), 3.
4. Preface to 2nd ed. of *Catiline* (1875); *HU,* 1:123.

A CONTRARY SPIRIT

1. Lis Jacobsen, "Ibsens sidste ord," *Ibsen-årbok* (1957–59), 79–92; Halvdan Koht, "Ibsens siste ord," ibid., 113–14.
2. Kjell Espmark, *The Nobel Prize in Literature: A Study of the Criteria Behind the Choices* (Boston, 1986), 18.
3. Michael Egan, ed., *Ibsen: The Critical Heritage* (London, 1972), 445.
4. George Rency, quoted in Hjalmar Pettersen, *Henrik Ibsen, the Norwegian Dramatist,* in *Contemporary and After Times Literature* (Oslo, 1928), 177.
5. Nicolas Ségur, quoted in Pettersen, *Ibsen, the Norwegian Dramatist,* 179. Ernest Renan (1823–92) was a French historian and philosopher.
6. Alfred Kerr, "Ibsens Tod," *Das literarische Echo* 8 (1905–6), 1297.
7. Carsten Svarstad, "Henrik Ibsens ordener og hederstegn," *Ibsen-årbok* (1957–59), 176–81.

8. Kerr, "Ibsens Tod," 1298.
9. Bergliot Ibsen, *De tre* (Oslo, 1949), 214.
10. Drachmann, *Breve*, vol. 2 (Copenhagen, 1965), 268.
11. August Strindberg, *En Blå Bok*, vol. 65 of *August Strindbergs samlade verk*, ed. Gunnar Ollén (Stockholm, 1997), 136, 143. Although Strindberg uses apocalyptic language, all his references are to particular people and utterances. See the commentary in *Blå Bok*, 555–56. C. L. Due, Ibsen's good friend in the early days, said Ibsen had "no ear for music whatever." Due, "Ibsen's Early Youth," *The Critic* 49 (1906), 38.
12. "Fear of the Light" ("Lysræd"); *HU*, 14:334.
13. Preface to 2nd ed. of *Catiline*; ibid., 1:119–20.
14. Letter to Ludwig Passarge, June 16, 1880; ibid., 17:187.
15. Maurice Bigeon, *Les Révoltés scandinaves* (Paris, 1894), 254.
16. Lorentz Dietrichson, *Svundne Tider*, vol. 1: *Bergen og Christiania i 40-og 50-Aarene*, 2nd ed. (Christiania, 1913), 368.
17. Speech in Christiania, March 23, 1898.
18. Ibsen, *Samlede Værker*, vol. 1 (Copenhagen, 1898), preliminary notice.

A DIVIDED SOUL

1. "The Conduct of Life," *Essays and Lectures* (New York, 1983), 1086.
2. *Van Gogh: A Self-Portrait*, ed. W. H. Auden (New York, 1963), 192.
3. *HU*, 19:411.
4. Ibid., 20:43.
5. Rudolph Lothar, *Henrik Ibsen* (Leipzig, Berlin, and Vienna, 1902), 123.
6. Shaw, *Pen Portraits and Reviews* (London, 1931), 143.
7. Einar Østvedt, "Gustav Adolph Lammers som modell til Ibsens Brand," *Ibsen-årbok* (1952), 68.
8. Henrik Jæger, *Henrik Ibsen 1828–1888: Et literært Livsbillede* (Copenhagen, 1888), 14.
9. Halvdan Koht, *Henrik Ibsen: Eit diktarliv*, 2nd ed. (Oslo, 1954), 1:11.
10. Philip E. Larson, *Ibsen in Skien and Grimstad: His Education, Reading, and Early Works* (Grimstad, Norway, 1999), 33.
11. Einar Østvedt, *Henrik Ibsen: Barndom og ungdom* (Skien, 1973), 66–67.
12. Ibid., 70–71.
13. Arne Duve, *Ibsen: Bak kulissene* (Oslo, 1971), 28, quoting an article in *Varden* (Skien), October 22, 1920. Also J. Brunsvig, "Ibsen-huset på Snipetorp," *Ibsen-årbok* (1953), 70.
14. The date of his leaving Skien has not been definitely established. See Halvdan Koht, "Når reiste Henrik Ibsen frå Skien," *Ibsen-årbok*, 1953, 56–62; and *HI skrifter*, 17 vols. (Oslo, 2005–10), vol. 12, *Kommentarer*, 69, 782.
15. Due, "Ibsen's Early Youth," 33–34.
16. H. Eitrem, *Ibsen og Grimstad* (Oslo, 1940), 24.
17. Due, "Ibsen's Early Youth," 37.
18. Ibid., 38.
19. H. Eitrem, "Henrik Ibsen—Henrik Wergeland," *Maal og Minne* (1910), 47–48.
20. *HI skrifter*, 12:35. This letter did not come to light until 1996; see Per Kristian Heggelund Dahl, "Nytt stoff om Ibsens mørke år," *Aftenposten* (Oslo), March 24, 1996.

21. Letter to Carl Johan Anker, January 30, 1858; *HI skrifter*, 12:102.
22. *HU*, 14:46.
23. Valfrid Vasenius, *Henrik Ibsens dramatiska diktning i dess första skede* (Helsingfors, 1879), 18; Østvedt, "Lammers som modell til Ibsens Brand," 68–91.
24. From the "Epic Brand," *HU*, 5:402–3.
25. *HU*, 10:170.
26. Eitrem, *Ibsen og Grimstad*, 111; Østvedt, *Ibsen: Barndom*, 90.
27. Oskar Mosfjeld, *Henrik Ibsen og Skien* (Oslo, 1949), 172.
28. Bergliot Ibsen, *De tre*, 73.
29. Ibid., 9–10, 75.
30. Edmund Gosse, *Henrik Ibsen* (New York, 1915), 3.
31. Francis Bull, *Traditioner och minnen*, translated by Ingeborg Essén (Stockholm, 1949), 163.

THE APPRENTICE

1. Due, "Ibsen's Early Youth," 35.
2. *HU*, 14:208.
3. Preface to 2nd ed. of *Catiline; HU*, 1:120.
4. Christopher Due, *Erindringer fra Henrik Ibsens ungdomsaar* (Copenhagen, 1909), 38–40; Due, "Ibsen's Early Youth," 37.
5. Sallust, *The War with Catiline*, trans. J. C. Rolfe (London and New York, 1921), ch. 5.
6. *HU*, 1:81, 88.
7. Ibid., 1:30.
8. Ibid., 1:114.
9. Hjalmar Hjorth Boyesen, *A Commentary on the Works of Henrik Ibsen* (New York and London, 1894), 21 (Boyesen's translation slightly revised); Bjørnson, "Gamle Heltberg," in *Samlede digter-verker*, vol. 8 (Christiania, 1920), 337.
10. See Ivo de Figueiredo, *Henrik Ibsen: Mennesket* (Oslo 2006), 112–13.
11. See *OC*, 2:32–36.
12. Ibid., 1:xxxi.
13. See Oddvar Bjørklund, *Marcus Thrane: Sosialistleder i et u-land* (Oslo, 1970), 50–51, 110–11; *OC*, 1: introduction.
14. Bjørklund, *Marcus Thrane*, 169–76.
15. *HU*, 1:321, 15:11.
16. *OC*, 2:131.
17. Jæger, *Ibsen*, 72–73.
18. *OC*, 2:120.
19. Jæger, *Ibsen*, 66–67.
20. *HU*, 14:143–47; vol. 21, pt. 1, xxix.
21. Einar Østvedt, *Et dukkehjem: Forspillet, skuespillet, etterspillet* (Skien, 1976), 46.
22. *HU*, 15:52.
23. These figures are uncertain. Perhaps as many as 195 copies survived. See *HI skrifter:* "Inledninger og kommentarer," 1:43–44.
24. Preface to 2nd ed. of *Catiline; HI skrifter*, 1:132.

THE FAILURE

1. Letter to Herman Laading, March 10, 1875; *HI skrifter,* 13:235.
2. Gösta M. Bergman, *Regi och spelstil under Gustaf Lagerbjelkes tid vid Kungl. teatern* (Stockholm, 1946), 174–75.
3. Gösta M. Bergman, *Lighting in the Theatre* (Stockholm and Totowa, NJ, 1977), 252–58; Terence Rees, *Theatre Lighting in the Age of Gas* (London, 1978), 6–19.
4. Roderick Rudler, "Ibsens teatergjerning i Bergen," in *Drama och teater,* ed. Egil Törnqvist (Stockholm, 1968), 60–61.
5. For an example of Ibsen as stage manager (*scen-instruktør*), see Laurence Senelick, ed., *National Theatre in Northern and Eastern Europe, 1746–1900* (Cambridge, 1991), 152–53.
6. See *The Oxford Ibsen,* ed. James Walter McFarlane, vol. 1 (London, 1970), 640–46.
7. John Paulsen, *Samliv med Ibsen: Nye erindringer og skitser* (Copenhagen and Christiania, 1906), 120. According to Suzannah Ibsen, Ibsen said Paulsen's memoirs would be "an invaluable source for later literary scholars, and, in that regard, classic" (*HU,* 19: 227).
8. Quoted in *Henrik Ibsens episke Brand,* ed. Karl Larsen (Copenhagen and Christiania, 1907), 44.
9. Ibsen spelled the name Susanna. See *HI skrifter: Brev,* 12:197.
10. *Oxford Ibsen,* 1:601–2; *HU,* 15:47–49.
11. *HU,* 15:43–46.
12. Ibid., 15:130.
13. For a list of plays staged at the Bergen theater between 1852 and 1857, see *Oxford Ibsen,* 1:647–48.
14. Koht, *Henrik Ibsen,* 1:74.
15. On *Lady Inger:* Bjørn Hemmer, "Fru Inger til Østeraad," *Ibsen-årbok* (1972), 93–108; Hjalmar Brendel, *Etiska motiv i Henrik Ibsens dramatiske ditkning* (Stockholm, 1941), 171–72; Vasenius, *Henrik Ibsens dramatiske diktning,* 124 ff.
16. *Oxford Ibsen,* 1:369.
17. In 1870 Ibsen disowned *The Feast at Solhoug,* but by 1883 he had reversed himself. See letter to Peter Hansen, October 28, 1870, and the preface to the 2nd ed. of *The Feast at Solhoug.*
18. See Otto Lous Mohr, *Henrik Ibsen som maler* (Oslo, 1953), 39–43.
19. *HU,* 2:306.
20. John Paulsen, "'Aftnerne i Arbinsgade': Utklipp av et etterlatt bind erindringer," *Edda* 43 (1943), 37–38.
21. Koht, *Henrik Ibsen,* 1:124.
22. Ibid., 1:125.
23. Ibid.
24. Martin Schneekloth, quoted in Ivo de Figueiredo, *Henrik Ibsen: Mennesket* (Oslo, 2006), 326.
25. Gosse, *Henrik Ibsen,* 85.
26. *HU,* 14:400, 390.

27. Letter to Peter Hansen, October 28, 1870. Ibsen read Kierkegaard while in Grimstad. See Brian W. Downs, *Ibsen: The Intellectual Background* (Cambridge, 1946), 79. Also Koht, *Henrik Ibsen,* 1:32, 65.
28. *Either/Or,* in Kierkegaard, *Samlede Værker,* ed. A. B. Drachmann, J. L. Heiberg, and H. O. Lange (Copenhagen, 1962–64), 2:274.
29. Fr. Ording, *Henrik Ibsen: "Kærlighedens Komedie"* (Christiania, 1914), 54 ff.; P. G. La Chesnais, "Ibsen disciple de Kierkegaard," *Edda* 34 (1934), 355–410; Jørgen Haugan, *Henrik Ibsens metode* (Copenhagen, 1977), 40–44; Francis Bull in *HU,* 4:130–32; *HI skrifter,* 4k:73–76.
30. Bull, *Traditioner och minnen,* 170.
31. Bergliot Ibsen, *The Three Ibsens: Memories of Henrik Ibsen, Suzannah Ibsen and Sigurd Ibsen,* trans. Gerik Schjelderup (New York, 1952), 172.
32. Letter to Peter Hansen, October 28, 1870.
33. Bolette Sontum, "Personal Recollections of Ibsen," *Bookman* (New York) 37 (1913), 252.

GOD'S STEPCHILD

1. Boyesen, *Commentary on the Writings of Ibsen,* 42–43.
2. Astrid Sæther, *Suzannah, Fru Ibsen* (Copenhagen, 2008), 98.
3. A[dolf] E[dward] Zucker, *Ibsen, the Master Builder* (New York, 1929), 81, 296.
4. Bull, *Traditioner och minnen,* 162.
5. Paulsen, *Samliv med Ibsen: Nye erindringer,* 60.
6. Gerhard Gran, *Henrik Ibsen: Liv og Verker* (Christiania, 1918), 1:153.
7. "Björnstjerne Björnson," in August Strindberg, *Samlade skrifter,* ed. John Landquist, 55 vols. (Stockholm, 1912–21), 17:238–39.
8. Fr. Ording, *Henrik Ibsens vennekreds: Det lærde Holland* (Oslo, 1927), 4.
9. Ibid.
10. Letter to Ludvig Daae, November 20, 1888.
11. Chr. Collin, *Bjørnstjerne Bjornson: Hans Barndom og Ungdom,* 2nd rev. ed. (Christiania, 1923), 1:233.
12. *Bjørnstjerne Bjørnsons brevveksling med danske 1854–1874,* ed. Øyvind Anker, Francis Bull, and Torben Nielsen (Copenhagen, 1970–74), 1:167.
13. Frederik Schyberg, *Dansk Teaterkritik indtil 1914* (Copenhagen, 1937), 222.
14. Letter to Clemens Petersen, c. July 25, 1857; in Bjørnstjerne Bjørnson, *Gro-Tid: Brev fra Årene 1857–1870,* ed. Halvdan Koht (Christiania and Copenhagen, 1912), 1:13.
15. Ibid., 1:xxiv.
16. Christian Gierløff, *Bjornstjerne Bjørnson* (Oslo, 1932), 195–96.
17. Collin, *Bjørnson: Hans Barndom,* 2:54.
18. Letter to Bjørnson, April 2, 1867; *Bjørnsons brevveksling med danske 1854–1874,* 2:123.
19. On Petersen and Bjørnson: Kari Hamre, *Clemens Petersen og hans forhold til norsk litteratur i årene 1856–69* (Oslo, 1945), 7–24; Schyberg, *Dansk teaterkritik,* 220–31; Gierløff, *Bjørnson,* 120, 195–96.
20. Letter to Petersen, March 5, 1859; Bjørnson, *Gro-Tid,* 1:76–77.
21. *HU,* 5:48.

22. Collin, *Bjørnson: Hans Barndom,* 2:145.
23. Ann Margret Holmgren, *Björnstjerne Björnson: Diktaren, hövdingen, politikern, människan,* vol. 1 (Studentföreningen verdandis småskrifter, no. 248; Stockholm, 1921), 43.
24. *HU,* 5:89.
25. Ibid., 5:146.
26. Ibid., 5:147.
27. Ibid., 5:45.
28. Ibid., 5:47.

PURITY OF HEART

1. Ivo de Figueiredo, *Henrik Ibsen: Mennesket* (Oslo, 2006), 319.
2. *HU,* 14:283, 284.
3. Letter to Peter Hansen, October 28, 1870.
4. Letter to Bjørnson, c. April 20, 1864; *Bjørnsons brevveksling med danske 1854–1874,* 2:13.
5. *HU,* 14:367.
6. Letter of January 28, 1865; *HI skrifter,* 12:175–76.
7. Letter of December 3, 1865; ibid., 12:195.
8. Einar Østvedt, *Henrik Ibsen og la bella Italia* (Skien, 1965), 72, 99.
9. Dietrichson, *Svundne Tider,* 1:338.
10. Letter of December 3, 1865; *HI skrifter,* 12:195–96.
11. Speech in Copenhagen, April 1, 1898; *HU,* 15:414–15.
12. Letter to Bjørnson, September 16, 1864; *HI skrifter,* 12:170.
13. Letter to Bjørnson, January 28, 1865; ibid., 12:176–77.
14. Letter to Magdalene Thoresen, December 3, 1865; ibid., 12:195.
15. Letter to Peter Hansen, October 28, 1870; ibid., 12:428.
16. Ibid.
17. Letter to Bjørnson, September 12, 1865; ibid., 12:182.
18. Ibid., 11k:726.
19. *Brand,* trans. G. M. Gathorne-Hardy (London and Seattle, 1966), 87–88. Gathorne-Hardy's translation is used throughout except where noted.
20. *En literair Anmeldelse,* in *Samlede Værker,* 14:79.
21. *HI skrifter,* 5k:302–3. Cf. Ibsen's letter to Brandes, July 15, 1869.
22. *Jäsningstiden,* in *August Strindbergs samlade verk,* vol. 20, ed. Hans Lindström (Stockholm, 1989), 271.
23. Letter to Peter Hansen, October 28, 1870.
24. Letter to Bjørnson, September 12, 1865.
25. Matt. 17:5.
26. *The Collected Works of Henrik Ibsen,* ed. William Archer, 13 vols. (New York, 1906–12), vol. 3: *Brand,* trans. and introduced by C. H. Herford, 90; *HU,* 5:239.
27. Matt. 4:16.

PEER GYNT

1. Letter to Bjørnson, September 12, 1865.
2. Letter to Bjørnson, March 4, 1866.
3. Letter to Clemens Petersen, March 30, 1866; Bjørnson, *Gro-Tid,* 2:190, 192.
4. *HU,* 14:242.
5. *Norsk biografisk leksikon,* 2:630.
6. *HU,* 16:136–37.
7. *Breve fra Riksarkivar Birkeland (1848–1879),* ed. Fr. Ording (Christiania, 1920), 117–19.
8. Letter to Birkeland, June 30, 1872; *HU,* 17:49.
9. Ording, *Ibsen: "Kærlighedens Komedie,"* 33 ff.; Ording, *Ibsens vennekreds,* 238; Gerhard Gran, ed., *Nordmænd i det 19de aarhundrede,* vol. 1 (Christiania, 1914), 446–47. The editors of *HI skrifter,* 12:327, question the animosity of Riddervold.
10. See *Henrik Ibsens episke Brand,* 40 ff.; Ibsen, *Tyve brev fra Henrik Ibsen: Utgitt i faksimile med innledning og oplysninger av Wilhelm Munthe* (Oslo, 1932).
11. Letter to Peter Hansen, October 28, 1870.
12. *HU,* 6:138.
13. Ludwig Passarge, preface to *Peer Gynt,* 2nd ed. (Leipzig, 1887).
14. Because there are so many topical allusions in the play, Ibsen believed that of all his works, up to 1880, it was "the least likely to be understood outside Scandinavia." Letter to Passarge, May 19, 1880.
15. Although H. Logeman's *A Commentary, Critical and Explanatory on the Norwegian Text of Henrik Ibsen's Peer Gynt* (Westport, CT, 1970, reprint of 1917 original) is mainly a philological study of the play, it takes note of the political background, seeing Peer as representing the average Norwegian (e.g., 169–74).
16. Clara Bergsøe, *Magdalene Thoresen* (Copenhagen and Christiania, 1904), 3, 19.
17. *Bjørnsons brevveksling med danske 1854–1874,* 2:356, 360.

PEER GYNT MEETS HEGEL

1. Letter to Brandes, June 26, 1869.
2. A. L. Andrews, "Ibsen's *Peer Gynt* and Goethe's *Faust,*" *Journal of English and Germanic Philology* (1914), 13:238–46.
3. Letters to Frederik Hegel, June 9, 1866, and March 8, 1867.
4. *Concluding Unscientific Postscript,* trans. David F. Swenson and Walter Lowrie (Princeton, 1941), 122–23.
5. Letter to Brandes, June 26, 1869.
6. *Being and Nothingness,* quoted in Mary Warnock, *Existentialism* (Oxford, 1970), 126.
7. Østvedt, *Ibsen og la bella Italia,* 61; Øyvind Anker, "Ibsen og Den skandinaviske forening i Roma," *Edda* (1956).
8. *HU,* 6:132.
9. Ibid., 14:402.
10. Ibid., 14:404.

11. *The Phenomenology of Mind*, translated by J. B. Baillie, 2nd rev. ed. (London and New York, 1931), 366–67; Hegel, *Werke*, vol. 2 (Berlin, 1842), 249.
12. Hegel, *The Philosophy of Fine Art*, trans. F. P. B. Osmarston (London, 1920), 2:74.
13. On "System" as being Hegel's system of logic, see Kierkegaard, *Concluding Unscientific Postscript*, 97–99, 101–3, etc.
14. *HU*, 6:199.
15. vv. 11433–52.
16. *HU*, 6:226.
17. vv. 12009–12; trans. Albert G. Latham.
18. Letter to Passarge, June 16, 1880.
19. Letter to Peter Hansen, October 28, 1870.
20. Letter to Edmund Gosse, April 30, 1872.
21. Letter to Passarge, June 16, 1880.

FALLING OUT WITH BJØRNSON

1. *Norsk Folkeblad*, November 23, 1867.
2. Letter of November 18, 1867; *Gro-Tid*, 2:244–45.
3. Georg Brandes, *Samlede Skrifter* (Copenhagen, 1899–1910), 3:271.
4. *Fædrelandet*, April 2, 1863.
5. Ibid., April 2, 1864.
6. Hamre, *Petersen*, 117, 126.
7. Letter of December 4, 1865; *HU*, 16:21–22.
8. Letter of March 30, 1866; Hamre, *Petersen*, 160–61; Bjørnson, *Gro-Tid*, 2:189.
9. Letter of March 9, 1867; *HU*, 16:180–81.
10. *Fædrelandet*, November 30, 1867; "Clemens Petersen," in *Omkring "Peer Gynt,"* ed. Otto Hageberg (Oslo, 1967), 40–47.
11. Letter of December 9–10, 1867; *HU*, 16:198.
12. Letter to Petersen, March 30, 1866; *Gro-Tid*, 2:189–90.
13. Letters of May 12 and July 11, 1866: ibid., 2:193, 198.
14. Letter of December 9–10, 1867; *HU*, 16:198–201.
15. Letter of December 28, 1867; ibid., 16:202.
16. Letter to Petersen, March 30, 1866; *Gro-Tid*, 2:190.
17. Henning Fenger, "Bjørnson og Georg Brandes før det moderne gennembrud," *Edda* 51 (1964), 87.
18. On this philosophical debate, see Brandes, "Den danske Literatur efter 1870," in his *Samlede Skrifter*, 15:191 ff.
19. Nielsen began his career as a supporter of Hegel's philosophy, which he saw as the basis for a new era in theology. He subsequently won the friendship of Kierkegaard, who was prepared to allow Nielsen to edit his papers after his death. However, in 1849 Nielsen published a work that assailed the speculative philosophy by using Kierkegaard's arguments without giving him credit or citing sources, and that directly attacked Bishop Martensen when Kierkegaard only wanted to use an indirect attack. Even after being turned out, Nielsen remained an ardent admirer of Kierkegaard.

20. Adolf Falkman in his article on Ibsen in *Illustreret Tidende*, January 27 and February 3, 1867, quoted by Francis Bull in *HU*, 6:43.
21. Hamre, *Petersen*, 43–44, 186, 211.

FALLING IN WITH BRANDES

1. Brandes, *Levned*, vol. 1: *Barndom og første Ungdom* (Copenhagen and Christiania, 1905), 176–78.
2. Brandes, *Samlede Skrifter*, 13:13–14.
3. Ibid., 13:17–20.
4. Letter of April 25, 1866; *HI skrifter*, 12:216–23.
5. Letter of June 26, 1869; *HU*, 16:249.
6. Brandes, *Levned*, vol. 3: *Snevringer og Horizonter* (Copenhagen and Christiania, 1908), 123.
7. Fr. G. Knudtzon, *Ungdomsdage* (*Memoirer og Breve*), ed. Julius Clausen and P. Fr. Rist, vol. 49 (Copenhagen, 1927), 164. Knudtzon gives the impression that Ibsen first learned about the controversy from him in 1867. This is demonstrably untrue, since Brandes and Ibsen were in contact with each other from April 1866. But Ibsen would have been eager to hear about the debate and probably pretended ignorance in order to draw out his visitor.
8. Letter of November 11, 1867; *Gro-Tid*, 2:242.
9. Letter to J. Collin, October 21, 1867; *HU*, 16:193.
10. Letter to Rudolf Schmidt, February 20, 1866; *Gro-Tid*, 2:185.
11. Quoted in Georg og Edv. Brandes, *Brevveksling med nordiske Forfattere og Videnskabsmænd*, ed. Morten Borup (Copenhagen, 1939–42), 4:xii. Petersen provided Bjørnson with the material used in this anonymous attack on Brandes; see Fenger, "Bjørnson og Georg Brandes," 101.
12. Letter to Ibsen, December 16, 1867; *Gro-Tid*, 2:261–66.
13. Letter of December 28, 1867; *HU*, 16:202.
14. See Bjørnson's letter to Fredrik Bætzmann, May 18, 1862, in "Brev fra Bjørnstjerne Bjørnson," *Edda* 32 (1932), 440.
15. For a summary of Bjørnson's thoughts at this time, see Jean Lescoffier, *Bjørnson, la seconde jeunesse* (Paris, 1932), especially 40, 60–62, 100–101.
16. Ording, *Ibsens vennekreds*, 33–36, 140 ff.
17. Letter of October 5, 1864; *Gro-Tid*, 2:142.
18. Letter of July 11, 1866; ibid., 2:199.
19. Hamre, *Petersen*, 198–201.
20. Letter to Bjørnson, December 9–10, 1867; *HU*, 16:201.
21. Ibid., 16:200–201.
22. Letter to Ibsen, December 16, 1867; *Gro-Tid*, 2:261.
23. *HU*, 16:199.
24. Letter to Ibsen, December 16, 1867; *Gro-Tid*, 2:261.
25. Letter to Petersen, March 5, 1859; ibid., 1:76–77.
26. Letter to Lina Bruun, August 15, 1870; ibid., 2:364.

27. See *OC*, 5:55 and 9:478, and Ording, *Ibsens vennekreds*, 227–29.
28. John Paulsen, *Samliv med Ibsen: Anden samling* (Copenhagen and Christiania, 1913), 13. Paulsen does not mention the date, but it may be conjectured on the basis of the following facts: (1) Bjørnson's remark was made in Denmark, and he was in Denmark in the fall and winter of 1867–68. (2) His remark was made at about the same time that Ibsen received Bjørnson's warm and gracious letter in the latter part of December 1867. (3) Ibsen said he received full confirmation of the incident in the summer of 1869, quite probably from Løkke, whom he spoke to at that time. The "full confirmation" implies that he had heard about the incident earlier. Halvdan Koht, in *Henrik Ibsen*, 2:19, also traces the cause of the rupture between Ibsen and Bjørnson to December 1867. There is further confirmation in the fact that Ibsen in February 1868 was planning a new play; evidently *The League of Youth* was taking shape in his mind.
29. Letter to Schmidt, December 27, 1869; *HU*, 16:265.
30. Letter to Brandes, June 26, 1869; ibid., 16:250.
31. *OC*, 9:19–20.
32. Letter to Bjørnson, December 9–10, 1867; *HU*, 16:199–200.
33. Erik Lie, *Erindringer fra et dikterhjem* (Oslo, 1928), 73.
34. 2:364.

THE LEAGUE OF YOUTH

1. December 16, 1867; *Gro-Tid*, 2:264.
2. Letter to Hegel, October 31, 1868; *HU*, 16:219. Brandes's book was published in the spring of 1868.
3. Letter to Hegel, December 22, 1868; ibid., 16:222–23.
4. Brandes had written his "Laeren om det Komiske" in the spring of 1866 in applying for a grant at the University of Copenhagen, and Ibsen heard about it at the time Brandes was working on it (letter to Hegel, October 31, 1868; ibid., 16:219). It was not published, however, until two years later, when he included the material in his *Aesthetic Studies* (Brandes, *Samlede Skrifter*, 12:99–141). His point of departure in analyzing comedy was a passage in Kierkegaard's *Philosophical Fragments* on the contradiction inherent in the human being, its two natures as the source of tension giving rise to wonder (*Samlede Værker*, 6:79–80). Applying this idea to the drama, Brandes came up with the commonplace that the essence of comedy lay in people and things being taken for their opposites: the coward appears as the braggart warrior and a graceless speech is greeted as beautiful.
5. Letter of June 26, 1869; *HU*, 16:249. The quote is from Holberg's *Jacob von Thyboe, or The Braggart Soldier*, act 2, scene 1.
6. "My next work will probably be a play for the theater [i.e., not a closet drama], and I hope it will not be long before I begin to work at it seriously" (letter to Hegel, February 24, 1868; *HU*, 16:206). "I have begun a new work that I hope to complete [this summer]" (letter to Bravo, June 22–25, 1868; ibid., 16:212). "My new drama (written for the stage and completely realistic . . .) is occupying all my thoughts" (letter to Hegel, August 20, 1868; ibid., 16:214–15). "I have been wrestling with it all summer without writing

anything down. Now the whole outline is finished and on paper" (letter to Hegel, October 31, 1868; ibid., 16:219). "In the autumn of 1868 when I moved from Italy to Dresden, I brought with me the outline of *The League of Youth* and wrote the play during the winter" (letter to Julius Hoffory, February 26, 1888; ibid., 18:194).

7. Letter to Hegel, October 31, 1868; ibid., 16:219.
8. The Norwegian constitution of 1814 stipulated that the privilege to vote (franchise) was granted to men who (1) were twenty-five years of age or older, (2) had resided in Norway for at least five years, and (3) were or had been civil servants, or had owned or leased registered land for at least five years, or were registered burghers or owned town property valued at no less than three hundred rigsdalers. It has been estimated that 45 percent of the male population over twenty-five years of age was entitled to vote in 1814. This was a remarkably high figure compared with that for other European countries at the time. (Stein Kuhnle, "Stemmeretten i 1814," *Historisk tidsskrift* 4 [1972], 373–90.)
9. J. E. Sars, *Norges politiske Historie 1815–1885* (Christiania, n.d.), 574–75.
10. Gustav Storm, "Norges politiske historie i det nittende aarhundrede," in *Norge 1814–1914: Tekst og billeder av norske forfattere og kunstnere*, ed. W. C. Brøgger et al. (Christiania, 1914), 1:36.
11. See Fredrik Stang, "Friele," *Samtiden* 28 (1917), 81–96, and Gierløff, *Bjørnson*, 166–69.
12. Søren Jaabæk consistently voted in the Storting as if the only aim of government was to reduce spending. His concern about Norwegian art and culture was so deficient that his taste was said to be entirely in his mouth. He had led the opposition to a national subvention for the Norwegian Theater in Bergen, had refused government support for the Latin schools while extending it to the people's schools, and had been the only legislator during the five-minute discussion on the bill authorizing an author's stipend to Ibsen to raise his voice against it.
13. Bjørnson, *Artikler og Taler*, ed. Chr. Collin and H. Eitrem (Christiania, 1912), 1:322.
14. The possible direct influence of Scribe's well-made plays on *The League of Youth* has been studied by William Archer, Henning Fenger, and Maurice Gravier. Archer ("Ibsen's Apprenticeship," *Fortnightly Review*, n.s., 75 [January 1904], 35) notes that the whole intrigue of the letters that makes rich capital sport in the fourth and fifth acts is a highly elaborated version of the letter incident in Scribe's *Mon Etoile*, which was staged in Bergen in 1855 while Ibsen was employed there. Archer also discusses Ibsen's use of quid pro quos and other devices of the well-made play (*Collected Works of Ibsen*, 6:xii–xiii). Fenger ("Det veldrejede og mondæne Teater," in *Teatrets Historie*, ed. Christian Ludvigsen and Stephan Kehler [Copenhagen, 1962], 236–38) provides an expert analysis of Ibsen's plot, showing its intimate relation to the Scribean well-made play. Fenger mentions Scribe's *La Camaraderie* (1837) in connection with the vote-getting plot, as does Gravier (*Ibsen* [Paris, 1973], 118). In both Ibsen's play and Scribe's a lawyer is the social climber; in both an election provides the business of the play; and in both the hero makes his way upward in spite of himself through the intrigues of a coterie. In Scribe's play the coterie is known as Jeune-France; in Ibsen's play, the League of Youth stands for Young Norway. The similarities appear too numerous to be dismissed as coincidences. Yet everything in Ibsen's play came from his observation of the Norwegian scene. In looking for comic material that would suit his purposes he may have recalled

or accidentally come upon Scribe's *Camaraderie* and been struck by its applicability to the Norwegian liberals. However, he spent the whole summer of 1868 unsuccessfully wrestling with ideas, and not until the Storting convened in October and Bjørnson began electioneering was Ibsen able to outline the plot.

15. Henrik Jæger, *Illustreret norsk Literaturhistorie* (Christiania, 1896), 2:667–68.
16. See Erik Bøgh's review of the 1876 production in Copenhagen of *The League of Youth*, in *Udvalgte Feuilletoner ("Dit og Dat") fra 1876* (Copenhagen, 1877), 289–92.
17. Letter to Lorentz Dietrichson, June 19, 1869; *HU*, 16:247. See also letter to J. P. Andresen, February 10, 1870; ibid., 16:274–75.
18. See Ibsen, *Efterladte Skrifter*, ed. Halvdan Koht and Julius Elias (Christiania and Copenhagen, 1909), 1:lxxix and 3:424; Koht, *Henrik Ibsen*, 2:20; Koht in *HU*, 6:343–44. Ibsen treated Lundestad less harshly than the other politicians because Ueland was a supporter of the union with Sweden. As a member of the Second Committee on Review of the Union Pact (Unionrevisionskommitten), he signed the agreement for a new pact; this earned him the scorn of the liberals. Also, Ibsen's friend Michael Birkeland was in sympathy with Ueland's policies (*OC*, 5:51). In his radical youth, Ibsen had satirized Ueland in the political squib *Norma* (1851).
19. *HU*, 6:421.
20. "Brev fra Bjørnstjerne Bjørnson," 530–31.
21. *Breve fra Riksarkivar Birkeland*, 191. Cf. letter from Bjørnson to Schmidt, October 23, 1869, in *Bjørnsons brevveksling med danske 1854–1874*, 2:287.
22. As for Ibsen's animosity toward Lie and his associates, see the letters to Schmidt, December 27, 1869, and to Michael Birkeland, June 30, 1872; *HU*, 16:264–65 and 17:48. Also Bjørnson's letter to Lina Bruun, August 15, 1870; *Gro-Tid*, 2:364. Ibsen had already caricatured Lie in *Peer Gynt*, as Peer the international capitalist and war profiteer in the opening scene of act four.
23. "Richter," *Norsk biografisk leksikon.*
24. Letter of August 8, 1869. In *Tidens Tegn*, March 7, 1931; quoted in *OC*, 9:24. Bjørnson recognized himself in certain manners of expression and in scenes like that in which Stensgaard leaps up on a table to address the throng; ibid., and Bjørnson's letter to Schmidt, December 27, 1869, quoted in Lescoffier, *Bjørnson*, 95.
25. Gierløff, *Bjørnson*, 319.
26. See Bøgh, *Udvalgte Feuilletoner*, 292.
27. Letter to Schmidt, October 27, 1869; *Bjørnsons brevveksling med danske 1854–1874*, 2:289.
28. Holmgren, *Bjornstjerne Björnson*, nos. 248–49, 2:12; Koht, *Henrik Ibsen*, 1:235–36.
29. *Ibsen*, 213–14.
30. E.g., Jæger, ibid., 213.
31. *Skrifter i Urval*, 9:191, quoted in *OC*, 9:36.
32. Letter to Lina Bruun, August 15, 1870; *Gro-Tid*, 2:363. Lescoffier in *Bjørnson*, 95, names Sverdrup as one of the models.
33. That Stensgaard's career was based in part on Bagger's was originally propounded by J. Brunsvig in *Fremskidt* (Skien), March 17, 1928; but as early as 1869 the satiric journal *Vikingen* (October 30) had noted that Ibsen had used people in Skien as models (*OC*,

9:23–24). Further discussion of Bagger's role in *The League of Youth* may be found in Halvdar Koht, *HU*, 6:344–45; Einar Østvedt, *Herman Bagger som redaktør of politiker* (Skien, 1932), 116–24; *OC*, 9:15–16; Mosfjeld, *Ibsen og Skien*, 85, 248–53; Brunsvig, *Henrik Ibsens barndom og ungdom og fødebyen i hans diktning* (Skien, 1952), 14–33; Koht, *Henrik Ibsen*, 2:16; and Østvedt, "Henrik Ibsen, politikken og staten," *Ibsen-årbok* (1954), 111–12.

34. Koht, *Efterladte Skrifter*, 1:lxxiv, and Koht, *HU*, 6:346. The fullest discussion of the resemblances between Hejre and Knud Ibsen is in Mosfjeld, *Ibsen og Skien*, 66, 70–71, 220–26 passim. Other models for Hejre have been suggested. Gerhard Jynge, drawing on old family reminiscences, said the merchant Jan Vibe was Ibsen's model (see Østvedt, *Ibsen: Barndom*, 212, quoting Jynge in *Tidens Tegn* [1928], no. 66). It should be noted that *vibe* means lapwing and *hejre* means heron. Mosfjeld also names as possible models Andreas Blom, a distant relation of Ibsen's (223), and an odd character named Hesler (225). As Mosfjeld remarks, Ibsen generally formed his characters out of his observations of several models. But "Daniel Hejre's history, character, and personality have undoubtedly had their origin in Knud Ibsen" (226). It has been suggested by Fredrik Stang ("Friele," 95) and Lescoffier (*Bjørnson*, 53) that a bit of Christian Friele, the editor of *Morgenbladet*, was to be found in Hejre. Possibly Friele figured in Ibsen's original plans and was replaced by Knud Ibsen when Skien became the setting for the political satire.
35. Bull, *Traditioner och minnen*, 243–44.
36. Mosfjeld, *Ibsen og Skien*, 223. Like Løvenskiold, Chamberlain Brattsberg resided mostly in Stockholm in his younger days (ibid., 250).
37. Jæger, *Illustreret norsk Literaturhistorie*, 2:666.
38. Letter to Peter Hansen, October 28, 1870; *HU*, 16:318.
39. The name Fjeldbo retains the basic sense of Birkeland, both conveying the idea of one who lives in the highlands (Koht, *Henrik Ibsen*, 2:19). To understand why Ibsen gave an esthete and city dweller the name Fjeldbo, one should read the poem "Paa Vidderne." This poem lends weight to the suggestion made by C. S. Nygaard (*Henrik Ibsen i hundredaaret for hans fødsel* [Copenhagen, 1928], 49) that Ibsen divided himself between Stensgaard and Fjeldbo. Birkeland coined the expression "dragge paa vidderne" ("roam the open spaces, the uplands"), meaning serve humanity but with aloofness. Koht (*HU*, 6:342) says that Stensgaard was first named Stenborg (stone fortress) in order to convey ironically what the man was not. Feeling that the name was too obviously satirical, Ibsen neutralized it to Stensgaard (stone house). But Stenborg would have been no more obvious and satirical than certain other names in the play. It is more likely that the name was changed to accentuate the difference between Fjeldbo and Stensgaard.
40. *HU*, 6:399.
41. *HU*, 6:471.
42. Ibid.

PARTICULAR INTERESTS

1. *Aftenbladet* (Christiania), July 27, 1857, quoted in *Efterladte Skrifter,* 1:lxxiii–lxxiv, where the editorial in question is ascribed to Ditmar Meidell.
2. Letter to Markus Grønvold, September 3, 1877; *HU,* 17:269.
3. Erich Eyck, *Bismarck und das deutsche Reich* (Erlenbach-Zürich, 1955), 2:268–69.
4. Letter to Hansen, October 28, 1870; *HU,* 16:318–19.
5. *Collected Works of Ibsen,* 6:xv.
6. Julius Lange in a letter to Brandes, June 10, 1868, in Brandes, *Samlede Skrifter,* 14:518.
7. Letter to Hegel, September 25, 1868; *Gro-Tid,* 2:288–89.
8. Schyberg, *Dansk Teaterkritik,* 255.
9. Letter to Magdalene Thoresen, November 19, 1867, in *Breve fra og til Johanne Luise Heiberg,* ed. Just Rahbek (Copenhagen, 1955), 2:8.
10. Gierløff, *Bjørnson,* 110, 123.
11. Hjalmar Hjorth Boyesen, *Essays on Scandinavian Literature* (New York, 1895), 10.
12. *Levned: Barndom,* 147.
13. Frederik Nutzhorn in a letter to Brandes, quoted in Fenger, "Bjørnson og Georg Brandes," 88.
14. Johanne Luise Heiberg, quoted in Holm Hansen, "Af 'Hvad jeg oplevede,'" *Tilskueren* (Copenhagen; November 1909), 389.
15. Letter to A. Linde, June 15, 1869; *HU,* 16:243.
16. Ibid., 16:227.
17. February 25, 1869; in *Gro-Tid,* 2:298.
18. Henning Fenger, *Den unge Brandes* (Copenhagen, 1957), 132.
19. *Bjørnsons brevveksling med danske 1854–1874,* 2:227.
20. Letter to Schmidt, March 17, 1869; ibid., 2:230.
21. Letter to Alexander Kielland, November 25, 1884; Bjørnson, *Kamp-liv: Brev fra årene 1879–1884,* vol. 2 (Oslo, 1932), 284.
22. Letter to Hegel, April 7, 1869.
23. Letters of March 17 and 18, 1869; *Gro-Tid,* 2:302–3.
24. Letter of July 15, 1869; *HU,* 16:251.
25. Letter of March 24, 1869; *Gro-Tid,* 2:305.
26. Letter to E. Stjernström, March 19, 1869; *Bjørnstjerne Bjørnsons brevveksling med svenske 1858–1909,* ed. Øyvind Anker, Francis Bull, and Örjan Lindberger (Oslo and Stockholm, 1960–61), 1:43.
27. Letter to Hørup, January 22, 1892, in *Bjørnstjerne Bjørnsons brevveksling med danske 1875–1910,* ed. Øyvind Anker, Francis Bull, and Torben Nielsen (Copenhagen and Oslo, 1953), 2:97.

OLD DEBTS REPAID

1. Robert Neiiendam, *Det Kongelige Teaters Historie,* vol. 1 (Copenhagen, 1921), 147.
2. *Illustreret Tidende,* February 27, 1870.
3. OC, 9:47–48.

4. Neiiendam, *Kongelige Teaters Historie*, 53.
5. Chr. K. F. Molbech, *Fra Danaidernes Kar* (Copenhagen, 1873), 442.
6. See Gertrud Nordström, "Den svenska urpremiären på Ibsens De ungas förbund 1869," in G. M. Bergman and Niklas Brunius, eds., *Dramaten 175 år: Studier i svensk scenkonst* (Stockholm, 1963), 241 ff.; and Georg Nordensvan, *Svensk teater och svenska skådespelare från Gustav III till våra dagar* (Stockholm, 1917–18), 2:258.
7. *Samlede Skrifter*, 13:379.
8. Quoted in Nordensvan, *Svensk teater*, 258–59.
9. Dietrichson, *Svundne Tider*, vol. 3: *Rom og Stockholm: 1862–1872* (Christiania, 1901), 328–29.
10. Molbech, *Fra Danaidernes Kar*, 444, 449.
11. Lescoffier, *Bjørnson*, 80; Ording, *Ibsens vennekreds*, 231.
12. Lescoffier, *Bjørnson*, 52.
13. Ording, *Ibsens vennekreds*, 231.
14. Lescoffier, *Bjørnson*, 53.
15. Letter to Richter, June 23, 1868; "Brev fra Bjørnstjerne Bjørnson," 529.
16. Jæger, *Ibsen*, 219–20; Jæger, *Illustreret norsk Literaturhistorie*, 2:669–70; and Reidar A. Marum, *Teaterslag og pipekonserter* (Oslo, 1944), 105–6. On the number of student demonstrators: Gierløff, *Bjørnson*, 232; and *OC*, 9:38, citing Peter Rosenkrantz Johnsen, *Passiar*, 47–55, and Kristofer Kristofersen, *Dagbladet* (Christiania), September 22, 1889. The account of the theater demonstration that Suzannah Ibsen gives in her letter to her husband, October 29, 1869 (see Bergliot Ibsen, *De tre*, 44), is somewhat garbled. She was residing in Dresden at the time and got her information secondhand.
17. Marum, *Teaterslag*, 1–11.
18. "Bifalds og Mishags-Yttringer i Theatret," *Prosaiske Skrifter* (Copenhagen, 1861), 6:310–14.
19. Whistling demonstrations in Norwegian theaters, beginning in 1856, were usually anti-Danish protests. See Ann Schmiesing, "The Christiania Theater and Norwegian Nationalism," *Scandinavian Studies* 76 (2004), 317–40.
20. Letter to Hegel, December 14, 1869; *HU*, 16:260.
21. Erik Lie, *Erindringer*, 73.
22. Letter of September 20, 1869; *Gro-Tid*, 2:325–26.
23. Letter of October 24, 1869; "Brev fra Bjørnstjerne Bjørnson," 537.
24. *HU*, 16:265.
25. Letter to Bjørnson, February 2, 1870; *Bjørnsons brevveksling med danske 1854–1874*, 3:4.
26. Letter of December 14, 1869; *HU*, 16:260.
27. Letter of April 20, 1870; *Gro-Tid*, 2:355–56.
28. Letter to Bjørnson, December 9, 1867; *HU*, 16:199.
29. Letter of November 30, 1869; *Gro-Tid*, 2:334.
30. Marum, *Teaterslag*, 108.
31. Gierløff, *Bjørnson*, 232.
32. Lescoffier, *Bjørnson*, 99.
33. *HU*, 6:474.
34. Letter to Bjørnson, December 28, 1867; *HU*, 16:203.

35. Speech to Norwegian students, September 10, 1874; ibid., 15:394.
36. Letter of September 18, 1867; *Gro-Tid,* 1:lxvii.
37. Letter to Hegel, October 31, 1868; *HU,* 16:219.
38. Letter of July 15, 1869; ibid., 16:253.

IBSEN IN COMMAND

1. Örjan Lindberger, "Ibsen och två svenska teaterchefer," *Nordisk tidskrift för vetenskap, konst och industri* 40 (1964), 377.
2. Hans Midbøe, *Streiflys over Ibsen og andre studier* (Oslo, 1960), 151.
3. *HU,* 14:409.
4. Letter to K. Janson, December 15, 1869; *Gro-Tid,* 2:341–42.
5. *Breve fra Riksarkivar Birkeland,* 190.
6. Letter to Magdalene Thoresen, May 29, 1870.
7. Letter to Lina Bruun, August 15, 1870; *Gro-Tid,* 2:363.
8. Letter to Bjørnson, December 28, 1867.
9. Letter to A. Klubien, September 9, 1870.
10. Letter to Ohan Demirgian, November 23, 1870.
11. Letter to Hegel, May 9, 1871.
12. Geir Kjetsaa, "Henrik Ibsen og Oscar von Knorring," *Ibsen-årbok* (1977), 22–45; Sven Eriksson, *Carl XV* (Stockholm, 1954), 270–371.
13. Letter to C. C. Hall, February 27, 1871.
14. Letter to Magdalene Thoresen, October 19, 1869; *Breve fra og til Johanne Luise Heiberg,* 2:43.
15. Letter to Gotfred and Margrete Rode, September 20, 1871; Bjørnson, *Brytnings-år: Brev fra årene 1871–1878,* ed. Halvdan Koht (Christiania, 1921), 1:30. Letter to Rodes, May 17, 1871; ibid., 16.
16. Ibid.
17. Letter to Hegel, May 5, 1870.
18. Letters to J. P. Andresen, February 10 and May 12, 1870.
19. Letter to Andresen, May 12, 1870; letter to Magdalene Thoresen, May 29, 1870.
20. Bjørnson, *Artikler og Taler,* 1:360–65.
21. Gierløff, *Bjørnson,* 257.
22. Peter Augustinus, *Signalfejden: Bjørnson og Danmark omkring 1870* (Aarhus and Copenhagen, 1914), 14. On the Signal Controversy, see Halvdan Koht, introduction to Bjørnson, *Brytnings-år,* 1:xxxv–xlv.
23. *HU,* 14:435.
24. Theodor Caspari, *Fra mine unge aar* (Oslo, 1929), 191–92.
25. *HI skrifter,* 14k:783.
26. *HU,* 14:419.
27. Paulsen, "'Afterne i Arbinsgade,'" 56.
28. *HU,* 15:353.
29. Ibid., 15:352–54.
30. Letter to P. F. Siebold, March 6, 1872; ibid., 17:24.

31. *HI skrifter,* 13:72; *vide* commentary, 13k:187–88. See Lothar, *Ibsen,* 89.
32. Letter to Brandes, April 30, 1873; *HU,* 17:86.
33. Letter to Johan Herman Thoresen, September 27, 1872; *HU,* 17:58.
34. Letter to Magdalene Thoresen, March 31, 1868; ibid., 16:208.
35. Dietrichson, *Svundne Tider,* 1:346–47; Kristian Magnus Kommandantvold, *Ibsen og Sverige* (Oslo, 1956), 12.
36. Letter to Fru Bjørnson, May 14, 1871; Bjørnson, *Breve til Karoline 1858–1907,* ed. D. B. Santreau (Oslo, 1957), 174.
37. Gustaf af Geijerstam, quoted in David Gedin, *Fältets herrar: Framväxten av en modern författarroll* (Stockholm, 2004), 5.
38. Letter to Laura Petersen, June 11, 1870; *HI skrifter,* 12:412.
39. *HU,* 14:350.
40. See Peter Vinten-Johansen, "Johan Ludvig Heiberg's Political and Social Thought," (PhD diss., Yale University, 1975), 103 ff. For a sampling of Heiberg's political views, see his *Prosaiske Skrifter* (Copenhagen, 1861–62), 1:19–20, 276–81; 4:401; 5:97–107, 215–16, 394; 6:267; 10:273 ff., 336, 347; 11:502.
41. Johanne Luise Heiberg, *Et Liv gjenoplevet i Erindringen,* 4th ed., rev. by Aage Friis et al. (Copenhagen, 1944), 4:428.
42. Knudtzon, *Ungdomsdage,* 214.
43. Letter to Lorange, April 4, 1872; *Breve fra Riksarkivar Birkeland,* 201.
44. *Henrik Ibsens sämtliche Werke in deutscher Sprache,* ed. Georg Brandes, Julius Elias, and Paul Schlenther (Berlin, n.d.), 10:465.
45. Letter to Birkeland, April 9, 1872; *HU,* 17:33.
46. Letter to Johan Herman Thoresen, September 27, 1872; ibid., 17:58.
47. "Ved Tusenårs-Feste" ("For the Millennial Festival"); *ibid.,* 14:454.
48. Letter to Hegel, February 16, 1871.
49. See F. U. Wrangel, *Minnen från konstnärkretsarna och författarvärlden* (Stockholm, 1925), 218–19. Knudtzon in *Ungdomsdage,* 109–11, 162, describes the change in Ibsen's appearance. The new cut of his beard can be seen in photographs reproduced in Francis Bull, *Henrik Ibsens Peer Gynt* (Oslo, 1947), 55, 58, 62. The overnight transformation in Ibsen that Emil von Quanten describes as occurring in 1864 was, if accurately remembered, only a foretaste of what was to come; see Erik Lie, *Erindringer,* 24–26.
50. Nordensvan, *Svensk teater,* 2:259.

THOSE LITTLE DEVILS

1. Garborg, quoted in Koht, *Henrik Ibsen,* 2:66.
2. Letters of February 17 and May 18, 1871. Herleiv Dahl, *Bergmannen og byggmesteren* (Oslo, 1958), provides the fullest discussion of the poems. The closest approximation to an annotated edition of the poems (prior to *HI skrifter*) is in *OC,* vols. 1, 2, 3, 5, 9 passim. Deserving special mention are the seminal articles by Andrew Runni Anderson, "Studies in Ibsen. I. The Poetic Themes in Ibsen's I Billedgalleriet; II. The Chronology and Composition of the Digte," *Scandinavian Studies* 2 (1914–16), 127–64. Anderson argued that the 1871 arrangement of the poems is significant and that the collection

should be regarded as a work belonging to 1870–71 rather than as an assemblage of poems from various periods. Other important commentaries: Paul Schlenther in *Ibsens sämtliche Werke*, 1:xix ff.; Roman Woerner, *Henrik Ibsen* (Munich, 1900–1910), 1:311–66; Johannes Mayrhofer, *Henrik Ibsen und seine Werke* (Trier, n.d. [1911]), 162–85; Kr. Elster, "Ibsens digte," in his *Fra tid til anden* (Christiania, 1920); Didrik Arup Seip, introduction to the poems in the Centennial Edition of Ibsen's works, *HU*, 14:9–41; and Daniel Haakonsen, "Henrik Ibsens lyrikk," *Edda* (1950), 135–53.

3. *HU*, 19:217.
4. John Paulsen, *Nye erindringer* (Copenhagen, 1901), says the poem is concerned with the death of Christopher Bruun's sister Thea. She died at the age of twenty-four after having exhausted herself caring for her tubercular brother (not Christopher). Further discussion is in Paulus Svendsen, "Henrik Ibsen's 'Borte,'" *Edda* (1957), 55–58, and H. Dahl, *Bergmannen*, 197–98.
5. *HU*, 14:378.
6. *Ibsen's Poems*, trans. John Northam (Oslo, 1986), 71.
7. Ibid., 72.
8. *HU*, 14:433.
9. Letter to Bjørnson, September 12, 1865.

ANTI-BRAND

1. *Ad egne Veje* (Copenhagen, 1884), 265–83.
2. Erich Eyck, *Bismarck and the German Empire* (London, 1950), 159.
3. "A Balloon Letter to a Swedish Lady," *HU*, 14:420.
4. John Paulsen, *Mine Erindringer* (Copenhagen, 1900), 162.
5. Letter to Brandes, September 24, 1871.
6. Letter to Birkeland, October 10, 1871.
7. *HU*, 5:321.
8. Letter to Bjørnson, March 23, 1884.
9. Letter to Brandes, February 17, 1871.
10. *HU*, 14:404–5.
11. Letter to Bjørnson, January 28, 1865; *HI skrifter*, 12:176.
12. Letter to Brandes, February 17, 1871.
13. Ibid. The idea that liberty is nothing but the continuing struggle for liberties may have come Ibsen's way from J. L. Heiberg's essay "On Human Freedom," according to La Chesnais in *OC*, 3:245–46 and 5:115. Erik Kihlman (*Ur Ibsen-dramatikens idéhistoria* [Helsingfors, 1921], 137 ff.) thinks Ibsen read this essay in 1850–51 without reading it thoroughly. But this would not have prevented him from reading it again and more thoroughly in the 1860s.
14. Letter to Brandes, February 17, 1871.
15. Letter to Brandes, September 24, 1871.
16. Letter to Brandes, December 20, 1870.
17. Letter to Brandes, February 17, 1871.
18. Ibid.

19. Ibid.
20. Ibid.
21. The Stirner quotations, with minor changes, are from John Carroll's translation, *The Ego and His Own* (New York, 1971). Not until 1902 did the well-read Brandes notice the influence of Stirner on Ibsen (Brandes, *Samlede Skrifter*, 17:315). P. W. K. Paterson, *The Nihilist Egoist: Max Stirner* (London and New York, 1971), 313, says Ibsen was "certainly" familiar with the ideas of Stirner but offers no evidence.
22. Letter to Brandes, April 4, 1872.
23. Letter to Brandes, December 20, 1870.
24. Alfred Austin, review of Matthew Arnold's poetry in *Temple Bar* (August 1869). Reprinted in Matthew Arnold, *The Poetry: The Critical Heritage*, ed. Carl Dawson (London and Boston, 1973), 207–8.
25. Irgens Hansen in *Dagbladet*, 1888, no. 86, quoted in J. B. Halvorsen, *Norsk Forfatter-Lexikon 1814–1880*, vol. 3 (Christiania, 1892), 20.
26. Letter to Johan Herman Thoresen, November 21, 1870.
27. Dietrichson, *Svundne Tider*, 1:360.
28. Letter to Dietrichson, May 28, 1869; *HU*, 16:237–38.
29. "Eine Rechtfertigung," printed in *Im neuen Reich* (November 1871); *HU*, 15:352–54.
30. Letter to Brandes, December 20, 1870.
31. *HU*, 14:419.
32. Letter to P. F. Siebold, March 6, 1872; ibid., 17:24.
33. Jonas Lie, letter to Bjørnson, September 4, 1875; in Erik Lie, *Jonas Lies Oplevelser* (Christiania and Copenhagen, 1908), 153.
34. Letter to H. Brøchner, August 10, 1874; Georg og Edv. Brandes, *Brevveksling med nordiske Forfattere*, 1:203.

THE PRUDENT REVOLUTIONARY

1. Letter to Brandes, March 6, 1870.
2. I follow Francis Bull and Henning Fenger in seeing Brandes as more influenced by Ibsen than the other way around in the period 1868 to 1871. See Bull, "Henrik Ibsen et Georg Brandes," in *Mélanges d'histoire littéraire générale et comparée offerts à Fernand Baldensperger* (Paris, 1930), 96–104 (also in Bull, *Studier og streiftog i norsk litteratur* [Oslo, 1931]), and Fenger, "Ibsen og Georg Brandes indtil 1872," *Edda* 51 (1964), 51:169–208. That the influence flowed the other way, from Brandes to Ibsen, is the argument of Paul V. Rubow, *Georg Brandes og den kritiske tradition i det nittende aarhundrede* (Copenhagen, 1931).
3. Brandes, *Levned: Et Tiaar*, 17.
4. Letter of December 20, 1870.
5. "Til Henrik Ibsen," in Brandes, *Samlede Skrifter*, 12:367; Fenger, "Ibsen og Georg Brandes indtil 1872," 188.
6. Brandes, *Levned: Barndom*, 380.
7. Letter of February 17, 1871.
8. Letter of February 22, 1871; Fenger, "Ibsen og Georg Brandes indtil 1872," 189.

9. Quoted ibid., 190.
10. Erik M. Christensen, *Henrik Ibsens realisme* (Oslo, 1985), 66.
11. Brandes, *Levned: Et Tiaar,* 56–57.
12. Leif Nedergaard, "Georg Brandes' forhold til Ibsen, Björnson, og Strindberg belyst gennem deres inbyrdes brevveksling," *Nordisk tidskrift,* n.s., 36 (1960), 17.
13. Fenger, *Den unge Brandes,* 208, 211.
14. *Illustreret Tidende,* October 20, 1871. Brandes did not include it in his collected works. It is reprinted in Fenger, "Ibsen og Georg Brandes indtil 1872," 194–98.
15. "Inaugural Lecture, 1871," trans. Evert Sprinchorn, in Eric Bentley, ed., *The Theory of the Modern Stage* (Harmondsworth, UK, 1968), 383.
16. Ibid., 395.
17. Ibid., 397.
18. P. Lauritsen, *Chr. Collin og Georg Brandes* (Copenhagen, 1958), 86–87.
19. Bertil Nolin, *Georg Brandes* (Boston, 1976), 35.
20. Brandes, *Emigrantliteraturen* in *Samlede Skrifter,* 4:173.
21. Letter of April 4, 1872.
22. Quoted in Fenger, "Bjørnson og Georg Brandes," 115–16.
23. Ibsen, letter to Brandes, July 23, 1872. Brandes, letter to Hans Brøchner, September 29, 1872; Georg og Edv. Brandes, *Brevveksling med nordiske Forfattere,* 1:172.
24. Brandes, *Levned: Et Tiaar,* 100.
25. "A Balloon Letter," *HU,* 14:423.

EMPEROR AND GALILEAN

1. Letter to Gosse, October 14, 1872.
2. Letter to Ludvig Daae, February 4, 1873.
3. William Henry Schofield, "Personal Impressions of Björnson and Ibsen," *Atlantic Monthly* 81 (1898).
4. *HU,* 19:229.
5. Lotten Dahlgren, *Lyran: Interiörer från 1870-och 80-talens konstnärliga och litterära Stockholm* (Stockholm, 1913), 272.
6. Dietrichson, *Svundne Tider,* 1:340.
7. Karl Warburg, *Carl Snoilsky: Hans lefnad och skaldskap* (Stockholm, 1905), 140–41.
8. Carl Snoilsky, *Samlade dikter,* vol. 1 (Stockholm, 1903), 98.
9. According to Christopher Bruun. See *OC,* 9:460.
10. Heine, "Ludwig Börne," in Heine, *Sämtliche Werke,* ed. Ernst Elster, vol. 7 (Leipzig and Vienna, n.d.), 24.
11. Letter to Brandes, September 24, 1871.
12. Letter to Ludvig Daae, February 23, 1873.
13. Brandes, *Levned: Et Tiaar,* 100–103.
14. *Levned: Et Tiaar,* 88–89.
15. *HU,* 7:244.
16. Dietrichson, *Svundne Tider,* 1:359.

17. *Lutetia,* trans. E. B. Ashton, in Heine, *Works of Prose,* ed. Herman Kesten (New York, 1943), 136–38. Ibsen, in his usual fashion, denied having read much Heine: "I have only once read through a volume of his travel books and his *Buch der Lieder.*" But he said this in 1867 (letter to Hegel, March 8, 1867), and it was only after that year that he was able to make any progress on his Julian drama.
18. "Jeg indesluttet står på en illusions ruiner," *Efterladte Skrifter,* 1:493. Later rephrased as "jeg våpenstekket står på en brusten drøms ruiner" in "A Balloon Letter."
19. Letter to Oscar von Knorring, November 2, 1870.
20. Letter to Johan Herman Thoresen, November 21, 1870.
21. Letter to Brandes, December 20, 1870.
22. *HU,* 15:344.
23. Letter to Ludwig Kugelmann, April 17, 1871.
24. Sven-Gustaf Edqvist, *Samhällets fiende* (Stockholm, 1961), 77.
25. Quoted in Tristram Hunt, *Marx's General: The Revolutionary Life of Friedrich Engels* (New York, 2009), 340. On contemporary politics in *Emperor,* see Chr. Collin, "Henrik Ibsens Fremtidsdrøm," *Samtiden* 17 (1906), 483.

IBSEN THE MYSTIC

1. Brandes, *Levned: Et Tiaar,* 100–103.
2. Ibsen, letter to Brandes, May 18, 1871.
3. Letter to Brandes, April 30, 1873.
4. *HU,* 7:98.
5. For Ibsen's knowledge of Neoplatonism, see S. Svensson, "Brand och den svenska göticism," *Edda* 30 (1930), 372–95. Rebutted by Carl David Marcus, "Ibsen och göticism," *Edda* 31 (1931), 81–97. Answered by Svensson, "Svar på 'Replik,'" *Edda* 31 (1931), 98–101. Ibsen became familiar with it when he first thought about the Julian play and read Julian's essays in the 1860s. See also Josef Faaland, *Henrik Ibsen og antikken* (Oslo, 1943), 252 ff. On sources for the Third Kingdom, see Paulus Svendsen, "Om Ibsens kilder til 'Kejser og Galilæer,'" *Edda* 32 (1932), 198–257.
6. Trans. Aaron Kramer in *The Poetry and Prose of Heinrich Heine,* ed. Frederic Ewen (New York, 1948), 112–13.
7. P.-Félix Thomas, *Pierre Leroux, sa vie, son oeuvre, sa doctrine* (Paris, 1904), 165.
8. Ibid., 181.
9. On Ibsen's knowledge of and familiarity with socialist and anarchist doctrine of the mid-nineteenth century, see Christensen, *Ibsens realisme,* 337 ff.

JULIAN AS IBSEN

1. *HU,* 7:77, 79, 81.
2. Rowland Smith, *Julian's Gods* (London and New York, 1995), 186.
3. *HU,* 7:102.
4. Ibid., 7:106.

5. Ibid., 7:154.
6. Edmund Gosse, *Studies in the Literature of Northern Europe* (London, 1879), 62.
7. *HU*, 7:156.
8. Ibid., 7:161–62.
9. Letter to Brandes, May 18, 1871.
10. Letter to Hegel, August 8, 1872; Halvdan Koht, "Korleis 'Kejser og Galilæer' vart skriven," *Ibsen-årbok* (1955–56), 114–25.
11. Brandes (1874), quoted in *HI skrifter*, 6k:256.
12. *HU*, 7:276.
13. Letter to Gosse, October 14, 1872. On autobiographical elements, especially Ibsen's early years, see Faaland, *Henrik Ibsen og antikken*, 172–79. On significant departures from facts, see *OC*, 9:535–50, and *Collected Works of Ibsen*, 5:xxxiii–xxxiv; *Oxford Ibsen*, 4:601–3.
14. Letter to Gosse, February 20, 1873.
15. Letter to Løkke, November 23, 1873; *HI skrifter: Brev*, 13:161–62.
16. Bernard Shaw, *Major Critical Essays* (London, 1932), 55.
17. Brandes, letter to Brøchner, September 29, 1872.
18. Letter to Bjørnson, December 9–10, 1867.
19. Letter to Brandes, September 24, 1871.
20. Ibid.
21. *HU*, 7:321–22.

CONCORDANCE OF OPPOSITES

1. Preface to the 2nd rev. ed. of *Catiline.*
2. Nicolas Cusanus, *Of Learned Ignorance*, trans. Fr. Germain Heron (London, 1954), 173.
3. Goethe, *Gespräche* (Artemis Ausgabe), 1:624. Cited in Jeremy Adler, "The Aesthetics of Magnetism: Science, Philosophy and Poetry in the Dialogue Between Goethe and Schelling" in Elinor S. Shaffer, ed., *The Third Culture: Literature and Science* (Berlin and New York, 1998), 68.
4. *HU*, 7:95.
5. Schelling, *Philosophie der Offenbarung*, in *Sämmtliche Werke*, ed. K. F. A. Schelling (Stuttgart and Augsburg), pt. 2, vol. 3 (1858), 436, 443, 454.
6. *HU*, 7:346.
7. Ibid., 89.
8. Ibid., 97.
9. "Bruno, oder über das göttliche und natürliche Princip der Dinge" (1802), in *Sämmtliche Werke*, pt. 1, vol. 4 (1859), 329.
10. *The Ages of the World*, trans. Frederick de Wolfe Bolman Jr. (New York, 1942), 109.
11. Letter to Hegel, July 12, 1871.
12. *Ages of the World*, 111.
13. *Die Weltalter* in *Sämmtliche Werke*, pt. 1, vol. 8 (1861).

14. This was not included in Ibsen's collected poems, but was published only after his death in *Efterladte Skrifter*; see 1:211, 2:163, and 3:444. See also *HU*, 7:339, 7:350, and 14:319. Halvdan Koht considered the poem as having a direct connection with *Emperor*: "Korleis 'Kejser og Galilæer' vart skriven," 116–17.
15. Schelling, quoted in E. D. Hirsch Jr., *Wordsworth and Schelling* (New Haven, 1960), 118.
16. Ibid.
17. See discussion in Rudolf Magnus, *Goethe as a Scientist*, trans. Heinz Norden (New York, 1949), 230–33.
18. Letter to Ludvig Daae, February 23, 1873.
19. *HU*, 304.
20. *HU*, 281.
21. Very little of this has any basis in the historical account or the known facts; Ibsen made up much of it. Julian was probably killed by a Persian soldier. An obviously biased Christian account says he was killed by "the lance of paradise, the lance of justice" (G. W. Bowersock, *Julian the Apostate* [Cambridge, Mass., 1978], 116).

ANOTHER TRIUMPH

1. *Concluding Unscientific Postscript*, 139–40.
2. Letter to Brandes, October 16, 1873.
3. Paulus Svendsen, "Emperor and Galilean," *Edda* 56 (1956), 338–50.
4. Letter to Brandes, September 8, 1873.
5. Dietrichson, *Svundne Tider*, 1:351, 354, 360.
6. Letter to H. E. Schirmer, November 19, 1873; Bjørnson, *Brytnings-år*, 1:168.
7. Quoted in Halvorsen, *Norsk Forfatter-Lexikon*, 3:57.
8. See accounts in *Morgenbladet* (Christiania; 1874), no. 252A; Halvorsen, *Norsk Forfatter-Lexikon* 3:21–23; and Einar Østvedt, *Henrik Ibsen som student og blant studenter* (Skien, 1971), 74.
9. Edith Pradez, "Henrik Ibsen's Return," *Academy* (October 10, 1874), 406.
10. Chr. Collin, "Henrik Ibsen und Norwegen," *Die neue Rundschau* 18 (July–December 1907), 1282.
11. *HU*, 15:392–95. Cf. the version given by Pradez, "Henrik Ibsen's Return," 406.
12. Letter to Hegel, September 16, 1874.

CHANGING TIMES

1. *HU*, 14:208–9.
2. Ibid., 14:325.
3. See letter to Hegel, September 15, 1876. For more on Ibsen's royalties, see Ibsen, *Letters and Speeches*, ed. Evert Sprinchorn (New York, 1964), 161–62, 191–95, 204–5.
4. Koht, *Henrik Ibsen*, 2:71.
5. *HI skrifter*, 6:247–48; Sæther, *Suzannah, Fru Ibsen*, 178–79.

6. Annie Wall, *Människor jag mötte* (Oslo, 1926), 52.
7. Strindberg, "Konstakademiens utställning 1877," in *August Strindbergs samlade verk*, vol. 7, ed. Per Stam and Bo Bennich-Björkman (Stockholm, 2009), 127–28.
8. Gunnar Ahlström, *Det moderna genombrottet i Nordens litteratur* (Stockholm, 1947), 80.
9. Letter of July 23, 1872.
10. Letter of June 30, 1872.
11. *HU*, 15:154, 136, 160, 159.
12. Letter to Gosse, January 15, 1874.
13. Ibid.
14. Brandes, *Henrik Ibsen* (Copenhagen, 1898), 64.
15. William Archer, *The Old Drama and the New* (Boston, 1923), 47.
16. Letter to Lucie Wolf, May 25, 1883.
17. Letter to Theodor Caspari, June 25, 1884.
18. Letter to Sophus Michaelis, January 2, 1899; *HI skrifter*, 15:462.
19. For a superb illustration of a drawing-room drama as staged by Montigny, see the oil painting by Adolph Menzel (in the Berlin National Gallery) of an 1856 production at the Théâtre Gymnase. For an account of Montigny's contributions, see Svend Erichsen, *Realismens gennembrud i parisisk teater i det nittende århundrede*, vol. 2: *Montigny og scenekunsten under Napoleon III* (Copenhagen, 1973).
20. Brandes, *Samlede Skrifter*, 14:267.
21. Letter to A. H. Isachsen, December 16, 1872.
22. Harald Noreng, *Bjørnsons skuespil på svensk scene* (Oslo, 1967), 80 ff.
23. *Det nya riket*, in *August Strindbergs samlade verk*, vol. 12 (Stockholm, 1983), 108–10.

THE PROBLEM PLAY

1. Alexandre Dumas *fils*, *Théâtre complet*, vol. 3 (Paris, 1893), 29.
2. Strindberg, "Björnstjerne Björnson," in *Samlade skrifter*, 17:240.
3. Örjan Lindberger, "Kring urpremiären på 'En Fallit,'" *Nordisk tidskrift för vetenskap, konst och industri*, n.s., 34 (1958), 156–57. See also Noreng, *Bjørnsons skuespil på svensk scene*, 80 ff.
4. Öppna brev till Intima teatern, in *Samlade skrifter*, 50:285.
5. André Antoine, *"Mes souvenirs" sur le Théâtre-Libre* (Paris, 1921), 129.
6. Strindberg, "Den litterära reaktionen i Sverige," in *Samlade skrifter*, 17:214.
7. Lindberger, "Kring urpremiären på 'En Fallit,'" 156–57.

PILLARS OF SOCIETY

1. In Fenger, "Ibsen og Brandes indtil 1872," 206.
2. *HU*, 14:447–49.
3. Strindberg, *Samlade skrifter*, 17:239.
4. "Björnstjerne Björnson," in *Samlade skrifter*, 17:240, 242.
5. Ibsen, *Efterladte skrifter*, 1:lxxxiv.

6. *HI skrifter*, 11k:834.
7. Letter to Hegel, October 23, 1875.
8. Letter of September 20, 1877; *HI skrifer*, 13:385.
9. Koht, *Henrik Ibsen*, 2:98.
10. *HU*, 8:142.
11. On the ending of the play as ironic, see, for example, Gunnar Høst, "Ibsens sammfunds-støtter," *Edda* (1947), 1–12, and James W. McFarlane, "Meaning and Evidence in Ibsen's Drama," *Ibsen-Årbok* 8 (1965–66), 35–50; as nonironic: Daniel Haakonsen, *Henrik Ibsen: Mennesket og kunstneren* (Oslo, 1981), 172–73, and Asbjørn Aarseth, *Ibsens samtidsskuespil* (Oslo, 1999), 55–58.
12. Letter, Edvard Brandes to Georg Brandes, November 30, 1877; Georg og Edv. Brandes, *Brevveksling med nordiske Forfattere*, 2:5–6.
13. "Den litterära reaktionen i Sverige," in *Samlade skrifter*, 17:216.
14. *Henrik Ibsens brevveksling med Christiania Theater 1878–1899*, ed. Øyvind Anker (Oslo, 1965), 18.

THE ROAD TO A *DOLL'S HOUSE*

1. Quoted in Ahlström, *Moderna genombrottet*, 120.
2. Bjørnson, *Artikler og taler*, 1:439–40.
3. Letter of February 17, 1871.
4. Ibid.
5. Brandes, *Samlede Skrifter*, 4:108.
6. The speaker has in mind the Christian sin of pride. St. Augustine said, "By craving to be more, man becomes less; and by aspiring to be self-sufficing [*sibi sufficere*], he fell away from Him Who truly suffices him." *The City of God*, trans. Marcus Dods (Edinburgh, 1871), book 14, chap. 13.
7. Carl Grimberg, *Svenska folkets underbara öden*, vol. 9 (Stockholm, 1924), 36–50.
8. John Bowden, *Norway* (London, 1867), 55, 118.
9. *HU*, 6:433.
10. Ibid., 8:154.
11. Marie Høgh and Fredrikke Mørch, eds., *Norske kvinder: En oversigt over deres stilling og livsvilkaar i hundredeaaret 1814–1914* (Christiania, 1914), 1:35–39.
12. Grimberg, *Svenska folkets underbara öden*, 9:46.
13. Bjørnson, *Samlede Digter-Verker*, ed. Francis Bull (Christiania and Copenhagen, 1919), 2:331.
14. Letter to Erik af Edholm, January 3, 1880.
15. *HU*, 8:442.

THE WOMEN BEHIND THE PLAY

1. Emil Reich, *Aus Leben und Dichtung* (Leipzig, 1911), 432.
2. Sæther, *Suzanah: Fru Ibsen*, 382.

3. Marcus Grønvold, *Fra Ulrikken til Alperne: En malers erindringer* (Oslo, 1925), 142.
4. February 6, 1872; quoted in Ellisiv Steen, *Den lange Strid: Camilla Collett og hennes senere forfatterskap* (Oslo, 1954), 154–55.
5. John Paulsen, "Erindringer," in Gerhard Gran, ed., *Henrik Ibsen: Festskrift i Anledning af hans 70de Fødselsdag* (Bergen, 1898), 36.
6. Paulsen, *Mine erindringer,* 97.
7. Paulsen, *Erindringer: Siste samling* (Copenhagen, 1903), 89.
8. Letter to Laura Petersen, June 11, 1870.
9. Letter of March 26, 1878.
10. Letter to Hegel, August 2, 1878; *HU,* 17:319.
11. This account based on Østvedt, *Et dukkehjem,* 104–21, superseding B. M. Kinck, "Henrik Ibsen og Laura Kieler," *Edda* 35 (1935), 498–543.
12. *HU,* 8:368.
13. Paulsen, *Samliv med Ibsen: Anden samling,* 60.
14. Gosse, *Henrik Ibsen,* 230.
15. Quoted in Østvedt, *Ibsen og la bella Italia,* 121.
16. Letter of December 30, 1879; Georg og Edv. Brandes, *Brevveksling med nordiske Forfattere,* 2:344.
17. Gunnar Heiberg's account, in *HU,* 8:259–60, 19:159–61. See also Østvedt, *Ibsen og la bella Italia,* 147–48.

THE WELL-MADE PLAY TRANSFORMED

1. Østvedt, *Et dukkehjem,* 205.
2. *The Scenic Art: Notes on Acting & the Drama, 1872–1901,* ed. Allan Wade (New Brunswick, NJ, 1948), 255.
3. Quoted in Archer, "'The Mausoleum of Ibsen,'" *Fortnightly Review,* n.s., 54 (1893), 84.
4. Strindberg, *En Blå Bok,* in *August Strindbergs samlade verk,* vol. 65 (Stockholm, 1997), 273.
5. Letter to Erik af Edholm, January 3, 1880.
6. Elizabeth Robins, *Ibsen and the Actress* (London, 1928), 14.
7. *Ibsens Nora vor dem Strafrichter und Psychiater* (Halle, 1907). See also Hermann J. Weigand, *The Modern Ibsen* (New York, 1925). On the hysterical Nora, see also Robert Geyer, *Étude médico-psychologique sur le théâtre d'Ibsen* (Paris, 1902), 37–39.
8. *The Theatrical "World" for 1893* (London, n.d.), 158.
9. *Giftas,* in *August Strindbergs samlade verk,* vol. 16 (Stockholm, 1982), 14.
10. Letter to Edvard Brandes, March 14, 1880; Georg og Edv. Brandes, *Brevveksling med nordiske Forfattere,* 2:349–50.
11. Paulsen, *Erindringer: Siste samling,* 110.
12. *Last Essays,* trans. Richard and Clara Winston (New York, 1959), 176.
13. *HU,* 8:360.
14. *Giftas,* 16:13–18.
15. Speech, May 26, 1898; *HU,* 15:417.

16. Ibsen, *Brev 1845–1905: Ny samling*, ed. Øyvind Anker, vol. 2 (Oslo, 1981), 119.
17. Herman Bang, *Kritiske Studier og Udkast* (Copenhagen, 1880), 220–23.
18. Shaw, *Our Theatres in the Nineties* (London, 1932), 3:132–33.
19. William Archer, in *Theatrical "World" for 1893*, 161.
20. Ola Hansson, "Eleanora Duse," *Tilskueren* (1893), 143–47. Also in Hansson, *Samlade skrifter*, vol. 10 (Stockholm, 1921), 303–10.
21. "Eleanora Duse" (signed Loris) in *Ord och Bild* 1 (1892), 237.
22. *HU*, 19:210.

THE GHOSTS AT ROSENVOLD

1. Halvorsen, *Norsk Forfatter-Lexikon*, 61.
2. J. P. Jacobsen, letter to Edvard Brandes, December 30, 1879; Georg og Edv. Brandes, *Brevveksling med nordiske Forfattere*, 2:344.
3. *Times Literary Supplement* (June 18, 1993), 25.
4. Quoted in Kinck, "Ibsen og Laura Kieler," 516.
5. Magdalene Thoresen, letter to Fredrika Limnell, February 12, 1880; Dahlgren, *Lyran*, 316.
6. William Henri Eller, *Ibsen in Germany 1870–1900* (Boston, 1918), 376.
7. P. F. D. Tennant, *Ibsen's Dramatic Technique* (Cambridge, 1948), 117.
8. Letter to Danish newspaper *Nationaltidende* (February 20, 1880). In *HI skrifter*, 14:24. For the text of Ibsen's revised ending, see Eller, *Ibsen in Germany*, 38–39.
9. Ibid., 36–38.
10. George [*sic*] Brandes, *Henrik Ibsen: A Critical Study With a 17 Page Essay on Björnstjerne Björnson*, trans. Jessie Muir, rev. William Archer (London, 1899; reprinted New York, 1964), 46–47.
11. Østvedt, *Ibsen og la bella Italia*, 132, quoting Georg Pauli.
12. William Archer, "Ibsen as I Knew Him," *Monthly Review* 23 (1906), 2.
13. This account draws on Fritz Hammer (= Michael Georg Conrad, the leading exponent of naturalism in Germany), "Mein Verkehr mit Henrik Ibsen," *Die Gesellschaft* 4 (October 1888), 741–46; John Paulsen, *Paa Vandring* (Copenhagen, 1882), 99–102; Paulsen, *Mine erindringer*, 136, 194; Paulsen, *Samliv med Ibsen: Nye erindringer*, 31–33; Reich, *Aus Leben und Dichtung*, 452; Henrik Jæger, "Henrik Jægers opptegnelser fra samtaler med Ibsen," in Midbøe, *Streiflys over Ibsen*, 158–60; Edward Payson Evans, "Ibsen's Home and Working Habits," *The Critic*, n.s., 13 (March 8, 1890), 122.
14. See Gran, ed., *Henrik Ibsen: Festskrift*, 294; *Nora*, trans. H. F. Lord (London and New York, 1882), vi.
15. Letter to Sophie Adlersparre, June 24, 1882.
16. *HU*, 9:136.
17. *HU*, 9:77–78.
18. Maurice Bigeon, "Profils scandinaves: Henrik Ibsen," *Le Figaro* (January 4, 1893), 3.
19. *HU*, 9:85.
20. Ibid., 9:71.

21. Ibid., 9:72–73.
22. Ibid., 9:136.
23. Ibid., 9:92.

SYPHILIS, THE UNMENTIONABLE DISEASE

1. Iwan Bloch, *The Sexual Life of Our Time in Its Relations to Modern Civilization*, trans. M. Eden Paul (New York, 1928), 393.
2. Quoted in Wilhelm Friese, ed., *Ibsen auf der deutschen Bühne* (Tübingen, 1976), ix.
3. Bertil Nolin, *Den gode Europén: Studier i Georg Brandes' idéutveckling 1871–1893* (Uppsala, 1965), 21–24.
4. *HU*, 9:105.
5. The English translation, trans. P. Albert Morrow, is dated 1881 but copyright 1880.
6. The Swedish edition, *Syfilis och äktenskap i föreläsningar hållna på Hopital Saint-Louis*, trans. Karl Malmsted, was published in 1882.
7. Alfred Fournier, *La syphilis du cerveau: Leçons cliniques recueillies par E. Brissaud*, 544, 550.
8. *HU*, 9:128, 106.
9. Ibid., 9:128; Fournier, *Syphilis du cerveau*, 68, 551.
10. *HU*, 9:104; Fournier, *Syphilis du cerveau*, 88.
11. Fournier, *Syphilis du cerveau*, 332.
12. Ibid., 129–31, 435–36.
13. Sander S. Gilman, ed., *Conversations with Nietzsche*, trans. David J. Parent (Oxford, 1987), 227–36. See also Deborah Hayden, *Pox: Genius, Madness, and the Mysteries of Syphilis* (New York, 2004), 172–99.
14. Henry Maudsley, *The Pathology of Mind*, 3rd ed. (London, 1879), 435; Fournier, *Syphilis du cerveau*, 550.
15. Fournier, *Syphilis and Marriage*, 141–42.
16. Letter to Molander, February 4, 1888; *August Strindbergs Brev*, vol. 7, ed. Torsten Eklund (Stockholm, 1961), 9.
17. *Correspondance de Georg Brandes*, vol. 2, ed. Paul Krüger (Copenhagen, 1956), 98.
18. "Samtale om 'Gengangere,'" *HU*, 19:162–63.
19. Fournier, *Syphilis du cerveau*, 7.
20. *The Traffic in Women*, 1917, quoted in Christopher Innes, ed., *A Sourcebook in Naturalistic Theatre* (London and New York, 2000), 202.
21. Fournier, *Syphilis du cerveau*, 84.
22. *HU*, 9:72.
23. "Urarva," in *Dikter på vers och prosa*, in *August Strindbergs samlade verk*, 15:21.
24. *HU*, 9:129.
25. Letter of October 18, 1883; "Ibseniana: Letters from William Archer to Charles Archer," *London Mercury and Bookman* 36 (October 1937), 535.
26. Vilhelm Alexander Bergstrand in *Ur Dagens Krönika*, quoted in Harald Elovson, "Livsglädje och levnadsglädje," *Edda* 30 (1930), 53–54.

PUBLIC ENEMY

1. Koht, *Henrik Ibsen,* 2:128.
2. Neiiendam, *Kongelige Teaters Historie,* 3:182.
3. See *Henrik Ibsens brevveksling med Christiania Theater,* 23.
4. *HI skrifter,* 14k:501.
5. See letter to Hegel, August 23, 1877.
6. Letter to Edvard Fallesen, October 5, 1877; *HU,* 17:275.
7. *Morgenbladet,* December 18, 1881.
8. Unsigned review in *Oplandenes Avis,* December 21, 1881; quoted in Ibsen, *Gengangere,* ed. Olaf Kortner (Oslo, 1965), 80–81.
9. Letter to Birkeland, June 30, 1872.
10. Letter to Hegel, October 25, 1880.
11. Letter to Sophus Schandorph, January 6, 1882.
12. Letter to Olaf Skavlan, January 24, 1882.
13. See *Ibsen-årbok* (1955–56), 131.
14. *OC,* 16:285.
15. Bjørnson, *Artikler og taler,* 1:476–77.
16. Letter to Brandes, June 8, 1882; *Kamp-liv,* 2:14.
17. Letter to Bjørnson, March 5, 1882; Erik Lie, *Jonas Lies Oplevelser,* 179.
18. Brandes, *Modern mænd* (1883); cited in Ahlström, *Moderna genombrottet.*
19. Quoted in Else Høst, *Vildanden av Henrik Ibsen* (Oslo, 1967), 12.
20. *Morgenbladet,* December 18, 1881.
21. Erik Lie, *Jonas Lies Oplevelser,* 258.
22. *Dagbladet,* December 14, 1881.
23. Elias Bredsdorff, "Georg Brandes og de politiske ideologier," *Tidskrift för Litteraturvetenskap* (Lund) 1 (1971–72), 200.
24. Letter to Brandes, January 3, 1882.
25. Letter to Hegel, January 2, 1882.
26. Letter to Schandorph, January 6, 1882.
27. Letter to Skavlan, January 24, 1882.
28. Letter to Hegel, March 16, 1882.
29. Letter to Skavlan, January 24, 1882.
30. Letter to Hegel, March 16, 1882.
31. Letter to Hegel, June 21, 1882.
32. Letter to Bjørnson, August 4, 1882.
33. Hans Heiberg, *"... født til kunstner": Et Ibsen-portrett* (Oslo, 1967), 230–31.
34. Erik Lie, *Jonas Lies Oplevelser,* 256, 254.
35. Letter to Hegel, September 9, 1882.
36. Koht, *Henrik Ibsen,* 2:134–35.
37. Friedrich Tramer, "Das Urbild für Ibsens Dr. Stockmann," *Neuphilologische Mitteilungen* 56 (1955), 20–27.
38. Øyvind Anker, "Scenekunst gjennom 150 år," *Dette er Norge* (1963), 3:178.

39. Letter to Hans Schrøder, December 14, 1882.
40. Letter to Schrøder, December 31, 1882.
41. *School* (New York, n.d.), 4.
42. Letter to Schrøder, December 24, 1882.
43. Letter to Schrøder, December 14, 1882.
44. Letter to Schrøder, December 31, 1882.
45. Letter to Brandes, January 3, 1882.
46. Letter to Otto Borchsenius, January 21, 1882.
47. Inscribed in an album presented to Leopold von Sacher-Masoch, December 12, 1882.
48. *Dagbladet,* January 3, 1882.

THE SLAIN PEGASUS

1. Zola, "From 'Naturalism in the Theatre,'" trans. Albert Bermel, in Bentley, ed., *Theory of the Modern Stage,* 365–66.
2. Ibsen denied being influenced by Dumas as regards dramatic form, "except that I have learned from his plays to avoid a number of quite serious mistakes and blunders that he is often guilty of" (letter to Brandes, October 11, 1896; *HU,* 18:386). He could hardly deny, however, that as regards content he was indirectly influenced by Dumas by way of Georg Brandes.
3. Charles Archer, *William Archer, Life, Work and Friendships* (New Haven, 1931), 182–83.
4. William Archer, "Ibsen as I Knew Him," 13.
5. W. Berteval, *Le Théâtre d'Ibsen* (Paris, 1912), half-title page.
6. Lothar, *Henrik Ibsen,* 126.
7. "'Lord William Russell' og dets Udførelse paa Christiania Theater," *HU,* 15:162.
8. *HU,* 14:311.
9. George [*sic*] Brandes, *Ibsen: A Critical Study,* 46–47.
10. Letter to Petersen, December 4, 1865; *HU,* 16:122.
11. Thomas Carlyle, *Sartor Resartus* (London, 1838), 228.
12. "Why the Arts Are Not Progressive?" in *The Collected Works of William Hazlitt,* ed. A. R. Waller and Arnold Glover (London, 1902), 1:164.
13. Bigeon, "Profils scandinaves: Henrik Ibsen," 3.
14. Quoted in F. W. J. Hemmings, Émile Zola (Oxford, 1953), 180.
15. Fergusson, *The Idea of a Theater* (New York, 1953), 161 ff.
16. *HU,* 9:113.
17. Ibid., 9:112.
18. Emile Faguet, "The Symbolical Drama," *International Quarterly* (Burlington, VT) 8 (1903–4), 335.
19. Fergusson, *Idea of a Theater,* 163.
20. Letter to Sophus Schandorph, January 6, 1882; *HU,* 17:450.
21. In Egan, ed., *Ibsen: The Critical Heritage,* 86.
22. Huneker, *Egoists: A Book of Supermen* (New York, 1909), 343.
23. In Egan, ed., *Ibsen: The Critical Heritage,* 99–100.
24. Ibid., 184.

THE WILD DUCK

1. *HU*, 9:137.
2. Ahlström, *Moderna genombrottet*, 429.
3. Ibid., 422.
4. Letter of June 12, 1883.
5. Letter to Hegel, June 14, 1884.
6. Halvdan Koht, introduction to Bjørnson, *Brytnings-år*, 1:xlv.
7. Letter to Caspari, June 27, 1884.
8. Anders Wyller, "Vildanden: En innledning og en kritikk," *Edda* 36 (1936), 278.
9. See Ingjald Nissen, *Vildanden—Rosmersholm—Hedda Gabler* (Oslo, 1973), 17–18.
10. *HU*, 10:151.
11. Letter to Schrøder, November 14, 1884.
12. Critic for the *Daily Telegraph*, quoted by William Archer, "The Humour of 'The Wild Duck,'" in *The Theatrical "World" of 1897* (London, 1898), 148.
13. Høst, *Vildanden av Henrik Ibsen*, 256.
14. Freud, *Civilization and Its Discontents*, trans. Joan Riviere (New York, 1930), 25.
15. Louis Desprez, *L'Évolution naturaliste* (Paris, 1884), 195.
16. Henry Maudsley, *The Physiology and Pathology of Mind* (New York, 1871), 300–1.
17. Georg Fasting, "Smaa minder om Bjørnson," *Samtiden* 24 (1913), 102.
18. Bull, *Studier og Streiftog*, 283.
19. Maudsley, *Physiology and Pathology*, 295.
20. "Själamord (Apropå Rosmersholm)" in *August Strindbergs samlade verk*, vol. 29 (Stockholm, 1985), 74.
21. Maudsley, *Physiology and Pathology*, 297.
22. *HU*, 10:170.
23. Ingard Hauge, *Den fremmede passajen* (Oslo, 1986), 135–45.
24. *HU*, 10:157.
25. Ibid., 10:136.
26. Ibid., 10:145.
27. Ibid., 10:86.
28. See Strindberg, *Gamla Stockholm*, in *Samlade skrifter*, 6:195.
29. Maudsley, *Physiology and Pathology*, 296.
30. Ibid., 304.
31. Ibid., 303–4.
32. Gustav Fredrikson, *Teaterminnen* (Stockholm, 1918), 221; Pelle Holm, *Bevingade ord och andra talesätt*, rev. ed. (Stockholm, 1962), 71–72.
33. *HU*, 10:64–65.
34. See Bernard Shaw, preface to *Three Plays by Brieux* (New York, 1914), xlviii.
35. Ronald Pearsall, *The Worm in the Bud: The World of Victorian Sexuality* (London, 1969), 225.

THE PAST RECAPTURED

1. Harald Grieg, *En Forleggers Erindringer*, vol. 1 (Copenhagen, 1958), 383–84.
2. *HU*, 10:170.
3. Maudsley, *Pathology of Mind*, 469.
4. Bull, *Vildanden og andre essays*, cited in Høst, *Vildanden av Henrik Ibsen*, 255–56.
5. Larson, *Ibsen in Skien and Grimstad*, 33.
6. Letter of December 9–10, 1867.
7. Bergliot Ibsen, *De tre*, 123.
8. Letter to Christopher Blom Paus, November 18, 1877.
9. Einar Østvedt, "Mørkeloftet og miljøet i 'Vildanden,'" *Ibsen-årbok* (1957–59), 93–108.
10. Carla Waal, "William Bloch's *The Wild Duck*," *Educational Theatre Journal* 30 (December 1978), 495–512.
11. Palle Lauring, ed., *Fjern og nær set gennem Illustreret Tidende* (Copenhagen, 1966), 102–3.
12. Bjørn Bjørnson, *Det gamle teater: Kunsten og menneskene* (Oslo, 1937), 104.
13. Ibid., 107.
14. Helena Nyblom, "Vildanden," *Ny svensk Tidsskrift* (January 1885), 65–69.
15. Quoted in Philipp Stein, *Henrik Ibsen zum Bühnengeschichte seiner Dichtungen* (Berlin, 1901), 26–27.
16. Shaw, *Our Theatres in the Nineties*, 3:138.
17. Per Lindberg, *August Lindberg: Skådespelaren och människan* (Stockholm, 1943), 146, 148.
18. Anker, "Scenekunst gjennom 150 år," 3:174. For specific examples of how traditional stage speech differed from ordinary speech, especially in the pronunciation of vowels, see Strindberg's 1874 appreciation of the Danish actress Fröken Dolcke in Strindberg, *Före Röda rummet*, ed. Torsten Eklund (Stockholm, 1946), 97–103.
19. Per Lindberg, *August Lindberg*, 146.
20. Letter to Schrøder, November 14, 1884.

THE DEPTHS OF THE SEA

1. *HU*, 7:282.
2. Emile Zola, *The Experimental Novel and Other Essays*, trans. Belle M. Sherman (1893; reprinted New York, 1964), 292.
3. *Critique of Judgment*, ¶ 79, "On the Necessity for the Subordination of the Mechanical Principle to the Teleological in the Explanation of a Thing as a Natural End."
4. *Experimental Novel*, 47.
5. *HI skrifter*, 16:494.
6. *HU*, 7:89.
7. In H. C. Andersen's tale "Agnete og Havmanden," the merman seduces Agnete and takes her down "paa Havsens Bund." In *The Vikings at Helgeland*, Ibsen uses the conventional *havets bund*.

8. Ernst Haeckel, *The History of Creation, or The Development of the Earth and Its Inhabitants by the Action of Natural Causes*, trans. E. Ray Lankester (New York, 1911), 2:54.
9. See Asbjørn Aarseth, "Ibsen and Darwin: A Reading of *The Wild Duck*," *Modern Drama* 48 (2005), 1–10.
10. *HU*, 8:390.
11. Zola, "Naturalism in the Theatre," in George G. Becker, ed., *Documents of Modern Literary Realism* (Princeton, 1963), 220–29.
12. *History of Creation*, 1:411.
13. *Sömngångarnätter på vakna dagar*, in *August Strindbergs samlade verk*, vol. 15 (Stockholm, 1995), 213.
14. On Ibsen as not hostile to Gregers, see Valborg Eriksen Lynner, "Gregers Werle—og Ibsens selvironi," *Edda* 28 (1928–29), 249–62.
15. *History of Creation*, 269–70.
16. Ernst Haeckel, *The Evolution of Man* (New York, 1899), 1:253.
17. *HU*, 11:164. The Haeckel source was noted by Koht and Elias in Ibsen's *Efterladte Skrifter*, 1:cvi.
18. *HU*, 10:143. Archer's translation is "plaguy integrity-fever" (*Collected Works of Ibsen*, 8:369).
19. *HU*, 10:115.
20. Ibid., 10:86.
21. *A Pair of Blue Eyes* (New York, 1928), 241–42.
22. *HU*, 10:132.
23. Lancelot Law Whyte, *The Unconscious Before Freud* (New York, 1962), 121.
24. "Sir Walter Scott," *Westminster Review* (January 1838).
25. Whyte, *Unconscious Before Freud*, 126.
26. Brandes, *Samlede Skrifter*, vol. 4 (Copenhagen, 1900), 428.
27. Quoted in Eduard von Hartmann, *Philosophy of the Unconscious*, trans. William Chatteron Coupland (London, 1931), 27.
28. Gerhard Stenzel, ed., *Die deutschen Romantiker*, vol. 1 (Salzburg, 1954), 616.
29. Ibsen, *Efterladte Skrifter*, 1:lxxvii.
30. Brandes, *Levned: Et Tiaar*, 281.
31. Taine, *On Intelligence*, trans. T. D. Haye (New York, 1875), 1:189.
32. Haeckel, *Evolution of Man*, 1:6.
33. Sir John Lubbock, *The Origin of Civilization and the Primitive Condition of Man* (New York, 1870), 360.
34. *HU*, 10:164.
35. *Psykologi i omrids* (Copenhagen, 1882), 87.
36. Ibid., 410–11.
37. Maudsley, *Physiology and Pathology*, 300.
38. Maudsley, *Pathology of Mind*, 344.

A VISIT TO NORWAY

1. Brandes, *Levned: Snevringer*, 29, 57.
2. Ibid., 59.
3. Ibid., 44–45.
4. Notes to *Wild Duck*; *HU*, 10:164.
5. *Levned: Snevringer*, 82–83.
6. Erik Østerud, "Den rosmerske adelighet og dybdepsykologien: En studie i Henrik Ibsens Rosmersholm," *Norskrift* 34 (1981), 7–11.
7. *Levned: Snevringer*, 143, 148, 124, 177.
8. Ibid., 80–82.
9. Østvedt, *Ibsen og la bella Italia*, 134.
10. Letter to Bjørnson, March 23, 1884.
11. Bjørn Bjørnson, *Det gamle teater*, 249–59.
12. *HU*, 15:422.
13. Ole Øisang, *Henrik Ibsen som radikaler: Ibsens samfundsopfatning og hans forhold til arbeiderbevegelsen* (Trondheim, 1928), 9.
14. *HU*, 15:407–8.
15. See George V. Plekhanov, "Ibsen, Petty Bourgeois Revolutionist," in Angel Flores, ed., *Henrik Ibsen* (New York, 1937), 38–39.
16. Grønvold, *Fra Ulrikken til Alperne*, 142–43.
17. Evans, "Ibsen's Home and Working Habits," 122. According to *HI skrifter*, 15k:79, Ibsen in 1888 purchased Grønvold's oil painting *The Workingman's Moving Day* (*Arbeidsmandens flyttedag*).
18. "Henrik Jægers opptegnelser fra samtaler," in Midbøe, *Streiflys over Ibsen*, 152.
19. Ibid., 153.
20. Østvedt, *Ibsen og la bella Italia*, 136–37.
21. Laura Kieler, *Silhouetter* (Odense, 1887), 13.
22. In Sigrid Arnoldon's guest book, August 30, 1891; *HU*, 15:380.
23. Jæger, *Henrik Ibsen*, 280.
24. J. P. Kristensen-Randers, "Hos Bjørnson og Ibsen: Et Par Samtaler og et Par Breve," *Tilskueren* (January–June 1917), 506.
25. Øisang, *Ibsen som radikaler*, 10–11.
26. O. Arvesen, *Oplevelsen og Erindringer fra 1830-aarene og utover* (Christiania, 1912), 130.
27. Letter to Snoilsky, February 14, 1886.
28. Letter to Klemming, September 18, 1879; Warburg, *Carl Snoilsky*, 235–36.
29. Letter to Magnus Lagerborg, October 29, 1883; R. G. Berg, ed., *Carl Snoilsky och hans vänner: Ur skaldens brevväxling* (Stockholm, 1917–18), 1:258.
30. Letter to Wirsén, 1882; cited in Harald Tveterås, "Ibsen og Snoilsky," *Norvegica: Minneskrift til femti-årsdagen for oprettelsen av Universitetsbibliotekets Norske avdelning* (Oslo, 1933), 148.
31. M. Prozor, "Carl Snoilsky," *La Nouvelle revue* (1897), 89, cited in Henry Olsson, *Den unge Snoilsky* (Stockholm, 1941), 200.
32. Gurli Linder, *Sällskapsliv i Stockholm under 1880 och 1890-talen* (Stockholm, 1918), 26.

33. Snoilsky, *Samlade dikter*, 4:124.
34. Letter to Kristiania Arbeidersamfund, September 28, 1885; *HI skrifter*, 14:309.
35. *HU*, 19:263.
36. *OC*, 13:430.
37. For Dietrichson's letter, see *HI skrifter*, 14k:425.
38. Letter to the Student Association, October 23, 1885; *HU*, 18:68–75.
39. Bjørn Bjørnson, *Det gamle Teater*, 250.
40. *HU*, 15:408.
41. Brandes, *Levned: Snevringer*, 146.

ROSMERSHOLM

1. Dietrichson, *Svundne Tider*, 1:371.
2. Letter of November 10, 1886.
3. Letter to Brandes, October 30, 1888.
4. Letter of February 14, 1886.
5. Letter to Lagerberg, July 29, 1885; Berg, ed., *Snoilsky och hans vänner*, 1:255–56.
6. The name Rosmersholm, it has been suggested, is a combination of the names of Snoilsky's two estates: Rosersberg and Vibyholm. Olsson, *Den unge Snoilsky*, 306.
7. Georg Brandes, *Store Personligheder* (Copenhagen, 1930), 152–53.
8. James Huneker, *Iconoclasts: A Book of Dramatists*, 95–96 (New York, 1905).
9. Letter to Sofie Reimers, March 25, 1887.
10. *Modern Ibsen*, 176.
11. Ibid., v.
12. *HU*, 10:416.
13. Maudsley, *Body and Mind*, 2nd ed. (New York, 1895), 80.
14. *HU*, 10:419.
15. Strindberg, "Själamord (A propå Rosmersholm)," in *August Strindbergs samlade verk*, vol. 29 (Stockholm, 1985), 73–82.
16. Julius Brand, "Henrik Ibsen," *Die Gesellschaft* 4 (December 1888), 1133.
17. Freud, *Civilization and Its Discontents*, 123.
18. *HU*, 10:424–25.
19. See Elias Bredsdorff, "Moralists versus Immoralists: The Great Battle in Scandinavian Literature in the 1880s," *Scandinavica* 8 (1969), 91–111.
20. *HU*, 10:397.
21. Brandes, *Levned: Et Tiaar*, 289–91.
22. Reich, *Aus Leben und Dichtung*, 454.
23. Whyte, *Unconscious Before Freud*, 166–67; Henri F. Ellenberger, *The Discovery of the Unconscious: The History and Evolution of Dynamic Psychiatry* (New York, 1970), 497.
24. *HU*, 10:413.
25. Sigmund Freud, "Some Character-Types Met With in Psycho-analytic Work," in Freud, *Collected Papers*, trans. Joan Riviere, vol. 4 (New York, 1959), 338. Freud's essay derives from Otto Rank, *Das Inzest-Motiv in Dichtung und Sage* (Leipzig, 1912), 404–5.
26. Freud, "Some Character-Types," 340.

27. *New Introductory Lectures on Psycho-Analysis,* in *The Standard Edition of the Complete Psychological Works of Sigmund Freud,* ed. and trans. James Strachey, 24 vols. (London, 1953–74), 22:67.
28. Letter to Bjørn Kristensen, February 13, 1887.
29. On the development of Ibsen's play from first notes to final draft, see Fritz Neumann, "Die Entstehung von Rosmersholm," *Edda* 17 (1922), 240–62, and 18 (1922), 37–68; and *OC,* 13:439–56.
30. *HU,* 10:428.
31. Auguste Ehrhard, *Henrik Ibsen et le théâtre contemporain* (Paris, 1892), 412, was the first to say that Brendel was Ibsen, the idealist. Brandes scoffed at the notion (*Cosmopolis* 5, 1897).
32. *HU,* 10:433.
33. *HU,* 7:311–12. The editors of *HI skrifter* misleadingly take Brendel's remark about sacrificing one's ear as an allusion to witchcraft and folk superstitions (8k:405–6). None of Brendel's other remarks point in this direction.
34. Paulsen, *Samliv med Ibsen: Anden samling,* 195.
35. *HU,* 10:436.
36. Ibid., 10:437.
37. Kihlman, *Ur Ibsen-dramatikens idéhistoria,* 226.

AFTER *ROSMERSHOLM*

1. Letter to Ann Margret Holmgren, December 8, 1886; *Bjørnsons brevveksling med svenske, 1858–1909,* 2:314.
2. Charles Sarolea, *Henrik Ibsen: Étude sur sa vie & son œuvre* (Paris, 1891), 54–55.
3. Julius Elias, "Ibsen-minner af hans tyske oversetter," *Samtiden* (1940), 403; Felix Philippi, "Theaterproben," *Velhagen & Klasings Monatshefte* 26 (1911–12), 75–76.
4. Archie Binns in collaboration with Olive Kooken, *Mrs. Fiske and the American Theatre* (New York, 1925), 194.
5. Letter of February 24, 1880; *Correspondance de Brandes,* vol. 3 (Copenhagen, 1966), 209.
6. *HU,* 15:410–11.
7. Valfrid Spångberg, *Adolf Hedin i Liv och Gärning* (Uppsala and Stockholm, 1921), 40–41.
8. Letter of November 4, 1887; Berg, ed., *Snoilsky och hans vänner,* 2:131.
9. Geijerstam, "Två minnen af Henrik Ibsen," *Ord och Bild* (March 1898), 115–24.
10. "Friedrich Nietzsche und der Naturalismus," *Die Gegenwart* 39 (1891), 209.
11. John Northam, "On a Firm Foundation—the Translation of Ibsen's Prose," *Ibsen-årbok* (1977), 86–87.
12. Jæger, *Illustreret norsk Literaturhistorie,* 2:708–9.
13. Charles Archer, *William Archer,* 157.
14. Paul Lindau, *Nur Erinnerungen* (Stuttgart and Berlin, 1916–17), 2:384.
15. Haeckel, *Evolution of Man,* 1:23.

16. Max Nordau, *Die conventionellen Lügen der Kulturmenschheit*, 12th ed. (Leipzig, 1886), 49.
17. Freud, *Complete Works*, 22:74; cf. 13:158.
18. Mrs. Alec Tweedie, "Henrik Ibsen and Björnstjerne Björnson," *Temple Bar* 98 (1893), 540.
19. *HU*, 11:164.
20. Harald Beyer, "To brev og et brevutkast av Henrik Ibsen," *Edda* (1947), 75; draft of letter (spring 1891) to Didrik Grønvold.
21. Alfred Sinding-Larsen, *Om Henrik Ibsen: Fruen fra Havet og Personerne deri* (Christiania, 1889), 14, 33. Originally in a series of articles in Christiania *Morgenbladet* published in December 1888.
22. Letter to Schrøder, February 5, 1887; *HI skrifter*, 14:389–90.
23. Letter to Schrøder, December 18, 1888.
24. *HU*, 11:164.

THE LADY FROM THE SEA

1. John Paulsen, *Reisen til Monaco og andre erindringer* (Christiania, 1909), 92.
2. Jorunn Hareide, "Ibsen's Drama—as Seen by Magdalene Thoresen," in *Proceedings, IX International Ibsen Conference, Bergen 5–10 June 2000* (Øvre Ervik, Norway, 2001), 374.
3. *HU*, 6:157.
4. Einar Østvedt, *Henrik Ibsen: Miljø og Mennesker* (Oslo, 1968), 126.
5. On Magdalene Thoresen, see ibid., 121–27; Bergsøe, *Magdalene Thoresen*; and Synnöve Clason, "Ibsens svärmor och 'Frun fra havet,'" *Svenska Dagbladet* (Stockholm) May 20, 1985.
6. Quoted in Francis Bull, *HU*, 11:27.
7. Jæger, *Illustreret norsk Literaturhistorie*, 2:692–93.
8. Brandell, *Vid seklets källor* (Stockholm, 1961), 94.
9. *The Freud-Jung Letters*, ed. W. Maguire, trans. R. Manheim and R. F. C. Hull (London, 1974), quoted in Brandell, *Freud: A Man of His Century*, trans. Iain White (Atlantic Highlands, NJ, 1979), 105. Typical of the psychoanalytic studies is Lionel Goitein, "The Lady from the Sea," *Psychoanalytical Review* 14 (1927), 375–419.
10. *HU*, 11:41.
11. Letter of May 17, 1888; *HI skrifter*, 14:473.
12. Passages from *Social Statics*, quoted in Charles Singer, *A Short History of Scientific Ideas to 1900* (Oxford, 1959), 512.
13. Letter to J. Hegel, September 26, 1888.
14. Elisabeth Davidsen, *Henrik Ibsen og Det kongelige Teater* (Copenhagen, 1980), 120.
15. Bjørn Hemmer, *Ibsen: Kunstnerens vei* (Bergen, 2003), 399.
16. Letter to Julius Hoffory, March 26, 1889; *HU*, 18:204.
17. Letter to Julius Hoffory, February 14, 1889; ibid., 18:201.
18. Ove Rode, "Ibsen-Ugen I Berlin," *Politiken* (Copenhagen) 76–77 (March 17–18, 1889).

19. Paul Binding, *With Vine-Leaves in His Hair: The Role of the Artist in Ibsen's Plays* (Norwich, 2006), 78–79.
20. Letter to Strindberg, December 5, 1888, quoted in *Strindbergs brev*, vol. 7, ed. Torsten Eklund (Stockholm, 1961), 197.
21. George [*sic*] Brandes, *Ibsen: A Critical Study*, 103.
22. Andreas-Salomé, *Henrik Ibsens Kvindeskikkelser*, trans. Hulda Garborg (Christiania and Copenhagen, 1893), 138.
23. Skram, "Moderne Forfattere," *Tilskueren* 6 (February 1889), 183–97.
24. Quoted in *HU*, 11:41.
25. Woerner, *Henrik Ibsen*, 2:367.
26. *Ibsens sämtliche Werke*, 8:xxxiii.
27. F. B. Averardi, "Eleanora Duse," *Theatre Arts* (September 1931), 773.
28. William Weaver, *Duse* (New York, 1984), 351.
29. Unsigned, "Il ritorno di Eleanora Duse: Assistendo ad una prova de 'La Donna del mare,'" Winifred Smith collection, Department of Drama and Film, Vassar College, trans. Vincent Giroud.
30. James Agate, *Red Letter Nights* (London, 1944), 71–72.

THE IMMORALISTS

1. Dietrichson, *Svundne Tider*, vol. 4: *Mellem to Tidsaldre* (Christiania, 1917), 295.
2. Letter to Nils Lund, March 4, 1887; *HU*, 18:129–30.
3. Dietrichson, *Svundne Tider*, 4:284–85.
4. Ibid., 4:286.
5. See Bredsdorff, "Moralists versus Immoralists," 104.
6. Letter to Drewsen, October 2, 1885; *Bjornsons brevveksling med danske 1875–1910*, 1:247.
7. Lauritsen, *Chr. Collin og Georg Brandes*, 1:125–26.
8. Bredsdorff, "Moralists versus Immoralists," 104, 107.
9. Letter to Paul Heyse, December 30, 1887; *Correspondance de Brandes*, 3:293.
10. Brandes, *Levned: Snevringer*, 219.
11. Letter to Heyse, December 30, 1887; *Correspondance de Brandes*, 3:293.
12. Frederick Böök, *Victoria Benedictsson och Georg Brandes* (Stockholm, 1949), 136.
13. Letter to Ellen Key, November 27, 1897; Georg og Edv. Brandes, *Brevveksling med nordiske Forfattere*, 7:173.
14. R. Thesen, "Bjørnstjerne Bjornson og Georg Brandes," *Festskrift til Halvdan Koht på sekstiårsdagen 7 de juli 1933* (Oslo, 1933), 320.
15. Böök, *Benedictsson och Brandes*, 275–76.
16. Ibid., 113.
17. Sten Linder, "Ernst Ahlgren och Georg Brandes," *Samlaren*, n.s., 16 (1935), 77.
18. Benedictsson, *Dagboksblad och brev*, ed. Axel Lundegård (Stockholm, 1928), 2:83, 114.
19. Quoted in Sten Linder, *Ibsen, Strindberg och andra* (Stockholm, 1936), 244.
20. Böök, *Benedictsson och Brandes*, 201.
21. Ibid., 283.

22. Linder, *Ibsen, Strindberg och andra*, 254.
23. Axel Lundegård, *Några Strindbergsminnen knutna till en handful brev* (Stockholm, 1920), 114–15.
24. Böök, *Benedictsson och Brandes*, 261–62.
25. First suggested by Li Bennich-Björkman, *Dagens Nyheter* (Stockholm), November 6, 1960.
26. Letter to Heyse, December 30, 1887; *Correspondance de Brandes*, 3:293.
27. Letters of January 11 and March 7, 1888; *Correspondance de Georg Brandes*, 3:448–49, 3:454, 3:455.
28. Brandes, *Nietzsche*, 43.
29. Brandes, "Friedrich Nietzsche," in Brandes, *Samlede Skrifter*, 7:643.
30. Nietzsche claimed (letter to Brandes, February 19, 1888) that he coined the term *Bildungsphilister*, but it had been used earlier by Gustav Teichmüller.
31. Letter to Brandes, December 2, 1887.
32. *Beyond Good and Evil*, section 265.
33. *Tilskueren* 7 (1890), 3.
34. Høffding, "Gensvar til Dr. Georg Brandes," *Tilskueren* 7 (1890), 130.
35. *Politiken*, April 11, 18, 25, May 2, 9, 1889.
36. *Tilskueren* 9 (1890), 7.
37. In *Politiken*, April 11, 18, 25, May 2, 9.
38. *HU*, 11:500.
39. Høffding, *Erindringer* (Copenhagen, 1928), 159.
40. *HU*, 11:512, 511, 506, 504.
41. Ibid., 11:511, 504.
42. Ibid., 11:503.
43. Ibid., 11:497.
44. Ibid., 11:504.
45. Ellen Key, *Ernst Ahlgren: Några biografiska meddeladen* (Stockholm, 1889), quoted in Haakonsen, *Henrik Ibsen*, 232.
46. Letter of January 5, 1889.
47. Georg og Edv. Brandes, *Brevveksling med nordiske Forfattere*, 6:248–49; Benedictsson, *Dagboksblad och brev*, 2:276–77.
48. Not in Centennial Edition. See Else Høst, *Hedda Gabler: En monografi* (Oslo, 1958), 82.
49. *HU*, 11:501.
50. Brandes, *Nietzsche*, 74.
51. Nietzsche, *The Will to Power*, ed. Walter Kaufmann (New York, 1967), 52–53.
52. *HU*, 11:512.
53. Ibid., 11:504.
54. Brandes, *Nietzsche* (New York, 1964), 108.
55. Interview, November 26, 1900; *HU*, 15:436.
56. On the philosophical similarities between Nietzsche and Ibsen, see Thomas F. Van Laan, "Ibsen and Nietzsche," *Scandinavian Studies* 78 (2006), 255–302.

THE UNSPOKEN *HEDDA*

1. Ehrhard, *Ibsen et le théâtre contemporain*, 446–47.
2. Bigeon, "Profils scandinaves: Henrik Ibsen," 3. In Maurice Bigeon's interview with Ibsen, conducted through an interpreter, Ehrhard's view of Hedda is mistakenly attributed to another critic, Jules Lemaître, who had a far lower opinion of her, calling her monstrously proud, above all laws, driven by a cerebral kind of jealousy, very capricious because of her pregnancy, and wicked because in mediocre souls wickedness becomes the best expression of strength. (Lemaître, *Impressions de théâtre, sixième série* [Paris, 1898], 52–54.)
3. *HU*, 11:511.
4. John Northam and Else Høst pioneered in the study of these visual elements in Ibsen's realistic plays, especially in *Hedda Gabler*, and others have followed in their footsteps (Northam, *Ibsen's Dramatic Method*, London, 1953; Høst, *Hedda Gabler*). Among further contributions to the subject are Sigmund Skard, "Else Høsts doktordisputas om Hedda Gabler," *Edda* 60 (1960), 24; Erik Østerud, "Lenestolsymbolet i 'Hedda Gabler,'" *Ibsen-årbok* (1960–62), 82–92; Northam, "Hedda Gabler," *Ibsen-årbok* (1968–69), 60–81; and James H. Clancey, "Hedda Gabler: Poetry in Action and in Object," in *Studies in Theatre and Drama: Essays in Honor of Hubert C. Heffner*, ed. Oscar G. Brockett (The Hague, 1972), 64–72.
5. See Northam, *Ibsen's Dramatic Method*, 132; Rannveig Åse, "'Fruen fra havet': En studie med utgangspunkt i den norske hørespillversjonen," *Ibsen-årbok* (1968–69), 151.
6. Letter to Kristine Steen, January 14, 1891.
7. Wolfgang Brachvogel, "'Hedda Gabler' in München," *Freie Bühne für modernes Leben* 2 (1891), 117–18; Davidsen, *Ibsen og Det kongelige Teater*, 177.
8. Ibsen, *Hedda Gabler*, French translation by M. Prozor (Paris, 1892), 5.
9. *On the Genealogy of Morals*, trans. Walter Kaufmann (New York, 1967), essay 2, section 16.
10. Ehrhard, *Ibsen et le théâtre contemporain*, 458.
11. *Truth*, April 30, 1891, quoted in Archer, "'Mausoleum of Ibsen,'" 85.
12. The similarities between the two plays were immediately apparent to knowledgeable critics; for example, Henrik Jæger, "Hedda Gablers forhold til tidligere skuespil af Henrik Ibsen," *Folkebladet* (Christiania, 1891), no. 2; Jæger, *Henrik Ibsen og hans Værker* (Christiania, 1892), 190; and Emil Reich, "Ibsen und das Recht der Frau," in *Jahresbericht des Vereins für erweiterte Frauenbildung* (Vienna, 1891).
13. *HU*, 4:94.
14. Arnold, *Culture and Anarchy*, ed. J. Dover Wilson (Cambridge, 1960), 102.
15. On the significance of the vine leaves, see Faaland, *Ibsen og antikken*, 74; Skard, "Else Høsts doktordisputas," 25–28, 49–50; Lis Jacobsen, "En trilogi: Studie over tre Ibsen'ske trylleord," *Edda* (1960), 53–70; Northam, "Hedda Gabler," 60–81; Eugene Webb, "The Radical Irony of Hedda Gabler," *Modern Language Quarterly* 31 (1970), 53–63.
16. Chapter 9, section 49.
17. See Harald Beyer, *Nietzsche og Norden* (Bergen, 1957–59), 2:36.
18. Lochmann, *Populære opsatser* (Christiania, 1891), 214. Among others who remarked

on the Nietzschean aspects of *Hedda Gabler* were Lemaître, *Impressions de théâtre,* 49–62 (a review that appeared originally in December 1891); J. A. Eklund, "Om 'Hedda Gabler' och 'esteticism,'" *Svensk Tidsrift* 2 (1892), 606–16; and Huneker, *Iconoclasts,* 101.

19. Quoted in F. E. Lea, *The Tragic Philosopher: A Study of Friedrich Nietzsche* (London, 1957), 319.
20. Ehrhard, *Henrik Ibsen,* 456.
21. Eklund, "Om 'Hedda Gabler' och 'esteticism,'" 613.
22. *Genealogy of Morals,* essay 1, section 11.

WORLD FAME

1. Letter of December 28, 1867.
2. Collin, "Henrik Ibsens Fremtidsdrøm," 485.
3. Koht, *Henrik Ibsen,* 2:69.
4. Hans Heiberg, "... *født til kunstner,*" 185–86.
5. *HU,* 19:168–69.
6. Otto Brahm, *Kritische Schriften,* vol. 1 (Berlin, 1915), 451.
7. Ibid., 1:452.
8. Franz Wallner, "Ibsens Freudentränen: Erinnerungen an die erste 'Gespenster'-Aufführung," *Die Deutsche Bühne* 20, no. 4 (March 13, 1928). See also Otto Brahm, "Ibsens Gespenster in Berlin," *Nation* (January 15, 1887), 106.
9. *Kritische Schriften,* 1:465.
10. Ibid., 1:460.
11. "Ibsens Gespenster in Berlin," 109.
12. Letter to Julius Hoffory, March 26, 1889.
13. "Ibsens Gespenster in Berlin," 107.
14. F. L. Lucas, *The Drama of Ibsen and Strindberg* (London, 1962), 20.
15. Adolph Paul, *Profiler* (Stockholm, 1937), 113.
16. Ibsen in conversation with Helene Raff, 1891; *HU,* 19:180.
17. Paulsen, *Nye erindringer,* 114–15.
18. Louise Dumont, in *Einiges über Ibsen: Zur Feier ihrer alljährlichen Mai-Festspiele herausgeben von der Ibsenvereinigung zu Düsseldorf* (Berlin and Leipzig, 1909), 22.
19. Symons, *Studies in Seven Arts,* 336–37.
20. Tor Hedberg, quoted in O. Wieselgren, "Svensk teater från 1500 till 1900," in *Svenska konstnärer inom teaterns, musikens och filmens värld,* ed. Einar Sundström (Stockholm, 1943), 52.
21. Geyer, *Etude médico-psychologique,* 11.
22. Georges Leneveu, *Ibsen et Maeterlinck* (Paris, 1902), 133.
23. "Über Henrik Ibsen und sein Dichtung 'Peer Gynt,'" in Otto Weininger, *Über die letzten Dinge* (Vienna and Leipzig, 1904).
24. Gosse, *Henrik Ibsen,* 239.
25. Huneker, *Egoists,* 317.
26. Shaw, "The Sanity of Art," in *Major Critical Essays,* 284.

27. Max Nordau, *Degeneration* (New York, 1895), 404, 400.
28. *Report from the Select Committee on Theatres and Places of Entertainment* (1892), in Irish University Press Series of British Parliamentary Papers: Stage and Theatre, vol. 3 (Dublin, 1970), 334.
29. *New York Tribune*, January 26, 1894.
30. Egan, ed., *Ibsen: The Critical Heritage*, 162, 229.
31. *Scenic Art*, 243, 249, 247.
32. Tweedie, "Henrik Ibsen and Björnstjerne Björnson," 540.
33. Lindau, *Nur Erinnerungen*, 2:384.
34. Leneveu, *Ibsen et Maeterlinck*, 197–98.
35. Mosfjeld, *Ibsen og Skien*, 181.
36. Sources for the above: Henrik Jæger, *Illustreret norsk Literaturhistorie*, 2:705–8; E. J. Goodman, "Dr. Ibsen at Christiania," *The Theatre* 26 (September 1, 1895), 146–49; Lindau, *Nur Erinnerungen*, 2:380–85; note to Roman Woerner, August 6, 1896 (*HI skrifter*, 15:358).
37. *HI skrifter*, 15:221.
38. "Profils scandinaves: Henrik Ibsen," 3. See photo portrait (1891) in *HU*, vol. 20, plate 103.
39. *Nur Erinnerungen*, 2:380.

NEW DIRECTIONS

1. Henrik Jæger, *Henrik Ibsen: Ein literarisches Lebensbild*, 2nd ed., trans. H. Zschalig (Dresden and Leipzig, 1897), 163.
2. See Pola Gauguin, *Krohg* (Oslo, 1932), 156–58.
3. Ibsen, *Brev: Ny samling*, 1:384.
4. *HU*, 11:356.
5. Zucker, *Ibsen, the Master Builder*, 234.
6. Siegfried Jacobsohn, in *Agnes Sorma: Ein Gedenkbuch*, ed. Julius Bab (Heidelberg, 1927), 54.
7. "Zur Kritik des Moderne" (1890), quoted in Brahm, *Kritische Schriften*, 1:468.
8. Brandes, *Essays: Fremmede Personligheder* (Copenhagen, 1889), 242–43.
9. "Fra det ubevidste Sjæleliv," reprinted in Knut Hamsun, *Artikler 1889–1928*, ed. Francis Bull (Oslo, 1965).
10. Hans Heiberg, "*. . . født til kunstner*," 274.
11. Knut Hamsun, *Paa Turné*, ed. Tore Hamsun (Oslo, 1960), 37.
12. Francis Bull, *Vildanden og andre essays* (Oslo, 1966), 41.
13. Letter to J. Collin, July 31, 1895; *HU*, 18:374.
14. Arne Duve, *Henrik Ibsens hemmeligheter* (Oslo, 1977), 46.
15. Interview with Jules Claretie (1897), in *HU*, 19:209; originally in *Le Figaro* (July 20, 1897).
16. *HU*, 19:154.
17. Letter to Prozor, November 14, 1892.
18. *OC*, 15:19–20.

19. Letter of January 17, 1892; Bjørnson, *Breve til Karoline*, 317.
20. Letter of May 26, 1894; *Breve fra Magdalene Thoresen 1855–1901*, ed. Julius Clausen and P. Fr. Rist (Copenhagen, 1971).
21. *OC*, 15:17.
22. Frederick Hegel, *Erindringen* (Copenhagen, 1946), 1:115.

WHO IS HILDA?

1. *HU*, 19:173.
2. Skard, "Else Høsts doktordisputas," 7.
3. Brandes, *Henrik Ibsen: Mit zwölf Briefen Henrik Ibsens* (Berlin, n.d. [1906]).
4. See Joan Templeton, "New Light on the Bardach Diary: Eight Unpublished Letters from Ibsen's Gossensass Princess," *Scandinavian Studies* 69 (1997), 147–70.
5. Quoted in Joan Templeton, *Ibsen's Women* (Cambridge, 1997), 235.
6. "New Light on the Bardach Diary," 169.
7. Templeton, *Ibsen's Women*, 247.
8. Letter to Bardach, October 15, 1889.
9. Letter of December 22, 1889.
10. Letter of February 6, 1890.
11. Letter of December 30, 1890.
12. Letter of March 13, 1898.
13. Letter of March 26, 1889.
14. Skard, "Else Høsts doktordisputas," 12.
15. Ibid., 18.
16. *HU*, 19:210; Skard, in "Else Høsts doktordisputas," 17.
17. Letter to Raff, November 30, 1889; *HI skrifter*, 14:583.
18. *HU*, 19:281.
19. Lindberg, *August Lindberg*, 315; *OC*, 15:19–20.
20. Bull, *Vildanden og andre essays*, 38.
21. Sontum, "Personal Recollections of Ibsen," 247–56. Details about Ibsen's spectacles, which have been preserved, can be found in Anne-Sofie Hjemdahl and Ane Haukebø Aasland, "Syn og sannhet," in *Ting om Ibsen*, ed. Anne-Sofie Hjemdahl (Oslo, 2006), 57–59.
22. Francis Bull, "Hildur Andersen og Henrik Ibsen," *Edda* (1957), 47–54.
23. *HU*, 14:462–63; trans. R. Ellis Roberts, in *Henrik Ibsen: A Critical Study* (London, 1912), 51.
24. Letter of January 7, 1893.
25. Letter to Hildur Andersen, October 5, 1893.
26. Ibsen, *Brev: Ny samling*, 2:121–22.
27. *HI skrifter*, 15:229–30.
28. Ibsen, *Brev: Ny samling*, 1:409–10.
29. *HU*, 19:173.
30. Ibid., 20:20.
31. Ibsen, *Brev: Ny samling*, 2:120–21.

32. Letter of May 7, 1895; *HU*, 19:376–77.
33. Letter of September 19, 1899; Ibsen, *Brev: Ny samling*, 1:466.
34. Bull, "Hildur Andersen og Henrik Ibsen," 54.
35. Gosse, *Henrik Ibsen*, 182; *Collected Works of Ibsen*, 13:185.
36. Romain Rolland, *Goethe and Beethoven*, trans. G. A. Pfister and E. S. Kemp (London and New York, 1931), 163–64.
37. *Tilskueren* (January 1895), 35–44.
38. Letter of February 11, 1895.
39. Werner Möhring, "Ibsens Abkehr von Kierkegaard," *Edda* 28 (1928), 67.
40. Heiberg, "*... født til kunstner*," 274.

THE STORY OF SOLNESS

1. *HU*, 12:65.
2. Both devils and trolls are referred to. The former are Christian demons; the trolls are Viking demons. In act one, Solness refers to devils, Hilda to trolls; in act two, the terms are used by both; in act three, Hilde refers to devils, and only Solness speaks of trolls. See Sandra E. Saari, "Of Madness and Fame: Ibsen's Bygmester Solness," *Scandinavian Studies* 50 (1978), 7.
3. M. Prozor, "Ibsens 'Lille Eyolf,'" *Ord och Bild* 4 (1895), 369.
4. Ernst Motzfeldt, "Af samtaler med Henrik Ibsen," *Aftenposten* (Oslo) (April 23, 1911).
5. Mathilde Schjøtt, *Efter Læsningen af "Byggmester Solness"* (Christiania, 1893), 6–7.

THE MAN BEHIND THE MASK

1. Hugo von Hofmannsthal, "Die Menschen in Ibsens Dramen," *Prosa*, vol. 1 (Frankfurt am Main, 1950), 109.
2. Motzfeldt, "Af samtaler med Henrik Ibsen"; trans. Michael Meyer, *Ibsen* (New York, 1971), 695.
3. Frank Wedekind, "Ibsen the Writer and Solness *The Master Builder*," translated by Christel Fjelde, in *Theater Three* 1 (Fall 1986), 94–103; originally in *Neue Zürcher Zeitung*, September 2–5, 1905.
4. Brandes, *Samlede Skrifter*, 18:200–201.
5. *HU*, 12:86.
6. Letter to Brandes, May 18, 1871.
7. Letter to Gosse, April 16, 1874; *Sir Edmund Gosse's Correspondence with Scandinavian Writers*, ed. Elias Bredsdorff (Copenhagen, 1960), 121.
8. See Brandes, *Samlede Skrifter*, 14:560.
9. Ibid., 14:559.
10. Ibid., 18:131.
11. See Erik M. Christensen, "Why Should Brandes Sabotage Ibsen in Germany?" in *Contemporary Approaches to Ibsen*, vol. 5 (Oslo, 1985), 81–98.

THE RETURN OF NORA

1. *OC*, 15:31.
2. *Dagens Nyheder*, May 23, 1890, signed G.E.
3. Ibid., May 24, 1890.
4. *HU*, 18:250.
5. Letter to Kieler, July 23, 1888.
6. Bjørn Bjørnson, *Det gamle teater*, 277–80.
7. Brandes, *Samlede Skrifter*, 18:127–28.
8. *Dagens Nyheder* 23 (May 11, 1890).
9. Ibid., May 14, 1890.
10. *HU*, 12:89.

SOLNESS AS SUPERMAN

1. Nietzsche, *The Birth of Tragedy and The Genealogy of Morals*, trans. Francis Golding (Garden City, NY, 1956), 77.
2. See Michael W. Kaufman, "Nietzsche, Georg Brandes, and Ibsen's Master Builder," *Comparative Drama* 6, no. 3 (1972), 169–86; and Michael Hinden, "Ibsen and Nietzsche: A Reading of *The Master Builder*," *Modern Drama* 15, no. 4 (1973), 403–10.
3. Key, "Ibsen's Individualism," quoted in Örjan Lindberger, "Ibsen, Ellen Key och kvinnorna," *Nordisk tidskrift för vetenskap, konst och industri*, n.s., 36 (1960), 108–9.
4. Brandes, *Levned: Snevringer*, 361.

CONQUERING FRANCE

1. Kela Nyholm, "Henrik Ibsen paa den franske Scene," *Ibsen-årbok* (1957–59), 77–78.
2. *HI skrifter*, 15:243.
3. Bigeon, "Profils scandinaves: Henrik Ibsen," 3.
4. M[ax] Harden, "Hedda Gabler und ihre Kritiker," *Die Gegenwart* 39, no. 8 (February 21, 1891), 125–26.
5. F. W. J. Hemmings, *Culture and Society in France 1848–1898* (New York, 1971), 241.
6. Brandes, *Samlede Skrifter*, 18:143–44.
7. Bigeon, "Profils scandinaves: Henrik Ibsen," 3.
8. Edgar O. Achorn, "Ibsen at Home," *New England Magazine*, n.s., 13, no. 6 (February 1896), 74.
9. Herman Bang, "Erinnerungen an Henrik Ibsen," *Die neue Rundschau* (December 1906), 1499.
10. *HU*, 19:210–11.
11. Letter to Emil Schreiner, December 3, 1900.
12. William Archer, "Ibsen's Craftsmanship," *Fortnightly Review*, n.s., 80 (July 1906), 113.
13. Shaw, *Our Theatres in the Nineties*, 1:78.
14. Interview with L. François in *La Revue d'Art Dramatique*, quoted in Frantisek Deak, *Symbolist Theater* (Baltimore, 1993), 204.

15. Letter to Emil Schreiner, December 3, 1900; *HI skrifter*, 15:532.
16. Per Lindberg, *August Lindberg*, 343.
17. Maurice Maeterlinck, "On the Master Builder," trans. Albert Bermel, *Theater Three* 1 (Fall 1986), 90–94. Originally in *Le Figaro*, "A propos de Solness le Constructeur" (April 2, 1894), 1. Revised later as "The Tragic in Daily Life."

LITTLE EYOLF

1. Heinrich Zschalig in Jæger, *Ibsen: Ein literarisches Lebensbild*, 277.
2. *HI skrifter*, 9k:383–87.
3. Ibid., 14k:36–37.
4. Quoted in McFarlane, ed., *Oxford Ibsen*, 8:320–21.
5. W. L. Courtney, "A Note on Ibsen's 'Little Eyolf,'" *Fortnightly Review*, n.s., 57 (January–June 1895), 284.
6. *HU*, 12:268.
7. Østvedt, *Ibsens barndom*, 114, 194–98.
8. Prozor, "Ibsens 'Lille Eyolf,'" 370.
9. Kurt Wais, "Henrik Ibsens Sinnbilder und die Krise seiner Jahrhunderts," *Edda* 56 (1956), 322.
10. *HU*, 19:203–4.
11. A. Collett, *Camilla Colletts livs historie* (Christiania, 1911), 196 ff.
12. John Paulsen, *Min første sommer i København* (Copenhagen and Christiania, 1908), 93.
13. Østvedt, *Et dukkehjem*, 210–11.
14. Ibid., 211–15.
15. Letter of May 3, 1889.
16. Letter to Collett, May 3, 1892; *HU*, 18:309–10.
17. Paulsen, *Min første sommer*, 91, 97.
18. Sources: Østvedt, *Ibsen og la bella Italia*, 133; Paulsen, *Mine erindringer*, 117.
19. *HU*, 12:206.
20. *HU*, 12:205.
21. Steen, *Den lange Strid*, 359.
22. Nordau, *Degeneration*, 338.
23. Chr[isten] Collin, *Kunsten og moralen: Bidrag til kritik af realismens digtere og kritikere* (Copenhagen, 1894), 90.
24. Ibid., 90–91.
25. Schofield, "Personal Impressions of Björnson and Ibsen," 570.
26. *Kunsten og moralen*, 302–3.
27. Ibid., 64.
28. Ibid., 53–54.
29. Ibid., 52–53.
30. Halvdan Koht and Julius Elias, "Forord" to Ibsen, *Efterladte Skrifter*, 1:cxiv–cxv.
31. *HU*, 12:281.
32. Ansten Anstensen, *The Proverb in Ibsen* (New York, 1936), 217.
33. *HU*, 12:211.

34. Ibid., 12:214.
35. Ibid., 12:242.
36. *Kunsten og moralen*, 53.
37. *HU*, 12:267.
38. Emil Reich, *Henrik Ibsens Dramen: Zwanzig Vorlesungen, gehalten an der Universitat Wien*, 7th rev. ed. (Berlin, 1910 [1909]), 427.
39. Zschalig in Jæger, *Ibsen: Ein literarisches Lebensbild*, 272.
40. *HU*, 19:204.
41. Sontum, "Personal Recollections of Ibsen," 252.

JOHN GABRIEL BORKMAN

1. Sontum, "Personal Recollections of Ibsen," 252.
2. Quoted by Zschalig in Jæger, *Ibsen: Ein literarisches Lebensbild*, 288.
3. Sperans, "Banquier-Symbolismus," *Sozialistische Monatshefte* 1 (1897), 87–97.
4. André Maurel, "Le nouveau drame d'Ibsen: Jean-Gabriel Borkman," *Le Figaro* (December 27, 1896), 5.
5. Egan, ed., *Ibsen: Critical Heritage*, 369.
6. Ibid., 360, 361.
7. Ibid., 364–65.
8. Quoted in Jæger, *Ibsen: Ein literarisches Lebensbild*, 291.
9. Cf. view of Zschalig, ibid.
10. Vilhelm Andersen, *Kritik: Teater* (Christiania, 1914), 86–87; Sigurd Høst, "Ibsen i tidens Kamp," in *Til Gerhard Gran 9. December 1916 fra venner og elever* (Christiania, 1916), 283.
11. *HU*, 12:86.
12. Reading the play as autobiography, Oscar Olsson (*Ibsens dramer* [Stockholm, 1937], 443–60) sees the publication of *Ghosts* as the beginning of Borkman's imprisonment.
13. Brandes, *Henrik Ibsen*, 84–85.
14. Christensen, "Why Should Brandes Sabotage," 89; and Christensen, *Henrik Ibsens realisme*, 52–60.
15. *HU*, 13:75.
16. Letter of June 25, 1884; *HU*, 18:27.
17. *HU*, 13:85.
18. Ibid., 13:87.
19. Ibid., 13:84.
20. Skram, "Moderne Forfattere," 194.

FOLDAL AND HINKEL

1. Schofield, "Personal Impressions of Björnson and Ibsen," 570.
2. *HU*, 13:79.
3. Ibid., 13:75.
4. *Collected Works of Ibsen*, 11:xxiii.

5. Boyesen, *Essays on Scandinavian Literature*, 215–16.
6. Letter to Brandes, October 3, 1896; Beyer, *Nietzsche og Norden*, 2:38.
7. Leo Berg, *Der Übermensch in der modernen Litteratur* (Paris, Leipzig, and Munich, 1897), 122–23. This book was in Ibsen's library.
8. Paulsen, "'Afterne i Arbinsgade,'" 57.
9. See Eugen Heinrich Schmitt, *Ibsen als Prophet: Grundgedanken zu einer neuen Ästhetik* (Leipzig, 1908), 217–18, 229–30.
10. Ernest Tissot, *Le Drame norvégien: Henrik Ibsen—Biörnstierne Biörnstierne* (Paris, 1893), 139–42.
11. Woerner, *Henrik Ibsen*, 2:233–35. See also the comments by Walter Kaufmann in his translation of Nietzsche's *Will to Power*, 52–54, and the commentary in *Correspondance de Georg Brandes*, 3:390–91.
12. Reich, *Ibsens Dramen*, 522.
13. Ibsen, *Brev: Ny samling*, 1:483.
14. Brandes, *Henrik Ibsen* (Copenhagen, 1898), 181.
15. *HU*, 13:106.
16. Francisque Sarcey, *Quarante ans de théâtre*, vol. 8 (Paris, 1902), 375.
17. Jules Lemaître, "Revue dramatique," *Revue des deux mondes* 139 (February 1, 1897), 699.
18. Birgitta Holm, *Victoria Benedictsson* (Stockholm, 2007), 178–79.
19. Speech of September 24, 1887; *HU*, 15:410–11.
20. George [*sic*] Brandes, *Ibsen: A Critical Study*, 64–65; originally in Brandes, *Henrik Ibsen* (Copenhagen, 1898), 92–93.
21. Vasenius, *Ibsens dramatiska diktning*, 143.
22. Brandes, letter of November 23, 1888; *Correspondance de Brandes*, 3:477.
23. Anders Uhrskov, *Christopher Bruun* (Christiania, 1916), 253.
24. Sontum, "Personal Recollections of Ibsen," 251.
25. Letter to Ola Hansson, January 2, 1897; *HU*, 18:391.
26. See Mark B. Sandberg, "John Gabriel Borkman's Avant-Garde Continuity," *Modern Drama* 49, no. 3 (Fall 2006), 340–44; Frederick J. Marker and Lise-Lone Marker, *Ibsen's Lively Art: A Performance Study of the Major Plays* (Cambridge, 1989), 200–1.
27. *The Authentic Librettos of the Wagner Operas* (New York, 1938), 445.
28. Patrick Carnegy, *Wagner and the Art of the Theatre* (New Haven and London, 2006), 111–13, with an illustration of the device.
29. *HU*, 13:124.
30. *HU*, 13:97.

SEVENTIETH-BIRTHDAY CELEBRATIONS

1. *Gosse's Correspondence with Scandinavian Writers*, 180.
2. *HU*, 15:414.
3. *Malmö-Tidningen*, April 7, 1898; *Lunds Dagblad*, April 7, 1898.
4. Francis Bull, "Ers Majestät, jag måste skriva Gengångare," *Röster i Radio* 49 (December 9–11, 1962).

5. Strindberg, letter to Geijerstam, October 23, 1898; *August Strindbergs brev*, ed. Torsten Eklund, vol. 13 (Stockholm, 1972), 23.
6. *HU*, 15:430–31.
7. Ibsen, letter to Geijerstam, October 4, 1898.
8. Albert Engström, "En intervju med Ibsen," *Skrifter av Albert Engström*, vol. 26 (Stockholm, 1945), 72.
9. Per Hallström, *Carl Snoilsky: En levnadsteckning* (Stockholm, 1933), 248.
10. *Malmö-Tidningen*, April 14, 1898.
11. Ibsen, *Samlede Værker*, 10:524; *HI skrifter*, 16:516.
12. Accounts from *Malmö-Tidningen*, April 13, 14, and 15, 1898.
13. See Ibsen, letter to Key, May 30, 1898.
14. Lindberger, "Ibsen, Ellen Key och kvinnorna," 102–9.
15. *HU*, 15:417.
16. Bergliot Ibsen, *De tre*, 177.
17. *HU*, 19:213.
18. "To My Brothers in Guilt"; ibid., 14:311.
19. William Archer, "Ibsen as I Knew Him," 19.
20. Letter to Moritz Prozor, March 6, 1900.
21. *Verdens Gang*, December 12, 1899; quoted in *HU*, 19:226.

A DRAMATIC EPILOGUE

1. *Verdens Gang*, December 12, 1899; quoted in *HU*, 13:206.
2. *HU*, 13:191, 19:215–16.
3. Per Lindberg, *August Lindberg*, 375–76.
4. Ibid., 375–77; Koht, *Henrik Ibsen*, 1:274.
5. *HU*, 19:215–20.
6. Francis Bull, ed., *Norsk Litteraturhistorie*, vol. 4 (Oslo, 1924), 450; Koht, *Henrik Ibsen*, 1:274; Didrik Arup Seip in *HU*, 13:191.
7. Shaw, *Major Critical Essays*, 111.
8. *HU*, 13:220–21.
9. Andreas Fibiger, in *Henrik Ibsen, En studie over Guds-linien i hans Liv* (Copenhagen, 1928), argues that Ibsen came to regard all his plays after *Brand* as a betrayal of the best in himself.
10. Letter to Kieler, November 24, 1891; *HI skrifter*, 15:155.
11. OC, 15:35; also Kinck, "Ibsen og Laura Kieler," 531.
12. Østvedt, *Et dukkehjem*, 216–21.
13. *HU*, 13:195–96.
14. Kinck, "Ibsen og Laura Kieler," 535.
15. H. Amsenck, *Sceneinstruktøren Herman Bang* (Copenhagen, 1972), 58.
16. Arthur Schopenhauer, *The World as Will and Representation*, trans. E. F. J. Payne (Indian Hills, CO, 1958), 1:8.
17. Letter to Rosa Fitinghoff, 17 April 1899.

18. Bodil Nævdal, "Hun ble kveldssolen i hans liv," *Aftenposten* (Oslo) December 24, 1988), 25. Cf. Sæter, *Suzannah, Fru Ibsen*, 306–7.
19. Huneker, *Egoists*, 335.
20. *OC*, 16:242; quoted in Ibsen, *Brev: Ny samling*, 465.
21. Letter to Edvard Brandes, March 1, 1899.
22. *HU*, 13:253.
23. Ibid., 13:254.
24. Cf. the similar view of B. M. Kinck, "Dramaet Brand: Opfatning og tolkninger," *Edda* 30 (1930), 81–95.

THE LAST YEARS

1. C. H. Herford, introduction to *Brand* (London, 1894), xv.
2. *Samlede Værker*, vol. 1, "Til læserne."
3. *HU*, 15:412.
4. Ibid., 19:212.
5. Letter to William Archer, January 13, 1890; *HI skrifter*, 15:12.
6. Letter to Fitinghoff, January 15, 1901; *HI skrifter*, 15:538–39.
7. *HU*, 15:440.
8. Zucker, *Ibsen, the Master Builder*, 281.
9. Arne Dvergsdal, "Den fatale historie," *Dagbladet* (May 23, 2006), 42–43; *HI skrifter*, 9k:206.
10. Bergliot Ibsen, *De tre*, 218; originally in Julius Elias, "Christianiafahrt / Erinnerungen," *Die neue Rundschau* (December 1906), 1459.
11. *OC*, 16:279–80.
12. Ibid., 16:280.
13. Bergliot Ibsen, *De tre*, 214.
14. Lugné-Poe, *Ibsen* (Paris, 1936), 94–97.
15. *HU*, 20:45.
16. Einar Østvedt, "Omkring Henrik Ibsens død 23 mai 1906," *Ibsen-årbok* (1955–56), 13.
17. Sæther, *Suzannah, Fru Ibsen*, 316.
18. Ibid., 334.
19. Preface to 2nd ed. of *Catiline*; *HU*, 1:123.
20. Gustaf af Geijerstam, "Ibsen der Mensch," *Die Schaubühne* 2, no. 26 (June 28, 1906), 725.
21. *HU*, 4:243.
22. C. H. Herford translation; *Collected Works of Ibsen*, 3:178. *HU*, 5:303.
23. Brandes, *Samlede Skrifter*, 18:137–38.

BIBLIOGRAPHY

Aarseth, Asbjørn. "Ibsen and Darwin: A Reading of The Wild Duck." *Modern Drama* 48 (2005).

———. *Ibsens samtidsskuespil.* Oslo, 1999.

Achorn, Edgar O. "Ibsen at Home." *New England Magazine*, n.s., 13, no. 6 (February 1896).

Adler, Jeremy. "The Aesthetics of Magnetism: Science, Philosophy and Poetry in the Dialogue Between Goethe and Schelling." In *The Third Culture: Literature and Science*, edited by Elinor S. Shaffer. Berlin and New York, 1998.

Agate, James. *Red Letter Nights.* London, 1944.

Ahlström, Gunnar. *Det moderna genombrottet i Nordens litteratur.* Stockholm, 1947.

Amsenck, H. *Sceneinstruktøren Herman Bang.* Copenhagen, 1972.

Andersen, Vilhelm. *Kritik: Teater.* Christiania, 1914.

Anderson, Andrew Runni. "Studies in Ibsen. I. The Poetic Themes in Ibsen's I Billedgalleriet ; II. The Chronology and Composition of the Digte." *Scandinavian Studies* 2 (1914–16).

Andreas-Salomé, Lou. *Henrik Ibsens Kvindeskikkelser.* Translated by Hulda Garborg. Christiania and Copenhagen, 1893.

Andrews, A. L. "Ibsen's *Peer Gynt* and Goethe's *Faust.*" *Journal of English and Germanic Philology* (1914).

Anker, Øyvind. "Ibsen og Den skandinaviske forening i Roma." *Edda* (1956).

———. "Scenekunst gjennom 150 år." *Dette er Norge* (1963).

Anstensen, Ansten. *The Proverb in Ibsen.* New York, 1936.

Archer, Charles. *William Archer, Life, Work and Friendships.* New Haven, 1931.

Archer, William. "The Humour of 'The Wild Duck.'" In *The Theatrical "World" of 1897.* London, 1898.

———. "Ibsen as I Knew Him." *Monthly Review* 23 (1906).

———. "Ibseniana: Letters from William Archer to Charles Archer." *London Mercury and Bookman* 36 (October 1937).

———. "Ibsen's Apprenticeship." *Fortnightly Review*, n.s., 75 (January 1904).
———. "Ibsen's Craftsmanship." *Fortnightly Review*, n.s., 80 (July 1906).
———. "'The Mausoleum of Ibsen.'" *Fortnightly Review*, n.s., 54 (1893).
———. *The Old Drama and the New*. Boston, 1923.
Arnold, Matthew. *Culture and Anarchy*. Edited by J. Dover Wilson. Cambridge, 1960.
———. *The Poetry: The Critical Heritage*. Edited by Carl Dawson. London and Boston, 1973.
Arvesen, O. *Oplevelsen og Erindringer fra 1830-aarene og utover*. Christiania, 1912.
Åse, Rannveig. "'Fruen fra havet': En studie med utgangspunkt i den norske hørespillversjonen." *Ibsen-årbok* (1968–69).
Auden, W. H., ed. *Van Gogh: A Self-Portrait*. New York, 1963.
Augustine, St. *The City of God*. Translated by Marcus Dods. Edinburgh, 1871.
Augustinus, Peter. *Signalfejden: Bjørnson og Danmark omkring 1870*. Aarhus and Copenhagen, 1914.
Averardi, F. B. "Eleanora Duse." *Theatre Arts* (September 1931).
Bab, Julius, ed. *Agnes Sorma: Ein Gedenkbuch*. Heidelberg, 1927.
Bang, Herman. "Erinnerungen an Henrik Ibsen." *Die neue Rundschau* (December 1906).
———. *Kritiske Studier og Udkast*. Copenhagen, 1880.
Benedictsson, Victoria. *Dagboksblad och brev*. 2 vols. Edited by Axel Lundegård. Stockholm, 1928.
Bentley, Eric, ed. *The Theory of the Modern Stage*. Harmondsworth, UK, 1968.
Berg, Leo. *Der Übermensch in der modernen Litteratur*. Paris, Leipzig, and Munich, 1897.
Berg, R. G., ed. *Carl Snoilsky och hans vänner: Ur skaldens brevväxling*. Stockholm, 1917–18.
Bergman, Gösta M. *Lighting in the Theatre*. Stockholm and Totowa, NJ, 1977.
———. *Regi och spelstil under Gustaf Lagerbjelkes tid vid Kungl. teatern*. Stockholm, 1946.
Bergsøe, Clara. *Magdalene Thoresen*. Copenhagen and Christiania, 1904.
Berteval, W. *Le Théâtre d'Ibsen*. Paris, 1912.
Beyer, Harald. *Nietzsche og Norden*. 2 vols. Bergen, 1957–59.
———. "To brev og et brevutkast av Henrik Ibsen." *Edda* (1947).
Bigeon, Maurice. "Profils scandinaves: Henrik Ibsen." *Le Figaro*, January 4, 1893.
———. *Les Révoltés scandinaves*. Paris, 1894.
Binding, Paul. *With Vine-Leaves in His Hair: The Role of the Artist in Ibsen's Plays*. Norwich, 2006.
Binns, Archie, in collaboration with Olive Kooken. *Mrs. Fiske and the American Theatre*. New York, 1925.
Bjørklund, Oddvar. *Marcus Thrane: Sosialistleder i et u-land*. Oslo, 1970.
Bjørnson, Bjørn. *Det gamle teater: Kunsten og menneskene*. Oslo, 1937.
Bjørnson, Bjørnstjerne. *Artikler og Taler*. Edited by Chr. Collin and H. Eitrem. Christiania, 1912.
———. *Bjørnstjerne Bjørnsons brevveksling med danske 1854–1874*. Edited by Øyvind Anker, Francis Bull, and Torben Nielsen. 3 vols. Copenhagen, 1970–74.
———. *Bjørnstjerne Bjørnsons brevveksling med danske 1875–1910*. Edited by Øyvind Anker, Francis Bull, and Torben Nielsen. Copenhagen and Oslo, 1953.

———. *Bjørnstjerne Bjørnsons brevveksling med svenske 1858–1909*. Edited by Øyvind Anker, Francis Bull, and Örjan Lindberger. Oslo and Stockholm, 1960–61.
———. "Brev fra Bjørnstjerne Bjørnson." *Edda* 32 (1932).
———. *Breve til Karoline 1858–1907*. Edited by D. B. Santreau. Oslo, 1957.
———. *Brytnings-år: Brev fra årene 1871–1878*. Edited by Halvdan Koht. Christiania, 1921.
———. "Gamle Heltberg." In *Samlede digter-verker*, vol. 8. Christiania, 1920.
———. *Gro-Tid: Brev fra Årene 1857–1870*. Edited by Halvdan Koht. Christiania and Copenhagen, 1912.
———. *Kamp-liv: Brev fra årene 1879–1884*, vol. 2. Oslo, 1932.
———. *Samlede Digter-Verker*. Edited by Francis Bull. Christiania and Copenhagen, 1919.
Bloch, Iwan. *The Sexual Life of Our Time in Its Relations to Modern Civilization*. Translated by M. Eden Paul. New York, 1928.
Bøgh, Erik. *Udvalgte Feuilletoner ("Dit og Dat") fra 1876*. Copenhagen, 1877.
Böök, Fredrik. *Victoria Benedictsson och Georg Brandes*. Stockholm, 1949.
Bowden, John. *Norway*. London, 1867.
Bowersock, G. W. *Julian the Apostate*. Cambridge, MA, 1978.
Boyesen, Hjalmar Hjorth. *A Commentary on the Works of Henrik Ibsen*. New York and London, 1894.
———. *Essays on Scandinavian Literature*. New York, 1895.
Brachvogel, Wolfgang. "'Hedda Gabler' in München." *Freie Bühne für modernes Leben* 2 (1891).
Brahm, Otto. "Ibsens Gespenster in Berlin." *Nation* (January 15, 1887).
———. *Kritische Schriften*, vol. 1. Berlin, 1915.
Brand, Julius. "Henrik Ibsen." *Die Gesellschaft* 4 (December 1888).
Brandell, Gunnar. *Freud: A Man of His Century*. Translated by Iain White. Atlantic Highlands, NJ, 1979.
———. *Vid seklets källor*. Stockholm, 1961.
Brandes, Georg. *Correspondance de Georg Brandes*. 4 vols. Edited by Paul Krüger. Copenhagen, 1952–66.
———. *Essays: Fremmede Personligheder*. Copenhagen, 1889.
———. *Friedrich Nietzsche*. London, 1914.
———. *Henrik Ibsen*. Copenhagen, 1898.
———. *Henrik Ibsen: Mit zwölf Briefen Henrik Ibsens*. Berlin, n.d. (1906).
———. *Levned*. 3 vols. Copenhagen and Christiania, 1905–8.
———. *Nietzsche*. New York, 1964.
———. *Samlede Skrifter*. 18 vols. Copenhagen, 1899–1910.
———. *Store Personligheder*. Copenhagen, 1930.
Brandes, Georg og Edv. *Brevveksling med nordiske Forfattere og Videnskabsmænd*. 8 vols. Edited by Morten Borup. Copenhagen, 1939–42.
Brandes, George [*sic*]. *Henrik Ibsen: A Critical Study With a 42 Page Essay on Björnstjerne Björnson*. Translated by Jessie Muir, revised by William Archer. London, 1899; reprinted New York, 1964.
Bredsdorff, Elias. "Georg Brandes og de politiske ideologier." *Tidskrift för Litteraturveten skap* 1 (1971–72).

———. "Moralists Versus Immoralists: The Great Battle in Scandinavian Literature in the 1880s." *Scandinavica* 8 (1969).

Brendel, Hjalmar. *Etiska motiv i Henrik Ibsens dramatiske ditkning.* Stockholm, 1941.

Brøgger, W. C., et al., eds. *Norge 1814–1914: Tekst og billeder av norske forfattere og kunstnere.* 3 vols. Christiania, 1914.

Brunsvig, J. *Henrik Ibsens barndom og ungdom og fødebyen i hans diktning.* Skien, 1952.

———. "Ibsen-huset på Snipetorp." *Ibsen-årbok* (1953).

Bull, Francis. "Ers Majestät, jag måste skriva Gengångare." *Röster i Radio* 49 (December 9–11, 1962).

———. "Henrik Ibsen et Georg Brandes," in *Mélanges d'histoire littéraire générale et comparée offerts à Fernand Baldensperger.* Paris, 1930.

———. *Henrik Ibsens Peer Gynt.* Oslo, 1947.

———. "Hildur Andersen og Henrik Ibsen." *Edda,* 1957.

———. *Studier og streiftog i norsk litteratur.* Oslo, 1931.

———. *Traditioner och minnen.* Translated by Ingeborg Essén. Stockholm, 1949.

———. *Vildanden og andre essays.* Oslo, 1966.

———, ed. *Norsk Litteraturhistorie.* Vol. 4. Oslo, 1924.

Carlyle, Thomas. *Sartor Resartus.* London, 1838.

———. "Sir Walter Scott." *Westminster Review* (January 1838).

Caspari, Theodor. *Fra mine unge aar.* Oslo, 1929.

Christensen, Erik M. *Henrik Ibsens realisme.* Oslo, 1985.

———. "Why Should Brandes Sabotage Ibsen in Germany?" In *Contemporary Approaches to Ibsen,* vol. 5. Oslo, 1985.

Clancey, James H. "Hedda Gabler: Poetry in Action and in Object." In *Studies in Theatre and Drama: Essays in Honor of Hubert C. Heffner.* Edited by Oscar G. Brockett. The Hague, 1972.

Clason, Synnöve. "Ibsens svärmor och 'Frun fra havet.'" *Svenska Dagbladet* (May 20, 1985).

Collett, A. *Camilla Colletts livs historie.* Christiania, 1911.

Collin, Chr[isten]. *Bjørnstjerne Bjornson: Hans Barndom og Ungdom.* 2nd rev. ed. Christiania, 1923.

———. "Henrik Ibsen und Norwegen." *Die neue Rundschau* 18 (July–December 1907).

———. "Henrik Ibsens Fremtidsdrøm." *Samtiden* 17 (1906).

———. *Kunsten og moralen: Bidrag til kritik af realismens digtere og kritikere.* Copenhagen, 1894.

Cook, Dutton. *On the Stage.* London, 1883.

Courtney, W. L. "A Note on Ibsen's 'Little Eyolf.'" *Fortnightly Review,* n.s., 57 (January–June 1895).

Cusanus, Nicolas. *Of Learned Ignorance.* Translated by Fr. Germain Heron. London, 1954.

Dahl, Herleiv. *Bergmannen og byggmesteren.* Oslo, 1958.

Dahl, Per Kristian Heggelund. "Nytt stoff om Ibsens mørke år." *Aftenposten* (Oslo), March 24, 1996.

Dahlgren, Lotten. *Lyran: Interiörer från 1870-och 80-talens konstnärliga och litterära Stockholm.* Stockholm, 1913.

Davidsen, Elisabeth. *Henrik Ibsen og Det kongelige Teater.* Copenhagen, 1980.

Deak, Frantisek. *Symbolist Theater.* Baltimore, 1993.
Desprez, Louis. *L'Évolution naturaliste.* Paris, 1884.
Dietrichson, Lorentz. *Svundne Tider.* 4 vols. Christiania, 1896–1917.
Downs, Brian W. *Ibsen: The Intellectual Background.* Cambridge, 1946.
Drachmann, Holger. *Breve,* vol. 2. Copenhagen, 1965.
Due, Christopher. *Erindringer fra Henrik Ibsens ungdomsaar.* Copenhagen, 1909.
———. "Ibsen's Early Youth." *The Critic* 49 (1906).
Dumas, Alexandre, *fils. Théâtre complet,* vol. 3. Paris, 1893.
Duve, Arne. *Henrik Ibsens hemmeligheter.* Oslo, 1977.
———. *Ibsen: Bak kulissene.* Oslo, 1971.
Dvergsdal, Arne. "Den fatale historie." *Dagbladet* (May 23, 2006).
Edqvist, Sven-Gustaf. *Samhällets fiende.* Stockholm, 1961.
Egan, Michael, ed. *Ibsen: The Critical Heritage.* London, 1972.
Ehrhard, Auguste. *Henrik Ibsen et le théâtre contemporain.* Paris, 1892.
Einiges über Ibsen: Zur Feier ihrer alljährlichen Mai-Festspiele herausgeben von der Ibsen-vereinigung zu Düsseldorf. Berlin and Leipzig, 1909.
Eitrem, H. "Henrik Ibsen—Henrik Wergeland." *Maal og Minne* (1910).
———. *Ibsen og Grimstad.* Oslo, 1940.
Eklund, J. A. "Om 'Hedda Gabler' och 'esteticism.'" *Svensk Tidsrift* 2 (1892).
Elias, Julius. "Christianiafahrt / Erinnerungen." *Die neue Rundschau* (December 1906).
———. "Ibsen-minner af hans tyske oversetter." *Samtiden* (1940).
Ellenberger, Henri F. *The Discovery of the Unconscious: The History and Evolution of Dynamic Psychiatry.* New York, 1970.
Eller, William Henri. *Ibsen in Germany 1870–1900.* Boston, 1918.
Elovson, Harald. "Livsglädje och levnadsglädje." *Edda* 30 (1930).
Elster, Kr. "Ibsens digte." In *Fra tid til anden.* Christiania, 1920.
Emerson, Ralph Waldo. "The Conduct of Life." In *Essays and Lectures.* New York, 1983.
Engström, Albert. "En intervju med Ibsen." *Skrifter av Albert Engström,* vol. 26. Stockholm, 1945.
Erichsen, Svend. *Realismens gennembrud i parisisk teater i det nittende århundrede.* Vol. 2, *Montigny og scenekunsten under Napoleon III.* Copenhagen, 1973.
Eriksson, Sven. *Carl XV.* Stockholm, 1954.
Espmark, Kjell. *The Nobel Prize in Literature: A Study of the Criteria Behind the Choices.* Boston, 1986.
Evans, Edward Payson. "Ibsen's Home and Working Habits." *The Critic,* n.s., 13 (March 8, 1890).
Eyck, Erich. *Bismarck und das deutsche Reich.* Erlenbach-Zürich, 1955.
———. *Bismarck and the German Empire.* London, 1950.
Faaland, Josef. *Henrik Ibsen og antikken.* Oslo, 1943.
Faguet, Emile. "The Symbolical Drama." *International Quarterly* 8 (1903–4).
Fasting, Georg. "Smaa minder om Bjørnson." *Samtiden* 24 (1913).
Fenger, Henning. "Bjørnson og Georg Brandes før det moderne gennembrud." *Edda* 51 (1964).
———. "Ibsen og Georg Brandes indtil 1872." *Edda* 51 (1964).

———. *Den unge Brandes*. Copenhagen, 1957.
———. "Det veldrejede og mondæne Teater." In *Teatrets Historie*, edited by Christian Ludvigsen and Stephan Kehler. Copenhagen, 1962.
Fergusson, Francis. *The Idea of a Theater*. New York, 1953.
Fibiger, Andreas. *Henrik Ibsen, En studie over Guds-linien i hans Liv*. Copenhagen, 1928.
Figueiredo, Ivo de. *Henrik Ibsen: Mennesket*. Oslo, 2006.
Fournier, Alfred. *Syfilis och äktenskap: Föreläsningar hållna på Hopital Saint-Louis*. Translated by Karl Malmsted. Stockholm, 1882.
———. *Syphilis and Marriage: Lectures Delivered at the St. Louis Hospital, Paris*. Translated by P. Albert Morrow. New York, 1881.
———. *La syphilis du cerveau: Leçons cliniques recueillies par E. Brissaud*. Paris, 1879.
Fredrikson, Gustav. *Teaterminnen*. Stockholm, 1918.
Freud, Sigmund. *Civilization and Its Discontents*. Translated by Joan Riviere. New York, 1930.
———. *New Introductory Lectures on Psycho-Analysis*. In *The Standard Edition of the Complete Psychological Works of Sigmund Freud*. Edited and translated by James Strachey. 24 vols. London, 1953–74.
———. "Some Character-Types Met With in Psycho-analytic Work." In *Collected Papers*. Translated by Joan Riviere. Vol. 4. New York, 1959.
Friese, Wilhelm, ed. *Ibsen auf der deutschen Bühne*. Tübingen, 1976.
Gauguin, Pola. *Krohg*. Oslo, 1932.
Gedin, David. *Fältets herrar: Framväxten av en modern författarroll*. Stockholm, 2004.
Geijerstam, Gustaf af. "Ibsen der Mensch." *Die Schaubühne* 2, no. 26 (June 28, 1906).
———. "Två minnen af Henrik Ibsen." *Ord och Bild* (March 1898).
Geyer, Robert. *Etude médico-psychologique sur le théâtre d'Ibsen*. Paris, 1902.
Gierløff, Christian. *Bjornstjerne Bjørnson*. Oslo, 1932.
Gilman, Sander S., ed. *Conversations with Nietzsche*. Translated by David J. Parent. Oxford, 1987.
Goitein, Lionel. "The Lady from the Sea." *Psychoanalytical Review* 14 (1927).
Goodman, E. J. "Dr. Ibsen at Christiania." *The Theatre* 26 (September 1, 1895).
Gosse, Edmund. *Henrik Ibsen*. New York, 1915.
———. *Sir Edmund Gosse's Correspondence with Scandinavian Writers*. Edited by Elias Bredsdorff. Copenhagen, 1960.
———. *Studies in the Literature of Northern Europe*. London, 1879.
Gran, Gerhard. *Henrik Ibsen: Liv og Verker*. Christiania, 1918.
———, ed. *Henrik Ibsen: Festskrift i Anledning af hans 70de Fødselsdag*. Bergen, 1898.
———, ed. *Nordmænd i det 19de aarhundrede*, vol. 1. Christiania, 1914.
Gravier, Maurice. *Ibsen*. Paris, 1973.
Grieg, Harald. *En Forleggers Erindringer*. Vol. 1. Copenhagen, 1958.
Grimberg, Carl. *Svenska folkets underbara oden*, vol. 9. Stockholm, 1924.
Grønvold, Marcus. *Fra Ulrikken til Alperne: En malers erindringer*. Oslo, 1925.
Haakonsen, Daniel. *Henrik Ibsen: Mennesket og kunstneren*. Oslo, 1981.
———. "Henrik Ibsens lyrikk." *Edda* (1950).
Haeckel, Ernst. *The Evolution of Man*. New York, 1899.

———. *The History of Creation, or The Development of the Earth and Its Inhabitants by the Action of Natural Causes.* Translated by E. Ray Lankester. New York, 1911.

Hageberg, Otto, ed. *Omkring "Peer Gynt."* Oslo, 1967.

Hallström, Per. *Carl Snoilsky: En levnadsteckning.* Stockholm, 1933.

Halvorsen, J. B. *Norsk Forfatter-Lexikon 1814–1880*, vol. 3. Christiania, 1892.

Hammer, Fritz (Michael Georg Conrad). "Mein Verkehr mit Henrik Ibsen." *Die Gesellschaft* 4 (October 1888).

Hamre, Kari. *Clemens Petersen og hans forhold til norsk litteratur i årene 1856–69.* Oslo, 1945.

Hamsun, Knut. *Artikler 1889–1928.* Edited by Francis Bull. Oslo, 1965.

———. *Paa Turné.* Edited by Tore Hamsun. Oslo, 1960.

Hansen, Holm. "Af 'Hvad jeg oplevede.'" *Tilskueren* (November 1909).

Hansson, Ola. "Eleanora Duse." *Tilskueren* (1893).

———. "Friedrich Nietzsche und der Naturalismus." *Die Gegenwart* 39 (1891).

———. *Samlade skrifter*, vol. 10. Stockholm, 1921.

Harden, M[ax]. "Hedda Gabler und ihre Kritiker." *Die Gegenwart* 39, no. 8 (February 21, 1891).

Hardy, Thomas. *A Pair of Blue Eyes.* New York, 1928.

Hareide, Jorunn. "Ibsen's Drama—as Seen by Magdalene Thoresen." In *Proceedings, IX International Ibsen Conference, Bergen 5–10 June 2000.* Øvre Ervik, Norway, 2001.

Hartmann, Eduard von. *Philosophy of the Unconscious.* Translated by William Chatteron Coupland. London, 1931.

Haugan, Jørgen. *Henrik Ibsens metode.* Copenhagen, 1977.

Hauge, Ingard. *Den fremmede passajen.* Oslo, 1986.

Hayden, Deborah. *Pox: Genius, Madness, and the Mysteries of Syphilis.* New York, 2004.

Hazlitt, William. "Why the Arts Are Not Progressive?" In *The Collected Works of William Hazlitt.* Edited by A. R. Waller and Arnold Glover. London, 1902.

Hegel, Frederick. *Erindringen.* Copenhagen, 1946.

Hegel, G. W. F. *The Phenomenology of Mind.* Translated by J. B. Baillie. 2nd rev. ed. London and New York, 1931.

———. *The Philosophy of Fine Art.* Translated by F. P. B. Osmarston. London, 1920.

———. *Werke*, vol. 2. Berlin, 1842.

Heiberg, Hans. "*. . . født til kunstner": Et Ibsen-portrett.* Oslo, 1967.

Heiberg, Johan Ludvig. *Prosaiske Skrifter.* 11 vols. Copenhagen, 1861–62.

Heiberg, Johanne Luise. *Et Liv gjenoplevet i Erindringen.* 4th ed., revised by Aage Friis et al. Copenhagen, 1944.

Heine, Heinrich. "Ludwig Börne." In *Sämtliche Werke.* Edited by Ernst Elster. Leipzig and Vienna, n.d.

———. *Lutetia.* Translated by E. B. Ashton. In Heine, *Works of Prose,* edited by Herman Kesten. New York, 1943.

———. *The Poetry and Prose of Heinrich Heine.* Edited by Frederic Ewen, translated by Aaron Kramer. New York, 1948.

Hemmer, Bjørn. "Fru Inger til Østeraad." *Ibsen-årbok* (1972).

———. *Ibsen: Kunstnerens vei.* Bergen, 2003.

Hemmings, F. W. J. *Culture and Society in France 1848–1898*. New York, 1971.

———. Émile Zola. Oxford, 1953.

Hinden, Michael. "Ibsen and Nietzsche: A Reading of *The Master Builder*." *Modern Drama* 15, no. 4 (1973).

Hirsch, E. D., Jr. *Wordsworth and Schelling*. New Haven, 1960.

Hjemdahl, Anne-Sofie, ed. *Ting om Ibsen*. Oslo, 2006.

Høffding, Harald. *Erindringer*. Copenhagen, 1928.

———. "Gensvar til Dr. Georg Brandes." *Tilskueren* 7 (1890).

———. *Psykologi i omrids*. Copenhagen, 1882.

Hofmannsthal, Hugo von. "Die Menschen in Ibsens Dramen." In *Prosa*, vol. 1. Frankfurt am Main, 1950.

Høgh, Marie, and Fredrikke Mørch, eds. *Norske kvinder: En oversigt over deres stilling og livsvilkaar i hundredeaaret 1814–1914*. 2 vols. Christiania, 1914.

Holm, Birgitta. *Victoria Benedictsson*. Stockholm, 2007.

Holm, Pelle. *Bevingade ord och andra talesätt*. Rev. ed. Stockholm, 1962.

Holmgren, Ann Margret. *Björnstjerne Björnson: Diktaren, hövdingen, politikern, människan*, vol. 1. Studentföreningen verdandis småskrifter, nos. 248–49. Stockholm, 1921.

Høst, Else. *Hedda Gabler: En monografi*. Oslo, 1958.

———. *Vildanden av Henrik Ibsen*. Oslo, 1967.

Høst, Gunnar. "Ibsens sammfundsstøtter." *Edda* (1947).

Høst, Sigurd. "Ibsen i tidens Kamp." In *Til Gerhard Gran 9. December 1916 fra venner og elever*. Christiania, 1916.

Huneker, James. *Egoists: A Book of Supermen*. New York, 1909.

———. *Iconoclasts: A Book of Dramatists*. New York, 1905.

Hunt, Tristram. *Marx's General: The Revolutionary Life of Friedrich Engels*. New York, 2009.

Ibsen, Bergliot. *The Three Ibsens: Memories of Henrik Ibsen, Suzannah Ibsen and Sigurd Ibsen*. Translated by Gerik Schjelderup. New York, 1952.

———. *De tre*. Oslo, 1949.

Ibsen, Henrik. *Brand*. Translated by G. M. Gathorne-Hardy. London and Seattle, 1966.

———. *Brev 1845–1905: Ny samling*. 2 vols. Edited by Øyvind Anker. Oslo and Bergen, 1981.

———. *The Collected Works of Henrik Ibsen*. Edited by William Archer. 13 vols. New York, 1906–12.

———. *Efterladte Skrifter*. Edited by Halvdan Koht and Julius Elias. 3 vols. Christiania and Copenhagen, 1909.

———. *Gengangere*. Edited by Olaf Kortner. Oslo, 1965.

———. *Hedda Gabler*. Translated by M. Prozor. Paris, 1892.

———. *Henrik Ibsens brevveksling med Christiania Theater 1878–1899*. Edited by Øyvind Anker. Oslo, 1965.

———. *Henrik Ibsens sämtliche Werke in deutscher Sprache*. Edited by Georg Brandes, Julius Elias, and Paul Schlenther. Berlin, n.d. (1898–1904).

———. *Henrik Ibsens skrifter*. 17 vols. Oslo, 2005–10.

———. *Ibsen's Poems*. Translated by John Northam. Oslo, 1986.

———. *Letters and Speeches*. Edited by Evert Sprinchorn. New York, 1964.

———. *Nora*. Translated by H. F. Lord. London and New York, 1882.

———. Œuvres complètes. Edited and translated by P[ierre] G[eorget] La Chesnais. 16 vols. Paris, 1930–45.

———. *Samlede Værker*. 10 vols. Copenhagen, 1898–1902.

———. *Samlede Verker: Hundreårsutgave*. Edited by Francis Bull, Halvdan Koht, and Didrik Arup Seip. 21 vols. Oslo, 1928–57.

———. *Tyve brev fra Henrik Ibsen: Utgitt i faksimile med innledning og oplysninger av Wilhelm Munthe*. Oslo, 1932.

Innes, Christopher, ed. *A Sourcebook in Naturalistic Theatre*. London and New York, 2000.

Jacobsen, Lis. "Ibsens sidste ord." *Ibsen-årbok* (1957–59).

———. "En trilogi: Studie over tre Ibsen'ske trylleord." *Edda* (1960).

Jæger, Henrik. "Hedda Gablers forhold til tidligere skuespil af Henrik Ibsen." *Folkebladet* (Christiania, 1891).

———. *Henrik Ibsen: Ein literarisches Lebensbild*. 2nd ed. Translated by Heinrich Zschalig. Dresden and Leipzig, 1897.

———. *Henrik Ibsen 1828–1888: Et literært Livsbillede*. Copenhagen, 1888.

———. *Henrik Ibsen og hans Værker*. Christiania, 1892.

———. *Illustreret norsk Literaturhistorie*. Christiania, 1896.

James, Henry. *The Scenic Art: Notes on Acting and the Drama, 1872–1901*. Edited by Allan Wade. New Brunswick, NJ, 1948.

Kaufman, Michael W. "Nietzsche, Georg Brandes, and Ibsen's Master Builder." *Comparative Drama* 6, no. 3 (1972).

Kerr, Alfred. "Ibsens Tod." *Das literarische Echo* 8 (1905–6).

Kieler, Laura. *Silhouetter*. Odense, 1887.

Kierkegaard, Søren. *Concluding Unscientific Postscript*. Translated by David F. Swenson and Walter Lowrie. Princeton, 1941.

———. *Samlede Værker*. Edited by A. B. Drachmann, J. L. Heiberg, and H. O. Lange. Copenhagen, 1962–64.

Kihlman, Erik. *Ur Ibsen-dramatikens idéhistoria*. Helsingfors, 1921.

Kinck, B. M. "Dramaet Brand: Opfatning og tolkninger." *Edda* 30 (1930).

———. "Henrik Ibsen og Laura Kieler." *Edda* 35 (1935).

Kjetsaa, Geir. "Henrik Ibsen og Oscar von Knorring." *Ibsen-årbok* (1977).

Knudtzon, Fr. G. *Ungdomsdage (Memoirer og Breve)*. Edited by Julius Clausen and P. Fr. Rist. Vol. 49. Copenhagen, 1927.

Koht, Halvdan. *Henrik Ibsen: Eit diktarliv*. 2nd ed. Oslo, 1954.

———. "Ibsens siste ord." *Ibsen-årbok* (1957–59).

———. "Korleis 'Kejser og Galilæer' vart skriven." *Ibsen-årbok* (1955–56).

———. "Når reiste Henrik Ibsen frå Skien." *Ibsen-årbok* (1953).

Kommandantvold, Kristian Magnus. *Ibsen og Sverige*. Oslo, 1956.

Kristensen-Randers, J. P. "Hos Bjørnson og Ibsen: Et Par Samtaler og et Par Breve." *Tilskueren* (January–June 1917).

Kuhnle, Stein. "Stemmeretten i 1814." *Historisk tidsskrift* 4 (1972).

La Chesnais, P. G. "Ibsen disciple de Kierkegaard." *Edda* 34 (1934).

Larsen, Karl, ed. *Henrik Ibsens episke Brand.* Copenhagen and Christiania, 1907.
Larson, Philip E. *Ibsen in Skien and Grimstad: His Education, Reading, and Early Works.* Grimstad, Norway, 1999.
Lauring, Palle, ed. *Fjern og nær set gennem Illustreret Tidende.* Copenhagen, 1966.
Lauritsen, P. *Chr. Collin og Georg Brandes.* Copenhagen, 1958.
Lea, F. E. *The Tragic Philosopher: A Study of Friedrich Nietzsche.* London, 1957.
Lee, Jennette. *The Ibsen Secret: A Key to the Prose Dramas of Henrik Ibsen.* New York, 1907.
Lemaître, Jules. *Impressions de théâtre, sixième série.* Paris, 1898.
———. "Revue dramatique." *Revue des deux mondes* 139 (February 1, 1897).
Leneveu, Georges. *Ibsen et Maeterlinck.* Paris, 1902.
Lescoffier, Jean. *Bjørnson, la seconde jeunesse.* Paris, 1932.
Lie, Erik. *Erindringer fra et dikterhjem.* Oslo, 1928.
———. *Jonas Lies Oplevelser.* Christiania and Copenhagen, 1908.
Lindau, Paul. *Nur Erinnerungen.* 2 vols. Stuttgart and Berlin, 1916–17.
Lindberg, Per. *August Lindberg: Skådespelaren och människan.* Stockholm, 1943.
Lindberger, Örjan. "Ibsen, Ellen Key och kvinnorna." *Nordisk tidskrift för vetenskap, konst och Industri,* n.s., 36 (1960).
———. "Ibsen och två svenska teaterchefer." *Nordisk tidskrift för vetenskap, konst och industri* 40 (1964).
———. "Kring urpremiären på 'En Fallit.'" *Nordisk tidskrift för vetenskap, konst och industri,* n.s., 34 (1958).
Linder, Gurli. *Sällskapsliv i Stockholm under 1880 och 1890-talen.* Stockholm, 1918.
Linder, Sten. "Ernst Ahlgren och Georg Brandes." *Samlaren,* n.s., 16 (1935).
———. *Ibsen, Strindberg och andra.* Stockholm, 1936.
Lochmann, E. F. *Populære opsatser.* Christiania, 1891.
Logeman, H. *A Commentary, Critical and Explanatory on the Norwegian Text of Henrik Ibsen's Peer Gynt.* Westport, CT, 1970, reprint of 1917 original.
Loris. "Eleanora Duse." In *Ord och Bild* 1 (1892).
Lothar, Rudolph. *Henrik Ibsen.* Leipzig, Berlin, and Vienna, 1902.
Lubbock, Sir John. *The Origin of Civilization and the Primitive Condition of Man.* New York, 1870.
Lucas, F. L. *The Drama of Ibsen and Strindberg.* London, 1962.
Lugné-Poe. *Ibsen.* Paris, 1936.
Lundegård, Axel. *Några Strindbergsminnen knutna till en handful brev.* Stockholm, 1920.
Lynner, Valborg Eriksen. "Gregers Werle—og Ibsens selvironi." *Edda* 28 (1928–29).
Maeterlinck, Maurice. "On the Master Builder." Translated by Albert Bermel. *Theater Three* 1 (Fall 1986).
Magnus, Rudolf. *Goethe as a Scientist.* Translated by Heinz Norden. New York, 1949.
Mann, Thomas. *Last Essays.* Translated by Richard and Clara Winston. New York, 1959.
Marcus, Carl David. "Ibsen och göticism." *Edda* 31 (1931).
Marker, Frederick J., and Lise-Lone Marker. *Ibsen's Lively Art: A Performance Study of the Major Plays.* Cambridge, 1989.
Marum, Reidar A. *Teaterslag og pipekonserter.* Oslo, 1944.
Maudsley, Henry. *Body and Mind.* 2nd ed. New York, 1895.

———. *The Pathology of Mind.* 3rd ed. London, 1879.
———. *The Physiology and Pathology of Mind.* New York, 1871.
Maurel, André. "Le nouveau drame d'Ibsen: Jean-Gabriel Borkman." *Le Figaro* (December 27, 1896).
Mayrhofer, Johannes. *Henrik Ibsen und seine Werke.* Trier, n.d. (1911).
McFarlane, James W[alter]. "Meaning and Evidence in Ibsen's Drama." *Ibsen-årbok* 8 (1965–66).
———, ed. *The Oxford Ibsen*, 8 vols. London, 1960–77.
Meyer, Michael. *Ibsen.* New York, 1971.
Midbøe, Hans. *Streiflys over Ibsen og andre studier.* Oslo, 1960.
Mohr, Otto Lous. *Henrik Ibsen som maler.* Oslo, 1953.
Möhring, Werner. "Ibsens Abkehr von Kierkegaard." *Edda* 28 (1928).
Molbech, Chr. K. F. *Fra Danaidernes Kar.* Copenhagen, 1873.
Mosfjeld, Oskar. *Henrik Ibsen og Skien.* Oslo, 1949.
Motzfeldt, Ernst. "Af samtaler med Henrik Ibsen." *Aftenposten* (April 29, 1911).
Nævdal, Bodil. "Hun ble kveldssolen i hans liv." *Aftenposten* (December 24, 1988).
Nedergaard, Leif. "Georg Brandes' forhold til Ibsen, Björnson, og Strindberg belyst gennem deres inbyrdes brevveksling." *Nordisk tidskrift för vetenskap, konst och industri*, n.s., 36 (1960).
Neiiendam, Robert. *Det Kongelige Teaters Historie.* Vol. 1, Copenhagen, 1921; vol. 3, Copenhagen, 1925.
Neumann, Fritz. "Die Entstehung von Rosmersholm." *Edda* 17 and 18 (1922).
Nietzsche, Friedrich. *The Birth of Tragedy and The Genealogy of Morals.* Translated by Francis Golding. Garden City, NY, 1956.
———. *On the Genealogy of Morals.* Translated by Walter Kaufmann. New York, 1967.
———. *The Will to Power.* Edited by Walter Kaufmann. New York, 1967.
Nissen, Ingjald. *Vildanden—Rosmersholm—Hedda Gabler.* Oslo, 1973.
Nolin, Bertil. *Georg Brandes.* Boston, 1976.
———. *Den gode Européen: Studier i Georg Brandes' idéutveckling 1871–1893.* Uppsala, 1965.
Nordau, Max. *Die conventionellen Lügen der Kulturmenschheit.* 12th ed. Leipzig, 1886.
———. *Degeneration.* New York, 1895.
Nordensvan, Georg. *Svensk teater och svenska skådespelare från Gustav III till våra dagar.* Stockholm, 1917–18.
Nordström, Gertrud. "Den svenska urpremiären på Ibsens De ungas förbund 1869." In *Dramaten 175 år: Studier i svensk scenkonst*, edited by G. M. Bergman and Niklas Brunius. Stockholm, 1963.
Noreng, Harald. *Bjørnsons skuespil på svensk scene.* Oslo, 1967.
Northam, John. "Hedda Gabler." *Ibsen-årbok* (1968–69).
———. *Ibsen's Dramatic Method.* London, 1953.
———. "On a Firm Foundation—The Translation of Ibsen's Prose." *Ibsen-årbok* (1977).
Nyblom, Helena. "Vildanden." *Ny svensk Tidsskrift.* Uppsala, January 1885.
Nygaard, C. S. *Henrik Ibsen i hundredaaret for hans fødsel.* Copenhagen, 1928.
Nyholm, Kela. "Henrik Ibsen paa den franske Scene." *Ibsen-årbok* (1957–59).

Øisang, Ole. *Henrik Ibsen som radikaler: Ibsens samfundsopfatning og hans forhold til arbeiderbevegelsen.* Trondheim, 1928.

Olsson, Henry. *Den unge Snoilsky.* Stockholm, 1941.

Olsson, Oscar. *Ibsens dramer.* Stockholm, 1937.

Ording, Fr. *Henrik Ibsen: "Kærlighedens Komedie."* Christiania, 1914.

———. *Henrik Ibsens vennekreds: Det lærde Holland.* Oslo, 1927.

———, ed. *Breve fra Riksarkivar Birkeland (1848–1879).* Christiania, 1920.

Østerud, Erik. "Lenestolsymbolet i 'Hedda Gabler.'" *Ibsen-årbok* (1960–62).

———. "Den rosmerske adelighet og dybdepsykologien: En studie i Henrik Ibsens Rosmersholm." *Norskrift* 34 (1981).

Østvedt, Einar. *Et dukkehjem: Forspillet, skuespillet, etterspillet.* Skien, 1976.

———. "Gustav Adolph Lammers som modell til Ibsens Brand." *Ibsen-årbok* (1952).

———. *Henrik Ibsen: Barndom og ungdom.* Skien, 1973.

———. *Henrik Ibsen: Miljø og Mennesker.* Oslo, 1968.

———. *Henrik Ibsen og la bella Italia.* Skien, 1965.

———. "Henrik Ibsen, politikken og staten." *Ibsen-årbok* (1954).

———. *Henrik Ibsen som student og blant studenter.* Skien, 1971.

———. *Herman Bagger som redaktør of politiker.* Skien, 1932.

———. "Mørkeloftet og miljøet i 'Vildanden.'" *Ibsen-årbok* (1957–59).

———. "Omkring Henrik Ibsens død 23 mai 1906." *Ibsen-årbok* (1955–56).

Passarge, Ludwig. Preface to *Peer Gynt.* 2nd ed. Leipzig, 1887.

Paterson, P. W. K. *The Nihilist Egoist: Max Stirner.* London and New York, 1971.

Paul, Adolph. *Profiler.* Stockholm, 1937.

Paulsen, John. "'Aftnerne i Arbinsgade': Utklipp av et etterlatt bind erindringer." *Edda* 43 (1943).

———. *Erindringer: Siste samling.* Copenhagen, 1903.

———. *Min første sommer i København.* Copenhagen and Christiania, 1908.

———. *Mine erindringer.* Copenhagen, 1900.

———. *Nye erindringer.* Copenhagen, 1901.

———. *Paa Vandring.* Copenhagen, 1882.

———. *Reisen til Monaco og andre erindringer.* Christiania, 1909.

———. *Samliv med Ibsen: Anden samling.* Copenhagen and Christiania, 1913.

———. *Samliv med Ibsen: Nye erindringer og skitser.* Copenhagen and Christiania, 1906.

Pearsall, Ronald. *The Worm in the Bud: The World of Victorian Sexuality.* London, 1969.

Pettersen, Hjalmar. *Henrik Ibsen, the Norwegian Dramatist.* In *Contemporary and After Times Literature.* Oslo, 1928.

Philippi, Felix. "Theaterproben." *Velhagen & Klasings Monatshefte* 26 (1911–12).

Plekhanov, George V. "Ibsen, Petty Bourgeois Revolutionist." In Angel Flores, ed., *Henrik Ibsen.* New York, 1937.

Pradez, Edith. "Henrik Ibsen's Return." *Academy* (October 10, 1874).

Prozor, M. "Ibsens 'Lille Eyolf.'" *Ord och Bild* 4 (1895).

Rahbek, Just, ed. *Breve fra og til Johanne Luise Heiberg.* Copenhagen, 1955.

Rank, Otto. *Das Inzest-Motiv in Dichtung und Sage.* Leipzig, 1912.

Rees, Terence. *Theatre Lighting in the Age of Gas.* London, 1978.

Reich, Emil. *Aus Leben und Dichtung*. Leipzig, 1911.

———. *Henrik Ibsens Dramen: Zwanzig Vorlesungen, gehalten an der Universität Wien*. 7th rev. ed. Berlin, 1910 (1909).

———. "Ibsen und das Recht der Frau." In *Jahresbericht des Vereins für erweiterte Frauenbildung*. Vienna, 1891.

Report from the Select Committee on Theatres and Places of Entertainment (1892). In Irish University Press Series of British Parliamentary Papers: Stage and Theatre, vol. 3. Dublin, 1970.

Ribbing, Seved. "Om den samtida dikten och dess förkärlek för sjukdomsskildring." *Ny svensk tidskrift* (1885).

"Il ritorno di Eleanora Duse: Assistendo ad una prova de 'La Donna del mare'" (unsigned). Winifred Smith collection, Department of Drama and Film, Vassar College. Translated by Vincent Giroud.

Roberts, R. Ellis. *Henrik Ibsen: A Critical Study*. London, 1912.

Robins, Elizabeth. *Ibsen and the Actress*. London, 1928.

Rode, Ove. "Ibsen-Ugen I Berlin." *Politikken* 76–77 (March 17–18, 1889).

Rolland, Romain. *Goethe and Beethoven*. Translated by G. A. Pfister and E. S. Kemp. London and New York, 1931.

Rose, Henry. *Henrik Ibsen: Poet, Mystic and Moralist*. New York, 1913.

Rubow, Paul V. *Georg Brandes og den kritiske tradition i det nittende aarhundrede*. Copenhagen, 1931.

Rudler, Roderick. "Ibsens teatergjerning i Bergen." In *Drama och teater*, edited by Egil Törnqvist. Stockholm, 1968.

Saari, Sandra E. "Of Madness and Fame: Ibsen's Bygmester Solness." *Scandinavian Studies* 50 (1978).

Sæther, Astrid. *Suzannah, Fru Ibsen*. Oslo, 2008.

Sallust. *The War with Catiline*. Translated by J. C. Rolfe. London and New York, 1921.

Sandberg, Mark B. "John Gabriel Borkman's Avant-Garde Continuity." *Modern Drama* 49, no. 3 (Fall 2006).

Sarcey, Francisque. *Quarante ans de théâtre*. Vol. 8. Paris, 1902.

Sarolea, Charles. *Henrik Ibsen: Étude sur sa vie & son œuvre*. Paris, 1891.

Sars, J. E. *Norges politiske Historie 1815–1885*. Christiania, n.d.

Schelling, Friedrich Wilhelm Joseph von. *The Ages of the World*. Translated by Frederick de Wolfe Bolman Jr. New York, 1942.

———. *Sämmtliche Werke*. 14 vols. Edited by K. F. A. Schelling. Stuttgart and Augsburg, 1856–61.

Schjøtt, Mathilde. *Efter Læsningen af "Byggmester Solness."* Christiania, 1893.

Schmidt, Rudolf. *Ad egne Veje*. Copenhagen, 1884.

Schmiesing, Ann. "The Christiania Theater and Norwegian Nationalism." *Scandinavian Studies* 76 (2004).

Schmitt, Eugen Heinrich. *Ibsen als Prophet: Grundgedanken zu einer neuen* Ästhetik. Leipzig, 1908.

Schofield, William Henry. "Personal Impressions of Björnson and Ibsen." *Atlantic Monthly* 81 (1898).

Schopenhauer, Arthur. *The World as Will and Representation*. 2 vols. Translated by E. F. J. Payne. Indian Hills, CO, 1958.
Schyberg, Frederik. *Dansk Teaterkritik indtil 1914*. Copenhagen, 1937.
Senelick, Laurence, ed. *National Theatre in Northern and Eastern Europe, 1746–1900*. Cambridge, 1991.
Shaw, Bernard. *Major Critical Essays*. London, 1932.
———. *Our Theatres in the Nineties*, 3 vols. London, 1932.
———. *Pen Portraits and Reviews*. London, 1931.
———. *Plays: Pleasant and Unpleasant*. London, 1898.
———. *The Quintessence of Ibsenism*. London, 1891.
———. *Three Plays by Brieux*, preface. New York, 1914.
Sinding-Larsen, Alfred. *Om Henrik Ibsen: Fruen fra Havet og Personerne deri*. Christiania, 1889.
Singer, Charles. *A Short History of Scientific Ideas to 1900*. Oxford, 1959.
Skard, Sigmund. "Else Høsts doktordisputas om Hedda Gabler." *Edda* 60 (1960).
Skram, Erik. "Moderne Forfattere." *Tilskueren* 6 (February 1889).
Smith, Rowland. *Julian's Gods*. London and New York, 1995.
Snoilsky, Carl. *Samlade dikter*. 4 vols. Stockholm, 1903–4.
Sontum, Bolette. "Personal Recollections of Ibsen." *Bookman* (New York) 37 (1913).
Spångberg, Valfrid. *Adolf Hedin i Liv och Gärning*. Uppsala and Stockholm, 1921.
Sperans. "Banquier-Symbolismus." *Sozialistische Monatshefte* 1 (1897).
Stang, Fredrik. "Friele." *Samtiden* 28 (1917).
Steen, Ellisiv. *Den lange Strid: Camilla Collett og hennes senere forfatterskap*. Oslo, 1954.
Stein, Philipp. *Henrik Ibsen zum Bühnengeschichte seiner Dichtungen*. Berlin, 1901.
Stenzel, Gerhard, ed. *Die deutschen Romantiker*. Vol. 1. Salzburg, 1954.
Stirner, Max. *The Ego and His Own*. Translated by John Carroll. New York, 1971.
Strindberg, August. *August Strindbergs Brev*. Edited by Torsten Eklund. Vol. 7, Stockholm, 1961; vol. 13, Stockholm, 1972.
———. *August Strindbergs samlade verk*. Stockholm, 1981–.
———. *Före Röda rummet*. Edited by Torsten Eklund. Stockholm, 1946.
———. *Samlade skrifter*. 55 vols. Edited by John Landquist. Stockholm, 1912–21.
Svarstad, Carsten. "Henrik Ibsens ordener og hederstegn." *Ibsen-årbok* (1957–59).
Svendsen, Paulus. "Emperor and Galilean." *Edda* 56 (1956).
———. "Henrik Ibsen's 'Borte.'" *Edda* (1957).
———. "Om Ibsens kilder til 'Kejser og Galilæer.'" *Edda* 32 (1932).
Svensson, S. "Brand och den svenska göticism." *Edda* 30 (1930).
———. "Svar på 'Replik.'" *Edda* 31 (1931).
Symons, Arthur. *Studies in Seven Arts*. London, 1906.
Taine, Hippolyte. *On Intelligence*. Translated by T. D. Haye. New York, 1875.
Templeton, Joan. *Ibsen's Women*. Cambridge, 1997.
———. "New Light on the Bardach Diary: Eight Unpublished Letters from Ibsen's Gossensass Princess." *Scandinavian Studies* 69 (1997).
Tennant, P. F. D. *Ibsen's Dramatic Technique*. Cambridge, 1948.
The Theatrical "World" for 1893. London, n.d.

Thesen, R. "Bjørnstjerne Bjornson og Georg Brandes." *Festskrift til Halvdan Koht på sekstiårsdagen 7de juli 1933*. Oslo, 1933.

Thomas, P.-Félix. *Pierre Leroux, sa vie, son oeuvre, sa doctrine*. Paris, 1904.

Thoresen, Magdalene. *Breve fra Magdalene Thoresen 1855–1901*. Edited by Julius Clausen and P. Fr. Rist. Copenhagen, 1971.

Tissot, Ernest. *Le Drame norvégien: Henrik Ibsen—Biörnstierne Biörnstierne*. Paris, 1893.

Tramer, Friedrich. "Das Urbild für Ibsens Dr. Stockmann." *Neuphilologische Mitteilungen* 56 (1955).

Tveterås, Harald. "Ibsen og Snoilsky." In *Norvegica: Minneskrift til femti-årsdagen for oprettelsen av Universitetsbibliotekets Norske avdelning*. Oslo, 1933.

Tweedie, Mrs. Alec. "Henrik Ibsen and Björnstjerne Björnson." *Temple Bar* 98 (1893).

Uhrskov, Anders. *Christopher Bruun*. Christiania, 1916.

Van Laan, Thomas F. "Ibsen and Nietzsche." *Scandinavian Studies* 78 (2006).

Vasenius, Valfrid. *Henrik Ibsens dramatiska diktning i dess första skede*. Helsingfors, 1879.

Vinten-Johansen, Peter. "Johan Ludvig Heiberg's Political and Social Thought." PhD diss., Yale University, 1975.

Waal, Carla. "William Bloch's *The Wild Duck*." *Educational Theatre Journal* 30 (December 1978).

Wais, Kurt. "Henrik Ibsens Sinnbilder und die Krise seiner Jahrhunderts." *Edda* 56 (1956).

Wall, Annie. *Människor jag mötte*. Oslo, 1926.

Wallner, Franz. "Ibsens Freudentränen: Erinnerungen an die erste 'Gespenster'-Aufführung." *Die Deutsche Bühne* 20, no. 4 (March 13, 1928).

Warburg, Karl. *Carl Snoilsky: Hans lefnad och skaldskap*. Stockholm, 1905.

Warnock, Mary. *Existentialism*. Oxford, 1970.

Weaver, William. *Duse*. New York, 1984.

Webb, Eugene. "The Radical Irony of Hedda Gabler." *Modern Language Quarterly* 31 (1970).

Wedekind, Frank. "Ibsen the Writer and Solness *The Master Builder*." Translated by Christel Fjelde. *Theater Three* 1 (Fall 1986).

Weigand, Hermann J. *The Modern Ibsen*. New York, 1925.

Weininger, Otto. *Über die letzten Dinge*. Vienna and Leipzig, 1904.

Whyte, Lancelot Law. *The Unconscious Before Freud*. New York, 1962.

Wieselgren, O. "Svensk teater från 1500 till 1900." In *Svenska konstnärer inom teaterns, musikens och filmens värld*. Edited by Einar Sundström. Stockholm, 1943.

Woerner, Roman. *Henrik Ibsen*. 2 vols. Munich, 1900–1910.

Wrangel, F. U. *Minnen från konstnärkretsarna och författarvärlden*. Stockholm, 1925.

Wulfflen, Erich. *Ibsens Nora vor dem Strafrichter und Psychiater*. Halle, 1907.

Wyller, Anders. "Vildanden: En innledning og en kritikk." *Edda* 36 (1936).

Zola, Emile. *The Experimental Novel and Other Essays*. Translated by Belle M. Sherman. 1893; reprinted New York, 1964.

———. "Naturalism in the Theatre." In George G. Becker, ed., *Documents of Modern Literary Realism*. Princeton, 1963.

Zucker, A[dolf] E[dward]. *Ibsen, the Master Builder*. New York, 1929.

CREDITS

FIGURES

Figure 1. Frontispiece; see p. iv
Figure 2. From Einar Ostvedt's *Henrik Ibsen og hans barndomsmiljo*, 2nd ed. Courtesy of Telemark Museum.
Figure 3. From Einar Ostvedt's *Henrik Ibsen og hans barndomsmiljo*, 2nd ed. Courtesy of Telemark Museum.
Figure 4. Owner: National Library of Norway.
Figure 5. Photographer: Eduard Larssen / Owner: National Library of Norway.
Figure 6. Used by permission of Audbjørn Rønning for Maihaugen, Stiftelsen Lillehammer Museum.
Figure 7. Photographer: Daniel Georg Nyblin / Owner: National Library of Norway.
Figure 8. Photographer: Fratelli d'Alessandri / Owner: National Library of Norway.
Figure 9. Photographer: J. Petersen / Owner: National Library of Norway.
Figure 10. Courtesy of Musikverket.
Figure 11. Artist: Julius Kronberg / Owner: National Library of Norway.
Figure 12. Photographer: ukjent, J. Leeb / Owner: National Library of Norway.
Figure 13. From Daniel Haakonsen, *Henrik Ibsen: Mennesket og kunstneren*, Oslo 1981.
Figure 14. Owner: National Library of Norway.
Figure 15. Courtesy of The Royal Danish Theatre.
Figure 16. Christian Krohg; Georg Brandes, 1879 © Photo: O Væring Eftf. AS, Norway.
Figure 17. Courtesy of The Royal Library.
Figure 18. Courtesy of The Royal Library.
Figure 19. Courtesy of Bonnier Rights.
Figure 20. Courtesy of VISDA.
Figure 21. From E. N. Tigerstedt, *Svensk litteratur-historie*, Stockholm 1953.
Figure 22. Photographer: Forbech, Ludvig. Oslo Museum / TM.T01062.

Figure 23. From Heinz Kindermann, *Theatergeschichte Europas*, Salzburg, vol. 8, 1968.
Figure 24. Lebrecht Music & Arts / Alamy Stock Photo.
Figure 25. From A *Source Book on Naturalistic Theatre*. Ed. Christopher Innes, London 2000.
Figure 26. Photographer: Jos, Albert. Oslo Museum / TM.T02949.
Figure 27. Photographer: Christian Gihbsson / Owner: National Library of Norway.
Figure 28. Image courtesy of Natur & Kultur publishing house.
Figure 29. Image courtesy of the Danish Royal Theater.
Figure 30. Photographer: Herman Hamnqvist. National Library of Sweden (Maps and Pictures) (Sv. P. Fitinghoff, Rosa Fa 1).

TEXT

"Ibsen and the Immoralists" first published in *Comparative Literature Studies* 9, no. 1 (1972), 58–79. Credit: © Penn State University. Used with permission.

"Science and Poetry in *Ghosts*" first published in *Scandinavian Studies*, 1979, vol. 51, no. 4, pp. 154–167.

"The Unspoken Text in *Hedda Gabler*" first published in *Modern Drama*, 1993, vol. 36, pp. 353–367.

"Syphilis in Ibsen's ghosts," Evert Sprinchorn, *Ibsen Studies* 4, no. 2 (2004), copyright © The Centre for Ibsen Studies reprinted by permission of Taylor & Francis Ltd, http://www.tandfonline.com on behalf of The Centre for Ibsen Studies.

INDEX

Page numbers in *italics* refer to illustrations. Works are by Ibsen unless otherwise indicated.

Aasen, Ivar, 39
Abildgaard, Theodor, 37, 38
"Abraham Lincoln's Assassination," 96–97, 163, 179, 187, 203
"Abydos," 211
Achurch, Janet, 292, 335, 479
Aesthetic Studies (Brandes), 122
"Afrodite och Sliparen" ("Aphrodite and the Grinder"; Snoilsky), 390
Aftenbladet (Norwegian newspaper), 118
Aftonbladet (Swedish newspaper), 276
Agate, James, 437
Albee, Edward, 2
Alberg, Ida, 493
Albertine (Krohg), 439
Almlöf, Knut, *132*
Almströmer, Jonas, 271–72
Ammianus Marcellinus, 201
Anckarsvärd, Ellen, 561
Andersen, Hans Christian, 44
Andersen, Hildur, 494–99, 515, 555, 573, 578
Andersen, Oluf Martin, 494
Andhrimmer (journal), 37, 58, 327
Andreas-Salomé, Lou, 433
Anno, Anton, 475
Ansichten von der Nachseite der Naturwissenschaft (Schubert), 377–78
Antigone (Sophocles), 96
Antoine, André, 259, 478
Antony and Cleopatra (Shakespeare), 457
"Aphrodite and the Grinder" ("Afrodite och Sliparen"; Snoilsky), 390
Archer, William, 336–38, 417; as critic, 293, 316, 318, 546, 547; Ibsen and Scribe linked by, 591–92n14; Ibsen described by, 298; as translator, 137–38, 274, 312, 313, 413, 479, 557; verse drama viewed by, 251
Arden, Mary, 28
L'Argent (Zola), 536
Arnesson, Nicholas, 62–63
Arnold, Matthew, 204, 305, 465
Arnoldson, Sigrid, 493
Art and Morality (*Kunsten og moralen*; Collin), 529–31
Asbjørnsen, Peter Christian, 39, 85
Asquith, Henry Herbert, 557

Atkinson, Brooks, 5
"At Port Said," 156–57
"Auf diesem Felsen bauen wir" (Heine), 218
Augier, Emile, 259, 270
Augustine of Hippo, Saint, 605n6
Les Avariés (Brieux), 307
"Awaken Scandinavians!," 89
Axelsen, N. F., 135, 327

Bagger, Herman, 128, 130–31
Bahr, Hermann, 487
Bakunin, Michael, 229
"A Balloon Letter to a Swedish Lady," 156, 162–63, 179, 186–87, 210
Balzac, Honoré de, 180
Bang, Herman, 516, 518–19
Bang, J., 313
A *Bankruptcy* (*En Fallit*; Bjørnson), 257–59, 261, 267
Bardach, Emilie, 490–93, 497–99, 570
Barrie, J. M., 557
"The Basis of Faith" ("Troens Grund"), 67–68
Bebel, August, 212
Becque, Henri, 516
Beerbohm, Max, 10
Bellini, Vincenzo, 38
Benedictsson, Christian, 442
Benedictsson, Victoria, 308, 442–45, 447, 452–53, 510
Berg, Leo, 547
"Bergmanden," 539
Den bergtagna (*The Enchanted*; Victoria Benedictsson), 510
Bernini, Gian Lorenzo, 70–71
Berteval, Walter, 404
Et besøg (*A Visit*; Brandes), 438
Between Battles (Bjørnson), 56
Beyond Good and Evil (Nietzsche), 453, 466
Beyond Human Power (*Over œvne*; Bjørnson), 347, 351
Bigeon, Maurice, 339, 483–84, 517
Birkedalen, Else Sophie Jensdatter, 88
Birkeland, Michael, 58, 83, 120, 133–34, 167–68, 249
The Birth of Tragedy (Nietzsche), 514
Bismarck, Otto von, 186, 189, 206, 210, 212, 248; Brandes's ingratiation with, 542–43; Catholic Church persecuted by, 188, 236; expansionism of, 136–37, 169, 179–80, 187, 209
Bjørnson, Bergliot, 489
Bjørnson, Bjørnstjerne Martinus, 9–10, 57, 67, 68, 72, 79, 274; boorishness of, 138–39; Botten-Hansen forced out of business by, 116–17, 130; Brandes vs., 115, 141, 197, 404, 440–41, 443, 449; Christianity renounced by, 269, 347; Collin praised by, 530; conservative attacks on, 145–46; declining popularity of, 159; German empire viewed by, 187; *Ghosts* defended by, 324, 332, 546; as heart of Norway, 56, 473; Ibsen contrasted with, 266; Ibsen's condescension toward, 60, 160; Ibsen's conflicts with, 102–10, 117, 121, 129, 139, 141, 146, 148–52, 154, 157, 159–60, 162, 164–65, 167–68, 204, 246; Ibsen's flattery of, 115–16, 119, 120, 327–28; during Ibsen's last days, 575–76, 577; Ibsen's reconciliation with, 268, 327; Ibsen supported by, 64, 81–82, 84, 117, 129, 545–46; Ibsen's view of, 61, 62–63, 164; Ibsen viewed by, 35, 102, 117–18, 120, 324, 353; as *John Gabriel Borkman* model, 545–46; *League of Youth* criticized by, 236–37; as *League of Youth* model, 128–30, 146, 147–48, 149, 151–52, 160; Learned Dutchmen disdained by, 117–18, 120, 133; liberal youth aligned with, 152; as pan-Germanist, 160–61, 164; as *Peer Gynt* model, 423–24; personal magnetism of, 56, 58, 69, 129, 152; Petersen linked to, 58–60, 114, 118, 138, 140; poetry collection by, 171, 177; political views of, 60–61, 71, 124, 125, 153, 248, 332, 473; realistic drama embraced by, 256–63; *Rosmersholm* criticized by, 412;

self-confidence of, 142; sexual double standard attacked by, 438; stipend awarded to, 83; Western Scandinavianism championed by, 119
Bleak House (Dickens), 274
Bloch, Iwan, 308
Bloch, William, 365, 366, 367
blocking, in theater, 42, 43
Blom, Andreas, 593n34
Blumenthal, Oscar, 433–34
Börne, Ludwig, 204
"Borte!" ("Gone!"), 173
Boström, Erik, 560
Botten-Hansen, Paul, 36–37, 58, 84, 116–17, 128, 130, 154
Boyesen, Hjalmar Hjorth, 404
Boyesen, Jacob, 21
Bradley, A. C., 4, 400, 557
Brahm, Otto, 475–76
Brahms, Johannes, 496
Brand, 4, 11, 12, 53, 69, 109, 154, 251, 363, 480, 532, 558, 578; anti-Teutonism in, 162, 186; Brandes's view of, 77, 113–15, 189, 556; critical and popular response to, 77–78, 103–4, 105–6, 113–15, 118, 248, 333, 454, 566; dualism mocked in, 115; as existential work, 94–95; family vs. ideals in, 19; female submissiveness in, 272; *Ghosts* contrasted with, 304; Ibsen's reconsideration of, 166, 179, 410; inspiration for, 71–73, 86; Nietzsche's influence on, 74, 547–48; publication of, 81–82, 83; royalties for, 565–66; sacrifice in, 75–79, 514–15; transvaluation in, 74, 80; women depicted in, 276
Brand, Julius, 402
Brandell, Gunnar, 426
Brandes, Edvard, 266, 345–46, 444, 510
Brandes, Georg, 90, 121, 180–81, 184, 186, 214, 245, 378, 405, 460, 499, 577; aristocratic radicalism articulated by, 448, 450, 547; Bjørnson vs., 115, 141, 197, 404, 446; Bjørnson viewed by, 139; *Brand* viewed by, 77, 113–15, 304; Collin vs., 528–30; dualism opposed by, 111–15, 190, 207; *Emperor and Galilean* viewed by, 224; as esthetician, 122–23, 189–90, 194; in Germany, 308–9, 382; *Ghosts* viewed by, 324, 332, 340; Ibsen described by, 205–6, 297–98, 454, 515; Ibsen's debates with, 215; as Ibsen's friend and champion, 102–3, 116, 139–40, 154, 308, 313, 394, 507, 579; Ibsen's poetry viewed by, 192, 193–94, 250; Ibsen's politics viewed by, 188, 189, 190–92, 517, 542–43, 551–52; Ibsen's symbolism denied by, 342; Ibsen's writings published by, 491, 562; *John Gabriel Borkman* viewed by, 548–49; Kieler denigrated by, 509–10; *Lady of the Sea* criticized by, 433; *League of Youth* praised by, 143–44; libel suit prompted by, 441; liberalism disclaimed by, 383; *The Master Builder* defended by, 505–6; materialism of, 264; as naturalist, 337–38, 340, 373, 440, 543; Nietzsche and, 416, 446–50, 453, 487, 529, 547, 552; political coalition envisioned by, 414; problem plays defended by, 256, 261, 507; as provocateur, 194–97; sexual exploits of, 140–41, 309, 441–45, 452; sexual freedom espoused by, 345, 438, 444, 547; as Shakespeare scholar, 547; Snoilsky criticized by, 390; as translator, 215, 273; women's status viewed by, 270, 310
Brand's Daughters (Laura Petersen), 276
Brentano, Bettina, 499
Brieux, Eugène, 307
Brøchner, Hans, 111
"A Brother in Need" ("En Broder i Nød"), 67
Bruun, Christopher, 11, 72–73, 347, 552, 577
Bruun, Lina, 72–73, 121
Bruun, Thea, 598n4
Bruzelius, Thure, 442
"Building Plans" ("Byggeplaner"), 31, 243–44, 528, 532

Bull, Dr., 576
Bull, Francis, 33, 576, 599n2
Bull, Ole, 39, 40, 45
Burckhardt, Jacob, 229
"Burnt Ships" ("Brændte Skibe"), 177, 486
"Byggeplaner" ("Building Plans"), 31, 243–44, 528, 532
Byggmester Solness. See *The Master Builder*
Byron, George Gordon Byron, Baron, 309

La Camaraderie (Scribe), 591–92n14
Cappelen, August, 39
Carlyle, Thomas, 339, 377
Catiline, 32–33, 63, 171
Catiline, 13, 27, 33–35, 36, 244
Cavour, Camillo Benso, Count of, 169
Cesarini, Giuliano, 228
Challenger expedition (1873–76), 372
Champfleury, 252
Charles XV, king of Sweden and Norway, 66, 83, 156, 184
Chekhov, Anton, 4, 16, 288, 307, 367, 478
Christian IX, king of Denmark, 558
Christian Ethics (*Den christelige Ethik*; Martensen), 215
Cicero, Marcus Tullius, 31–32
Civilization and Its Discontents (Freud), 352–53, 402
Claretie, Jules, 519
Coleridge, Samuel Taylor, 377
Collett, Camilla, 275–76, 278, 285, 296, 394, 525–28, 532
Collin, Christen, 528–31, 533
A Commentary on the Works of Henrik Ibsen (Boyesen), 404
Common Sense About the War (Shaw), 164
Comrades (Strindberg), 404, 559
Concluding Unscientific Postscript (Kierkegaard), 95
Conrad, Georg, 395
Constantine I, emperor of Rome, 201, 220, 222
Die conventionellen Lügen der Kulturmenscheit (Nordau), 419
Les Corbeaux (Becque), 516
Correggio, Antonio da, 70, 83
Courtney, W. L., 523
Crawfurd, Georgiana, 26, 32
Creditors (*Fordringsgäre*; Strindberg), 516
Critique of Judgment (Kant), 371–72

Daae, Ludvig, 58, 145, 146, 388
Dagbladet (newspaper), 114, 268, 296
Dagens Nyheder (newspaper), 509–10, 512
La Dame aux Camélias (Dumas), 256
Dano-Prussian War (1864), 100, 184, 209; cultural parallels to, 93, 95, 96, 98; domestic politics and, 124–25; Ibsen's disillusionment with, 66–67, 68; *Peer Gynt* inspired by, 89, 90, 92, 97, 101, 137
Dansk Maanedskrift, 114
Dante Alighieri, 100
Darwin, Charles, 237, 372–75, 427, 428, 449; Brandes's view of, 197; Ibsen and, 197, 305, 354, 371, 425; religious views threatened by, 304–5, 323, 347
David, Caroline, 140
David, Ludvig, 113
Degeneration (Nordau), 479, 529
Delescluze, Louis Charles, 223
Delphine (de Staël), 270
Demirgian, Ohan, 156, 158
"De satt der, de to—" ("They Sat There, the Two of Them—"), 495–96
The Descent of Man (Darwin), 304, 373
Desprez, Louis, 398
Dickens, Charles, 274
Dictionary of Norwegian Authors (*Norsk Forfatterleksikon;* Halvorsen), 509
Dietrichson, Lorentz, 143, 162, 165, 170, 171, 201, 396, 438; Collett praised by, 526; *Emperor and Galilean* esteemed by, 207–8; as Ibsen's Stockholm guide, 155–56; naturalism condemned by, 388, 394, 439–40; students' invitation to Ibsen and, 391–93, 397, 409, 439

Dikter på vers och prosa (*Poems in Verse and Prose*; Strindberg), 250
Disraeli, Benjamin, 248
"Ett dockhem" (Strindberg), 274
Dolcke, Fröken, 612n18
A Doll's House (*Et dukkehjem*), 43, 252, 476, 479; characterization in, 284–86; Christian elements in, 337; critical and popular response to, 294, 296, 299, 320, 333, 434, 486, 533, 542; Darwinian allusion in, 373; ending of, 289, 296–97, 299, 322, 335–36; expurgations of, 296–97; feminist message of, 1, 3, 275, 280, 290, 347, 404, 438, 526, 562; forged-signature device in, 287–88, 335, 509–11; French premiere of, 516; *Ghosts* as response to, 299–301, 308, 345; philosophical themes in, 291; publication of, 296; real-life models for, 283, 291, 294–96, 301, 508, 510–13, 526, 567–68; sexuality and temptation in, 286, 337, 480; tarantella scene in, 288, 289, 292, 335, 336, 339, 340; title of, 274; visual elements in, 336; as well-made play, 284, 287, 335–37; *When We Dead Awaken* linked to, 565; writing of, 251, 280–81, 289
Don Carlos (Schiller), 61
Dostoyevsky, Fyodor, 517
"Doubt and Hope," 27
Douglas, Ludvig, 560
Drachmann, Holger, 12, 345, 383
Dualism in Our Newest Philosophy (*Dualism i vor nyeste Filosofi*; Brandes), 114
Due, Christopher L., 26, 31, 497
Et dukkehjem. See *A Doll's House*
Dumas, Alexandre, *fils*, 256, 270, 335
Dumont, Louise, 477
Dunker, Bernhard, 128–29, 145
Duse, Eleanor, 3–4, 292–94, 336, 398–99, 434–37, 277, 577

Ebbell, Clara, 26
Echegaray y Eizaguirre, José, 10
"Edderfuglen" ("The Eider Duck"), 238
Edgren, Anne Charlotte, 452
Edholm, Erik af, 156
The Editor (*Redaktøren*; Bjørnson), 259, 267, 268
Edward VII, king of Great Britain, 388
Les Effrontés (Augier), 259
The Ego and His Own (*Der Einzige und sein Eigentum*; Stirner), 182–83
Ehrhard, Auguste, 456, 464, 467
Ehrlich, Paul, 310
"The Eider Duck" ("Edderfuglen"), 238
Elias, Julius, 562
Eliot, T. S., 235
Emerson, Ralph Waldo, 16
Emigrantliteraturen (*Literature of the Emigrants*; Brandes), 196, 270
Emperor and Galilean, 197, 206, 222, 229–32, 250, 371, 409–10, 532, 548; atypicality of, 200, 237; autobiographical elements in, 199, 207, 214, 219, 225–27; critical response to, 236–37; epic scale of, 200–201, 227; Ibsen's high regard for, 199–200; mysticism of, 215–16, 372, 375; philosophical elements in, 199, 216, 227–28; publication of, 171, 236; Third Kingdom underlying, 217–19, 220–21, 223, 224, 232, 233, 414–15; world politics mirrored by, 201–2, 204–5, 208, 214, 217, 218–19, 232–33
The Enchanted (*Den bergtagna;* Victoria Benedictsson), 510
An Enemy of the People, 137, 333, 366, 481, 517, 544, 575–76; casting of, 331–32; Ibsen's independence asserted in, 346; indignation and humor combined in, 330, 344; inspiration for, 327–28, 329
Engels, Friedrich, 213, 229
Engström, Albert, 559
Die Entstehung des Gewissens (Rée), 405
Ernst Ahlgren (Key), 452
Die Erziehung des Menschengeschlechts (Lessing), 218
Ethics (Høffding), 449, 450, 451

Eugen, prince of Sweden, 560
L'Evolution naturaliste (Desprez), 398

Fædrelandet (newspaper), 58, 66, 111, 116, 118, 119, 161–62, 345
Faguet, Emile, 342
"A Fallen Star" (Andreas Munch), 324, 392
En Fallit (*A Bankruptcy*; Bjørnson), 257–59, 261, 267
La Famille Benoiton (Sardou), 259
"Far Away" ("Langt borte"), 262
Farmers' Friends (Bondevenner), 124, 125, 129
The Father (Strindberg), 549
Faust (Goethe), 92–93, 99, 100, 199, 478
Fear and Trembling (Kierkegaard), 52
Fearnley, Thomas, 39
"Fear of the Light," 34
The Feast at Solhoug (*Gildet paa Solhoug*), 48–49, 551, 552, 558
Feilitzen, Urban von, 433
Fenger, Henning, 591–92n14, 599n2
Fergusson, Francis, 338, 340
Feuerbach, Ludwig, 108, 111, 182–83
Filosofi of Teologi (*Philosophy and Theology*; Høffding), 111
Le fils naturel (*The Illegitimate Son*; Dumas), 256
First International, 203–4
Fischhof, Alfred, 493
Fiske, Minnie Maddern, 414
Fitinghoff, Rosa, 570–73, 576
Flaubert, Gustave, 449
Fontane, Theodore, 365
Fordringsgäre (*Creditors*; Strindberg), 516
For Idé og Virkelighed (journal), 139, 171
"For the Millennial Festival" ("Ved Tusenårs-Fest"), 169
Fournier, Alfred, 310–13, 315
Fra de stummes lejr (*From the Camp of the Voiceless*; Collett), 276
"Fra det ubevidste Sjæleliv" ("From the Unconscious Life of the Soul"), 487
Fra Kristiania-Bohêmen (*From Christiania's Bohemia*; Jæger), 439
Franco-Prussian War (1870), 160, 179, 190, 209–10, 223
Frederik VII, king of Denmark, 66
Fredrikson, Gustaf, 143, 356–57
Freud, Sigmund, 352–53, 418, 425; collective mind theorized by, 419; guilt vs. happiness viewed by, 402; Oedipal theory of, 407–8; *Rosmersholm* and, 404, 407, 426; the unconscious theorized by, 406
Friele, Christian, 124, 146, 593n34
From Christiania's Bohemia (*Fra Kristiania-Bohêmen*; Jæger), 439
From Skåne (Benedictsson), 442
From the Camp of the Voiceless (*Fra de stummes lejr*; Collett), 276
"From the Unconscious Life of the Soul" ("Fra det ubevidste Sjæleliv"), 487
Fru Inger til Østraat (*Lady Inger of Østraat*), 47–48, 49, 244, 561
Fru Marianne (Benedictsson), 444
Für Darwin (Müller), 378

Garborg, Arne, 237, 325, 438, 440
Garibaldi, Giuseppe, 203
Gauguin, Paul, 16, 391, 521
Geijerstam, Gustaf af, 415–16, 428, 452, 559, 578
Georg II, duke of Saxe-Meiningen, 321, 475
Germinal (Zola), 339–40
Die Gesellschaft (journal), 395
Ghosts, 3, 14, 245, 251, 390, 427, 516, 558; autobiographical elements in, 301, 304; classical tragedy evoked by, 304, 305–6; controversy surrounding, xi, 1, 307, 320–23, 325–26, 332, 333, 344–47, 357, 359, 439, 474–75, 533, 542; defenders of, 324, 475–76, 526, 560; as *Doll's House* response, 299–301, 308, 345; euthanasia plea in, 316, 320, 322, 342, 343–44, 439; fire symbolism in, 340–43, 525; French

and German elements in, 47; late point of attack in, 315; light vs. darkness in, 13, 43, 302–3, 368; past bearing on present in, 459; performance history of, 321, 473; sacrifice in, 302, 318, 319, 347, 409; sexuality and peril in, 27, 303, 314, 438; syphilis in, 307–15, 320–21, 322, 341–43, 371, 439, 480, 533
Giftas (*Married*; Strindberg), 332–33
Gildet paa Solhoug (*The Feast at Solhoug*), 48–49, 551, 552, 558
Gladstone, William, 248, 388
A Glass of Water (Scribe), 335
Gloersen, Kristian, 387
A Glove (*En hanske*; Bjørnson), 438, 441, 446
"Godt mod" ("Good Cheer"; Bjørnson), 177
Goethe, Johann Wolfgang von, 9, 70, 199, 225, 229, 232, 499, 548; Bjørnson linked to, 59–60; Dante's influence on, 100; Ibsen influenced by, 92–93, 99; Ibsen's opposition to, 92, 95, 96, 99; works and grace viewed by, 74
Goldman, Emma, 291, 311
Goncourt, Jules, 312
"Gone!" ("Borte!"), 173
"Good Cheer" ("Godt mod"; Bjørnson), 177
Gosse, Edmund, 51, 199, 250, 313, 344, 478, 557
Götterdämmerung (Wagner), 51
Götzen-Dämmerung (*The Twilight of the Idols*; Nietzsche), 466
Götz von Berlichingen (Goethe), 59–60
Gravier, Maurice, 591–92n14
Great Eastern (ship), 263
"A Greeting in Song to Sweden" ("Sangerhilsen til Sverige"), 262
Grieg, Edvard, 11, 39, 177, 244, 497
Gröbner, Ludwig, 491
Grønvold, Marcus, 386, 533
Grundtvig, Elisabeth, 440, 453
Grundtvig, Nikolai Frederik Severin, 152; Bjørnson's support for, 114, 115, 117, 160–61; Kierkegaard vs., 108; wide influence of, 90, 109, 117, 120
Gude, Hans Fredrik, 39
"The Gully" ("Kløftet"), 171

Haeckel, Ernst, 372–76, 378, 379, 418, 425, 427
Hærmændene paa Helgeland (*The Vikings at Helgeland*), 50–51, 53, 168, 171, 244–45, 464, 548
Håkonsson, Håkon, 60–62
Halvorsen, Jens Braage, 509
Hamlet (Shakespeare), 4, 405, 456
Hamsun, Knut, 487–88, 518, 521
En hanske (*A Glove*; Bjørnson), 438, 441, 446
Hansson, Ola, 293, 416
Hansteen, Aasta, 273–74
Harald the Fairhaired, 167, 169
Hardy, Thomas, 377, 557
Harring, Harro, 38
Harrison, Jane, 557
Hartmann, Eduard von, 378
Hauch, Carsten, 111, 194, 196
Hauptmann, Gerhart, 475
"I havsnød" ("A Ship in Distress"), 66
Hazlitt, William, 339
Hebbel, Friedrich, 50
Hedberg, Franz, 143
Hedda Gabler, 4, 111, 476, 487, 492–93, 502; characterization in, 456; divided stage in, 458–60, 463, 468–70; French influence on, 516; mixed reception of, 486; Nietzschean elements in, 450–51, 453–55, 460–62, 466–67, 469; past bearing on present in, 461; realistic drama's conventions and, 456–57; real-life models for, 450–52, 455; symbols in, 521; Viking spirit in, 460–62, 464–65, 470; visual elements in, 457–58; as well-made play, 453
Hedin, Adolf, 415
Hegel, Frederick, 489

Hegel, Frederik, xi–xii, 139, 150–51, 154, 322, 536
Hegel, Georg Friedrich, 109, 218, 231, 378; Heine vs., 229; Ibsen's changing views of, 216–17; Kierkegaard vs., 93, 95, 98, 99, 108; *Peer Gynt*'s repudiation of, 92, 93, 95–96, 97, 98; political compromise viewed by, 96, 108; sublation theory of, 208; wide influence of, 92, 108
Heiberg, Gunnar, 568–69
Heiberg, Johan Ludvig, 60, 147, 598n13; democracy mistrusted by, 166, 180; as Hegelian, 108, 109, 166; Ibsen likened to, 166; Scribe admired by, 47; traditionalism of, 59
Heiberg, Johanne Luise, 138, 139, 143, 144, 159, 165, 167
Heidenstam, Verner von, 487, 559
Heine, Heinrich, 204, 208–9, 217–18, 229
Heinessen, Mogens, 85, 86
Hellesylt, Ingeborg, 86
Hennings, Betty, 291–92
Henrik Ibsen (Rose), 404
Henrik Ibsens Keiser og Gaililær (Garborg), 237
"The Heroic Ballad and Its Significance for Literature" ("Om kjæmpevisen og dens betydning for kunstpoesien"), 47
Hettner, Hermann, 47
Heyse, Paul, 395, 414, 448
Hirschholm, Niels Jørgen, 23
History of Creation (Haeckel), 374, 378
Hitler, Adolf, 163, 181
Høffding, Harald, 111–12, 115, 379–80, 394, 448–51
Hoffory, Julius, 492
Hofmannsthal, Hugo von, 505
Holberg, Ludvig, 2, 58, 93, 122
Holst, Rikke, 45, 49, 53, 173
Høst, Else, 338
Hugo, Victor, 11, 48
Huneker, James, 4, 344, 399, 404, 478, 572
Hunger (*Sult;* Hamsun), 487
Huxley, Thomas Henry, 374
"Hvita frun" ("The White Lady"; Snoilsky), 390–91

"I Billedgalleriet" ("In the Picture Gallery"), 51, 63, 83
Ibsen, Hedvig (sister), 29–30
Ibsen, Henrik Johan: aims vs. capabilities viewed by, xii, 4–5, 578; aloofness of, 12; anarchism averred by, 11, 517–18, 542–43; anger as motivation for, 122; aristocracy of the spirit envisioned by, 414–15; awards and accolades coveted by, 156–59, 169, 226, 243–44, 245–46, 249, 333, 385–86, 473–74; birthplace of, *20;* bitterness of, 28–30, 68–69, 71–72, 133, 167–69, 177, 206, 245; Bjørnson contrasted with, 266; Bjørnson's conflicts with, 102–10, 117, 121, 129, 139, 141, 146, 148–52, 154, 157, 159–60, 162, 164–65, 167–68, 204, 246; Bjørnson's rapprochement with, 268; Bjørnson's success envied by, 259–60, 261; Bjørnson viewed by, 61, 62–63, 164; Brandes viewed by, 114; casting preferences of, 331–32; characters visualized by, 420; childhood of, 17, 19–24; Christiania students addressed by, 237–40, 506; Collin's criticism of, 529; commercial successes and failures of, 2, 47–49, 56, 82, 102, 267, 294, 296, 299, 320–23, 325–26, 333, 433, 434, 536; commitment vs, noncommitment and, 88–89, 152–53, 263; conservatives' approbation sought by, 58, 132, 154, 165; as constitutional monarchist, 117; criticism dismissed by, 325–27; Dano-Norwegian language favored by, 39, 98, 155; darkness congenial to, 13; Darwinism and, 197, 305, 354, 371, 425; death and funeral of, 9–11, 576, 577–78; determinism opposed by, 427; dialogue stressed by, 252–53, 413; dramatic conflicts unresolved by, 2–3; drinking habits of, 298; *Emperor and Galilean* esteemed by, 199–200; estheticism viewed by, 177–78, 205;

estrangement from parents conceded by, 363–64; extramarital flirtations and affairs of, 490–99; farmers disdained by, 180; feminist sympathies disclaimed by, 290–91, 562; finances of, 40, 55, 81–84, 119, 205, 266, 485; French and German drama contrasted by, 46, 249; German language ability of, 136, 274; Germany viewed by, 96, 162, 185–88, 198; Goethe opposed by, 92, 95, 96, 99; growing self-confidence of, 84–85; habits and routines of, 298–99, 481–83; Hegelianism embraced by, 216–17; hypersensitivity of, 28; illegitimate son of, 26–27, 88; images of, 57, 65, 85, 247, 483; importance of, 1, 480; inner conflicts of, 17–18, 19, 25, 28, 75, 134, 198, 201, 204, 208, 236, 270, 291, 337, 344–45, 352, 360, 541; intellectual curiosity of, 214; in Italy, 70–72; journal copublished by, 26–27; Kierkegaard's influence on, 52, 77, 92–96, 98–100, 107, 117, 184, 454; in labor movement, 37; literary renown sought by, 5, 71–72, 82, 103, 251; logical conflicts in work of, 80; marriage viewed by, 25–26, 52; masochistic streak of, 184; medical career ambitions of, 24–25, 27; as nationalist, 68, 86, 101; national theater launched by, 39–40; Nietzsche's influence disavowed by, 455, 547–48; nihilistic turn of, 192–93, 197–98; Norwegian resettlement rejected by, 395; at Norwegian Theater, 54–55; painting career considered by, 24, 39, 70, 336, 359–60, 367, 431, 457; pan-Germanism embraced by, 162–64; parents' financial troubles and, 19, 28–30, 75, 87, 133, 360–62; Parnassian self-image of, 267, 301; Clemens Petersen and, 67, 141; Laura Petersen and, 276–80; philosophical ideas dramatized by, 227–28; "photographic" technique of, 121, 125, 127, 130, 153, 250, 338, 363; physical ailments of, 13–14, 488; physical appearance of, 18, 44–45, 169–70, 206, 297–98, 484, 572; poetry abandoned by, 250, 251; poetry volume compiled by, 172–77, 184–85, 191; political views of, 11, 117, 180–81, 183–84, 198, 206–7, 248–49, 326–27, 329–30, 332, 347, 383–87, 391, 396, 473–74, 517–18, 542–43; problem plays of, 263–67; reading vs. viewing public and, 322; realistic acting furthered by, 367, 476–77; religious background and views of, 11, 24, 25, 79, 182, 577; retrospective technique used by, 399; revealing by concealing favored by, 126, 562; revisions by, 171; Scandinavian Society in Rome addressed by, 281–83, 289; Schleswig-Holstein dispute viewed by, 65; seventieth birthday celebration for, 557–62, 568; sexual repression and, 53; Shakespeare's career parallels to, 28; as social climber, 36, 44, 58, 120, 131, 133, 149, 153, 157, 169–70, 243–44; solitude of, 297; spiral staircase theory of history formulated by, 187, 205, 211, 217, 235; stage design advanced by, 367–68; state and nation viewed by, 179–82, 183, 191, 203, 208, 211–13, 216, 223; stipends awarded to, 83–84, 249; in Stockholm, 155–56; students' invitation declined by, 391–94, 397, 439; suicide contemplated by, 55–56, 88; symbolism employed by, 249–50, 337–44, 348, 501–3, 506–7, 513, 518; Third Kingdom envisioned by, 217–19, 220–21, 223, 224, 232, 233, 414–15, 427–28, 450, 453, 513, 515, 533, 539, 541, 543, 550, 552, 555–56, 567, 578–79; at university, 35–36; women depicted by, 272–73, 276; works' trajectory viewed by, 14, 15, 360, 575; writing career chosen by, 27, 31; writing technique of, 281

Ibsen, Johan (brother), 28, 29

Ibsen, Knud (father), 19, 20–24, 30, 131, 361, 363, 593n34

Ibsen, Marichen Altenburg (mother), 18–19, 20–21, 29

Ibsen, Nicolai (brother), 24
Ibsen, Ole (brother), 29, 130
Ibsen, Sigurd (son), 70, 185, 323, 493, 496, 498, 525; as diplomat, 387, 494; marriage of, 489; as translator, 536
Ibsen, Suzannah. *See* Thoresen, Suzannah
The Ibsen Cycle (Johnston), 95
The Ibsen Secret (Lee), 338
The Iceman Cometh (O'Neill), 2
Iconoclasts (Huneker), 404
"I Høsten" ("In the Autumn"), 31
The Illegitimate Son (*Le fils naturel*; Dumas), 256
Illustreret Nyhedsblad, 116–17
Im neuen Reich (journal), 163
Inferno (Strindberg), 558, 559
"In the Autumn" ("I Høsten"), 31
"In the Picture Gallery" ("I Billedgalleriet"), 51, 63, 83
Isaachsen, Andreas, 26

Jaabæk, Søren, 124
Jacobsen, Jens Peter, 237, 281, 289, 295, 304, 373
Jacob van Thyboe (Holberg), 58, 123
Jæger, Hans, 430, 438–39, 440, 451
Jæger, Henrik, 130, 386, 417, 426
James, Henry, 286, 480, 523, 537, 557
Janson, Kristofer, 351
Jaspers, Karl, 95
Jensen, Else Sofie, 26
Joachim of Flora, 216, 217–18, 232
John Gabriel Borkman: autobiographical elements in, 535–36, 538–41, 543–44, 553–56, 564; critical and popular response to, 536–37; effectiveness of, 538; Nietzschean elements in, 548; real-life models for, 538–39, 542–43, 545–46; sexuality in, 548–49; Wandeldekoration employed in, 554; younger generation in, 546–47, 550
Johnston, Brian, 95
Jonson, Ben, 28
Josephson, Ludvig, 244, 252
Joyce, James, 235
Julian (the Apostate), emperor of Rome, 85, 86, 200, 202, 219; as Ibsen's alter ego, 201, 205, 214, 221–26; nineteenth-century politics and, 211, 213; philosophical studies of, 216, 217, 220
Jung, Carl Gustav, 426
Jynge, Gergard, 593n34

Kainz, Josef, 475
Kant, Immanuel, 371–72
Kautzon, Martin, 495
Kerr, Alfred, 10, 11
Key, Ellen, 259, 452, 514, 561–62
Kieler (Petersen), Laura, 565; as *Doll's House* model, 283, 291, 294–96, 301, 508, 510–13, 526, 567–68; Ibsen approached by, 276–78; Ibsen upbraided by, 568, 569; marriage of, 278–79; as *Master Builder* model, 509, 574; personal and professional troubles of, 279–80; religiosity of, 510
Kieler, Victor, 278–80, 567–68
Kielland, Alexander, 325, 384
Kierkegaard, Søren, 47, 229, 424, 551; Abraham's sacrifice viewed by, 100; Angst conceived by, 99, 107; Brandes influenced by, 82, 94; *Brand* inspired by, 76–77, 96; compromise disdained by, 96, 108, 109; conflicting human natures viewed by, 590n4; existentialism foreshadowed by, 94, 95; Hegel criticized by, 108; Ibsen influenced by, 52, 77, 92–96, 98–100, 107, 117, 184, 454
The King (*Kongen*; Bjørnson), 268
Kjæmpehøien (*The Warrior's Barrow*), 36
Kjaer, H. S., 384–85
Kjærlighedens Komedie. See *Love's Comedy*
Kleist, Heinrich von, 180, 184, 378
Klemming, Gustaf, 389
"Kløftet" ("The Gully"), 171
Knudsen, Tormod, 20
Knudtzon, Bertha, 441

Knudtzon, Frederik Gotschalk, 589n7, 597n49
Koht, Halvdan, 566, 590n28, 603n14
Kongen (*The King;* Bjørnson), 268
Kongs-emnerne. See *The Pretenders*
Kragh, Niels, 424
Krohg, Christian, 394, 439, 440
Kronberg, Julius, 246, 247
"Kunsten Magt" ("The Power of Art"), 40
Kunsten og morale (*Art and Morality;* Collin), 529–31

Laading, Herman, 42, 44
The Lady from the Sea, 376, 416–17, 422, 476, 494, 523, 526; acclimatization in, 426, 428, 430, 431; ambiguous ending of, 433; casting of, 434–37; characterization in, 420–21, 423; critical and popular response to, 432–34, 544; divided set in, 457; esthetic contradictions of, 432; *Rosmersholm* compared to, 429, 430–31; sea symbolizing mind in, 418–19, 423, 426
Lady Inger of Østraat (*Fru Inger til Østraat*), 47–48, 49, 244, 561
Lame Hilda (Bjørnson), 59–60
Lammers, Gustav Adolph, 29
Landstad, M. B., 39
Lange, Julius, 121, 353, 507
"Langt borte" ("Far Away"), 262
Larsen, A. C., 111
Lassalle, Ferdinand, 203
Laube, Heinrich, 252, 253
The League of Youth, 41, 125–38, 149, 151–53, 159, 165, 166, 327, 361; conservatives' admiration of, 156, 333; critical vs. popular response to, 143–48, 170, 260, 508; everyday speech in, 250, 256; polarizing effect of, 152, 157, 167; women's independence in, 272–73
Learned Dutchmen (social circle), 58, 84, 116, 124; Bjørnson's disdain for, 117–18, 120, 133; Ibsen esteemed by, 118; political views in, 117
Lee, Jennette, 338
"Lefve Kejsaren!" ("Long Live the Czar!"; Snoilsky), 202
Le Gallienne, Eve, 286
Lemaître, Jules, 550, 620n2
Leroux, Pierre, 218–19
Leschetizky, Theodor, 495
Lescoffier, Jean, 593n34
Lessing, Gotthold Ephraim, 217–18, 225
Lie, Jonas, 149–51, 167, 249, 394, 426, 577; Botten-Hansen pressured by, 116, 128; *Ghosts* defended by, 324; Ibsen's resentment of, 150, 168; as *League of Youth* model, 128, 327, 328
lighting, in theater, 42–43, 367–68
Limnell, Fredrika, 156, 162, 165, 186–87, 510
Lindau, Paul, 297, 434, 484
Lindberg, August: in *Brand*, 565–66; as director, 366; in *Ghosts*, 316, 317, 321, 474, 560; Ibsen praised by, 560–61; in *John Gabriel Borkman*, 540; in *The Master Builder*, 519; *The Wild Duck* viewed by, 366–67
Lindeman, Ludvig, 39
Literature of the Emigrants (*Emigrantliteraturen;* Brandes), 196, 270
Little Eyolf: autobiographical elements in, 525, 527, 528, 531–33, 541; change and maturation in, 524–25, 533; commercial success of, 522; inscrutability of, 524, 527, 531; as morality play, 531; real-life model for, 526–27; weaknesses of, 523, 534–35, 536, 538, 554, 564
Lochmann, Ernst Ferdinand, 427, 428, 466
The Logic of Basic Ideas (Høffding), 112
Løkke, Jakob, 58, 120, 155, 171–72, 225, 507
Lombroso, Cesare, 529
Long Day's Journey into Night (O'Neill), 2
"Long Live the Czar!" ("Lefve Kejsaren!"; Snoilsky), 202
Lorange, Johan, 167
Løvenskiold, Severin, 21, 23, 30, 37, 131, 361

Love's Comedy (*Kjærlighedens Komedie*), 63, 84, 171, 244, 248, 323, 333, 477, 578; *Brand* linked to, 71; critical and popular response to, 56, 103; Kierkegaard's influence on, 52, 93; love vs. marriage in, 50, 53
Lubbock, John, 379
Ludwig II, king of Bavaria, 475
Lugné-Poe, 432, 517, 518–19, 521
Lundegård, Axel, 444–45, 559

Macbeth (Shakespeare), 4, 405
Madigan, Elvira, 467
Mænd af Ære (*Men of Honor*; Kieler), 509–13, 567
Maeterlinck, Maurice, 520, 521
Main Currents in Nineteenth-Century Literature (Brandes), 310
Manderström, Kristoffer, 165, 388
Mantzius, Karl, 149
Married (*Giftas*; Strindberg), 332–33
Martensen, Hans Lassen, 215
Marx, Karl, 166, 212
Mary Stuart (Bjørnson), 138
The Master Builder (*Byggmester Solness*), 14, 480, 511, 517, 530, 538, 558, 574; artistic creativity as subject of, 499–500; Brandes's influence on, 507; *Brand* linked to, 514–15; irrationality and happenstance in, 502–3, 518; *The Lady from the Sea* linked to, 494; *Little Eyolf* contrasted with, 523–24; Maeterlinck's view of, 520; Nietzsche's influence on, 514; self-assuredness of, 490; as self-portrait, 485, 488–89, 505–7, 508–9, 513, 521, 525, 527–28, 563; tower symbol in, 496, 501, 504, 506, 521, 528; younger generation feared in, 482, 519
Maudsley, Henry, 353–54, 356, 361, 380–81, 425
Maximus of Ephesus, 217, 218, 220, 221, 224, 226, 228–29, 232–34
McFarlane, J. W., 312
"Med en Vandlilje" ("With a Water Lily"), 173
Melpomene (*The Tragic Muse*; Michelangelo), 71
"A Memory from Molde" ("Ett mine från Molde"; Snoilsky), 391
Men of Honor (*Mænd af Ære*; Kieler), 509–13, 567
Michelangelo Buonarroti, 70–71, 81, 152, 190
Midsummer Eve (*Sancthansnatten*), 47–48, 49
Mignon (Thomas), 497
Mill, John Stuart, 194, 215, 273, 275, 447, 449
"Mindets Magt" ("The Power of Memory"), 239
"Ett mine från Molde" ("A Memory from Molde"; Snoilsky), 391
Miss Julie (Strindberg), 430, 432, 445, 453, 510
Modern Breakthrough (*Det modern gennembrud*), 194, 352, 529, 544, 556
The Modern Ibsen (Weigand), 399–400
Moe, Jørgen, 39
Molière, 538, 554
Moltke, Helmuth, Graf von, 179, 184, 187, 210
Mommsen, Christian Matthias Theodor, 9
Mon Etoile (Scribe), 591–92n14
"Money" (Benedictsson), 442
Monrad, M. J., 248
Montigny, Adolphe Lemoine, 252, 254–55
Moore, James, 344
Morgenbladet (newspaper), 162, 259, 388; Bjørnson attacked by, 145–46; conservatives linked to, 120–21, 151, 157, 165, 268; Ibsen championed by, 118; monarchist slant of, 116; Reform Association assailed by, 124
Mosfjeld, Oskar, 593n34
Müller, Fritz, 378
Müller, Henrick, 21
Munch, Andreas, 118, 324, 392

Munch, Edvard, 315–16
Munch, P. A., 39, 168
"Mun unge Vin" ("My Young Wine"), 172–73
Murger, Henri, 569
Murillo, Bartolome, 83
Murray, Gilbert, 557
Murray, John, 372
"My Young Wine" ("Mun unge Vin"), 172–73

Napoleon III, emperor of the French, 204, 209
Neoplatonism, 216, 217
"Nero's Golden Palace" ("Neros gyllene hus"; Snoilsky), 203
Nessler, Viktor, 497
New Criticism, 338
The New Kingdom (*Det nya riket;* Strindberg), 253–54
The Newly Married Couple (*De Nygifte;* Bjørnson), 274
New Romanticism, 544
The New Scientific View (*Den nyere Naturanskuelse;* Lochmann), 427
Nicholas of Cusa, Cardinal, 228–29, 230, 232, 233
Nielsen, Lars, 26
Nielsen, Martinius, 565, 566
Nielsen, Niels Peter, 26
Nielsen, Rasmus, 138, 451; Bjørnson denounced by, 161; Brandes's criticism of, 111–14; faith and knowledge reconciled by, 108–15, 117, 153; Young Denmark aligned with, 139
"Nielsen's Philosophy and the Grundtvigian View" ("R. Nielsens Philosophie og den Grundtvigske Anskuelse"; Schmidt), 115
Niels Lyhne (Jacobsen), 304
Niemann-Raabe, Hedwig, 252, 296
Nietzsche, Friedrich, 4, 235, 405, 406, 460, 466, 479; Brandes's proselytism for, 416, 446–50, 453, 487, 547; *Brand* influenced by, 74; existentialism foreshadowed by, 95; *Hedda Gabler* influenced by, 450–51, 453, 454; *The Master Builder* influenced by, 514; posthumous reputation of, 455; syphilis of, 312, 454
Night of the Retreat (*Tilbagetogsnatten;* 1864), 98
Nilson, Randolph, 60
Det nittende Aarhundrede (journal), 262
Nobel Prize, 9–10, 577
Nordau, Max, 419, 478–79, 529, 530
Nordenfelt, Vilhelm, 272
Norma, 38, 165
Norma (Bellini), 38
Norske arbeideres forening (Norwegian Workers' Union), 264
Norske Huldre-Eventyr og Folkesagn (Asbjørnsen), 85–86
Norsk Folkeblad, 105, 116, 124, 130, 149, 151
Norsk Forfatterleksikon (*Dictionary of Norwegian Authors;* Halvorsen), 509
Northam, John, 338
North German Confederation, 185
Norwegian Association, 60
Det nya riket (*The New Kingdom;* Strindberg), 253–54
Nyblom, Helena, 365
Den nyere Naturanskuelse (*The New Scientific View;* Lochmann), 427
Nygaard, C. S., 593n39
De Nygifte (*The Newly Married Couple;* Bjørnson), 274

Oedipus Rex (Sophocles), 33, 408
Oken, Lorenz, 230, 374
Olaf Liljekrans, 39, 49
"Om kjæmpevisen og dens betydning for kunstpoesien" ("The Heroic Ballad and Its Significance for Literature"), 47
O'Neill, Eugene, 2, 19
"On Human Freedom" (Johan Ludvig Heiberg), 598n13
"On J. L. Heiberg's Death" ("Ved J. L. Heibergs Død"), 166

On the Genealogy of Morals (Nietzsche), 405, 416, 446, 450, 453
"On the Heights" ("Paa Vidderne"), 52, 53, 172, 176; estheticism and detachment in, 25, 51, 63, 72, 79, 166, 177; Kierkegaardian element in, 93
"On the Mother of the Gods" (Julian), 216
On the Origin of Species (Darwin), 304–5, 373
Oscar II, king of Sweden, 265, 268–69, 390, 559, 561
Our Mutual Friend (Dickens), 274
An Outline of Psychology (*Psykologi i omrids;* Høffding), 379–80
Out of Work (Grønvold), 386
Over œvne (*Beyond Human Power;* Bjørnson), 347, 351
Overskou, Thomas, 44

"Paa Vidderne." *See* "On the Heights"
Une Page d'amour (Zola), 367
A Pair of Blue Eyes (Hardy), 377
Paradiso (Dante), 100
Paris Commune (1871), 196, 211–13, 217–19, 223, 247–48
La Parisienne (Becque), 516
Parsifal (Wagner), 478, 554–55
particularism, 137, 152, 153
Pauli, Georg, 325
Paulsen, John, 276, 584n7, 590n28
Paus, Christopher Blom, 24, 28, 29, 363
Peer Gynt, 11–12, 21, 114, 116, 136, 185, 350, 549, 554, 556; autobiographical elements in, 87–88; Bjørnson's view of, 118, 126; *Brand* compared to, 19, 89, 92, 93, 100; commercial success of, 102; commitments avoided in, 88–89, 152–53; critical response to, 103–6, 353, 478; Dano-Prussian War linked to, 89, 90, 92, 97, 101, 137; Darwinism and, 197, 305, 371; Egyptian setting in, 97, 156; farmers depicted in, 384; *Faust* likened to, 92–93; Grieg's incidental music to, 39, 244; as philosophical drama, 92–101, 107–8, 154; real-life models for, 351, 388, 423; sexual peril in, 27; Teutonism refuted in, 162; women depicted in, 276; writing of, 5, 86–87, 251
Petersen, Clemens, 338; Bjørnson linked to, 58, 114, 115, 118, 138; as dualist, 108–10; Ibsen and his works viewed by, 67, 103–7, 116; mixed reputation of, 138–39; physical appearance of, 59; sex scandal and exile of, 140–41
Petersen, Laura. *See* Kieler (Petersen), Laura
Phèdre (Racine), 456
The Phenomenology of Mind (Hegel), 97
Philippi, Felix, 412–13
Philosophical Fragments (Kierkegaard), 590n4
Philosophy and Theology (*Filosofi of Teologi;* Høffding), 111
The Physiology and Pathology of Mind (Maudsley), 353–54
Pigott, Edward Smyth, 479
Pillars of Society (*Samfundets støtter*), 38, 269, 273–74, 294, 322, 327, 516, 526; complexity of, 265; popular success of, 267, 481, 508, 532, 542; shortcomings of, 266; topicality of, 263–64, 335; women's emancipation in, 270, 273, 276
Pinero, Arthur Wing, 557
Piper, Hedvig, 388
Pius IX, Pope, 204
Plimsoll, Samuel, 263
Ploug, Carl, 119, 138, 161, 345
Plutarch, 203
"A Poem for the Klingenberg Festival" ("Sang ved Festen paa Klingenberg"), 66
Poems in Verse and Prose (*Dikter på vers och prosa;* Strindberg), 250
"The Polish Volunteer" ("Den polske frivillige"; Snoilsky), 202
Politiken (newspaper), 522
Poulsen, Emil, 350
"The Power of Art" ("Kunsten Magt"), 40

"The Power of Memory" ("Mindets Magt"), 239
The Pretenders (*Kongs-emnerne*), 61, 123, 146, 159, 161, 166, 363, 547–48, 560; autobiographical elements in, 62–63; *Brand* linked to, 72; censorship of, 144; critical response to, 67, 103, 148, 309; publication of, 171, 176, 244; sources of, 39
The Prince of Homburg (Kleist), 378
Prozor, Moritz, 338
Prudhomme, Sully, 9
Psykologi i omrids (*An Outline of Psychology*; Høffding), 379–80

Quanten, Emil von, 597n49
The Quintessence of Ibsenism (Shaw), 404
Quo Vadis? (Sienkiewicz), 10

Racine, Jean, 47, 456
Raff, Helene, 491, 493, 497–99, 570
Raphael, 70–71, 83
Redaktøren (*The Editor*; Bjørnson), 259, 267, 268
Rée, Paul, 405
Reform Association (Reformoreningen), 124
Reich, Emil, 548
Reich, Wilhelm, 406
Reimann, J. A., 25
Reimers, Sophie, 403
Réjane, Gabrielle-Charlotte, 516
Renaissance (Heidenstam), 487
Renan, Ernest, 236, 449
Das Rheingold (Wagner), 230
Rhodes, Cecil, 538–39
"A Rhymed Letter to Fru Heiberg" ("Rimbrev til Fru Heiberg"), 167, 250
Ribbing, Seved, 307
Ribot, Théodule, 418, 425, 428
Richter, Jean Paul Friedrich, 378
Richter, Ole, 128, 130, 135–36, 149, 154
Riddervold, Hans, 84, 323
Rigoletto (Verdi), 48
Riis, Fanny, 283
"Rimbrev til Fru Heiberg" ("A Rhymed Letter to Fru Heiberg"), 167, 250
Der Ring des Nibelungen (Wagner), 81, 464
The Robbers (Schiller), 34, 60
Robertson, T. W., 258, 331
Robins, Elizabeth, 287, 464, 468, 557
Rode, Ove, 392, 431–32
Rodin, Auguste, 566
Le Roi s'amuse (Hugo), 48
The Romantic School in Germany (*Den romantiske Skole i Tyskland;* Brandes), 196
Rose, Henry, 404
Rosmersholm, 479–80, 567; characterization in, 400–401, 404–5; critical and popular response to, 410, 412, 544; *The Lady from the Sea* compared to, 417, 422; morality controversy in, 404; Oedipus myth retold in, 408; performance problems of, 413–14; psychological insights in, 397–98, 401–2, 405–9, 412, 425; retrospective technique in, 399; sacrifice in, 410–11; Snoilsky as model for, 396–97, 401, 403, 408
Rudolf, Crown Prince of Austria, 467
Russell, Bertrand, 1
Ruuth, Ebba, 390, 396, 397

Saint-Simon, Henri, 213
Sallust, 32
Samfundets støtter. See *Pillars of Society*
Samvittighed og Videnskab (*Science and Conscience*; Larsen), 111
Sancthansnatten (*Midsummer Eve*), 47–48, 49
Sand, George, 272
"Sanger-hilsen til Sverige" ("A Greeting in Song to Sweden"), 262
"Sang ved Festen paa Klingenberg" ("A Poem for the Klingenberg Festival"), 66
Sarcey, Francisque, 549

Sardou, Victorien, 259, 335
Sars, J. Ernst, 268, 394
Sartor Resartus (Carlyle), 339
Sartre, Jean-Paul, 95
Scènes de la Vie de Bohème (Murger), 569
Schelling, Friedrich Wilhelm Joseph von, 218, 229–33, 372, 378
Schiller, Friedrich, 34, 47, 59–61, 225, 227, 378
Schlenther, Paul, 562
Schmidt, Rudolf: as dualist, 110, 111, 115, 139; Ibsen's poetry praised by, 179; as journal publisher, 139, 141, 149–51; Petersen's sex scandal and, 140, 141
Schofield, William Henry, 199
School (Robertson), 331
Schopenhauer, Arthur, 378, 440, 569–70
Schubert, Gotthilf Heinrich von, 377–78
Schulerud, Ole, 26, 35, 40
Science and Conscience (*Samvittighed og Videnskab*; Larsen), 111
Scott, Clement, 537
A *Scrap of Paper* (Sardou), 335
Scribe, Eugène, 45, 47, 48, 334, 335, 508, 591n14
"The Sea Bird" ("Søflugen"; Welhaven), 354
"The Servant Brother" ("Den tjenanden brodern"; Snoilsky), 390
Seven Weeks' War (1866), 136
Shakespeare, John, 28
Shakespeare, William, 405, 456, 478, 547; good vs. evil in, 4; Ibsen's career parallels to, 28; *Sonnets* of, 172
Shaw, George Bernard, 1, 4, 18, 164, 292, 331, 478, 519, 557; Archer's view of, 417; childhood of, 16–17, 23; Ibsen's works viewed by, 78, 225, 296, 335, 366, 404, 479, 566; limited readership of, 2; stage directions of, 481
"A Ship in Distress" ("I havsnød"), 66
Sibbern, George, 98
Sienkiewicz, Henryk, 10
Signal Controversy (Signalfejden), 161
"Signals in the North," 161–62, 164, 187
Sigurd Jorsalfar (Bjørnson), 161
Sigurd Slembe (Bjørnson), 83
Silhouettes from Travels at Home and Abroad (*Skyggebilleder fra Rejser i Indland og Udland;* Drachmann), 383
Sinding, Stephen, 18
Skram, Erik, 433, 544
Skule, Earl, 61–62, 63
Snoilsky, Carl, 425, 559–60; aristocratic background of, 202, 389; divorce and remarriage of, 390, 397, 403; Ibsen's dispute with, 165; as poet, 388–89, 390–91; radical sympathies of, 202–4, 390, 397; as *Rosmersholm* model, 396, 401, 408; Third Kingdom viewed by, 415, 428
"Søflugen" ("The Sea Bird"; Welhaven), 354
Sohlman, August, 66
Sontum, Dr., 494, 553, 576
Sontum, Helene, 41, 494, 534
Sophia, queen of Sweden, 559
Sophocles, 34, 96, 399, 408
Sparre, Sixten, 467
Spencer, Herbert, 425, 428, 429
Stabell, A. B., 38
Staël, Madame de (Anne-Louise-Germaine), 270
Stages on Life's Way (Kierkegaard), 52
Stang, Frederik, 84, 146, 248
Stang, Fredrik, 592n34
Stanislavsky, Konstantin, 255, 367, 476, 478
Stendhal, 180
Stirner, Max, 182–83
Stjernström, Edvard, 252–59
Stousland, Hedvig, 576
Strauss, David Friedrich, 108
Strindberg, August, 4, 93, 258, 274, 313, 390, 430, 432, 510, 516; Benedictsson's suicide attempt and, 444–45; Bjørnson and Ibsen contrasted by, 267; Bjørnson viewed by, 56, 257, 262–63; Brandes linked to, 440; *Brand* viewed by, 78;

childhood of, 17; creation theory satirized by, 374–75; A *Doll's House* viewed by, 286, 290; drawing-room drama satirized by, 253–55, 259; Ibsen avoided by, 558; Ibsen viewed by, 12–13, 246, 332–33; Nietzsche and, 448; recklessness of, 326; *Rosmersholm* viewed by, 402; sexual views of, 438, 573; theatrical conventions of, 478; verse drama criticized by, 250; women's role viewed by, 291, 453–54, 517, 549
Strodtmann, Adolf, 309–10
Strodtmann, Henriette, 309–10
The Subjection of Women (Mill), 194, 273, 275
Sult (*Hunger*; Hamsun), 487
Sverdrup, Johan, 123–25, 130, 149, 151, 153, 154
Swedenborgianism, 12
Symons, Arthur, 344
Synnøve Solbakken (Bjørnson), 56, 59
Syphilis and Marriage (Fournier), 310
La Syphilis du cerveau (Fournier), 310–11

Taine, Hippolyte, 190, 378, 406, 425, 427
"Tak" ("Thanks"), 176–77
Tartuffe (Molière), 538, 554
Teichmüller, Gustav, 619n30
Templeton, Joan, 491
Tennyson, Alfred Tennyson, baron, 305, 309
"Terje Vigen," 173–74, 176
La Terre (Zola), 339
Testament from America (Harring), 38
"Thanks" ("Tak"), 176–77
Thaulow, Fritz, 391, 394
Thaulow, Harald, 328–29
Le Théâtre d'Ibsen (Berteval), 404
Thérèse Raquin (Zola), 398, 405
"They Sat There, the Two of Them—" ("De satt der, de to—"), 495–96
Thiers, Louis Adolphe, 211–12
Thomas, Ambroise, 497
Thompson, Wyville, 372
Thomsen, Grímur Thorgrimsson, 424
Thoresen, Hans Conrad, 45, 424–25
Thoresen, Magdalene, 50, 68, *91*, 296, 423–26, 498, 526; characters modeled after, 90, 423, 425; literary salon led by, 49, 67
Thoresen, Marie, 276
Thoresen, Suzannah, 49, 53, 70, 88, 277, 279, 417, 423, 526, 547; asexuality of, 52; Bardach accepted by, 489, 491, 492, 497–98; during Ibsen's last days, 576, 577–78; Ibsen's marriage to, 45, 54–55, 424, 489, 493, 496, 498; Petersen's impressions of, 67; physical ailments of, 486; plays inspired by, 50; women's role and, 275–76
Thrane, Marcus, 37, 38
Thus Spake Zarathrusta (Nietzsche), 416, 446, 455
Tiberius, emperor of Rome, 203
Tidemand, Adolph, 39
Tilbagetogsnatten (Night of the Retreat; 1864), 98
"Til de Genlevende" ("To the Survivors"), 166
"Till de Medskyldige" ("To My Brothers in Guilt"), 69, 338
"Til men Ven Revolutions-Taleren!" ("To My Friend Who Talks of Revolution"), 181, 415
"Til Noget in Norge" ("To Something in Norway"; Drachmann), 383
Tilskueren (journal), 450
"Den tjenanden brodern" ("The Servant Brother"; Snoilsky), 390
Tocqueville, Alexis de, 180
Tolstoy, Leo, 4, 9, 479, 517
"To My Brothers in Guilt" ("Till de Medskyldige"), 69, 338
"To My Contemporaries" (Ploug), 345
"To My Friend Who Talks of Revolution" ("Til men Ven Revolutions-Taleren!"), 181, 415
"To Something in Norway" ("Til Noget in Norge"; Drachmann), 383

"To the Survivors" ("Til de Genlevende"), 166
The Tragic Muse (*Melpomene;* Michelangelo), 71
Tree, Herbert Beerbohm, 557
Tristan und Isolde (Wagner), 478
"Troens Grund" ("The Basis of Faith"), 67–68
Der Trompeter von Säkkingen (Nessler), 497
The Twilight of the Idols (*Götzen-Dämmerung;* Nietzsche), 466

"Uden Navn" ("Without a Name"), 165
Ueland, Ole Gabriel, 123, 165
Det unga Tyskland (*Young Germany;* Brandes), 487
"Upon the Sovereign Sun" (Julian), 216
Der Ursprung der moralischen Empfindungen (Rée), 405
Utilitarianism (Mill), 215, 447

Vaillant, Auguste, 517
van Gogh, Vincent, 16, 521
Vasenius, Valfrid, 552
"Ved J. L. Heibergs Død" ("On J. L. Heiberg's Death"), 166
"Ved Tusenårs-Fest" ("For the Millennial Festival"), 169
Verdi, Giuseppe, 48
Vetsera, Marie, 467
Vibe, Jan, 593n34
The Vikings at Helgeland (*Hærmændene paa Helgeland*), 50–51, 53, 168, 171, 244–45, 464, 548
Vinje, Aasmund Olavsson, 36–37, 40, 130, 155
A *Visit* (*Et besøg;* Brandes), 438
Voltaire, 32

"The Wages of Virtue" (Strindberg), 438
Wagner, Richard, 42, 478, 494, 497; Ibsen likened to, 81, 230, 375, 464, 479; philosophy and drama interwoven by, 375; time and space interwoven by, 554; Viking legends exploited by, 50–51, 464
Wallenstein (Schiller), 227
Wallner, Franz, 475
The Warrior's Barrow (*Kjæmpehøien*), 36
Weber, Joseph, 378
Wedekind, Frank, 505–6, 513
Weigand, Hermann J., 399–400
Weininger, Otto, 478
Welhaven, Johan Sebastian, 39, 171, 354, 527
Werenskiold, Erik, 18
Wergeland, Henrik, 39, 152, 275
When We Dead Awaken, 9, 13, 557–74, 576, 578
"The White Lady" ("Hvita frun"; Snoilsky), 390–91
Whitman, Walt, 140
Who's Afraid of Virginia Woolf? (Albee), 2
Wiehe, Vilhelm, 143–44
The Wild Duck, 1, 4, 12, 19, 43, 344, 476, 558; autobiographical elements in, 17, 22, 23, 29, 359, 360–65; biblical language in, 355–56; critical and popular response to, 351–52, 365–66, 434, 544; Darwinism in, 373–77; earlier works compared to, 347–48, 349, 360, 361; eyesight and blindness in, 349, 354–55, 357–58; heredity in, 357; homosexual hints in, 348; idealism vs. realism in, 353, 354; lighting in, 367–68; loft symbol in, 369–71, 372, 406, 418, 419, 459; long scene change in, 258; psychology of the unconscious in, 379; as realistic theater, 366; self-absorption in, 349–50, 351; suicide in, 365, 368, 369; women's psychology in, 380–81; writing of, 347
Willemer, Marianne von, 499
William I, German emperor, 136, 187, 209, 211
Winter, William, 479
Winter-Hielm, K. A., 171
Winterhjelm, Hedwig, 317
Wirsén, Carl David af, 560

"With a Water Lily" ("Med en Vandlilje"), 173
"Without a Name" ("Uden Navn"), 165
Woerner, Roman, 548
Wolf, Lucie, 365
The World as Will and Representation (Schopenhauer), 569–70
Wulfflen, Erich, 288

Yeats, William Butler, 173, 532
Young Denmark, 118, 120, 125, 138, 139, 141, 154, 179
Young Germany (*Det unga Tyskland*; Brandes), 487
Young Norway, 118, 120, 125, 138, 154
Youth (Garborg), 438

Zacconi, Ermete, 434–36
Zola, Emile, 405, 479, 516, 536; Ibsen's view of, 339–40, 342–43, 383, 517; impressionism promoted by, 367; as naturalist, 325, 334, 339, 371–72, 373, 398, 430, 487; notoriety of, 325; symbolists vs., 521